D0376100

This bear has been reading the dictionary & is quite tired, poor bear! But he can put in a marker & read no more.

This bear has just made a good joke — So he is writing it down in his note-book that he may not forget it.

A drawing from one of Leslie Stephen's letters to Mrs W. K. Clifford; the 'tired' bear reading a dictionary refers to his own indefatigable labours on the *DNB*.

LESLIE STEPHEN

The Godless Victorian

NOEL ANNAN

The University of Chicago Press

Chicago and London

The University of Chicago Press, Chicago 60637
The University of Chicago Press, Ltd., London

95 94 93 92 91 90 89 88 87 86   5 4 3 2 1

Library of Congress Cataloging in Publication Data

Annan, Noel Gilroy Annan, Baron, 1916–
    Leslie Stephen: the Godless Victorian.

    Bibliography: p.
    Includes index.
    1. Stephen, Leslie, Sir, 1832–1904—Biography.
2. Authors, English—19th century—Biography.
3. Atheists—Great Britain—Biography.   I. Title.
[PR5473.S6A88   1986]   828'.809 [B]   85-24714
ISBN 0-226-02106-8 (pbk.)

To George Rylands

A drawing from one of the letters Leslie Stephen sent to the children of Mrs W. K. Clifford, written as if from one dog to another.

CONTENTS

ILLUSTRATIONS

Leslie Stephen aged twenty-eight, 1860
Leslie Stephen by Julia Margaret Cameron
Leslie Stephen by G. C. Beresford, 1902 (*Hulton Picture Library*)
Minny Thackeray by Julia Margaret Cameron, 1862
Leslie Stephen with Minny, *c.* 1867–8
Anny Thackeray, 1875
Leslie Stephen with Alpine guide Melchior Anderegg,
    c. 1870
Leslie Stephen with his dog Troy, 1875
Fitzjames Stephen; drawing by G. F. Watts (*National
    Portrait Gallery*)
James Russell Lowell (*National Portrait Gallery*)
J. K. Stephen
Julia Jackson aged fourteen
Julia Stephen by Julia Margaret Cameron (*National
    Portrait Gallery*)
Leslie and Julia Stephen, 1892
Talland House, St Ives
Sir Leslie Stephen with his daughter Virginia, by
    G. C. Beresford, 1902

PREFACE

When I returned from Germany after the war to take up my fellowship at King's College, Cambridge, I intended to write a book about the Victorian agnostics. One day Richard Braithwaite, the philosophy don there, said to me, 'Have you seen that the Le Bas Prize this year is set on Leslie Stephen?' It so happened that a month or so earlier a family friend, James MacGibbon, had quite independently sent me a bundle of photostats of Leslie Stephen's letters to Charles Eliot Norton and had suggested that I write about him, adding that he would be glad to publish anything I might write. I thought to do so would have the advantage of concentrating my mind and enable me to publish a book far sooner than the tome I had planned.

I then learnt what luck it is to have a good publisher. My draft was concerned exclusively with Stephen's place in the history of ideas. James MacGibbon told me that I must start with a biographical introduction. I had no intention (nor have I now) of replacing F. W. Maitland's masterly commemorative biography; but I thought I should go to Sussex to see if there were papers which would modify Maitland's account. The material in Leonard Woolf's possession was not available, but Vanessa Bell with great generosity lent me the manuscript of the autobiography Stephen wrote for his children, now published under the name they gave it, *The Mausoleum Book*; and such papers and photographs as she had she put at my disposal. So I was able to put Stephen's own account of himself beside the portrait of Mr Ramsay which Virginia Woolf drew in her novel *To the Lighthouse*. Maitland, whom professional historians revere perhaps above all other Victorian historians, had told his successor how to write about his friend: 'He is too big for one sort of writing,' he said, 'and too dear for another'; and he added, 'Someone will some day do for him what he to our admiration did for many others: illustrate in a small compass his life by his books, his books by his life, and both by their environment.' This I tried to do.

It is now over thirty years since my book was published and it has long been out of print. Curiously enough at the time I was writing it several American scholars of about my age were writing doctoral dissertations on some aspect of Stephen's work; and these I have now been able to consult. But it was not until the opening of the Bloomsbury archives that a mass of new biographical material became available, much of it meticulously edited by Quentin and Olivier Bell. Meanwhile various libraries in the United States acquired papers which had been in Leonard Woolf's possession, and these too have been subjected to minute scrutiny by a new generation of American scholars. All this time a prodigious number of books, monographs and articles on the Victorian age poured from the presses and were recorded by that invaluable periodical, *Victorian Studies*. So when I retired from being vice-chancellor of the University of London, I at last had the time to examine the work of many of these scholars and rewrite my book on Stephen.

The new book is still not a biography. Undoubtedly one could be written if only because some of the new items which have come to light show that Maitland, writing when he did, felt himself unable to do more than allude to them. Like many Victorians Leslie Stephen was an indefatigable letter writer. The letters he wrote to his first and second wives would fill a volume in themselves. But I still believe that his writings are of greater interest than his life and that to understand Stephen is to understand Evangelical morality and Victorian rationalism, the strongest influences of the age. He is the dominant in Victorian tonality. I have always admired G. M. Young's advice to historians to go on reading until you can hear people talking, and when I have had to analyse what Stephen wrote, I have let him speak as far as possible in his own voice.

Someone may ask whether I have changed my view of Stephen. Not essentially. When I first wrote, I showed he was a demanding husband and an exacting father; and the new evidence has confirmed that judgement. He sometimes enjoyed posing as a philistine and where women and their capabilities were concerned he really was a philistine. I think a little worse of his particular brand of rationalism and a little better of his achievements as editor, critic and moralist than I did. Thirty years ago I failed to do justice to him as an historian of ideas; and in particular to his contention, so different from that of his master, John Stuart Mill, that literary genres and fashions, even ideas themselves, are generated by forces at work in society rather than springing, like Pallas Athene, from the head of their progenitor. His virtues still seem to me to outweigh his defects. I always admired him and I still do.

But I have another ambition. I have tried to contribute more to the history of ideas itself and this time set Stephen in a wider constellation of ideas: in particular those of the German Renaissance of the eighteenth and nineteenth centuries which has been as important for Europe today as the Italian Renaissance was in the sixteenth and seventeenth centuries. Many of the hares which Stephen started are still running strongly in our day; and if we have to course them in different country from his, it is worth seeing where they started and the track they have now taken. Some may be alarmed. Is this whig history in which the context of Stephen's ideas is disregarded and they are approved if they point to our times or patronized if they do not produce happy descendants? Does it claim that there can be such a phenomenon as disinterested theoretical writing and deny that any disquisition upon theology or politics or literature must be part of a design to gain power? The reader must judge. But I hope that my lack of enthusiasm for structures or *mentalités* and my interest in occasionally suggesting where the perennial arguments about our condition are being conducted today will not deter those who want to understand the way our ancestors felt, reasoned and lived.

25 December 1983   NOEL ANNAN

ACKNOWLEDGEMENTS

My greatest debt is to Quentin Bell and Angelica Garnett for permission to quote from material and use photographs of which they own the copyright. I have enjoyed the stimulus of Quentin Bell's own writing and a friendship lasting over many years.

My next heaviest debt is to Professor John W. Bicknell of Drew University, New Jersey, the *doyen* of Stephen studies. That he put his unpublished doctoral dissertation at my disposal is only one of his kind deeds. We have corresponded for long and he has put me on to many letters and documents which I might otherwise have missed. I should also mention the help I have obtained from reading the unpublished doctoral dissertations of other American scholars, in particular Drs John J. Timmerman, S. A. O. Ullmann, Floyd Tolleson and Edwin Sheen. For material on Stephen's editorship of the *Cornhill* I am indebted to Professor Oscar Maurer; and of the *Dictionary of National Biography* to Mr Alan Bell.

I am also indebted to Professor Jane Marcus of the University of Texas at Austin for inviting me to take part in the centenary celebrations of the birth of Virginia Woolf. She sent me numerous published and un-published papers and introduced me to the work of other young American scholars who had been working on Virginia Woolf and who generously have given me permission to see and quote from their dissertations or papers: such as Professor Jeffrey von Arx, Professor Katherine C. Hill-Miller, Professor Virginia Hyman, Dr Jane Lilienfeld, Dr Leila Luedeking and Professor David Ross. I owe a special debt to Dr Martine Stemerick whose dissertation on the Stephen family I have read. I have learnt much from discussing her sources with her and she was generosity itself.

I owe much to Professor Sheldon Rothblatt who invited me to stay for a month at the University of California at Berkeley, to Professor Alex Zwerdling of the same university and to Professor Phyllis Rose of Wesleyan University, Connecticut, for discussing with me their work on

Virginia Woolf.

I am grateful for permission to quote from material in the possession of Mrs Edward Norman-Butler; Dr Daniel Waley, Keeper of Manuscripts at the British Library; Mr A. E. B. Owen of the University Library of Cambridge; Dr Mattie U. Russell of the William R. Perkins Library, Duke University, North Carolina; Mr Rodney G. Dennis of the Houghton Library, Harvard University; and Dr Lola Szladits of the Berg Collection, New York Public Library. I want to thank Mrs Christopher Dilke for providing some of Leslie Stephen's charming drawings from his letters to her grandmother, Mrs W. K. Clifford. I am indebted to many friends and colleagues for help, comment and suggestions which I have acknowledged, where possible, in the notes at the end of the book.

Mr John Gross and my editor Miss Elizabeth Burke read my manuscript and I am in their debt for their wise comments. I owe a general debt of gratitude mounting over the years to Sir Isaiah Berlin; and in particular for lending his unpublished lecture on Joseph de Maistre. Professor Michael Hill of Victoria University, Wellington, kindly sent me some relevant sociological studies and Professor E. S. Paykal of the Department of Psychiatry of St George's Hospital Medical School sent me papers he has published on manic depression.

I must also thank Mrs Elizabeth Ackermann for typing my manuscript which demanded all her skills to decipher and check; my one-time classics tutor at Stowe, Mr Patrick Hunter, who in his eighties read both the manuscript and the proofs; and to Mr Douglas Matthews, Librarian of the London Library, for many kindnesses and for compiling the index.

Finally I must once again thank my mentor Dr George Rylands. He did not this time read the whole book twice in draft and in proof, but he read two chapters and as ever gave that severe but affectionate criticism which is, perhaps, the only kind of criticism which helps one to write less badly.

And I do not forget what I owe to my dear wife.

Leslie Stephen
13 a. 97

Chapter One

❦❦❦

THE EARLY YEARS

The Victorian Intellectuals

When Andrea Mantegna chose to paint St Jerome, a favourite subject of early Renaissance artists, he did not picture him, as others did, aged but vigorous, calmly contemplating folios of theology as he sat in his study, his little dog beside him, or in the open air, guarded by his lion. He chose instead to paint St Jerome in the wilderness. In the foreground looms a massive rocky mountain which provides a cell, but in the distance one can see the sunny smiling landscape laced with twisting roads along which a hermit would plod to end his days in penitence among these crags. Before his cell the saint sits wrapped in melancholy. His eyes are cast down so that he looks at what lies at his feet, the symbol of worldly pride and power – his cardinal's hat. All that appears to sustain him are his books, two of which await him on a stone which serves as a table while he grasps a third. The saint is at the end of his days.

Some such picture is conjured up when people think today of Leslie Stephen. Beresford's photograph of a gaunt old man staring out into space, the tyrannical, demanding, selfish father of Virginia Woolf, comes first to mind rather than the photograph of the alert, wiry figure, full of force and apparently about to put a question, which his wife's aunt Julia Cameron took. We are accustomed to summing people up when their career is over because we imagine that only then can we form a judgement on a man's contribution to his times; but we will get a truer picture if we see people at the height of their powers when their achievements, or indeed their failures, are still before them.

When in 1862 he resigned his tutorship at Cambridge because he had lost his faith and turned to write for the periodicals he was 30. By the time he was 40 he had been made editor of the *Cornhill Magazine* and had begun to publish the articles which established him as the first literary critic in England of that relatively new form of art, the novel. While in the editorial chair he wrote his classic on eighteenth-century English thought.

When he was 50 in 1882 he became the first editor of the *Dictionary of National Biography*, the great work to which Rosebery gave a prime-ministerial accolade, calling it 'the monumental literary work of Her Majesty's reign . . . each new examination of its volumes only increases my admiration and amazement'. A pioneer Alpinist, a walker to whom 40 miles in a day was a stroll, in his prime he was thought by some who heard his sardonic aphorisms and asides to be an unsociable porcupine. But nothing so earthbound as a rodent conveys the right image. In his need for solitude he resembled far more a sure-footed ibex as he leapt from rock to rock in the lonely landscape where his imagination ranged ever ready to impale an opponent on his horns.

We may prefer to think of him as the notable critic and editor but that was not how he wished to be remembered. Were he alive today there is little doubt what he would have regarded as his greatest achievement. A Victorian who came of age in the middle of the nineteenth century and lived to see it end, might not be as bewildered by the present times as some might think. He would find parliamentary institutions and their relation to the law and the judiciary familiar. He would recognize in the manoeuvres of the United States and Soviet Russia to buttress or extend their zones of influence the perennial exercise of power which the great nations of his age displayed. The debates about the creation of wealth or the mitigation of poverty by self-help or by collective intervention would be commonplace, and he would not be amazed by the decline of some social groups such as the squirearchy and the rise of others such as the trade unions. No doubt he would be astonished by the advances in technology, extensions though they are of the industrial revolution with which he was so well acquainted. No doubt he would comment on the decline of deference to rank or wealth and the more easy-going manners between classes and age-groups while recognizing that a variegated working class still continued to exist. But he would certainly notice one great change in the cultures of his times and ours. No longer do most men and women acknowledge God to be their Father.

Leslie Stephen would have been the last to claim that the secularization of public life was brought about by intellectuals such as himself. But he would have judged his most notable achievement to have shown that it was possible not to believe in Christianity, yet to live a virtuous life. Shortly after he became an agnostic he wrote: 'I now believe in nothing, to put it shortly; but I do not the less believe in morality etc. etc. I mean to live and die like a gentleman if possible.'

Was he a gentleman? That word caused nerve-racking embarrassment to Victorians. When in one of Trollope's political novels Lady Mary Palliser pleads with her father, the Duke of Omnium, to be permitted to marry Mr Frank Tregear, she argues, 'He is a gentleman.' 'So is my private secretary,' the Duke testily replies. 'The curate of the parish is a gentleman, and the medical man who comes here from Bradstock, the word is too vague to carry any meaning that ought to be serviceable.' To have been to a public school was not a necessary qualification; but unless you belonged unequivocally to a noble family, to have been to a university, or by some means to have acquired professional status, was almost a requirement. The first half of the nineteenth century saw a new group defined by its status beginning to form in society. This was an aristocracy of intellect. Certain families established an intellectual ascendancy and began to share the spoils of the professional and academic worlds between their children. These children intermarried and formed a class of able men and women who drew into that circle people of intellectual distinction. The same blood could be found appearing among the headmasters of the public schools and the fellows of Oxford and Cambridge colleges; the same tone of voice could be heard criticizing, teaching and leading middle-class opinion in the periodicals; and whenever it was possible to argue that posts in the public service (for example in Whitehall) should be filled by open competition rather than by patronage, these families would insist that competitive examinations in academic subjects were the best test of ability.

Most of these families rose by time-honoured methods. The younger son of a line of yeoman farmers or country parsons went into trade or industry and flourished. His children fell under the spell of evangelical religion which inspired them with moral purpose and reminded them, when their time came to raise a family, of their duty as parents to teach their children diligence and responsibility. Or they came from Quaker families moving slowly up the social scale into banking or brewing – or chocolate. Or they owned businesses and as men of means supported parliamentary reform and studied philosophic radicalism. As a result the next generation was able to compete successfully for the prizes of school and university life, and the learned professions were open to them. They had to work for their honours: examinations disciplined their minds and forced them to show their mettle. But their intellect was trained principally at home where from childhood they were accustomed to hear their fathers and uncles discussing abstract questions with their friends. They talked a common language, shared similar experiences which enabled them to develop intimate friendships with each other; and what then could be more natural than to marry the sister of one's friend?

Thus through the century these clans began to form: the Wedgwood-Darwin connection, the Butlers, the Vaughans and the Hodgkins. Leslie Stephen was born into one of the most famous connections, the Clapham Sect. The Clapham Sect was the derisive name which Sydney Smith conferred on that circle of well-to-do men who struggled to abolish the slave trade; organized evangelical philanthropic societies; and by their enthusiasm for humanitarian causes inspired such men and women as Shaftesbury and Florence Nightingale. Leslie's father wrote that the group consisted of the sons of men who had been thought enthusiastic fools. But though they too were as strong as their fathers in the faith, they were never afflicted by the narrow piety of those Evangelicals who, as a sign of the purer light, despised the fruits of the intellect. They were businessmen with sound incomes and wide interests. Wilberforce was a man of charm and breeding who disliked a gloomy Sunday. Zachary Macaulay corresponded with Madame de Staël, Broglie and Chateaubriand. Granville Sharp learnt in his youth as a draper's apprentice 'to love the Quaker, to be kind to the Presbyterian, to pity the Atheist, and to endure even the Roman Catholic'; and perhaps this descending scale of compassion had something to do with winning for himself the position of patriarch of the anti-slave movement. Henry Thornton was a vastly able man, a banker who also understood the theory of finance and wrote a treatise of such excellence that Bentham abandoned his enquiries into the matter. Nor was he the kind of Protestant who divorced his religion from his business activities. He spoke in Parliament against the unequal pressure of taxation on rich and poor and 'raised his own contribution to the level of his speech' by giving six-sevenths of his income to charity until he married, after which he gave one-third.[1]

The members of the Clapham Sect had begun to intermarry before they settled there. William Wilberforce and Henry Thornton shared an aunt, and the Thorntons were allied through the Sykeses to the Babingtons. One of Thomas Babington's sons married a niece of Mrs Thornton, another married Eleanor Elliott who was a granddaughter of Henry Venn, and a sister married Thomas Gisborne. Babington himself married the sister of Zachary Macaulay whose daughter married Sir Charles Trevelyan. Thus when Leslie Stephen's father married Jane Venn he became a kinsman of all these families. His elder brother was, like their father, a lawyer, and the author of 'Stephen on Pleading', his younger brother, Sir George Stephen, an author, and his sister became the mother of an editor of the *Observer* and of A. V. Dicey, professor of law at Oxford and author of a classic in days gone by, *Law and Public Opinion in England*.

[1] Other prominent members of the Sect were: the Venn family; Charles Simeon, the famous Cambridge preacher; E. J. Eliot, brother-in-law of Pitt; Lord Teignmouth, devout but temporizing Governor-General of India; Sir R. Inglis, Chairman of the East India Company; Sir William Smith, art-connoisseur and opponent of religious disabilities; Lord Glenelg, Secretary of the Colonial Department (1835–9); Robert Grant, Glenelg's brother, who championed the cause of Jewish emancipation; and Charles Bradley, who held an incumbency in Clapham from 1829 to 1852 and was father by two marriages of a score of children, including G. G., F. H., and A. C. Bradley, and Margaret Woods, author of the excellent short novel, *A Village Tragedy*.

Leslie Stephen's brother, Fitzjames, became as well known as Leslie – a Saturday Reviewer and the author of a powerful attack on John Stuart Mill's conception of liberty. He ended his days a judge of the High Court. His daughter became principal of Newnham and the wife of one of his sons was a great-niece of Florence Nightingale and a niece of the poet A. H. Clough whose sister had been the first principal of Newnham.

Leslie Stephen himself married into a vast clan. His second wife was the aunt of H. A. L. Fisher, Warden of New College and President of the Board of Education in Lloyd George's administration. Fisher's wife was the great-niece of F. H. and A. C. Bradley and his sister married the historian F. W. Maitland, who was Leslie Stephen's official biographer. Another sister of Julia Stephen married a Vaughan and their son became headmaster of Rugby and took as his wife a daughter of John Addington Symonds whom Leslie Stephen counted among his friends.

Julia Stephen married twice. George Duckworth, her son by her first marriage, married a daughter of the fourth Earl of Carnarvon (father of the discoverer of Tutankhamun's tomb); Evelyn Waugh married one of the earl's graddaughters, divorced her and married a second. By Julia's marriage to Leslie Stephen she had Vanessa, the wife of Clive Bell, Virginia, the wife of Leonard Woolf, Thoby who died young and Adrian who married Karin Costelloe, the sister of Ray Strachey and hence related to the Strachey family, the Wedgwoods, the Pearsall-Smiths, to Bertrand Russell and Bernard Berenson. To bring the tale down to the present day, Vanessa Bell's second son, Quentin, professor of the history and theory of art at Sussex University, married the daughter of the keeper of prints and drawings at the British Museum and granddaughter of the Fabian Sydney Olivier. Vanessa's daughter Angelica by Duncan Grant married David Garnett whose father Edward was the keeper of printed books at the British Museum and whose mother Constance by her translations virtually introduced Russian literature to England. One of Angelica's daughters married the son of Ralph Partridge, the author and friend of Lytton Strachey. This boy's mother was Frances, the sister of Tom Marshall, professor of sociology at London, and of Ray, the first wife of David Garnett. David Garnett's eldest son by Ray became a publisher and married the offspring of the union between Professor Bruce Dickens and the daughter of Professor Sir Herbert Grierson.

Where did these people fit into English society? The term 'intellectual aristocracy' was first coined by a Stephen – by J. K. Stephen, the son of Fitzjames – though he seemed to imply in his defence of compulsory Greek in Littlego, the entrance examination to Cambridge, that anyone who had surmounted this hurdle had 'obtained entrance into a favoured class'. They may indeed have done so, but attribution of the term 'intellectual' to those who in those days somehow scraped through to read for a pass degree in the intervals of rowing or playing cricket strains credulity. They were a status group. The real intellectual aristocracy never confused themselves with the real nobility and ruling class. They were often stern critics of the manners and morals of their betters. Henry Thornton smiled satirically when he heard his brother was giving a breakfast party for Queen Charlotte and her daughters in his exquisitely embellished villa. 'We are all City people and connected with merchants and nothing but merchants on every side,' he said; and the subsequent failure in business of this brother, who died under an assumed name in New York, may have seemed to him like a judgement on such luxurious display. They can justly be called intellectual not merely by their reading, their pursuits and their jobs. They were intellectual because they measured others by their mental and moral attributes, not by wealth or birth.

They can also be called aristocratic because they felt ultimately secure; secure that their standard of values was correct; secure in that they were above grinding economy, seediness and niggling. They saw no reason to imitate the manners of any other class and therefore they inherited the natural ease of manner (in their case the self-confident tone of voice in which they addressed the public) which characterizes an aristocracy. Distinct as they knew themselves to be from the nobility, some of them were kinsmen of aristocratic families. One or two might marry a girl from an aristocratic family, such as the Lytteltons; one of Julia Stephen's aunts married Lord Somers and one of her sisters married a son of the Duke of Beaufort. The Babingtons were country squires who descended from a duchess, the Stracheys and Trevelyans were cadet branches of old west-country families.

The British Victorian intelligentsia were not alienated or excluded from the ruling class nor were they subject to interference by the State. They did not, as did the intelligentsia in France, so often feel obliged to polarize themselves and identify either with the party of order or the party of liberty. Nor did they, as in Russia, face the consequences of living under a despotism, nor as in Germany did they as professors become officials of the State. Instead they have been accused of being part of the Establishment.

That accusation is too facile. In the nineteenth century many things set them apart from the governing class. The very word Establishment provides a clue to one estranging influence in that in the eighteenth century it was a term meaning the Church of England as established by law, 'our happy establishment in Church and State', a partnership intended to keep down Dissent and keep out Roman Catholics. These intellectual families did not belong to either the High and Dry or the Low and Slow parties in the Church. Moreover, as a class, they were too interested in obtaining reforms which many in the ruling classes resisted: in the universities, to name only three, the removal of religious tests, the abolition of celibacy as a requirement for a fellowship and the development of the natural sciences. It took time for them to acquire posts of influence even in the professions which were peculiarly theirs; and for the new professions of colonial administration, public schoolmastering, museum curatorship or journalism to be recognized as the counterparts of the old professions of divinity, law and physic. It was not until the 1870s that their Bill of Rights, the Trevelyan-Northcote report of 1853 which recommended throwing the leading posts in the civil service open to competitive examination, was implemented.

They found therefore no difficulty in being both in harmony and at times at odds with the ruling class. Shirley Letwin convincingly argued that this was what characterized an English gentleman and that in Trollope's novels we can see how this habit of neither rushing to extremes nor allowing oneself to be governed by doctrinaire policies was one of the hallmarks of gentlemanly behaviour. Leslie Stephen, radical, utilitarian and positivist though he was, exhibited to a fault the traits of the group into which he was born; and it is all the more interesting to see how the Stephens acquired this status.

Leslie Stephen's Forebears

The Stephens, like the Gladstones, descended from Scots farmers and had to make their way in the world. One of them came south to make his living as a small merchant, and sailing from Bordeaux in 1752 with a cargo of wine was shipwrecked at night on the Isle of Purbeck. Lashing the four survivors together he climbed the sheer cliff-face in the stormy darkness with them behind him. He was put up for some weeks by the local excise officer with whom he had a common interest in preventing the local inhabitants plundering the wreck. The hospitality proved fatal for the host. His young guest ran off with his daughter. Stephen tried to make his way in London, but his business failed, he landed in a debtors' gaol and there became the first of the family to publish. His pamphlet, *Considerations on Imprisonment for Debt*, cited Magna Carta as an authority for proving that to send debtors to prison was both foolish and illegal, and he denounced the famous Tory judge Lord Mansfield with such vehemence that when he tried on his release to be called to the bar, the Benchers of the Inns of Court rejected him as a low fellow. He set up as a somewhat shady partner to a solicitor but never came to anything.

His second son did. Towards the end of his life, very much as Leslie Stephen was to do in the manuscript which his children called *The Mausoleum Book*, Jem Stephen wrote his memoirs. Thrown on the world by his father's improvidence, frustrated in his attempts through schooling to master Latin and Greek which would enable him to rise, passionate like his father in argument, which involved him as a boy in fights and as a young man in duels, he somehow scraped together a legal education. He had other passions than anger. Susceptible to girls from the age of 10, he fell in love at 14 with his future wife, Nancy Stent, who loved Jem so tenderly that she broke with her father and rejected the suit of her guardian's son for his sake. Only her brother stood by her and he, a naval lieutenant going to sea, asked his friend Jem to plead his own suit with a friend of Nancy. What happened then was startling. 'I have been told', Stephen wrote, 'that no man can love two women at once; but I am confident that this is an error.' He had an affair with the girl, who bore him a son – later to become for sixty years a blameless country parson – but never lost Nancy's sympathy or affection. Plain she might be compared with her luscious rival, but Nancy had the better intelligence, taste and understanding of her lover's tortuous behaviour and tortured heart. Nancy finally married him clandestinely and Stephen left for the West Indies to join his elder brother who had inherited money from their uncle. There his wife followed him and they raised their family.

This is where the story ends in the memoirs. By the time he wrote them Jem Stephen was a strong Evangelical and he had one object in view. He wanted his children to acquire a particular piece of knowledge. They should learn from his account how Divine Providence works. Providence is not concerned solely with the fate of nations. God also watches over every twist and turn of a man's life. Stephen's tale is as much the sociology of a soul, an analysis of its relations with the forces operating upon it, as a narrative of his youth. Time and again the Lord chastises him, refuses to listen to his prayers and thwarts his designs even when they appear to be good and generous; but it is all for his eventual good. Stephen shows the difference between being a Christian and being in a state of grace. Of his youth he wrote, 'I feared God, and thought sometimes that I loved him. I was far from neglecting private prayer and generally if not always attended public worship regularly on the Sabbath.' But he took no credit for this. If he abstained from sin it was from prudence or fear, not 'from a desire of God's favour'. He knew that he sinned and suffered because he knew. One of the few matters of taste on which Stephen dissented from Wilberforce was on the relative merits of Cowper and Young as religious poets. Stephen preferred Young's *Night Thoughts*, no doubt because Young recognizes that God teaches rebellious man through suffering to renounce his life of misery. 'Among thy list of blessings infinite Stands this the foremost, that my heart has bled!' Nevertheless the moral of the *Memoirs* comes straight from Cowper. Behind a frowning providence God hid a shining face.

Stephen's account of his remorse, guilt, self-disgust and misery during his youth, still more the workings of the heart reminds one of Richardson's novels. His generous impulses were neither unctuous nor hypocritical. Aged 21 he went one evening to the Coachmakers Hall to one of those societies, such as exist today, where the young imitate parliamentary procedures and train themselves in the art of politics. There was a debate on the question of negro slavery. Jem's impromptu speech brought the house down – and it was the spectacle of his holding the audience in the palm of his hand which made the girl who became his mistress fall in love with him. What he saw in the West Indies – two terrified negroes accused of rape on worthless evidence before a hectoring judge, condemned and burnt alive – reinforced his horror of slavery. He began to correspond with Wilberforce and, his legal practice prospering, returned in 1794 and immediately sought him out. He set up house in Clapham and two years later, on Nancy's death, married Wilberforce's widowed sister. Pamphleteering indefatigably he entered the House of Commons, and Spencer Perceval, the Prime Minister, an Evangelical and supporter of the anti-slavery lobby, became his intimate friend. He died in Stephen's arms when shot down in the lobby of the House; and Stephen visited his assassin in gaol to pray with the criminal.

Jem Stephen was an inflexible man. As a boy he had thought of going to join George Washington, yet he perhaps more than any single man was responsible for the war with the United States in 1812. Partly out of interest in thwarting the slave trade, he devised the famous Orders in Council of 1807, which were aimed at stopping the evasion, by ships flying a neutral flag, of the restrictions which Britain was applying to the trade of her continental enemies. This, far more than the impressment of her sailors, brought America into the war. His adherence to the anti-slavery cause was equally inflexible. He would reproach Wilberforce for any act of courtesy shown to the opposition, and particularly detested Whigs who refused to support him on the slavery issue; but he wept at Fox's grave because 'however wrong in his general politics, he had been a true and zealous abolitionist'. He was right in judging that by Tory support alone would the slave trade be abolished, but that did not deter him from applying for the Chiltern Hundreds in 1815 when Liverpool would not adopt his scheme of registration which he believed essential to prevent the reintroduction of the slave trade in the West Indies. Though still rough in his ways and heated in his language, Stephen, by this time a fervent Evangelical, was accepted without question by the Clapham Sect; and as a Master in Chancery he had risen in the world to an assured position. Thus, although James Stephen himself lacked polish, his friends were distinguished. His children, contemporaries of the Wilberforce boys and of the young prodigy, Tom Macaulay, listened to the conversation of men who were public figures with a great taste for discoursing on moral and religious topics.

It was the Master in Chancery's third son, James, who clave most strongly to the traditions of Clapham by marrying into the Sect and by becoming their chronicler. On his mother's death his father married Wilberforce's sister, but being then 11 years old he was spared the more rigorous side of his stepmother's educational theories; for she was a woman who held that a child ought to have read Bishop Butler's *Analogy* – the greatest English theological work of the eighteenth century – before the age of seven. His father sent him to Trinity Hall and bequeathed him to the care of an evangelical don, Joseph Jowett, great-uncle of the future Master of Balliol, an elegant Latinist and Professor of Civil Law, noted, as it was said, for the perennial freshness of his interest in young men.[1] But the younger Stephen was not impressed with his education. The 'three or four years during which I lived on the banks of the Cam were passed in a pleasant, though not a very cheap, hotel. But had they been passed at the Clarendon, in Bond Street, I do not think that the exchange would have deprived me of any aids for intellectual discipline or for acquiring literary and scientific knowledge.' Young Stephen was called to the Bar and since his father was able to transfer some of his clients to him, the briefs began to pile up in his chambers. In 1814 he married the daughter of John Venn, Rector of Clapham. The Venns had been clergymen since the reign of Elizabeth and they stood at the centre of the Evangelical movement within the Church of England.[2] The sanguine temperament of the Venns matched the parvenu energy of the Stephens, and while the second James Stephen had inherited the thin skin and quick temper of the Stephens, Jane Venn possessed the common sense and cheerfulness of her own family. It was from their marriage that Leslie Stephen was born on 28 November 1832, barely a month after the death of his grandfather, the Master in Chancery.

By the time James Stephen reached maturity the great days of Clapham appeared to be over. Evangelicalism was gaining ground everywhere and the party had already one bishop in the House of Lords. The slave trade had (in theory) been abolished and the struggle over the administration of the Act had been won. But there still remained work to do. Could not the slaves in the British Colonies be freed? Stephen had combined a practice

---

[1] It was Jowett who composed, or rather arranged from Handel, the Cambridge chime, now known throughout the world as the chime of Big Ben.

[2] John Venn's father, Henry, can almost be said to have invented the Clapham Sect. The contemporary of Whitefield and Wesley he was, like them, much moved by Law's *Serious Call*, and during his curacy at Clapham spread the light to Henry Thornton's father. His book, *The Complete Duty of Man*, was accepted by all Claphamites as the classic exposition of Evangelical theology. Charles Simeon was his disciple and inherited his eloquence. His son, John, returned to the scene of his father's first triumphs and was rector of Clapham from 1792 to 1813.

at the bar with an appointment in the colonial department to advise on legislation. In 1825 the work proved too heavy and he gave up the bar to become Counsel to the Colonial Office and Board of Trade and for twenty-two years he laboured in Colonial affairs, to become one of the great colonial administrators of the age. Permanent civil servants soon learn to despise those whom the fortunes of politics set over their heads. Politicians appear to fall neatly into the two categories of knaves or fools whose desires are to be thwarted or humoured as occasion serves. Stephen displayed all the weary contempt of the able civil servant for his chiefs, and in addition his very virtues excited envy and fear. An encyclopaedic memory gave him command over the details of the politics, administration and constitution of all the colonies, and the various Secretaries of State who flitted briefly in and out of office were compelled to rely on his fabulous comprehension. Members of Parliament began to complain that here was a man who had not won his power in the political arena and yet was able to influence governments. For Stephen was an official with a policy: whereas the Government's policy was to 'meliorate' the position of the slaves, Stephen intended to free them. When, therefore, at about the time of the Reform Bill the agitation to free the slaves, led by Zachary Macaulay, was bound to lead to legislation, strong feelings were expressed that Stephen should have no hand in the matter. The Secretary of the Colonies, Lord Stanley, determined that he would keep the permanent official in his place. He rejected Stephen's counsel, intimated that he himself was a man of ability and let it be known that he had decided to draw up the bill himself. But Stephen was to have his revenge. The task proved quite beyond the powers of the nobleman, and on a Saturday morning Stephen was summoned to do the job at top speed. He returned home; began to dictate that afternoon; worked for the first and last time in his life over Sunday; and laid the draft bill in sixty-six clauses before his chief on the Monday morning. Far from diminishing, his influence grew and became sadly apparent during the four-year tenure of office by the amiable and guileless Claphamite, Lord Glenelg. Just before Glenelg was appointed, the Under-Secretary to the office, whose work had been done by Stephen for years, complained to Lord Melbourne that his subordinate was trying to supplant him. 'It looks devilishly like it,' replied the Prime Minister – and left it at that. Two years later, during Glenelg's period of office, the unfortunate man resigned and Stephen took his place as Under-Secretary. The nickname of Mr Over-Secretary Stephen is intelligible.

Omniscience and high rectitude do not endear a man to his lesser contemporaries. Crabb Robinson had noted that Stephen, as a youth, spoke of his worldly prospects 'with more indifference than was perhaps right in a layman', and described him as a 'pious sentimentalist and moralist'. He did not conceal the fact that he thought his own policies right and those of his opponents iniquitous; and this was more than usually irritating because his mind, trained to appreciate legal and moral distinctions, seeded objections like weeds to choke his opponents' proposals and bred innumerable arguments to fertilize his own proposals. That good man Lord Aberdeen was his admiring minister but thought him 'the most unpopular man in Europe. I do not quite know why. Perhaps something in his treatment of inferiors was the cause.' His ministers found themselves too often arguing from a brief which was so subtle that it confused rather than convinced their colleagues. 'The truth is,' he said to his subordinate, Henry Taylor,[1] who was urging him to take the simple course of action in some matter, 'the truth is I am *not* a simple man.' He was not. He knew men thought him odious, and he had a nervous trick of talking with his eyes half shut that made him seem maddeningly condescending. His shyness took the form, as shyness sometimes does, of inordinate loquacity. Taylor tells how Stephen once brushed off a caller by talking to him without pause for breath for half an hour and bowed him out of the room before the man had uttered a word.

An official's unpopularity, however, is rarely explicable simply in terms of his personality, and the abuse which Stephen endured was partly created by the changing relations between the permanent officials and ministers of the Crown. Whereas it had been possible for the former to be regarded as superior clerks in the eighteenth century, an age of legislative reforms transformed their status. We accept the preparation of bills by the bureaucracy as inevitable today and think that a minister is entitled to tell his permanent officials of the general idea of a new measure and to expect them to implement it *in toto*. The fiction that the minister formulates policy and that his Civil Servants execute it is preserved only by the Civil Service itself. In fact the senior officials not only direct day-to-day policy, but by their familiarity with the problems of their department lay down long-term policy. In their view it is for the minister to indicate that he wants the policy to be changed, and only by hard work and political insight can the minister see what changes should be made and how they are to be effected. In Stephen's time this had not begun to be recognized. Ministers did not take kindly to that sort of hard work, and even Gladstone complained that he had been sent to school again to study figures when he was appointed to the Board of Trade. Nevertheless the old days of staffing Whitehall with gentlemen by patronage and supporting them by clerks and messengers were passing. Statistics were almost becoming popular in times when Anti-Corn Law League

---

[1] Sir Henry Taylor (1800–86) played for years an important role in the Colonial Office. He wrote an Elizabethan pastiche drama, *Philip Van Artevelde*, which at one time had a certain *réclame*, and an admirable treatise on the art of rising in politics, entitled *The Statesman*.

pamphlets lay on the drawing-room tables of the middle classes. The man who prepares and can handle statistics has the measure of the amateur statesman who has never learnt the technique of criticizing them and, in general, the official who prepares the details of a legislative measure necessarily is the master in argument. Government was gradually becoming more professional, and more dependent on the expert.

The new experts were formidable men. There was Edwin Chadwick who defeated a multitude of vested interests to set up the first factory inspectorate, reform the Poor Law and create a new system for improving public health. There was Charles Trevelyan who was recalled as Governor of Madras for defying the government of India in its attempt to cut public expenditure but who returned to hold one of the most senior administrative posts. They were men of inexhaustible energy, of disinterested probity, of indefatigable industry; but tact, compromise and suavity were foreign to their natures. They had the strength of mind to establish principles for dealing with the problems they were set; but once formed they could admit no others and closed their mind because the administrative structure they had invented seemed to them the only feasible way of dealing with the problem. Chadwick's Poor Law replaced a ramshackle and extravagant contrivance; but he remained impervious to the outcry that his reform was harsh and inhumane. Trevelyan could not be shaken in his view that the government on his advice was doing all that was feasible to relieve famine in Ireland. For Stephen as for them opponents were to be denounced as the agents of vested interests. So indeed many of them were – the white community in the colonies and their lobby in Parliament. Even so, the Colonial Governors who had to execute Stephen's policies were not always obscurantists. Reformers often expect that the measures into which they have thrown so much energy and spirit must achieve not only the legal and administrative changes which they propose but also that change of heart vital to the success of a measure. Stephen saw his great bill for the liberation of the slaves as the end of the campaign when it was really the beginning. He remained impervious to the despatches from the West Indies which complained that the problem of slavery began only after its abolition – that the transition from slavery to freedom was not just a change in legal status effected by a stroke of the pen, but a social process. 'As the question at present stands,' wrote a Governor of Trinidad some years later, 'a race has been freed, but a society has not been formed.' Biased as many of them were, Stephen's critics were making valid points which could not be met by clever drafting or by sapient memoranda.

He was certainly one of the founders of Victorian imperialism. 'Mr Mother-Country Stephen' had had the foresight to envisage self-governing Dominions and wrote in 1850, 'No reasonable man would ever affirm broadly and generally that a mother-country ought at some time or other to part with her colonies. . . . We emancipate our grown-up sons but keep our unmarried daughters, and our children who may chance to be ricketty, in domestic bonds' – the domestic metaphor came all too naturally to him. For did he not preside over a patriarchal home which resounded to his measured tread as he dictated to his wife, to his sister and later to his daughter like a latter-day Milton? Nevertheless, those who see the harsh imperialist overseas as a reflection of the patriarch at home should recollect that for years the word 'enemy' for him was synonymous with the West Indian white settlers, and he saw his life work as the 'mitigation, if not the prevention, of the cruel wrongs which our country has inflicted on so large a portion of the human race'.

There was, however, a darker side to Stephen's nature. In 1824 the strain of combining a practice at the bar with his duties as a civil servant had proved too much, and he suffered his first nervous breakdown. Then in October 1832 the bitterness of the struggle to pass the bill to emancipate the slaves brought on a second nervous collapse. Fourteen years later to the month his eldest son, Herbert, the apple of his eye, died of typhoid at Dresden. As Stephen crossed the threshold of his house on his return from Dresden with his son's body his daughter fell about his neck and heard him say, 'God has been very good to us, my child'; but his faith could not win the contest with his grief and he mourned his son as David wept over Absalom. His vitality waned, and a year later he had another attack so severe that his doctors and close friends advised him to retire prematurely from the Colonial Office.

Not that he accepted that he was ill. He preferred to say, 'when illness, or perhaps I should rather say, when the decided advice of my medical attendants, constrained me to relinquish my office in Downing Street'. Some put this illness down to long years of personal vendettas. As a civil servant he could not reply. 'I don't know what is the feeling that makes me abhor all praise while yet nobody more desires to be praised,' wrote this unhappy man. He felt unappreciated. The harder one slaved, the odder politicians thought it that one did not slave harder. 'You will write off the first joint of your fingers for them, and then you may write off the second joint, and all they will say of you is: "What a remarkably short-fingered man!" ' he wrote bitterly. In the world of letters work was judged on its merits: in politics expediency and the innocuous proposal were the governing criteria. He was too puritanical to enjoy society. 'Unless I am much mistaken, frivolity of discourse, mere talk for talk's sake, is one of the most besetting sins of our generation.' He declined the entrée to Holland House. In later years he might be found at one of Macaulay's breakfasts with Monckton Milnes, Charles Buller, the Wilberforces, Hallam, Milman and Thirlwall, enjoying the brilliance of the talk though finding it undeniably frivolous. But, in general, if clever men wished to see him, they could come to his house. And they did come. James Spedding, one of the early Apostles, Nassau Senior, the economist (a next-door neighbour), John Stuart Mill, and Greville, the diarist, were glad to listen to his flow of conversation. John Austin, the utilitarian jurist, his literary wife and their remarkable daughter, Lucy, who kept a skull and a rifle in her bedroom, were also frequent callers. Stephen, however, liked best the simpler Clapham company of his brothers-in-law, Henry and John Venn, the Diceys and Garratts and his own brothers.

But there was more to the breakdowns than unsociability and unpopularity. He had bad thoughts. They were not brought on by fears for his faith or by misfortunes in his career. He looked too deep into his soul. He wrote to his wife during one of their temporary separations that solitude was 'quite as bad as dissipation': it induced castle-building. 'Living alone I am sometimes oppressed by myself. I seem to come too closely into contact with myself. It is like the presence of an unwelcome visitor. . . . Yet I suppose everyone has now and then felt as if he were two persons in one, and were compelled to hold a discourse in which soliloquy and colloquy mingled oddly and awfully.' 'There stands upon my chimney-piece here a clock, tick, tick, ticking from morning till night. Each tick, when I listen to it, sounds like a knell.' Stephen lived perilously close to the border where sanity dissolves into insanity.

Childhood

Leslie Stephen grew up in a house in what is now Hyde Park Gate, in a Kensington still separate from London where children could stroll through country lanes and where deer nibbled the grass in Kensington Gardens, which was surrounded by a high wall. He was the fourth of a family of five children. Herbert was a good deal his senior, and the second child, a daughter, died in infancy before Leslie was born. James Fitzjames dominated him, but he had an adoring young sister, Caroline Emilia (Milly), at his beck and call. His mother jotted down the marks of his infant disposition – aged one 'he seemed to have no fear at all', later he was 'rather violent in his temper and if displeased will cry most loudly but in a moment will change to kindness and affection'. He first disliked learning anything but at four took to Watts's catechism. He burst into tears if reproached, he would not hear stories with unhappy endings, he hid his face rather than look upon a picture of the Crucifixion, and the ending of *Erlkönig* had to be changed before he could hear it. He adored listening to poetry and would repeat it to himself long after he had been put to bed, humming the lines or, as he called it, 'playing the band'. So potent was the effect that his whole frame would shake while it was being read, and these transports of emotion exhausted his slender reserves of energy.

His mother spoiled him. Leslie was her favourite. His delicacy made him irritable, and in fact he had throughout his life a flaming temper. Years later his sister-in-law recollected some story she had been told of Leslie hurling a flower-pot at his mother and his family being astonished that no one seemed to be able to control him. He was already a pacifist. His cousin, Edward Dicey, who grew up with him, said that his first memory was of Herbert lifting them both on to a billiard table and telling them to fight. Both refused. 'He has a passion for flowers,' his mother wrote. 'He is always drawing . . . has long conversations with the beasts of Noah's ark and [didn't like books] that went *wiggling* from one subject to another.' His mother, who taught him his early lessons, noticed that he was bright at arithmetic; but she also marked how languor and pallor stole over his face after a bare half-hour. Eventually a doctor was consulted who diagnosed that great Victorian malady, incipient brain-fever, and prescribed a regimen of Brighton – and no more poetry. 'Associating with grown-ups', he opined, 'was as bad for his mind as feeding on turtle and venison would be for his body – the great object should be to tranquillize the mind' as he was in danger of becoming effeminate. Leslie's father was never a man to shirk the call of duty: he moved the whole family to Brighton and travelled down from London for the week-ends. It was less inconvenient than it might have been, for Fitzjames was already there at a private school run by an Evangelical clergyman. Leslie joined him there and was rewarded by readings of the *Arabian Nights* in place of *Marmion*.

The pious air of an educated upper-middle-class Evangelical family in the last century is breathed no more today. The descriptions of an Evangelical childhood left by Stephen or G. W. E. Russell belie the more publicized memories of gloomy severity or cruelty recorded by Ruskin, Samuel Butler or Augustus Hare. The Stephen children led happy, gentle lives. Christianity flowed about them and they bathed in it. There were no fervid prayer meetings, no witch-hunting for sins, no probing the heart and titillating the conscience, no tense expectation of the moment when each child should announce that he was saved and demand that his elders should celebrate his conversion. The children were never troubled by the thought of their mother waiting for them to receive an 'illumination'. They learnt to pray at her knee, to join every morning and evening in family prayers, to read the Bible as the best of all story books. The children believed that Jesus lived because their parents talked to him each day; and their conviction that Jesus was journeying through the world, but always at hand, was extraordinarily vivid – as if another member of the family were living under the same roof. They followed the events of his life through the Church year – the long slow weeks of Lent, leading to Passion week when the story of how he passed each day was retold, to the great culmination of Good Friday when Jesus redeemed mankind and made his offer of salvation to them. All this appeared to them as but yesterday. But they learnt more than a religion of emotion. The Catechism, simple theology and family prayers stamped their imagination with the graver and more terrible images of the Christian faith. Hell existed and God punished sinners. Not that such a fate awaited them. They were children and Jesus loved them. How then, asked their mother, could they offend their dearest Friend by fits of temper and obstinacy? No doubt religion often went to their heads. All children are at some time or other prigs and the form that the priggishness takes depends on their upbringing. Leslie was no exception. He once refused to ride on a donkey to church because it was sinful to make the beast work on Sunday and enjoyed the feeling of sanctity as his father argued vainly to persuade him that such views were extreme. It was exactly such priggishness that Sir James Stephen was determined to eradicate. He would not have his children grow up patent Christians, formalists and cheats. They were to be taught that morality is not to be found by obeying a set of rules. Life was a continual effort to do one's duty to other people. The children were brought up to notice that their father was a man of principle. 'Did you ever know your father to do a thing because it was pleasant?' his mother asked Fitzjames, who replied, 'Yes, once – when he married you.' But it was true. Sir James Stephen was inexorably suspicious of pleasure. He drank little; ate the lightest of meals; and asking himself once why it was that he continued to take snuff and receiving no satisfactory reply, ceremoniously emptied the box out of the window. 'He once smoked a cigar,' wrote Leslie, 'and found it so delicious that he never smoked again.' Home life was austere. They went neither to theatres nor dances, but here again their father was at pains to point out that such pursuits were not sinful, although for people like themselves they were not 'convenient'. On no account were they to lay up as treasure to themselves that they were better than others. The Stephen household was more liberal than most Evangelical households at that date; and the customary apparatus of instruction, the penny-bank, the missionary stories, the charitable work among poor children and the Sunday School, were quietly ignored. Their sense of duty was so ingrained that they believed themselves to be living the freest of lives. The Stephen boys noticed something else about their father: they saw that he never exposed his heart.

This fear of an excessive display of the Christian virtues may have determined Sir James Stephen's choice of a public school for his sons. Arnold was at that time at the height of his fame at Rugby and Sir James might have been expected to send his sons there; indeed he took Fitzjames with him to see Arnold, but decided in favour of Eton. Whether he felt that Rugby encouraged boys to become prigs, or whether he feared the reproaches of his more solid Evangelical relatives to whom Arnold's intellectual Christianity was suspect, is not clear. More probably he doubted the doctor's sanguine verdict on Leslie's health after the boy had been a year at Brighton. The doctor had advised a boarding school 'to have the sugar taken out of him', but Sir James had other ideas. He saw that Leslie was still delicate and he had heard of the abuses at public schools.[1] To ensure that his boys would not be contaminated, and since Leslie was still only nine and a half, he decided to take a house at Windsor, from which he could commute to London, and his sons attend Eton as day-boys. He accordingly called on Dr Hawtrey, the headmaster, outlined his scheme and asked whether there was any prejudice against day-boys. Dr Hawtrey sagely shook his head, and on 25 April 1842 both boys entered the school.

Experts in one field are all too ready to take on trust the judgements of experts in another field. The headmaster's *ipse dixit* was enough for Sir James Stephen, whereas the most casual enquiry would have told him that day-boys, as they always have been in boarding schools, were despised. The public schools for the past twenty years had been redefining the term 'free education'. At Shrewsbury small tradesmen who demanded that their sons should be educated free or at low cost in the local grammar school had been defeated by first Butler and then Kennedy, headmasters who interpreted a free education to mean a liberal training in classical scholarship and not instruction in book-keeping. This was less true of Eton which had in the eighteenth century established its claim to educate the sons of the ruling class, but it still counted for something. A day-boy was suspect because he might be the son of a Windsor grocer or footman at the Royal Household who was attempting to break into the upper classes by insisting that his sons be educated in their home town. Young boys exaggerate the prejudices of their parents, and at Eton in the 1840s the length of the journey which a boy made to the school each half-year was thought to be directly correlated with the breadth of the paternal acres. The Eton authorities, moreover, mistrusted Sir James Stephen. He was a reformer, an occult power behind Royal Commissions, and an Evangelical. Eton despised reform, loathed interference and belonged to the High and Dry party in the Church. If Sir James's first consideration was the well-being of his sons, he could not have taken a more disastrous

[1] Sir James feared for the spiritual health of his sons as they passed out of the influence of the home. Giving thanks to God for Herbert's safe return from his first spell of duty in the Royal Navy, a service then famous for its repertoire of profanity, he told his wife, 'He has brought back with him less (at least so it seems) of the contagion of that fearful calling than my fears had foreboded. He has returned with his affections active and simple.'

decision than to send them to an Oppidan house as day-boys.

Both Fitzjames and Leslie were bullied systematically from the day they arrived. College was the place for poor boys or the sons of Windsor parents, not the Oppidan houses, which were reserved for gentlemen; and this fact was driven into their heads and bottoms.[1] They were unprepared in every way for such treatment. They had not been brought up in some high-spirited upper-class family, they were middle-class boys who had been taught to converse seriously, to read omnivorously and to admire Scott and Wordsworth; they now found themselves in an exceptionally aristocratic house, their companions boys who preferred field sports to such pursuits. As a day-boy Leslie rose at six, read the Bible at his mother's side, and returned home each evening to prepare the next day's lessons, so that to the end of his time at Eton he never made a single friend. He was too small and fragile to be able to defend himself. Living at home, however, shortened the hours in which he was exposed to bullying, and the tough Fitzjames did something to protect him though, as Leslie said afterwards, he fought other boys so often that his bill each term for top-hats must have been phenomenal. At all events it was no use looking to Dr Hawtrey for help. Hawtrey was a humane man who deplored violence and once told a sixth-former that it was bullying that turned Shelley into 'a perfect devil'. But he was a snob; bullying was a tradition, and tradition was sanctified; and his appeals to the boys' better nature delivered in an eccentric pronunciation were ridiculed. In Hawtrey's defence it should be said that even Arnold despaired of boyish brutality, for though Arnold hoped to turn out Christian gentlemen, he thought it beyond his powers to make Rugbeians Christians while still at school.

By the standards of the day an Eton education was sound, and a high proportion of prizemen and classics who took first-class honours at the University were Etonians. Etonians enjoyed a reputation for a quick brilliance and elegance in their classical work, and above all a peerless ability to turn out elegiacs. A good copy of verses was the summit of achievement. Beginning in the lowest forms by stringing nonsense words together to imprint scansion upon the mind, an Eton boy would show up a copy of longs and shorts once or twice a week for the five or seven years of his schooldays, so that classical prosody was drummed into him until it became second nature. But other schools had begun to outstrip Eton. The

[1] They were fortunately preserved from the torture endured by small boys at the hands of the Sixth Form in Long Chamber in College into which they were locked with their fag-masters from 8 p.m. to 8 a.m. secure from any interruption by a master. So appalling were the conditions of bad food, dirt and squalor under which they lived that the year before the Stephens went to Eton, only two candidates presented themselves to election to College although thirty-five places were vacant. During their time in the school, new lodgings were built for Collegers and under Provost Hodgson the horrors of Long Chamber gradually mitigated. Fitzjames Stephen was years later to plead in the Ecclesiastical Courts for a Colleger, Rowland Williams, accused of writing a heretical essay in *Essays and Reviews*, who was literally scalped in Long Chamber through being tossed in a blanket and remained disfigured for life.

Etonian scholar could master grammatical forms, but the pupils of Vaughan at Harrow or Kennedy at Shrewsbury were learning philology. Shrewsbury boys, in particular, were famed at the university for their minute scholarship and mechanically perfect Greek iambics, and for a precision of mind which left its mark on everything they touched: so much so that they were noted for a special aptitude at whist which they played with astonishing accuracy and expressionless countenances. Hawtrey had begun to reform the classical curriculum but, as one might expect, in the most discreet manner, and the changes he effected were designed rather to lower the number of boys in a class than to broaden their knowledge. He did his best, however, to instil respect for a good composition or set of verses, he encouraged the teaching of ancient history, and since he spoke excellent French and fair German and introduced allusions from these languages into his lessons, he may have conveyed to a few of his pupils that the Muses inhabited other countries than England, Greece and Rome.[1]

But Hawtrey's teaching touched only the Upper School, so that neither Leslie nor Fitzjames ever benefited as they both left the school too young. Leslie was clever at his work and went up the school rapidly, but the Eton curriculum did not suit his talents. Mathematics other than elementary arithmetic was not even compulsory. French was a subject which he picked up at home. The teaching of modern history or literature or even English grammar was unknown. The *Edinburgh Review* commented in 1845, 'A Parliamentary return of all that is taught at Eton during ten years of pupilage in the nineteenth century – what books are read, even at the head of the school, Ovid, Virgil, Horace and Homer – ought (if anything can) to surprise the public into some uneasiness on the subject'; and the writer added that matters were not much better elsewhere in that Arnold had introduced remarkably few changes into the public school courses of study. It was at a later date that the admirable practice was introduced of sending boys to their tutor for private reading which might include English literature. Leslie had no such luck. He lodged with Dr Balston, and Dr Balston was a single-minded man. 'If you do not take more pains,' he said to Fitzjames, 'how can you ever expect to write good longs and shorts? If you do not write good longs and shorts, how can you ever be a man of taste? If you are not a man of taste, how can you ever hope to be of use in the world?'

Handsome, kindly, unimaginative and conservative to a degree which delighted the Eton boys as much as it was to astonish the Public School Commissioners when some years later in 1862 they took evidence from

[1] His attempts, wrote A. D. Coleridge, 'were received with broad smiles and vague incredulity'. 'The modern Germans', said he, 'have borrowed from Homer's ἴφθιμος γυνεζ eine wackere Frau.' Inextinguishable laughter. *Hawtrey*: 'What on airth is there to laugh about?'

him as headmaster, Edward Balston had only one criterion for judging a boy. Could he do well what he, Balston, had done as a boy – could he construe and repeat Latin and Greek poetry by heart, could he learn the syntax in the Eton grammar and extract books? To study a book of Virgil, or a play by Sophocles, to read Livy or Thucydides as living authors would be dangerous and, according to Dr Balston, unlikely to improve a boy's taste. He was not a tyrant, his devotion to the ever-increasing number of pupils in his house was exemplary, although he considered armchairs too great a luxury for them. He failed with Leslie as he had failed with Fitzjames. At the end of 1846 when Leslie was just 14, he was prizeman of his division and had been moved up to Upper Division, Fifth Form. But this did not satisfy Dr Balston. He wrote to Sir James complaining that, while Leslie was diligent and well-behaved, his elegiacs were a disgrace and his compositions lacked polish. Without taste, Dr Balston repeated, the boy could not appreciate beauty. Sir James, with memories of Leslie's voracious appetite for poetry, thought that he responded to beauty better than most boys of his age, and had the courage to do what few fathers dare. He had already taken Fitzjames away when he discovered that he was unhappy, and now he removed Leslie on the grounds that if Eton could not in four years ground his son in elegiacs, to persevere was stupid. Dr Balston went his way unmoved and twenty years later had the satisfaction of resigning as headmaster rather than sanction the reform of the curriculum recommended by the Public School Commissioners.

Both boys had hated their schooldays but they reacted differently. On the day that he left, Fitzjames tore off his white tie, stamped it into the mud and slouched into the ante-chapel to scowl at the boys as they entered. But in later life, like so many Englishmen, he revised his opinion and thought that bullying had made a man of him. 'I was on the whole very unhappy at Eton,' he admitted, 'and I deserved it; for I was shy, timid, and I must own cowardly'; he liked to recall the time when he realized that the only salvation for a boy lay in his fists, 'the process taught me for life the lesson that to be weak is to be wretched, that the state of nature is a state of war, and that *Vae Victis* is the great law of Nature'. When the day came he sent his son, the immortal of the Wall Game, J. K. Stephen, to College. Leslie was more critical. He refused to worship at the shrine of the public schools and thought their teaching was contemptible. 'The average lad of eighteen who comes up to the Universities from one of our great places of education shows a negation of all useful knowledge which is, in its way, a really impressive phenomenon.'

Nor did he condone the savage discipline of the public schools. The famous headmaster of Shrewsbury from 1866 to 1908, H. W. Moss, once gave a boy eighty-eight strokes which led to a question in the House of

Commons and a poem in *Punch*. He himself remembered at Eton receiving at the hands of the Lower Master a flogging 'so unjust that I am even now stung by it' – remembered the shame and pain of being held down on the block, his shirt-tails lifted, his bare bottom exposed. In the 1870s there was a celebrated scandal at Winchester, the case of the 'Tunded Macpherson' in which prefects inflicted thirty cuts quite unjustly on a senior boy: a friend of the boy's father wrote to *The Times*, and within a few days that newspaper and the *Daily Telegraph* were deluged with letters complaining of the appalling thrashings inflicted on their sons by prefects. (The Headmaster took action to stop this cruelty and, though he rightly refused to expel the prefect responsible after the public outcry, his description of him as a 'good and gentle boy' aroused some surprise.) Stephen took this opportunity to speak about the tortures suffered by small boys and the honest Dobbins of *Vanity Fair*; bullying would not be stopped until men stopped 'dwelling more fondly upon their schooldays in proportion to the remoteness of their memory'. 'Universities and schools', he wrote, 'calmly speak of producing great men when all that can safely be said is that they have not put an end to them.' On the other hand, he thought that, bad as it was, a public school was the best English education available, and he would not have gone so far as many intellectuals in the first third of this century who declared that the only reason for enduring a public school was that it made the rest of one's days comparatively happy since no disaster later in life could ever parallel the horrors of adolescence. Leslie Stephen believed in discipline and self-reliance. Latin grammar was as necessary as physical exercise; force, vitality, energy, manliness had a better chance of surviving at a public school than elsewhere. In other words he realized that it was not entirely Eton's fault that companionship in games and walks – sunny summer afternoons and eating enormous teas in winter – had been denied to him.

On another curious point Leslie and Fitzjames were also agreed. However tough Eton might have been, it was satisfyingly free from moral uplift. The Chapel Services taken by the Provost and Fellows were so dry that no boy ever connected the religion he professed in Chapel with the life he led in the school. Indeed it was difficult at times to perceive the slightest connection between the two in the sermons which were preached to them. 'The subject of my discourse this morning, my brethren, will be the duties of the married state', droned one old fossil, and his discourse, it need hardly be said, bore no resemblance to those frank talks delivered by housemasters of the present age. The lack of religious zeal was later to excite earnest enquiries from the Public School Commissioners. On this point, at any rate, Leslie Stephen saw eye to eye with his old tutor. Dr Balston did not want to run the risk of a sermon in which one phrase might swerve from the canons of good taste. Asked when he was headmaster whether he did not think that preaching was an excellent means of influencing the boys, 'No,' he replied, 'I was always of opinion that nothing was so important for boys as the preservation of Christian simplicity.' Stephen saw that, though one might raise an eyebrow at his tutor's assumption that the young thugs who boarded with him had remained in a state of primitive innocence, there was much to be said for the kind of honesty which did not pretend that religion was connected with the ordinary boy's life of cribbing, lying, cheating, elegant stealing and brutality. He personally deplored the famous Rugby earnestness and disliked boys 'who conceive themselves to have imbibed a moral as well as a social superiority, and who go through the world ever afterwards as volunteer missionaries, brandishing their exalted moral sense in the face of all spectators'. Eton was free from cant. The Alma Mater was a bloated old harridan, boisterously merry, unashamedly dirty, who did not try to conceal her failings by sneaking off to the conventicle to thank God that she was better than others. This is an odd tribute to pay to one's school, but more interesting than most.

Until he went up to Cambridge Leslie studied with private tutors and spent a few terms at King's College London, where he attended F. D. Maurice's lectures to improve his mathematics. More and more able young men spent a year or two there before entering the old universities, but the majority of the students were hard-working middle-class boys of London parents. The painful lack of refinement that marred Leslie's elegiacs was less of a handicap and he also learnt modern languages and history. But his attendance was fitful. His health was still erratic. He remembered the summer of 1848 when he was sixteen as a long holiday of sickness. At Bruntisland on the Firth of Forth he used to 'lie on the grass and look at the gulls and the seals . . . but I spent most of my time in bed sometimes with leeches on and my bones still shiver when I think of it'. The next year he spent the autumn and winter at Torquay reading Greek and Latin by himself and German with his sister. There was a humiliating interlude in a gymnasium swinging Indian clubs; and his sister's dancing-mistress lent him a chest-expander. Leslie at this time was a tall, lanky boy who had outgrown his strength, awkward and unwilling to open his heart to a soul. Despite his parents' care, despite his Windsor Park pony and his Chinese mice, his boyhood had been lonely. He adored his mother but he found his father unapproachable. Fitzjames remained his father's favourite, for Fitzjames held independent views, spoke his mind, damned the consequences, but garnered parental wisdom. Always in Leslie's youth the figure of Fitzjames loomed above him; broad and strong, successful and competent, knowing his own mind and already the friend of the best men of his generation at Cambridge. In contrast Leslie felt that fellows thought him a muff. The dull days, however, were drawing to an end. He was to leave his family and go to Cambridge. He would return to his first love, mathematics, and serve at a court where common sense and logic were king and queen and where that odious flunkey, Good Taste, was told to kick his heels in an ante-chamber. He would have a room of his own and a chance to make some friends. Even so there were risks. He was to read for honours in an exacting subject; and devout relations prayed, with good reason and no lively hope, that he might survive the Cambridge climate. His health persuaded Sir James that the intellectual competition of his brother's college, Trinity, with its blue ribands of freshman and scholarship examinations and prizes would overstrain him, so he was entered for his father's old college, Trinity Hall. In the Christmas term of 1850, when he was still 17, Leslie took up residence in college; the chest-expander was left in a cupboard at home.

Undergraduate and Rowing Man

It may sound odd that Leslie's parents feared that reading for an honours degree would overtax his strength but their anxiety was well founded. Undergraduates at Cambridge fell academically into two sets: men who read for honours in mathematics or classics,[1] and the majority or *polloi* who read for a pass degree and 'went out in the poll'. It was no surprise to see able men take the poll examination.[2] Sir James Stephen had taken the alternative course of going out in law and Fitzjames, having twice failed to win a Trinity scholarship – an examination taken during under-graduate residence – decided to go out in the poll since his failure had ruined his chance of a Fellowship at his College. Most reading men spent at least seven or eight hours a day at their books, so that work for an honours degree required a healthy constitution and above all, as Leslie Stephen was later to judge, intellectual vigour.

Indeed the Mathematical Tripos was designed partly to test exactly how long a man had worked each day. All questions in every paper were compulsory and more were set than a man could reasonably be expected to answer within the time. They consisted of propositions, or *bookwork*, and problems, and the trick was to know the bookwork by heart and dash it down on paper as quickly as possible to leave the maximum time for the

[1] The Moral Sciences and Natural Sciences Triposes, created in 1851, attracted very few men at this time.

[2] Before 1849 any man who wished to sit for the Classical Tripos had first to be classed, i.e. qualify as a Junior Optime, in the Mathematical Tripos. There was always a number of unfortunate classics who failed to be classed in mathematics and were consequently debarred from attempting the Classical Tripos; their only course was to go out in the poll. Macaulay was one of those who were 'gulfed'. After 1849, a man needed only to qualify for an ordinary degree in mathematics or to obtain a first class in the poll examination to be allowed to take the Classical Tripos. Even so, a man whose studies had been interrrupted by illness or other troubles would very likely abandon his hopes of an honours degree and take the poll examination.

problems. For instance, there were seventy-five propositions in Conic Sections alone which might be set, and yet not more than seven would be likely to appear in the examination. A hard-working man would learn the lot by heart in order to be safe. In Stephen's time, the papers were spread over eight days amounting to forty-four and a half hours' work in all. During the first three days candidates were examined in elementary subjects and forbidden to use analytical geometry or the calculus; there was a short interval while the weaklings were weeded out; and all who passed were then permitted to sit for the second part of the examination. A good Wrangler, or first-class man, could be expected to *floor* the bookwork in the early papers and tackle nearly all the problems. The trial of knowledge and ability came in the second part. But it was still primarily a test of wide knowledge rather than of skill and ingenuity, for the examiners reckoned that only twelve hours of the forty-four and a half should be spent on problems. Much of the preparatory work consisted of practising manipulations which would increase the rate of solving and writing out the solutions of propositions. Part of the test lay in the speed at which a candidate could work, and this in turn depended on how fast he could make his pen skim over the sheets of paper. Hence it paid to learn endless propositions by heart so that not a moment would be wasted in the examination room in thinking them out. The reckless were soon entangled in horrid snares. A good man, tempted to try too many questions, would lose marks for accuracy; another, tackling problems which were worth more marks, would get bogged, and fail to score enough marks on the bookwork. The Tripos was a trial of memory and nerves.[1]

True to their sporting instincts the English had contrived to turn even the university examinations into an athletic contest. Everything depended on marks, and the year Leslie Stephen took the Tripos, the candidates were each given a slip of paper on which marks were assigned for bookwork and riders in order to indicate the relative difficulty of the different questions. Candidates were arranged in the class list in strict order of merit from the Senior Wrangler down to the last Junior Optime

[1] The scope of the papers was about as wide as the present Mathematical Tripos Part II except that there was more optics and astronomy, far less analysis and, of course, no thermodynamics. But the type of work required was greatly different. The Tripos in Stephen's time was designed for the hard and fast worker. Far more bookwork was demanded and the problems were not nearly so remote from bookwork as they are today; in fact no man who had gone thoroughly over the ground would find himself faced with a problem which could not be related to a similar problem in his books, whereas today a Junior Optime who relied on bookwork would have no hope of answering some of the problems which demand ingenuity and a certain degree of originality of mind. It is more difficult to compare the Cambridge mathematical student of the 1850s with his contemporaries at the Polytechnique; but the most sanguine estimate in favour of the English suggests that, while the first ten Wranglers might be the equal of the Frenchmen, the average undergraduate reading for honours was below the continental standard.

or holder of the Wooden Spoon; and below him lay the hapless men who were *gulfed*, or allowed degrees, and those who were plucked outright. It soon became known who were in the running for the top places in the first class. You studied 'Calendar', as it was called, just as bookies study form, and bets were laid on the favourites. Weeks before the examination the pundits would know how the best men had been shaping, what their coaches predicted and how their health had been standing up to the long grind. A rumour would fly about that a small-College man had made wonderful progress during the vacation and that the Johnian and Trinity bloodstock had better sharpen their pace. The great Whewell was defeated for the place of Senior Wrangler by an obscure man who had 'run dark' and, it was rumoured, had thrown Whewell off his guard by professing to go hunting and really alighting to read mathematics at some distant village. As they came into the straight, men would work fifteen hours a day or more and their coaches would spot likely questions and urge them on to a final spurt; one or two would strike it up as high as twenty hours a day in the last week and totter into the examination room with flasks of ether or brandy in their pockets. Examination day dawned in the first week in January and prospective Wranglers prayed for a mild spell of weather. For if there was a sharp frost the Senate House would be so cold that a good man might get *frozen up*, his hands so blue that he could not write at speed, and valuable marks would trickle away before he could recover. The Peterhouse outsider would be seen to be writing for dear life, and the sight would throw his Trinity rival off his stroke. When the great mathematician, Arthur Cayley, took the Tripos in 1842 his rival from St John's was seen ostentatiously to leave the Senate House a full hour before the end of the allotted time for the paper. A friend rushed up to his rooms that evening, 'Cayley! Cayley! they tell me Simpson floored the paper this afternoon in two hours. Is it so?' His backers had no cause for alarm; the future Senior Wrangler, who was soaking his feet in a tub, replied imperturbably without altering his position, 'Likely enough he did. I floored it myself in two hours and a half.' College loyalty ran high and tutors and gyps would pick up gossip about the fortunes of their men; the coaches would prognosticate; and the punters hedged. A long fortnight intervened and then the results were posted. There was money in it for the victors. The first ten Wranglers stood an excellent chance of a Fellowship even at Trinity and St John's; a man from a small College could hope for a Fellowship if he were placed among the Wranglers. A high Wrangler could set up as a coach with propriety and a first or second Wrangler had a testimonial of ability that would open doors for him in London. Leslie Stephen estimated the value in hard cash of a high place at about five thousand pounds in all.

Such was the career on which Leslie embarked, and so far from his health breaking under the strain it steadily improved and troubled him no more. At the end of his first year he won a scholarship at Trinity Hall and had obviously settled to his work. His next task was to choose a good coach. College teaching was inadequate and tutors spent their hours of instruction ramming the elementary propositions into the heads of the average undergraduates. A flier went to an outside coach whose reputation rested on his record of successes. A good coach could work up a clever man whose training had been neglected, or cram a man of good memory but no great brilliance, or drive a nimble-witted fellow by cracking his whip. Much depended on him, and many men preferred a coach with a rough tongue who would slang his pupils to victory. The great coaches flung part of their personality into their best men and worked through them. Probably because he was a small-college man, Stephen was not accepted by the leading coach of the day, William Hopkins, who in twenty-two years of teaching produced 175 Wranglers of whom seventeen were top of the examination.[1] He chose instead to go to the Johnian, Isaac Todhunter, and in the vacation was tutored by his cousin, James Wilberforce Stephen, a Fourth Wrangler. Todhunter was a character: quaint, crotchety, sour, uncouth, surrounded by cats and canaries, he worked with true mathematical precision: Chapel at 7.30, pupils from 8.15 until 3 o'clock, a walk which never varied until dinner at 4, and from 5.30 to 10 another stream of pupils. Leslie Stephen wrote:

> He lived in a perfect atmosphere of mathematics; his books, all ranged in the neatest order, and covered with uniform brown paper, were mathematical; his talk, to us at any rate, was one round of mathematics; even his chairs and tables strictly limited to the requirements of pupils, and the pattern on his carpet, seemed to breathe mathematics. By what mysterious process it was that he accumulated stores of miscellaneous information and knew all about the events of the time (for such I afterwards discovered to be the fact) I have never been able to guess. Probably he imbibed them through the pores of his skin. Still less can I imagine how it came to pass that he published a whole series of excellent educational works. He probably wrote them in momentary interstices of time between one pupil's entering his sanctum and another leaving it.

Todhunter lived for his work, and though he told his wife on their wedding-day that his devotion to mathematics melted beside the love he bore her, he nevertheless introduced her to Hamilton's Quaternions on their honeymoon. Stephen went to him twice or three times a week for catechetical lectures and was stirred to compete against his fellow pupils by Todhunter's weekly papers. Todhunter stopped him from holding office in the Cambridge Union though he could not stop him speaking in debates. 'Push on. Push on,' his coach would say, and Leslie pushed on to

[1] Hopkins's successes were so habitual, writes Winstanley, that when on one occasion his highest man was only eighth Wrangler, his servant, according to report, remarked 'Master ain't placed this year'.

such effect that he turned himself into a reasonable mathematician. After a labour of ten terms he took the Tripos and was placed twentieth in the list of Wranglers or half-way up the first class out of a field of 143 men.

It was a sound performance, since he had the bad luck to strike a particularly brilliant year. The Senior Wrangler was E. J. Routh who later far outshone both Hopkins and Todhunter as a coach and produced an astonishing list of successes among his pupils.[1] The Second Wrangler was the genius Clerk Maxwell who first reduced the properties of the electromagnetic field to exact measurement and discovered that the velocity of the transmission of the forces in this field was the same as that of light – a discovery which Einstein declared was the most important in physics since Newton's time. The place immediately above Stephen was occupied by Aldis Wright, the editor of Shakespeare. But Stephen defeated his cousin, Edward Dicey, who later became editor of the *Observer*, and the future Lord Hartington, and sundry budding archdeacons. His triumph duly brought its reward, though it was a reward which later proved to be double-edged. Stephen naturally hoped for a Fellowship, but another Trinity Hall man who stood above him in the list of Wranglers had prior claims and was at once elected to a lay Fellowship. The college, however, was determined not to lose sight of Stephen who, they thought rightly, had the makings of a good college tutor. It so happened that another Fellowship at this moment fell vacant; Stephen's name was put forward and he was elected at Christmas 1854. The award was of the type which required the holder to take Holy Orders.[2] And this he duly did in the following year.

He still found it difficult to meet people easily. As an undergraduate he kept a bullfinch in his room to sing to him and was known by his contemporaries as 'a tall, gaunt, and shy man who read mathematics, and hovered on the edge of a conversation without boldly taking his part'. But he was fast coming out of his shell. In the Union debates he spoke frequently and but for Todhunter's remonstrances would have held office in his third year. Politics had begun to interest him and as a radical he displayed the contempt for the conservatism of his elders which a young man ought to show. Although he still belonged to a small circle of men mostly in his own college, the Diceys were another link with the university world. He began to develop his own style of talk; he would express his

[1] For twenty-four consecutive years a pupil of Routh was Senior Wrangler. He produced twenty-eight Senior Wranglers in all and hundreds of his pupils were placed in the first class.

[2] Not all Fellows were compelled to take orders; all but two in Trinity and all but four in St John's were so obliged, but in Trinity Hall only two out of twelve were clergymen. The remainder were usually absentee lawyers who resided twelve days a year at Christmas for audit. The University Commission of 1852 pointed out that this was sanctioned by practice rather than by the College statutes which seemed to lay down that certainly four and probably eight of the twelve Fellows should be in orders; but that as the statutes were so obscure they ought to be revised. This was accomplished in 1860 with Stephen's help.

opinion with the utmost vigour, and then relapse into silence, ready to pulverize some sententious judgement in a sentence. Not all who met him approved. He was ambitious to be invited to join the Apostles; his brother had been an active member and two of Leslie's friends belonged to the society; yet no invitation came. Henry Jackson believed that a new generation of the brethren – Montagu Butler, Farrar, Roden Noel – kept him out because they disliked Fitzjames; but as we shall see there may have been another reason. Intimate friendship came hard to one who was as shy as he was, but his shyness was a symptom of something far more crucial. Something in his personality grated on his intellectual equals and made them feel that he was not of their own flesh and blood.

They were right. Stephen did not care to be an intellectual. Above him loomed the ghost of Fitzjames's reputation and Leslie had to lay it before he could be himself; and as so often happens, the ritual of exorcism transformed the exorcist.[1] He was not disturbed by his brother's mental prowess with which he knew that he could compete on equal terms. His father certainly thought him the cleverer of the two. But he was ashamed of his nervous sensibility and boyish ill-health. Throughout his life he despised weakness in any form. Weakness must be overcome: he admired his cousin, Albert Dicey, for 'the triumph of an active intellect over a ridiculously incapable body'. Stephen wanted to appear to his contemporaries as an athlete who incidentally owned a competent thinking-box. So he went in for the river. True, he rowed badly and though he still continued to row when a young don he could never rise higher than the second boat. His triumphs were achieved as a coach when Trinity Hall went head of the river in 1859 and again in 1862. None could rival his wind and fire and his long legs could keep up with the boat mile after mile along the tow-path as the crew paddled down the river towards Ely. Clad in a filthy shirt and grey flannel trousers with a large purple patch in the seat, and damning the eyes of any cox on the river who did not give way, the Rev. Leslie Stephen was a sight to make Victorian eyes blink. The fact that he had taken Holy Orders did not disturb him a whit. His great-grandfather Henry Venn a few days before he was ordained in 1747 had played for Surrey against All England and at the end of the match gave his bat away to the first comer saying, 'I will never have it said of me, Well struck Parson.' Leslie belonged to a different generation, and it is he as much as Charles Kingsley who should be regarded as the founder of muscular Christianity. He was also a formidable athlete, a great walker for whom a stroll to London and back to attend a dinner was nothing

---

[1] Leslie Stephen nursed no feeling of resentment against his brother whom he honoured and whose biography he wrote. The book, however, betrays his lack of sympathy with Fitzjames's mind which was in politics more searching than his own. It gives the impression of a man sparring at a distance from his opponent; parrying and feinting skilfully enough but never squaring up to him.

extraordinary. He once challenged a friend to run three miles while he himself walked two and won by 230 yards. Stephen invented the athletics match between Oxford and Cambridge, and won the mile in 5.4 minutes and the two miles in 10.54. He challenged another friend, 'Friday' Thornton, to run to Baitsbite along the tow-path while he leapt over ditches and plunged through hedges cross-country on the other side of the river, and was beaten only in the last 30 yards. One day the Vicar of Eaton Socon complained that 'his parish had been invaded by four lunatics who, he was told, were clergymen from Cambridge'. It was Stephen with some friends testing his muscles on yet another feat of endurance. Sir James Stephen's careful plan to send Leslie to a small college so that he should not overtax his strength had somehow miscarried; the delicate boy had turned himself into a fanatical athlete.

Rowing remains such a popular pastime at the universities because it gives the otherwise physically inept what they want but cannot get from games. The happiest hours of rowing are when it is over; the sensation of having overcome the weariness and desperation which afflict an oarsman in rowing a course produces after the event an extraordinary quality of pleasure. The will has triumphed over the body. This pleasure is also strongly tinged with the emotion of enduring hardship with one's friends. In rowing, far more than in cricket or football, where a star player may win a match, nothing can be achieved without team spirit. The art of rowing in an eight is to make the boat run smoothly and this depends as much on the psychology as on the physique of the crew. Weeks of coaching may improve individual oarsmen yet the boat may deteriorate, since its progress depends on the crew's state of mind. This is the point where the boat-club is so important. The crew eat together in Hall; as an essential to success, they are encouraged to consider themselves superior to their fellows; and a good oar may be dropped from the club if he does not fit in. This intense feeling of comradeship and reliance upon each other makes the boat run smoothly – so that if one man relaxes the pressure of his feet on the stretcher or brings his oar through too high, the other members of the crew almost unconsciously deviate from their normal stroke so as to prevent the boat from rolling or running in jerks.

The real leader of the boat is the coach; for though stroke dictates the rate of striking, he is quite unable to increase the boat's speed unless the crew are so co-ordinated that they immediately respond. The coach's job is to get the men into the proper attitude of aggressive self-confidence so that they overcome in a race their natural feeling of exhaustion and despair. The crew must believe in victory not only during the race but throughout training. In rugger a first XV will nearly always beat a second XV simply because the individual skill and knowledge of the players is superior. But a second boat will often beat a first boat in a trial because the second boat, knowing that to be beaten is no disgrace, rows without nerves, while the first boat fears defeat, knowing that victory will not heighten their prestige. Everything therefore depends on the coach. He must be tyrant enough to be obeyed without question, persuasive enough to prevent sulkiness or loss of self-respect, sensible enough not to demand perfection in the early stages when the boat is running poorly and before the crew can see the results of hard work, and careful enough not to bring the crew on too fast. For if he does the crew goes stale and conjures up groundless doubts and fears which take weeks to eradicate. The coach is virtually a member of the crew and plays upon it like a minstrel on his harp.

Stephen has a place among the great rowing coaches. He may have rowed badly but he knew how it should be done. He could invent ingenious analogies and similes to catch his crew's imagination; he knew when to slang a man and when to praise; and his fertile mind was always thinking out new ways of improving rowing technique so that he never grew stale. He defended the sport on the grounds that none other demanded such skill, pluck and rigorous training. Never mentioning the coach he gave all credit to the captain of the boat who had to enforce discipline for long weeks yet display exceptional diplomacy in choosing and sometimes changing the order in the boat. Bow, an unpopular man, will be said to have won his place through favouritism; Two displays a new symptom or injury each day; Five is rumoured to be breaking training in a pub; Cox may have a head on his shoulders but why should the crew carry someone a stone overweight? 'There is in every crew someone who makes it a favour to row.' Yet of all fanaticisms is not this the most harmless and does it not draw men together 'when their affections are most malleable and most cohesive'? Rowing gave Stephen the pleasure of intense comradeship; coaching gave him in addition the delights of leadership. It gave him self-confidence and the pleasurable knowledge that others had confidence in him as well. This was what he was to require during the rest of his life. He had subdued his sensitiveness and could count himself one of those 'manly affectionate fellows' whom he had learnt to admire at Trinity Hall. During his years at Cambridge no fitter epitaph could have been designed for him than that of the first rowing man in literature, Elpenor in the Odyssey: 'Fix upon the mound of my grave the oar that in life I pulled among my comrades.'

Stephen felt that he had triumphed over his nature; but as so often happens the price of the triumph was not realized until many years later. An instalment, however, had to be paid almost at once. The transmogrification into a tough lost Stephen friends in a place where people are too often judged by the company they keep. Trinity Hall was not distinguished academically or socially. It was filled with amiable young men of whom the brightest intended to be lawyers and the remainder came to Cambridge to enjoy themselves. Night after night Stephen's rooms were filled with the din and jargon of rowing men comparing the form of the boats. 'You took me for a sanctimonious prig, and I took you for a rowing rough, and I don't know which was nearest the mark', a contemporary told him in later years. He was not aggressively anti-intellectual but indicated strongly that affairs of the mind should be kept like a kettle on the hearth humming a private song to itself, to be displayed only when some public occurrence had stoked the fire so fiercely that the kettle had to blow off steam. His utterances on such occasions were explosive and delivered with a solid portion of contempt for the opinions of all concerned – himself included. This apparent contempt for other men's opinions in a discussion, even for the value of discussion itself, had probably led the Apostles to reject him. Yet though he disappointed the Apostles, Trinity Hall rejoiced. The undergraduates saw that their tutor's heart was in the College and, what was more, in their personal pursuits. It was Stephen who presided at Bump Suppers and wrote the College Boating Song, and they noticed that his enthusiasm was more frenzied than their own when the boat went head of the river. 'I shall never forget the joy with which he caught hold of my hand and shook it,' said the stroke of the boat on that occasion. 'He very nearly upset us all into the river, and, if I had not used some strong language, I believe he would have done so.'

Undergraduates could forget that he was a parson, for Stephen was ready to take the lead in every new enthusiasm. He was president of a club for walking called the Boa-constrictor, he himself being known as the Old Serpent. At the time when Tennyson was calling Riflemen to form, Stephen enrolled as a Volunteer and his rooms resounded to the crash of arms drill. Happily the idlest undergraduate in the College, whose rooms were below the tutor's, did not miss his opportunity and sent his gyp to present his compliments to Sgt Stephen and beg him to conduct 'Order Arms' with a little less noise as his studies were being disturbed. Moreover, the undergraduates saw him as their champion; though he was in authority he deflated it by referring to the Master as 'old stick-in-the-mud', and by despising openly the fusty, dusty dons who opposed rowing and athletics because young men enjoyed them. The freedom with which he expressed his views somewhat scandalized the senior tutor Ben Latham, who winced to see a College official galloping round Parker's Piece in some race and losing so many garments in the process that parsonical decency was imperilled. But it was Stephen and not Latham who was the major influence in the College during the 1850s. Not that he adopted any of the subtler means by which a tutor can achieve popularity. His letters to pupils were models of forthright bluntness, and if they could not see the affection that lay behind them *tant pis pour eux*. He loved to talk, as he put it, nonsense to undergraduates and mistake it for philosophy. What he meant was that he talked about ideas and serious subjects – not just about politics and the boat. Keen intellect – generous enthusiasm – warm heart – were the words which the undergraduates forty years on used to describe him. Nor did he rely on formal entertainment but bawled at them across the court to bring their own commons and have tea with him. He was a character. At one time he developed a partiality for dried figs and carried a box of them about with him to friends' rooms where he would perch on a table swinging his legs and munching.

Stephen set a new fashion in dons and must take his place beside schoolmasters, such as Warre of Eton and Bowen of Harrow, who fastened athleticism upon Victorian youth in order to keep them out of mischief. They were so successful that by 1870 criticism of the cost to parents of games-playing at the public schools and the universities and of the harm it did to the boys' studies was vented in *Punch* and the *Saturday Review* which formerly had been sympathetic to manly feats. 'Their brief day of general favour is over,' Stephen observed, 'and we are now going through the familiar process of breaking in pieces the idol we had set up.' Reviewing a novel by Wilkie Collins in which, horror of horrors, the villain was a marvellous athlete and physical specimen who indulged in seduction, blackmail, intent to murder and wife battery, Stephen protested mildly that Collins laid on his colours pretty thickly. But he consoled himself as a muscular non-Christian that 'the sect, indeed, flourishes and spreads as ever'. It spread because there was method behind the apparent madness of 30-mile Sunday walks and College athletics. It was not entirely unreasonable, for the majority of under-graduates were not and never would be interested in the dreary curriculum of the poll degree. Stephen described himself in his under-graduate days as a wearied and disgusted wayfarer along the lanes of mathematics, and the poll men retched at learning gobbets of Paley's *Evidences of Christianity* and the first three books of Euclid by heart. Treated by the University as schoolboys, spending the minimum of time at lectures, resorting to the grossest type of cramming, hemmed in by restrictions, with few diversions to break the routine of Chapel and Hall, they were devoured by ennui and refused to behave as adults. What else was there to do except drink at inns, gamble at Newmarket and pick up tarts in Barnwell; or, by way of change, to bowl over old ladies when out for a spin in a gig and break windows and each other's heads in a hooligan rag? So all freshmen went down to the river to learn to row and, after dark, 'harmonic evenings' took place in the tutor's rooms where feats of strength would be performed. It was his antidote to 'loafing'. 'I think loafing a euphemism,' wrote Henry Jackson to Maitland about those days. 'You speak of the Hall as not dissolute. It was very dissolute in 1860.' Stephen's cult of athleticism was a palliative for the recurrent disease of student boredom. But he had other remedies in mind; and one of these was the reform of the examination system.

The Radical Don

In each generation the mass of undergraduates need someone who will fight their battles against the purists and disciplinarian scholars. Dons are always ready to teach those undergraduates who are going to get a First. They are not so ready to admit that at least half their pupils, who will never be scholars, also deserve to be considered and taught something which will sustain them in their adult life. The Victorian poll-man no doubt was a difficult creature to teach. Stephen knew his needs better than most dons, but he came up against the familiar academic argument which runs: 'No one should leave the university with a degree unless he has been examined in such and such a topic.' There was Dr Paget who clamoured for the inclusion of hydrostatics among the subjects for poll-men, contending that 'if hydrostatics were not required, then Bachelors of Arts might go down without knowing the difference between a thermometer and a barometer, and without knowing how to describe the common pump.' There was Dr Joseph Mayor who bewailed the fact that the proposed changes in the poll degree would deprive men of the spirit of Greek *mousike* or moral and aesthetic appreciation; and casting a baleful glance at Stephen declared that the changes were inspired by 'pestilent muscular Christianity'. There was Henry Fawcett, Stephen's greatest friend in the university, who believed in mental discipline: he admired the old Tripos examinations precisely because they were narrow, and thought that young men should train their brains, as acrobats train their muscles, and learn the whole technique of back-somersaults and hand-stands before trying to swing and soar on the trapeze of the intellect.

These were the kind of arguments which Stephen had to meet and, though he failed to convince the opposition, his proposals seem in retrospect sensible. We pretend, argued Stephen, to educate the poll-man. Well then, let it be an education and not a soulless farce which undergraduates regard as a stinking bog to be crossed by hiring a crammer. Away with Dr Mayor and his pretensions that a few classical texts swotted with curses will sweeten the imagination of poll-men with *mousike*. Let us rather give them a general course of history and geology and the spirit of the classics. Let them study accountancy which might persuade the parents of the commercial classes to send their sons to Cambridge. Above all, do not stigmatize the poll-man as a lower form of vertebrate life. Open the Tripos to him by providing a pass class.

An examination (the poll) from which all the best men are by their nature excluded, infallibly produces a low standard among the examinees. The poll system does not simply assume that one man is stupider than another. It deliberately stamps half our students as intellectual pariahs. It writes down every man an ass who can't pass an honours examination . . . The truth is that all poll examinations will be defective as long as they are entirely divorced from the honour triposes.

Why did Stephen fail in his attempted reform? Partly because his suggestion to incorporate the poll degree in the Tripos was not particularly happy; to open the Tripos to pass men would have inevitably lowered the standard of the honours schools without humanizing the content of the pass degree. Yet it is interesting in these days when secondary education has moved towards the comprehensive school and a common curriculum in the first public examination, to find Stephen using the argument that the segregation of the clever and able from the average or backward leads to a decline in standards and a contempt for learning among the latter who most need to have their standards raised. It is also interesting to see him in 1870 declaring that men who read honours had been bribed by the lure of prizes and fellowships worth two or three thousand pounds obtained in the end by a handful of Wranglers and clever classicists to read a subject which four-fifths would never touch again in their lives. 'If their minds have been taught they have not been filled.' They ought to take honours degrees in which they would study several subjects. Instead of giving bribes the University should be creating adequately paid professorships for men such as Jowett who influenced generations of young men. At present 'the universities do not themselves set the example of reverencing intellectual cultivation above everything'; and for those who can't win prizes, they openly say don't work, play. These very arguments still rumble round universities today.

The decisive cause of his failure was, of course, the form of academic self-government at Cambridge. Any institution which relies on taking executive decisions on nearly all important topics by a vote of all its members will enjoy a semi-paralysed existence. Then, as now, the resident senior members of the university combined a deadly power of dialectic with astonishing stamina and obduracy in debate. The ingenuity in argument, the subtlety in drawing distinctions, the dexterous pre-varications, the imperative reasons for procrastination, perpetually bewilder and confound the novice in university politics. The leaders of opinion in Cambridge were all convinced that reform must come; but since each was also convinced that he alone could propound the exact solution, the proposals of syndicate after syndicate went down into the dust. Perhaps it was natural that all the reformers, Stephen included, set their sights too low, for the relations between the universities and Church and State were changing too rapidly for them to catch a glimpse of the target. There was also a third cause which made reform singularly difficult: the deplorably low level of the average schoolboy's education. Very little could be done until the university and the colleges followed Trinity's lead in establishing an entrance examination, thus forcing the public schools to raise their standards; and this they could not do because they restricted entry as far as possible to the sons of gentlemen and rejected in disgust the continental ideal of the career open to talent.

This, indeed, was the crux of the matter. The universities of every country unconsciously assume a purpose in the education they provide. German universities in the nineteenth century assumed that nothing was more important than the increase of knowledge and tried to bind the best brains of each generation to the grindstone of research. In France the universities and Grandes Ecoles during the 1840s forged an examination system designed to provide a standard of qualification for the professions including that of teacher in the State schools. Oxford and Cambridge were peculiar in that they assumed that their first duty was to educate the governing class for service in Church and State. Not that there was anything as crudely purposive as special courses of study in politics or commerce – only recognized branches of scholarship were allowed; but before their eyes was the ideal of the educated gentleman who left the university to take his place in the world of affairs. The ideal was no better or worse but born of a different social tradition from that of other countries and other times. It was expressed, not in the courses of study provided, but in the selection of entrants and in the attitude to learning.

Stephen found fault with the English ideal. He had no sympathy for Fawcett's delight in a narrow curriculum. He wished to broaden the field of studies not only for the poll-man but for those who read for honours. Unlike many dons he recognized that admirable scholarly disciplines existed, each with its own techniques and publications, other than classics and mathematics and the newly founded and despised triposes of the Natural and Moral Sciences. Whatever garden of knowledge you choose to study is surrounded by a wall. The wall is the technique of the subject and to climb it means inevitable drudgery. Why not climb walls which protect gardens of roses rather than force young men to climb those which land them in a plot of cactus? In a series of four articles, contributed to *Fraser's Magazine* after he had left Cambridge, he raised more fundamental questions. Stephen was appalled at the lack of a learned class at Oxford and Cambridge. No one cared if a good man left or stayed, and if he stayed he had to submit to vows of celibacy or take Holy Orders or engage in hack coaching. 'Most of the working men of the place are so steeped in the wearisome details of teaching, enforcing discipline, and administering the college funds, that they have absolutely no time for pursuing an independent course of study.' More professorial chairs could be endowed if the financially wasteful system of independent college teaching were abandoned; and this was unlikely to happen so long as professors remained remote from the undergraduate curricula, their lectures 'sprinkled by a few eccentric individuals who have the singular desire to improve their minds'. To compare Oxford and Cambridge with the intense intellectual activity of German universities would be humiliating. And why was this? Because Cambridge's educational values were wrong. Fawcett liked to boast that Cambridge treated Fellowships as prizes for those who won the tripos races without any nonsensical regulations about research attached to them. But, according to Stephen, this very system of competitive triposes and prize fellowships, often held *in absentia*, was ruinous. It turned triposes into tests of mental agility; examiners were so frightened of cramming that any subject which could be got up was excluded; and nearly all subjects of interest can, of course, be got up – after a fashion. Stephen felt that the mania for testing ability, a quality required for the ordinary kind of worldly success, had so maimed the Cambridge ideal of education that any suggested improvements in the system were judged by the degree to which they increased the spirit of competition for honours and prizes. No wonder English lawyers and theologians were so notoriously narrow-minded.

In this respect Stephen was ahead of his colleagues. 'In the sixties', wrote Maitland, 'he was already advocating the reforms effected by the second Royal Commission in the eighties.' Stephen did not demur, however, at the restriction of entry to the sons of gentlemen. To criticize a past generation for not accepting what we ourselves have only just accepted as normal is supercilious folly; and to argue that Stephen should have advocated open entrance examinations and have crusaded for the abolition, not only of the religious tests but also of the unspoken class tests, would be to ask him to step out of his own generation into our own. G. M. Young has said that the Oxford and Cambridge ideal of the educated gentleman was almost the sole barrier against an all-encroaching materialism and professionalism; and certainly it did much to make earnest people of all classes think of education as something valuable in itself and not as a short cut to political power or crude self-advancement.

Stephen was not at fault in his acceptance of the ideal. But he was at fault in interpreting its possibilities. He wanted dons to be more learned and undergraduates to be given the chance to benefit from this learning, but he did not hope that this would change the character of the undergraduate. On the contrary, he was satisfied with the young men as they were. For Stephen himself was subtly tainted with the English contempt for culture and the world of ideas. Learning and literature were well enough, but what Stephen feared was the atmosphere of mind that they generate in the young. Were there not weeds and deadly nightshade, mandragora and fennel, hidden among the flowers of learning which only an adult mind could distinguish and reject? He had visited Heidelberg after taking his degree and the experience confirmed him in his notions of insular superiority: the only other man he had seen sculling on the Neckar was an Englishman. He thought the English undergraduate, playing cricket and rowing, infinitely superior to duelling philosophizing German louts or spindly French intellectuals arguing about politics and art. And so he informed Matthew Arnold that the English had every right to call themselves 'the best breed in the universe' because there weren't many better. What nobler type of boy was there, for instance, than Tom Hughes's young brother, Harry, whose funeral sermon Stephen preached at Trinity Hall when he broke a blood vessel at athletics and died young? True, it had taken all Stephen's powers to push him through his examinations, yet 'without any special intellectual capacity, he somehow represented a beautiful moral type . . . absolutely unselfish . . . so conspicuously pure . . . so unsuspicious of evil in others . . . sweet and loyal in his nature . . . [which inspired among other undergraduates] profound respect, at least, for the beauty of soul that underlay the humble exterior'.

It is right to tell the clever and the successful not to despise the simple and unaffected, but a different matter to set up such young men as the ideal. Like so many of his contemporaries Stephen worshipped 'character' as a Kantian Thing-in-itself, and failed to realize that character, unless instructed by the intelligence or informed by the emotions, is liable to be exerted on the side of injustice and intolerance. Guts and open-heartedness without some knowledge of the world are not enough, and to believe that 'manly and affectionate fellows' could 'fight a good battle in the world' was to glorify will-power as an end, not a means, and to forget that education means opening, as well as training, the mind. 'I don't care a straw for Greek particles, or the digamma,' mused Tom Hughes's Squire Brown when he sent Tom to Rugby. 'If he'll only turn out a brave, helpful, truthful Englishman, and a gentleman, and a Christian, that's all I want.' But you cannot produce Stephen's or Squire Brown's ideal unless you acknowledge the value of *mousike*, even though you may not define it in terms of Dr Mayor, and of the digamma. Stephen's ideal among intellectual undergraduates was the hard-headed man who stood for no nonsense – a type too often blind to the subtler kinds of sense. Mockery, affectation, frivolity and extravagance are also ways in which young men criticize life, and Stephen would not have been at home in Matthew Arnold's set at Oxford in the 1840s. He was determined to admire nothing and, though men were none the worse for taking time off to read literature or talk politics, he advised them to 'stick to your triposes, grind at your mill, and don't set the universe in order until you have taken your bachelor's degree'. To this he allowed one exception. In politics the young were to be given their head: he himself in his old age did not regret his youthful republicanism. 'A man should be ashamed rather of not having felt in his youth the generous impulses which make him sympathize with whatever appears to be the cause of progress.' He would have understood the motives which led his grandson, Julian Bell, to abandon pacificism and, though no Communist, drive an ambulance in the Spanish Civil War, in which he lost his life: his grandson exemplified 'what a young man ought to become – an enthusiast for the newest lights, a partisan of the ideas struggling to remould the ancient order and raise the aspirations of mankind'.

Stephen was known at Cambridge as a radical and an ardent party man. The genial toughs whom he taught were insufficient for his needs; he sought intellectual companionship and found it in the circle which centred upon Henry Fawcett. Two years Stephen's junior at Cambridge, Fawcett moved to Trinity Hall shortly after coming into residence and was elected a Fellow in 1856. He later became Professor of Political Economy, entered Parliament and served in the administration of 1880 as Gladstone's Postmaster-General where he introduced the parcel post. The two men became close friends, and after Fawcett was accidentally blinded by his father in a shooting accident, Stephen cared for him with feminine tenderness. In those days, wrote Stephen, there were two main circles among the younger men, the literary set who read Tennyson, *Jane Eyre* and sometimes Browning; and the more serious thinkers who discussed *Sartor Resartus* or followed F. D. Maurice as liberal theologians. Fawcett would have nothing to do with the aesthetes, and denounced Carlyle as reactionary and Maurice as muddle-headed; he set himself up as a descendant of the Philosophic Radicals. His mind was uncommonly clear and he admired Cambridge teaching for its distrust of obscurity and ambiguity. 'This shallow stuff does not go down here, does it ?' he used to say. Leslie Stephen fell under his spell and together they declared war on what they called 'dyslogistic' words such as sentimentalism and declamation. Anyone who denounced them as philistines was told roundly that this 'was a name which is best definable as that which a prig bestows on the rest of the species'. The universities were traditional in politics, and though Cambridge had long-standing connections with the Whigs, radicals were few and far between. Blindness had not dimmed Fawcett's high spirits; six foot three and broad in proportion, he rode to harriers and skated fifty miles in a day across the Fens. Together the two firebrands, as young dons should, enjoyed themselves at the expense of the Old Guard. They fastened in particular upon Dr Geldart, the Master of Trinity Hall, an ancient megatherium, who liked his bottle in the evening and asked only to be left in peace. By now he resembled a barnacled dreadnought, straddled by salvoes from port and starboard, his young radical colleagues on the one hand and on the other his wife, a formidable Mrs Proudie of the Evangelical persuasion. One day she sent her husband into a College meeting with strict instructions not to permit F. D. Maurice to preach in St Edward's Church which was in the gift of the College, on the grounds that he held lax views on the subject of Eternal Punishment. Stephen and Fawcett guessed what had happened and innocently enquired the exact nature of the allegedly heretical passages. The Master, unable to make a signal to base, foundered with all hands, and to their delight Maurice preached. Far from disliking him, the rebels regarded Dr Geldart with unassailable affection; and when some years later in 1874 he lay on his death-bed Fawcett visited him and so invigorated the old gentleman that he called for a bottle of port and his fishing tackle to the infinite scandal of Mrs Geldart who forbade a repetition of the visit.[1]

Fawcett's good-natured hard-headedness, however, provided a mingy diet. Uninterested in science, theology or the arts, he was the kind of utilitarian who gloried in using the felicific calculus like a sickle and preached free trade, co-operatives, social equality of the sexes, and the removal of religious tests. He was in spirit nearer to James Mill than to John Stuart Mill. Intellectually Stephen lost by his attachment to Fawcett nearly as much as he gained. Maitland told Henry Jackson that what surprised him about the Stephen of those days was 'his willingness – or more than willingness – to hear Fawcett talk for six hours a day'. He was the only man who could shut him up. "Don't talk like a damned fool, Fawcett," he shouted down the table at an Ad Eundem club dinner when Fawcett was holding forth 'in a somewhat affected and unreal manner . . . which cleared the air'. Maitland came to believe that such was his shyness in the 1850s that he could get on only with the rumbustious. By the 1860s he was self-confident and went electioneering when Fawcett stood for a seat as a Radical. (He won neither at Cambridge nor at Brighton because a Liberal split the vote.) At Brighton Stephen edited a halfpenny newspaper with a new edition every few hours. 'You are the rummiest lot that ever came to Brighton' said the awed sub-agent. His appearance gave

[1] Mrs Geldart found it most difficult to get her husband into a seemly frame of mind. 'I don't know why it is,' she complained, 'but I can't get poor dear Charles to take any interest in the arrangements for his funeral.' As a good Evangelical she waited anxiously for her husband's last words which would indicate that his thoughts were fixed on higher things, but Dr Geldart remained lamentably alloyed with the dross of this world. Feeling the death pangs hard upon him, the flame lit up for the last time. 'You will let the undergraduates have some of the old sherry,' he gasped, and thereupon expired. Mrs Geldart, writes Thomas Henry Thornely, was so appalled that she called for an autopsy and joyfully exclaimed, when the surgeons proclaimed that there was evidence that the Master's mind had become unhinged at the end, 'Clearly not responsible! Clearly not responsible!'

no clue to his profession and the agent who pressed him to stand himself at the next election was struck dumb when his hero replied, 'Damn your soul, Sir, don't you know I am a parson.' He did, however, succeed in getting Fawcett re-elected a Fellow of Trinity Hall when he had got the chair of Political Economy and had married. It was not easy, but Stephen enjoyed a tussle with Ben Latham who was trying to get Fawcett's re-election delayed. Latham twisted and turned but 'I can be very insolent when I choose and I was' – and the opposition gave in for 'sheer want of pluck'. His dislike of Latham never vanished: he distrusted him.

In the formative years Fawcett drove Stephen so far towards the centre of the circle that he never quite had the strength in maturity to struggle towards the periphery. A great critic should stand to one side of his age so that he can see it in perspective. When we think of Dr Johnson or Matthew Arnold or Tocqueville, we can appreciate the advantage a critic enjoys who is not committed to any one of the prevailing ideologies which the majority of men unconsciously choose. The critic should draw a distinction between an attitude and an answer to life. The former is a process of thought. It may rest on a highly dogmatic structure such as Christianity, but the critic will be aware of his duty to revalue, re-open his mind, and keep the antennae of his sensibilities as responsive to new experience as possible. He will always be rearranging old material in new shapes, never satisfied that like Browning's Grammarian he has settled Hoti's business or properly based Oun; he will avoid slipping into a mechanism of thought which does the job for him like an adding machine; and he will judge every new problem on its own merits and not equate it with some similar experience in the past. The latter – the answer to life – is not to be despised. It is essential to politicians who would be unable to conduct their business without it. It assumes that the major questions are settled once and for all and that all change is in effect a modification of the prototype on the floor of the factory. It provides firm ground for the controversialist and by no means implies inferior capability. Still, it is less helpful to a critic. Stephen was handicapped by his early allegiance to the utilitarian system and it was some time before he disentangled himself from Fawcett's influence. Despite their similarity of outlook, there was, however, a noticeable difference between them. Fawcett believed that the best way of learning a subject was to lecture on it. One evening, he announced after Hall, 'Now, I am interested in Socrates, and want to know more about him, so I am thinking of giving a lecture upon him.' 'But, Fawcett,' said Stephen, 'have you read his works?' 'No, but I mean to.' Stephen, on the other hand, was steadily reading philosophy. By 1860 he had read Mill and Comte, Kant and his English adapter Sir William Hamilton, Hobbes and Locke, Berkeley and Hume and most of the main intellectual works of the day; but since his secret activity was unknown to most of his contemporaries they were somewhat surprised when he was appointed in 1861 to examine in the comparatively newly created Moral Sciences Tripos.[1] This interest in philosophy was in the end to cut short his career in Cambridge.

Stephen's Christianity had never been fervent. He had never adhered to the Evangelical party whose foremost members, by the middle of the century, were noted for their piety and philanthropy rather than for their intelligence, and whose committee men were often despicable bigots with a taste for persecution. Even his father had fallen out with them. After his retirement from the Colonial Office, Sir James Stephen had published a volume of essays in one of which, like Tennyson, he faintly trusted the larger hope that sinners *might* in some remote aeon be relieved of their suffering in hell. This hapless blunder was seized upon by people outside as well as inside the Evangelical camp. Shortly after Sir James's retirement the Prime Minister on Macaulay's advice appointed him in 1849 to the Regius Professorship of Modern History at Cambridge and the con-servative party sniffed at the appointment. Would not Sir James now be in a position to pervert the youth of the country? Dr Corrie, the Master of Jesus College, wagged his head at Archdeacon Hardwick. 'Who would have thought we should have seen a live Gnostic walking about the streets of Cambridge? You know, my friend, in healthier times he would have been burnt.'[2] In 1851 Dr Corrie returned to the charge. 'These are dangerous times when an atheist walks about the streets of Cambridge in cap and gown, my friend, in cap and gown!' Accordingly in Leslie's second year as an undergraduate a Grace was offered at a congregation to enquire into Sir James's beliefs and probe for *falsa doctrina*, though the Grace was not put to the Senate. Two years later, in 1853, F. D. Maurice, whose lectures Leslie had attended in London, was bitterly attacked in the Evangelical press for holding similar views and was expelled from King's College, after a series of shabby interviews with the Principal, Dr Jelf. This treatment of two men whom he knew to be deeply religious naturally turned Leslie towards the moderates.

The interesting fact about the episode of Sir James Stephen's religious

---

[1] This tripos included philosophy, political economy, jurisprudence and some history. The office of examiner could hardly be described as exacting since in 1860 there were no candidates at all, and in the first nine years of its institution only sixty-six men took honours.

[2] Dr Corrie was famous for such remarks. When a Dr Donaldson, whose edition of the *Book of Jashar* Corrie had condemned, complained that the Master appeared willing to re-light the fires of Smithfield, Corrie remarked, 'In these economical days he would not be considered worth the faggots'. He could never make up his mind which he disliked most, a radical or a ritualist. Born in 1793, he wielded considerable power in the Church. For thirty-two years he was an excellent tutor of St Catharine's but on failing to be elected Master he was given the Mastership of Jesus College. He also held a lonely Fen living. Dr Corrie was of a reverent though practical frame of mind. Bishop G. F. Browne, visitor of the living, was somewhat disturbed, on going early one morning to the church, to identify a pungent smell which hung inside it. The verger explained: 'Rector doesn't mind smell of gunpowder. He won't have pigeons flappin' about in t' church, not he.' Corrie died, aged 92, in 1885.

beliefs was not that a protest was made, but that the Grace was never put to the Senate. In Cambridge religion was never the issue that it was in the Oxford of Newman and Bishop Wilberforce. Stephen wrote that

The average Cambridge don of my day was (as I thought and think) a sensible and honest man who wished to be both rational and Christian. He was rational enough to see that the old orthodox position was untenable. He did not believe in hell, or in 'verbal inspiration' or the 'real presence'. He thought that the controversies on such matters were silly and antiquated, and spoke of them with indifference, if not with contempt. But he also thought that religious belief of some kind was necessary or valuable, and considered himself to be a genuine believer. He assumed that somehow the old dogmas could be explained away or 'rationalized' or 'spiritualized'. He could accept them in some sense or other but did not ask too closely in what sense. Still less did he go into the ultimate questions of philosophy. He shut his eyes to the great difficulties and took the answer for granted.

Church-going was to perform an edifying ceremony, not to state one's beliefs; and in this spirit Stephen was ordained.

There was more to it than that. Edward Dicey, his earliest and oldest friend, who had been at King's College London with Leslie, believed that Sir James Stephen had made things difficult. Like his son after him, Sir James was haunted by fear of penury and thought Leslie would not succeed in any branch of life in which competition was keen. He distrusted journalism as a paying profession and told Leslie that if he left Trinity Hall he must live at home. Dicey even wondered whether he urged Leslie to take Orders because he himself required reassurance – and indeed Sir James's letters show how inadequate he realized he was in apologetics and how troubled he was by his own generosity of mind which accepted that men such as John Stuart Mill could abandon Christianity and yet be good.

But this is not how Leslie's sister Milly saw the matter. She was the only one of the Stephen children who lived a spiritual life, and she knew Leslie more intimately than anyone at this time in his life. She lamented that Leslie was never able to speak frankly to his father. (As a boy he addressed him as 'Sir', whereas Dicey called his father 'Governor'.) When Leslie was an undergraduate and his father came up to deliver his professorial lectures, Leslie often proposed, much to Sir James's pleasure, that they should go for walks together; but his father (to whom conversation was a monologue) found him 'very inarticulate and very reserved'. According to Milly, Sir James tried 'again and again' to talk to Leslie about taking orders but was baffled by his reticence.

Nor was it surprising that he was baffled. All good Evangelicals believed a man must show that he had a 'vocation for what we had been accustomed to think of as the most sacred of callings'. Milly was startled when her brother told her,'the fact is that you are naturally religious and I am not'. The day before he was ordained, with much courage she taxed him about his state of mind, 'and the only reply I got was, "Oh, never mind – it's all right" '. Milly thought him 'curiously immature at that age and indeed he seemed strangely boyish to the end' – a shrewd comment. His soul was not communing with God: it was in the boats. Dicey too warned him he was as unfit for a clerical career as Dicey himself: Leslie did not resent this frankness and thanked him for his advice. The truth was that he wanted to stay at Cambridge and taking Orders was the only way to do it. 'I took this step', he reproached himself later, 'rather – perhaps I should say very – thoughtlessly. I was in a vague way a believer in Maurice or in what were called Broad Church doctrines. My real motive was that I was very anxious to relieve my father of the burden of supporting me.' That was not entirely true. Stephen wanted to be independent of his family. But he became a clergyman more in order to become a tutor and inculcate young men with the principles of 'fearing God and walking a thousand miles in a thousand hours'. It was a higher ideal than the routine acceptance of a Fellowship as a prelude to a College living leading possibly to a Deanery, but it was much lower than the standards set and practised in Oxford under the influence of the Tractarians.

For this there was a reason. Religious parties were weak in Cambridge and few young Fellows asked themselves where they stood. The 'Sims' or Evangelicals who garnered souls were much despised, partly for snobbish reasons as many of them were sizars and poor undergraduates. The Cambridge Camden Society, whose stratagem for restoring the Round Church had been unmasked as a ritualist plot hatched by the ecclesiologist J. M. Neale,[1] was no longer a force, and the Oxford Movement had not taken root in Cambridge. Stephen recorded that one undergraduate at Trinity Hall turned his gyp-room into an oratory with candles and flowers, but declared that he was exceptional. Even infidelity in the 1860s caused little comment. 'One of our fellows', Stephen noted in a letter, 'wrote a book the other day to prove under a very thin veil, that Christianity was a degenerate kind of Gnosticism. Nobody has taken any notice of it, and if he does not insult people's feelings, nobody will.' In a largely clerical society party loyalties and enmities were inevitable, but they were on the level of gossip and university politics rather than of serious disputes about fundamentals. Stephen was thought to be a rather modern clergyman concerned more with ethics than theology, and the sudden collapse of his faith came, therefore, as a shock even to his

[1] J. M. Neale (1816–66) was a leading Ritualist at one time inhibited from officiating in his diocese by his bishop. The promoter of Anglican sisterhoods, he is best known as a hymnologist: in the first edition of *Hymns Ancient and Modern* one eighth of the total were his translations or original hymns.

intimate friends.

He had been ordained in 1855 and a curiously inexplicable interval elapsed before he took priest's orders in 1859 shortly before his father died; the fact that he became a fully fledged parson shows that he had no serious doubts until after that date. Indeed in 1860 he advised Alfred Ainger to be ordained, and the following year was still, so his mother thought, reading the service 'in an impressive and beautiful manner'. Yet by the summer of 1862 he found himself unable any longer to conduct the chapel services. He informed the Master, who went into conclave with the Fellows of the college. Apparently almost all were unanimous in desiring to retain Stephen as tutor until his doubts resolved themselves one way or another, but a senior Fellow feared for the undergraduates' morals, and Stephen resigned immediately; so far from bearing any malice he rightly thought that under the university statutes, it was the only proper course – and chuckled when shortly afterwards the stern arbiter of morals went off with the wife of one of his friends and mother of six and had to resign *his* fellowship. Fawcett managed to convince his colleagues, quite wrongly, that Stephen's fellowship need not lapse with the tutorship and he therefore continued to hold the offices of bursar and steward and coached the boat. But these pursuits soon appeared futile. His prospects of university office were now ruined.

We shall see later what led to this change of mind. For it was a change of mind rather than a change of heart. 'From the age of fifteen,' wrote John Henry Newman in his *Apologia*, 'dogma has been the fundamental principle of my religion; I know no other religion; I cannot enter into the idea of any other sort of religion; religion, as a mere sentiment, is to me a dream and a mockery.' Stephen agreed with Newman. Facts he had learnt from Fawcett were facts, and if the dogmas of Christianity did not correspond to them, then those dogmas were false and should be rejected. The scales fell from his eyes. As a child Noah's Ark had been his favourite toy; now, like Bishop Colenso, he found that 'it was wrong for me to regard the story (of the Flood) as a sacred truth'. He told himself, wrongly as Maitland judged, that he had never had any faith to give up.

It all seems straightforward. And then suddenly one comes across a sentence which his younger daughter wrote in a memoir of her father. 'Fred Maitland once hinted to me that he thought of suicide.' One of his friends told Maitland that Fawcett said he was with Stephen late one night discussing his troubles and that 'when he quitted him Stephen's state of mind was such that Fawcett entertained serious fears he might cut his throat during the night'. It *may* have been so – and yet it sounds more like a figure of speech typical of that over-emphatic way of speaking which Stephen and Fawcett cultivated. If Fawcett had really believed Stephen was likely to kill himself he would have stayed the night with

him. Later in life, however, he may have forgotten just how anguished he
was. Robert Romer did not forget. 'The pain he suffered was very acute
. . . he knew what grief it would cause to his family.' It was not the shock
of disbelief which struck at his heart. How could he look his mother in the
face, how could he appear to other men what to him was always the test,
an honourable man? He knew that people whom he loved and respected
would be offended. The mortification was intense. As tutor of Trinity
Hall he was known to the undergraduates as a man who above everything
despised humbug, mental and physical laziness, indecision. Yet here he
was, having only the other day taken priest's orders which enabled him to
celebrate Holy Communion, now confessing his inability to believe what
he then professed. Shame made Stephen wish he were dead. He could not
bear to give up the life of the unconventional tutor beloved by the
undergraduates, to give up being something which he longed all his life to
be even if it was expressed in such trivial forms – a leader of men. He
wanted if possible – how few do not? – to have it both ways. Even after he
had resigned the tutorship he was still preaching in 1863 but the two years
he tried to continue as a don were wasted years. Looking back on that
time he was to reflect how odd it was that he, always so anxious about his
prospects, his future, his financial plight, should never then have worried
about his career or taken a thought for the morrow. 'I must get
enthusiastic about something,' he told his sister. 'I have got enthusiasm in
me, but it won't come out.' The truth, as he realized later, was that he was
in those days without ambition and had formed no picture of what his life
was to be or what he wanted to do with it.

No one should underestimate the honesty of the step he took. No one
should exaggerate its importance. Stephen possessed after his father's
death a small private income and he was able to live at his mother's house
in London. Both in temperament and character he was better able to
sustain the change in circumstance than Arthur Clough who had resigned
his tutorship at Oxford in 1848. He had not alienated all his friends in
Cambridge nor was he likely to suffer social ostracism in London where a
freethinker was by no means unique. Moreover, his resignation did not
excite an immediate reaction in favour of toleration in the university. In
1867 Fawcett admitted that the resident members who wished to abolish
the religious tests, whereby only Anglicans could hold Fellowships, were
still in a minority. The dons remained obdurate until Parliamentary
agitation forced them to change their tune. As they saw bills defeated by
ever-decreasing majorities or voted to be read again but shelved owing to
the dissolution of Parliament, they realized that the change must come, so
that by 1869, when Henry Sidgwick resigned spectacularly from Trinity,
the battle was won, even though two more years were to pass before the
university tests were finally repealed. Stephen's action had no direct

political effect. But it had a moral significance, and this subtly affected the political atmosphere. In 1870, testifying before the House of Lords, that wise clergyman and scholar, Bishop Lightfoot, saw that the tests were creating a prejudice in the minds of undergraduates against the religion they were meant to protect. 'They see a man prepared to sacrifice his material interests for the sake of conscientious scruples, and it begets a sort of sympathy for non-belief.' Lightfoot saw further. 'It is impossible to shut one's eyes to the fact that a flood of new ideas has been poured in upon the world, and that at present they have not found their proper level; minds are unsettled in consequence, and young men often do not like to pledge themselves to a very distinct form of religious belief.' Lightfoot had for long opposed the repeal of the tests, but the dignified and high-minded resignations of men such as Stephen convinced him of the *justice* of the reform. Whatever Lightfoot's attitude had been, the tests would eventually have been repealed, but the manner of their repeal owed something to Stephen and his followers. Unless the opposition is convinced that their opponents are governed by the same considerations of seriousness and principle, government by consent becomes impracticable. Taken at its lowest, Stephen's self-sacrifice compelled his opponents to retreat gracefully lest they outlawed themselves in the eyes of public opinion. Though it is necessary on some occasions to assault one's opponents brutally, good behaviour in politics tends in stable times to breed good behaviour. Stephen's action was an example to others, a pronouncement that it is immoral in all circumstances to bow down in the House of Rimmon when a free choice lies before you. Like many other nonconformists who have sacrificed their position for their principles, he deserves praise.

Chapter Two

MAKING A REPUTATION

A Radical in Politics

Leslie Stephen was barely 30 when he left Cambridge, and he had no difficulty in persuading himself that the change in his situation was for the better. Had he continued to remain in Cambridge he declared that he would soon have been covered in a blue mould of premature senility. London was a tonic which restored one to health. It was a new experience to be insignificant. At Cambridge 'I walked about in a gorgeous cap and gown, and everyone I met took off their hats to me. Now in London I find that people don't instinctively recognize me. I can walk down the Strand without causing any visible sensation.' Stephen's ironic references to Cambridge were not sour grapes; most young dons who tear themselves away from the numbing embrace of that insatiable being, who is at once their mother and their bride, never regret the step they take. Cambridge, Stephen thought, was all too pleasant a place for a bachelor. He lived in a delightful set of rooms with no regular working hours, long holidays and leisure; friends were within a stone's throw; gossip, the ritual of Hall and wine, the walks and sports, the curious avenues of enquiry down which he ambled were all amiable ways of wasting time. He floated down the years as serenely as the new-mown grass from the lawns which College gardeners cast into the river. Visitors to Oxford and Cambridge may imagine that the quiet quadrangles and courts provided the perfect atmosphere for scholarly research. They picture the don seated at his desk, piled high with folios, rising occasionally and pacing across the cobblestones to check a reference in the library, breaking his labours only to swallow a few mouthfuls of cold meat at the hour when deference must be paid to the demands of the flesh; is it fancy, as they saunter past sets of panelled rooms on a drowsy afternoon, half drugged by the scent of flowers and the hum of summer insects – is it fancy or does he not hear the scratch of a learned quill on foolscap? And is not this sound to be heard in room after room, in college after college? – so that tomes of learning were being delivered one after another to the press and thence to library shelves?

But in mid-Victorian Cambridge it was quite otherwise. The legend which Abraham Flexner propagated in the 1930s that the ancient universities in England were no more than finishing schools came oddly at a time when Cambridge led the world in research into physics and neural physiology; but the gibe reflected what in Stephen's time had been so. The demands of tuition, of academic rituals and politics, of sociable gatherings and of administering not only the university but the colleges in meetings, where the joys of debate were matched only by the delight of elucidating why certain Fellows had voted which way and for what reasons, inhibited the urge to publish. In mid-Victorian Cambridge there was little or no incentive to do so. Some dons were too indolent; others curled up like snails at the thought of their colleagues' comments; some who might have published possessed too acute a sense of their own limitations in the face of German and French scholarship and were repelled by the sight of books written by those who had yet to acquire such a sense. In the 1860s in England the most interesting works in those subjects which were later to be incorporated within university studies, such as economics, anthropology, politics and indeed much of the natural sciences, were not being written in universities. Had Leslie Stephen stayed in Cambridge he would never have become a literary critic or a controversialist and, like Mark Pattison, he might never have completed his researches on eighteenth-century thought.

He still enjoyed the companionship of College life: he not only remained a Fellow until he married but he would go up to Trinity Hall to collect his dividend or stipend as a Fellow at Christmas and take part in the rituals of the place. In 1866 he was to be found walking thirteen miles in three hours on the way to Newmarket for lunch and back for dinner to dispel the excesses of Christmas Eve dinner in Hall. There were long evenings of jolly talk with Romer, Wolstenholme and Fawcett. He dined with the Vice-Chancellor whom he called Greasy Jem to distinguish him from the Master of Peterhouse, Dismal Jemmy; and, challenged to predict the religion of the future, froze the company by saying that if he could do that he would claim to be the Messiah himself. Conversationally he was an *enfant terrible* much given to irony and chaff about parsons and dogma, a good man to sit next to in Hall and often invited out. The next year he came up again at Christmas and drew his fellowship dividend of £120 – £47 less than the previous year – for the last time.

The sociability of those days was to fade. Ten years after he had resigned his fellowship on marriage and when his first wife was dead he wrote to the woman who was to be his second wife that he once 'smoked and drank to general satisfaction. Now I have learnt to loathe the kind of thing which I then enjoyed. I would rather have my books and my pipe by myself than meet the most attractive party of dons or London people. I am a sort of harmless misanthrope.' His disillusion with celibate Cambridge had set in before that. There were too many young Fellows about in Cambridge baulked by 'the stolid incumbent refusing with unreasonable obstinacy to exchange the vicarage for the graveyard'. Writing to Norton in 1875 about people he had known there, he said:

Some are dead; one cut his throat a week before I went there, leaving a wife and three children without a penny; another whom you know, W. G. Clarke, has softening of the brain and spends all his time at the station watching the trains; others, like Thomson (*sic*) of Trinity, are utter fogies; one or two more are turning grey and bitter and are entangled in long engagements with no hopes of marriage; another has taken to drinking and utterly disgusted me by coming to dinner to meet me and my wife in a state of palpable intoxication. Monroe has finished his big book on Lucretius for a wonder and has since devoted himself exclusively to furnishing his rooms. Sidgwick is the man who is thought to be the best of the lot; and Sidgwick has also published his big book on ethics, which I take to be a monument of wasted ingenuity and now spends his time on investigating 'spiritualism'! Heaven save the mark! He sickened me with his silly ghost stories: but he really is honest and clever and well-meaning: so I ought not to abuse him. The only persons whom I thoroughly liked were Jebb the public orator and Mrs Jebb: but Mrs Jebb is an American lady and so is naturally unlike Cambridge and indeed thoroughly charming. I always like Americans.

In London he lived with his mother and sister in Porchester Terrace. Some scholars have thought this odd. Is it not significant and sinister that his excessive love for his mother induced him to return to the womb? The truth is that it is not significant at all. It was perfectly natural that Stephen who, if not destitute, needed to earn an income, wanted to make his mother's life less lonely and to chaperone, if need be, his sister; after all he was not intending to live with a mistress. (After his second marriage his stepsons although in their twenties regarded his house as their home even after the death of their mother and sister.) Leslie Stephen was induced to write by two common incentives, want of money and boredom. Believing (wrongly) that his parson's orders prevented practice at the Bar – a profession he in any case found unattractive – he resolved to supplement his income by journalism.

Here again Leslie was in luck. His brother Fitzjames was not only a flourishing barrister but one of the leading journalists in the London periodicals. Fitzjames had married in 1855 the daughter of the Evangelical vicar of Harrow, J. W. Cunningham, who edited with diminishing success the *Christian Observer*. Fitzjames became editor and wrote articles for this sober journal to improve his style, though he admitted that 'kind old Mr Cunningham' had to insert some phrases to flavour them with the spice of unction expected by the faithful.[1] To support his family he turned to London journalism and worked his way to become in the 1860s possibly the most distinguished of all the talented contributors to the *Saturday Review*. He was a master of the slashing, exuberant, contemptuous style which made the paper the outstanding intellectual periodical of the day. It was he who introduced Leslie to the editor, John Douglas Cook, and very soon Leslie was writing two articles a week, the one a review and the other a middle on any subject from Poor Law Amendment to Parisian Criminals or the Redundancy of Women. Cook took all he could get, and in 1867 gave Leslie a yearly retaining fee of fifty guineas as a wedding present. Nor was Leslie confined to the *Saturday Review*. Within a month of his settling in London a new afternoon paper costing twopence, the *Pall Mall Gazette*, was founded, and Fitzjames saw to it that an article by his brother appeared in the second number. Here Leslie was again writing in the company of the élite. Trollope, Kingsley and Matthew Arnold contributed to the literary side and Froude, G. H. Lewes and he wrote on politics. The young newspaper which Thackeray had hoped would be a journal written by gentlemen for gentlemen flourished and, incidentally, engaged Engels as its war correspondent during the Franco-Prussian war. In 1866 Leslie also began to write for the *Cornhill* which had been edited by Thackeray, and in addition sent a fortnightly letter on English politics to the New York *Nation* containing descriptions of debates in the House of Commons and some excellent character studies of its members.

His normal routine from 1865 to 1871 of three or four articles a week gives some idea of his capability. He possessed the gift of Victorian concentration. Snorting, groaning and scribbling marginalia, he would seem to idle through a book. Then, taking up a pen and lying almost recumbent in a low rocking chair which he tipped to and fro as he wrote in a small nervous hand, he would complete an article of six thousand words often at a sitting. 'It is one of my weaknesses', he wrote, 'that I cannot work slowly; I must, if I work at all, work at high pressure.' Stephen subscribed with evangelical fervour to the Victorian gospel of work. His grandfather and great-grandfather in their youth were driven beyond prudence by their sexual appetite. Evangelicalism taught Leslie's father and himself to master that appetite and to divert the craving into bouts of intense work. Indeed Leslie's leisure pursuits of walking and mountaineering commanded just as intense application as his writing.

He enjoyed journalism and was adept at catching the tone of the paper

---

[1] More than one view was expressed about the character of Fitzjames's father-in-law. Fanny Trollope savagely caricatured him in *The Vicar of Wrexhill*; on the other hand the Duchess of Beaufort wrote: 'It is so delightful to think of having for our companions throughout the endless ages of eternity such men as Mr Cunningham.'

to which he was contributing. But he had to be careful, since his religious views and his politics were not those of a gentleman writing for gentlemen. 'Stephen and I', wrote John Morley, himself making his name on the *Saturday Review*, 'were shut out from political writing, for we were both of us in politics inexorable root and branch men', and they were warned off controversial subjects especially as the owner of the paper was a High Churchman. If Stephen wished to air his agnosticism he had to take to the pages of *Fraser's Magazine*, edited by J. A. Froude. In 1866 he began to publish on religious subjects in other periodicals, but it was not until Morley took over the *Fortnightly Review* that he found one sufficiently radical to suit his taste. Meanwhile, he pressed on with his own private reading. He contemplated an essay on the United States, but abandoned the idea and settled down to long evenings of philosophical study and annotation, Spinoza, Hegel, Comte, Strauss and Renan.

Amid this mass of work the fortnightly letters to the New York *Nation* entertained him most, which was not strange because Stephen had visited the United States at the height of the Civil War. In 1863, tired of the snobbery of the Confederate supporters at Cambridge, he had determined to go to the North and see for himself at first hand American democracy at work. Leslie Stephen was one of the very few intelligent Englishmen who found the United States sympathetic. Still riled by the independence of the colonies, despising Americans as low-bred boors, a generation of English travellers from Harriet Martineau to Dickens confirmed their countrymen in their attitude of superiority. Stephen realized only too well that this upper-class dislike of the North sprang from dread of democracy. 'The whole affair is looked upon in this country as a breakdown of democracy; that is one of the main causes of the absence of sympathy (for the North),' one of the leader writers on *The Times* noted. Would it not be proved if the North was defeated, that the best form of government was a stable aristocracy of landowning peers and squires, leavened by a number of bankers and merchants and a few men of exceptional intelligence? If this was proved, then movements for extending the franchise were manifestly inexpedient and possibly seditious. Led by *The Times*, upper-class opinion was solid for the aristocratic Free Trade South, which was portrayed as menaced by a corrupt, protectionist democracy, while the North was accused of hypocrisy because their President would not take the stump in favour of emancipation. The North could find support only in the industrial areas of England. When the Federal army ran Russell, the pro-Unionist *Times* correspondent, out of the country, enraged by his accurate reporting of the rout of Bull Run, the last English journalist of importance who might have done something to educate public opinion disappeared; and Delane was at liberty to substitute an editorial policy of animosity against the

North in place of a cogent examination of the facts. *The Times* represented official English opinion for Americans, and Stephen therefore underwent something of an ordeal on his visit. As an hereditary Claphamite he naturally favoured the abolition of slavery, but could not convince Americans, especially after Lincoln's proclamation in favour of emancipating the slaves, that Englishmen did not regard the issue of slavery as crucial. He could point to the fact that John Bright and Morley supported the North and that a fellow radical, Goldwin Smith, had addressed large sympathetic meetings at which *The Times* was hissed, but he had to tell his hosts that Englishmen were incapable of understanding the constitutional issues at stake. Delane saw to it that the North should get no quarter. The evicted Russell declared, 'As I from the first maintained the North must win, I was tabooed from dealing with American questions in *The Times* even after my return to England.'

To visit a country in time of war, more especially of civil war, is a delicate matter. The easy course is to flatter one's hosts by telling them what they want to hear, but it is even easier to scatter unintentional insults by laying one's finger on their obvious weakness which they by a Freudian process have conveniently forgotten. The way in which Stephen was accepted shows what strength of character he possessed and how his integrity impressed his hosts. He prided himself on his tough 'realist' attitude to politics which enabled him to see that 'the North are destroying slavery, not because they are abolitionists, but because the South depends on slavery. That seems to me as plain as two and two makes four.' His shrewd observations during his trips to New York, Washington and the battle-front enabled him to understand American democracy better than other Englishmen. He was English enough to think that American statesmen were an inferior breed – by which he meant that Jefferson and Hamilton were not the equal of Burke and Canning – and to admit surprise that Lincoln was 'more like a gentleman to look at than I should have given him credit for from his pictures'; and when some years later he contributed to a volume of essays in 1867 advocating a second Reform Bill, he was careful to point out that the abuses of democracy which the English always triumphantly pointed to in America were purely indigenous.[1] Corruption in American public life disgusted him, but it took more than average cleverness to see that machine politics was a concomitant of the continual flow of illiterate immigrants who looked to the local bosses for protection; and he added that subtler means of financial and social inducement to procure favours were not unknown in

[1] Stephen made a number of simple points. He began by saying that democracy need not necessarily swamp intelligence. How could Congress bulge with cultivated statesmen when the general level of culture in the country was so low? He himself was prepared to rely on the snobbery of the English electorate, even with full enfranchisement, to return a sound quota of the sons of the aristocracy to the House of Commons for some time to come.

England. Stephen was a sensible traveller in that he knew that a few months spent in a country is just long enough for a man to misunderstand everything of importance, and he resisted Fawcett's appeals to pour out a flood of radical pamphlets on his return. He realized that Englishmen were likely to remain ignorant of America, but he could not forgive the men whose duty it was to lighten that ignorance; and two years after his return he attacked *The Times* in a long and brilliant pamphlet under the worldly-wise anonymity of initials. It was irrelevant, Stephen declared, whether *The Times* were right or wrong about the causes and progress of the war. 'But I contend that I have proved . . . that it was guilty of "foolish vituperation", and as I am weak enough to think anything a serious evil which tends to alienate the freest nation of the old world from the great nation in the new . . . I contend that I have proved *The Times* to be guilty of a public crime.' And he spoke as he did 'to withdraw our countenance from the blustering impostor who has been speaking all this time in our name without any due authority'. Stephen was right. Where there is a serious conflict of interest between two nations, fervent appeals to the principles of friendship and fair play tend to bring morality in politics into disrespect, because people apprehend that the issues cannot be solved by a simple appeal to the rights and wrongs of the case; but where, as in the case of Britain and the United States, there was no fundamental political rivalry, *The Times* had done wrong to embitter relations needlessly between the two countries. Its factious policy brought retribution in the shape of a lasting distrust by Americans of British foreign policy.

Stephen's American tour gave him something more than the satisfaction of a good nonconformist in championing the right. So far we have seen him as a man with many younger cronies but few intimate friends; deeply attached only to Fawcett or to some odd Cambridge fish such as Joseph Wolstenholme, a mathematician and walker who had the gift of being able to spout thousands of lines of poetry by heart, as the evening fell and the pair of them pounded the last ten miles of the grind back to Cambridge. But now he was beginning to develop a talent for friendship. As he grew older he shunned acquaintances, and the friends he made became devoted to him, so that in their correspondence a great warmth of affection breathes through the written word. In America he made three friends in particular. The closest in the end proved to be Charles Eliot Norton of Harvard, and another was the young Oliver Wendell Holmes, later the great Justice of the Supreme Court. The third came from the same milieu, and their letters to each other reveal what Stephen sought and found in friendship.

This third friend was James Russell Lowell, to whom Stephen presented a letter of introduction from their common friend Tom Hughes. Of the bluest blood in New England, a scion of Boston, Lowell was then the acknowledged high priest of culture in Cambridge, Massachusetts. His career had all the auguries of brilliance; the cleverest young man of his class, rusticated from Harvard for excessive vitality and bumptiousness, he had redeemed himself by a dazzling success at the age of twenty-nine with the Yankee folklore of *The Biglow Papers*. His inherited conservatism melted on his marriage to a New England beauty, Maria White, who was the centre of a circle of young radical Abolitionists. Rejoicing in his ancestry and Americanism, Lowell was overflowing with bitterness against the insults of British opinion. 'England *can't* like America do what she or we will,' he wrote to Stephen after his visit. 'But I think the usages of society should hold between nations, and see no particular use in her taking every opportunity to *tell* us how disagreeable and vulgar we are'; and he spoke with pride and sorrow of his cousins and nephews who had fallen in the war and asked Stephen whether they were the sort of men *The Times* had in mind when it referred to Federal officers as blackguards. In Stephen, however, Lowell found more than a sympathetic Englishman. Here was a fellow bookman who could cap his quotations. Lowell was already the doyen of American letters with all the Bostonian faculty for snubbing a hick. 'Who in the world ever heard of the Claudian Emissary?' exclaimed the young novelist Howells, exasperated by Lowell's omniscience. 'You are in Cambridge, Mr Howells,' came the chilling reply. Stephen was spared this side of Lowell's tongue, and he noticed that Lowell was peculiarly sensitive to his listener's state of mind and possessed an 'awkward power of penetrating one's obscurer feelings . . . so acute that he was naturally secure from ever becoming tiresome. Of all the qualities that make an agreeable companion, certainly one of the chief is an intuitive perception of the impression you are making.' Cambridge, Mass., learnt to commune with Cambridge, Eng. In Lowell's study at his large Georgian house, Elmwood, the two men would sit, attired in velvet jackets and puffing at pipes, hour after hour, submerged in an intimate silence to be broken by a comment on some point which would lead to a barrowload of volumes, scored with pencil marks, being scattered over the floor in search of a reference. Calderón, Boccaccio, Dante – Lowell had read them all and could nod to authors in most dead and living languages. This was the kind of scholar Stephen could admire, tossing hay in the meadow by morning, knowing every bird and flower by name, revelling in Yankee speech and drinking whisky-toddy by night. Grunts of pleasure greeted Lowell's jocular verse and erudite puns, and when the visit ended they parted with a long, strong handshake at the corner of the road under the lamp which both men looked back to with emotion till the end of their days. It was to Lowell's house that Stephen hurried on his second visit to America in 1868 when his wife had fallen ill, and it was to Stephen that Lowell went to recuperate from his official duties during his appointment as Minister to the Court of St James in the 1880s. Lowell stood godfather – or, as Stephen preferred to say, in quasi-sponsorial relation – to his daughter Virginia, and Stephen obeyed a summons to Elmwood to visit him for the last time in 1890, the year before he died; he had invited Stephen because he thought him 'the most lovable of men'.

What were the causes of this affinity? Their common Puritan stock had much to do with it. They both shied from indecency in literature and judged that a biographer had betrayed his trust if he unveiled any weakness which should have been left in modest obscurity. Great was Lowell's rage when Froude asserted that Carlyle was impotent and that the great prophet's marital life was a model of incompatibility. Stephen said he was equally shocked; to publish such stuff now was 'a needless outrage'. Lowell deplored the fact that 'biography, and especially that of men of letters, tends more and more towards these indecent exposures . . . There are certain memoirs, after reading which one blushes as if he had not only been peeping through a key-hole but had been caught in the act.' Stephen echoed him in his review of the published Browning love letters. Sometimes it is almost impossible to distinguish between the two voices in the Elmwood study, especially when they mourn to each other the loss of their wives; each of them has sacred places to which they would fain make pilgrimage – the heavily sardonic phraseology is identical. Their attitude to sinful pleasure was also similar; commenting on Stephen's essay about the New England Calvinist theologian, Jonathan Edwards, Lowell wrote, 'If he had only conceived of damnation as a spiritual state, the very horror of which consists (to our deeper apprehension) in its being delightful to who is in it, I could go along with him altogether.' Stephen was, also, just the man to be taken in by the false honesty, the overripe confession spoken in a deprecating, mock-modest tone that is the sincerest form of self-flattery, which Lowell so often employed; as when Lowell admitted that he had as a young man put a pistol to his head but did not have the courage to pull the trigger, 'of which I was heartily ashamed, and am still whenever I think of it'. This kind of revelation would convince Stephen that his host was a manly fellow, too brave to commit suicide, but too honest not to admit that fear to some extent deterred him.

It is possible that he was also taken in by Lowell's professed radicalism. Lowell soon forgot his youthful attacks on law, order, and the Constitution. He believed in a Bostonian conception of democracy which was fast passing, if, indeed, it had ever existed. He told Tom Hughes that he would never give up a thing if it had roots, and Stephen noted that in the Civil War the barb which festered in Lowell's mind longest was the English assumption that all Americans were low-bred immigrants. On his return from his diplomatic mission abroad, Lowell bewailed the state of American democracy, ruined by corruption and the Irish; it was a 'kakistocracy rather, for the benefit of knaves at the cost of fools'. Insensibly he moved closer to the ideals of the country he had so bitterly criticized. As Minister in London he found himself at home, admired for his after-dinner speeches and courtly felicities, a natural hidalgo. He could still see through the English and pray Americans to retain some of their dynamic vulgarity, and he was astonished by the innuendoes of certain low-bred politicians that he had been bought by English culture. 'These fellows', he complained, 'have no notion what love of country means. It is in my very blood and bones. If I am not an American, who ever was?'

Lowell was indeed an American but of a special caste. What Stephen took to his heart was less America than New England. The last of a line of Cambridge Brahmins when the strain was running thin, Lowell's youthful rebellions had always been a little forced, as ill-fitting as his poetical effects were contrived, and after his wife's death, Harvard reclaimed him as a professor and tamed her wayward son. His poems echoed every poet in turn. Economics, trade unions, science ('I hate it as a savage hates writing, because I fear it will hurt me somehow'), were all anathema. Stephen's agnosticism disturbed him. 'I find no fault', he wrote, 'with a judicious shutting of the eyes' and he complained that Stephen seemed to think that there was something dishonest as well as undignified in drifting about on the hencoop after Science had scuttled the old ship of Faith. He liked to lie in an intellectual easy chair and guzzle books, adhering 'to the old notion of literature as a holiday'. When Lowell could not lean on the word genius, he was undone. Deprecating originality in anything which he was unfamiliar with, he was imprisoned by the good-form standards of his own class. Mercifully, however, few people select their friends for their intellectual merits alone. Reading between the lines of Stephen's letters to Lowell, we detect a certain reserve: Stephen praises Lowell's writing primarily for evoking memories of Elmwood. Stephen understood better than Lowell the way he related to the world; and they ended their days in different political camps.

Unlike Lowell there was a sense in which Stephen remained a radical all his life. It is worth while pausing to gauge what kind of a radical he was. Until now the common-rooms of the ancient universities had been associated in people's minds with insensate conservatism. In the 1860s there was a significant change in Oxford and Cambridge. Mill became the most widely read philosopher, and much to Robert Lowe's disquiet first the Quarterly, then the Athenaeum and the Contemporary Review noted the emergence of a new kind of radical don. Morley boasted that in future radicalism would have support in the ancient universities; and in 1867

Stephen was one of those, his cousin A. V. Dicey and Bryce among them, who contributed to a volume called *Essays on Reform*. But Stephen was a radical with a difference. He would not subscribe to the confident dogmas of the left. Of his target he was certain enough. 'It would be hard to say that the majority of English landlords have not attended pretty fairly to their interests as a class or that they have not, on the whole, been distinctly opposed to all the great causes which have lately attracted the sympathy of European intelligence.' There must be some change to enlarge the electorate and permit Parliament to represent other interests. Stephen judged that in 1867 out of 658 seats in the House of Commons, 500 were held by the landed interest of which 326 were directly connected with the aristocracy. Two members alone could be said directly to represent working-class interests. But he did not proceed triumphantly to declare that the case for reform was therefore self-evident. He wanted to convince his readers that men of intelligence and character would be returned to a reformed Parliament. First he agreed that the familiar arguments against democracy were justifiable enough when one considered the United States, especially in those States which had just been established in the West; but for many reasons the low level of intelligence and probity among Congressmen would not be replicated in Britain. The fact that John Stuart Mill had been returned in a large popular constituency such as Westminster confirmed the experience in France where men of intellectual distinction had been returned in numbers. Nor need the aristocracy tremble. Englishmen dearly loved a lord – even a radical lord such as the future father of Bertrand Russell, Lord Amberley. They deferred to the rich and the socially eminent because by and large all classes liked the established order of things. Enlarge the electorate and aristocratic rule would still persist, and so would the nobility's monopoly of patronage. No new order which could capture the imagination of the masses was remotely in sight.

Nor was the new gleaming machinery of democratic reform likely to make all that difference. The ballot box would not regenerate mankind. Proportional representation was not worth the candle. 'We confess to a general prejudice against reforming mankind by clever arithmetical dodges.' 'The more we apply the scientific spirit to the investigation of social problems the more we are struck with the essential continuity of history and the impossibility of introducing spasmodic change.' In passages which recall the theory of society he was later to construct Stephen reiterated that societies are not assemblages of mechanical parts but composed of living tissue which changes organically – and slowly. Why then bother to effect conscious reforms of the franchise? Stephen appears almost to have made out the case which his political opponent, Robert Lowe, argued, for leaving well alone.

But then came the case for reform. 'Men may not have been made equal by being called equal but the masses of men were encouraged in the great virtue of self-respect.' It might be true that for generations to come the upper classes would still be ruling for a simple reason: power went to those who controlled the wealth of the country. It might appear to be wise, as Frederic Harrison said, that experts should rule and members of Parliament should refrain from meddling in the details of legislation. But in the end 'rough popular methods' were necessary. To ignore the need for reform 'tends directly and energetically to increase that profound division of classes which is one of the great evils of the time'. If it became common for some working-class members of Parliament to be returned, it would be a cheap price to pay for filling the social gulf: if trade unionists never sat in the legislature, they would look to other means of getting their voice heard. Still, Stephen was no great democrat. He looked to parliamentary reform as the means to deflect the vested interests who encouraged Britain to remain an inefficient country with a scandalous record in public education. But the way the Reform Bill passed with Conservatives voting against their principles and Liberals divided and muddled sickened him.

These are wise words, words appropriate to the temper of the times, words which express both concern for working-class interests and for the election to Parliament of Platonic guardians to initiate measures which the governing class would be too indolent or self-interested to introduce themselves. But they are not words to set the Thames on fire. The British electorate has never had much regard for Platonic guardians. Nor was there much place for them in a House of Commons that would be exposed to the insults and buffooneries of Lord Randolph Churchill or Lord Hugh Cecil. Stephen retained his contempt for aristocratic rule and the deference which sustained it. He sparred with the ancient universities and public schools, took off the mufflers to attack Governor Eyre and called the Anglican church 'the church of a class, an inveterate foe to the new social hope as we know her to be to new scientific truth'. The spectacle of the bishops, the Whigs and the Tory squires throwing out time and again legislation which would have curbed the vested interests of rank and possessions enraged him.

In this he parted company with the two well-known jurists, his cousin A. V. Dicey and his fellow Alpinist, James Bryce. Their books *Law and Public Opinion* and *Modern Democracies* resemble spits of sand already engulfed by the tide of the new radicalism. They feared what intellectuals often fear, that the shift in power towards the lower classes will destroy the quality of life which they as intellectuals hold most dear. Of the band of intellectual radicals of the 1860s only Stephen's close friend John Morley stayed the course. It would be wrong to picture Stephen as satisfied by the second Reform Bill and the legislation of Gladstone's first administration. On the contrary: he became more gloomy and thought the government of the country was becoming more and more a 'mere branch of stock-jobbing. Everywhere the division between classes widens instead of narrowing.' He admired Bismarck more than Gladstone. The Liberal Education Act was to his mind ruined by the sectarianism of the churches whose power instead of declining seemed to be stronger than ever. Gladstone seemed imprisoned by pressure groups and party hacks. Where were the new institutions and ideas needed for the new age? Stephen thought Liberalism was applying the wrong remedies.

Young radicals often find that in middle age their causes, once apparently so unachievable, one by one drop off the tree like ripe apples. They find themselves with groaning baskets and are unwilling to gather more: the apples remaining on the tree look sour and likely to turn their stomachs. The crudity of reformers repels them; and certainly by 1874 Stephen found Fawcett's optimism unbearable and thought that but for the accident of their sojourn at Cambridge they would never have become friends. He lost interest in politics because he saw that the principles which he had applied with such zeal in the 1860s had degenerated into formulae and that he lacked the ability to give them new meaning. Liberal principles were merely 'pretexts for acting in a convenient way'; when British trade needed peace, Liberals were Quaker pacifists; when foreign competition turned Britain imperialist, Quaker precepts were condemned as cowardly. He agreed with Morley that politics were not an art or a science but a dodge, and he commended Bagehot's 'good, sweeping, outrageous cynicism' and his dictum that illusion is a necessity in politics. Lamenting in his old age the decay of the Gladstonian programme of peace, retrenchment and reform, Stephen wrote:

> We are sometimes invited to regret the insensibility of Englishmen to 'ideas'. The regret may be softened by the reflection that in politics an idea means a device for saving thought. It enables you to act upon a little formula without taking the trouble to ask whether it be or be not relevant to the particular case.

Stephen disliked a life in which illusions and compromise were the realities, and principles were appearances. Unlike Lowell, who was bewildered by the developments in American politics, Stephen knew that he was temperamentally unsuited to the game and was wise enough not to waste his energies on a frustrating pursuit. And also, unlike Lowell, his sympathies were nearly always instinctively with the little man and against the Establishment. Jeffrey von Arx may well be right in thinking that disillusionment with practical politics goaded Stephen to turn to political theory and the discovery of the laws governing social development. After the débâcle of Syracuse Plato wrote the *Laws*.

The First Marriage

The Leslie Stephen who settled in London in 1865 was still recognizable as the boy who had gone up to Cambridge fifteen years before, though in the United States he had grown a beard, the bright red straggling growth with which he was afterwards to be inseparably connected in people's minds. He still inwardly distrusted himself. Freed from celibate university life, and now in his middle thirties, he wanted to marry. But who – surely no one – could wish to marry him? 'I was shy, diffident, and fully impressed with the conviction acquired at Cambridge that I was an old don.' Bachelors, especially Cambridge bachelors in those days, were apt after the age of forty to go one of two ways. Either they became old maids, fussy, prudishly and primly garbed, valetudinarians whose cupboards bulged with tonics, pills and lotions; or they gyrated in orbits of ever wilder eccentricity, their trousers supported by string, their socks attached to combinations by paper-clips, their rooms an asylum, the walls padded by decades of unread newspapers and letters from scholars long since dead. Receipted bills were filed by flinging them up on the top of wardrobes, forgotten mutton chops mouldered beneath a mountain of discarded research, and some ancient beldam forbidden to disturb the dust of ages eventually became the sole companion of their dying years. Such visions of the future appalled Stephen and inspired him to look about before he should be 'dried up into a hopeless mummy, "walking about to save funeral expenses", and with a soul that ought to rattle like a dried pea in a pod'. He hoped he was not too far gone to be revived, but feared that no girl would look at him.

At this time two young ladies were much on the mind of literary hostesses in London. William Makepeace Thackeray had died in 1863 leaving two daughters, Anne Isabella and Harriet Marian, living by themselves in Onslow Gardens. In March 1865 they lunched with Lady Stephen, and in June Leslie and his sister with Fitzjames and wife took them by train to Henley where they hired a boat and rowed down the river to Maidenhead. Leslie also met the sisters at the house of his father's successor at the Colonial Office, Herman Merivale, and of George Smith, the publisher of Thackeray. Mrs Gaskell saw Leslie and the Thackeray girls together at the latter house and prophesied that he would marry. The two sisters were by no means alike. Anny's face was round and plain, her figure short and dumpy, and conversation poured from her in floods: vivacious and entertaining, she was already hatching a clutch of novels. Of Minny, on the other hand, her father wrote that at 21 she was 'absurdly young for her age for she still likes playing with children and kittens and hates reading and is very shy tho' she does not show it and very clever tho' she does not do anything in particular and always helps me out of scrapes which I am getting into'. Thackeray had given them a cosmopolitan upbringing: they could both handle French and German with some competence. Minny grew up to be a beauty. 'Her beautiful bronze hair, brilliantly white teeth and delicate complexion . . . gave one the impression of the most exquisite freshness' – thus one of her friends described her. 'One day she would look like the young girl she really was, and on the next twenty years older, so varying were her moods and expressions . . . She was one of those people who do not *like*; they love and are beloved in return.' It soon became obvious that Leslie was taken with her, but how was he to be made to conquer his diffidence and be brought up to the mark? There was a Mrs Huth – wife of the rich bibliophile and friend of Thackeray who bought the new house the novelist had built just before his death for £2,000 more than Thackeray had paid in building it – who had taken a special fancy to Minny. Mrs Huth was a great lionizer, and had worshipped Buckle whose works she vainly tried to make Minny read. But she was also, like many Victorian matrons, an inveterate matchmaker. She suspected what was up, put what Minny called 'corkscrew' questions, but took no offence when Minny declined to be decanted. Since she was going to Switzerland, she invited the two sisters to go with her to Chamonix, and Minny shamelessly badgered the party to move on to Zermatt where she knew Leslie was staying. Stephen walked towards his fate. 'One of my sacred places ever afterwards was a point where the road winds round a little bluff near Täsch. Thence I descried the party approaching on mules . . . and walked back with them to Zermatt . . . I began to know that my fate was fixed.' Nevertheless, he displayed a certain hesitation in meeting it and hastened away to keep a date with Bryce, the historian, in Vienna, where also, incidentally, he began his long friendship with George Meredith. Back in London in the autumn he waited but could not bring himself to decide. Then, hearing a rumour that the Thackeray girls were annoyed with him for not calling, he pulled himself together. The day came when 'I lunched by myself at the Oxford and Cambridge club, thought over the whole affair in a philosophic spirit and went to 16, Onslow Gardens.' He proposed and was accepted. Mrs Huth congratulated herself and set about with no success at all to lionize Herbert Spencer; everyone rejoiced; and on 19 June 1867 Leslie and Minny were married in a seemly but rather unusual manner, described by Leslie's mother as 'a most original wedding – at 8 o'clock in the morning . . . nobody invited, but a large number of friends and acquaintances assembled'.

They went for their honeymoon to the Alps and the spirited letters which they both wrote to Anny showed the joy they found in each other. Minny declared that crossing three passes in a day was well enough but for the fact that it was obligatory to eat a meal of bread and honey at the top of each. Leslie teased her for saying that she had seen the place where the Rhine flows into the Rhone 'showing the effect of crossing three passes on a weak mind'. She called him Lez and he nobly restrained himself from climbing more than one or two Alps. But she was content to be left to read in the hotel and to make uninhibited comments on her reading. 'Poor old Queen, what a time the Prince must have had with her,' was her comment on the Queen's life of Prince Albert. 'I am trying not to look out of the window,' she wrote to Blanche Warre-Cornish, 'for if I do I shall see the Matterhorn with the moon shining on it and you can't think how horrid it looks, like a great hooky sort of gleaming ghost. I always think it will come and poke its great hook nose into the window.' Despite the phallic inference which some might read into this sentence the honeymoon seems to have held no terrors. 'It is the greatest nonsense to say that new married couples are shy and miserable,' Minny reported. It was too hot to go to Venice – though two years later they went there and Minny declared that Leslie found it 'scrumptious' – but they went to Milan which Leslie found shabby and dirty and he took against the dandies whom, he said, he would not touch with tongs. On their return to London, they set up house in Onslow Gardens. Stephen had had to endure the usual quizzing from Fawcett and other friends. 'Miss Thackeray is the youngest, isn't she, Stephen? Yes. Does she write, as well as her sister? No. Doesn't she write occasionally? No. Doesn't she help her sister to write? No. Wouldn't she write well if she did write etc. etc. etc. which I succeeded in stopping by inextinguishable laughter.' A letter of his survives scribbled with the point of a fork on the menu of a dinner of the Political Economy Club, 'My dearest Minny, I am suffering the torments of the damned from that God-forgotten Thornton, who is boring on about supply and demand, when I would give anything to be with you. He's not a bad fellow, but just now I hate him like poison. O-o-o-o-o-o-oh!'

'I feel like a frozen animal that has been taken in and thawed by benevolent people,' Stephen wrote. He cooed over Minny entranced with his new and frightening acquisition. She was an English rose, a Victorian girl untouched by education, 'pure-minded,' he said, 'as happily many are pure-minded, and free from any taint of coarseness or conceit or self-consciousness which destroy the true ring of the natural affections'. She had a peculiar charm of her own, wayward and changeful and quaintly picturesque. Her mind was untrained but her intuition was sharp and the good sense of her judgements perpetually astonished her husband – after he had decided to act contrary to her advice.

Love for Stephen was a simple emotion. Passion, obsession, delusion could never steal upon him unseen, breed about his heart and possess him.

The fascinating and alluring, and those attractions which are mysteriously generated by the temperament and physique, were alien to his nature and repelled him. Love meant devotion: to adore and to be adored. Minny not only adored him and did her best to make him wear slightly less tattered clothes on holiday, but she also got on with her mother-in-law and with Fitzjames, to whom when he was codifying the law in India she wrote artless letters like a brook flowing over stones. There was the behaviour of Leslie's dog Troy who had had his nose scratched in a maul, 'I never knew such a dog for getting into mischief'. There was her cat Turkey who drank Troy's milk and boxed his ear, 'I never knew such an impudent cat'. There was the weighty problem of going to church. Somehow they never went: Anny believed, but invariably found herself at the point of going too busy with other matters, whereas although 'I enjoy going to Church . . . and from force of habit like the hum of the service . . . on the whole I can't believe it can be right to go and join in a service in which I don't believe.' In 1868 Leslie took her to America which she liked but by the end of the trip got tired of being so civil and on her best behaviour. She thought, so she said, of bringing back a small black boy and told herself that she must go out and smell a few as she would not want guests to rush from her house when Buttons opened the door, though she believed that the smell had gone since they had been abolitioned. Her wit was very much of her class and time: as is ours.

Stephen regarded his wife as a soothing creature who would dissipate worry, attend his needs and bend to his will, but discovered to his surprise that Minny had a determined chin. She would not kow-tow to her sister-in-law. One day she would be bright and determined, on another grey and stiff; she was in fact growing up fast and the use of her natural intelligence was giving her confidence. Moreover he had another cross to bear. Since for reasons of Victorian propriety Anny was living with them at Onslow Gardens, Stephen found that he had also married a sister-in-law. He might have managed Minny alone, but Anny was beyond his control. She had the habit 'which I cannot unreservedly applaud' of looking on the bright side of things. Gay, utterly haphazard, for ever in a muddle, she was unable to distinguish facts from her own interminable fancies. She wrote novels – but were they, Leslie asked himself, as good as they should have been? 'Once when a story of hers was published in Australia, the last chapter got into the middle and nobody found out – in Australia, at any rate.' The Stephens decided that her Irish blood had somehow overpowered her father's strain: they would tame and reform her. They told her she was a sentimentalist and erratic; Fitzjames advised her on a systematic course of reading, 'Macaulay, Gibbon, etc. It was well meant advice, but,' said Leslie, 'I could afterwards have told him, utterly useless.' Fitzjames reviewed one of her stories by comparing her to Jane

Austen 'with ponderous insistence upon the negative merits' of Anny's tiny offering. It was then that Minny spoke up. 'Fitzy', she exclaimed, 'does not see that Anny is a genius!' Anny and Minny were by no means pliable, and since Minny sided with her sister, Leslie found himself to his chagrin only half her master. 'Anny and Minny used to call me the cold bath from my habit of drenching Anny's little schemes and fancies with chilling criticism.' The weighty analysis he applied to destroying a chapter of Buckle had no relevance in his sister-in-law's world. More than ten years after he had known her, he was still trying to reform her by telling her that if she must write about Madame de Sévigné she must first be a 'thorough critic', next study French history in depth, then read all the memoirs of the time and finally sort out the bibliographical problems of the period.

But there was worse to come. Anny not only muddled her facts, she muddled her figures. She was, he complained, far too generous and 'imprudent in money-matters'. Why, she even went so far as to spend the money that she earned from the publication of her stories. Worse, she could not pay her share of the household expenses and often led Minny into making rash purchases. He made scenes with her over unpaid bills, she promised to amend, but somehow the promises slipped her mind. Sometimes she roared with laughter and flipped a coin at him. And then she *would* talk in the evenings when he wished to be silent, and of these occasions he said in self-defence, 'she was always the aggressor'. Stephen could be memorably silent, and the arrival of guests was no deterrent. 'I am, I think, the most easily bored of mankind,' he offered as an excuse, and the cheerless obmutescence which would descend about him was an omen of a sudden exit to his study leaving his wife to cope as best she could with the guests. Edmund Gosse has described one of these evenings. Indeed, he could hardly forget it. Bidden with Robert Louis Stevenson to dine, the two young aspirants hurried round expecting to meet the literary world of London. Instead they were greeted by the Stephens and Anny Thackeray. Their host remained bowed and speechless throughout the whole of dinner and, at first bewildered, they found themselves mesmerized into a similar state of oral paralysis. It was left to Anny to burble away in an unbroken monologue. But when she exclaimed, 'Indeed I tell my maid everything', even Minny was moved to say, 'Oh yes, Anny, and we do wish you wouldn't,' while the gloom fell again over the company and Anny's silvery laughter rang round the dining-room. Yet, although the companionship of a sister-in-law is not the natural recipe for a successful marriage, Leslie was proud of his wife and content. In the spring of 1868 Minny had a miscarriage and in December 1870 when she gave birth to a daughter, Laura, the child had to be wrapped in cotton wool for more than a month. They called her Meemee, and Stephen

rejoiced in the happiness of the family life. Writing to Holmes, he said,
'Did you ever remark what a beautiful object a small baby is? I never did
before, but I see it now. As for a mother and child in the attitude of a
Madonna, I can only say that the sight goes some way to reconcile me to
papists.'

Family life forced him to work even harder at his journalism, and
though enjoyable he began to find it unsatisfying, for at the back of his
mind an idea for a large scholarly work was germinating. He ground
away on the *Saturday Review*, sneering at virtue and enthusiasm, as he
put it, but the routine became meaningless. Ought he to live on bread and
water and produce a *magnum opus* establishing certain everlasting laws
of human nature until somebody else proved the contrary, or ought he to
have an occasional glass of champagne and write only leading articles
which did not prove anything in particular? His family urged him once
again to read for the Bar and he ate dinners in a desultory fashion hoping
that nothing would come of it. Conveyancing, at which so many
Wranglers excelled, he regarded as a dodge; and the mystical inner
coherence of the Common Law which English lawyers regard as superior
to justice, did not rejoice the heart of the moralist. But there were lights on
the horizon. In 1871, however, it was suggested that he might take on the
editorship of *Fraser's Magazine* in Froude's place; he consulted George
Smith who promptly offered him the *Cornhill*. *Fraser's* would have given
Stephen the greater scope. But he chose the *Cornhill* probably for two
reasons. Thackeray had been its first editor when it appeared in 1860 and
naturally Minny and Anny were pleased to keep the family connection.
The *Cornhill*, moreover, had rocketed to success and was the oustanding
magazine of the 1860s. It paid its contributors handsomely and the salary
of £500 a year which George Smith offered Stephen not only exceeded
what Longman could pay but it enabled him to give up some of his
journalism so that he could settle to the task of writing the book which
was to become *The History of English Thought in the Eighteenth
Century*. He brought out the first number in March of that year.

Editor of the Cornhill

The *Cornhill* was a family magazine, published monthly, and designed
for the drawing-room tables of the upper-middle class. Thackeray had
left no one in doubt what audience he had in mind. 'At our social table we
shall suppose the ladies and children always present; . . . we shall listen to
every guest who has an apt word to say, and I hope induce clergymen of
various denominations to say grace in their turn.' Or as Stephen put it, 'an
unprecedented shilling's worth . . . limited to the inoffensive'. 'What can
one make', he grumbled, 'of a magazine which excludes the only subjects

in which reasonable men can take any interest: politics and religion?'
Stephen was not, however, a man to quarrel with his fate and the mixture
was handed out as before. Nor was the mixture to be as bland as
Stephen's deprecating words suggest. Nearly all the major mid-Victorian
novelists, poets and critics contributed and Stephen could claim to have
nursed Henry James, Hardy, Symonds and Robert Louis Stevenson to
fame. In the best tradition of English literary editorship he trained his
contributors to write better and think more clearly. James Sully recalled
that he made him rewrite whole chapters; W. E. Norris said that 'he
would scrawl all over one's tidy manuscripts'; and Stevenson's most
renowned essays were improved by his unflattering criticism. Moreover,
Stephen began to break with the tradition of anonymity. Full-length
serialized novels still remained anonymous but verse and short stories
were signed and many pieces carried initials. He accepted, as editors of all
but the most austere of magazines must, that the readable must often take
priority over the profound. He did not disdain to publish forty articles on
astronomy by Richard Procter, an adept popularizer of science; and the
novels of Mrs Oliphant, Mrs Lynn Linton and his friend James Payn were
more to his readers' taste than to his. George Smith had formerly
frequently interfered in editorial policy and in 1874 vetoed the inclusion
of Meredith's *Beauchamp's Career* on the grounds of unreadability. But
he gave Stephen a free hand and encouraged him to publish his reflections
on some English classics. From that sprang the twenty-seven articles
which were later published as *Hours in a Library*. He published sixty
articles in all during his time as editor.

'The editor', wrote Stephen with characteristic irony some years later,
'is regarded by most authors as a person whose mission is the suppression
of rising genius and as a traitor who has left their ranks to help their
natural enemy the publisher.' An editor is inevitably a censor if only to
protect his proprietor from the operation of the law of libel. Society,
whether through the sanctions of the State or through the pressures which
can be exerted by the market, will always impose some limitations on
freedom of expression: and they will be most severe upon that medium
which seems to be most influential. In the eighteenth century Walpole
thought the theatre was so potentially inflammatory that he imposed a
censorship upon plays. In our own times first the cinema and then
television was subjected to censorship, whether by the State or by public
agencies or by commercial interests. In Victorian times it was the novel,
and its medium for dissemination in monthly instalments, the periodical,
which felt censorship most severely. The censorship which existed in
Victorian times was the censorship of the market. A magazine which
offended its readers went bankrupt. *Fraser's* lost readers from county
families for publishing Kingsley's *Yeast* and for his verses denouncing the

game laws; Trollope was sacked by *Good Words* under pressure from
Evangelical fanatics; and Thackeray in the *Cornhill* had to stop further
publication of Ruskin's denunciations of orthodox political economy.
Leslie Stephen was compelled in this atmosphere to safeguard the
interests of his proprietor.

Even Matthew Arnold was assailable. Arnold had sent Stephen *Culture
and Anarchy* and *St Paul and Protestantism* because the *Cornhill* 'both
pays best and has much the largest circle of readers'. The beginning of
Literature and Dogma followed but in September 1872 Stephen wrote to
Minny: 'Rather vexatiously Mat. Arnold has sent in an article which I
must read before it goes in because it is supposed to be heterodox and I
can't get back tomorrow night.' This was the chapter which dealt with
miracles and which Stephen judged impossible for the *Cornhill* to
publish. Arnold had been allowed some latitude, but an unknown writer
such as James Sully was forbidden to mention Schopenhauer because the
ordinary reader might vaguely scent infidelity in a German name.

Nor did Stephen hesitate to tell Hardy that his heroine in *The Trumpet
Major* married the wrong man. 'I replied', said Hardy, 'that they mostly
did.' 'Not in magazines,' he answered. He deluged Hardy with apologetic
requests when three lady subscribers wrote to complain of an improper
passage in a serial of one of his novels. *May 1875*: 'Delete "amorous"
substitute "sentimental".' *August*: 'I may be over-particular, but I don't
quite like the suggestion of a close embrace in the London churchyard.'
October: 'Remember the country parson's daughters. *I* always have to
remember them. I think you have much improved the rose-leaf incident.'
Hardy expostulated to his editor, pointing out that after the publication
of the book *The Times* had commended one of the very passages Stephen
had suppressed, and Stephen was reduced to irritated silence till he closed
the interview by saying that he spoke as an editor and not as a man, and
that Hardy had not more consciousness of these things than a child. He
broke the connection with Hardy in 1877 because he feared that the
opening situation in *The Return of the Native* might develop into
something 'dangerous' for a family magazine.

How far was Stephen a weary but worldly-wise editor who bore the
disdain of his authors because he could read the reactions of his public?
Or how far were the excisions which he excused on editorial grounds
agreeable to him on personal grounds? Oscar Maurer has made a spirited
defence of his editorial policy and cited Stephen's own wry acknowledgement that, whether one liked it or not, defiance of convention, such
as Ouida's overblown novels, produced greater absurdities than the
insular and emasculated works of English fiction. The conventions which
editors followed were not their invention: they were rooted in English
society itself and its deep puritan traditions. The contention that morality

is formed by society's lies, as we shall see, at the heart of Stephen's thought. But if Stephen admitted, as he could hardly fail to admit, that public opinion emasculated contemporary literature, his letters and phrases in his writings when he was a free man and no longer an editor suggest that he found no overpowering repugnance in indulging the taste of the *Cornhill's* subscribers. He pitched into the Fleshly School of Poetry and echoed the ritual denunciations of the treatment of sex in French novels. Writing of an obscure author, Margaret Veley, he said, 'the end of her novel was painful whereas most readers – and I do not say they are wrong – like things to be made pleasant'. Some of the rejections and excisions which he made on editorial grounds he would have justified as expediency: but the code of his times was agreeable to him for personal reasons.

During the 1870s Stephen's mind was preoccupied with religious controversy. This was the decade when suddenly a flood of books and articles appeared criticizing conventional Christianity, and Stephen published in *Fraser's* and the *Fortnightly* most of the articles he wrote as an advocate of agnosticism. They were by tradition unsigned but in 1873 his *Essays on Freethinking and Plainspeaking* appeared as a book under his name. He had nailed his colours to the mast and he more than once declared that some of those, particularly the Broad Churchmen, who still kept the old ensign flying on the halyard, were guilty of flying a flag of convenience. He might have been expected to have been, if not among the founding members, certainly among the first, of the Metaphysical Society; but he was not. This was a discussion club founded by almost his exact contemporary, James Knowles, who was soon to become the enterprising editor of a magazine of liberal churchmanship, the *Contemporary Review*. Knowles was a striking contrast to Stephen. An architect, he was a connoisseur of the arts, admired the pre-Raphaelites, disliked biography which he regarded as a form of gossip, dined out everywhere and acquired the reputation of a witty conversationalist – which is done by being a good listener. Knowles was a brilliant editor; and when by publishing W. K. Clifford's *Ethics of Belief* in the magazine he upset his pious publisher, he broke with him and founded the best of all the late Victorian periodicals, the *Nineteenth Century*. The Metaphysical Society was intended to be a meeting-place for those thinkers who genuinely desired to clear their minds and exchange views about the truth of religion and its relation to science. The original members ranged from Manning and W. G. Ward to Huxley and Tyndall, from R. H. Hutton and Gladstone to Henry Sidgwick and Frederic Harrison. It first met in 1869 and a number of Stephen's friends including George Croom Robertson, the Professor of Logic at University College London, were elected before he belatedly joined the Society in 1877. By that time the members were exhausted and given to bickering, and Leslie formed a low view of its proceedings.

Why yet again, as with the Apostles, was Leslie Stephen not regarded as an automatic choice for membership? He had already made his name by 1869 as a radical but he had shown that he was not a narrow party man. The warmth with which his friends regarded him became a byword in later years. There are two possible explanations. The first is that after marriage he was no longer a clubbable man. It could no longer be said of him, as Johnson said of Savage, that 'at no time of his life was it any part of his character to be the first of the company that desired to separate'. He was already acquiring his reputation for being formidably silent and noting how easily other men made fools of themselves. So admirably ordered was his mind that he found other men's offerings inconsequential and maundering. Then, secondly, he was one who got on better with his juniors than with his contemporaries. He was, in fact, a thwarted leader of men, never happier than when coaching the boat at Cambridge or taking the lead on a twenty-mile walk, leading his team of contributors to the *Cornhill* and even more the historians compiling the *Dictionary*, guiding, correcting, encouraging them, the indisputable head of the concern. He stood somewhat at an angle to his own generation.

Yet he wanted people to know where he stood on these matters, and in 1875 he performed a symbolic act. One spring day he asked Thomas Hardy to call on him in his study no matter what hour, and late that night, after the long climb up the stairs to the top of the house, Hardy found Stephen pacing up and down the room. The only light was a solitary lamp on the reading table. The dressing-gown which Stephen was wearing over his clothes accentuated his height so that he looked like a seer in robes as he passed in and out of the shadow, the lamp illuminating his prophetic face each time he passed the table. On it there lay a document. It was a deed by which Stephen renounced his Holy Orders and Hardy had been called to witness his signature. Like most men who are fighting for a matter of principle Stephen was depressed by the lassitude, indifference and ignorance of intelligent men to what he conceived to be the vital issues, and as usual with reformers he was disappointed most with the followers in his own camp. He told Charles Eliot Norton that alone among free-thinkers he found Huxley and Morley fully sympathetic. He felt isolated in his agnosticism. Apart from a whiff of grapeshot from the Broad Churchmanship of the *Spectator*, most journals refused to notice his book of essays. He was perpetually astonished at the hardiness of the most exotic of Anglican plants; in the 1860s he commented on a lawsuit brought against the Ritualists to decide 'what clothes they may wear, and the only way of deciding it is [to find out] what clothes people wore in the days of Charles I'; and ten years later he found the same disputes flourishing as he watched his brother defend Ritualist priests in the courts, and solemnly argue whether the sacramental bread should be cut thick and square or round and thin. 'And David Hume has been dead for a century! I blush for my race!' Such matters seemed to him grotesque and he let them pass to concentrate his attack on the main theological defences of the Church. Later in life he was to fret that his plain speaking might have wounded someone's feelings, just as in his literary criticism he argued that disagreeable topics should be excised from novels for the same reason; but at the time he was vexed that he seemed to make no impression on the public's hide. Whether or not he gave offence, he was received socially without visible embarrassment on the part of his hosts. The circles in which he moved were unalarmed, and he complained that some of them regarded his controversial activities as an aberration and himself as a 'respectable radical, partly misled by female influences and given to chaff the parsons'. The positive effect of his preaching was somewhat limited. An old family acquaintance, Archdeacon Allen, wrote to him in pain and fury to protest against his book and then sent Stephen's civil reply to Newman demanding chastisement. Newman declined to enter into another controversy and returned the letter. Crying vengeance the Archdeacon touted both Stephen's and Newman's letters around and eventually tried to involve William Thompson, the Master of Trinity. The Master lived up to his reputation for sardonic humour by ignoring the Archdeacon's demand and by offering instead to buy Newman's letter for the beauty of its style which he valued at seventy shillings. The baffled Archdeacon accepted in despair, and the only tangible result which Stephen could see that his book had achieved was that the Zanzibar Mission was that amount the richer by the Archdeacon bestowing his blood money upon it.

The Death of Minny: the Engagement to Julia

When in 1874 his mother, Lady Stephen lay dying, Leslie wrote to Anny: 'The best thing I ever did in my life was marrying Minny: for you and she have made the last seven years a mine of happier relations between us all than any years before.' A year later Minny was dead. Stephen received a shock from which he never fully recovered. Minny had fallen ill during pregnancy, and in the summer of 1875 he took her to Switzerland to recuperate. She suffered both there and on the journey back 'much discomfort', but he wrote cheerfully to Norton that they were no longer anxious. One November night she fell into convulsions, lost consciousness and died the next day on Stephen's forty-third birthday. He never celebrated his birthday again. 'I would have died for her with pleasure,' he told Lowell. 'I scarcely ever saw a cloud upon her bright face . . . Well, so long as I can work and help two or three people near me, I can feel life tolerable; but the old charm has gone.' More than the old charm had vanished. He was plunged into appalling gloom; he no longer dined out; he took no pleasure in any activity and was set fast to become a recluse. Old Cambridge friends complained that they had to dig him out if they wanted to see him and the flow of letters to Lowell and Holmes diminished to a trickle. He resigned from the Cosmopolitan and the Century Club, where he used to meet fellow radicals and anti-clericals such as Frederic Harrison; and though he kept up with Morley, he saw him only occasionally. In his distress he leant upon two women, one a young widow, Julia Duckworth, a next-door neighbour, and the other Anny Thackeray, who for eighteen months stayed with him to keep house. Anny remained devoted to her brother-in-law and was almost impervious to the difficulties of his temperament, but how she endured him at this time is hard to fathom. Just as he misjudged Minny's power of common sense, he could not recognize that though Anny's conversation sounded reckless and her mental processes might differ from his own, she often made sound judgements on matters which lay within her province. She knew how to bring up a tiny girl. Yet directly she took charge, he began to interfere; he told a foolish German nurse, who slyly made trouble between them, to disobey Anny's instructions, which led to a row, and Julia Duckworth had to intervene and tell him to behave sensibly.

Money also continued to be a cause of friction. Stephen preened himself on his generosity. He was proud of the fact that he gave Anny a house costing five hundred pounds and prouder still when, some years later, he declined her offer of eight hundred in repayment and accepted only four hundred.[1] Anny, however, flouted all his conceptions of sound finance, and he had to defend himself against criticism:

At this time, a time I need hardly say of deep melancholy to me, some of Anny's friends thought, not unnaturally perhaps, that I was wanting in consideration for Anny. Her old and affectionate, though not very judicious, friend, Mrs Brookfield, reproved me for worrying Anny about money matters. I was able to make a very simple statement of facts which showed that I was not substantially to blame on that head. I cannot say with equal confidence that I was not occasionally irritable upon details and I find that I made a scene soon afterwards when Anny brought me some unexpected bills. Julia spoke to me more to the purpose about my want of temper, as we met each other one day; and I took a turn with her in Kensington Gardens where I had the sense to confess my shortcomings and make promises of amendment.

The attitude of men to money is often so bizarre and diametrically

[1] Stephen had his gains as well as his losses by his connection with the Thackeray family. He gained the MS of *Vanity Fair*, the illustrated MS of *Lord Bateman*, and a dowry for Laura which later reverted to his family.

opposed to their other characteristics that to generalize from it is mad. Open-handed characters display the meanest streaks, and it is interesting that English novelists on the whole shy away from this awkward theme while the French attack it with gusto. Stephen would lend to young scholars in need and was not thought by his friends to be stingy; and unexpected bills deposited gaily by a spendthrift are alarming to a family man. Yet he seems from time to time to have convinced himself that his family was on the point of bankruptcy. In his last years he plagued his daughter Vanessa's life by accusing her of overspending on the kitchen books so that she was forced to enter into collusion with the cook to falsify the accounts. Any odd expense in the family was always greeted by a declaration that it would end by them all 'shooting Niagara to ruin'. He staggered his family once by announcing that he had only a bare thousand pounds in the bank. The story got about in the London clubs that poor old Stephen was ruined and Edmund Gosse made discreet enquiries preparatory to obtaining a grant from the Civil List. He discovered that the story was true only if one omitted to include securities and his income, and by the bank Stephen meant his current account. This preoccupation with money in the family circle arose partly from his determination to make it clear that those dependent on him were really dependent and partly from his desire for gratitude and appreciation. The subconscious process runs: if I can impress upon them that but for me they would be in the workhouse they will love me and appreciate my talents all the more.

Yet there was also something fine in Stephen's attitude to money. He despised it. He despised it at a time when the middle classes were beginning to ape the nobility in the ostentatious spending of money and when they too began to judge people not merely by the wealth they owned or had made but by their conspicuous consumption. Stephen shared the belief that money was corrupting society. The belief was expressed in Henry James's *The Awkward Age*, Trollope's *The Way We Live Now* and Ouida's *The Massarenes*. All he wanted was enough to enable him to write without too much drudgery of reviewing. He even looked wistfully at the Mastership of Trinity Hall when Geldart died in September 1874 though he knew he could never be appointed and Latham deservedly would get the post. Some critics have found it easy to sneer at Stephen or at his daughter Virginia Woolf for expecting to live as *rentiers* sheltered lives in which they were free to write as they pleased. On the contrary: they deserve to be praised for refusing to be seduced from their calling as writers into shallow ways of increasing their incomes which by the middle-class standards of their times were modest. Some months before Minny died Stephen wrote a letter to Anny which sets out what he felt:

I have received your letter and it has made rather an odd impression upon me. I can't help relieving myself by writing you a bit of a sermon. My temper is so bad that when we talk I always put you out and never succeed in expressing myself properly. Perhaps I shall do better on paper. Anyhow I shall try.

My text is this; you say you want to write because you want some money. That is the sentiment which shocks me. I would try to say why, though you know pretty well, and indeed George Eliot told you, some of what I mean.

You admit that you ought to do your best to make people about you happier and better. You have two qualifications, you have some money and some genius – say cleverness if you like it better. You ought to make both go as far as you can. How do you actually manage your life? You throw away your money so recklessly that you don't in the least know how much you have spent nor on what you have spent it. It is simply muddled away. If you spent half as much with discretion you would give away as much as you do now and make it go three times as far. Spending money is an art which wants care and discretion and you utterly refuse to give either. Then you get into difficulties and have to write at a moment's notice in hot haste and without waiting till your mind is full. You are making yourself into a pump instead of a spring, and, if you will go on at this rate you must end by pumping yourself out. I can't bear to think of it. Every fool has money; there are not half-a-dozen people who have your genius in England; and you are taking yourself to market and wasting your talents in order to spend more money and to less purpose than hundreds of people with half your means. When I see good powers thrown away it is positive pain to me. It hurts me to see J. F. S. slaving to death to keep up an expensive house. It is in my opinion simply wicked, though I have no right to throw the first stone. And yet his work is of a kind which doesn't suffer like yours, his arguments may be a little the worse for his haste; but they produce substantially the same effect. Your art is in danger of being seriously injured. Why will you keep all your good sentiments about the evils of worldliness for your novels and leave none for your life? Doesn't your father preach of the wickedness of sacrificing ourselves to the world? Don't you agree with him? Why don't you act up to it? You and I are living three times as expensively as we need and making our lives a burden by over-strain – why can't we pull in and be content to be as poor as nine nine nine out of one thousand people round us?

You do this because you are unselfish, because you like to give away money. But half the trouble would enable you to make the money go twice as far; and enable you to live quietly, work thoroughly, and live a reasonable life. You fancy that your novels do not do more good than your charity. You are wrong. Good literature has an immense influence. George Eliot has influenced people more than if she had given away millions, and you can do the same if you like.

How can we get out of it? I have made up my mind. I won't make more money than I can make by good work and a reasonable amount of labour. We shall then be forced to pull up somehow, whether we like it or not. We shan't like it; but it must come. Minny and Meemee and I can live for £1,000 or £1,200 a year, for millions of people do it. I won't make more. As for you, I will tell you what I think. Make up your mind to two things; always to pay ready money and to live for a moderate sum. Make yourself an allowance and then you can't exceed it. You will have to cut off some of your habitual indulgences, charitable and otherwise, for a time; but you will find that life is quite as agreeable and at any rate much more usefully employed.

Amid this gloom a startling event took place which, though it first upset Stephen, was in fact again to bring happiness into his life. Anny had begun to see much of a charming boy, Richmond Ritchie,[1] who had just gone up to the university, and she set her cap at him to such effect that he was swept off his feet by her gaiety and high spirits. Rumours of an attachment began to circulate, and then,

> at last the catastrophe occurred. To speak plainly I came into the drawing-room and found Richmond kissing Anny. I told her at once that she ought to make up her mind one way or the other: for it was plain that as things were going there could be only one result. She did, I think, make up her mind and informed me of her engagement that afternoon. As Anny was, I think, seventeen years older than Richmond it was clear that a long engagement would be very undesirable. She could not afford to waste time.

His inhibitions were understandably aroused, since Anny was not only so greatly older but Richmond Ritchie's cousin. The engagement invoked a major family row in which he was much blamed by the Ritchies who accused him of promoting the match and making it possible by forcing Richmond to enter the public service in order to support his wife-to-be. 'The fact was that if they hated the marriage, I positively loathed it. I could not speak of it to Julia without exploding in denunciation.' Julia Duckworth, however, told him that his behaviour merely showed that he was jealous of Ritchie's happiness and did not want his household broken up by Anny's disappearance. There was, however, another familiar reason: Stephen was upset by the marriage of a middle-aged woman to a young boy, and as is common in such cases he made a moral judgement to express an aesthetic revulsion. He showed the same horror when Robert Louis Stevenson married a wife twenty years older than himself.

Directly Anny had taken the decision Stephen insisted that the marriage should take place without delay. He induced Richmond to leave the university without taking his degree and sit at once for the India Office examination. Anny had different ideas. She proposed to leave Onslow Gardens and set up house on her own before she got married. Stephen might have been expected to fall in with this idea, for he disliked having Richmond about the house. 'It is very awkward', he wrote to Anny, 'to be a third person and especially an unsympathetic third person.' But he could not sanction a move which might offend propriety. He told Anny that he owed a duty to Minny to care for her happiness – which in fact he was well on the way to destroying. 'You never did and never will understand me in the least,' he complained. 'I loathe bores and despise sentimentalism and dislike over-demonstrativeness.' Wounded at being deserted, affronted by Anny's choice, buffeted between the Ritchies and

---

[1] Richmond Ritchie later became KCB and Permanent Under-Secretary at the India Office, dying before his wife in 1912.

Anny in whose best interests he believed himself to be working, his life was a misery until the wedding. When it took place Emily Ritchie noted: 'Poor Leslie looked very deplorable, and Julia Duckworth who wore the thickest black velvet dress and heavy black veil, and gave the gloomiest, most tragic aspect to her side of the chancel.'

So he and Anny parted. To the end of his life he continued to see her and correspond. 'If anyone compared our letters,' Leslie wrote to her, 'they would say it was like a dove talking to a gorilla.' He knew his faults and she her provoking ways; but neither would allow the sermons and grumpiness on his part or the disorganized, gay impracticality on her part to affect the fondness which had grown up between them. For every letter of reproof which he sent her there were dozens of affectionate gossip. A few years before he died he wrote to her:

> It is often strange to me to think of our past history. I have not been always all that I ought to have been to you: but I know at least now all that you have been to me and these last years will be cheered and soothed by your wonderful goodness to me. If I don't say so often, in so many words, you know what I feel inside my cantankerous outside.

In the year after Minny's death it looked for a time as if Stephen was going to let himself dwindle into a self-tortured misanthrope in love with his own condition of sorrow. He almost enjoyed telling Norton that his pleasure in friendship had withered and he deliberately nursed his unhappiness. He recorded that the Christmas after Anny married neither George Smith nor Morley invited him to their home and he ate Christmas dinner alone. His sister Milly rushed to his assistance, but she loved not wisely but too well. Leslie thought 'she was too like me to be helpful'. Whatever he said she agreed with; if he was in doubt she fell into utter perplexity; if he was sad, she wept. 'Tears always came too easily to her . . . though affectionate she was a most depressing companion.' Towards the end of her life, as we shall see, she gained her independence, but after three weeks her health broke down and she retired to her own house. In the midst of this domestic chaos suddenly all was to change.

During his two years as a widower Stephen had on more than one occasion, as we have seen, relied on Mrs Duckworth for comfort and advice. Once again it was the Hughes family who had in the first instance introduced them, when Tom Hughes's sister had told Leslie before he married Minny that he ought to consider Julia Jackson carefully. Julia was then a young girl of ethereal beauty whom Burne-Jones had chosen as the model for his painting of the Annunciation. Her mother had been one of the seven Pattle sisters famous for their good looks and descended from a dashing French nobleman who had settled in India after the Revolution. Stephen first met Julia at a picnic at Little Holland House, which belonged to her uncle Thoby Prinsep, who patronized the arts and took both Burne-Jones and G. F. Watts at different times into his household. 'The house', wrote Stephen, 'had a character of its own. People used to go there on Sunday afternoons; they had strawberries and cream and played croquet and strolled about the garden, or were allowed to go to Watts's studio and admire his pictures . . . And there used to be Leighton and Val Prinsep and his friends who looked terribly smart to me.' In a word, Stephen found it not his sort of world and both the Prinseps and he were a little shy of each other.[1] Everyone danced attention upon Julia; she had proposals from Holman Hunt and the sculptor Woolner, and Stephen dared hardly think that she would cast her eyes in his direction. When she became engaged to Herbert Duckworth, he remembered how, when they were both undergraduates at Cambridge, he had heard Duckworth described as 'the perfect type of public school man' and 'felt a sharp pang of jealousy'. This confirmed Stephen in his self-distrust and convinced him that such beautiful creatures as Julia Jackson were not for crotchety intellectuals like him. But Duckworth died in 1870, leaving his widow with three small children. 'I was only twenty-four,' she told Stephen, 'when life all seemed a shipwreck', and when Stephen found himself in the same predicament they were drawn to each other. She was still strangely and exquisitely beautiful with wide, wise eyes which had seen suffering, eyebrows that lifted naturally away to the temples, and an expression sad and poetical; and he remembered how even when he married Minny he had been keen to make a good impression on Julia. Julia had known the Thackeray girls, and in the early 1870s had invited Leslie and Minny to stay in the country. Living in the next street she had dropped in to see the Stephens on the evening of 27 November to see how Minny was; and she had left the Stephens together because she felt that someone burdened with a sorrow such as hers had no right to intrude on their happiness. The next day she heard Minny was dead.

Both Leslie and Julia were bruised by their calamities and took time to discover how to be healed, and perhaps at first they both felt that re-marriage was too easy and cut across the duties which Julia felt she owed to their children and Leslie to his sister-in-law. She helped him and Anny move into 11 Hyde Park Gate South, but that summer when he stayed in lodgings at Seaford to be near Mary and Herbert Fisher she kept out of his

---

[1] Not because the Prinseps were aesthetes. Val Prinsep, on the contrary, could bend a poker in his hands and despised 'artistic effeminacy'. To a lady gushing that a sky in one of his paintings was too beautiful, he replied, 'Yes, madam, I thought I had got in a rummy effect.' D. G. Rossetti, who loathed him, wrote:

> There is a big artist named Val,
> The roughs' and the prizefighters' pal.
> The mind of a groom, and the head of a broom,
> Were nature's endowments to Val.

way for fear she bored him. She soon, however, found herself discussing
Anny's engagement to Richmond: she stood up for Anny and lost her fear
of Leslie. Anny's decision to marry Richmond Ritchie made their
marriage possible. But it was his favourite pastime that saved Stephen
from the slough of despond; the Alps told him he was cured. He went to
Switzerland in the winter for the first time, and he returned renewed. In
War and Peace Prince Andrey, after the death of his wife, the little
princess, sees an old gnarled oak obstinately leafless in the early spring
and concludes that life for him and the oak is over. On the return journey
from the Rostovs' country estate he sees the oak's branches, no longer
menacing, but covered in foliage; which brings back to his mind that
night when he heard Natasha, leaning out of her bedroom window in
ecstasy at the beauty of the spring moonlight, chattering to Sonia and
begging her to share her joy. And Prince Andrey learns that life renews
and says to himself, 'No, life is not over at thirty-one.' So Stephen
regained self-confidence from Nature and became 'capable once more of
a strange feeling of – what shall I call it? – of something like joy and
revival'.

Julia's feelings were slower to change. She had decided, her daughter
Virginia guessed, to consecrate the pitifully short years of her marriage as
golden years when she 'exulted in a world of pure love and beauty'. Both
she and Leslie luxuriated in their grief and some will judge that their
mourning was a form of self-indulgence and of self-dramatization. Julia
flung aside religion and became a passionate disbeliever – it was indeed
through reading articles of Leslie's that her interest in him was aroused
although she liked the articles better at first than the man. Having grown
up among the intelligentsia, she had chosen to marry a simple, handsome,
conventional charmer; now she was being drawn back into the circles
which she had almost deliberately quitted. At first she resisted, convinced
that all that was left for her was a life dedicated to the service of others and
hallowed by suffering. But soon their relationship began to change. They
were no longer two suffering beings in sight of each other sailing like ships
at sea on different courses. One of the ships began to tack swiftly towards
the other. 'I was walking into town one day past Knightsbridge barracks
when I suddenly said to myself, "I am in love with Julia!"' At the
beginning of 1877 he sensed that she was discovering that 'something less
repulsive was concealed by my alarming outside'. He laid siege to her.
Practised *coureurs* importune their prey by lavishing flowers every day.
Stephen showered her with letters. He wrote daily, sometimes twice. In
February as she was leaving a dinner party he slipped a note into her hand
declaring that he loved her 'as a man loves the woman he would marry'
and told her he would put his future in her hands. He realized, he said,
that she could not love him and, if she so wished, would never speak of

love again. Julia told him that marriage was out of the question but she was happy for them to be on terms of the closest friendship because, as she admitted frankly, she had such affection for him. 5 April: 'I am afraid of going on writing. I feel I might say something silly.' 6 April: 'I will try to perform a feat – to write to you without saying for the hundredth time the one thing that I am inclined to say' (four sheets follow). 'There, dear, I have said nothing about it, have I?' On 7 April he proposed in the morning letter, followed it with another that afternoon, and sent a third that night. 8 April: 'You have given me a good blowing-up this morning, dear, and I doubtless deserve it.' 10 April: 'Your letter has come – the dreaded letter! . . . don't imagine me – as I fancy you do – to be a sublime philosopher.' She had refused him; and another vast screed from Stephen followed her refusal.

Re-reading her letters of that month in his old age Stephen saw that

she already loves me tenderly: she dreams of me and thinks of me constantly: and declares that my love is a blessing which lightens the burthen of her life. But this feeling is blended with a fear of the consequences to me. She feels that she is making me more restless; my position is a trying one; she remembers how she has herself thought of women who had men 'devoted' to them, who gave nothing and took everything . . . I suggested that we might continue to live as we were living and yet go through a legal form of marriage, which would give me the right to be with her as much as I desired. She at once pronounced the scheme to be – as of course it was – impracticable.

Soon she found it impossible to give him up (as her mother urged she should if she could not make up her mind to marry him). Julia wrote,

If I could be quite close to you, and feel you holding me, I should be content to die. Knowing what I am, it is no temptation to me to marry you from the thought that I should make your life happier or brighter – I don't think I should. So if you want an answer, I can only say that as I am now it would be wrong for me to marry . . . All this sounds cold and horrid – but you know I do love you with my whole heart – only it seems such a poor dead heart.

With skill, tenderness and sympathy Leslie went along with whatever analysis she made of her own state of mind: but he was adamant that he was the sole judge of his. 'I entreat you . . . never again to tell me in a letter that your affection does me harm . . . Tell me as often as you please that you can never be my wife. That does not sting me, though of course I would rather hear the contrary . . . But the other thing . . . affects me as if you had given me your hand and put a pin in it.' Sometimes she misunderstood his letters. There was one in July in which he said how much he wanted women to be as well educated as men. 'I dont want my little Laura – or your Stella for that matter – to be a mere young lady.' Julia flared up and Leslie next day expostulated, 'You speak as if I were a schoolmaster who values people for the place they could take in a tripos. Education is a good thing . . . but I like people for what they are and not for what they have got.' Then gently he added, 'I love you because your ways of feeling about people are always congenial.' Two days later they were again on the best of terms.

Not all their letters were about their state of mind. Stephen wanted sometimes to explain what he was and he did this by commenting on his contemporaries. 'No, dear,' he wrote, 'Ruskin does not admire me one bit . . . He has never read my books and would hate them if he did . . . He paws me, but he paws everybody. It is his unctuous way.' 'The fact is,' he said in another letter, 'that to talk to Ruskin is like walking amongst eggs.' Or again, 'You ask me whether Mat Arnold is not affected. Of course he is – a lump of affectation though I don't think he was affected when he wrote *Empedocles*. But he has genius under the affectation and some people have not.' And occasionally he let that sharp-edged humour which his friends treasured show its face. 'I did, however, remember a cheerful dream which I had a night or two ago that Mrs Brookfield was burnt to death.'

Mrs Brookfield was an exceptionally tiresome gossip; but there were others who did not approve of Leslie's suit. Julia's aunt. Mrs Cameron, the marvellous pioneer photographer, had a scheme of her own. Her daughter had died and what could be more suitable than for Julia to marry the widower, Charles Norman? She was scornful of Leslie, 'tall, wrapt in gloom, appealing for pity and dazzling her niece by his vast intellect'; and several of *his* friends had hopes that he would marry Julia Marshall who had been taken with him ever since he made friends with her when she came out to Switzerland to see her brother's grave after he had been killed on a climb. But Mrs Cameron had a heart and she altered her opinion of Leslie when she heard him recite the *Hymn to Proserpine* and *Omar Khayyám* and concluded that he was not a block, a stone, a worse than senseless thing. Julia's mother, too, saw what poetry meant to him and began to realize that his emotions were at least as strong as his intellect and that he was not looking for a housekeeper or a receptacle for self-pity but for a woman to love and that he had found one to worship. Gradually Julia's defences crumbled. She first asked Stephen to decide for her. He refused: 'The worst thing that could happen would be that she should become my wife and find that she had been mistaken.' He wrote to her: 'There is no hurry. You may think of me as I think of Troy (my old collie) – a nice kind loving animal who will take what I give and be thankful.' That autumn he talked of engaging a housekeeper and Julia realized that this might lead to separation. Could she 'come to life again'? Should she not keep herself solely for her children? Should she not abandon hopes of a new life, accepting that she was drowning and let herself sink? Not Constant's Adolphe or Fromentin's Dominique examined their feelings with more energy or doubt than did these two lovers. Slowly Stephen's strategy of letting her discover that she too must not live for the past worked and led to her surrender. On 5 January 1878 they went over the same ground apparently fruitlessly; and then as he rose to go she looked up at him and said, 'I will be your wife and will do my best to be a good wife to you.' Ten days later she wrote, 'My darling one, I feel most commonplace and quiet. The only think I can't quite believe is that we are not yet married.' That happened on 26 March 1878. Lucy Clifford left an account of their wedding: 'I shall never forget them. They both looked tall and grave and thin, as if they remembered a world of sorrow and understood ours, and were half-ashamed of their happiness.'

Chapter Three

◈◈◈◈◈◈

THE MAN OF LETTERS

The DNB *and the Alps*

Happiness once again fell upon Stephen like a May shower; but, burnt by the desert sun of solitude and anguish, he had learnt to change his ways. His love for Minny had been protective, jocular, cosseting. In Julia he recognized a deeper and more sensitive character than his own and one who had borne sorrow, as he would have wished to bear it, but could not. He worshipped her with unalterable devotion – 'Good God, how that man adores her,' said Henry James, and Meredith told Stephen's daughter, 'He was the one man to my knowledge worthy to have married your mother.' Indeed, worship was what he sought in marriage: a living image before whom he could pour out the flood of devotion that could find no outlet in religion. He idealized her and longed to sacrifice himself for her – which in the day to day routine of home life he was quite incapable of doing. In one of the letters which he wrote to Julia imploring her to marry him, he said:

> You must let me tell you that I do and always shall feel for you something which I can only call reverence as well as love. *Think* me silly if you please. Don't *say* anything against yourself for I won't stand it. You see, I have not got any Saints and you must not be angry if I put you in the place where my Saints ought to be.

In this period, so full for Stephen of domestic happiness and sorrow, he wrote the works on which his fame as a scholar and thinker rests. During his first marriage he had been writing a long essay on the religious thought of the preceding century and this grew in scope until he published in 1876 *The History of English Thought in the Eighteenth Century* in two volumes totalling 925 pages. The subject had been suggested to him by an essay on some aspects of the religious thought of that century, the only contribution to *Essays and Reviews* which was uncontroversial. It was by Mark Pattison, then smarting from his rejection for the rectorship by the fellows of Lincoln who disliked his devotion to scholarship and his liberal theology. Before he had finished Stephen had analysed the thought of the Deists and the orthodox apologists, the political, moral and economic theories of the age as well as, briefly, its imaginative literature. It still stands as a major contribution to scholarship and in a sense will never be superseded. He followed this work up with another tome, and from 1876 to 1882 he worked on *The Science of Ethics*. These were the years too when much of his best literary criticism was written.

The year 1882 marked a new phase in his life. George Smith broke the news to him that autumn that the *Cornhill* was running at a loss and that the circulation had dropped from 25,000 monthly to 12,000 during Stephen's editorship. Part of this fall was due to causes beyond Stephen's control. The popularity of the periodical, and in some cases its striking success, encouraged publishers to found new magazines. Publications such as *Temple Bar* (1860), the *Argosy* (1865), *Belgravia* (1886), *Tinsley's Magazine* (1867) and the new look given to the *Gentleman's Magazine* after 1868 all drew away those readers who took the *Cornhill* as light entertainment. Some of its serious readers were persuaded to change their allegiance to *Macmillan's Magazine* (1859), the first serious shilling monthly, the *Fortnightly* (1865), the *Contemporary* (1866) and *Nineteenth Century* (1877). Stephen was in fact now trying to run a magazine which fell between two stools. It was neither challenging and controversial enough to command the support of the intelligentsia and its literary articles were too weighty for the drawing-room readers. A good editor should have a flair for sensing changes in public taste and should be able to hold in his mind the spectrum of the public whom he is trying to satisfy. Preoccupied by his own writing and not one who enjoyed the gossip of London literary circles or studying his competitors, Stephen was too content to run in the old grooves. 'I do not fancy myself to be a good judge of public taste,' he confessed, and he wrote to Smith telling him that he was 'deeply vexed to think that my rule has been so prejudicial in the commercial sense'. Smith turned the editorship over to one of Stephen's friends and contributors, James Payn, to enjoy whose romances, as Stephen once said, one had to be unsophisticated. Payn had served his apprenticeship as editor of *Chambers's Journal* and he soon transformed the *Cornhill*. Henry James and Symonds no longer graced its pages and Rider Haggard, Conan Doyle and Stanley Weyman spun their yarns.

George Smith had concealed from his editor that the magazine had been running at a loss, and he did not make the change until he had something in mind for Stephen. He now decided to invite Stephen to edit a vast new project of his own devising, the *Dictionary of National Biography*. He had originally planned a compendium of universal biography but 'from that wild attempt', he admitted, 'I was saved by the knowledge and sound judgment of Mr Leslie Stephen'. Stephen guessed that the difficulties attending the birth and delivery of a national biography were grave enough. The past was already littered with the corpses of infant dictionaries which had perished at the tender age of the third or fourth letter of the alphabet. He had first to ask himself which names to include. By printing twice a year in the *Athenaeum* the names which he and correspondents considered worthy and asking readers to suggest additions Stephen hoped to escape the charge of editorial partiality. He next decided that names which were only names should not qualify; legendary figures should continue to exist in limbo. He also drew a distinction between biography and bibliography; the mere fact that a man had published a book did not qualify him for inclusion. But he wanted to inclúde everyone whose 'career presents any feature which justifies its preservation from oblivion'. Sportsmen as well as statesmen should feature and he later claimed that 'malefactors whose crimes excite a permanent interest have received hardly less attention than bene-factors'.

He then had to pick his team of contributors. In doing so Stephen had always to think of time – the enterprise was financed by an individual and delay could kill it. He tended therefore to choose men who would make much of the horse they were to mount or at least men who worked in the same stable. He circulated to them his own article on Addison as a model – and the *Quarterly* in a nit-picking criticism of the plan of the Dictionary acknowledged that it was a model 'full of details, yet clear and concise'. His contributors were kept on a tight rein. In a circular he told them that he must be an autocrat but hoped to be a considerate autocrat. They were told to complete their articles within six months, curb irrelevance, verbosity and pedantry. But to be in sympathy with their subject was not enough. The most famous rule of all was the injunction to keep eulogy within bounds; 'No flowers by request' as Alfred Ainger put it. And so the venture got under way.

Then the nightmare began and letters arrived in dozens. He was haunted by families with requests to include obscure kinsmen. The inevitable clergyman wrote enclosing a list of 1,400 hymn-writers each of whom was entitled to a place. The bombardment of the editor by those with candidates for a place was matched by the explosions of grief from those whose kinsman had been included but justice not done to his semi-divine attributes. The wife of an Indian army officer paced up and down in the office wringing her hands. 'My dear husband', she sobbed, 'slew with his own sword fourteen sepoys . . . All India rang with the deed; and there is not a word of it in his biography! Oh! Oh!' Meanwhile the contributors, antiquarians and bookworms in the vanguard, moved in to the assault. 'The wild beasts at Ephesus were but a type of the unreasonable herd of antiquarians who struggle over my body,' he wrote to Norton. Yet one of the minor triumphs of the Dictionary was Stephen's success in taming the pedants. True, in the first volume he was not aware of all the possibilities, and when one looks up King Alfred one is greeted with the entry 'Alf- see Aelf-', and the harmonious names of Elgiva and

Elfrida have been transmogrified into Aelfgifu and Aelfthryth. This mania for Anglo-Saxon spelling had been imposed on Stephen by the arch-pedant, E. A. Freeman, and there was a danger that the ordinary reader would fail to find many Anglo-Saxon names when their customary spelling had been so changed. But Freeman was not to enjoy his triumph long. The vision of a line of kings, such as Athelstan and Ethelbert, stretching out to the crack of doom and masquerading in diphthongs, so seared Stephen's eyeballs that he was prepared to risk a breach with the professor rather than let unnatural orthography prevail and common sense perish. He accordingly proposed a compromise: that names would be found under their ordinary spelling and their scholarly aliases inserted in brackets. Freeman would have none of it: was it not an insult to his championship of our Saxon heritage? He would resign rather than contribute an article on Athelstan spelt with an A. Stephen accepted the resignation with alacrity and the professor departed in a huff.

Stephen let two years elapse between the inception and the publication of the first volume. That volume was delayed. Alarmed on reading the proofs at the number of misprints, George Smith insisted that his young nephew Robert Musket should scan the volume for errors. Stephen was not best pleased that the birth of the great enterprise was delayed from Michaelmas until Christmas, but he had to admit that he was a poor proof-reader and that Smith's explosion of wrath was justified. Worse was to follow. Smith detected that one article bore a suspicious resemblance to one in the Encyclopaedia Britannica. Its author, a Presbyterian Doctor of Divinity, Alexander Grosart, had already written Stephen unendurable letters complaining that lives which were 'his' by right had been given to other contributors: he even wrote Stephen a sonnet of abuse. Now this man had endangered the publication of the first volume by breaching copyright and Stephen was mortified to have to acknowledge that Smith was again in the right. Mercifully the proprietors of the Encyclopaedia behaved generously; an acknowledgment to them was inserted in the text; and Stephen gave Grosart 'such a kick as has knocked him altogether out of time'; when Grosart finally conjured up a reply it contained 'a contemptible mixture of whine and bray, poor wretch'.

Thereafter a volume was published on each quarter day with astonish-ing regularity. Giving its continental competitors a start of as much as twenty-five years in some cases, the British Dictionary outran them all. Stephen was able to sustain the pace because he led a team. Scots and Irish historians, orientalists and old India hands, Anglican and non-conformist scholars were enlisted as specialists in their fields. The total number of contributors was 653, but three-fourths of the work was done by a mere hundred. The great names of Victorian historiography were there and gave of their best: Tout, Round, Poole and Mary Bateson were among the medievalists; Creighton, Pollard, A. W. Ward, Gardiner and Firth tackled the sixteenth and seventeenth centuries. Tout, Pollard and Firth each contributed the equivalent of one volume and Ward's articles came to about two-thirds. Tout confessed that although he was already a young professor, 'like many Oxford men of my generation I approached historical investigation without the least training or guidance in historical method, and felt very much at a loss how to set to work. The careful and stringent regulations which [Stephen] drew up, and the brusque but kindly way in which he enforced obedience to them, constituted for many of us our first training in anything like original investigation.' Nor did Stephen regard himself solely as an editor. He wrote the lives of most of the major poets and writers. By the end he had written 378 biographies 'almost any one of which might have earned an American PhD degree', Alan Willard Brown mournfully remarked. It was not merely concern for his patron's purse which made Stephen press on; he had an example before his eyes. The first two volumes of the Rolls series, the medieval records still in private hands, had appeared in February 1858 only eleven months after the decision was taken to publish and in the same year a further thirteen volumes were added; volumes continued to appear at the rate of three or four a year, though the level of editing was uneven and far below the standard Stephen set. The Victorian intelligentsia may not have been professionals but they worked hard.

Such a task of organization could not be borne by one man, and Stephen had the good judgement to pick an excellent assistant in Sidney Lee. Stephen edited the first twenty-six volumes, Lee the remaining thirty-seven and also brought out the supplements of 1901 and 1912. The Dictionary as originally planned took fifteen years to complete. The planning was Stephen's work; but much of the credit is due to Lee who proved to be his superior as an editor. Lee had greater patience and stamina to check and re-check proofs, and he was able to eliminate some of the inaccuracies and misprints which had crept in, and which were ruefully acknowledged in 278 pages of Errata. Lee was in the position to benefit from the mistakes of earlier volumes, and he was also able to entice more contributors. As the Dictionary's fame mounted, the list of those anxious to contribute and share in the triumph grew.

For it is a triumph. This Dictionary of 29,120 lives in 63 volumes, *monumentum aere perennius*, is Stephen's most enduring bequest to posterity. German and French scholars generously admitted the Dictionary's superiority to their own national compendiums. It was an enterprise free from literary log-rolling and the worst features of seminar research. Moreover, the state of English historiography at that time must not be forgotten. The *English Historical Review*, born in 1868, passed its infancy fast asleep. The history schools in the older universities at last were beginning to turn out able scholars, but the editors could not fall back on a regiment of academic historians and cadres of PhDs trained in the methods of research. In this respect England was far behind Germany and France. As a result there was a good deal of unevenness in the contributions and the disparate treatment of sources which more professional editing might have eliminated. But greater professionalism would have led to delay and dullness. The Dictionary was spared *Historismus*. For Stephen's greatest rule was that each life was to be readable, a biography in itself, not a compendium of sources or a disquisition by a scholar on disputed points. Contributors were encouraged to enliven their style, and Stephen followed his own advice. In writing George Eliot's life he described Tito, the hero of *Romola*, as one of her 'finest feminine characters', which drew from a phlegmatic reviewer the comment that presumably Romola herself was meant. Maitland observed: 'A Dictionary should not be strewn with such mantraps.'

The *DNB* is a monument to the Victorian age. It is a monument to private enterprise. No State subvention was sought or offered, no Academy or learned society sponsored it. George Smith was one of those remarkable entrepreneurs of the age who as a young man had rescued his family firm from bankruptcy, a finance house with an import and export business as well as a growing interest in publishing, by working often until three or four in the morning or, on occasions when the Indian mails had to be caught, for thirty-two hours at a stretch sustained by mutton chops and green tea. By so doing and by a far-sighted speculation in Apollinaris ('Queen of the Table Waters') he made a fortune. He gave his editors complete confidence: if things went wrong, he never blamed them but cursed the general perversity of things. As someone who despised fops and humbug, Stephen was particularly dear to him. The older he grew the more Smith revered and enjoyed helping literary men and women, and he resolved that the Dictionary should be his gift to English literature. Leslie Stephen wrote that Smith's famous generosity to Thackeray or George Eliot could be disparaged as being astute business, but no one could disparage his generosity to the Dictionary and its contributors. On an outlay of £150,000 he expected to lose £50,000 and in the end he lost £70,000. No doubt he could finance the loss by his other publishing successes, as indeed is done by publishers today; but today people expect such an enterprise to be funded by universities, private foundations and by research grants from the State.

Does the Dictionary, however, do justice to that age and does it reflect, as its sponsor and editors intended it to do, the nation's greatness? Stephen himself admitted that it was not truly professional, but he owed a duty to George Smith to publish it within a time limit. Some may be surprised that considering private enterprise had financed the venture so few businessmen were included. The criticism is fair so long as one remembers that English economic history had scarcely seen the light of day and that the Victorians drew a distinction, however prejudiced and unreal it may seem to us today, between those who served the State whether or not they made money out of it, and those who simply made money. If a businessman, or for that matter a landowner, went into politics, then he had claims to be a national figure; but if he stayed in his counting-house or factory or on his estates, then he was judged to be concerned solely with his own prosperity: how far the prosperity of his business enhanced that of the country was ignored. Stephen's judgement inevitably reflected the assumptions of the times, and these sometimes coincided with his own prejudices. Veils were drawn over sexual delinquency; and if Louise de Keroualle crept in, famous courtesans such as Skittles Walters did not make it even after 1920. Nor for that matter did all that number of women of the most exquisite virtue; and for that not only were the laws and conventions of Western Europe responsible but, as we shall see, Stephen had his own view of the contribution which women should make to the life of the nation. It was, perhaps, unwise of Stephen not to include a saint after whom a well-known town had been named. But when St Alban's life appeared in the Supplement his biographer – having recorded how on his way to execution the waters of a river parted so that the saint might cross dry-shod, how a spring suddenly gushed from the top of the flower-covered hill where he was beheaded, and how after his martyrdom his executioner's eyes dropped out – felt bound to add, 'Doubt has been cast on this narrative.' No wonder the editor looked askance at such speculative material.

The two-volume Supplement was not, of course, filled with the names of those who had by error been omitted. It consisted overwhelmingly of biographies of those who had died during the planning and publication of the original volume. The number of rectifications, such as Sir Thomas Erpingham, the Lancastrian soldier, are neither numerous nor startling. But one rectification catches the eye. Jem Belcher, the boxer, who appears in the Supplement, was the darling of the fancy, as well as of the Corinthians, but one may for instance search in vain for his contemporary Tom Faulkner, the fast bowler; or for other working-class heroes, such as footballers and music-hall artists, to say nothing of many of the early trade unionists. David Cannadine declared that the *DNB* did not in fact fulfil Sidney Lee's claim to 'satisfy the commemorative instinct of all sections of the nation'. But when he continues by criticizing the readiness with which Stephen permitted contributors to pass moral judgements he is on weaker ground. Stephen would have had to step outside his age to omit moral judgements, but he did not follow the most famous moralist among Victorian historians. Only a couple of years after the *DNB* was launched Lord Acton delivered his well-known rebuke to Bishop Creighton. 'I know you do sometimes censure great men severely,' Acton wrote. 'But . . . I cannot accept your canon that we are to judge Pope and King unlike other men . . . Power tends to corrupt and absolute power corrupts absolutely. Great men are almost always bad men, even when they exercise influence and not authority . . . If we debase the currency for the sake of genius or success or reputation . . . then History ceases to be a science, an arbiter of controversy, a guide to the wanderer.' Creighton replied, 'You judge the whole question of persecution more rigorously than I do. Society is an organism, and its laws are an expression of the conditions which it considers necessary for its own preservation . . . Nowadays people are not agreed about what heresy is; they do not think it a menace to society, hence they do not ask for its punishment: but the men who conscientiously thought heresy a crime may be accused of an intellectual mistake, not necessarily a moral crime.' Stephen had the good sense to follow Creighton. Acton's dictum makes history incomprehensible.

It was the *DNB* more than any other of his labours which led to Stephen being made a Knight of the Bath, but it is refreshing to see that the great monument of his labours attracted an impudent dog or two to cock a leg. In 1901 an ingenious and anonymous parody appeared entitled *Lives of the Lustrious*, A Dictionary of Irrational Biography edited by Sidney Stephen and Leslie Lee. There was W. W. Astor who 'owing to a curious aversion from anything suggesting stars or stripes is never known to lift his eyes at night, all the servants on his estate are restricted to check trousers and eagles are peremptorily refused permission to nest in the Cliveden woods'. There is Mr Hall Caine who lives at Greta Castle 'where his windows have recently been doubled to shut out the booming of the Atlantic, which otherwise he considers a satisfactory ocean'. Best of all there is Henry James:

James, Henry
Six-shilling Sensationalist, was born at Hangman's Gulch, Arizona, in 1843. This favourite author, whose works are famous for their blunt, almost brutal directness of style and naked realism, passed his early years before the mast, and is believed at one period of his career to have sailed under the skull and crossbones. Mr Henry James turned to the pen for a livelihood, and under a variety of pseudonyms produced in rapid succession a large number of exciting stories, the most popular of which are probably *The Master Christian*, *The Red Rat's Daughter*, *The Mystery of a Hansom Cab*, *The Eternal City*, and *The Visits of Elizabeth*.
Authorities: Jacobite Papers; Daisy and Maisie or The Two Mad Chicks.

Stephen's name was known to many Englishmen who were never likely to consult the *DNB*. He was one of the heroes of the new sport of the upper-middle class in mid-Victorian England, the conquest of the Alps, when the exploits of great climbers were followed with almost the same avidity as those of cricketers in the succeeding generation. Although Rousseau was the first (in Stephen's words) 'to set up mountains as objects of human worship', and pioneers such as Albert Smith were climbing in the 1840s, the golden age of mountaineering did not begin till the 1850s when the French railways reached Basel and Geneva, and Switzerland came to be hardly more than a day's journey from London and the fare less than ten pounds. The London lawyer or businessman, the don or clergyman, could reach their playground quickly and cheaply and the sport itself was inexpensive: in 1855 a single climbing expedition with five porters and three guides cost a couple of friends only four pounds each. In true English fashion the enthusiasts formed a club; and though Stephen was not one of the original members of the Alpine Club, founded in the autumn of 1857, he was elected in 1858, became President in 1865, edited the *Alpine Journal* from 1868 to 1872, and spent some twenty-five holidays in the Alps. Stephen was one of the protagonists in the days when the great peaks fell one by one before the skill of these pioneers in a new kind of exploration. The technique of the sport was still in its infancy and there was no question of selecting well-known climbs or ice-walls as tests of skill; conquest was all and climbers had to pick their own routes to the summits. Stephen was the first man to climb the Schreckhorn and could claim a number of other peaks as his own. Everyone spoke of him as one of the great climbers of his day; better perhaps on ice and snow than on rocks, but a master of both; a climber who delighted in long, steep snow slopes, as well as in cutting steps, and able to manage the loose scree of the Bietschorn. His long legs, like a pair of compasses, moving at the slow, steady, guide's pace, his great reach, his power of resistance to cold and fatigue, and his sanguine temperament, gave him great advantages. Unlike some of the brotherhood he was opposed to guideless climbing and he chastened the English Alpinists by telling them that a third-rate guide was always superior to a first-rate amateur. This was untrue and, in any case, Stephen nearly always climbed with the three best guides in Switzerland.[1] But the remark is characteristic of Stephen's dislike of boasting and his habit of denigrating his accomplishments. As an Alpinist he was the soul of orthodoxy: that is to say he loudly condemned climbers racing each other up mountains, and frequently did it himself.

[1] One of them, Melchior Anderegg, became a privileged person and was twice invited to England. He pained Stephen by declaring that the vista from the railway carriage of the endless chimney-pots of South London was a finer sight than any Alpine horizon; but his preference for the waxworks at Madame Tussaud's to the splendours of Westminster Abbey entranced his host.

Stephen went to the Alps to climb and for no other reason. Ruskin might stay in the valleys to worship and sketch and curse the vulgarity of the mountaineers rushing home 'red with cutaneous eruption of conceit, and voluble with convulsive hiccough of self-satisfaction'; but, though Ruskin in London was 'one of the people who frightens me to death, and makes me want to sink into my shoes and forces me to be sulkily silent', in the Alps he was a figure of fun, an absurdity who criticized Stephen for the sacrilege of smoking a pipe on the top of a peak. Nor had Stephen much use for the other body of opinion – the scientists – who had done much to advance Alpine adventure. He rallied them for toiling up the slopes laden with clinometers, barometers and prismatic compasses, 'fanatics who by a reasoning process to me utterly inscrutable have somehow irrevocably associated Alpine travelling with science'; the physicist Tyndall, who was second only to Huxley as a publicist for science, was so offended by such remarks that he resigned from the Club. Stephen was single-minded in his devotion to the point of rudeness. He cut Olive Schreiner, the South African novelist, when she was staying at the same hotel, simply because she was a celebrity. One day H. A. Morgan, explaining why he could not accompany Stephen on a climb, was interrrupted by a young lady who most inappropriately began asking details of the excursion Morgan had promised to arrange for her. 'I see what you prefer, to coming with me over the mountains!' Stephen snapped, and with a look of contempt strode down the path to Zermatt. He was always a jealous lover.

The charms of mountaineering resemble those of a great courtesan; in addition to her physical attractions, and the raptures she inspires, she possesses that indefinable quality of mystery which, once felt, binds her devotees to her helplessly for life. It is a power which is exerted with peculiar poignancy over intellectuals. Mountaineering makes it possible for the intellectual to experience things which would otherwise be impossible: danger, intense comradeship, manliness, physical pain in pursuit of a tangible objective, and the sensation of being at one with Nature. Psychologically the intellectual is always conscious of his isolation. He is not at one with the human race: the world is forever out of joint and he is conscious that he cannot escape. Remove him from civilized society and plant him in the silence of the snows and his neuroses fall from his back like Christian's burden – but in this Pilgrim's Progress Evangelist carries not the Bible but the Book of Nature in his hand. Stephen was a Wordsworthian. He communed with Nature and Nature 'helped' him. That was why he insisted on climbing in silence, not in order to cogitate on the march, but so as to bathe his mind in the healing springs of Alpine scenery. His indignation with Fitzjames was boundless when, on the only occasion the brothers climbed together, Fitzjames talked *Saturday Review* all the way to the top and down again. Sometimes his silence was due to natural causes; when one of his party chaffed him as they were starting on a long ascent at 2 a.m. in a cold mist, he announced, 'I hope no one's such a fool as to suppose I'm in a good temper at this hour in the morning.' More often his silence was of a depth that struck his companions more forcibly than words. His most valiant Alpine friend and the only European apart from his guides whom Stephen ever got to know, the French painter Gabriel Loppé, described how on Titlis, 'Tout vibrait à nos yeux tant notre émotion était profonde . . . Stephen silencieux, remuait à peine les lèvres pour dire à son neveu le nom de quelques unes de ces grandes cimes qui font l'orgueil de la Suisse. Trois-quarts d'heure furent bien vite écoulés, il fallut partir; chacun reprit son piolet, et nous descendîmes en silence.'

Stephen was a Wordsworthian – which is a very different thing from being Wordsworth. He communed with Nature but also came to achieve, to walk farther and faster than other men, to conquer mountains. He liked to note the varieties of flowers and plants, or to identify the other peaks visible from the summit. Whereas Wordsworth's eye was a kind of hole in the head through which the impressions he received from Nature passed directly to his heart, Stephen's was a categorizing eye; it was as if he needed a direct contact with things in order to make him human again after living too long with people. Achievement is the essence of mountaineering. Climbing gives, to those who need it, the reassurance that they are men – men still capable of defeating the tyranny of life. Stephen's youthful determination to be an athlete was a rationalization of a more deep-seated fear: a doubt whether he was capable of achieving anything. Mountaineering gave Stephen the chance to announce to the world that he gloried in the struggle for existence. It was no accident that he chose mountaineering as the background of his profession of faith. In *A Bad Five Minutes in the Alps* he pictures himself hanging over a precipice and asking himself the value of life. As he hangs on the ledge, knowing that he will, as his joints crack, be hurled into eternity, what is there left to believe in? Christianity, proclaiming the utter sinfulness of man and threatening damnation, is at once dismissed. Pantheism, either of the new scientific or ancient Eastern variety, is also unsatisfactory; the assertion that the self on death merges with Nature and is, as Omar Khayyám declares, no more than a bubble among a million similar bubbles poured by the eternal Saki from his bowl, affronts our sense of individuality. And if this is too pessimistic, the Religion of Humanity is too optimistic. Is it not brash to proclaim that each man plays his part in helping the human race to progress? 'Humanity will blunder on pretty much as it did before . . . [it] was too big and distant, and too indistinctly related to me, to lift me for one minute above the sense of that awful personal crash which was approaching so speedily.' No: at such a time all creeds fail us.

The one suggestion which was of some sort of use came from a different and very undignified source. Years ago I had rowed and lost a race or two on the Thames, and there was a certain similarity in the situations, for there comes a time in a losing race when all hope has departed, and one is labouring simply from some obscure sense of honour. The sinews of the arms are splitting, the back aches, and the lungs feel as though every blood-vessel in them were strained almost to bursting-point. Whatever vital force is left is absorbed in propelling the animal machine; no reason can be distinctly given for continuing a process painful in a high degree, dangerous to the constitution, and capable of producing no sort of good result; and yet one continues to toil as though life and happiness depended upon refraining from a moment's intermission, and, as it were, nails one's mind – such as is left – down to the task. Even so the effort to maintain my grasp on the rock became to me the one absorbing thought; this fag end of the game should be fairly played out, come what might, and whatever reasons might be given for it.

Fight the good fight and you will live; and if you must die, then look back with pleasure and pride at the strife. Mountaineering dramatizes the struggle for life. 'The game is won', writes Stephen, 'when a mountain-top is reached in spite of difficulties; it is lost when one is forced to retreat.'

Through mountains Leslie Stephen could relate to destiny and fate. 'He would roll a large rock down a precipice and imagine that he was that rock,' wrote Bruce Haley. Stephen apprehended Nature through his whole body, pitting his strength against the mountains, aware of their magnitude and power compared with his own puny shape. But the pygmy conquers the giant. Geographers measure Nature in figures, mountaineers measure her through their muscles. The struggle gives one an electrifying sense of one's own identity. But mountaineering is not just a trial of endurance. Greater even than on the river is the emotion of comradeship.[1] For here, more than glory is at stake, it is life or death, and the rope round your waist speaks of the friends above you and below on the rocks who will save your life in the certainty that you will as willingly lay down your life for them. Those friendships last longest in which two men have endured and suffered danger together; no matter how often they quarrel in later life, neither can forget the intense emotion they have experienced together. The monotonous regularity of regimental re-unions, so inexplicable to wives, at which a man forgathers with old acquaintances, with whom he has in civilian life nothing in common, testifies to the strength of the bonds which unite men who have once faced danger together – or who imagine that they did. For the Victorians

---

[1] There is an affinity between the physical and psychological adjustments which a crew must make in rowing to get the boat to run smoothly, and those which mountaineers make when roped together on a climb.

mountaineering was one of the few ways in which pacifist liberals could experience emotions similar to those they envied in soldiers and mariners. 'An Alpine journey', wrote the pioneer J. D. Forbes in the *Quarterly Review* of 1857, 'is perhaps the nearest approach to a campaign with which the ordinary civilian has a chance of meeting.' Danger, indeed, is one of the physical pleasures of life; and if men cannot obtain it in one way they will invent new ways of finding it. Alpine comradeship was at once a freemasonry and an opportunity for Stephen to relax, joining in rags and stump-cricket or playing *fly-loo* in some little inn with his companions and the guides, 'which means that everyone puts down a piece of sugar and a ten-centime piece before him, and the one on whose sugar the first fly settles, gets the money'. The Victorian public school mystique of games permeated the Alpine brotherhood and influenced their attitude to the sport. Play is sanctified if it can be shown to be work – work which teaches a moral lesson. 'Properly speaking,' said Carlyle, 'all true Work is Religion.' Writing of an ascent of Mont Blanc, made in the company of Huxley and two other friends, John Tyndall confessed: 'We were about to try our strength under unknown conditions, and as the various possibilities of the enterprise crowded on the imagination, a sense of responsibility for a moment oppressed me. But as I looked aloft and saw the glory of the heavens, my heart lightened, and I remarked cheerily to Hirst that Nature seemed to smile upon our work. "Yes," he replied, in a calm and earnest voice, "and, God willing, we shall accomplish it." ' Stephen, the apostle of the religion of work, subscribed to the doctrine of vicarious labour through play.

G. M. Young judged that Stephen did much to make mountaineering respectable in England by showing that it was not a series of foolhardy pranks but a laborious, hardy and ennobling pursuit. He also canonized it as the great pursuit for the introspective: the pursuit which helps to solve the problem which sometimes besets them – how to show that they are good-hearted fellows when they lack the skill and grace to play games or the accuracy, upbringing and inclination for field sports. Climbing bolsters the ego; no mountaineer can be a muff. It would be ridiculous to suggest that every climber takes to the mountains to nurse his neuroses, and the early Alpinists were drawn to Switzerland for a variety of reasons: the Italian princesses, for instance, who made some well-advertised climbs, originally went there to hunt ibex and chamois. But in Stephen's case there was more to it than a love of Nature or adventure, and behind his Alpine essays lurks a strange uneasiness. He worshipped the emotions he had experienced in certain places, not Nature. Yes, the emotions themselves; Stephen was an Alpine sentimentalist first and last, and he luxuriated on his memories. Like the road junction under the lamp where he clasped Lowell's hand, which was sacred, so was the trysting place with Minny at Täsch sacred; Wengen Alp was sacred – the list of holy shrines in fact was interminable. He was in love with his own feelings and would indulge for hours in nostalgic recollection. If you carefully seal an emotional experience into a bottle of preserves, you will find when you open it in wintertime that it tastes different from fresh fruit; there is a sugary almost sickly taste and something will have to be done to disguise it. He often disguised his sentimentality by making jokes.

Some of the jokes are excellent. S. A. O. Ullmann selected some of Stephen's essays hitherto buried in the periodicals of the past and chose two examples of Stephen at his best. Nothing could exceed the ease, the charm, the modesty of his account of the assault on Mont Mallet; of the frustrations and excitements of the climb; and of his amusement about the deviousness of guides. Was it the jealousy of the Swiss guide Melchior Anderegg that made the French guides declare that the glacier was 'a collection of horrible crevasses, seracs swept by avalanches, falling stones and I know not what else, defying the skill of the bravest guides', when in fact the glacier turned out to be 'of the most domestic and pacific nature, a glacier so mild that, as somebody said of a small earthquake, "you might stroke it"; a glacier which we traversed from top to bottom at a jog-trot, and which barely deserved the ceremony of a rope'? Nothing could reveal better than Stephen's essay 'A Substitution for the Alps' the gap which was beginning to yawn between the old Alpinist of his generation to whom a climb meant at most a night out on the mountain with the minimum of equipment and a return to a comfortable inn for dinner and talk, and the new generation of climbers in the Himalayas who resembled generals marshalling an army of porters in support of an assault party of Gurkhas. The mountaineer had become a 'Moltke, toiling at his desk . . . instead of a simple-minded barbarian chief rushing out for a day's raid'. Stephen preferred the Alps to Everest and K2 because, awe-inspiring in their loneliness as the Alps are, they are part of a civilized landscape. 'Mont Blanc never looks so lovely to me as when it shows itself across the Lake of Geneva as the guardian of the dwelling-place of a people.' Whereas the Himalayas 'for countless ages have wasted their beauty on a few wandering bears and ibexes . . . these strange monsters rise in the region of thin air, to which comes nothing living except some luckless butterfly, carried up by a gale to be frozen in eternal snow, so deserted that Mr Conway was pleased to get down again to a place where he was once more bitten by mosquitoes'. This badinage was his to command: what does it matter if on another occasion he declares that Mont Blanc is best seen from above the snow-fields which feed the Glacier du Géant?

But there is another Stephen in the Alps whose jocularity becomes facetious. Facetiousness springs from the desire to conceal, from being ashamed to expose one's emotions. It is also an attempt to have things both ways. Stephen liked to show that he was moved by the Alps, that they alone could stir him to blaze forth in a purple passage. No sooner, however, has he launched himself on a flight of fancy than, 'I am verging on the poetical'; down comes the balloon and he brings himself ostentatiously to earth. We all applaud – here is a man who can do the tall talk and yet is on our level. How excellent to shrug off the scientists by saying in wretched weather on the top of a mountain, 'As for ozone, if any existed in the atmosphere, it was a greater fool than I take it for.'

There are, however, some fine passages in the *Playground of Europe* in which Stephen can match the great Victorian word-painters. He did not compete with them; indeed he deplored Ruskin's rococo imagery. He preferred to paint the Alpine scenery in separate strokes of purple, almost meticulously, and to awake in his reader that emotion, so familiar to the mountaineer, of man's insignificance among these lonely peaks which seem to echo Obermann's cry, 'Eternity, be thou my refuge!' The following is an extract from 'Sunset on Mont Blanc' which Stephen thought to be his best piece of prose:

And suddenly began a more startling phenomenon. A vast cone, with its apex pointing away from us, seemed to be suddenly cut out from the world beneath; night was within its borders and the twilight still all round; the blue mists were quenched where it fell, and for the instant we could scarcely tell what was the origin of this strange appearance. Some unexpected change seemed to have taken place in the programme; as though a great fold in the curtain had suddenly given way, and dropped on to part of the scenery. Of course a moment's reflection explained the meaning of this uncanny intruder; it was the giant shadow of Mont Blanc, testifying to his supremacy over all meaner eminences. It is difficult to say how sharply marked was the outline, and how startling was the contrast between this pyramid of darkness and the faintly-lighted spaces beyond its influence; a huge inky blot seemed to have suddenly fallen upon the landscape. As we gazed we could see it move. It swallowed up ridge by ridge, and its sharp point crept steadily from one landmark to another down the broad Valley of Aosta. We were standing, in fact, on the point of the gnomon of a gigantic sundial, the face of which was formed by thousands of square miles of mountain and valley. So clear was the outline that, if figures had been scrawled upon glaciers and ridges, we could have told the time to a second; indeed, we were half inclined to look for our own shadows at a distance so great that whole villages would be represented by a scarcely distinguishable speck of colouring . . . By some singular effect of perspective, rays of darkness seemed to be converging from a point above our heads to a point immediately above the apex of the shadowy cone. For a time it seemed that there was a kind of anti-sun in the east, pouring out not light, but deep shadow as it rose. The apex soon reached the horizon, and then to our surprise began climbing the distant sky. Would it never stop and was Mont Blanc capable of overshadowing not only the earth but the sky? . . . But rapidly the lights went out upon the great army of mountains; the snow all round took the livid hue which immediately succeeds an Alpine sunset, and almost at a blow the shadow of Mont Blanc was swallowed up in the general shade of night . . . We were between the day and the night. The western heavens were of the most brilliant blue with spaces of transparent green, whilst a few scattered cloudlets glowed as if with internal fire. To the east the night rushed up furiously, and it was difficult to imagine that the dark purple sky was really cloudless and not blackened by the rising of some portentous storm . . . In that strange gloom the moon looked wan and miserable enough . . . and but for her half-comic look of helplessness, we might have sympathized with the astronomers who tell us that she is nothing but a vast perambulating tombstone, proclaiming to all mankind in the words of the familiar epitaph, 'As I am now, you soon shall be!'

On other occasions the purple passages seem to be a little too carefully constructed and accurately phrased. His inferior, Kingsley, described wild Nature better. Stephen could rarely manage such writing because he did not think like an artist; he usually gives a memorandum of possibilities.[1]

The Sunday Tramps was the other athletic fraternity to which Stephen belonged and which he founded after his second marriage. He, and the lawyer Frederick Pollock, and Croom Robertson, the first editor of the philosophical journal *Mind*, were in the habit of taking long Sunday walks and began to invite others. Eventually the Tramps numbered sixty strong though usually not more than ten came out on any one Sunday. The fellowship lasted for fifteen years and chalked up a score of 252 walks.[2] Among the members were the philosopher James Sully and the Positivist James Cotter Morison; Scrutton and Romer represented the law, F. Y. Edgeworth economics, W. P. Ker criticism, Maitland history and Robert Bridges poetry. Twenty miles was an average stroll and the rule of the order was high thinking and plain living.[3] Sometimes, however, they would be fêted at dinner on their way home by Frederic

[1] Famous as he was, there were occasions when his fame was shrewdly gored. Mrs W. K. Clifford recalled an occasion in Switzerland when a parson and fellow-guest in their hotel did them some service which she wished to acknowledge. 'I thought I was in some fashion paying back the parson's kindness when I invited him to meet Leslie. But that parson, bless you, had never heard of Leslie and to my horror I heard him say, "Oh, yes, Mr Stephen, I like some Radicals, I assure you. Now there was Mr Fawcett – did you ever come across him?" Leslie gave a grumpy "Yes". I settled myself at the tea-table and said firmly, "Oh, but you forget that Mr Stephen is Mr Fawcett's biographer." "Indeed?" said the parson in a benevolent voice, "Do you do much writing, Mr Stephen?" Leslie gave a grunt, and I put in, "Mr Stephen is editing a little Dictionary", and as that produced no response I added, "The Dictionary of National Biography", for I felt bound to boast a little when I saw my poor friend being sat upon. "Indeed," beamed the parson, "It must be very interesting." The thread of the conversation wandered to the scenery, "There are beautiful walks about here," said the parson, and then he asked the shepherd of the Sunday Tramps in a kind of patronizing manner, "Do you care for walking, Mr Stephen?" Leslie was too much squashed even to answer, and again I struggled to the rescue with "Mr Stephen is a great walker and a little stroll of twenty miles before breakfast is nothing to him." "Indeed!" said the parson incredulously. "Ever do any climbing?" '

[2] The Tramps were revived in the first years of this century with the blessing of Pollock and others of the old fraternity. G. M. Trevelyan was a prominent member.

[3] Stephen came by his walking honestly. His grandfather, the Master in Chancery, on his seventieth birthday walked twenty-five miles to breakfast, thence to his office and back home on the same day.

Harrison, Darwin, Tyndall or George Meredith; but Stephen discouraged such sybaritic festivities. On a twenty-mile walk he spoke once to the young philosopher, Samuel Alexander; and that was to point out Morley's house which they were *not* going to visit. He was the general of all expeditions, summoning his troop by cryptic postcards, planning the strategy of the walks, studying the ordnance survey for short cuts to catch a London train that would land them home for a late dinner, and generally maintaining order and discipline. It satisfied his foible for leadership and his delight in ordering the practical affairs of other men, who he liked to assure himself were unpractical bunglers. Mrs Clifford has described the scene of a dinner at the Tyndalls where the Tramps stopped before setting out on the last lap for home. 'Leslie sat at the head of the table and did his autocracy with an occasional grunt or groan if someone said something absurd, but we all knew him to be in his glory. Afterwards we had coffee in Tyndall's study upstairs and then Leslie looked round and said to himself so that all who were near him could hear, 'I must sweep these creatures off', and five minutes later the Tramps were striding down the road two by two, Leslie's tall figure erect and unfaltering, a pace or two in front.'

Leslie and Julia

Leslie Stephen's marriage to Julia changed his life and brought his friends once more into it. Neither he nor Julia had social ambitions. Although their maids whispered that they were 'well connected', since Julia's first cousins were the Duchess of Bedford and Lady Henry Somerset (the daughter-in-law of the Duke of Beaufort), the Stephens had no desire to be received at Woburn or Badminton; and as Lord Henry Somerset, and his younger brother Lord Arthur, who was a central figure in the Cleveland Street Scandal, had both on different occasions been compelled to fly the country for fear of being prosecuted for homosexual offences, they were even less inclined to court these grandees. Leslie made great play with the fact that he shunned society. Julia was at home on Sundays but Leslie would often rush from the room, particularly at the sound of music. In his own house he would stamp and groan if someone outstayed his welcome and once when an old friend droned on he said audibly to himself, 'Oh Gibbs, what a bore you are!' (Gibbs was somewhat cast down and Julia made Leslie apologize.)

He was blind to the visual arts, did not care for sightseeing and was unhappy in Bohemia. 'I have always been shy of artistic people who inhabit a world very unfamiliar to me,' he confessed to his children. Nature, not art, was Stephen's goddess. For this insular Englishman France by and large was a disagreeable corridor to Switzerland. He detested catechizers who tried to pry quotable opinions out of him. When his tall spare figure entered a drawing-room, hostesses feared that a blight would wither the conversation. As Augustine Birrell remarked, Stephen's favourite wind was due east. He was silent because he was thinking about his next article, about the past, about some tangle in the writing of some philosopher long dead. Watts's portrait pictures him meditating, far away. Morley used to tell the story, as an example of Stephen's 'refusal to magnify an incident into an event', of how they spent one Sunday together alone in the country and how Stephen just as he was leaving remarked: 'I suppose you have heard that the French army has surrendered at Sedan and the Emperor is a prisoner?'

In fact Leslie was more sociable than legend allowed. Julia introduced him to the Little Holland House set and he found Burne-Jones and Watts less intimidating than he feared. There was scarcely a literary figure whom he did not know: Tennyson, Carlyle, Arnold, George Eliot, Trollope, Meredith were all in varying degrees on friendly terms with him. This did not mean he toadied to them. He could be satirical about the worshippers at Tennyson's shrine or in George Eliot's bower; he thought Trollope just the man to write Thackeray's life because 'he will be stupid but kindly'; he disliked Arnold's 'rhymeless and to my taste jolting and uncomfortable metres,' and even more what he regarded as his humbug about Greek and Roman civilization. He had for a radical such as himself a discerning respect for Carlyle, recognizing that Carlyle too had been a radical, as much a destroyer of the shams of upper-class society as he was in his latter days a lampooner of democracy. He knew just how to write the sort of letter which might extract an article from George Eliot on a subject of his choice – neither too flattering nor obsequious but sincere in its evident acceptance of the unique place she held in English intellectual life. As we have seen he was a patron through his editorship of younger writers and men of letters such as Gosse – his one regret was that his friendship with Robert Louis Stevenson failed to ripen, entirely, he thought, through his own fault.

Indeed the recluse of the last years, shrouded in gloom, is nothing like the man in his prime of life. ' "I shall be glad when all this dining out is over, Ginny," he said to his daughter as he stood under the lamp in the hall waiting to go out to dinner,' but she had the impression that he liked it. He gave dinner parties for eight or ten, with many courses and different wines. He liked pretty women, Virginia thought.

I can see him taking a lady downstairs on his arm; and laughing. He cannot have been as severe and melancholy and morose as I make him out. He must have made conversation and told anecdotes, and he had, now I come to think of it, a little card case and went calling, like other Victorian gentlemen, of a Sunday afternoon . . . He must have been an attractive man of fifty: a man who had four small children, and a beautiful wife; a man who came into the drawing room in evening dress and marched off down to dinner with Mrs Gosse, or Lady Romer, or Mrs Boon, or Lady Lyttelton just as he presided over the London Library meetings and went to the Ad Eundem dinner at Oxford or Cambridge . . . He had great charm for women, and was often attracted as I could tell from something gallant and tender in his manner by the young and lovely. The name of an American, Mrs Grey, comes back to me, and my mother somehow conveying to me that I might tease him, as I extricated crumbs from his beard, about 'flirting with pretty ladies'. These were the words used; and he looked at me, not angry, for I was only acting a parrot; still I remember the sudden shock, then he controlled what might have been a snort; and said something emphatic, as if to show me he would stand no jokes about that . . . All the same I like to remember, for it gives humanity to his austere figure, that he was so struck, so normally and masculinely affected by Mrs Langtry's beauty, that he actually went to the play to see her. Otherwise he never went to the play.

Friendship for Stephen was an act of private communion. Once when he and Maitland marched over the Cornish moors, Leslie remained silent all day: but Maitland said, 'I felt we had become friends.' It was characteristic of Stephen that, when he was broken by Minny's death and spent his days in solitude, he roused himself to make one new friend who needed friendship and was enduring a harder fate than himself, the brilliant mathematician, William Kingdon Clifford, at that date almost at his last gasp from consumption. It was Stephen who got up a subscription to send him to Madeira in the vain hope that he might recover.[1] Naturally many of his friends were among the rationalists, Croom Robertson the logician at University College London being a favourite. But he prized, far more than conformity to his brand of heterodoxy, poetic imagination among his friends. He knew thousands of lines of poetry by heart and cared no more than when he was a tot of startling onlookers by reciting them aloud to himself. He was formidable. He was impressive. When he entered a room, he changed what was said and felt there. For young men such as his nephew H. A. L. Fisher or the King's classical scholar Walter Headlam who were putting out to sea Stephen was a lodestar by which one navigated. His sincerity, honesty and integrity were proverbial – and so were his eccentricities. He was more than the sum of his qualities. No one was left in any doubt what he thought of things – or of themselves. 'Out he would come,' said his daughter, 'with some fact or opinion, no matter who was there. And he had very strong opinions; and he was extremely well-informed. What he said was most respectfully listened to.' He was in fact a fine talker – not in general conversation when he would

[1] He continued after Clifford's death in 1879 to look after his widow and family, who often stayed at his house in Cornwall. Lucy Clifford was the author of *Mrs Keith's Crime*, a novel which created a certain stir, and of a number of children's books: one of her stories, 'The New Mother' in *Anyhow Stories*, is a classic of the Victorian nursery.

say little (though he timed his snorts admirably) but alone when he would talk of books, poetry, prize-fighting, philosophy, the Alps and the iniquities of contributors to the Dictionary. He talked excellent French and reminded Gabriel Loppé of the 'English eighteenth-century novelists with their humour and their good sense'. He liked talking about people and their oddities – in the last year of his life he was roaring with laughter over the memoirs of Squire Mytton.

Of all his friends Meredith, Morley, Charles Eliot Norton and Maitland were the dearest: Meredith, accepting that man is Earth-born and at one with Nature, with his creed of cultivating joy and laughter, with his belief that action and feeling unlock all gates and that action and feeling proceed from the brain; and the young radical Morley of the *Saturday* and *Fortnightly* Reviews, who was one of the few men Stephen could bear to see after Minny's death – with his belief in reason and freedom of the mind, and with a capacity for kindness that impressed two such dissimilar men as Herbert Spencer and Gladstone; and who in turn years later was to say that among all his friends Stephen moved him most since Stephen had such uncanny powers of sympathy. He got to know Norton in 1868–9 and again in 1872–3, when he was in London. Norton was the most faithful of his American correspondents, described by Maitland as 'father confessor to English literary gents'. Here was an art historian who praised the age of Giotto and Dante and saw in Renaissance art (St Peter's dome being 'swollen with earthly pride') the offspring of corrupt politics and lax morality. Here again was an American gentleman who disliked the form democracy was taking there, thought American football brutal, and spoke his mind about architecture in Cambridge to such effect that a Harvard sophomore, on being asked why he thought a certain building important, replied 'It has not yet been condemned by Charles Eliot Norton.' As for Maitland, his distinction of mind was so evident and his admiration and affection so touching that Stephen was to say 'I think no *man* is so fond or as pleasant to me in every way.' Friends were there to give him love: he expected to take at least as much as he gave in friendship. Thus when Leslie Stephen came to write the *Mausoleum Book* and describe for his children his life with their mother, he chose a curious but characteristic sequence. He chose to record the deaths of those who through kinship or friendship were nearest to him, milestones along the black road on which he was travelling until he reached the most terrible tombstone of all which stood over Julia's grave. He acknowledged that his children might think it odd but explained that his solitude as a widower was all the more intense 'because so few of those with whom I started and upon whose sympathies I could have counted survive to care for me'.

Like other women Julia had found Leslie terrifying at first, but he told her that she had a side to her character scarcely less formidable: 'if she looked at me as I had seen her look at some people, I would sink into the earth'. To the intellectual aristocracy she seemed the ideal wife. Her beauty was noble, her expression pensive, her grief in widowhood unassuageable and her devotion to her husband and children inexhaustible. She brought Leslie three step-children: her elder son George Duckworth on whom she particularly doted, her daughter Stella to whom as a girl she was excessively severe, and her younger son Gerald to whom, being delicate, she gave special attention. She was to bear Leslie four children in the five years between 1879 and 1883: Vanessa, Thoby, Virginia and Adrian; and again in the dreamy, forgetful youngest son she found a special joy, calling him her 'joydé'. She had the gift of combining genuine tenderness with firmness towards children so that they always knew where they were and what was expected of them, and their father boasted that she never had to punish them. She could heal a child's wound before it could fester, read thoughts before they were uttered, and her sympathy was like that of the touch of a butterfly, delicate and remote.

As if running a house for a demanding husband and eight children were not enough, Julia Stephen would help anyone who knocked at her door: the bereaved, the sick, her mother crippled with rheumatism who wrote her two or three letters a day; old friends of Leslie who by this time had become bores and whom few would solace; young suitors for whom the course of love was not running true, including those whom Stella rejected. She remembered anniversaries, she invented treats for her multitude of nieces and nephews and cousins, she sometimes made the running on a committee: when a memorial to Lowell could not be erected in Westminster Abbey because he was an American, she saw to it that he was commemorated in the Chapter House. She did not hesitate to pillory in the *Pall Mall Gazette* the guardians of St George's Workhouse in Fulham for giving in to the temperance movement and cutting off the half-pint of beer which the inmates got. She was in turn attacked for indiscretion and deceiving the public, but she accepted public controversy to be inescapable. Day after day she made immense rounds by bus – shopping, calling, visiting hospitals and workhouses – returning home exhausted. Day after day the pile of letters and calls for help, all to be answered, grew more daunting. 'Ah, thank Heaven,' she would exclaim on a Saturday, 'there is no post tonight', and Leslie would look up from his book, press her hand and plead with her, 'There must be an end of this, Julia.' But there never was.

She was not only solicitous. She was shrewd and practical. Julia's single publication is lost in oblivion yet it reveals her character as surely as Virginia Woolf's portraits. It is about nursing and called *Notes for Sick Rooms*. 'I have often wondered', she asked, 'why it is considered a proof of virtue in anyone to become a nurse. The ordinary relations between the sick and the well are far easier and pleasanter than between the well and the well.' Jane Marcus wondered whether she was ever a little guilty about her power over the ill. Julia advised nurses to hide troubles from their patients and even to 'lie freely'. Her book was imaginative in that it brought to mind all the details unobserved by the sage, combining an exquisite sensibility towards other people's sufferings with exceedingly practical advice on how to alleviate them. 'The origin of most things', she begins, 'has been decided on, but the origin of crumbs in bed has never excited sufficient attention among the scientific world' – and from there she analyses the almost impossible task of getting rid of them.[1] From the snuffing of candles, their arrangement, and the position of looking-glasses, to the techniques of bed-baths and of administering enemas, everything is discussed, from the point of view of the sufferer, with irony, detachment and common sense.

Alexander Zwerdling noticed how little her unpublished essays resemble the wispy figure of Mrs Ramsay. You do not become a nurse, wrote Julia, to get wages or freedom, or to become a heroine or a slave. You conform to rigid rules and unvarying schedules because you recognize that to serve is the highest expression of your nature. You do not become an agnostic to follow your husband. 'In the acceptance or rejection of a creed let the woman be judged as the man.' Her children's stories are tales of the disappointments restless, rebellious children suffer who try to escape from the routine of the nursery: such terrible

[1] 'Among the number of small evils which haunt illness, the greatest, in the misery which it can cause, though the smallest in size, is crumbs. The origin of most things has been decided on, but the origin of crumbs in bed has never excited sufficient attention among the scientific world, though it is a problem which has tormented many a weary sufferer. I will forbear to give my own explanation, which would be neither scientific nor orthodox, and will merely beg that their evil existence may be recognized and, as far as human nature allows, guarded against. The torment of crumbs should be stamped out of the sick bed as if it were the Colorado beetle in a potato field. Anyone who has been ill will at once take her precautions, feeble though they will prove. She will have a napkin under her chin, stretch her neck out of bed, eat in the most uncomfortable way, and watch that no crumbs get into the folds of her night-dress or jacket. When she lies back in bed, in the vain hope that she may have baffled the enemy, he is before her: a sharp crumb is buried in her back, and grains of sand seem sticking to her toes. If the patient is able to get up and have her bed made, when she returns to it she will find the crumbs are waiting for her. The housemaid will protest that the sheets were shaken, and the nurse that she swept out the crumbs, but there they are, and there they will remain unless the nurse determines to conquer them. To do this she must first believe in them, and there are few assertions that are met with such incredulity as the one – I have crumbs in my bed. After every meal the nurse should put her hand into the bed and feel for the crumbs. When the bed is made, the nurse and housemaid must not content themselves with shaking or sweeping. The tiny crumbs stick in the sheets, and the nurse must patiently take each crumb out; if there are many very small ones, she must even wet her fingers, and get the crumbs to stick to them. The patient's night-clothes must be searched; crumbs lurk in each tiny fold or frill. They go up the sleeve of the night-gown, and if the patient is in bed when the search is going on, her arms should hang out of bed, so that the crumbs which are certain to be there may be induced to fall down. When crumbs are banished – that is to say, temporarily, for with each meal they return, and for this the nurse must make up her mind – she must see that there are no rucks in the bed-sheets.' Is not the tone of voice similar to that in her daughter's essays?

truthfulness may explain why children preferred wilder fantasies.

People spoke of her as perfect and the marriage as perfect; but, of course, nothing is perfect. She and Leslie decided to teach their children in the nursery; but Leslie was too much of a Wrangler to understand how to teach simple arithmetic and to the end her daughters counted on their fingers. They were both too quick-tempered and unadaptable in their methods to be good teachers. Nor did Julia see to it that the French and Swiss governesses taught her children foreign languages instead of learning theirs. She prided herself that until just before her death no servant ever gave notice except to get married but she was astounded, as we shall see, when one tweeny in an outburst told her that the state of the servants' quarters made her life a misery. She was a little too anxious, perhaps, to proffer help, a little too inclined to plot; not all her matchmaking was wise. She could not believe that anyone could do menial tasks for her husband and children better than herself, and in this she was right; but that is not a sufficient reason for not engaging a nurse in illness. She was, Virginia Woolf admitted, 'impetuous and a little imperious'; she pandered to Leslie's fetish for economy and was for ever saving time. Perhaps the demands their father made on her left too little time for her children, and perhaps they occasionally wondered whether they, too, were one of her self-imposed tasks as she hurried away to leave them for her demanding mother or some sick dependant. Julia herself had written, 'the art of being ill is no easy one to learn, but it is practised to perfection by many of the greatest sufferers'; and though some blame Leslie for grudging the time she spent nursing her mother, Mrs Jackson was an experienced valetudinarian and Leslie saw that those visits exhausted Julia. There was never enough time to do all the duties she imposed upon herself and in the end she was 'to sink, like an exhausted swimmer, deeper and deeper into the water'.

Nevertheless her relationship with her husband was perfect – if by that we mean that whatever each gave was freely given. Perhaps Julia did not often tell him how much she adored him, and husbands and wives need to tell each other aloud how much they dote. But in this case there was no need to do so as they had other means of telling each other, 'by their gestures, their glances of pure and unutterable delight in each other'. In her letters she called him by the endearments of Wowski or Wummy. She would not have married him if she had not believed she could worship him; and she did worship him. He worshipped her so much that he had to resort to the language of religion to describe his devotion. In a reminiscence written for her nephews well before she published her first novel Virginia Woolf found how hard it was to describe her mother without turning her into the marble angel of Leslie's *Mausoleum Book* – the book he wrote for Julia's children. Virginia told her nephews that

Julia had lived a life of service to others but that they should not confuse it 'with that "mischievous" philanthropy which other women practise so complacently and often with such disastrous results'. She helped people to discover what they really meant or felt because she understood how they were placed and what therefore they were free or not to do. It was not what she did but how she did it, discovering incongruity in unlikely situations and having 'a constant sense of the mystery which encircled' people's lives. She animated people to do and say things they would never have done had she not stirred them. Nor was her concern only for family friends: the conductor on the bus would be asked in winter why the company provided no straw for him to stand on, 'Your feet must be cold.' Agnosticism taught her to live intensely for the event of the moment: the future was futile. Her imagination set fire to her words so that, in that most inarticulate of situations when children are being seen off on a journey, she would make up stories about the other passengers and keep them laughing.

She could say sharp things – teasing things too – and smile at her husband's ways. But it was her delight, not her duty, to do all trivial chores for him so that he could be a great man – as she always assured her children that he was. Younger by fifteen years, she felt genuine humility before him without doubting that her own work of helping others as well as him was important. In everything that mattered they were in perfect sympathy with each other. She knew Leslie was tormented by the thought that he was a failure who had not quite made it, had not fulfilled himself; and she told him not to be excessively modest, took care to repeat compliments she had heard and learnt how to praise him with discrimination. But she did not let him walk over her: she issued invitations on the spur of the moment to old and young alike and kept the house alive, pressing friends to stay for dinner even if it brought groans from her unsociable husband.

The Stephens lived at 22 Hyde Park Gate, a cul-de-sac off Kensington Gore. This is how Virginia Woolf, in the last year of her life, remembered her home:

The servants' sitting room in the basement was at the back, very low and very dark; there was an ottoman covered in shiny black American cloth along one wall; and a vast cracked picture of Mr and Mrs Pattle covered the wall above it. I remember a very tall young man with tight trousers strapped over the instep, and white socks. It was relegated to the room because it was so big, so cracked, so bad – compared with the Watts portraits upstairs. One could hardly see it – who was the woman? I cannot see her – or anything else; for the creepers hung down in front of the window, in summer strung with hand-shaped semi-transparent leaves. There was an iron trellis to support them, and outside the little dust-smelling, patchy square of wall-circled back garden. I remember the wood cupboard in the passage; piled with bundles of fire wood tied with tarry string; once when I rummaged there for a stick to whittle, two eyes glowed in a corner; and Sophie warned me that wild cats might have lived there. The basement was a dark insanitary place for seven maids to live in. 'It's like Hell', one of them burst out to my mother as we sat at lessons in the dining room. My mother at once assumed the frozen dignity of the Victorian matron; and said (perhaps), 'Leave the room'; and she (unfortunate girl) vanished behind the red plush curtain which, hooped round a semi-circular wire, and anchored by a great gold knob, hid the door that led from the dining room to the pantry.

It was in the dining room, at the long baize covered table, that we did our lessons. My mother's finger with the opal ring I loved pointed its way across French and Latin Grammars. The dining room had two little windows filled with bottle glass at one end. Built into the alcove was a heavily carved sideboard; on which stood a blue china dumb waiter; and a biscuit tin shaped like a barrel. The room smelt slightly of wine, cigars, food. It was lit also by a skylight, one pane of which lifted in a wind and made me shiver, lest it should crash on our heads. Round the walls hung Sir Joshua engravings; in the corner on a pedestal of mottled yellow marble stood the bust of the first Sir James – an eyeless white man. It was a very Victorian dining room; with a complete set of chairs carved in oak; high backed; with red plush panels. At dinner time with all its silver candles, silver dishes, knives and forks and napkins, the dinner table looked very festive. A twisting stair case led to the hall. In the hall lay a dog, beside him a bowl of water with a chunk of yellow sulphur in it. In the hall facing the front door stood a cabinet with blue china; and on it a gold faced clock. In the hall was a three cornered chair; and a chest in which rugs were kept; and on this chest was a silver salver deep in visiting cards; and a plush glove for smoothing the silk of George's and Gerald's top hats; and I also remember nailed over the fire place a long strip of chocolate coloured cardboard on which was written: 'What is to be a gentleman? It is to be tender to women, chivalrous to servants.' What else I cannot remember; though I used to know it by heart. What innocence, what incredible simplicity of mind it showed – to keep this cardboard quotation – from Thackeray I think – perpetually displayed, as if it were a frontispiece to a book – nailed to the wall in the hall of the house.

The two drawing rooms opened out of the hall; the front and the back drawing room. The front, facing the street, was comparatively light; the Watts portrait of father faced the door, a flattered, an idealized picture, up to which father would lead admiring ladies; and pause and contemplate it, with some complacency. But 'Lowell said it makes me look like a weasel', he once said. There was the grand piano upon which Christmas presents were stood; and Stella's writing table in the window; and the round table in the middle, which, when supplemented by a small folding table which has followed me, unwelcomed, even to Monks House, made the tea table. The tea table, the very hearth and centre of family life, the tea table round which sat innumerable parties; on which, when Sunday came – the tea table's festival day – pink shell plates were placed, full of brown Sunday buns, full of very thin slices of white and brown bread and butter.

The tea table rather than the dinner table was the centre of Victorian family life – in our family at least. Savages I suppose have some tree, or fire place, round which they congregate; the round table marked that focal, that sacred spot in our house. It was the centre, the heart of the family. It was the centre to which the sons returned from their work in the evening; the hearth whose fire was tended by the mother, pouring out tea. In the same way, the bedroom – the double bedded bedroom on the first floor was the sexual centre; the birth centre; the death centre of the house. It was not a large room; but its walls must be soaked, if walls take pictures and hoard up what is done and said, with all that was most intense, with all that makes the most private being, of family life. In that bed four children were begotten; there they were born; there, first, mother died; then father died, with a picture of mother hanging in front of him. The house mounted in three roomed storeys above that bedroom. Above father's and mother's bedroom floor were the three bedrooms of George, Gerald, and Stella; above their bedrooms our night and day nurseries; above that the great study with its high ceiling of yellow stained wood; and the servants' bedrooms. There were different smells on different landings of that tall dark house. One landing smelt perpetually of candle grease; for on a high cupboard stood all the bedroom candles. On another half landing was the water closet; with all the brass hot water cans standing by a sink. On another half landing was the solitary family bath. (My father all his life washed in a yellow tin bath with flat ears on which the soap stood.) Further up, was a brown filter from which once the drinking water presumably was supplied: in our day it only dripped a little. At that height – it was on the study half landing – carpets and pictures had given out, and the top landing of all was a little pinched and bare. Once when a pipe burst and some young man visitor – Peter Studd? – volunteered help and rushed up stairs with a bucket, he penetrated to the servants' bedrooms, and my mother, I noted, seemed a little 'provoked', a little perhaps ashamed, that he had seen what must have been their rather shabby rooms. My father's great study – that study had been built on, when the family grew – was a fine big room, very high, three windowed, and entirely book lined. His old rocking chair covered in American cloth was the centre of the room which was the brain of the house. He had written all his books lying sunk in that deep rocking chair; which swung up and down; for it was so deep that his feet were off the ground. Across it lay his writing board; with the sheets of foolscap always folded down the middle, so that he could make corrections in the margin. And there was his fine steel pen and the curious china inkpot, with a well lidded, out at the side. All his books were dipped out of that well on the point of Joseph Gillott's long shanked steel pens. And I remember the little flat shield that his pen had rubbed smooth and hard on the joint of his forefinger. Minnie's portrait by Watts – a charming shy face – nestling away, not noble, not heroic, but shy and sweet, hung over the fireplace; and in the corner by the window stood a stack of rusty alpenstocks. From the three long windows one looked out over the roofs of Kensington, to the presiding church of St Mary Abbots, the church where our conventional marriages were celebrated – and one day standing there father saw an eagle. It was, I thought, like him that he knew it for an eagle at once; and at once verified the fact, from the paper, that it was an eagle that had escaped from the Zoo. He would not make up stories about wild eagles flying over London.

In 1881 on a walking tour Stephen discovered St Ives and saw a house

owned by the Great Western Railway to let in what he called the very toe-
nail of England. The railway had reached the town that year and it was
still a little town with steep little streets, without hotels or villas. The
distance was such that it could never be more than a summer holiday
home. It stood on the hill outside the town with a garden surrounded by
hedges of escallonia, full of purple jacaranda; and from a grassy mound
there was a view across the bay. The curves of the bay 'flowed in and out
to the two black rocks at one end of which stood the black and white
tower of the Lighthouse'. This was where each summer the family moved
for a holiday of garden cricket, of long walks on the moors – regarded by
the young children as a penance – or to look for cowrie shells on the beach
or occasionally to go fishing in a lugger; and when they made for home,
Leslie would say, ' "Show them you can bring her in, my boy," and Thoby
with his blue eyes very blue and his mouth set, sat there bringing us round
the point into harbour'.

There was no lack of guests at Hyde Park Gate and Talland House:
Julia was given to inviting people on the spur of the moment. Whom
might you have met at the Stephens? Poets and writers of the older school
such as Meredith, or of the younger such as Henry James. Burne-Jones,
G. F. Watts and Millais were often there; John Addington Symonds and
his daughter Madge were welcome guests – Leslie, who considered
married homosexuals as blackguards, being presumably unaware that
Symonds's relations with Alpine guides were more than somewhat
different from his. There were younger scholars such as Frederick
Pollock, Maitland or W. P. Ker: among thinkers Haldane and Croom
Robertson were frequent visitors. You would not have met acquaintances
such as Herbert Spencer or Froude whom Julia detested. Naturally there
were Positivists such as Frederic Harrison or James Cotter Morison.
Among the Positivists, Vernon Lushington's wife Jane was a great
favourite, and Julia made a famous match between their beautiful
daughter Kitty and Leo Maxse. Indeed there were a lot of young people
around. Leslie liked the young if they were intelligent and not on the
make. Leonard Woolf remembered meeting him in Thoby's rooms in
Trinity and being alarmed at having to talk to him by shouting into his
ear-trumpet, when every word he said produced an ever deepening
expression of sorrow. But oddly enough he found his terror evaporating.
Stephen's charm, his natural distinction, his exquisite sense of what the
young might be feeling and, above all, the humour and the laughter
showed that, as they were courteous enough to appreciate him, he had no
difficulty in appreciating them.

What did that eminent Victorian look like? 'A striking, indeed a
magnificent figure,' Virginia Woolf thought:

well dressed in his Hill Brothers clothes; a swallow tail coat; very lean and tall
and bent, with his beard flowing so that his little scraggy tie scarcely showed. His

chin I think retreated; perhaps his mouth, which I never saw, was a little looselipped; but his forehead rose and swelled; his skull was magnificent, with a little dent over the arch of the brain, that he made me feel once; and though his eyes were very small, with hairy eyebrows hanging over them, they were pure bright forget me not blue. His hands were beautifully shaped; and he wore a signet ring with his double eagle crest engraved on a pale blue stone. As a trifling sign of his indifference to appearances, he went on wearing the ring when the stone was lost. He must have put on his clothes automatically, to the sound of poetry, I expect; the waistcoat was often unbuttoned; sometimes the fly buttons; and the coat was often grey with tobacco ash. He smoked pipes incessantly as he wrote, but never in the drawing room. There he sat in his own chair, with a little table beside him on which was a lamp and two or three books, and . . . as my father read he kicked his foot up and down, and twisted and untwisted the lock behind his ear. He was always absorbed; often seemed completely unconscious of his surroundings; and lived by rote – that is always at a certain moment would be up and off – up stairs to work, out to walk; every Saturday to visit James Payn; or off to some meeting. And out of doors he strode along, often shaking his head emphatically as he recited poetry, and giving his stick a flourish. He wore a billy cock hat always, which sat rather oddly upon that great head with the thick bush of hair flowing out on either side.

The Stephens brought up their children along conventional Victorian lines. The discipline of the nursery and the schoolroom ruled their lives when they were tiny. Stephen called them the ragamice. 'I can always call up their little faces especially Virginia's,' he wrote to Julia. 'I see her eyes flash and her sweet little teeth gleam.' As they grew older they spun fancies about them as parents will; Thoby was to be Lord Chancellor, Virginia a writer, Adrian – well, he was more puzzling to Stephen since he 'always seems so infantile for his years though he is certainly intelligent'. Their father read to them – not merely *Tom Brown's Schooldays* and *Treasure Island* but all Jane Austen, Hawthorne, Carlyle's *The French Revolution*, and the thirty-two volumes of the Waverley novels which once he had completed he would begin again at the first. He drew sketches of animals in their books – and his own. If one of their toy boats sank in the Round Pond and it was retrieved, he would re-rig it with his own hands chortling at the pleasure it gave him. He shattered the peace of several homes with his shout of 'Rats!' as he recited the Pied Piper of Hamelin. And he could sulk over a game of raversi with little Ethel Clifford: 'She would beat me, confound her, I never like being beaten.' It was not an ecstatic family, in which cousins and kinsmen and rounds of visits or travel wove patterns which made the tapestry of childhood glow through the rest of their lives; but neither was it grim and cheerless like many middle-class upbringings.

There was one matter in particular on which Leslie and Julia saw eye to eye. That was the status of women. What at the beginning of the century had seemed to be the eccentricities of Mary Wollstonecraft had become by mid century 'The Woman Question'. Stephen did not share the views of his friends at Cambridge. C. B. Clarke told how at 'a dinner at Wolstenholme's rooms, in Christ's, there were present Horne, . . . and others: we discussed the emancipation of women. L. Stephen did not chime in. We reached the point when we agreed we would give women votes for Members of Parliament. At this point Stephen stood up at the dinner table and said, "I wish I had somebody's head here in a mortar," which he energetically pounded, "it makes one wild to listen to you fellows drivelling radicalism . . . To give women votes – why, it might save the Church of England for a quarter of a century" '. Yes, women were less afraid than men to make sacrifices of conscience but if women were to acquire influence they must become more sceptical and not 'buy peace of mind at the expense of truth and liberty'. Yes, women should be properly educated; but as they were not and formed part of the mountain of prejudice, why put the cart before the horse and give them votes before they were qualified to express opinions? Votes for women were part of that 'happy millennium when ladies will compete with men for success in the learned professions'. When in 1897 there was a Grace in the Senate House at Cambridge to grant women full membership of the university, Stephen did not go up to vote. He did not care for emancipated women. George Eliot was one thing; Olive Schreiner another. He met 'the wonderful Miss Schreiner' in Switzerland in 1887, 'a pretty, black-eyed, tiny woman of 25 or so who has written the African farm' and was 'a desperate free-thinker'. All at first went well; then after two days he judged 'she is clever, but I should guess hard and conceited'; and after a fortnight, he learned 'she disapproves of marriage and thinks that everybody should be free to drop everyone else – I should drop *her* like a hot potato'.

Julia Stephen was even more decided than he. Octavia Hill was her close friend and in 1889 she signed her Appeal Against Female Suffrage as did that formidable young woman, the future Fabian, Beatrice Potter. Julia shared Leslie's view – and, as we shall see later, it was the view held by the vast majority of their contemporaries – that men and women played different roles in life, roles conditioned by their physiology as well as their education. She had every right to pride herself on her household management and her efficient management on other matters than her family. But she considered a woman's duty was to serve – to serve her husband, her children, her parents and kinsmen and those in need. She delighted to play what Meredith called the part of princess to a patriarch.

The 1880s were years when Stephen came into his own. He began to write biographies. Each generation has its Great Author series and the English Men of Letters series was then getting under way: Leslie contributed the volumes on Swift, Pope, Johnson, George Eliot and at the very end of his life on Hobbes. Fawcett got him to stand for the newly created Clark Lectureship at Cambridge: he got it and delivered twenty lectures in the May Term of 1884. Fawcett may have hoped that Trinity or some other college might offer him a fellowship; or the University would create a chair for him; but Stephen thought the enterprise worthless and whatever plots Fawcett may have laid vanished when Stephen's old friend died at the end of that year. The inevitable occurred. Stephen took on the task, in addition to his editorial labours on the Dictionary, to write Fawcett's life, as he was to do in the next decade for his brother Fitzjames and for J. R. Green. He was also doing the research for the biographies in the Dictionary which he himself had undertaken to write. No one should imagine Stephen regarded this as a chore. To him such research became after a time a delight. 'No man', he wrote, 'is a real reading enthusiast until he is sensible of the pleasure of turning over some miscellaneous collection, and lying like a trout in a stream snapping up, with the added charm of unsuspectedness, any of the queer little morsels of oddity or pathos that may drift past him . . . I do not know that one can find a much better hunting-ground than the dictionary.'

In 1884 he wrote to Julia, 'When I am by myself I always begin thinking what poor stuff all my writing is . . . the practical moral is that I may as well do dictionary work as anything else.' Some scholars are at heart modest men and for partly that reason undertake chores of editing learned periodicals, and commenting upon other scholars' work in manuscript. A letter to Austin Dobson in 1887 shows what a meticulous scholar he was and how detailed were the references which he would give to a contributor. But the editorial work on the Dictionary was in the end to crush him. Once the enterprise got under way many hours were spent in cursing the handwriting and prolixity of the contributors. In 1885 he took no holiday, his own handwriting grew spidery and difficult to read, and the headaches which racked him after Minny's death returned. Throughout his letters the execrations roll like thunder. 'That damned Dictionary is about my bed and spies out all my ways, as the psalmist says' . . . 'I am knee-deep in dictionary and drudgery' . . . 'A hideous package from the Dictionary has come which I have not yet had the courage to open' . . . 'The damned thing goes on like a diabolical piece of machinery, always gaping for more copy, and I fancy at times that I shall be dragged into it, and crushed out into slips.'

His friends, accustomed to his groans and delighting in his outbursts of invective against some obtuse contributor, laughed at the act Stephen put on for their benefit. But his wife did not laugh. She loathed the Dictionary and saw that it was killing Leslie. Even at its inception in November 1882 he had bad nights, and in the year 1884 he seems to have been filled with self-doubt. In March he thought that 'Hours in a Library and all that kind of stuff is not my real taste and therefore I can produce only third-rate work': hence he was justified in taking on the Dictionary. Five months later he thought, 'I have done just enough in another way to show that I could have done something decent if I had not wasted myself', and he spoke to Julia of his depression which 'only comes by fits chiefly a dodge to get a rise out of you'. Each Christmas George Smith sent Mrs Stephen an elegant box of sweets and in her letter of thanks in 1885 she told him how worried she was about Leslie's state of mind. She wrote to the same effect after Christmas in 1887 recalling how Leslie had described a night in which 'the Dictionary came upon me in the most ghastly manner'. In 1888 she told Smith he had had a week of bad nights.

Stephen's breakdown was serious. He had never known what it was not to sleep well. During the worst of the attacks he still slept, but woke up convinced that he had not. He tossed and turned and 'I would sometimes lie awake in a fit of "the horrors" – in a state, that is to say, of nervous excitement and misery', convinced that he would not sleep again that night. Julia was there to soothe him and get him off to sleep – at the cost of broken nights and loss of strength on her part and daytime irritability on his. He had already made over the management of their financial affairs to her and he admitted that having delegated he began to pick holes in her management and nag that the family would soon starve as he was nearly broke. Stephen did not give up the Dictionary without a struggle: to quit seemed to him equivalent to striking his colours. First he allowed Lee's name to appear as co-editor, and even when Lee finally took over, biographies continued to flow from his pen. In 1899 he wrote: 'I went to the B. Museum on Saturday and I hope I did the last bit of drudgery[.] I began with Addison seventeen years ago, and now have done Young.' Julia was not only firm: she was resourceful. Tactfully she encouraged him to go ahead with a large-scale project on which he could work at his own pace – the three-volume analysis of the English Utilitarians. He needed her reassurance that he was regarded as a man of some account. When he was courting Julia, he told her that he heard himself described as a notorious penny-a-liner and thought there was a 'horrible plausibility in the description'; and later he asked her to tell some young man that 'it would be more virtuous to starve or take a public house' than earn a living by journalism. The fear that he had dissipated his talents by attempting to fill too many roles continued to haunt him.

Stephen need not have feared. After Matthew Arnold's death in 1888 he was regarded as the first man of English letters and an eminent Victorian. His eminence can scarcely be in doubt. When he rendered his account he had written five volumes of histories of thought, the five books in the English Men of Letters series, three full-length Life and Letters biographies, two short books of reminiscences, and well over a hundred and fifty long articles and introductions. The most important of these articles he gathered together in three volumes of controversial rationalist publications, three volumes of literary criticism, and four volumes of biographical studies. There was also his only purely philosophical work on ethics. Interspersed were his articles for the *DNB* together with a mass of more ephemeral journalism. Finally, just before he died he tried to set out the theory of what he had been trying so often to do in individual articles – namely to relate literature to the society in which it was born and which must in his view inevitably characterize it: he has indeed been called the pioneer of the sociological study of literature. And like many of his contemporaries he was an indefatigable correspondent. There was indeed in the last two decades of the century no one who could match both the enormous range of his reading and an intellectual power under perfect control which expressed itself in a fluent, sinewy style. In the break-up of the mid-Victorian world of letters he symbolized the stable formidable past. Honours began to shower upon him. Trinity Hall made him an Honorary Fellow. Harvard, Cambridge, Oxford and Edinburgh in turn presented him with honorary degrees, and it was at this time that he was elected President of the London Library. He received these awards, declared Sir Walter Raleigh in the first Leslie Stephen Lecture delivered in Cambridge, with amused gratification. The world considered that despite the labour and sorrow that are the common lot of man, he had passed a fortunate life.

The Last Sad Years

But the judgements of the world, as we know, are not worth much. Thomas Hardy told Sidney Lee that 'I have always felt that a tragic atmosphere encircled Leslie Stephen's history and was suggested in some indefinable way by his presence.' Hardy's uncanny instinct had not deserted him. For not only did death hang over the Stephens, as it did over all Victorian families. Madness hovered in the air. They used the word 'thin-skinned' to describe their irritability and manic drive to work. Leslie's father, it will be remembered, had three nervous breakdowns and referred to his 'power of going mad' as if he possessed an over-drive in the gears of his psyche. Leslie himself was in a high state when he decided he could no longer call himself a Christian and again when the Dictionary took its toll. In his own family he had suffered a particularly agonizing blow when it dawned upon him that his daughter Laura was not naughty or recalcitrant but mentally retarded; and eventually she had to be cared for in a special part of the house. Then in the 1880s disaster overtook his favourite nephew, J. K. Stephen. Handsome, companionable, ebullient,

J. K. S. combined the common sense of the Stephens with uproarious wit, was (and still is) the toast of College at Eton for his prowess at the Wall Game, was a Fellow of King's and the author of *Lapsus Calami*, a collection of dazzling parodies which were the talk of London. Leslie admired him as his own son and witnessed the distressing spectacle of seeing him, too, gradually lose his reason. When visiting friends near Felixstowe he was hit on the head by one of the sails of a windmill which worked a pump. Soon after he began to suffer from fits of wild excitement and depression; at times apparently normal, he would suddenly make violent scenes; the committee of his club were compelled to post a policeman at the door to restrain him forcibly from entering. He also at this time began to make violent advances to Stephen's step-daughter, Stella Duckworth. Virginia Woolf remembered him charging into the nursery and skewering a loaf of bread with his sword-stick. But Julia declared that she would never shut her door on 'our Jem', and he continued his visits until the day when the specialist, Sir George Savage, advised confinement. He starved himself to death in an asylum in 1892, the promise of his youth blasted in early years. His father, Fitzjames, was broken by this experience. When Leslie said good-bye to him one day, he noticed for the first time that his hand was no longer crushed by Fitzjames's strong grip. Two years after his son's death, Fitzjames followed him to the grave. Senility overwhelmed him, and he had the mortification of being advised to retire from the Bench after a disgracefully biased summing-up against a woman who he told the jury, without evidence, was an adulteress and that an adulteress by nature was likely to commit murder. But so long as Julia was with Leslie to minister to all his wants and soothe him in his depression he remained unshaken.

Then disaster struck. Julia Stephen came down with influenza early in March 1895. She seemed to get better and the Duckworth children left for the Continent in April. Suddenly life began to drain from her. The family doctor talked of rheumatic fever and the Duckworths hurried home. To the end she trained and cherished her children. 'Hold yourself straight, my little Goat,' were her last words to Virginia as her daughter crept in terror from her bedroom. She was only 48 when she died on the 5th of May, and as the children were brought to the bedroom to kiss their mother's cheek while her body was still warm, Leslie staggered past brushing them aside groaning with grief. Kinsmen and friends came and went, the household lamented and wailed, and the children were brought in yet again to kiss their mother's face now marbled in death. Maitland wrote him a letter which tells how his younger friends felt for him. 'I have an irrepressible wish, however foolish and wrong it may be, to touch your hand and tell you in two words that I think of you . . . Believe that it is (let me say it) with something of filial love that I think of you and write these useless words.'

Today among the English intelligentsia prolonged prostration would be deprecated as embarrassing and as a pathetic inability to come to terms with the inexorable laws of biology. Everything in the day of death is played in the key of C major, so as to diminish pain – the obsequies become a thanksgiving service for the life of the departed and no allusion may be made to the anguish of those who suffer for fear of an unseemly outburst of woe. No one, except conceivably on the day of the funeral, wears black, and the ghastly confederation of mutes, widow's weeds, crape, mourning rings, gloves for the pall-bearers and nodding plumes for the horses who drew the hearse and carriages have vanished as too unsightly a reminder of gloom and doom. Affliction has become a displeasing physical condition, like a colostomy, to be concealed and if possible never mentioned. As a result, that loyalty to the memory of her first love and husband which lacerated Julia, and Leslie's passionate devotion to Julia's spirit seem startling and incredible. Yet when Herbert Duckworth died, Julia used to lie on his grave. Who lies on their lover's grave today? No doubt people when bereaved suffer as deeply as they ever did, but does our love continue for those who died long after they are dead as intensely as Stephen's love did? Perhaps he loved her more volubly in death than in life – and that is a criticism; but to those who consider that his grief was excessive, his explanation is irrefutable: the heart stood up and answered, 'I have felt'.

Some will consider that, having discarded the consolations of religion, he had brought his hopelessness upon himself. But however much good Victorian Christians reassured themselves that their beloved was in a better country and in a better state of spiritual health, they seemed no less inconsolable. Stephen wrote of his loss in an address, 'Forgotten Benefactors', which he gave to the South Place Ethical Society. It was useless, he said, trying to prove that the very thing for which we offer consolation has not happened. The pain persists and when it lulls almost at once revives. True nobility in character means turning grief to account; and this is possible if we recollect that our forgotten benefactors are those who live obscure lives – our wives and mothers, those who knit families together. Stephen may have had in mind the end of *Middlemarch* where George Eliot defends her heroine by saying that, though Dorothea's strength 'spent itself in channels which had no great name on earth', the growing good of the world depended on unhistoric acts by those who 'lived faithfully a hidden life, and rest in unvisited tombs'. Such people, Stephen thought, wield power after they die. The memory of what they approved of or sympathized with is so vivid that we act as if they still lived and were there to guide us.

The rest of his life he decided to consecrate as a memorial to Julia.

Unfortunately in remembering her he forgot everyone but himself. His grief cut to the bone, but he luxuriated in the pain and expected his family to minister to him as Julia had done, all the more so as he now was suffering. Indoors he would walk up and down the room, gesticulating, crying that he had never told their mother how he loved her. Then Stella would fling her arms around him and protest. Most of his life he had had women to attend to his wants and soothe him – his mother, Minny, Anny, Milly, Julia – and now his step-daughter Stella as of duty bound was to fill the breach. But she was already being wooed by a handsome young lawyer with political ambitions. Stella had refused Jack Hills once at St Ives and he went off, if not to the jungle to shoot tigers, to Norway to fish; but he returned, determined to win her, and was at Hyde Park Gate the night before Julia died. He was not to renew his suit at St Ives. In the past two years Stephen had been worried, with two sons of public school age, by the expense of keeping a summer place. Now that he could never endure to visit it again he told his stepson, George, to sell Talland House at once. In its place Stephen took a house in 1896 at Hindhead, and there on a warm summer's night Jack and Stella walked about the garden until the rest of the family had gone to bed. Next morning they announced their engagement. Jack Hills had not got on well with his worldly, snobbish mother whose intellectual aspirations extended no further than friendship with that bookman of bookmen, Andrew Lang; and he had become a special protégé of Julia, which should have commended him to Leslie. 'We must all be happy,' Leslie commanded, 'because Stella is happy.' Despite this good resolution Leslie resented Stella leaving him as he had resented Anny's engagement, and began to abuse Jack to his own children. Jack's name, he said, cut him like the smack of a whip, and he contrived to make the wedding arrangements, always a nerve-racking affair, more frenetic than they need have been. He began to make trouble, the 'ladies were called in'. They called him (behind his back) a monster of selfishness. Virginia remembered those days as 'mostly arguments, denunciations of father'. But though Stella married, dutiful as ever she and Jack settled three doors off and Stephen paid her a daily visit. Then in April on her return from the honeymoon Stella fell ill with appendicitis; and when that summer she became pregnant, the doctors decided to operate. She died the next day.

Stephen's behaviour was all the more outrageous because Stella had taken upon her shoulders all her mother's household duties. Leslie would do nothing for himself. Stella had to buy the underclothes, pay the bills and listen to complaints that she had ordered fish too often that week. What was more alarming and exhausting, she had to tend Virginia's first symptoms of madness. Virginia became anorexic, irritable, spiteful and terrified of strangers or travelling in London. Moods of frenzied excitement were succeeded by fits of depression. Sir George Savage was called in. His diagnosis in some way resembled Stephen's views on women because it derived from the same premise, namely that women have weaker minds as well as weaker bodies. In puberty they developed to a milder or more dangerous extent a disease called hysteria which inflamed the imagination so that it could lead to insanity. Education, certainly prolonged mental activity, was not healthy for growing girls: it was as unnatural as stuffing Strasbourg geese. 'If a promising girl is allowed to educate herself at home,' he opined, 'the danger of solitary work and want of social friction may be seen in conceit developing into insanity.' Yet by the medical standards of the time Savage was in advance of his profession. He argued that patients who came from neurotic stock were more likely to 'go out of their senses' periodically but not necessarily 'out of their minds'. He also isolated several of the associated symptoms which were to alert those who were to care for Virginia throughout her life, such as the relation of attacks of instability to menstruation or to attacks of influenza.

Savage already knew something of the family history. He had treated J. K. Stephen and he may have learnt more from Leslie: not perhaps about Sir James's three breakdowns or of his claims that he had the power of going mad at will. But Leslie may have told him of the delirium which in 1894 had seized Thoby at his prep school as he was recovering from influenza. He had tried, screaming, to the terror of the other boys, to throw himself out of the window; and Thoby had another attack at home a month later. Thoby went back to school where there were grown men to cope with any repetition of the attack. But in Hyde Park Gate there was only Stella, and she was forced to police Virginia and see that she followed Savage's regime – a regime she hated. Reading books and study would, according to the theory of the day, drain energy from her reproductive system. So a spade should be bought for her to make a little garden, she must be forbidden to study (though she was not by her own admission deprived of books), she must take to her bed when menstruating and drink plenty of milk and eat food which her rage against her mother for dying and her father for tyrannizing made it impossible for her to digest. In fact Stella modified the regime – they read German together and translated George Sand – but Virginia also went on·the endless round of good works and visitations and during those drives Stella would quiz her sister about her health. Virginia was understandably forbidden to see Stella when Stella fell ill, and that made her own illness worse. Yet curiously enough it was Stella's death that brought freedom. Dr Seton might once again prescribe Sir George's regime of milk and no lessons. But now there was no one to enforce it. Vanessa refused. Leslie would not have dreamt of doing so: he would not have considered it his concern.

The remaining years of Stephen's life were tragic for him and his family. Visitors to the house now found a gaunt old man vainly trying to catch his children's chatter and insisting they shout their jokes in his ear-trumpet. He demanded that everyone should acknowledge how pitiful was his plight. The ladies who called obliged. His own children did not. He wanted the Duckworth boys to like him though he admitted 'it is hard for a lad to feel at ease with a grisly old skeleton like me'. They were now grown up and they gallivanted in second-class fashionable society. The sensible, easy-going, dependable Thoby was away first at Clifton and then at Trinity, Cambridge. Stephen's two daughters were at that stage of adolescence when they had to assert their own individuality if they were to exist in their own right. Unlike the placid Stella, schooled by her mother to a life of service, they were determined not to be enslaved. Adrian never cared for that remote being, his father, and was at this time afflicted with losing within eighteen months both his mother and his substitute mother. Stephen wanted over-much that his spirit should live on in his sons; he was impatient of theirs. Writing to Norton about the son whom his wife most adored, he said, '[Adrian] is a very attractive, simple little fellow but oddly dreamy and apt to take a great deal of interest in the things which are most impractical'. The boy, then, must be made to be practical. Adrian in revenge taught himself to imitate his father's voice and, safe in the knowledge of his father's deafness, would strike up before all the family at dinner in the hope of making his brother and sisters giggle; the device worked to perfection until the day when he performed in a growler and discovered that among the peculiar properties of that vehicle was a quality which turned it into a gigantic ear-trumpet, so that his father heard every word. Moans issued from the deeply distressed Stephen, 'Oh, my boy, my boy!' With the merciless insight of children they seized on their father's failings, in particular his habit of dramatizing the insignificant into the cosmic. Once as he passed their room stumbling upstairs to his study they heard him talking to himself: 'I wish I were dead . . . I wish I were dead . . . I wish my whiskers would grow.'

His daughters had more right to resent their father's tyranny. Thoby could not see why Virginia disliked having to accompany him on his afternoon walk round the Serpentine, up to Marble Arch and back to the Round Pond; but then he was not present on Wednesday at lunch when Vanessa presented the week's accounts. Nor, she knew, would her father have behaved as he did had Thoby presented them. He behaved as he did because Vanessa was a girl, and her sister left a memorable account of the horror of Wednesdays.

The books were presented. Silence. He was putting on his glasses. He had read the figures. Down came his fist on the account book. There was a roar. His vein filled. His face flushed. Then he shouted, 'I am ruined.' Then he beat his breast. He went through an extraordinary dramatization of self-pity, anger and despair. He was ruined – dying . . . tortured by the wanton extravagance of Vanessa and Sophie. 'And you stand there like a block of stone. Don't you pity me? Haven't you a word to say to me?' and so on. Vanessa stood by his side absolutely dumb. He flung at her all the phrases – about shooting Niagara and so on – that came handy. She remained static. Another attitude was adopted. With a deep groan he picked up his pen and with ostentatiously trembling fingers wrote out the cheque.

This was wearily tossed to Vanessa. Slowly and with many groans the pen, the account book were put away. Then he sank into his chair and sat with his head on his breast. And then at last, after glancing at a book, he would look up and say half plaintively, 'And what are you doing this afternoon, Ginny?'

Never have I felt such rage and frustration.

That was not her sole cause of frustration. Years later she was to complain to Vita Sackville-West, 'But then think how I was brought up; mooning about alone among my father's books; never any chance to pick up all that goes on in schools – throwing balls; ragging; slang; vulgarity; scenes; jealousies.' She resented the fact that no money was spent on sending Vanessa and herself to school. She resented being excluded from that great male preserve. Did it never cross her father's mind that she too might enter the world apparently reserved for Thoby and his friends? Other Victorian fathers might be only dimly aware of the existence of the women's colleges or think of them as suitable only for such dazzling creatures as Frances Ramsay, second wife of the Master of Trinity, who had been placed above the Senior Classic in the Tripos. But Leslie's own niece, Katherine Stephen, had become Principal of Newnham and he knew some of the pioneers of girls' education. The truth is that for years a ding-dong debate had reverberated through Stephen's household about girls' education. It had begun over Laura, who was unable to learn much. Trying to come to terms with her backwardness, Leslie declared: 'I am infinitely more anxious that Laura should have a noble character than that she should learn anything whatever. I prefer health to learning.' But did he? For this letter to Julia was his *amende honorable* for a letter he had written her the previous day. This was the one in which he declared that women should be:

> as well educated as men . . . enough to be able to make her living by it, if it is of the paying kind, or to be an authority on it, if not . . . I hate to see so many women's lives wasted simply because they have not been trained well enough . . . I don't want my Marme [Laura] – nor your Stella for that matter – to be a mere young lady . . . It makes me angry to see how people are wasted. If (but don't breathe a whisper of this) Anny had been educated at all, so as to have some rudimentary perceptions of what is meant by systems or by thinking, she might have done something incomparably more telling than she can ever do now.

This was not at all what Julia wanted to hear. If Anny was uneducated, 'I am quite sure you have no idea how utterly uneducated I am . . . it requires all my faith in you to believe with such views on female education you can care for me', and his letter had 'depressed her utterly'. Julia wanted Stella – and Vanessa and Virginia after her – to become 'part of myself' and dedicate themselves to a life of service. 'To serve is the fulfilment of woman's highest nature': the models for her children were to be Florence Nightingale, Mrs Humphry Ward and Octavia Hill. In the midst of wooing Julia Leslie was all too ready to give in; and his daughters were brought up to suit Julia's ideas rather than his. Mothers usually do have the last word where their daughters' education is concerned, and Stephen could excuse himself for, in bringing up their daughters as they did, he and Julia were in no way eccentric or niggardly. Dip into Victorian memoirs and novels and it is plain that they did for their children what the vast majority of parents in their walk of life did: the boys were sent to public school and the girls were taught at home. It is true that the Stephens dispensed with the customary English governess for their daughters and taught them the three Rs themselves; but foreign governesses were employed and first Walter Pater's sister and then Janet Case came to teach Virginia Greek as well as Latin. The scheme worked well enough for Vanessa who was not one for books and wanted only to go to art school. It worked in a sense well enough for Virginia who read far more books than she would ever have read had she been placed under Miss Beale or Miss Buss.[1] Beatrice Potter had much the same education as Virginia. Her rich father never considered sending her to Oxford or Cambridge, but he paid the expenses for several of her poor cousins to go there. Neither Miss Potter nor Miss Stephen was intended to make a career when they grew up. On the other hand for a girl of pinched parents a degree might mean all the difference between being a teacher or a secretary and being a governess.

There was another reason why her father might have hesitated urging Virginia to work for Cambridge. He would have doubted after her first mental breakdown whether she could stand the strain. Although she resumed attendance at lectures in King's College London in the autumn of 1897, he may well have thought that passing examinations would have brought on another attack. Could she indeed ever at that stage have passed them? Would she ever have mastered enough maths to pass Littlego, the entrance examination to Cambridge; and disliking as she did

[1] The headmistresses of Cheltenham Ladies' College and North London Collegiate respectively: of whom the plaintive rhyme was written by one of their pupils,

Miss Buss and Miss Beale
Cupid's darts do not feel:
How different from us
Miss Beale and Miss Buss.

the technical side of history, would she have relished unravelling the mysteries of medieval institutions such as Chancery and the Wardrobe? She enjoyed later in life watering the tender plant of her grievance, but the ironical, teasing glance which she always gave to Cambridge, academies and other pious institutions of learning was provoked by her conviction that such places crush imagination and fail to bring the gift of translating emotion into words.

And yet she was deprived; and she had a grievance. For there is little doubt that Leslie Stephen never contemplated any other future than the one he and Julia chose. Money probably came into it; it usually did when Stephen took decisions. He had just had to give up the editorship of the Dictionary and its stipend, and for many years to come British parents of the professional classes to their shame were to save on their daughters' education. 'He spent', said Virginia, 'perhaps £100 on my education.' But there can equally be little doubt that the decision was a joint decision by Leslie and Julia. They were by no means paid up members of the radical movement embracing all its tenets from temperance to the wearing of rational female dress such as bloomers. Julia wanted her daughters to develop their accomplishments; she took pride in their childish achievements such as the family newsletter, the *Hyde Park Gate News*; but to her the destiny of women was the life of service. She was harder on Stella, whom she did not love, than on George or Gerald. Sure enough Stella developed into the girl of her dreams, beautiful, dutiful and altruistic. This was what the generation who venerated George Eliot held up as the ideal. It was an ideal Leslie Stephen was all too ready to accept, since it enabled him to assume that after Stella's death Vanessa and Virginia would continue to regard as their first duty to minister to his own needs.

The years after their mother died were desolate years for the children. No Cornwall, no bustle and coming and going of guests, none of the irony, merriment and invention which Julia created so spontaneously. Only the Stygian gloom which hung over their father's study. Only the emotional demands he made upon them for sympathy and reassurance. But on one charge Stephen stands acquitted. Admirers of his daughter have declared that he gave her 'ambivalent messages' or 'confused signals' so that she was bewildered and did not know which way to turn. Nothing could be further from the truth. His children acknowledged that they knew precisely what he thought, what he wished, what he valued. What was more he did not have double standards about freedom of choice. His children were free to choose their bent or obey the dictates of their heart. After Stella's death Jack Hills in a state of sexual frustration began to court Vanessa who was by no means indifferent. George Duckworth was appalled. Not only the Church but the law forbade the marriage of a deceased wife's sister: of course they could evade the prohibition by

marrying abroad; but the scandal – his career – Virginia's marital
prospects – *his own* marital prospects – his stepfather must intervene!
Stephen refused. It was up to Vanessa to make up her mind. She did so.
The truth is that in Vanessa her father met his match. Throughout her life
she was to go her own way just as her father did; was as determined to get
it as he was; was as emotionally dependent on the great love of her life
Duncan Grant as he was on Julia; and had as demanding a relationship
with her daughter as Julia had had with Stella.

The daughter who suffered most at Leslie's hands is usually forgotten.
This was Laura. That wretched mite could not respond to Leslie's
teaching or her nurse's training and it took long for it to dawn on Leslie
that she was congenitally backward. After Minny's death Anny had been
in charge of her and tried kindness. Leslie objected that she treated little
girls as though they were angels. She seemed to think that if 'she was
sentimental enough about them, all would come out right'. The fur flew
and Julia, then only a friendly neighbour, once again had to intervene to
restore peace. When Anny left to get married Milly took over. Milly
believed that 'in practice we all know that fear and love can scarcely be
altogether separated; a reason the more for giving fear its proper place'.
This good Evangelical doctrine impressed Leslie: it also impressed poor
Laura who found her screaming got her nowhere. When Julia became her
step-mother discipline grew even stricter, and Laura was fourteen before
he and Julia faced the truth. There was a pathetic scene once when Anny
paid a visit and the child ran to her laughing and beaming to hug the only
grown-up whom she could remember had shown her love. Parents can be
forgiven if they are slow to admit to themselves that one of their children
is not mentally normal. But when Leslie knew Laura could never grow up
– for when Laura found herself among the Duckworth children the little
girl found the strain too much for her, and she relapsed into baby-ways
and apathy – he put her as far as possible out of his life. The memory of
those days when he tried to teach her to read and he would lose his
temper, the succession of governesses and the eventual committal to an
asylum ate into him. He did not shirk his financial responsibilities but he
could hardly bear to see her, let alone show affection. That was women's
work. Martine Stemerick observed that after Stella's death he appointed
his niece Kate to be Laura's guardian, and he warned Thoby that some
day he would have to assume responsibility for his half sister. For him a
bitter chapter was closed; but for Laura?

In the dark days of his last years some crumbs of comfort came
Stephen's way. He was appointed a Trustee of the National Portrait
Gallery, though three years later he had to give it up as he was too deaf to
follow the business at meetings. The speeches he had to make over the
celebrations on the completion of the *DNB* drew groans from him, and

he had to endure a dinner with the Prince of Wales to which he, Lee and George Smith were invited. Such invitations reassured him that he was not forgotten – though a morning without post convinced him that he had no friends left. He was pleased to be among the founder fellows of the new British Academy, and American learned societies too paid their tributes by electing him to foreign membership. Finally he received a letter in the spring of 1902 from the Prime Minister informing him that the Sovereign 'had it in mind' to appoint him a Knight Commander of the Bath in the Coronation Honours list and asking whether Mr Stephen would accept.

Mr Stephen was at first disinclined to accept – it was not altogether an appropriate honour, he thought, for a 'literary gent'. To the connoisseur the British system of honours is as delicate in its nuances as it is intriguing in its singularity. During Queen Victoria's reign merit in literature and scholarship had been less conspicuously rewarded than in painting or music: Disraeli had offered a knighthood to Tennyson and the GCB to Carlyle but both had refused; novelists were regarded as entertainers; and when Tennyson was made a peer his isolation among the other literary giants was all the more conspicuous. Edwin Arnold, who wrote leaders for the *Daily Telegraph* and was author of the epic poem 'The Light of Asia', John Seeley, the historian and author of *Ecce Homo*, and Richard Jebb, the classical scholar, had received knighthoods, but those for Arnold and Jebb were given for political services rendered. The sole recipient in Leslie Stephen's walk of life was Sir Walter Besant, the co-author of numbers of all-too-popular novels, founder of the Society of Authors and a public benefactor who had built his People's Palace of the East End, in no way Stephen's intellectual equal. Stephen may have looked wistfully towards the new honour created for the Coronation, the Order of Merit; but he had always formed a just estimate of his own abilities. Numbers of scholars and intellectuals hesitate, as Stephen did, to accept a title, but they usually put it about that their families overcame their reluctance. Certainly Thoby and the family did so, by using the time-worn argument that refusal to accept would suggest to the world that the honorand in his vanity had expected a higher honour to have been offered him. Did not the honour glorify not merely Stephen himself but the profession of intellectual journalism – did it not mark the journey of the man of letters from the squalor, in which that bright, sottish master of scholarly insult, William Maginn, Thackeray's mentor and editor of *Fraser's*, had dwelt, to the Alpine height which Stephen had climbed? What was more this was no mere knighthood such as had been bestowed on Walter Besant. The KCB was awarded to those who had done the State some service, such as the great Librarian of the British Museum, Anthony Panizzi. Was it not a subtle recognition of the King's personal interest in the Dictionary? Was it not perhaps an indication of the new

Prime Minister's goodwill, a salute from Sidgwick's brother-in-law, Arthur Balfour?[1] 'I told him he was leading us all,' wrote Haldane to his daughter, 'and he smiled and said, "You will all of you make me vain." ' During these last years he still continued to work. The mammoth study of the Utilitarians in three volumes was completed. J. R. Green's widow persuaded him to write a memoir and publish her husband's letters. His sense of the absurd was as keen as ever when he wrote 'Did Shakespeare Write Bacon?' and his clarity of mind and strength undimmed when he wrote on Pascal in 1902, a study he had been working on for at least five years since Virginia heard him deliver a lecture on Pascal in 1897 ('Father too deep for the audience, very logical and difficult for the ignorant . . . to follow'). He would write in a nursing home: his book on Hobbes was literally born between the sheets. For in April 1902 his doctors diagnosed cancer of the bowel – induced perhaps by the self-torment and guilt he felt as he accused himself of not having loved Julia enough. His surgeon advised him to wait until the end of the year before they operated. Undaunted he composed his Ford Lectures which told his successors what direction he thought literary research ought to take; but he was so weak that his nephew Herbert Fisher had to read them for him at Oxford. When too weak to write he continued to read. Not until his articles for the *National Review* appeared in 1903, which were collected and issued years after his death as *Some Early Impressions*, was there a decline in his powers. 'I have seen the list of the books which were to be brought to him from the London Library,' Maitland recalled.

It began with the names of Réville, Martineau, Brunetière, Flint, Vauvenargues, Vandal, Sabatier, Chateaubriand, Sorel, Pater, Ostrogorski, W. Watson and Dostoievksy. Some of our biblical critics are there and Emile Zola. Then when other books failed, he fell back on the old, old story. Need I name it? He told his nurse that his enjoyment of books had begun and would end with Boswell's 'Life of Johnson'.

His friends had been dying fast about him – Sidgwick, Croom Robertson, Dyke Campbell, the old bore Frederick Gibbs, and in the pages of the *Mausoleum Book* he tolled the bell for each of them. By the close of the year the end was in sight, and too weak to write he dictated to Virginia: 'I shall write no more in this book. I have been growing weaker, and I fancy I shall do no more work . . . I have only to say to you, my children, that you have all been as good and tender to me as anyone could be during these last months and indeed years. It comforts me to think that

[1] In fact when Edward VII wanted to honour the liberal churchman, James Knowles, the editor of the *Contemporary Review* and the *Nineteenth Century* and founder of the Metaphysical Society, who was a personal friend of the King, he made him a Knight of the Victorian Order which was in his own gift. Balfour may have had some influence but the Honours List was prepared and published in Salisbury's last months as Prime Minister.

you are all so fond of each other that when I am gone you are better able to do without me.' On Christmas Eve he no longer had the strength to recite by heart, as he always had, Milton's *Ode on the Nativity*. But that spare long wiry body would not give in. Death seemed certain to come in January but to the exhaustion of his daughters he lived on. Throughout the year he had watched death approaching with open and curious eyes. Huxley had told Morley that he found his dislike of the thought of extinction increasing as he got older and nearer the goal; another rationalist, Herbert Spencer, was much troubled at the end by the Immanence of Space and was in such a state of nerves, Stephen wrote to Norton, 'that he can only talk to anyone for three and a half minutes by his watch and then must be kept from . . . exciting topics'; Stephen himself remained calm and awaited annihilation. Just before he died he wrote to bid farewell to George Meredith. Meredith, also at the end of his days, replied:

My dearest Leslie – Your letter gave me one of the few remaining pleasures that I can have. I rejoice in your courage and energy. Of the latter I have nothing left. Since last September I have not held a pen, except perforce to sign my name . . . We who have loved the motion of legs and the sweep of the winds, we come to this. But for myself, I will own that it is the Natural order. There is no irony in Nature.

Leslie Stephen died early on the morning of 22 February 1904. He was cremated at Golders Green, Frederick Pollock noted, to a modified Anglican rite in which the Beatitudes replaced St Paul's vindication of the resurrection of the dead from his first letter to the Corinthians. Frederic Harrison was 'rather scandalized', but Pollock thought the service in no way odd as Stephen had been married twice in church.

Six months later those children, the 'better able to do without' him, moved to the unfashionable squares of Bloomsbury. That summer for the first time Virginia was visited by her Eumenides and heard those terrible voices.

Chapter Four

✍✍✍

WHAT WAS HE REALLY LIKE?

Portraits and Photographs

Sitting on the floor, surrounded by a medley of paintings, drawings, sketches, and exposures, Stephen's biographer is bound to gaze at two of them with particular intensity because they are not snapshots but portraits by novelists. Virginia Woolf's portrait of her father in *To the Lighthouse* was inspired by a rage which had simmered for over twenty years since the days at Hyde Park Gate. She resented his treatment of Vanessa so fiercely because her sister was the first and dearest love of her life, her heroine; independent, courageous, the leader of their friends in Bloomsbury, just as her father had been among his; someone who would not be cowed by a parent, a stepbrother or a lover; a pioneer who struck out a career for herself and followed without a qualm a way of life even though it dismayed her father's circle and most of her own class. Virginia Woolf's Mr Ramsay is utterly insensitive to the feelings of those immediately about him. He resents his limitations as a scholar and vents his chagrin upon his children. His damning utilitarian insistence on factual accuracy, that whether they like it or not the weather will change and the expedition to the Lighthouse will be ruined, takes the joy out of every childhood fancy and expectation. He is forever jawing with equally unimaginative friends about so-and-so who is a 'first-rate man' and so-and-so who is fundamentally unsound: these alpha-minded, dreary academic categories are meaningless in the only world that matters – the world of human beings who breathe and suffer and love. 'The crass blindness and tyranny in him', which makes him fling a plate through the window at breakfast because he finds an earwig in the milk, which forbids him ever to praise his youngest son and makes his son hate him, is described with desolating intensity as Mr Ramsay rows Cam and James to the Lighthouse. 'To pursue truth with such astonishing lack of consideration for other people's feelings, to rend the thin veils of civilization so wantonly, so brutally, was to her so horrible an outrage of human decency.' Can a man find truth, truth of any value, when he has maimed his feelings, the antennae with which he can sense other people's emotions? It is not that Mr Ramsay ignores his family for the company of shuffling, sniffling old savants like Mr Carmichael; he makes unreasonable emotional demands upon them. He considers himself to be pitied, a man whose career has been wrecked by his marriage and eight children and who is owed affection and sympathy to sustain him in his great loss. He demands to be told that he is genuinely suffering. 'Sitting in the boat he bowed, he crouched himself, acting instantly his part – the part of a desolate man, widowed, bereft; and so called up before him in hosts people sympathizing with him; staged for himself as he sat in the boat, a little drama.' The high-minded moralist turns out to be a ruthless egoist determined to exploit his own suffering and force his family, who are unable to escape, to suffer with him.

Stephen had signed the warrant for his arrest in the book he wrote for his children. When she sat down to write her novel, Virginia Woolf deliberately did not consult the *Mausoleum Book* from which the portrait of Mr Ramsay derives. She did not need to do so. The passages were engraved on her heart. That manuscript which Stephen wrote the year after his wife died was meant to tell his children something about their mother and does indeed contain a mezzotint of her. But far more revealing was the charcoal sketch in the background of the autobiographer himself. The man of integrity who hated sentimentality and gush assuaged his grief by compounding an electuary of sentimentalism. The death of each friend was noted, the narrowing circle, the anniversaries of desolation and the happiness that could be no more. Stephen's sentimentality was all the more striking because he diagnosed the emotion in others unerringly and defined it as a mood in which we make 'a luxury of grief and regard sympathetic emotion as an end rather than a means – a need rightly despised by men of masculine nature'. Sentimentalism, the enjoyment of emotion for its own sake, is no more a vice than many other similar moods such as nostalgia. But it is often a cloak, a perfumed shroud, donned to conceal the stink of vice, of secret and unknown sins, such as cruelty and coarseness. Stephen was neither cruel nor coarse but his sentimentality concealed his fear – that people would blame him for Julia's death or put it about that he had brought her unhappiness.

In his relations with Minny and Julia he adopted two of the classical attitudes of people who demand to be loved: 'People do not really like me, so I will retreat from society and secure myself from any rejection which would mortally wound me'; and, 'You ought to love me because I suffer and am helpless.' He played games with Julia and knowingly resorted to tactics and ploys to extort motherly indulgence. Leila Luedeking says that

'He pleaded ... he was weak, sickly, helpless, nervously irritable, sensitive, shy, easily upset, easily bored', and demanded to be cared for and protected. 'There was an accusation in it: "If I am unhappy, ill, bored, you are to blame." And there was an implied threat, "You'll regret it if you deny me what I need and want." ' Admitting his faults, he puts them down – and then tries to justify them. Moods of self-recrimination are followed by explanations of his conduct designed to persuade himself that he was misunderstood. Guilt wells from his pen. He has only to write of Julia and he is pursued by 'hideous morbid fancies' which haunt him that he was at times unkind to her, 'fancies which I know to be utterly baseless and which I am yet unable to disperse by an effort of will. I must live them down.' But he cannot, and the memories return to lie with him at night. 'All this comes back to me – trifles and things that are not quite trifles – and prevents me from saying, as I would so gladly have said, that I never gave her anxiety or caused her needless annoyance.' What the trifles were we know. They once had a tiff over sitting up late. Or he would reproach her if a child were late for dinner: he spoke as if it were certain the child had been killed or maimed in an accident. What the more than trifles were we can only guess.

Two allusions in the *Mausoleum Book* to dead men show what was on Stephen's mind. In his account he tells the story of his brother-in-law, Halford Vaughan, on whom George Eliot should have modelled Casaubon. Vaughan let people know that his *magnum opus* had been destroyed by a servant, but Leslie suspected he had destroyed it himself – which would have been no loss, he thought, if one was to judge from Vaughan's three-volume collection of marginalia on Shakespeare, 'some of the most singular instances of misapplied ingenuity that I ever saw'. But Vaughan's real tragedy was not in his study but in his bedroom. His wife, Julia's sister, worshipped him as a genius and this 'strange, self-willed, proud recluse, absorbed in his own futile studies . . . rarely unbent or condescended to caress her'. Stephen acquitted himself of this fault. But he was all too aware of the revelation Froude made in publishing Carlyle's *Reminiscences* which showed how harshly Carlyle had treated his wife and how bitterly she resented it. Both the Stephens thought Froude had gone beyond his instructions in using this material, but Leslie said, 'If I felt I had a burthen upon my conscience like that which tortured poor Carlyle, I think I should be almost tempted to commit suicide.' That was why both in life and in his manuscript he appealed to his children to tell him that he bore no resemblance to Carlyle.

But then we reach those parts of the *Mausoleum Book* which are less explicit. Stephen knew that he lacked foresight. Had he not years ago thoughtlessly taken Holy Orders without asking himself what he really believed? And now he had failed again to foresee the strain which the demands which he and others had made would have upon his wife's health. Stephen set out to rebut this charge; and again with some justice because if his breakdown in health over the Dictionary and his demands for support had drained Julia's strength so did the demands of others which she insisted on meeting. Nevertheless, the apparition of the tyrant of the hearth, repenting too late but avid for absolution, hangs over the *Mausoleum Book*.

There was another hostile witness in the family. His doting sister, Milly, at last wriggled out of her cocoon. She was a classic victim of Victorian masculinity. When Sir James left the Regius chair at Cambridge to teach at Haileybury she fell in love with a student there; but he never proposed to her, he may never have known of her passion, and suddenly he was posted to India. As a dutiful Victorian daughter, she looked after her parents and nursed her mother through her final illness. She was fat, she was ugly, she was excruciatingly dull and had adopted all Leslie's views, leaving the Church of England and publishing a book in 1871 called *The Service of the Poor* in which she warned that the family as an institution depended for survival on the unpaid labour of unmarried daughters who should not be seduced into sororities or colleges or, worse still, convents. Women needed their brothers. 'You cut yourself off from what most strengthens the mind' if you leave the family. But in 1890 she showed she had been changing her opinions. In that year she published *Quaker Strongholds* and described in that natural, readable style in which all Stephens wrote, her conversion to the Society of Friends. Her brother slightingly described this as 'another little book of hers'.[1] Now 'Julia's death laid bare the chasm between Leslie and me.' She decided she had been exploited. 'The action of the spoilt child in him often had to me the effect of unkindness.' She had noticed that streak of childishness in him long ago when he was about to be ordained and others noted it too. Gabriel Loppé was amused that Stephen refused a cake specially baked for him because it had too few sultanas in it. The next day another cake was baked – this he accepted: 'I like cake with the plums nearer together.' A little pout. Milly now regarded her former opinions about women to be mistaken. The Quakers provided the example of a community which did not harm the family and in which one could establish 'a nunnery of one'; and she harked back to the time when she and Anny used to lecture university students on the joys of spinsterhood and declared that unmarried daughters might find it hard at first to break from the family but 'an admonition or two, a gently affixed label of eccentricity, and the

---

[1] At the beginning of this century Caroline Stephen moved to The Porch, a cottage in Cambridge. The Cambridge Hegelian, McTaggart, said that had women then been deemed eligible to be elected to the Apostles, she alone would have been worthy of the honour. It must be admitted that this has been said about a number of women.

thing is done'. Leslie, she thought, was too obsessed by the triumphs of public life. When she came to write their father's life, she stressed his spiritual development, not his triumphs or defeats at the Colonial Office.

And then, turning over the likenesses, the biographer comes across the other portrait of Stephen by a novelist. Meredith's impression, Vernon Whitford, in *The Egoist*, cannot compare with Mr Ramsay. Meredith was too absorbed in creating his monster, Sir Willoughby Patterne, to do more than throw off a sketch of his friend. The deflationary man of few words is there and, as he was honest, he deflates himself first. When Miss Middleton puts the equivalent of the luckless parson's question, 'Do you care for walking?', Mr Whitford replies that he has been strolling for the past nine and a half hours principally to work off his own bad temper. The dependable Stephen is also acknowledged when young Crossjay Patterne says of his tutor, 'I like him because he's always the same and you're not positive about some people. Miss Middleton, if you look on at cricket, in comes a safe man for ten runs. He may get more, and he never gets less.' That equable decency was part of his character.

Certainly one should also stand on an easel the admirable portrait painted without tell-tale *pentimenti* by the greatest English historian of his day in the last year of his short life. Maitland never touched any subject without transforming men's notions of their past; and yet we know that when he wrote Stephen's biography he could not bring himself to believe the stories Stephen's daughters told him of their father's violent temper. Or one looks at the negatives Lowell and Charles Eliot Norton provide, or at the prints supplied by dozens of friends who had such affectionate memories of him – and then one hears a voice saying, 'He did by instinct all the little things a woman likes.'

It is his daughter's voice. Virginia Woolf never intended the portrait of Mr Ramsay to be the whole story. She created in her novel a symbol of Victorian domestic life and of the power of fathers to make 'people do what they did not want to do, cutting off their right to speak'. But on the centenary of her father's birth Virginia Woolf gave a very different account in an article she wrote for *The Times*. She spoke of the gift of amusing his children when they were tots by drawing animals or telling stories or reading aloud. He might be old-fashioned in his views about the vice of luxury or the sin of idleness, and he rebuked Vanessa for smoking cigarettes though he smoked pipe after pipe. But she was free to choose to attend art school and Virginia was free to study Plato under Walter Pater's sister and read at will in his unexpurgated library. 'Freedom of that sort was worth thousands of cigarettes.' It might never have crossed Leslie Stephen's mind that Virginia should go to a university but he had marked out a future for her quite different from that he had in mind for Stella. She could be his literary heir, and that meant an education in history and biography. Recorded in a little diary she kept during 1897 are the books he chose for her to read when she was fifteen; Froude's *Carlyle*, Creighton's *Queen Elizabeth*, Lockhart's *Life of Scott*, Carlyle's *Reminiscences*, James Stephen's *Essays in Ecclesiastical Biography*, J. R. Lowell's *Poems*, Campbell's *Life of Coleridge*, Carlyle's *Life of Sterling*, Pepys's *Diary*, Macaulay's *History*, Carlyle's *French Revolution*, Carlyle's *Cromwell*, Arnold's *History of Rome*, Froude's *History of England* and his own *Life of Fawcett*. These books he expected her to discuss with him – 'But my dear, if it's worth reading, it's worth reading twice.'

Moreover, he taught his children never to accept the judgements of good form. 'At the end of a volume my father always gravely asked our opinion as to its merits, and we were required to say which of the characters we liked best and why. I can remember his indignation when one of us preferred the hero to the far more life-like villain.' They learnt from him to recognize selfish and trivial opinions. 'A lady, for instance, complained of the wet summer that was spoiling her tour in Cornwall. But to my father, though he never called himself a democrat, the rain meant that the corn was being laid; some poor man was being ruined; and the energy with which he expressed his sympathy – not with the lady – left her discomfited.' It was not his reserve which impressed his children so much as the vigour with which he felt, his love of clear thinking and his hatred of the stock response. 'He had a way of upsetting established reputations and disregarding conventional values that could be disconcerting, and sometimes perhaps wounding, though no one was more respectful of any feeling that seemed to him genuine.'

These were the qualities which made Meredith and others love him. He won for himself a privilege often denied to the old: young men, for instance Desmond MacCarthy, enjoyed his company and were kind to him. His friends knew that he valued them for their qualities, not for their abilities, and that once accepted they would not be dissected and discarded. He despised personal gain and all devious ways of influence or persuasion; and if this magnanimity took him a pace or two out of the world, he was a figure 'who lived a very real life in the minds of men like Walter Headlam or Herbert Fisher; . . . a man with a standard they often referred to'.

Virginia Woolf's Last Portrait

The image of her parents for ever rose before Virginia Woolf's eyes and time and again she returned to write about them. She had written on her father's death to Maitland and in 1907, partly as an exercise in teaching herself how to write, she set down some reminiscences for Vanessa's children. These were concerned more with her mother than with her father though she did not conceal in her Latinized prose her resentment against him. Twenty years later came *To the Lighthouse*, after which she thought she had laid their ghosts. But then came the turn-over article in *The Times*, and during the bombardment of London in 1940 she was writing draft after draft of the article which was to be published years later, 'A Sketch of the Past'. 'I am obsessed with them both unhealthily', she wrote in her diary, and her other writings sometimes contain allusions to them. In an address, for instance, which she gave to a women's rights society she described her irritation with her mother's selflessness:

> She was intensely sympathetic. She was immensely charming. She was utterly unselfish. She excelled in the difficult arts of family life. She sacrificed herself daily. If there was chicken, she took the leg; if there was a draught she sat in it – in short she was so constituted that she never had a mind or a wish of her own, but preferred to sympathize always with the minds and wishes of others. Above all – I need not say it – she was pure.
>
> . . . And when I came to write I encountered her with the very first words. The shadow of her wings fell on my page; I heard the rustling of her skirts in the room. Directly, that is to say, I took my pen in my hand to review that novel by a famous man, she slipped behind me and whispered: My dear, you are a young woman. You are writing about a book that has been written by a man. Be sympathetic; be tender; flatter, deceive; use all the arts and wiles of our sex. Never let anybody guess that you have a mind of your own. Above all, be pure . . . Had I not killed her she would have killed me. She would have plucked the heart out of my writing. For, as I found, directly I put pen to paper, you cannot review even a novel without having a mind of your own, without expressing what you think to be the truth about human relations, morality, sex.

In 'A Sketch of the Past' Virginia drew her mother. But there was another draft which she never lived to incorporate in the her memoir in which she described her father. It was her last effort to come to terms with him before she killed herself and she categorized him as three fathers; the sociable father, the writer father; and the tyrant father. She realized that her feelings about him were formed at an age when she could know little of the sociable father; though as a child she 'had many a shock of acute pleasure when he fixed his very small very blue eyes upon me and somehow made me feel that we were in league together'. The writer father she knew better, the father who 'gave his little amused, surprised snort when he found me reading some book which no child of my age could understand'. The image of the writer father was stamped on a steel engraving captioned 'Cambridge Intellectual'. The plate remained unbroken throughout her life: she knew the likeness all too well, G. M. Trevelyan and Charles Sanger were struck from it. She measured others against them, the more brittle of second-generation Bloomsbury, and often found them wanting. But respect that engraving as she did, she found it too literal and exact for her liking.

> There are no crannies, or corners to catch my imagination; nothing dangles a spray at me . . . I find not a subtle mind; not an imaginative mind; not a suggestive mind. But a strong mind; a healthy out of door moor striding mind; an impatient, limited mind; a conventional mind entirely accepting his own standard of what is honest, what is moral, without a shadow of doubt accepting this is a good man; that is a good woman . . . obvious things to be destroyed – headed humbug; obvious things to be preserved – headed domestic virtues.

At times she admired her father's writing, for instance on Pope: 'very witty and bright without a single dead sentence in it'. 'Yet he is not a writer for whom I have a natural taste. Just as a dog takes a bite of grass, I take a bite of him medicinally.' The father she remembered all too well was the tyrant father.

> It was like being shut up in the same cage with a wild beast. Suppose I, at 15, was a nervous, gibbering, little monkey, always spitting or cracking a nut and shying the shells about, and mopping and mowing, and leaping into dark corners and then swinging in rapture across the cage, he was the pacing, dangerous, morose lion; a lion who was sulky and angry and injured; and suddenly ferocious, and then very humble, and then majestic; and then lying dusty and fly pestered in a corner of the cage.

How did this apostle of reason justify his unreasonable behaviour? Virginia Woolf believed that her father was following a convention of the time, set by Carlyle and Tennyson. They were men of genius; and men of genius had fits of positive inspiration and wore long hair, great black hats, capes and cloaks and were ill to live with. 'It never struck my father, I believe, that there was any harm in being ill to live with.' The genius let himself fly and after such an outburst became according to convention touchingly apologetic. He took it for granted that the women of the house would accept his apology, that he was exempt because of his genius from the laws of good society. That was how her father behaved – as a man of genius. But he behaved fraudulently. He knew he was not. ' "Only a good second class mind", he once told me as we walked round the croquet lawn at Fritham.'

Once again Virginia Woolf's deduction is documented by Stephen himself. Her father's determination never to lie to himself convinced him that he was a failure and that nothing he had done would be long remembered. Writing in the *Mausoleum Book* Stephen said,

> Had I – as I often reflect – no pretext for calling myself a failure, had I succeeded in my most ambitious dreams and surpassed all my contemporaries in my own line, what should I have done? I should have written a book or two which would have been admired by my own and perhaps by the next generation. They would

have survived so long as active forces, and a little longer in the memory of the more learned, because they would have expressed a little better than other books thoughts which were fomenting in the minds of thousands, some abler and many little less able than myself. But putting aside the very few great names with whom I could not in my wildest fancy compare myself, even the best thinkers become obsolete in a brief time, and turn out to have been superfluous. Putting my imaginary achievements at the best, they would have made no perceptible difference to the world.[1]

The honesty of this judgement must give us pause. Glancing at the career of the greatest of all Victorian dons, Stephen noted that Jowett was always able to believe in his own achievements. Jowett, as he cryptically put it, had 'not known the greatest happiness': he had not married and begot children. But he had acquired a derivative immortality from his College, and knew that his work would be carried on by his chosen successors. This enviable frame of mind enabled him to retain the illusion which the old usually lose that 'anything you did at your best had any real value, or that anything you can do hereafter will even reach the moderate standard of the old work'. Stephen would not accept this illusion, and his honesty is touched with the annihilating ruthlessness of Turgenev's hero Bazarov, 'If you've made up your mind to mow down everything, don't spare your own legs.'

Psycho-Biography

Does Stephen's demand to be treated as a genius, even though he knew he was not one, explain his character as Virginia Woolf thought it did? She may have answered to her satisfaction the riddle about her father which she put to herself, but she does not answer ours. Was she not too like him to judge? Had she sailed further on that endless voyage out and asked why men use that word genius and what they mean by it, she might have seen an image rise from the sea which resembled both her father and herself. Catherine Earnshaw's marvellous discovery in *Wuthering Heights* rings in one's ears. 'Nelly, I *am* Heathcliff! He's always, always in my mind; not as a pleasure, any more than I am a pleasure to myself, but as my own being.' Virginia was in a real sense, as Vanessa was not, flesh of his flesh and bone of his bone. She and her father were both tall and gaunt, great walkers. She could not think with his clarity, logic and power, but like him she could turn a judicious, readable review; he could never rise to her imaginative heights, but like her he responded in poetry to words and

---

[1] Cf. *To the Lighthouse*, Pt. I 'And his fame lasts how long? Is it permissible even for a dying hero to think before he dies how men will speak of him hereafter? His fame lasts perhaps two thousand years. And what are two thousand years? (asked Mr Ramsay, ironically, staring at the hedge) . . . His own little light would shine, not very brightly for a year or two, and then would be merged in some bigger light, and that in a bigger still.'

rhythms. Both were charmers when they chose to be. Both burnt with rages; she inwardly, her rage emerging in spite and malice; his like a volcano hurling rocks and molten magma into the air, freeing him thereafter from it. Money threw both into panic. Neither ever stopped working – Leonard Woolf thought Virginia worked fifteen out of a sixteen-hour day. Both were put on the rack by unsympathetic reviewers of their work. They both leant on women to give them support – Virginia on Violet Dickinson, Madge Vaughan and Vita Sackville-West. For both rejection and disappointment made existence insupportable.

When Katharine Hill made this comparison, she noticed how Leslie considered Virginia his literary heir and she was struck by her resemblance to her father. On her ninth birthday Leslie wrote to Julia, 'She is certainly very like me I feel', and years later Virginia told Vita Sackville-West, 'I was more like him than her I think; and therefore more critical; but he was an adorable man, and somehow, tremendous' – remembering perhaps that she had surprised Vanessa in the nursery by telling her that she preferred her father to her mother. Stephen judged that she 'will really be an author in time' and set about training her adolescent mind. That training took the form of giving her reading lists in history and biography since he had already formed the view that 'history will be a good thing for her to take up as I can give her some hints'. Poetry and novels were already her inheritance: almost as long as she could remember her father had read aloud to his children. She learnt from her father's pioneering work on the relation of literature to society and anyone who reads her essays can see how closely she followed his line. When she explained how to read a book she followed the advice her father had given to the students of St Andrews many years ago. What was more, she expressed in practice in her novels her father's theory that only through experiment in literature can writers keep literature alive and reflect the shifts in class structure and historical change which the society in which they live is experiencing.

This excellent analysis, so full of sense and sensibility, did not overlook the oppressive regime which Leslie inflicted on his daughter. On the contrary, it alluded to his jealousy, self-indulgence and histrionics, his demands for reassurance and the final exhausting trial of nursing him in his last illness which led Virginia to write in her diary the sentences quoted so often that had he lived longer 'His life would have entirely ended mine. What would have happened? No writing, no books; – inconceivable.' Phyllis Rose gets it right when she says that 'with men he was rational and analytical. Women, creatures of emotions as the Victorian myth had it, were for Leslie emotional wastebaskets.' But again, like Katharine Hill, she agrees that it was no bad thing to be born into a house where the best writers and thinkers of the day passed in and out and where writing was a normal human activity. Father and daughter, so astonishingly alike in temperament, differed, however, in one respect. Virginia went mad. Her father did not.

But was he not near to madness? It is at this point that the analysts of the psyche step in and claim to answer our riddle. Virginia Hyman compared Stephen's anxieties to his daughter's state of manic depression. The first tell-tale anxiety she identified is Stephen's behaviour towards Laura. Was not his delay in recognizing that Laura would always be retarded odd and was he not too ready to conclude that her childhood schizophrenia came through her grandmother Isabella Thackeray? Stephen tried to rebut this charge by declaring that not only Isabella was mad – she went into deep post-natal depression after Minny's birth, which followed a miscarriage – but her sister was 'so queer as to be almost on the borders of sanity'. But the Stephen family also had a history of mental instability. Leslie himself admitted he was all too like his father, skinless, over-sentimental and nervously irritable. It apparently never struck him that his boundless demands for sympathy and reassurance resembled the last years of his father who too had insisted that his children should show their concern as old age engulfed him, and had resorted to flattering his favourite son Fitzjames in order to get the attention he thought was his right. Leslie's father's nervous breakdowns may have made him fear that Julia's death would cause him to collapse as his father had done. The 'hideous morbid fancies' which he had to 'live down' may have been the fear that he himself would go mad. Did he, when in the night the fit of the horrors seized him, see himself gibbering in an asylum? Perhaps he dreaded he would be gripped by an evil which he himself had defined – for in *The Science of Ethics* he had declared that Nature had 'but one precept, "Be Strong" ' and conversely 'but one punishment, decay culminating in death and extirpation'. 'The one evil' is 'the weakness that leads to decay'.

The manic depressive trail has been followed several leagues further by Katharine Hill. She discovered in Stephen's melancholia the classic symptoms of guilt in the grief-stricken survivor during mourning depicted by Freud in 'Mourning and Melancholia': the self-reproaches, the abasement, the demands for sympathy which can in the end overwhelm 'the instinct which constrains every living thing to cling to life'. Leslie Stephen did not commit suicide as his daughter did; but it crossed his mind as a possibility. Now, melancholia, Katharine Hill continued, is but a stage removed from manic-depression. There is convincing evidence that some kinds of manic-depressive illness are transmitted genetically and the Stephen family seemed to inherit this tendency. One of the symptoms is unreasonable anger; and this Leslie Stephen exhibited throughout his life and especially after Julia's death when his anger at being left alone was matched by another symptom of mourning: guilt at surviving which makes the survivor blame himself. Infants predisposed to this disease make demands upon their mother which, especially in a large Victorian family, she cannot fulfil. Hence they tend to be jealous of their siblings and later in life to resent any attention which the substitute for their mother gives to others. In the case of the Stephen males the substitute mother was their wife. Did not Leslie make immense demands on his own mother and later grudge the time and care Julia bestowed on her ever-growing horde of beneficiaries? Did not Virginia resent, and was not Adrian incapacitated by, their father's overwork and illness brought on by editing the Dictionary which took their mother away from them to nurse him? And does not this account for the rage which swept over Leslie and his daughter, sometimes vented on others, sometimes internalized and driven back on themselves, which emanated in exaggerated self-reproach and 'morbid fancies'?

If the theory accounts for the anger, it also should account for that ceaseless quest for approval which becomes for the manic depressive a matter of life and death. And so it goes on to do. The rupture of the primary bond with the mother, which engenders anger that becomes internalized, forces manic depressives to try to recreate the situation where they are dependent on their mother and hence rely abnormally on maintaining good relations with others. Anthony Storr goes so far as to say that for them rejection and disapproval are a matter of life and death – without approval self-esteem sinks so low that rage becomes uncontrollable and suicide a possibility. Manic depressives never get it right in their human relations. Either they become overbearing and assertive or else submissive and ingratiating. 'This certainly describes Leslie Stephen,' Katharine Hill concludes, 'the character who is "the most lovable of men" to James Russell Lowell but who terrorizes his daughter Vanessa over the weekly accounts.' This too explains his excessive sensitivity to bad reviews of his books since the manic depressive 'feels the fate of his books to be tied up physically and mentally with his own fate'. He will express in his books resentment of his parents for depriving him of love in infancy but he will also try to make restitution for the harm he has done to his parents. Did not Leslie and Virginia dedicate themselves to writing the lives of the obscure, the forgotten benefactors, to pardon their offence to Julia?

What are we to make of this? There are few things more exhilarating than giving a theory a good run on an afternoon walk. When the theory of significant form was at its most mesmeric, Max Beerbohm drew a cartoon of Clive Bell saying to Roger Fry, 'I always think that when one's been carrying a theory too far, then is the time to carry it a little further'; and Roger Fry replying, 'A *little*? Good heavens, man! Are you growing old?'

After Katharine Hill's analysis no one will need further convincing that some of Virginia Woolf's manic-depressive symptoms can be discovered in her father's behaviour; and her comparison of father and daughter is as revealing as it is stimulating. But to discover in the symptoms every trait of behaviour which must inexorably follow the typology of the manic-depressive as laid down by Freud, Kraepelin and Storr is to become obsessed by theory. Neither Leslie Stephen nor Virginia Woolf was excessively jealous of their siblings nor did they differ from other Victorian children of their class who lived in the nursery and learnt that their father's work came first. Stephen's first wife was not a Dorothea Brooke or a Bella Wilfer: when they married she was more like Dora Copperfield. So far from resenting Julia's charitable work, Leslie was proud of it and remonstrated in the mildest terms with her for helping too many lame dogs over stiles. Stephen's grief over his wife's death may appear excessive to some: but it would not have appeared so to the German Latinist Eduard Fraenkel, a man renowned for his meticulous, professional, unemotional scholarship, who the day after his wife died took his own life. Indeed no epithets could be less appropriate than overbearing and assertive for Virginia Woolf, unless they be submissive and ingratiating for Leslie Stephen.

The application of the human sciences to history and biography has led to marvellous illuminations, but, blinded by the light, its devotees can fall into some fearful snares, gins and pitfalls. Generations of Marxist historians, but more especially the famous concatenation of talent which gathered in the *sixième section* of the Ecole Pratique des Hautes Etudes in Paris, have tried to expel from history the individual politician, soldier, entrepreneur, engineer and thinker as they use the techniques of the human sciences to describe agrarian or urban conditions created by geography, the vagaries of climate, land and sea routes, demography, migration, systems of exchange, food supplies, the availability of precious metals and commodities, the technology of ships, roads, mines, trade and manufactures, and the formation and movement of social classes. In such a vision of history the individual, if he is permitted to make an appearance at all upon the stage, is a mere agent of these impersonal forces. No doubt he has some idiosyncrasies of his own but in the scale of human endeavour these idiosyncrasies count for nothing. Similarly the biographer is drawn into a powerful magnetic field where the techniques of experimental psychology used on rats convey the impression that men and women are condemned by behavioural patterns to react in stereotyped ways to events; or where clinical psychoanalysis suggests that the contradictions in people's lives can be explained by revealing those subconscious desires which determine their behaviour.

This drive to discover behavioural laws, or if not laws the inner springs

which motivate our actions, has been intensified by the triumphs of the
novel. The greatest triumph of the novel has been the revelation that the
intentions behind an action may be nullified by the nature of the agent. An
act which a man believes he is doing out of kindness in fact turns out to be
engendered by quite other motives. The novelist is always confronting us
with characters who imagine they are acting from one set of motives but
whose wills drive them along a different road. Moralists such as that
prudential philosopher, Mr Square, in *Tom Jones*, having spent the
afternoon laying down the laws of virtue, are caught in the evening in an
outrageous position with a chambermaid; worldly adventurers such as
Kate Croy and Merton Densher succeed in their plots but acknowledge
defeat because the memory of the girl they have wronged haunts them;
the rake and bully, Dolohov, is revealed as a devoted son and tender
brother of a hunch-backed sister. A voice nags us that if we will only dig
hard enough we will penetrate the surface of the conscious will and of
appearances and reach the 'real' person, the inner core of a man's nature,
whose unconscious motivation will explain his behaviour. That will be
the person the biographer is searching for and whom his reader will want
to know. Nor can it be doubted that the unconscious and people's
instinctual drives condition how they behave. And what more conclusive,
more scientific, way is there to understand their behaviour, so it is argued,
than by using the typology of the psychological sciences and by removing
stratum by stratum the layers of personality until we reach the primal
rock – the primal scream – which determines the way a man or woman
behaves?

There is in the human sciences a predisposition – though no more than
that – to determinism. The notion that men resemble flies struggling
vainly in the cobweb of historical causation is not tenable for a
biographer. Gandhi, Weizmann or de Valera stamped with something of
their own personality the State each helped to create and which, had he
not existed, would have taken a different shape. Matisse not only saw an
odalisque in a different way from Ingres: he made people see the human
form in a way which no one could have predicted. Psycho-biography
starts with an ideal type and it intends to show the subject of the
biography displaying traits identical to those which research has shown
to be a common pattern of behaviour. Richard Ellmann complained that
if that were to be established conclusively, all the biographer could do
would be to act as a Greek chorus confirming what the gods, or in this
case the analyst, had decreed. The differences between human beings are
at least as important as their similarities. Were their anatomy not highly
similar medical science could not exist. But physical attraction, the
expression of charm, depend upon minute differences in bone structure
and tissue: did not Pascal say that the whole face of the world might have

been changed if Cleopatra's nose had been shorter? So it is with the psyche. Behavioural types have been identified since before the days of Humours. Important as it is to understand why a man's character is as it is, we also want to see how it develops, how it flowers, what shape his talents take. How was it that he took this path rather than the one which his class or his psychic type should have predisposed him to take? People act from many motives and it is by no means self-evident that their subconscious drives are always the most powerful.

Human behaviour cannot without falsehood be described as a structure made up of impulses, drives and delusions which in turn is subject to the overpowering pressures of the impersonal forces in society; so that human beings are flies struggling and stuck to the fly-paper without choice or sense of direction. What people do and say may well disguise their true motives, but their actions and words are not merely symptoms of deeper causes for their behaviour. Control has to be exercised, from the first infant control over the most primary actions of weeping, drinking and excretion, but control is not imposed solely by external forces. The will and conscience play their part. Greatest among the attributes which make for free will is man's self-knowledge – knowledge not only of his own self but of the way the self relates to the community he inhabits. He is capable of deciding how far he should rebel against the morality of his world or how far he should accept the numerous conventions and norms which make life in the world possible.

The Triumphant Will

We must reject determinism. We can accept that some typologies seem partially to fit Leslie Stephen but it is far more important to stress where he breaks out of the mould. To become preoccupied with the sub-conscious in the hope that by digging ever deeper we will discover what the man 'is', will lead us to neglect his conscious will. It is an error to regard Stephen's conscious will as a delusion, a mere mask for the hidden man. It is an error to conclude that the mould of the hidden man cannot be broken by a conscious act of will. Some men and women, contemplating themselves with contempt, decide to conquer their weakness and abandon a style of life they have come to loathe. In fact in rare cases what a man is may be of less importance than what he tried to become. The Evangelical philanthropist, Lord Shaftesbury, was a man of ungovern-able passions – was by temperament proud, imperious, dictatorial, resentful and ambitious; but his life was the story of how he mastered these passions by 'the constant, stubborn, unrelenting dedication of his life to God'. Many of Evelyn Waugh's acquaintances after some appalling scene or calculated insult may have doubted whether his conversion to

Catholicism had changed him at all for the better. But Waugh declared that without God's grace he would scarcely have been human. The same is true of Stephen and is the key to his character. As a young man he was driven on by his Evangelical upbringing to search his soul for faults. He tried to change himself. He believed his hypersensitivity to be a weakness and determined to conquer it. The very thought of suffering pained him. He refused ever to visit a hospital; he could not bear to hear the word dentist mentioned. During the Crimean and again in the Boer War he lay awake at night fancying he could hear the guns on the battlefields and he would go out of his way to avoid seeing newspaper posters carrying news of the slaughter. But hypersensitivity, he thought, saps a man's will to go out into the world and do his duty. It must be held relentlessly in check. In check only. Leslie did not follow his brother Fitzjames in equating toughness of mind with the determination never to be taken in by any argument which rested on humanitarianism or common decency. He was not one of those realists who pride themselves in coming to harsh conclusions and end in defending shabby, inhumane actions by others. Leslie grew up a liberal and made himself a courageous, outspoken liberal. The titles of two of his books record his victory over himself. He would not be a weakling but would engage in free thinking and plain speaking. Like Newman, he too would write his apologia – for being an agnostic. He would swim against the current of his time, and remind his contemporaries of the good sense and equability of the eighteenth century. He knew he was prone to sentimentalism: well then, he would decry it. He knew he was thin-skinned: he would tell the muffs that no one cared a pin for their moanings and it was better to stand up and take what came.

One of his defences against hypersensitivity was hard work. Work brings forgetfulness in fatigue. All the Stephens ruined their health through overwork, a symptom of a deep-seated family neurosis. Leslie declared that he had never in his life worked hard except when taking his degree, adding, 'the only reason why I ever get anything done is that I do not waste time in the vain effort to make myself agreeable'. In that there was nothing eccentric. Scores of intellectuals are incompetent at small-talk, avoid social functions and live a private life within their own secret garden. His method of work was markedly manic. It is, however, significant that he was not able to work at the slow, deliberate, patient pace that is needed for such tasks as proof-reading and indexing.

Another of his defences was humour. Humour is one of man's most valuable weapons against the weariness of the world. Some people use it as a defence against mental exertion and laugh problems away which they would rather not face; others expose the weaknesses of their fellow-men to restore their belief in themselves. Stephen's humour was renowned for being deflationary, sardonic, wry: guaranteed to take the stuffing out of cherished old armchairs and *chaises-longues*. Not everyone relished his asides. But the humour which curls round the pages of his essays resembles the eddy which seeps into a rock pool making the seaweed dance and the anemones open. It was characteristic of Stephen to open a lecture on Matthew Arnold by admitting that he did not know him so well that examples of his felicities at once came to mind. 'At one of my meetings with him, indeed, I do remember a remark which was made and which struck me at the moment as singularly happy. Unfortunately it was a remark made by me, and not by him.' The fact that he enjoyed the company of the young did not deter him from saying, 'Perhaps the most offensive type of human being in the present day is the young gentleman of brilliant abilities and high moral character who has just taken a good degree.' He questioned emotional clichés and bequeathed the deprecating glance to his children in Bloomsbury. Some high spirits too: as when he compared dons to toads since 'with an unpromising exterior they both sometimes bear a precious jewel in their heads', or watching the forecourt of King's College Chapel before matins he said, 'I see the surpliced congregation gathering to form the picture which suggested to Tennyson "six hundred maidens clad in purest white" (I can't say that is precisely what they suggest to me).' No one saw himself more clearly in a comical light. On himself as a young tutor teaching a class of rowing men New Testament Greek: ' "Hallo! Easy all. Hard word there. Smith, what does it mean?" "I don't know," says Smith. "No more don't I. Paddle on all." ' Above all, his humour protected him against self-righteousness. Stephen realized that a moralist, who keeps before his eyes a goal of personal perfection, is always in danger of being a prig; the number of times he mentions that word in his essays betrays his own anxiety to avoid the charge. Humour, in this connection, is the art of seeing oneself and one's ideals in relation to other human beings. Not only to human beings: to the whole scale of human endeavour. One reflexion which never failed to comfort him was that it is ridiculous to be self-important and put too high a value on your achievements. By these means he hoped to win a victory over himself.

Did he succeed? No victory is won without casualties; and there will be those who will question whether it was a victory. 'It is impossible', wrote Hazlitt, 'for those who are naturally disagreeable to be otherwise . . . A vain man who is endeavouring to please is only endeavouring to shine . . . An irritable man who puts a check on himself only grows dull and loses spirit to be anything.' Certainly many men and women turn themselves through their efforts to reform into censorious and conceited purists. They injure themselves more than they would have done had they plodded on unregenerately as before. That is not true of Stephen. What is true is that he knew in his heart that his athletic feats on the track, on mountains or on moors intended to prove that he was no longer a weak and sensitive schoolboy proved nothing. His body learnt to endure hardship but his nature remained raw and sensitive. In this Hazlitt is right: both Shaftesbury and Stephen failed to become the person they set out to be because men had certain temperamental strains which they cannot breed out of themselves. He was indeed a free thinker and plain speaker but there was within him a deutero-Stephen who whispered in his ear that all was in vain. No sooner had he laid down a critical canon than he regarded it quizzically, despairingly. It was not that, in Van Wyck Brooks's phrase, he adopted an Indian-giver style of criticism that took back with one hand what he had granted with the other; but one can hear a sigh of disbelief that anything that he had written was really worth the reader's time.

That he did not make himself 'agreeable' to masses of acquaintances mattered not at all. But it mattered much in the family. He acknowledged that he was fidgety and troublesome, 'and even when alone in my family, I am sometimes as restless as a hyaena'. When taxed he made promises to mend his ways and failed. But sincerity depends on the relation between our words and our thoughts, not between our beliefs and our actions. It is not the measure of men's success or failure but the *manner* in which they try to change themselves which is important. Most people's domestic life is an odd hotch-potch. The spectacle of Stephen promising his wife 'to make amends' and failing to do so, and pleading with his children to exonerate him from behaving as badly as Carlyle did, is sad. Men and women are to be pitied; and we ourselves too.

Stephen dreaded that his inner life, his sensitivity, would be exposed. 'I only met him once when he was an old man visiting his sister in Cambridge,' said E. M. Forster. 'He said little. Then he noticed that I was looking at him and he turned away.' He made a virtue of hiding his feelings under a cloud of gruffness. Hardy once wrote in his diary: 'Called on Leslie Stephen. He is just the same or worse; as if dying to express sympathy, but suffering under some terrible curse which prevents his saying any but caustic things, and showing antipathy instead.'

But Hardy also remembered the first time he had met Stephen. He had asked him why he had chosen to live in a new street in Kensington with the pavements hardly laid and the road not yet rolled. Stephen replied that 'he had played as a child with his nurse in the fields hard by, and he fancied living on the spot, which was dear to him . . . I felt then that I liked him, which I had first doubted. The feeling never changed.' That was why Stephen loved to walk round Kensington Gardens and Hyde Park where, wrote his daughter, allowing her fancy free rein, 'as a little boy his brother

Fitzjames and he had made beautiful bows to young Queen Victoria and she had swept them a curtsey'. In the Gardens he had as a child recited *Marmion*; now with his daughters he would shout Newbolt's *Admirals All* at the top of his voice to the astonishment of nannies and park-keepers. He had affection for the quiet things in life.

In fact his defences were paper thin. His friends knew that he was not ashamed to feel deeply; and his feeling ran into good channels. He adored both Minny and Julia and each knew it. Those tender and terrible simplicities of life – marriage and death – brought him joy and anguish, and he did not hide them. Today men are more shy, less ready, than the Victorians to dwell upon touching instances of babies moving into childhood, and children into adolescence; and being less ready and also less absorbed by the family, do men experience such joy as Stephen felt? Women are wiser. He exploited his grief by demanding the impossible from his children, and held conventional ideas about the place of women which someone of his generous political instincts might have been expected to reject. In doing so one feels he was not without guile. Looking at Watts's portrait one feels that the lower lip of that passionate mouth is beginning to tremble and Stephen is on the verge of tears. He is shamelessly appealing for love and protection. There will always be women who love men for their failings and weakness. Candida sticks by Morrell because she pities the strong man whose defences have collapsed.

The quirks of his personality cannot define him. If we want a visual image to catch the grandeur and hardness of his character, the oddness and complexity of the man, we should see him climbing up the slopes and rocks scaling the Alps that towered above him. In 1897 when Thomas Hardy saw the Schreckhorn, 'then and there I suddenly had a vivid sense of him, as if his personality informed the mountain, gaunt and difficult, like himself . . . As I lay awake that night . . . I felt as if the Schreckhorn were Stephen in person; and I was moved to begin a sonnet to express the fancy.'

> Aloof, as if a thing of mood and whim,
> Now that its spare and desolate figure gleams
> Upon my nearing vision, less it seems
> A looming Alp-height than a guise of him
> Who scaled its horn with ventured life and limb,
> Drawn on by vague imaginings, maybe,
> Of semblance to his personality
> In its quaint glooms, keen lights, and rugged trim.
>
> – At his last change, when Life's dull coils unwind,
> Will he, in old love, hitherward escape,
> And the eternal essence of his mind
> Enter this silent adamantine shape,

And his low voicing haunt its slipping snows
When dawn that calls the climber dyes them rose?

This, then, is how we shall view him – as a peak set in the mountain range of a certain tradition of thought. Leslie Stephen's life is primarily of interest for the light it throws on his intellectual development and his writing is most valuable when judged in relation to the Victorian ethos. We think of him today as a fine biographer or as an historian of ideas. But no one should doubt what he considered was his claim, not to fame for he knew that was not his to grasp, but to modest recognition by generations to come. That was his demonstration that if belief in the dogmas of Christianity waned, there was still a morality as peremptory which men and women should accept if society was to improve. In the labyrinth of his conceptions of right and wrong we shall find the man for whom we are searching.

Chapter Five

⟪⟫⟪⟫⟪⟫

EVANGELICALISM

The Spirit of Evangelicalism

Evangelical morality was the single most widespread influence in Victorian England. It powerfully influenced the Church of England, was the faith of the Methodists, and revived the older nonconformist sects; it spread through every class and taught simple comprehensible virtues. The peremptory demand for sincerity, the delight in plain speaking, the unvarying accent on conduct, and the conviction that he who has attained a Higher Truth must himself evangelize, leap from the pages of Stephen's books and proclaim him a child of the Evangelical tradition. The intellectual heritage of Evangelicalism has been too readily forgotten. The stream of missionaries, the philanthropy of Wilberforce and Shaftesbury, the soldierly piety of Outram, Havelock and Gordon, come easily to mind; but it is too often assumed to be a religion with a theology simplified to the point of banality which calls men to action rather than strengthens their minds – the enemy of intelligence and learning. Those who so argue may recall the ranting of Edward Irving; the bitter, partisan, persecuting spirit of the Evangelical organ, the *Record*; the religious revivalism of the 1860s and 1870s which stirred the working classes; Primitive Methodism and the Salvation Army. Yet, in fact, there were throughout the century numbers of men and women of distinction and depth of mind who were proud to call themselves Evangelicals: even in Oxford, the home of High Churchmanship, the achievements, both in their undergraduate days and later in life, among the Evangelicals were remarkable. Half the men and much of the enthusiasm of Tractarianism were of Evangelical origin, and recent research has shown how inter-woven the two movements were in the early days of the Oxford Movement. Certainly the older group of Evangelicals, led by the Clapham Sect, were masters of the closely reasoned argument, and could draw the finest of moral distinctions. The members of the Sect, as Sir James Stephen put it, were 'well instructed in spiritual dynamics'. Sobriety and regularity were their watchword, emotionalism and violent language their bane. What then was the faith which Leslie Stephen inherited in his childhood? The demands of the faith were simple. Man must experience God. He must evangelize among his fellow-men. He must listen to God's word; and since God speaks through the conscience, this meant following the inner light wherever it shone.

What kind of God did the Clapham Sect worship and how could one experience him? The Claphamites took their lead in theology from their fellow member, Charles Simeon, the disciple of old Henry Venn, who inclined rather to Whitefield's Calvinism than Wesley's Arminianism. It was a moderate and joyful Calvinism which assumed that no man could say how many or whom God would elect and that it was the duty of his evangelists to go into the fields and feed his sheep. To the strict Calvinists the Doctrine of Assurance was paramount. You must be assured that you yourself are saved, and if you want to be assured that someone else is saved you had better see how he conducts himself, how he speaks, whom he befriends and where he goes rather than ask whether he does good works. But the Clapham Sect were not so narrow. Wilberforce was emphatic that the assurance of salvation was not the most important of spiritual attributes. It is true that man is so utterly sunk in Original Sin, so depraved that he hates his God, shuts his ears to God's call, and his eternal soul stands in peril of death. But all is not lost; Christ died for him on the Cross and this can be his salvation. 'The offer' made by Christ to sinful man is ever open and he can 'close with it' at any time. If he allows God's grace to open his heart to his Saviour, the pains of hell shall not prevail; but if, stiff-necked and obdurate, he plunges downward all unheeding, then eternal punishment shall be his reward. The Evangelicals were acutely aware of the distinct Persons of the Trinity. Their vision of God was expressed in the final scene of the first part of *Faust* where Mephistopheles cries in triumph over Gretchen, '*Sie ist gerichtet*'. '*Gerettet*' proclaims the voice from above. God is both a judge and a saviour. In majesty and wrath, he comes to judge the world but at his side sits Christ who can intercede. In the most famous of all Evangelical hymns the Calvinist Toplady wrote:

> Whilst I draw this fleeting breath,
> When my eyestrings break in death,
> When I soar through tracts unknown,
> See Thee on Thy Judgment-Throne;
> Rock of Ages, cleft for me,
> Let me hide myself in Thee.

So far from being a Paleyan Deity who proves his existence to men by the ingenious mechanism of Nature, the Evangelical God is a God of miracles. The conversion of every soul by his evangelists is a miraculous sign of his mercy. But Christ's compassion must not turn man's gaze away from the awful vista of his Father's Judgement Seat. Man is to be judged by other-worldly standards. The God of the Clapham Sect was an ambivalent God who, however open to intercession by his Son, had to weigh each soul in the balance. By God's holiness the Evangelical meant God's need to judge and, in his mercy, forgive sin; sometimes he might show his judgement in this world as when he worked mightily through wars and plagues caused by inevitable human wickedness. Thus, though the atoning power of Christ's sacrifice was the central doctrine of Christianity, God's judgement – indeed his duty to judge – remained the final reality. If this duty to judge lay so heavily upon their Maker how much more did it weigh upon his children? In the light of this belief Evangelical parents guided their sons and daughters from infancy to distinguish between right and wrong, the good and the wicked, the precious and the worthless. Throughout his life Leslie Stephen never doubted that a man was saved in a moral sense so long as he recognized that it was his duty to exercise his judgement.

Such was the God to whom they prayed. But it was not enough to appreciate that this was the Grand Design. The Evangelicals demanded more – they declared that a man could be saved only if he had experienced God's grace. A man could be certain that God's message of salvation was intended for him personally only by experiencing the moment when grace descended. That moment was his conversion. When a man acknowledged his helplessness, when overwhelmed with the horror of his mortal corruption he cast his sins at the feet of his Redeemer, when he begged Christ to bear the burden as he had promised to his Father on the Cross, then, in a flash, that man might stand upright; not assured indubitably of a place in heaven – for God's grace might depart and he could yet slide back into the mire of worldliness – but confident in the knowledge that Christ had changed his heart and that he was now, and almost certainly would be, numbered with his saints. God must have touched the heart so that a man *experienced* his own sinfulness and the power of his Saviour. To know God was an emotional experience as well as an intellectual conviction. Theology, the arrangement of syllogisms, the creation of principles and philosophies, were fundamentally valueless: no structure of thought could make the design of creation intelligible. The raw stuff of emotional experience was the proof of God's existence. And so a young Evangelical who developed a turn for philosophy was likely to be drawn towards the Utilitarians who professed to base their conclusions on an empirical examination of human experience. Both Evangelicals and Utilitarians, Leslie Stephen noted, regarded their own version of verifiable experience as final and both were opposed to the study of metaphysics.

To the experience of conversion the Evangelicals added the daily experience of God – the day-to-day meditation in the silent bedroom, Bible in hand, led a man to know Christ as a friend. The surest test of a redeemed Christian was the earnestness and length of time he spent in prayer. It was in prayer that they learnt to train their conscience. High among the tenets of the faith was the injunction that no human intermediary, no priest or State servant, should dare to intervene between man and his Maker and usurp God's majesty in his dealings with another human being. A sincere man's conscience must be, at the last, the measure of his actions. It must be free to enable him to follow the prompting of the Holy Spirit. How else can he claim to be a moral being, how can he claim God's mercy, unless his actions are his own, and not those dictated to him by the external spiritual authority of a visible Church? The Evangelical appeals to the inner light within him for guidance. The Protestant stakes all on the relationship between the soul of the agent and the Judge. Protestantism is a creed for supermen – for men so secure in God's grace that they cannot stumble.[1] The particular glory of the faith is that at best its disciples are taught to follow the truth in their hearts. But the dangers are obvious. In a letter to Moncure Conway about his state of mind in 1823, Francis Newman explained, 'I was an Evangelical, but like plenty of Evangelicals beside, both now and then, was resolved to follow the Truth *whithersoever it led me*; and was always indignant when told "you must believe this or that", or you will find it "will lead you further". "*If* that time comes, I shall go further" was my uniform reply.' It was this spirit which led so many of the best brains among the Evangelicals to go further and to secede from the party.

Evangelicalism challenged at every point the way of life of the upper classes. Aristocracies live by a code. They ask whether a man is brave, generous, well-bred, and fanatically loyal to his kin and kind; and they detest sneaking opportunists, cagey trimmers, toadies and those who reason why. The way to ensure that one's actions are never squalid is to act instinctively by the light of honour – and if that means to act recklessly without thought for the consequences of one's actions, well, that is better than acting with calculation according to the rules of the counting-house. The Evangelicals never tired of putting this code in the pillory. Was it an accident, they asked, that sport and dances were inseparable from profanity and profligacy? What was honour but inflated self-conceit so that the nobility treated the faintest disagreement as a slight? Reckless-ness led to gambling, gambling to the duel, the duel to murder. They particularly abhorred the sin of pride, 'the passion which strikes the deepest root in the breast of a Nobleman'. There was a test which

---

[1] The great Durkheim, in his famous essay on suicide, inferred that the rate of suicides was higher among Protestants than among Catholics because Protestantism placed the full weight of responsibility on the individual's shoulders.

Evangelicals applied to those they met. Were they 'becoming serious'? Seriousness was thought to be the best evidence that a man was not merely a nominal Christian but one who professed his faith and acted upon it. It meant conquering the world, living in it but not belonging to it. Self-denial, humility, moral as distinct from physical courage, and self-control were the virtues which afforded the best evidence of salvation.

On another issue also the Clapham Sect distanced themselves from the upper classes. They were men of property, conservative in politics and well-connected with Parliament, the Church, the City, the colonial service, the universities and the army and navy. But as Evangelicals they had little faith in institutions. All institutions were created by sinful men: what hope could they hold out of regenerating society? The Established Church was indeed a blessing because it provided religious education for the poor and created an atmosphere in which oaths in the witness-box should be regarded as sacred and conventions accepted of the kind which must exist if order is to prevail. To the Clapham Sect the Prayer Book was especially dear – Simeon said that he was never nearer to God than when reading it. But loyal as they were to the Anglican Church they had a higher loyalty – to the Invisible Church. The Invisible Church of Christ was composed of all those who had closed with the offer of salvation, whether Anglicans or Dissenters. Beside it the Erastian Church of the High and Dry party appeared trivial. Reform of the Church was an Evangelical ideal but not reform through commissions, canon law or convocations. The only way to accomplish reform was to change the hearts of the clergy and then of their congregations. Wilberforce was adamant that Dissent in 'unsteepled places of worship' was an evil, but he would have agreed with Simeon that if Dissent flourished in a parish it was because the pulpit was occupied by 'a light and trifling clergyman'. One of the reasons Geoffrey Best argues, why Evangelicals, the Clapham Sect being no exception, puzzled people, who sometimes admired but more often disliked them, was because they refused to give their loyalty to institutions. We have seen how Jem Stephen resigned his seat because Liverpool would not move on the abolition of the slave trade; Henry Thornton before him voted against Pitt 'so that if my Master had come again at that moment, I might have been able to give an account of my stewardship'. Prime Ministers and Chief Whips turn up their noses at such concern for personal rectitude; but this notion – that a man's first loyalty is to an ideal rather than to his kinsmen or to the State and its institutions – was one of the most important which the Clapham Sect bequeathed to their intellectual descendants.

But a living religion cannot be expounded point by point. To explain his views, Sir James Stephen told Carlyle, he would have to write an autobiography:

to tell of opinions inherited – of the diversities between the paternal and maternal inheritance – of the friends of my youth who, one after another, went down into the grave in the full maturity of the Christian life, and of the Christian faith – of the friends of my later years, in whom the ripening of faith was a tardy and imperfect process – of many books read, which all in turn left me still to search – of the vicissitudes of life, which taught me much not to be found (or not to be found by me) in any books – of Biblical studies and meditations – of habitual exercises of devotion, public, domestic and private – of the reaction on my own mind of the lessons I had to convey to my children – and of influences silently, imperceptibly, yet progressively exerting themselves over my interior self which . . . have wrought that self into a persuasion (that is a heart conviction) from which in this life, I can never now be divorced – a persuasion that the Bible, or rather the greater part of it, is, in some real though indefinable sense, the Word of God – the persuasion that, between the life and death of Jesus Christ and our own reconciliation to God, there is an indispensable, though (I confess) a perfectly inexplicable relation . . . – the persuasion of a real, though wholly incomprehensible, intimacy (amounting almost to unity) of life, and being, and nature between parents and their children, and their more remote posterity – the persuasion thence resulting of an ancestral corruption of our whole race – and the persuasion that, by the adoption of our nature, Jesus Christ has broken the otherwise indissoluble bonds which link us all to sin, and to sorrow, the child of sin.

To draw out this creed of mine into any series of dogmatical propositions . . . is quite beyond my power. My convictions are, I know, less strong than my persuasions. I am living, or trying to live, more under the guidance of an invisible hand, and under the impulse of indefinable motives, than in submission to any logic, or body of evidences, or weight of authority. If I were of the Society of John Wesley, I should say I am living by my experiences . . . My creed has for its foundation, superstructure and summit, the sense of unworthiness – of my own personal and individual unworthiness. But yet I think myself bound . . . to tell you as distinctly as I can, that however remote I may be from the character of a Christian, I am bound by links stronger than death to him from whom that holy name is derived.

Evangelicalism, then, is a religion for men of this world. It demands that men shall labour to save their brothers' souls. But how can one evangelize without becoming contaminated by worldly wickedness? How has a man the audacity to show other men their sins knowing all the time that he himself is sinful?

Study the private papers of the Evangelicals and the answer is clear. Henry Thornton of Clapham left a diary which contains the daily entries of his solitary communing. It is a diary of a man in this world, not of it. He does not seek to merge the soul with the One, and to lift himself out of the complexity of human existence into the stillness of the infinite where the soul can join itself to God. His religion is a practical religion dealing with practical affairs, and Christ his wise counsellor. A man may work in the world and return with clean hands provided that he is constantly introspective. Each day Thornton examines his life according to the commandments laid upon him by God's Book. Has he lived according to the Law? How can he amend his acts to follow it more closely? Scrutiny of his actions leads him to resolve to control his will. For the human will yearning after the pomps and vanities of the world must die and become Christ's will. The past is renounced, the old selfish private will dies, and the regenerated will takes control. This state of mind leads, all too often, to a man denying that the old will ever inhabited his body.[1] But the strength and self-confidence such a belief gives a man is fabulous. Moreover, it redeems him from guilt. Regarded purely as a therapy, Evangelicalism can be a most potent healer. Justified by his faith in Christ, a man is freed from all *ultimate* doubt. He may wrestle with his conscience and search his heart for shortcomings in his everyday life. But, unlike a man who believes in justification partly by works and never therefore quite knows what the score is – who never knows how many of his bad actions have atoned for his good actions – the Evangelical's mind is at rest on the ultimate question of salvation. The knowledge that God does not forget his saints gives him the strength to labour in the vineyards of the world.

From Clapham to Bloomsbury

Thus the Clapham Sect had the confidence to change the world. They acted in the spirit of the collects for the last Sunday in Trinity and the first in Advent; with their wills stirred up by God, they put on the armour of light, and learned to live in the world and yet to despise its values. Secure in the experience of their conversion they were untroubled by the distractions and vices of London society. They had seen the obstinate defenders of the slave trade, Nelson among them, retire shattered. High and Dry and latitudinarian Anglicans hindered and sneered at them, yet they saw their cause everywhere gaining ground. Unpopularity and derision often sour zealots and turn them into cynics or fanatics, but an unpopularity which gradually evaporates into success and something like approbation is a tonic. The Clapham Sect saw that sincerity paid, and they acquired the habit of going against the grain of their times. Their

---

[1] Leslie Stephen fell into this Evangelical state of mind when he ruminated over the religious crisis that led to his agnosticism. 'I was not discovering that my creed was false, but that I had never really believed it' and 'I . . . became convinced among other things, that Noah's flood was a fiction (or rather convinced that I had never believed it).' Maitland commented on these passages that if you have to 'discover' or to 'become convinced' of the falsity of the story of Noah's Flood, then you have really believed it however baseless the belief may have been. It is an interesting example of how a highly scrupulous mind can deny after 'conversion' that it held certain beliefs which have become morally odious.

sincerity sprang from their determination not to let outward circumstances dictate their actions. When the time came for Leslie Stephen to evangelize on behalf of the North in the American Civil War or to propagate agnosticism, he appeared to have inherited a double portion of the Clapham spirit.

He also acquired another quality peculiar to the Clapham Sect, namely the sense of belonging to a chosen body. Sydney Smith was wrong in calling them a sect, for a more orthodox body of men never stepped. They were not a sect but a coterie. Leslie's father admitted that they were a close-knit society up in arms if one of their number was attacked and unsparing in their judgements of individuals outside the clique. They dipped their tongues in vinegar and delighted to smell out a sham. Zachary Macaulay was renowned for his eager frankness and zeal in admonishing his friends and he expected no less from them. An officer who met Zachary Macaulay was rash enough to say that swearing was a practice which harmed no one. Macaulay was on him like a knife, and subsequently 'feared he might have been offensively strong on the subject'; but he rejoiced to hear that the officer a little later swore no more and 'has become exceedingly restless and uneasy about that and other matters'. Again, visiting a sick friend who said he could not fix on any particular sins, Macaulay 'was at no loss to remind him of numberless particular sins, of the commission of which I myself had been a witness. I set them before him with all their aggravations.' Or, again, a young lady 'showed some very striking marks of a vain mind': whereupon Macaulay spoke his. 'The young lady did not altogether relish my plain but, I am sure, friendly expostulation.' Later he noticed she had put off 'her monstrous, misshapen dress ... and her lowly looks were, I hope, no fallacious indication of a humbled mind'. Macaulay expected his friends to be equally zealous with him. 'Mr Thornton's letter, in which were only eight lines, was long enough to give me the satisfaction of knowing that he had nothing particularly to blame; a negative, but from Henry Thornton no mean, praise.' Thornton's great-grandson, E. M. Forster, recorded how a young bride, who married into the family, said thoughtfully: 'If there were a spot upon the glorious Sun himself, the Thorntons would notice it.'

The censoriousness of Thornton and Macaulay was intensified by their belief that every moment of time, every word, every friendship, were accountable to God. This self-awareness, this contempt for the opinions of all outside the charmed circle, are the marks of a coterie. There are, however, advantages in clannishness. To belong to a set in which integrity and intelligence are blended, whose members criticize each other vigorously, and which can claim to be educating the country, inoculates a man against the evils of snobbery and the itch to simulate fashionable opinion. The Stephens were content to remain where they found themselves in society: what need was there to climb higher when they were at the top? Had Jem Stephen tried to do so his second wife, Wilberforce's sister, would have reproved him. 'O! She was the friend of my soul. She told me frankly all my faults,' he said; and for him this was cause for praise, not the explanation of an unhappy marriage. The Stephens lived a public life, but they forswore the lures which public life dangles in front of men, inveigling them to shuffle off their principles. And there was, of course, within the Sect a circle even more important in their eyes to spiritual development, the family itself. Leslie Stephen learnt to base his whole ethical system on the family. 'The degree in which any ethical theory recognizes and reveals the essential importance of the family relation is, I think, the best test of its approximation to truth,' he wrote in an essay in which he answered the question which Johnson posed: which had done the most for humanity, Dr Johnson or his poor dependant, the doctor Levett?[1] Obscure creatures like Levett, answered Stephen, really inherit the Kingdom of Heaven; a writer should pray to be obscure for fear of being demoralized by public applause. Humanity owed the greatest debt to the most obscure of all beings in the eyes of the world, wives and mothers, who by their self-sacrifice shape the lives of their husbands and children. So deeply had the Evangelical tradition of the family as the natural centre of worship affected Stephen that he founded the moral health of society upon the institution of the family in his *Science of Ethics*.

Leslie Stephen's thought, therefore, was hewn in Evangelical rock. He relied on experience rather than on a metaphysical vision of the world. He was not shy of preaching as it was the most natural of all duties. He was certain that he ought to make judgements when he criticized. And he looked to his conscience to guide him when doing all three. So much he had gained; but he also rejected part of the tradition. How did Evangelicalism fail him?

Stephen was fortunate in his Clapham upbringing, for the Claphamites exhibited the best side of Evangelicalism. Its dimmer lights, like Thomas Gisborne, might at their brightest exhibit only 'a grave and cheerful complacency', but its leaders were men of strength and character, and Stephen would not confuse them with the rank and file of the Evangelical party at the time when he was a young man. For by that time the heroes of his grandfather's generation were dead, and his father lamented 'Oh

[1] This was the question which provoked the lines in Johnson's poem on Levett which Stephen declared he could hardly read without tears starting to his eyes:
His virtues walked their narrow round,
Nor made a pause, nor left a void;
And, sure, the Eternal Master found
The single talent well-employed.

where are the people who are at once really religious, and really cultivated in heart and in understanding, the people with whom we could associate as our fathers used to associate with each other?' The natural successors to the Clapham Sect had gone into other fields and by the middle of the century the Evangelical party had become for Thackeray a byword for bigotry and a narrow, sneaking morality. Even their great chief, Shaftesbury, confessed, 'I have received from the hands of the [Evangelical] party treatment I have not received from any other. High Churchmen, Roman Catholics, even infidels, have been friendly to me; my only enemies have been the Evangelicals.' The doctrine of the regenerated will, in the mouths of men less humble and honest than Thornton, encouraged hypocrisy and double-dealing; for it is not every man who can lead a changed life while partaking of the normal pleasures of the world. Pusey noted that belief in the regenerated will led some Evangelicals to speak of their past sins as if they had been committed by another. 'Every man', said Keble, 'was his own absolver', and pharisaically those 'born again' looked down on anyone who did not use Evangelical jargon. The initiate had only to mention 'judgements' on sinners, which he had witnessed, or speak with a rapt look about his 'seals', or converts, which proved that he was 'owned', or of a child who had merited a 'gracious' whipping, and he was accepted as saved in low Evangelical circles. The doctrine that good works were *evidential* – or in other words an excellent indication that one was of the Elect enjoying perpetual sanctification through the Holy Spirit – exaggerated the importance of worldly success in the eyes of the petty-minded. The close connection between cash and religion, pharisaism and cant, was the legacy of an emotional religion when it was professed by the ruck of those classes in society who were learning the value – and it was a real value – of respectability.

Far more serious was the growing distrust by Evangelicals of the intellect and the imagination. 'Parents know not what they do,' wrote that popular Protestant writer, Charlotte Elizabeth Tonna, 'when from vanity, thoughtlessness or overindulgence, they foster in a young girl what is called a poetical taste.' The Stephen family would have laughed at her for declaring that when she read *The Merchant of Venice* she 'drank a cup of intoxication under which my brain reeled for many a year'; but there was an Evangelical saying, 'Literature is inimical to spirituality if it be not kept under with a firm hand'. Benjamin Gregory recalled how he crushed the love of literature he had gained at his Methodist school and after his conversion refused to read any but devotional books. Indeed there had always been an incipient doubt about the value of learning for its own sake. Leslie's great-grandfather, Henry Venn, had opposed the study of the Hebrew text of the Old Testament and had said, no doubt with the intention of discouraging degrading religious controversy, 'Never on any account, dispute. Debate is the work of the flesh.' 'The cultivation of the intellectual powers', said Dean Close, 'can of itself have no tendency towards moral or spiritual good.' Canon Storr went as far as to say that the Evangelicals cared little for the pursuit of truth for its own sake, and the wisest of all the Victorian nonconformists, R. W. Dale, the Congregationalist minister in Birmingham, admitted that Evangelicals cared only for those truths directly related to salvation. Truth was an instrument for placing men permanently in the right relation to God.

The faults in the rock ran even deeper. Evangelicalism does not satisfy an intellect which asks for knowledge of God apart from personal experience. Directly the sinner is convinced that he is at one with God, no further intellectual effort is required. This led the Oxford Noetics to condemn it as a belief which fostered spiritual pride, Sir James Stephen to deplore its formalism and Dr Arnold to declare that Evangelicals were good Christians of low understanding, bad education and ignorance of the world. It did not matter that Evangelicalism gave no metaphysical explanation of the riddle of the universe. But it did matter that the one problem it professed to answer – namely the existence of evil in the world – was so often handled in such a gross manner. The redemption of man was treated, Gladstone declared, as a joint stock transaction between God and man with Christ as the broker. One acquired 'a saving interest in the Blood of Jesus'. It was a religion whose phraseology was of this world; this made it easier for the uneducated to understand but more difficult for the cultivated to remain inspired. Evangelicalism appeals to the heart but it makes a *rational* appeal. Once a man has closed the deal with God, he is free to rejoice and does not have to justify his state of mind by searching through dogmas. God is recognized by the depth of an emotional experience rather than through the comprehensiveness of belief. The very clarity of Evangelicalism was its undoing. It rested on two stones, the truth of the Bible and the experience of conversion; the Bible was already under attack; and the social milieu in which the children of Clapham lived differed from that in which their middle-aged fathers had received the miracle of conversion. And, as time went on, the Evangelical party in the Church, lashed into a lather by the excesses of the Ritualists, became more and more bigoted so that Archbishop Magee could refer to one of their societies as 'Persecution Company Ltd'.

Too often an Evangelical clergyman came into a parish not to send peace but a sword. They divided their flock into sheep and goats, and harsh were the words they used about the reprobates. Too often novelists found them easy to caricature and their ingratiating humility appears in the shape of Uriah Heep, or their worldly ambition hidden beneath the usual formularies appears in Barsetshire in the form of Mr Slope. But

Trollope gave a more telling account of Evangelical divisiveness in his portrait of the Rev. Mr and Mrs Stumfold in *Miss Mackenzie*. The *Christian Observer* made no bones about it. 'We believe that little good is done in a parish until a clergyman divides his auditors into two classes – those that serve God, and those that serve Him not; so there may be no mistake in men's minds upon so momentous a subject.' So much had changed by the middle of the century from the heyday of the Clapham Sect. Evangelicalism was no longer a stirring of conscience and a quickening of heart and action within a tiny minority in the Church of England. It had become associated in men's minds with a party – a partisan party – making up for whatever it lacked in suppleness of manoeuvre by dogged determination to impose its own interpretation of holiness upon society as a whole. On all sorts of issues, which in the days of Simeon and Wilberforce were fluid, it now was rigid. Sympathy for godly Dissent had now become a form of ecumenical Protestantism to the intense distaste of High Churchmen who stood on the principle of the apostolic succession in the priesthood. Devotion to the Prayer Book had now become a fanatical adherence to the Church Establishment as a safeguard against the pretensions of the Tractarians. The organization of the Establishment had now become both a device to institutionalize evangelism and to thwart other parties within the Church. The Church Pastoral Aid Society and the Simeon Trust, which bought advowsons to ensure an Evangelical succession in a parish, were detested by other clergymen as caucuses for spreading bigotry. Even their charitable activities took the form of a wounding spear-head which Evangelicals drove into the side of society, and their desire to change people's lives, especially their Sabbatarianism, made more enemies than it won them friends. Bit by bit they imposed their manners upon the clergy and often upon urban society.[1] But though duchesses might grace the platforms of their public meetings, the Evangelical clergy, fatally for their reputation, all too seldom counted many indisputable gentlemen among their numbers – and even fewer learned gentlemen. These were some of the reasons why Evangelicalism failed to make a fresh appeal to the descendants of the Clapham Sect.

In the Clapham Sect we can observe an interesting example of an hereditary intellectual strain. Each generation renounced their father's beliefs but the spirit of the coterie was so strong that there remained an outlook, an attitude, not unlike that of the Sect itself. The second generation of Claphamites witnessed the first defections. It was the

[1] By mid century the fox-hunting squarson was vanishing, no clergyman would go to the theatre or opera and many refused an invitation to a dance. Samuel Wilberforce upbraided a young parson in his diocese for hunting: he replied that it was not more worldly than a ball at Blenheim which Wilberforce had attended. 'Ah!' said the Bishop, 'but I was never within three rooms of the dancing.' 'Oh, if it comes to that,' replied the clergyman, 'I am never within three fields of the hounds.'

Evangelicals in the Oxford Movement such as Newman and Faber, who
went over to Rome; the sons of High Churchmen, Pusey and Keble,
remained firm. Among the Claphamites the Wilberforces seceded in
droves. Three of the four sons of William Wilberforce and both his sons-
in-law became Roman Catholics. Samuel alone remained in the Anglican
Communion and lived to see his daughter and her husband go over to
Rome; and even he returned to the Evangelical fold, says Tom Mozley, as
a brand plucked from the burning, but with the smell of burning strong
upon him. Shaftesbury had Zachary's son, Lord Macaulay, publicly
chastised for negativism in a lecture delivered on Macaulay's death by the
celebrated Methodist preacher, Dr Punshon; and among Macaulay's
papers was found a quotation from Conyers Middleton: 'But if to live
strictly and think freely; to practise what is moral and to believe what is
rational, be consistent with the sincere profession of Christianity, then I
shall acquit myself like one of its truest professors' and Macaulay added
'Haec est absoluta et perfecta philosophi vita.' Sir James Stephen was a
liberal Evangelical, and though he told his children that they should treat
atheists as men who had insulted their dearest friend, he himself remained
on cordial terms with John Stuart Mill and Austin. This was a falling-off
from the days when William Wilberforce prosecuted a wretched printer
whose name appeared on a blasphemous publication. 'The freedom with
which the vessel swings at anchor, ascertains the soundness of her
anchorage,' he proclaimed, but he was careful not to put any undue strain
upon the chains. He explained to Fitzjames:

I am profoundly convinced of the consistency of all the declarations of scripture,
but I am as profoundly convinced of my own incapacity to perceive that they are
consistent . . . I am not here to speculate but to repent, to believe and to obey; and
I find no difficulty in believing, each in turn, doctrines which seem to me
incompatible with each other. It is in this sense and to this extent that I adopt the
whole creed called evangelical. I adopt it as a regulator of the affections, as a rule
of life and as a quietus, not as a stimulant to inquiry.

Fitzjames commented that this kind of humility came so close to irony
that he found it hard to separate them. Leslie summed up his father's
position by saying that he wore the uniform of the old army though he
had ceased to bear unquestioning allegiance.

If the second generation of Clapham were laxer, the third would have
shocked their grandparents inexpressibly. Florence Nightingale, granddaughter of Sir William Smith, was bitterly attacked for Puseyism by that
odious Scots bigot, Alexander Haldane, who edited the Record. John
Venn, the Cambridge logician, took Holy Orders but in 1883 renounced
them.[1] A. V. Dicey remained a Christian but cared less than nothing for
dogma. He even doubted the value of the Broad Church movement and

[1] His religious convictions remained, however, fundamentally unshaken and later in life he said that
he realized that he could have stayed in the Church.

thought that Dean Stanley had lost much by remaining a clergyman. Sir George Otto Trevelyan followed his uncle Macaulay and left Christian theology alone; he admired Henry Sidgwick's theism but he kept aloof from the struggle between rationalism and religion because he feared that much good might perish in it. Fitzjames Stephen sympathized with Lady Grant Duff in her perplexity over the proper course to take in bringing up her children. 'My wife and I', he wrote, 'take a very definite line with our children . . . We take them to church and have family prayers which my wife reads.' He could hardly have read them himself. In a letter to Sir William Hunter in 1873 he was explicit.

As to my theological opinions, I should have thought that they were as plainly intimated in the last chapter of my book (*Liberty, Equality, Fraternity*) as was necessary. However, if you care to know more explicitly what I think, it is just this. I do not believe the New Testament narrative to be true. To my mind, the whole history of Christ, in so far as it is supernatural, is legendary. As to Christian morals, I cannot regard them as either final or complete. As to natural religion, I think its two great doctrines – God and a future state – more probable than not; and they appear to me to make all the difference to morality. Take them away and epicureanism seems to me the true and proper doctrine. This will hardly be news to any one who has read what I have written with discernment.

The change in the fourth generation is more startling. By the beginning of this century the intellectual revolt against Christianity had been superseded by an ethical revolution far more profound in its consequences. The name of the Bloomsbury circle will always be associated with this revolution, and on the surface there seems to be little to connect Leslie Stephen's daughters, Vanessa Bell and Virginia Woolf, or Henry Thornton's great-grandson, E. M. Forster, with the Clapham Sect. On the surface only. Bloomsbury, like Clapham, was a coterie. It was exclusive and clannish. It regarded outsiders as unconverted and was contemptuous of good form opinions. Remarks which did not show that grace had descended upon their utterer were met with killing silence. Like the Claphamites they criticized each other unsparingly but with affection. Like Clapham, Bloomsbury had discovered a new creed: the same exhilaration filled the air, the same conviction that a new truth had been disclosed, a new Kingdom conquered.[1] Bloomsbury assumed that

---

[1] In a paper, entitled *Old Bloomsbury*, Vanessa Bell pointed out that the original circle, which gathered in Brunswick and Gordon Squares between 1904 and 1915, had ceased to exist many years before the term became fashionable and other people inherited its name and reputation. The original members were Vanessa Bell, Virginia Woolf, Thoby and Adrian Stephen (the four children of Sir Leslie); Clive Bell and Leonard Woolf; J. M. Keynes, Duncan Grant and Roger Fry; Desmond and Molly MacCarthy; Lytton, Oliver, Marjorie and James Strachey; Saxon Sydney-Turner, musician and civil servant; H. T. J. Norton, mathematician and don; and on occasions E. M. Forster and Gerald Shove, who was a Fabian and a Cambridge economist, and married F. W. Maitland's daughter, whose great-aunt was Julia Stephen.

Thoby Stephen, Bell, Woolf, Turner and Lytton Strachey had all met at Trinity where in 1899 they founded the Midnight Society which met on Saturdays to read plays and poetry at that hour. Keynes was brought into the circle through Strachey and Woolf, and Grant was cousin to the Stracheys. Lady Strachey knew the Stephens well through her friendship with Anny Ritchie. This was the original nucleus.

worldly values were grotesquely stupid and wicked. Its members despised wealth, power, popularity and success and were sharp to notice whether someone was on the make. For this reason both Clapham and Bloomsbury infuriated polite society and drew upon themselves a good deal of envious spite. The two sets, of course, held very different views about laughter. The Claphamites were cheerful but only Wilberforce can be said to have known the meaning of the word humour. Bloomsbury's sense of humour was exceedingly highly developed – it was fantastical, gay, satirical, ironic; they were at one with A. V. Dicey when he said, 'It is better to be flippant than dull.' They combined extreme frivolity with extreme seriousness. Because they did not fall into the academic error of confusing seriousness with solemnity, it did not follow that they were not in earnest. They took the aesthetic movement out of the hands of Oxford dilettantes and gave it backbone; with the help of G. E. Moore's philosophy they created an ethical justification for art for art's sake. Both Clapham and Bloomsbury were circles which influenced the outlook of succeeding generations. They were each in their time responsible for justifying a new way to live by specific notions of what was good and what worthless.

Bloomsbury, moreover, had its religion. In his memoir, *My Early Beliefs*, J. M. Keynes – himself of Nonconformist stock – described it. 'Our religion closely followed the English puritan tradition of being chiefly concerned with the salvation of our own souls . . . We claimed the right to judge every individual case on its merits, and the wisdom, experience and self-control to do so successfully. This was a very important part of our faith.' From G. E. Moore's ethics they learnt that nothing mattered but 'states of mind'. A state of mind such as being in love, or apprehending beauty, was to be judged by its intrinsic value and without regard to its consequences, and salvation was to be obtained by 'communion with objects of love, beauty and truth'. Whether the state of mind created by such communion was good or bad was a subject for long discussion in which Moore's celebrated technique of rational analysis was used to decide whether the disputants were asking the right questions or discussing the same things. Whereas it had been customary in utilitarian ethics to assume that goodness could be explained in terms of pleasure, Moore discarded this part of the tradition and denied that the amount of pleasure promoted by a state of mind was any criterion for its goodness. In the early days his disciples went even further and tended to argue that a good state of mind so far from being pleasurable was nearly always painful. Intensity, passion, creation, produced pain; yet were they not the most admirable of qualities? It was therefore thought to indicate a very low state of mind if one argued that the amount of pleasure produced by an action had any connection with its goodness or badness.[1]

Thus far the argument followed orthodox puritan lines, but at this point it took a turn towards heterodoxy. Like puritans in the past who had emphasized personal salvation they were in danger of falling into the heresy of Antinomianism. If you are convinced that it is your duty to follow the inner light and to purify your state of mind without reference to any worldly standard, you begin to despise the world so strongly that you ignore your own relation to it; the world may call your actions sinful but to you they are not, because they proceed from a mind at one with God. If, moreover, you are among the Elect, the unconverted are hardly in a position to criticize you. Were they Antinomians? In Keynes's recollection the undergraduates who sat at Moore's feet and later became the Bloomsbury circle denied that there was any close connection between *doing* good and *being* good; and they did not follow Moore's precept that the rightness of actions depended on the eventual good which they produced. Leonard Woolf, as one of those undergraduates, believed Keynes's memory was at fault. He recalled endless discussions about the consequences of one's actions even to the extent of relating these actions to practical politics. In either case the religion was inspired by a determination to make truthful statements within the framework of common sense.

Their religion was also as strongly concerned with experience especially, wrote Desmond MacCarthy, 'those parts of experience which could be regarded as ends in themselves'.

Morality was either a means to attaining those goods of the soul or it was nothing – just as the railway system existed to bring people together and to feed them, or the social order that as many 'ends' as possible should be achieved. These ends naturally tied themselves down to personal relations, aesthetic emotions and the pursuit of truth. We were perpetually in search of distinctions; our most ardent discussions were attempts to fix some sort of a scale of values for experience. The tendency was for the stress to fall on feeling rightly rather than upon action . . . Nor were we particularly interested in the instincts or the will compared with the play of the intelligence. What was the will but a means, a servant? Or what were the instincts but the raw stuff out of which the imagination moulded a life worth contemplating?

The fourth generation of the Clapham Sect naturally repudiated the moral code of their forefathers. The doctrine of original sin was replaced by the eighteenth-century belief in man's fundamental reasonableness, sanity and decency. They cut the painter which had attached Leslie Stephen to Evangelical sexual constraints, tossed overboard any form of

---

[1] This was an intellectual judgement which had little direct effect on their habits. Sir James Stephen's resolve never to smoke another cigar because he found his first so pleasant would have been frostily received.

supernatural belief as so much hocus-pocus, and set their sails in the purer breezes of contemplation. And yet one can still see the old Evangelical ferment at work, a strong suspicion of the worldly-wise, an unalterable emphasis on personal salvation and a penchant for meditation and communion among intimate friends.

From Calvinism to Rationalism

The Evangelical tradition ran strong in Leslie Stephen's veins. What did he himself think of his heritage? Not much. His heart lay with the eighteenth-century clergy who thought that religion was part of reason. How could one compare the teaching of Whitefield or Newton with the civilized discourses of the Deists, when Whitefield's one ambition was to induce an ignorant miner to give up drink by preaching the consoling truth that, if he did not, he would burn everlastingly; or when Newton's way of comforting the agonized poet Cowper was to stop him translating Homer and set him to compose hymns which inflamed his religious mania? And yet, here was a fascination, a mystery. How was it possible for a man of intellect to believe the appalling doctrines of the Calvinists – that God tossed infants with glee into the bottomless pit and swept heathens and Christians in their millions to the eternal fires reserving for himself only a handful of the Elect? Rummaging in the curiosity-shop of the past, Stephen paused to examine Jonathan Edwards, the eighteenth-century New England divine and one of the most powerful of all Calvinist theologians. This curio had described himself as a man who had 'a constitution in many respects peculiarly unhappy, attended by flaccid solids; vapid, sizy, and scarce fluids; and a low tide of spirits'. So remorseless were his edicts against pleasure, his diatribes against children as 'young loathesome vipers', and his descriptions of the 'exquisite, horrible misery' of the damned among whom most of his congregation would be numbered, that finally even the children of the Pilgrim Fathers could bear no more and ran him out of town. Yet Edwards possessed an exceptionally acute mind and his book on the freedom of the will argues the case for predestination with almost excessive ingenuity and faces every major theological problem. How could the boy who had found so many objections to the doctrine of God's sovereignty and the Elect have come in manhood to accept this ghastly doctrine as 'infinitely pleasant, bright and sweet'? Stephen noted that Edwards was not a mere fanatic. Beneath the crust of his religious belief was hidden a profound moral sense. Edwards distinguished between those human affections which harmonized with the Divine Will and those which were discordant. No outward sign – no vision, no transport of delight, no miracle, no words – could prove a man to be virtuous, for virtue is to love God for his own sake. The only way a man could guess that a fellow human being had been born again was if he observed him love Christ without a thought for heaven or hell, and humble himself publicly. Stephen thought virtue depended on two conditions. Did John Jones's actions help other people to lead good lives and did those actions measure up to the highest standard of conduct? Next he asked what were Jones's motives for his actions. Only if he could be judged to act for the love of doing good for its own sake and not for some favour or reward, could we say that he is virtuous. These were the exact criteria demanded by Jonathan Edwards. Stephen thought that he deserved to be remembered for this revelation alone.

Stephen's long analysis of this Calvinist should have led him to realize that Protestantism no less than Catholicism can be a highly logical and morally satisfying structure, provided, of course, that the existence of God and its major dogmas are not questioned. But in other essays Stephen applauded Protestantism for an entirely contradictory virtue. By insisting that a man must follow his own conscience, Protestantism made it possible for a really intelligent man to be done with the whole business. 'Protestantism in one aspect', Stephen wrote, 'is simply rationalism still running about with the shell on its head.' So far from it being a religion with a logical structure, Stephen described it as common-sense morality with a carapace of superstition. Protestantism compels a man to examine first principles, Catholicism demands a blind acceptance of dogma. Stephen assumed without argument that Protestantism was a revolt by liberals against the authoritarianism of the Catholic church. The movement away from rites to sermons, from sacraments to extempore prayer, must be a revolt towards reason and away from incantation. Such a judgement was crude Macaulay. The connection between Protestantism and freedom of thought or the development of science is a highly complicated subject and this kind of generalization distorts history. Whether a Catholic or a Protestant determined like Francis Newman to 'go further', depended on his temperament and upbringing, not on the nature of his religious belief. Every generation is faced with certain questions which seem to be of paramount importance. Each has to ask itself whether the religion in which they have been brought up will be able to provide answers to those questions. Stephen was so anxious to convince himself and others that in the evolution of ideas Protestantism was merely a stage on the road to the discovery of new truths – among them the falsehood of Protestantism – that he did not analyse what were the questions which this religion attempted to answer and how far it failed or succeeded in doing so. Nor can we plead that he was only following the historiography of his age. His fellow rationalist, Thomas Huxley, refused to be taken in by Stephen's thesis. To replace Transubstantiation by Consubstantiation was not, Huxley thought, a sign of liberal thought: 'One does not free a prisoner by merely scraping away the rust from his shackles.'

The apparent contradiction in Stephen's thought can be explained by his view of human nature. In his view the Protestant, whose religion tells him to develop and rely ultimately upon his private judgement, *ought* to become a rationalist. How then are we to account for the fact that Jonathan Edwards's acute mind did not lead him to this conclusion? Had those flaccid solids and vapid sizy fluids disturbed his balance of mind? Possibly. But more probably, thought Stephen, because he had the misfortune to be a backwoodsman living out of the current of European thought: by nature a German professor accidentally dropped into the American forests. An emancipated European would face no such difficulty. Let us, therefore, examine the system of thought which Stephen believed had emancipated mankind. Let us look at the second great influence on his life, the impact of British rationalism on his mind at Cambridge: and let us also see how the rising tide of a new tradition of thought, German transcendentalism, began to lap at the rocks below the cliffs on which he stood.

Chapter Six

❦❦❦

BRITISH RATIONALISM

The German Renaissance

No one can appreciate the nineteenth century, or indeed our own times, unless he realizes that we live in the shadow of a Renaissance as brilliant and dominating as the Italian Renaissance. Despite all reinterpretations of history the Italian Renaissance still stands as one of the most astonishing outbursts of human creativity which transformed the culture of Western Europe in the sixteenth and seventeenth centuries. But it is arguable that the explosion of genius which burst in Germany and Austria in the eighteenth and nineteenth centuries was even more startling than what had occurred during the Italian Renaissance: the originality was as striking and the political and intellectual influence more profound. As in the Italian city states the towns of the German princelings who had for so long been pawns in the manoeuvres of the Great Powers nurtured the composers, the poets, philosophers and scholars who were to challenge the Europe of *l'âge de raison*. The movement was not, as in Italy two centuries before, heralded by a revolution in the visual arts, although the ravishing extravagances of Neumann, Zimmermann, the Fischers or the brothers Asam in the baroque churches which they built or decorated – or Schinkel's grave simplicity at the turn of the century – were notable achievements. German art was to find its expression in music rather than painting and after the compositions of Bach, Telemann and Scheidt, for two hundred years no decade passed without composers of genius emerging to dominate classical and romantic music, some of them supremely pure musicians such as Mozart or Schubert but many great, self-conscious artists such as Beethoven or Schumann or Wagner or Mahler burning to interpret the ideas of their times.

For it was the ideas of the German awakening which became as exciting to Germans as the ideas of the Enlightenment and of 1789 had been to Frenchmen. Kantian ethics, philosophic idealism, the justification of nationalism, the need for man to find his identity and having found it to

express himself, the interpretations of freedom, the heart-rending concern about the nature of man's will, the awareness of ineluctable conflicts
between equally valuable principles such as the Dionysian and the
Apollonian, between the *naïv* and the *sentimentalisch*, between reason
and understanding, between the will to power and the ideals of
renunciation and self-annihilation, are only a handful of the concepts
which were to change the way men and women interpreted life. The
galaxy of talent rivalled the humanists of the Italian Renaissance. Some of
them towered over their European contemporaries as did Kant and
Goethe, or were profoundly original minds such as Herder and Hegel,
some were humanists such as Lessing, Schiller and Winckelmann, others
philosophers of aesthetics such as Schelling or of religion such as
Schleiermacher and Feuerbach. There were optimists who followed
Fichte, and pessimists who favoured Schopenhauer, there were romantics
such as the unhappy young Kleist or the brothers Schlegel, and skilful
scholars engaged on Biblical exegesis, in particular those in the famous
theological faculty at Tübingen. They worked within the framework of a
body of ideas which seemingly continued ever to expand as one mind
struck sparks from another and changed men's notions about the
authenticity of history, about the relation of the natural sciences to
theology and about the place of the German nation in Europe and the
world. The dynamism of German culture began to be matched by the
efficiency of German industry and organizing skill. The geographical and
economic position in Europe of the German powers proved to be too
great a challenge to German statecraft; and having done more than their
share to provoke the First World War, they were left shattered after their
defeat in the second, which their leader had instigated. The prodigious
energy which had been released in the German Renaissance still glowed
and enabled the German people to rebuild their countries; but the strange
flame of originality and invention, which in the past had been fed so often
by German Jews, now scarcely flickered in a Europe of small states
dominated by America and Russia.

Yet German modes of thought still retain their vitality. As when a star
explodes, highly radioactive particles continue to be hurled into space.
For years British historians of ideas have contrasted with the English
liberal tradition the glorification of the State by Hegel, which buttressed
Prussian autocracy, or Nietzsche's heroic vitalism which they believed
inspired so many iniquities in Nazism, or Marx's dialectical materialism
which justified the so-called dictatorship of the proletariat and the
totalitarian State. Such genealogies, although not entirely false, do not
begin to do justice to the fecundity of the ideas of these thinkers, and a
case can be made out, and indeed was made out by the Israeli political
thinker J. L. Talmon, for totalitarianism being the child not of German

idealism but of the French Enlightenment. German thought can just as legitimately be regarded as the forerunner of pluralism – for did not Herder declare the overwhelming importance of self-expression and hence of the need to recognize that men belong to different cultures, different groups, each unique and unassimilable to the others, each with its own language and style of life, each inspired by its own history?

The revolt of the German thinkers against what they regarded as the soulless, precise, mechanical technocrats of the French Enlightenment is the theme of many of Isaiah Berlin's most penetrating articles. Out of their denial that one system or one ideology could possibly claim the loyalty of men who belonged to different cultures with different history came another insight: that people become obsessed with the problems of identity and status if they do not know who they are and where they stand in relation to others. Germans did not have the same secure sense of their identity as had the inhabitants of the great nation states of France and Spain, Russia or England. They were not even confident about their language. Günter Grass pictured German writers meeting after the Thirty Years War at Telgte to discuss what the German language was – unthinkable in the lands of Malherbe, Cervantes or Milton. No wonder the theory of alienation, worked out in this century by the Frankfurt School, which assumes men to be estranged from industrialized society because they are treated as just another cog in the machine constructed by technocrats and planners, sprang from the German thinkers of the eighteenth and nineteenth centuries; as did Weber's classic work on the sociology of bureaucracy or Freud's analysis of the 'rational' mind. Existentialism was another vision of life which emerged between the two world wars from German thought, and it is paradoxical that France, having seen Germany subdued after these two wars, should herself have been overcome by her ancient foe in the world of ideas. The mother of Cartesian clarity and logic has renounced her child and succumbed, Sartre in the role of pander, to the embraces of Heidegger and later to the delectable obscurities of structuralism or to various *marxisant* interpretations of life. What are *mentalités* but the children of Freud and Marx?

Perhaps the most disturbing of the multitude of ideas which the German awakening brought together and released was the contention that reason was not one and indivisible but consisted of two distinct and unbridgeable processes. Mathematics, history and religion were man-made and hence susceptible to formal analysis: whereas the natural sciences lay in another world and required totally different techniques to unravel their mysteries. Nor could there be much doubt which form of reason was superior. Faust found that magic, not science, gave him a picture of the macrocosm. Kant's distinction between Pure and Practical Reason, or Jacobi's between *Verstand* and *Vernunft*, were concepts fundamental to the enterprise of undermining the crude rationalism of the past. It was this division which permitted German scientists to make their discoveries without disturbing what had now become the generally accepted matrix of thought. German science was as renowned as German music or philosophy in the German Renaissance. Helmholtz, Hertz, Ohm, Röntgen, Liebig, Johannes Müller and Loeb had their counterparts in Britain and France. But science was better organized and supported in Germany. Poor as Germany and Austria were in comparison, the succession of great scientists culminating at the beginning of this century in Max Planck, Einstein and Heisenberg was better assured. So accepted had Kant's way of interpreting thought become that materialism as popularized by Ludwig Büchner had more influence outside than inside Germany. In Germany the discoveries of science made less impression on the minds of intelligent people because the conclusions which people drew from them had been anticipated by the conclusions of the philosophers and, in particular, by the historians who were themselves disciples of the philosophers.

The Historians and Christianity

The historical movement resembles a battlefield painted by Uccello. Amid the confusion of horsemen and their steeds the terrible lances and banners of the hosts draw precisely the lines of recession to create a hitherto undreamt of depth and space through the art of perspective: though who is friend or who is foe remains obscure. Historians who seem to belong to one school often borrow their ideas from those who might be described as their opponents so that any summary is bound to be in some respects misleading; but there were in the main three schools or ways of analysing the past.

The first of these derived from eighteenth century rationalism, and was to continue chastened but unrepentant at least until the days of J. B. Bury at the beginning of the twentieth century. It claimed to be scientific in that its premises were based on the axioms of human nature. 'Man, generally speaking', Voltaire had said, 'was always what he is now.' Man's history was the story of the triumphant march of his mind; as he achieved greater technical control over his environment his political and social institutions improved. Civilization was the goal; and if we look we can see that, admittedly with many deplorable setbacks and certainly not uniformly in every part of the globe, man has become more civilized – indeed it was the mission of the enlightened to civilize the less fortunate. That was why Bossuet believed that history was in effect the history of Europe. Facts, curiously enough for rationalists, were not the most important part of history. The most important part was the elucidation of the objective and universal laws of progress. But the historian also had to celebrate the individuals whose achievements as lawgivers, destroyers of archaic societies, or creators of new ideologies, scientific hypotheses or technological inventions had led the human race forward. This was the tradition which dominated historical studies in England when Stephen was a young don; but it should be realized that to this tradition, with some modifications, belonged not only romantic historians such as Scott or Tories such as Hume or Hallam, but the Whig historians as well, Macaulay, Grote and James Mill whose *History of British India* was not intended to analyse Indian culture but to determine how far along the road to civilization the sub-continent had moved. Tennyson pictured history as recording how freedom slowly broadens down from precedent to precedent.

This quasi-sociological version of the past came to be regarded with the utmost horror and contempt in Germany. German historians determined no longer to regard the past as a unilinear story. It was a cycle of opposing cultures which rose, flourished and waned, each valid and by no means inferior to those which succeeded it. The historian's duty was to compare these cultures, not to warm to the illegitimate task of evaluating them and pronouncing one to be superior to another. Nor should one conceive of events as being caused by some statesman or soldier willing that this or that should happen. Customs, religion, art, language were the unconscious ways in which a people expressed themselves: religion was not a crude superstition imposed upon men by crafty priests nor were laws yet another instance of their rulers' skill in preserving their own interests. The role of the historian was to explain the past in terms of itself, not of the present. By 1790 it was axiomatic among German intellectuals that no man with any pretensions to learning asked whether Christianity was true or false. Kant had shown that the truth of religion could never be proved or disproved by pure reason. What was debatable – and very fierce the debates were – was whether a society in which religion was important was a good or a deplorable society.

Christianity, however, is a religion which begins with dates and facts; and by the time Stephen was a young don the nature of evidence – and hence the truth or falsity of Christianity – had obstinately elbowed its way onto the centre of the German stage. One of the books Stephen read which was published just about the time he went up to Cambridge came from Tübingen and showed him how the critical treatment of sources had changed the way the Bible should be interpreted. This was F. C. Baur's *Paulus*. Baur distinguished between the sources emanating from the narrow Judaizing party of the early disciples and those of a much later date inspired by the world-wide religion of St Paul such as the Fourth Gospel which emphasized the Incarnation and Christ's divinity. There

was also Strauss's *Life of Jesus* – another product of Tübingen – which
Stephen almost certainly read before he began himself to write intellectual
history. It too declared that Christian dogmas remained untouched by the
destruction of Christian legends. It too exposed eighteenth century
rationalist interpretations of Scripture, whereby miracles were treated as
superstitious accounts for which natural explanations could be found.
After showing how the ancients had faced the same problems of
interpreting religious events in the same fashion as modern scholars,
Strauss concluded that argument about the facts of Christ's life was
irrelevant and that the miraculous in Scripture was not fiction or
exaggeration but myth. The story of Jesus's life simply embodied as myths
spiritual truths about human experience. He therefore made it clear that if
rationalists of the old school could glean no comfort from his analysis nor
could apologists of the old school. Strauss gained his reputation by his
vast learning and also by his command of Hegelian epistemology. He had
no use for theologians who thought they could pick up a technique here,
an idea or two there and somehow leave matters as they had been a
generation ago. With that mordant irony so characteristic of Goethe or
Thomas Mann, indeed of the German mind, Strauss said: 'Not everybody
can pulverize Christianity and Newtonian science so as to mix them.
Most men end up with sausage; the meat is orthodoxy, the fat is
Schleiermacher, the spice, Hegel.'

   Churchmen in Britain found themselves much like Christian in the
Valley of the Shadow of Death teetering on a hellish narrow path between
the Ditch of positivist rationalism on the one side and the Quag of
German idealist Biblical interpretation on the other. The German
intelligentsia, indeed the Lutheran pastors, were more receptive to new
ideas than their British brethren. They were more compact as a class,
more accustomed to academic methods of discussion, their universities
more numerous and the curriculum less narrow. Many of the Anglican
clergy were used to interpreting Scripture almost cabalistically, wrench-
ing Old Testament prophesies out of their context, and explaining the rise
and fall of civilizations as instances of God visiting his wrath upon erring
peoples in much the same way as they spoke of 'judgements' falling upon
individuals or nations or upon the wicked city of Paris. Anglican
clergymen were thrown into confusion when they encountered this new
Revelation. A bishop of Lincoln wished 'all Jarman philosophy at the
bottom of the Jarman ocean'. This desire for a second Flood was
comprehensible because, however contemptuous the German trans-
cendentalists were of the history of Voltaire and Gibbon or the theodicy
of Leibniz, and however confident in abandoning the trenches and
foxholes of the classic defences against deism and infidelity, they had
thrown up their new epistemological redoubts and historiographical

parapets on what appeared to be enemy ground, so that an Anglican bishop might justly wonder which side they were on.

H. J. Rose, a High Churchman from Cambridge, was in no doubt that they were the enemy. He had heard at Göttingen Eichhorn's celebrated lecture on Balaam's ass and returned to write a diatribe against those critical methods which Michaelis long ago had fashioned and which now his 70-year-old pupil was making fashionable. Rose could not understand how one could reject miracles yet believe in the honesty of those who related them, nor how ministers of Christianity who denied the divine inspiration and historical accuracy of the Bible could teach it to children without hypocrisy. Alarmed at what he heard, the young Pusey left Oxford to go to Germany. He too attended Eichhorn's lecture and was disgusted by what probably by then had become an overripe performance. 'I heard a titter going through all the room, and I saw only one person who was grave.' But Pusey was amazed by Eichhorn's erudition and he got to know other scholars: Pott, Bunsen and, in Berlin, Schleiermacher himself. 'This will all come upon us in England,' he observed, 'and how utterly unprepared for it we are.' He accordingly wrote a criticism of Rose's book and a partial defence of German scholarship. But Pusey had not yet learnt how to marshal a case; he got into trouble with the Bishop of London and failed to convince Rose, or for that matter anyone else, when he tried to show what might and might not be valuable in the higher criticism. It goes without saying that if the High Church were troubled, the Evangelicals were horrified to see Jesu, the sinner's friend, disappear under a welter of interpretations in the quest for the historical Jesus. Nor were Broad Churchmen in depicting Jesus as a teacher of ethics any better pleased in being brought up short by commentaries upon the darker eschatological sayings of Christ.

One tiny circle of learned and discerning clerics mediated German historiography and, even more remarkably, studied Vico. Duncan Forbes called them the Liberal Anglicans: Henry Milman, Connop Thirlwell, Julius Hare, Thomas Arnold and his pupil Arthur Stanley. Hare wrote a *Vindication of Niebuhr's History of Rome*, Thirlwell translated Schleiermacher, and from their pens came histories of Greece and Rome, of the Jews, of Christianity and of the Eastern Church. They argued from Vico that states and nations go through cycles and decline as they become what rationalists call more civilized. They delighted in the complexities and contradictions in history. Miracles presented no insuperable difficulty: they happened in so far as they were believed to have happened. But Arnold died in his forties, Thirlwell became a bishop, Milman and Stanley respectively Deans of St Paul's and Westminster. They were a little too scrupulous, too disinclined to cause one of those scholarly rumpuses which generate animosity but by their very exaggeration make people reassess what they have hitherto taken to be true. They were eclipsed by someone who conveyed as cloudy an impression of German historiography as Coleridge had of German philosophy. For whereas Coleridge had little talent for abstract ideas, Carlyle was a genuinely original and disturbing thinker.

Leslie Stephen read Guizot, Grote, Tocqueville, Buckle and a good deal of American history during the 1850s, but the historian who shook up his mind was Carlyle. That grim, grotesque humour, that determination to destroy shams, that command to men to work not whine, accept and not reject the world, spoke to Stephen's condition. He venerated Carlyle and told Oliver Wendell Holmes that he was 'a really noble old cove and by far the best specimen of the literary gent we can at present produce'. His respect was not reciprocated. Stephen told Norton that 'I regret very much my position to the old prophet but I cannot help it. Whenever I see him it is the old story: I like him, indeed I might say, I feel a strong affection for him but he always rants at me . . . I think that he dislikes me.' Carlyle dismissed him as a mechanistic positivist and Stephen was irritated by Carlyle's illiberalism and the 'rather pestilential nonsense' he talked. But of his influence he was in no doubt. 'You might return from the strange gloom and splendour of the *French Revolution* or *Sartor Resartus* revolted or fascinated; but to read it with appreciation was to go through an intellectual crisis; and to enter into this spirit was to experience something like a religious conversion. You were not the same man afterwards. No one ever exercised such a potent sway over the inmost being of his disciples.' Stephen misunderstood Carlyle – he described him as manly and simple, not the happiest of epithets. But neither did other Victorians understand him. It was not until historians related Carlyle to Wagner and Nietzsche, the heirs of German transcendentalism, who dispensed with what Carlyle called Coleridge's accumulation of 'formidable apparatus, logical swim-bladders, transcendental life-preservers and other precautionary and vehiculatory gear' (i.e. philosophical concepts), that Carlyle could be seen to be at once a reactionary and a revolutionary. He was an aberration in European thought.

Stephen accepted that Carlyle was not an historian in the German mould; historical method, as Niebuhr or Ranke defined it, he never employed: and 'in opposing the necessary logic of intellectual development, his hero-worship and theory of right led to arbitrary and chaotic results.' But Stephen was convinced that 'Carlyle's impetuous and vehement assertion of certain great social, ethical and political principles was of the highest value'. Carlyle wanted history to burn with imagination just as Coleridge wanted poetry to be fired by the imagination rather than by fancy. Mill in his well-known essay on Bentham and Coleridge admitted that his own school, the Utilitarians, who professed to base their interpretation of human behaviour upon experience, rejected history; and that with a little good will the utilitarians might fill in gaps in their philosophy by borrowing from Coleridge. Shortly after the publication of the essay Mill reviewed Michelet's *History of France* and astonishingly enough praised the prince of romantic historians for his scientific ability in combining poetry, reliability and ingenuity in interpretation to illuminate the general laws governing order and causation in historical phenomena. For trying to reconcile the two traditions in thought Mill has been praised by literary critics as different as Basil Willey, F. R. Leavis, Raymond Williams and Dorothea Krook. All praise him for recognizing that the life of the spirit could not be ignored; all welcome his recognition that happiness cannot be attained by making it the direct and sole end in life; all see in Mill what a philosopher might be if he would only expose himself to the full experience of literature and life that criticism analyses.

Stephen would have none of this. Trained as a mathematician he delighted in disentangling arguments and showing precisely where they led or where they contradicted each other. If Mill could not accommodate imagination, perhaps even religion, within his philosophy, then he should have modified his philosophy. There is in fact an inevitable antagonism between the cultural mode of thought which critics employ and the operations of empirical philosophy and the social scientist. The artist, the metaphysician and the critic who judges them, are all demanding a single vision of life, whereas the empiricist is placing life under the lens so that he can study its component parts. In retrospect we can see that it was at this time that social philosophy was splitting itself up into new autonomous academic disciplines which no longer could be subsumed under a super-theory of knowledge. All they could do was occasionally to lighten each other's darkness. Alfred Marshall's *Principles of Economics* contains many praiseworthy passages about thrift and self-reliance. The evil of poverty inspired him to consider how wealth could be redistributed. None of these moral reflections affected the logic of his economic theory; and indeed Marshall fought at Cambridge to detach economics from the moral science tripos. Keynes believed that capitalism was inefficient and unemployment a blot upon the good life; but the validity of his *General Theory* did not rest on moral considerations. Stephen was right to declare that the traditions of thought which descended from transcendentalism and intuitionism could not be reconciled with the *System of Logic*. After describing Mill's failure to join the two together in holy matrimony, he explains why in the last paragraph of his second volume on the utilitarians which consists of a single sentence: 'They did not love each other.'

In his writings Leslie Stephen often returned to the astonishing insularity of the English in the early nineteenth century, their sublime ignorance of the German language and their indifference to German thought and literature. He put it down to a temporary paralysis of speculation from the time when George III began to reign. 'The deist railed no more; and the orthodox were lapped in drowsy indifference.' He wrote his own account of the few pioneers who realized that something remarkable which ought to interest cultivated minds had occurred. Since he wrote many charts have been made of the channels through which German ideas percolated, often much diluted, through Coleridge and Carlyle, through two of the Apostles at Cambridge, Julius Hare and John Sterling, and through George Eliot and her translations of Strauss and Feuerbach. Certainly in the last decades of the century there seemed to be some signs that German transcendentalism was influencing British speculation. At Oxford idealism in the mild form T. H. Green gave it, or full-bloodedly in Bradley and Bosanquet, became the fashionable philosophy and even Cambridge produced an idealist in McTaggart. Matthew Arnold popularized the notion of *Kultur* even if it was very different in its overtones from Burckhardt's conception of an age expressing its spirit through religion, art and politics in an articulated and analysable way. Certainly, too, the concept of self-realization took root and stood at the centre of most of the English philosophical justifications of socialism or of promoting welfare by State intervention.

At first sight the chasm between German transcendentalism and the British tradition of empirical rationalism seemed to be unbridgeable. Much of German thought had grown out of the search for a national identity, for an explanation why Germans with a culture so deep-rooted and spiritually powerful remained so divided, alienated, enfeebled. The explanations given were profound, ingenious, far-ranging, some justifying absolutism, others class warfare, others nationalist warfare, others the cult of the self, others an elite of supermen or of dedicated artists remote from the *canaille* of democratic society. Most of these visions of society, such as those swirling in the mind of Nietzsche or Wagner, with all their dazzling insights into man's nature or the neuroses of industrial society, did not contain any picture which related the vision to political realities still less to political action. The poet, Stefan George, lived to see to his horror ideas which he held dear being translated into action by the Nazis; just as a generation later the miserable coward Marcuse recoiled and disowned the black revolutionaries or student leaders who declared they were putting his explicit ideas into practice. The British had no problem about national identity. They did not need to ask who they were or whether they existed as a nation. Their most notable philosophers ever since the Reformation had never failed to concern themselves with the practical political questions of obligation, legitimacy, or the limits which impersonal forces impose upon governments, or for that matter the limits which philosophy faces in making meaningful statements about politics. They regarded the British constitution and parliamentary democracy as a supreme synthesis of speculation and action, flexible enough to absorb notions such as universal suffrage yet sturdy enough to withstand revolutionary radicalism. To argue that T. H. Green's definition of positive freedom was superior to Mill's negative freedom was not to assert something about the soul or Nature, or nobility or aesthetics or the role of intellectuals: it was a prosaic argument about the duty of the State to interfere in certain limited spheres which affect the life of the citizen. Leslie Stephen never conceded an inch of ground to German speculation which in his eyes was scarcely concerned with the world of politics and fact. 'In short,' he said, 'Hegel is in many things little better than an ass.' That is not the seemly judgement one would expect from an historian of ideas; and it reminds one of James Mill's comment: 'I see clearly enough what poor Kant would be about.' But Stephen always regarded himself as a working utilitarian and one should no more expect him to genuflect to the Absolute or the Real Will than one would expect Russell or Moore to do so. What was the tradition which he inherited and how did he modify it?

The Rationalist Method of Advancing Knowledge

'The young men who graduated in 1850 and the following ten years', said Stephen, 'found their philosophical teaching in Mill's *Logic*, and only a few daring heretics were beginning to pick holes in his system . . . Hour after hour was given to discussing points raised by Mill as keenly as medieval commentators used to discuss the doctrines of Aristotle.' The same was even true of Oxford at that date exhausted by theological controversy. 'It is Mill', wrote a contemporary historian of philosophy, 'that our young thinkers at the Universities, our young shepherds on the mountains consult, and quote and swear by.' Soon his work had become the standard text at both universities. The *Logic* was one of those books which capture the mind of a generation. By explaining the relation between the logic of the natural and social sciences it gave young liberals the same kind of assurance that Marxist dialectic gave in the years between the two world wars to young radicals. Experts may pick holes in such books, but long before they make the road impassable readers have crossed the bridge into new territory and have outflanked them. At the end of his life Stephen still considered the *Logic* to be the most important manifesto of utilitarian philosophy and upon it he ordered his own opinions.

The key to the *System of Logic* is the title. Before Newton and Locke formal logic was the test of the truth or falsehood of propositions and philosophers used to construct absolutely true statements and then demonstrate that their own arguments were couched in similar terms. After Locke formal logic all but disappeared. In Scotland it ceased to be taught in the universities except as an appendage to the 'mental science' which Locke had invented, or as the 'natural logic' of common sense which demonstrated how reasoning actually takes place without examining the internal relationships between the sentences which are the product of this reasoning. In Cambridge logic was replaced by Newtonian mathematics and it survived only at Oxford as a despised part of Aristotelian study. In 1637 Descartes had written disparagingly of the syllogism, and following him Locke said:

> This way of reasoning discovers no new proofs, but is the art of marshalling and ranging the old ones we have already. The forty-seventh proposition of Euclid is very true; but the discovery of it, I think, not owing to any rules of common logic. A man knows first, and then he is able to prove syllogistically. So that syllogism comes after knowledge, and then a man has little or no need of it . . . And if a man should employ his reason all this way, he will not do much otherwise than he, who having got some iron out of the bowels of the earth, should have it beaten up all into swords, and put it into his servants' hands to fence with, and bang one another.

Philosophy for Locke therefore was a *scientia scientiarum*, synthesizing all knowledge and eliminating human vagary and prejudice because it was based on hard facts. Mill in his wisdom saw that this contempt for logic had led to much of the confusion in the rationalism of his father's generation. He had already in 1828 replied to an article extolling the lost art by Whately, the most vigorous mind of the Oriel Common Room in its great days, but Mill was uninterested in the old Aristotelian logic which Whately was revising. His own plan was far-reaching. It was nothing less than a scheme to establish the logic of the natural and the social sciences together.

Mill had no use for the syllogism. Reasoning of the kind: All men are mortal, Socrates is a man, therefore Socrates is mortal, did not increase knowledge, because if you accepted the premise, *ipso facto* you accepted the conclusion. Knowledge could be increased only by reasoning inductively from particular instances to a generalization. Generalizations of this kind could be called true because they were shorthand descriptions of perceived facts. Mill did not refute Hume. No doubt Hume was right to assert that we could never be certain that an induction was true since one vital fact, which was an exception to the rule, might have been overlooked: but he replied that if the whole method of induction was invalid, then all science would be false, which was absurd. The uniformity of Nature ensured that scientific laws were true, and the uniformity of

Nature was not an *a priori* axiom but an empirical generalization proved by scientific laws.[1] The circularity of this argument did not disturb Mill. He declared that the only method of enquiry which would yield truth was the scientific method, for it alone was capable of showing that certain conclusions and no others could be drawn from a particular series of experiments unless one assumed that Nature was not uniform; and though Hume was right in denying that we could discover the *necessary* relation between cause and effect, we were nevertheless justified in talking of those causes and effects which we could perceive.

But induction is inapplicable to the social sciences: the sands of society are too vast and shifting to admit experiment followed by inference and generalization. Mill was dissatisfied both with his father's simple interpretation of society as a collection of individuals each bent on his own happiness and with Macaulay's pseudo-empirical criticism of his father's methods. Mill followed the lead of the first avowed sociologist, Auguste Comte, and declared that the laws of society could be found by the historical or 'inverse deductive' method. They would not be 'true' in the sense that inductive scientific laws were true. But they could be checked against other laws, found by the 'direct deductive' method, in such social sciences as Political Economy and what Mill called Ethology or the science of national character. Mill agreed with Comte that what changed society was not economic or other kinds of impersonal forces, but *ideas*. Every change in society was preceded by a change in men's beliefs or store of knowledge. Truth for him existed in palpable form. At one time he thought it was like seed which needed to be sown and germinate in the mind. Later he thought it was composed of hard and gritty particles which needed to be put in a philosophical centrifuge to be separated from error. Truth mounted at compound interest. 'The progress of opinions is like the advance of a person climbing a hill by a spiral path which winds round it, and by which he is as often on the wrong side of the hill as on the right side, but still is always getting higher up.' Throw opinions into the market square and let men debate them: truth will emerge. That was why Mill argued that a government which suppressed discussion assumed itself to be infallible. That was why he deplored social disapproval as the anaesthetist of intellectual life.

The rationalists made a further claim for themselves. They, not the theologians, were more likely to persuade men to behave better and improve society. 'Our business here', Locke had said, 'is not to know all

---

[1] The agnostics used Hume to defend themselves against the charge of materialism. They did not declare, like the German materialists, that the universe could be explained solely in terms of force and matter, because the only impression we gain of the outside world is through our senses: space and time are merely mental forms imposed upon chaotic sense impressions. Therefore, God *may* exist and miracles *may* occur. But the agnostics then turned to Mill's argument from the uniformity of Nature and declared that both these contingencies are so unlikely, that we are justified in rejecting them.

things, but those which concern our conduct. If we can find out those measures whereby a rational creature put in that state, which man is in in this world, may, and ought to govern his opinions depending thereon, we need not be troubled that some other things escape our knowledge.' From associationist psychology arose the notion that human nature could be changed for the better. Since every human thought sprang from individual experience, education alone was needed to make him good and sensible. Reward and praise a child when he did good; punish and blame him when he was naughty; and by the association of ideas he would grow up instinctively to realize that his own happiness depended on the degree to which he promoted the happiness of others. As human nature changed society's evils would be remedied; and each generation would inherit a less corrupting environment. By playing a double ruff through dummy and his own hand, man would eventually win game and rubber.

Throughout his life Mill was engaged in trying to re-establish the unity of truth. That was why he tried to reconcile Coleridge to Bentham and overhauled utilitarianism. Whether a philosopher succeeds in transforming the way people think depends in part upon his ability to convince them that what he says conforms to unanswerable principles. When Locke argued that ideas were attracted to each other by the two forces of observation of the outside world and 'the internal operations of our minds, perceived and reflected on by ourselves', he reminded his contemporaries of Newton's universe in which the planets were attracted to each other by force of gravitation. The world of inanimate matter and of human beings seemed to be governed by the same laws; the economics of the physiocrats, the conclusions of jurisprudence, the discoveries of the psychologists could be explained in terms of forces reacting upon each other. In a similar manner Mill created for his followers the vision of a coherent world; and from him Leslie Stephen inherited three propositions.

There are not different modes of thinking but different premises from which you can argue. The dichotomy between heart and head, faith and reason, is inadmissible. Second, science alone can give us true propositions. Science is conceived as a system of absolute and inflexible rules which scientists discover. Third, beyond scientific truth, illuminated brightly, there lies a prairie of knowledge over which the shadows lengthen and merge into perpetual night on the horizon. In the foreground the shadows are receding as social scientists till the soil and gather in their first crops. But on the horizon lies barren soil useless to cultivate. There one may discern the corpses of many thousands of books on ontology and the nature of God. Why should we further waste our energy on such vain attempts to reconcile theology and facts through metaphysics? Let us rather work on land which will provide us with knowledge and in due time harvest the fruits of a complete science of society. 'When this time shall come, no important branch of human affairs will be any longer abandoned to empiricism and unscientific surmise: the circle of human knowledge will be complete, and it can only thereafter receive further enlargement by perpetual expansion from within.'

The Reply of the Intuitionists

A university is not a monolithic society like a club, nor an adversary assembly like Parliament, nor a convention of graduated opinions like a chamber of deputies. There were bodies of orthodox churchmen at Cambridge who considered their doctrines to rest on reason, no less than the followers of Mill. The burly Master of Trinity, William Whewell, of whom Sydney Smith said that science was his forte and omniscience his foible, and who had published works on mathematics, mechanics, mineralogy and chemistry, was better equipped than Mill to analyse scientific method, and he took Mill to task for misinterpreting what he had written on the logic of induction. There was no logic of induction, Whewell replied. A scientist did not discover unalterable laws. He experimented and tested hypotheses to see whether they were true. Scientists were fallible and today's hypotheses could be discarded tomorrow. 'Scientific discovery must ever depend upon some happy thought, of which we cannot trace the origin . . . No maxims can be given which will inevitably lead to discovery.' The scientist must be a genius. Whewell had all the scorn of the true scientist for the notion that 'an inquirer of a truly inventive mind need come to the teacher of inductive philosophy to learn how to exercise the faculties which nature has given him'. Mill, however, held out the promise that scientific method could be taught and there might come a time when human progress would no longer depend on Whewell's man of genius. (This argument rumbles on in our own times in the works of Popper, Kuhn, Feyerabend, Lakatos and Maxwell.) Yet Stephen when he came at the end of his life to re-examine the point between Mill and Whewell, saw Mill, like most of his contemporaries, as the prophet of modern scientific method and Whewell as belonging to some older and discredited tradition. He did so because Whewell had adopted Kant's conclusion that when by experiment a scientist did in fact discover a scientific law, it was a law of a different order from axioms in mathematics and logic. Whewell himself did not maintain that scientific laws could be known *a priori* but he proclaimed the existence of 'fundamental ideas' which enabled men to penetrate the meaning of phenomena in nature. Whewell had in fact attached his admirable analysis of how scientists research to the prevailing British doctrine of innate ideas.

Stephen was well acquainted with this doctrine, and was unimpressed by Mill's opponents. None of them, not even Whewell, who was concerned almost entirely with the philosophy of science, understood Kant. They did not speak the language of German idealism because they were first cousins of the philosophic radicals. Both the intuitionists and the rationalists claimed descent from the tradition of Newton and Locke. Locke had given birth to two schools of psychology; the associationist school to which the rationalists belonged and the intuitionist school. The intuitionists asserted that judgements and perceptions, not ideas, were primarily important. If we were to think at all, we had to accept that certain principles of necessary truth existed. These were metaphysical axioms such as, 'Whatever begins to exist, must have a cause which produced it'; or logical axioms, or grammatical axioms or even axioms of taste. There were also principles of contingent truth such as, 'Everything of which I am conscious exists' or 'Those things which I distinctly remember really did happen'. From these principles the 'fundamental laws of human belief' could be deduced. Man was endowed with special faculties which distinguished him from the beasts of the field by enabling him intuitively to perceive the difference between right and wrong and the truth of these principles. The intuitionists were divided from the rationalists on only one fundamental issue, namely the nature of mind.

The insularity of the intuitionists impeded the understanding of the one philosophical system which could have armed Protestants against the rationalists. Kant had built for those who believed in God a new and formidable base camp but it was many years before Anglicans were willing to bivouac there. Ever since the Civil War Anglicans had argued that faith must rest in reason. Yet Kant purported to have destroyed the rationalism of Newton and Locke and in the process had also exploded the 'rational' metaphysics of the orthodox defenders of Christianity in England and Scotland. The intuitionists pretended to find something useful in Kant, but Henry Crabb Robinson was right when he predicted in 1803 that the alliance of these philosophers with the Kantians 'will be more out of love to the result than out of a genuine and adequate perception of the abstract truth of the system, and it is possible that this school will be among the last to accede to the new doctrines'. In fact the intuitionists, whose philosophy was a canonization of the moral plati-tudes of the club and coffee-house, soon realized that Kant undermined them. After all why was there any need, they asked, for an autonomous theory of ethics constructed by a German? Bishop Butler in his *Analogy* had given us a perfectly adequate English model. Coleridge, whose name conjures up those first gropings of Englishmen towards German philosophy, never understood Kant. René Wellek, the historian of Kant's influence in England, concluded that Coleridge 'simply did not seem to have the ability to conceive in thinking what he felt he should confess and preach as a person. He made a philosophy out of this incapacity, a philosophy of the dualism of the head and the heart. With a serene indifference to the inconsistency involved, he kept much of the architectonic of the mind as it was laid out by Kant, preserving only the negative part of Kant.' No doubt Coleridge had a seminal mind; no doubt he influenced many poets and reasoners, F. D. Maurice among them. Indeed Mill himself admitted that it was Coleridge who had persuaded him in 1840 that Locke's theory of mental science must be overhauled. Coleridge transmitted a poetic vision rather than a philosophic doctrine when he translated Kant's Practical Reason as Imagination. His influence, which appears so great in literary history, was not such as would have affected a young rationalist at Cambridge. How dependent the defenders of religion were on the tradition which they shared with the rationalists can be seen in the Bampton Lectures of that orthodox theologian J. B. Mozley. On the question of miracles he followed Hume like a dog snapping at his heels and in the end biting the hand that fed him; but intellectually Mozley was Hume's servant. Even W. G. Ward, the Catholic convert, remained astonishingly faithful to the kind of argument in which intuitionists and empiricists engaged. Until F. H. Bradley elaborated his Idealist ethics, until Oxford expounded Hegelianism in the 1880s and Anglo-Catholics drew on the armoury of Rome, the rationalists held the philosophic initiative; their opponents produced no work which could give as satisfying an answer as the *Logic* to the relations of scientific truth, economic laws and moral obligation.

There had been in fact one last attempt in Edinburgh to shore up the once famous school of Scottish philosophy. Leslie Stephen left a memorable picture of Sir William Hamilton, impressive in appearance, delightful with children, magnanimous in controversy yet 'with a mental rigidity which made him incapable of compromise . . . A queer vein of pedantry ran through the man. A philosopher ought surely not to spend two years unearthing a baronetcy.' Stephen described how his lectures were repeated for twenty years without alterations and his notes on other philosophers, for instance on Reid, consisted of chains of quotations. 'He gave a list of 101 authorities from Hesiod to Lamenais with quotations in which an appeal is made to common sense. He might have collected a thousand . . . It was natural enough that Hamilton should note an unfavourable opinion of mathematical study expressed by Horace Walpole; but a grave citation by Horace Walpole as an authority upon mathematical studies would have amused nobody more than Walpole himself.' Hamilton had made his reputation in 1829 by reviewing Cousin and welcoming Kant's destruction of 'rational' metaphysics. But

Hamilton still wanted to preserve the Scottish common-sense intuitionism on which he had been suckled, and he therefore fell into a series of
confusions deeply painful to a convinced Kantian. The confusions
resembled the prospectus of a new limited liability company issued by an
asset stripper who tries to persuade investors that the merging of two
companies will increase the wealth of both concerns whereas he is secretly
determined to sell off whatever he finds it unprofitable to take over.

Yet, as happens from time to time, a disciple emerged who chose the
most fatal part of Hamilton's argument on which to base his own
apologetic for Christianity. H. L. Mansel, an Oxford don, came to the
agreeable conclusion that if Kant had now destroyed reason an end
should be put to vain speculation about the nature of God. In 1858 he
published his Bampton Lectures and called his book *The Limits of
Religious Thought*. Mansel seems to have developed a taste for philosophy at an early age. As a child he used to say, 'My foot, my hand, but
what is *me*?' Mansel argued that every object is known only as it relates to
other objects. There can be no knowledge of the Infinite because the
Infinite has no limits whereas every finite object is limited by its relation to
other objects. God is the infinite: therefore we cannot know God. Reason
will tell us nothing about God. Why then should we be surprised if some
Christian dogmas appear to us unreasonable or even immoral? At this
point some of his audience may have wondered how, if reason is so
fallible, we know that God exists. Here Mansel abandoned Kant and fell
back upon the intuitionists, basing his case on axioms and 'special
faculties'. We know God exists because we are dependent on him – which
is why we pray – and because our sense of moral obligation, given to us by
God, presupposes a moral lawgiver. We know he exists because our
reason tells us there is an Unknowable and our intuition and common
sense create moral imperatives which proclaim his existence. 'It is our
duty', he said, 'to think of God as personal; and it is our duty to believe
that He is Infinite. It is true that we cannot reconcile these two
representations with each other': but if our frail reason creates contradictions for ourselves, none exist, we may be sure, for God.

Mansel's lectures were a triumph. He was hailed as a major metaphysician and even the College servants, it is said, thronged to St Mary's
to hear him.[1] But the triumph was ephemeral; like undisciplined cavalry
his lectures opened the way to defeat by their victorious charge and were,
in fact, the last Anglican attempt to found Christianity solely by calling
upon philosophy. Mansel was not a first-rate metaphysician: 'C'est un
disciple qui ressemble à un maître,' was Nédoncelle's judgement. F. D.
Maurice was aghast at the suggestion that God was unknowable, and J. B.

---

[1] On the other hand the verger of St Mary's was said to give thanks that after hearing University
sermons for thirty years he still remained a Christian.

Mozley hit the mark when he wrote in a letter of October 1858 that the lectures 'seem to me a blunder though a clever blunder'. Pringle-Pattison commented that, if the inventors of those instruments did not themselves do evil, the first man to use them would surely cut his fingers. Huxley with characteristic vigour said that Mansel reminded him of 'the drunken fellow in Hogarth's contested election who is sawing through the signpost at the other party's public-house, forgetting he is sitting at the other end of it'. The retribution came in 1865 when Mill published his *Examination of Sir William Hamilton's Philosophy*. If I am asked to believe, he argued, that the principles of God's government are so beyond our comprehension that they are not sanctioned (in Mansel's phrase) by 'the highest human morality which we are capable of conceiving', then I will refuse to worship such a God. 'I will call no being good, who is not what I mean when I apply that epithet to my fellow-creatures; and if such a being can sentence me to hell for not so calling him, to hell I will go.' Mansel's rejoinder in defence did him no good. The future economist, Alfred Marshall, who had just taken his degree at Cambridge, said that it 'showed me how much there was to be defended'. When Stephen dismissed the philosophy of intuitionism, he was thinking of Mill's criticism of Hamilton. He read Kant in German during the winter of 1859–60, but he never criticized Kant's text itself; and no wonder since his opponents had hardly begun to read it themselves. He read Gotthard Lechler's work on the English deists published in 1841, but he missed F. A. Lange's *Geschichte des Materialismus* (1866) though his friend Morley consulted it when writing about Voltaire. In 1877 Stephen was to write to Norton praising Lange's book which, he said, 'overpowers me. He is dead, poor man, but he wrote such a book as I would have written if I could.' Stephen was more aware than most of his contemporaries how far removed from the British or indeed the French tradition of thought was that which had grown up in Germany. He acknowledged that German philosophy transformed the methods and interests of German historians and hence of the way the Bible was interpreted; but he was not to be seduced from the British empirical tradition. He was indeed to show some contempt for the man who had been among the earliest to display an interest in German idealist philosophy.

The Cambridge Mind

As always for Stephen logic alone never carried the day. There was a moral quality in the type of mind he admired and which he associated particularly with Cambridge. To illustrate it he resorted to a simple stratagem. Just as Matthew Arnold described what he meant by the grand style in Homer by quoting Francis Newman's translation to show what it was not, so Stephen drew a portrait of the greatest of Oxford dons to illustrate the Cambridge mind.

Even today in our more mobile society where easier social relationships and a less rigid class structure have ironed out so many distinctions, one can still perceive faint signs of those temperamental differences which struck Stephen. In his day the contrast was clear. No Cambridge man can ever compete at Oxford. Directly he sets foot in that city he is aware that he is wearing hobnail boots. Of a coarser and rougher texture, a country cousin from a tranquil backwater, he is whipped on his arrival into a dialectical whirligig. He starts one of those frank, intimate, disinterested Cambridge discussions which are intended to clear the mind – and the words are whisked out of his mouth and tossed in the air by jugglers like so many coloured balls until, bemused by the wit and elegance of the display, he falls into a helpless and unnoticed silence. Oxford is a worldly society where a gate from All Souls opens straight on to London. He cannot discuss politics because in some strange fashion London politics are discussed in terms of Oxford politics and, indeed, appear in the minds of his hosts to be identical. He is a provincial. The very gossip is more pungent and obscure, the savours more delectable, the quadrangles and gardens more orchidaceously romantic. He finds himself among High Churchmen, whose piety is spiced with irony, and who do not hesitate to perform the pleasurable duty of biting the benighted, in a manner which makes his Latitudinarian ears tingle. Nor can he well discuss literature since, accustomed as he is to emending classical texts after the fashion of Bentley, he is lost in a maze of metaphysical and literary allusions. Aesthetic theories are spun like webs about him and poets' names whizz through the conversation like shuttlecocks; true, all the poets are Cambridge men but that does not mean that he is any better able to discuss them in the Oxford manner.[1] He likes to take the text, construe the meaning and analyse the poem itself, but as he listens to the talk he reflects lugubriously that his hosts' theories are not susceptible of analysis. For them the poem is an excuse for propounding a philosophy of life, for explaining the inner meaning of poetry, art and life itself. Spinning in circles of ever widening generalizations, he dimly apprehends that Oxford men are asking him to unify religion, aesthetics and morality into a comprehensive metaphysic – can he not hear the call, asks the most

[1] Witness the lamentable figure which three Apostles, Hallam, Monckton Milnes and Sunderland, cut when they debated in the Oxford Union that Shelley was a better poet than Byron. 'The Oxford young gentlemen,' wrote James Pope-Hennessy, 'seemed as elegant and unconcerned as their room, and lounged about the fireplace with provoking sang-froid. Worst of all, they alleged that they had never heard of Shelley, and one of them even pretended to think that the Cambridge contingent had come over to support the claims of Shenstone, and that the only line of that poet he could call to mind was one running: "My banks are well furnished with bees." '

persuasive and cultured of all Oxford voices, 'to the true goal of all of us, to the ideal, to perfection'? Will he not admit that beauty is but truth seen from the other side and that all the science of Tübingen (and of Cambridge) is inferior? Why is he not prepared to swear allegiance in this home of lost causes to at least one – which almost certainly, if supported by worldly-wise Oxonians, is not lost? Is there no teacher or prophet to preach a philosophy of life at Cambridge?

The answer to the last question, said Stephen, is simple. There is none. Cambridge appears to be inhabited by nonentities whereas the history of nineteenth century Oxford is the history of its preachers: Whately, Thomas Arnold, Keble, Newman, Jowett, Ruskin, Pater and T. H. Green. To these names there are no Cambridge analogues. Stephen allowed that against Gladstone 'with his great abilities somewhat marred by over-acuteness and polish,' all Cambridge could set was the clear and energetic, but limited, intellect of Macaulay. By the mystery, charm and hypnotism of their personalities the Oxford prophets cast a spell over the young, fascinating, enthralling, tearing the heart out of their disciples. Rugbeians venerated Dr Arnold, Newman inspired passionate party loyalty, Balliol men were devoted to Jowett, because these teachers were regarded as great souls at work in the world. This spectacle, commented Stephen, provokes a faint nausea in Cambridge men. They prefer to keep the soul in its place for fear it may breed fads and enthusiasms. Back again, safe and snug in his provincial den, the Cambridge man consoles himself by saying that prophets are half humbug and produce disciples who will be wholly humbug. Let us stop talking for effect and return to studies which are precise and yield tangible results. Above all, let us not attach ideas to a man. To criticise a man's ideas dispassionately is next to impossible if he inspires a Movement. The Cambridge don who, like Stephen, was prepared to give up his time to young men would be their friend, within certain limits their guide, but never their philosopher. In Cambridge ideas were hammered into principles to be judged empirically. The Oxford craving for prophets in Stephen's view weakened the already tenuous hold which Oxford retained on impartial philosophic enquiry. And the man who weakened it most was Benjamin Jowett.

Benjamin Jowett, elected to a Fellowship at Balliol while still an undergraduate, tutor for twenty-eight years and Master for twenty-three, stood in a class by himself. His intellectual achievements were considerable; he introduced Hegel to Oxford, stimulated the study of early Greek philosophy and by his translations made Plato's spirit walk again in England. In mid-Victorian times he was harried by Tractarian bigots for his Broad Church principles which were, as much as anything, inspired by his hatred of persecution. But Jowett was, beyond all else, an incomparable teacher of young men. Statesmen, diplomats, civil servants,

proconsuls, professors, philosophers, historians, men of letters, passed
through his hands, and to each Jowett imparted the secret of hard work
and determination to succeed. His pupils were sometimes paralysed by
his shyness and made aware of the dignity he attached to his position.
Every sentence they spoke was expected to carry weight, and unmeaning
remarks were quenched by a chilling reply. His methods of teaching were
Socratic – he would pause, poker in hand, and search his man with a
question, and so on round the class to show to what logical absurdities
sloppy thinking leads. Despising lectures, he put his pupils through the
old catechetical mill and sharpened their wits on the grindstone of
construe. Yet, though he deplored young men wallowing in poetry and
distrusted the influence of T. H. Green's metaphysics, he widened his
pupils' literary horizon. They were left with the impression that Jowett
thought both poetry and metaphysics important, though they were never
quite sure what he himself believed. 'The charm was enhanced', wrote
Pater, 'by a certain mystery about his own philosophic and other
opinions'; and in the introductions to his translations of Plato, Jowett did
not do much to unravel the mysteries of Platonic thought. The secret of
his power lay rather in a kind of slow magnetism. His cherubic features,
his bell-like voice, his power to declaim verse beautifully, drew undergraduates and friends ineluctably to him. He did not let them slip; they
were pursued with sympathetic letters demanding to hear that they were
doing themselves justice. He not only wanted his pupils to succeed, he did
his best to put their feet on the rung of the ladder to success by filling the
Master's Lodge in term time with celebrities who might well help his
pupils in later life. As he grew older, he sympathized with undergraduate
pleasures. As early as 1879 Balliol held a college ball. ('A ball –
attachments – matchmaking – matchmaking in College - most inappropriate' muttered a doddering old Fellow.)[1] He supported the Oxford
University Dramatic Society to the fury of his enemy, Freeman, who
spluttered with indignation against this 'portentous rage for play-acting'.
Nothing was put before the College. It was his life, his child; and as the list
of first classes grew longer and longer Balliol was acknowledged beyond
dispute to be academically the most distinguished college in Oxford.
Somewhat naturally this bred envy and malice, and Jowett was often
attacked. He was not above enticing a clever man from another college or
indulging in sharp practice in university politics. 'Parnell is not in it with
him in obstruction', commented a member of the Hebdomadal Council.
By the time he became Master of Balliol in 1870 he was exposed to
assaults from both flanks. The old conservatives still regarded him as the
arch-liberal in theology; and now that academic reform had taken the
place of ecclesiastical questions as the centre of controversy, Jowett, who
opposed professorial lectures and research, was regarded by the younger

---

[1] Henry Sidgwick opposed a similar proposal at Trinity College, Cambridge.

Liberals as a man who had had his day. He was an indifferent scholar and, indeed, despised the whole business: 'How I hate learning!' he once admitted. Nor had the young conservatives much use for him. The youthful historian and Tory, Charles Oman, thought he was 'a noted and much detested figure', representing 'modernism, advertisement, an autocratic pose, and a tendency to push the importance of his College beyond the limit of its undoubted merit'.

Perhaps it is now becoming clearer why towards the end of his life Stephen chose the publication of Jowett's biography as the occasion to examine him as the antithesis of the Cambridge mind. He acknowledged that Jowett did far more for his men than all the Heads of Houses in Cambridge put together, nor did he minimise the affection in which Jowett was held, and he added – from Stephen high praise – 'The core of the man's nature was sweet, sound, and masculine.' Moreover, Jowett avoided the intellectual tyranny which Newman exercised over his pupils and he encouraged his undergraduates to root among the pearls that he cast before them and select whichever they regarded as valuable. 'You might not learn anything very definite, but you were subject to a vigorous course of prodding and rousing, which is perhaps the best of training for early years.' But when Stephen considered his man seriously, he passed a measured but hostile judgement. The agnostic first laid his finger on the Broad Churchman's equivocations. In Jowett's hands Christianity appeared to demand no more than a recognition of the moral beauty of Christ's life and a murmured hope that he was divine. How could a man transform dogmas, which he admitted were repulsive, into metaphors, allegories, analogies and rhetoric, when theologians had interpreted them as literal truths for eighteen hundred years? Aged 40 when the *Origin of Species* and *Essays and Reviews* were published, Jowett, so Stephen held, was not too old to change his views. On these grounds Stephen's attack might appear partisan; Broad Churchmen could claim that John Stuart Mill had urged them to continue to sign the Thirty-Nine Articles, even though they did not believe in them, in order to prevent the Church falling into the hands of fanatics; and Arnold's revision of Christianity appeared to Stephen feeble but sincere. Why did Stephen decline to accept Jowett's plea of sincerity?

Stephen thought Jowett an intellectual coward. Jowett used history to escape from his duty to decide how far any philosophy was true.[1] Had

[1] At the time of Jowett's maturity the game of using history as a stick of dynamite to blow up a system of thought was in full swing. German theologians employed history in one way to demolish orthodox Christianity by the higher criticism of the Bible. In another way conservative theorists employed history to oppose liberalism. Savigny and Maine in jurisprudence, and the Austrian school in economics, were attempting to destroy Bentham and Adam Smith by appealing to tradition and showing that deductive systems have no objective validity and are merely the product of their age. Games can be played only if one never questions the rules; and this particular pastime is endurable so long as one does not ask what *kind* of history is being used. Directly the selection of historical facts and hypotheses is seen to be arbitrary, and 'tradition' becomes what the author wants it to mean, one loses interest. Jowett was playing the game of darkening wisdom with history by declaring that, since most philosophies had some good in them, there was nothing to choose between the lot of them.

Jowett been a thoroughgoing relativist, had he had the courage to say that Christianity, Hegel, and ethics, were all to be judged *sui temporis* and that no absolute truth existed, Stephen to some extent would have agreed. But Jowett was a Judas to his profession. He opposed Mark Pattison's scheme for endowing research, not so much because Oxford education would suffer, but because he condemned scholarship and learning. He genuflected before the altar of philosophy in the sight of the world but in private he sneered at it. 'Logic', his pupils quoted, 'is neither a science nor an art, but a dodge' – small wonder that there was so little logical connection between his own thoughts. He was an intellectual harlot masquerading beneath the bombazine of a high-minded ethic. True, he had dabbled in Hegel, who led to 'some interesting points of view not really so much better than others', and Stephen despised him precisely because he was a dabbler. He never made it clear whether he thought Hegel was true or false; *he* did not care for truth at all. Stephen paused to make a point. ' "He stood", said one of his pupils, ". . . at the parting of the ways", and he wrote, one must add, "No thoroughfare" upon them all.'

Had Jowett not deliberately stopped thinking from fear, in Stephen's view, he must have left the Church and taken the hard decision to leave his college as Henry Sidgwick and Stephen himself had done at Cambridge. But Stephen suspected that there were other than purely spiritual reasons which kept Jowett in the Church. In a moment of worldly ingenuousness Augustine Birrell criticized Stephen's judgement on Jowett and asked:

Why should [men] sell out of a still going and dividend-paying concern when they have not the faintest idea where to look for another investment for their money? Where was Jowett to go if he gave up Balliol? . . . So he stayed where he was and Balliol got new buildings and a new cricket ground, and turned out a number of excellent young fellows warranted to come and go anywhere except to the gallows and the stake.

Stephen, however, admired men who would go to the stake for their beliefs, with the hoots of society ringing in their ears. He had once met in America the abolitionist, Garrison, 'who was dragged through the streets of Boston for preaching abolition [of slavery] and was only saved by the police with great difficulty'. Stephen thought Garrison a muddle-headed pacifist, but, 'it is impossible not to feel some respect for a man who has been dragged through the streets by a rope'. Jowett was not of such mettle, nor were his pupils. Stephen should have quoted from Stendhal: 'Good birth . . . destroys those qualities of the spirit which make people be sentenced to death.' Jowett would not have advised any of his pupils to risk the gallows or exclusion from polite society and the seats of power. What was it, asked Stephen, that induced him to remain a clergyman and become Master of Balliol? Snobbery. Stephen's irony was not aroused by

Jowett's preference for well-bred and titled young men; nor even by Jowett's pleasure at hearing that Tennyson had mentioned his name to the Queen or his thinking the Crown Princess of Prussia 'quite a genius' when she visited him *incognita* to talk philosophy. It was Jowett's calm assumption that the criterion of merit was worldly success. It was his conviction that anyone who had been at Balliol but had failed to make a mark in the world had somehow insulted him and was worthless. Stephen despised Jowett for being all things to all men and for commending 'a good sort of roguery' which consisted in never saying a word against anybody however much they might deserve it. Was not his friendship slightly tarnished? Did he not care less for the man than for his achievements?

Such was Stephen's indictment; but though scrupulously presented, it is the case for the prosecution. For instance, Jowett's biographers argued that it was the sight over the years of so many wasted lives, of squandered talents, that made Jowett so insistent on success. Geoffrey Faber denied Jowett was a sceptic – he believed in a personal God and in the validity of Christ's teaching about that God. It was cheap of Stephen to sneer at dons such as Jowett or W. G. Clark at Cambridge for cultivating poets and novelists and to insinuate that they lionized the literary world in order to show that a don was not by nature incapable of acquiring a pretty taste in verse and fiction. Nevertheless the essay on Jowett is an epitaph, if not on Jowett, then on Stephen's own career at Cambridge in which he implicitly says that it is the duty of a tutor not to batten on his pupils, or court their praise, or pose as a wise adviser and then reject them when they will not follow that advice, or to live his life through them; but to help them when they are in need, to inspire them with a love of enquiry, to show clearly what he believes and values himself; and then to leave them to judge for themselves. The essay also reveals Stephen's vision of the Cambridge mind – a mind in firm control of the heart. 'The intellect is very well in its way, but the heart is God's especial province,' said Lord Shaftesbury, and Stephen was to reply, 'The "heart" is not another kind of reason . . . but a name for emotions which are not reason at all.' Cambridge did not despise generous feelings; as Alfred Marshall declared (in a phrase to which Jowett took strong exception), her dons tried 'to increase the number of those whom Cambridge, the great mother of strong men, sends out into the world with cool heads but warm hearts'. But warm hearts by themselves are not enough, and Stephen thought that 'one's conscience may be a dangerous guide unless it condescends to be enlightened by patient and impartial enquiry'.[1] Cambridge instilled this quality by

---

[1] It was all very well, wrote Stephen, for Ruskin to thunder away against classical economics but where was the lightning? Nassau Senior and Fawcett believed that scientific enquiry had established certain laws: laws cannot be charmed away by rhodomontade. Stephen claimed (though he can hardly have believed such a naive excuse) that Thackeray stopped publication in the *Cornhill* of *Unto This Last* simply because Ruskin scouted that spirit of scientific enquiry which alone convinces experts that the purpose is serious.

honouring mathematics. 'As a mere intellectual toy mathematics is far
ahead of any known invention,' said Stephen. 'To have been in love with
some women is, we are told, to have received a liberal education . . .; a
three years' flirtation with mathematics is supposed to produce the same
effect . . . Our minds have been strengthened and prepared for dealing
with other subjects.' The queen of the sciences, the paragon of reason
fired by the imagination, mathematics trained the mind to argue with
rigour and economy. Mathematics always gave an answer; even though it
satisfied a limited enquiry to a previously hypothesized question, still it
was an answer. Stephen, Sidgwick,[1] Clifford, Marshall and Venn all came
to philosophy through mathematics and gravitated to empiricism.
Metaphysics flourished in Oxford, the home of Aristotle. It was no
accident that whereas Oxford at the end of the century became the home
of German idealism, Cambridge nurtured Bertrand Russell's logic which
employed Boolean algebra.

   And yet on one matter German idealism and scientific rationalism
coincided. Both gave within a single framework an explanation of the
way the universe worked. Hegel conceived of the world as a place which
passed through distinct epochs. In each epoch man came closer to
understanding how to overcome the constraints of geography, climate
and material circumstances; and in so doing he liberated himself and
discovered the only true freedom, the determination to master his fate.
When Carlyle announced that the universe was not 'dead and de-
moniacal, a charnel-house with spectres; but godlike and my Father's', he
did not mean that he had rediscovered revealed religion. It was his way of
echoing Hegel's notion of freedom. Science, too, so its publicists declared,
could give a similar answer to those who wanted to hear it. Although, as
we shall see, some despaired because blind chance played so great a part
in evolution, evolution suggested to others that development was not a
mere game of hazard. Life moved from the simple to the complex and
from lower to higher forms. By the end of the century there were Bergson,
Bernard Shaw and Wells speaking of a life force directing the human race.

   Stephen made some very proper distinctions. The Germans it was true,
had a theory of evolution; but it was evolution through the operation of
the dialectic 'in which each stage of history represents a moment of some
vast and transcendental process of thought' – and this seemed to him 'to
be mere mysticism or intellectual juggling'. Evolution which 'managed by
some illegitimate process to give a crude generalization from experience
the appearance of a purely logical deduction . . . was really opposed to
science'. The time, however, was to come 'when evolution would present
itself in scientific form'. What Stephen did not perceive was that both

[1] Sidgwick was, of course, a classicist, but he had also had to sit for the mathematical tripos and in the
year that he was placed top of the Classical Tripos, he was also thirty-third wrangler.

German transcendentalism and his own scientific rationalism claimed to analyse human experience by a single set of interlocking principles. The reason he did not perceive it was this. He had found in his reading at Cambridge a rationalist who like the German idealists provided an explanation of human development but unlike them was anchored within the rationalist scientific tradition. This was the verbose, humourless systemizer, Auguste Comte.

Chapter Seven

🙟🙟🙟

THE RHETORIC OF TRUTH

The Theorists of the Evolution of Society

Leslie Stephen believed that the laws which govern the development of society could eventually be discovered. In his search he was first attracted by Comte's explanation; but Comte's theory did not show how in reality such laws operated. Suddenly in England there appeared a man who did so. Darwin actually showed how species develop; and therefore, using his methods, it should be possible to demonstrate how society should develop. What was needed, Stephen concluded, was plain speaking, which rationalists had up till then been most unwilling to do. Not to speak out plainly and say which beliefs were likely to impede and which accelerate human progress was to betray truth; truth was a unity and whatever conflicts with scientific laws must be exposed as error.

Stephen did not swallow Comte whole: for Comte was not an isolated figure any more than were the German thinkers who followed Kant and Herder. He belonged to that succession of indefatigable French utopians stretching back to Fénelon and Mably of whom the most astonishing were Fourier and Saint-Simon. In rows of volumes these men set out their claims to have discovered the laws governing the development of society and depicted in exhaustive detail the precise shape it should take when men at last were prepared to change their institutions out of respect for these laws. For instance in Fourier's ideal co-operative which he called the Phalanstère even the children – divided by age into *nourrissons*, *bambins* and *poupons* (who in turn were sub-divided into *pouponnais*, *pouponnards* and *pouponnâtres*) – would be engaged in useful work. Since children revel in dirt, two thirds of the boys and one third of the girls would do the work which their elders found distasteful and would labour in the slaughter-houses or clean the streets. The other children who could be presumed to prefer neatness would look after pigeons and flowers and correct their parents' bad pronunciation.

Saint-Simon was not so confident a futurologist. He believed in government by experts who should learn at school mathematics rather than classics, but he understood that the conclusions which experts reached would not always be palatable to their fellow citizens. As the first technocrat he did not blench. These conclusions should become political decisions because they would be based on scientific knowledge. There was no other kind of knowledge: religion was what men in the past had thought to be true – a kind of pre-scientific knowledge. But that did not mean religion was a vanishing anachronism. It merely needed to be given a new aim. Religion should be directed to make men happy in this world instead of the next and should reconcile them to the technological inventions which might put them personally out of work but would raise the general standard of living.

Comte's thought derives almost wholly from Saint-Simon. Even the famous law of the three stages, which in his role as Solon he claimed to have invented, came from Turgot through Saint-Simon's teacher Burdin. Scholarly summaries of Comte's thought, while reminding the reader that Comte was the father of sociology, somehow fail to convince their own writers, let alone their readers, that Comte's merits entirely compensated for his defects. But the tribute has to be paid. Otherwise why did Mill respect Comte so sincerely and why did he declare that his inverse deductive method in the *Logic* derived from Comte? Why did George Eliot venerate him and why was she reading his *Discours Préliminaire* in her decline less than a month before she died? Why for that matter in the 1850s did Stephen read him and why was he pained when Sidgwick unfairly took him to task for exaggerating the influence of Darwin and underestimating Comte? – indeed, why did he say (though one cannot rule the remark out as an example of Stephen's deft irony) that had he been at Oxford he might have become a Positivist?

There were two practical reasons why Comte impressed the younger generation. Unlike his predecessors Comte was no socialist. He was a notable conservative believing in order as the prerequisite of progress. He was not a de Maistre but a modern conservative who welcomed the industrial revolution and the dissolution of the *ancien régime*. Moreover, he had the sense to separate the six volumes of his philosophical theorizing which appeared between 1830 and 1842 from the political schematization in four volumes which were published ten years later. His theory also appeared to be candid. Comte was the first to analyse how scientific method could be applied to the social as well as the natural sciences. He understood the distinction which is crucial to empirical philosophy between the way we refer to physical objects and the way we refer to ideas and concepts. It was this which endeared him to Mill. Comte's scrupulous exploration of the philosophy of science is not a series of arbitrary assertions, masquerading as axiomatic truths. Like

Pope, Comte pictured the universe as governed by laws which remain hidden until man discovers them. But when God said let Newton be and all was light, what precisely did Newton do? Comte said that Newton and all scientists first formulated hypotheses and then saw if their observations fitted those hypotheses. If not they modified or discarded them. Unless men discovered the correct way to reason, nature's laws would remain hid in night.

The pass-key to understanding the world was the law of three stages. Man first explained the world theologically by ascribing events to the will of God, next metaphysically by replacing God with principles and forces, and now was on the point of being able to explain it by 'positive' or scientific means. Once upon a time men thought that opium induced sleep because God willed it; then they thought that opium contained a soporific principle; today all a physiologist could do was to observe, analyse and experiment and admit that at present he could not account for it at all. (Comte would have welcomed modern pharmacology.) Merely to observe facts was not enough. That was crude empiricism. Men must put forward theories. And that was why progress depends ultimately on the human mind. Much of Comte's energy was spent in formulating ways in which the human mind would not be permitted to lay down arbitrary laws but would work on genuine scientific lines.

To do so men would have to subdue their individual wills and subordinate their activities to the laws of social evolution. Evolution is another name for that collective wisdom of Humanity which binds the past to the future. Liberty as the English used the word was anathema to Comte. Certainly concepts such as the sovereignty of the people, equality, freedom of thought had enabled mankind to discover the evolution of thought and see the dawn of the scientific age. But they would soon be dangerous irrelevancies. Who needed freedom of conscience any longer to understand the laws of astronomy and physics? One by one each scientific discipline, including in the end politics itself, would render up its secrets and be explicable. The laws which governed them would be established and, once established, the general will of intellectuals – what Comte called 'public reason' – would decide what was debatable and what had once and for all been decided as being for the good of Humanity present and to come.

How was such public agreement to be reached? Comte was mum. It is indeed exceedingly hard for political theorists to appear convincing at this point. In our times John Rawls suggests that social harmony and reform will come about through the public becoming better informed. They will be ready to accept constraints only if it is possible to show how in a regime of liberty and equality such constraints would have been willingly accepted by citizens. The Frankfurt School speak of breaking the chains of technology and bureaucracy which imprison us. So do Foucault and other members of the Dadaist school of philosophy. Habermas declares, like Rousseau, that the chains are shackles we made ourselves, our false 'legitimating beliefs', by which we justify to ourselves repression and evil. Free our consciousness and the chains will fall to our feet. The chains, according to Habermas, were those forged by Comte, the chains of a positivist belief in scientific laws. And yet Habermas in a sense is as Comtist as Comte. For, having established to his satisfaction that what Comte believed to be the final and 'positive' state of thought is only another form of metaphysics, he then elaborates a new way of thinking, a new kind of knowledge, not merely scientific or hermeneutic but derived from the critical study of texts – a rabbinical pursuit – which will enable everyone to understand what is really for the good of society: just as through psychoanalysis self-knowledge enables us to live with our guilt and repressions.

It is not quite true that Comte ignored the legitimacy of government. He maintained that capitalists, and in particular bankers who were most skilled of all in the mysteries of capital transactions, could alone rule. He accepted that the working class would need to be persuaded that their decisions were just. Of course they would be just because they would be based on scientific knowledge. Still, even though the general pattern of positivist society was for ever fixed, Comte accepted that as new knowledge came into being there could be room for further discussion. After all, the new knowledge might not be recognized for what it was by the mass of men. So there was need for a mediator, a final arbiter in disputes between capital and labour. This mediator was to be the church of Humanity. The new church would be responsible for harmonizing scientific and moral ideas with the harsh realities of life and would reconcile human beings to the truth that rights are indistinguishable from duties.

Believing as he did that intellectuals change the world, Comte became the evangelist of the expert. From their scientific understanding experts rather than democratically elected politicians should govern – a thesis not entirely displeasing to the English intellectual aristocracy who were tiring of being governed by jaunty Whigs and by Tory squires. Like Arnold he thought society was in as great a danger from intellectual anarchy as it was from the suppression of free enquiry. That was why he spent his life trying to prove that politics was susceptible to the same scientific treatment as physics and astronomy. It is not surprising that Beatrice Webb in her teens was much taken with Comte, or that E. H. R. Pease, the first secretary of the Fabian Society, acknowledged how in the 1880s Comte's religion appealed to the young intelligentsia. If experts were needed to design a bridge or manufacture a product 'guided by antecedent knowledge', surely society could not be reorganized without a similar theoretical framework. Comte gave his adherents the same confidence that nowadays systems analysis, cybernetics and cost benefit analysis give to some. The experts would divine the shape of the future by scientific observation of the past: the artist would get the masses to accept their findings by exercising imagination. Imagination, Comte thought, was not a quality appropriate to scientific activity; but it was singularly felicitous when it came to writing propaganda, a role which he thought eminently suitable for artists.

Comte could never have won George Eliot's heart had he not been a moralist – Mill called him 'a morality-intoxicated man'. He deduced that religion performed a function in society; and if religion in its present form became obsolete, steps would have to be taken to replace it. One of the objects of the new religion was to curb selfishness and promote altruism; and it was this conviction that altruism can be kindled through social institutions, such as the family, and that true happiness can be found only through altruism, that became the core of agnostic faith. Leslie Stephen subscribed to this faith. In his thirties he even went so far as to claim a place for the new religion in the organization of society. But he drew an inference from Comte quite different from that of his contemporaries. It was an inference which Durkheim two generations later was to make with incomparable force. If religion or a society's morality performed a social function and bound society together, perhaps social forces interacting upon each other and not men's ideas were the agents of change and progress. If impersonal forces determined change, then ideas were merely the audible reaction human beings made when change came about. He reached this conclusion because the scientific description of evolution and evidence in other fields seemed to him to put beyond a shadow of doubt the conclusion that natural laws of selection determine how all species including that of *homo sapiens* develop.

Stephen left his enemies to criticize Comte; but he did not hesitate to criticize certain English thinkers who appeared at first sight to be thinking on the same lines as Comte. Stephen was not to be taken in by works, however full of learning, simply because they were written by rationalists. Lecky, he thought, was 'apt to throw out wide generalizations and then apparently to lose sight of them'. But perhaps this was a welcome relief in that people must have become weary of 'gentlemen who include in a single glance a period of a thousand years or so, and extract from the complex history of politics and morals, and philosophy and religion, some half-dozen definite dogmas forced upon us at the point of the pen'. Lecky never really addressed himself to the consequences of what he wrote whereas, whatever criticism could be made of Comte, the sage of Positivism created a coherent system of thought.

One of the gentlemen Stephen had in mind was Lecky's predecessor Henry Thomas Buckle. In 1857 there appeared the first volume of his *History of Civilization in England* which in the next twelve years went through four editions. It was the work of a polymath who went neither to school nor to university, who read indefatigably, could speak eighteen languages by the time he was 30 and was to die in his early forties travelling in the Levant. Buckle reduced history to a science by subsuming all phenomena under laws. Geography gave certain laws, statistics even more laws. For instance, Buckle argued that since the statistics of suicide showed little variation in its incidence, and since the resolution to kill oneself was surely the most personal and decisive of human actions, free will was an illusion. Men were subject to such laws but unfortunately two of their most powerful springs of action, the love of money and the love of knowledge, had been hampered by protectionism. Free trade and free thought were two sides of the same coin but the currency was devalued by the machinations of protectionists, namely men's rulers and their priests. Of course history was a bewildering labyrinth of facts but who can doubt that it must be susceptible to fixed laws?

How, Stephen asked, did Buckle silence the doubters? He gave meaning to the facts by explaining a tendency as the spirit of the age and making the spirit of the age the explanation of the tendency. Sometimes Buckle argued that in Europe man was more powerful than nature: at other times that nature was more powerful than man. Was it any wonder that enthusiastic young ladies went about 'panting for wider generalizations'? As a sample of Buckle's historiography Stephen cited him on the Reformation. Henry VIII divided the spoils of the Pope and his satellites the monks with the people, whereas François I divided the spoils of his clergy and his people with the Pope. 'Similar explanations', said Stephen sardonically, 'are to be had in abundance from whips of parliamentary parties . . . but when they profess to be the philosophy of history, the obvious remark is that they are no explanation at all.' For Stephen, Buckle exemplified 'that curious tone of popular complacency which was prevalent some thirty years ago when people held that the devil had finally committed suicide upon seeing the Great Exhibition, having had things pretty much his own way till Luther threw the inkstand in his face . . . Protection had been abolished yesterday and war was to be abolished the day after tomorrow.' Comte, thought Stephen, had a far clearer view of history as a process of organic development.

Nevertheless there was to be published in 1859 a book which convinced Stephen that some day, some time, tentative provisional laws governing human nature and behaviour could be discovered and that they would be 'scientific': not perhaps in quite the same way that Newton could be said to have propounded laws governing the physical universe, but in the way that biologists, having classified the species, conjecture how they came to be as they are. Comte showed how it might be done. Darwin showed how it could be done.

The Influence of Darwin

Science in mid-Victorian England had scarcely begun to be taught. No wonder, in a country where individual initiative and the demand of the market were expected to supply engineers. Science, then as now, was feared. Ruskin feared it would corrupt craftsmen. Newman and Arnold feared it would impoverish the mind if it filled the school curriculum. But for years science had been extending the dimensions of history both back into the past and forward into the future. As early as 1836 Boucher de Perthes had argued that mankind and mammals now extinct were contemporaries. Geology and biology told the history of the earth before man existed: physics foretold the end of the earth when, devoid of kinetic heat, it would spin frozen round an extinct sun. No single publication, however, could rival in its effect the *Origin of Species*. Darwin's work compelled intellectuals to reconsider the whole European tradition of metaphysics stretching from Plato to the eighteenth century.

The metaphysical significance of evolution has been analysed by Arthur O. Lovejoy in his classic work in the history of ideas, *The Great Chain of Being*. Lovejoy traced the fortunes of a complex of three ideas which for two thousand years gave pattern and coherence to European metaphysics, but desiderated not one but two Gods. The one was a transcendental, other-worldly Idea or Ground, self-sufficient, apart from time or space, uniting all eternal Ideas, a self-contained perfection, needing nothing to complete or to realize itself. But since the contemplation of such a remote disinterested Being satisfied few and could not explain the peculiar scheme of things in this world, or why the world exists, still less how it changes, another God was required. This was a God whose essence required a world teeming with living creatures, immanent in the processes of nature and related to our sense of space and time. These two conceptions of God, though logically opposed, were united by Plato in the *Timaeus* by the device of emanationism: the Transcendental God, the goal of all desires, was perfect Good and therefore envious of nothing; hence he would wish everything to be as he is, and he accordingly overflowed into the imperfect and projected himself into the universe. He realized himself by creating successively all possible kinds of being for all time, and all these beings were connected to each other ranged in hierarchical order as an infinite number of links in a chain. A rational world was now established; and the presence of evil was explicable by the fact that the different species of being were all imperfect, each with its distinct qualities and defects: even though Nature, red in tooth and claw, permitted one species to hunt and kill another, the hunted had far better have lived and partaken of the Divine Perfection than never to have existed at all. All cosmological and ontological structures in European religion were raised on this metaphysical foundation.

At the end of the seventeenth and during the eighteenth century, a factor hitherto relatively unimportant – Time – impinged upon human consciousness, and the idea of the chain of being had to be reinterpreted to include the notion of progress. It was accordingly modified by arguing that all creatures tended toward God and drew ever nearer to him during time. Being finite they had to be able to perfect themselves since to be static was to deserve extinction. Perfection was to be attained through eternal alteration and evolution. The Chain of Being, as Lovejoy put it, was temporalized. Though for a time the unity of the fundamentally dualistic God was held together, the contradiction in it became more and more apparent. There was a Creator who, being always the same and acting in accordance with changeless perfect reason, could generate only one Creation to express his perfection. There was also, however, a temporalized God whose created world was essentially different at one time from what it was at another. The order of things in time now began to conflict with man's conception of the eternal aspect of things. As Natural Theology was spread by such divines as Paley, the God of this world was emphasized at the expense of the Transcendental Idea and Absolute God. Soon there began to creep in the heterodox conception that God himself was part of the time-process and, no less than the species he had created, was not yet fully self-realized – was not himself fully perfected.

Yet the belief in an orderly and rational universe might have continued for some time longer had not a new principle been introduced into metaphysics by the Romantic Revival. This was the principle of diversity. Most eighteenth-century metaphysicians accepted the principle that all conceivable species had been created and were fulfilling themselves because God could not have created a world lacking one or more of His inventions. They believed that the universe was ordered rationally in accordance with a few simple laws accessible to man's reason; and even if man's reason was too limited to apprehend the full truth, they did not doubt that every species was sanctioned by a Divine reason, however many species there were or were yet to be discovered – the greater the number the greater God's glory. The links of the chain of Nature had to hold together because the world was internally determined by necessary truths and bound in a fixed relationship to the Absolute God. This belief in the rationality of the world was shaken by the Romantic discovery of diversity. The Romantics denied that all beings must strive towards one

ideal of perfection: perfection resided in their essential difference and the
world was enriched by these differences. Diversity replaced universality
as the principle governing the universe – a diversity which would not fit
into a rational scheme of things, for every rational scheme impaired the
ideal of perfection. For the Romantics even untruth was a valuable
addition to diversity; though some poet's dream might be an illusion, the
world was that much the richer, the Creator more fully realized; *le moi*
and the unique work of art or imagination were more valuable than any
rational whole.[1]

Thus when the question is put, as Stephen often put it: why had the
work of eighteenth-century scepticism to be done all over again in the
nineteenth century – why Hume and Voltaire appeared to have argued in
vain – one answer is that an age-long metaphysical explanation of life on
earth was being challenged. Voltaire may have rejected the notion of
gradation between species but he retained the conception of a rational
universe. The Deists degraded Christ but they accepted traditional
metaphysics. In the nineteenth century, however, not only Christian
theology but a metaphysical theory of the Creation and the processes of
Nature which had existed from the time of Plato was called in question.

Since a century and a half of evolutionary hypotheses preceded
Darwin, why did the *Origin of Species* have such an effect? Partly because
Darwin became in a lesser degree what Newton was for his age: the man
who had discovered the laws governing a wide but circumscribed field of
enquiry on which lesser or less lucky minds had been working for many
years. Partly because the hypothesis of natural selection, derived from
Lyell's geology and Malthus's demography, appeared to have been
achieved by employing Newton's methods faithfully. To readers of the
Logic a fruitful new hypothesis was now available to be applied
deductively to social problems. Just as Newton's prestige was enhanced
by the respect accorded to mathematics, so Darwin rose on the breezes of
the prestige won for the natural sciences by the staggering discoveries of
the astronomers, physicists, chemists, geologists and statisticians.[2]

But the real significance of the *Origin of Species* lay in its apparent

[1] Not that the Romantics showed any lack of fertility in conceiving gods. But the gods of Schlegel,
Schleiermacher, Schelling, were heretical creations in the sense that Kant's God was not. Kant too had
temporalized Being, and progressive diversification and development was for him the supreme law of
Nature. But he believed that a species could not develop beyond a certain point and, when self-realized,
was eliminated in order that the links in the Chain of Being may still conform to each other: cosmic
egregiousness was unthinkable because Kant assumed the universe to be rational. *Per contra* the
German Romantic philosophers dispensed with the rational cosmos, or rather they dispensed with one
part of it. The Hegelian Absolute resided *inside* the universe – it was not an Idea of Ideas existing quite
apart from force and matter.
[2] The unwillingness of scientists such as Lyell, or Darwin himself, to accept the principle of organic
evolution added to their reputation for scrupulosity. Huxley admitted that, before Darwin published,
he opposed the hypothesis for lack of evidence and looked askance at its advocates.

THE RHETORIC OF TRUTH   201

contradiction of orthodox metaphysics. Darwin introduced the idea that *chance* begot order. Fortuitous events, not planned or rational but fortuitous, resulted in a physical law: the process of natural selection, achieved by minute accidental variations in the species, broke the principle of internal determinism so that the links in the Chain of Being fell apart. Chauncey Wright, the American naturalist and philosopher, pointed out that the very title of Darwin's book implied a reversal of orthodox metaphysics. ' "Origin" now means how things go from one determinate appearance to another ... the word "species" now means not an absolute, but a comparative fixity of character, [so that in Darwin] the two terms appear with modern non-scholastic meanings.' Thus the *Origin of Species* made the world seem less, not more, rational, and the universe a creation of blind chance, not a 'block-world' (in William James's phrase) created by an other-worldly Master Mind. Attempts naturally were made to escape from the disagreeable situation of existing in a mechanistic world without a mechanic;[1] intelligent theologians absorbed evolution by the doctrine of Immanence; and Henry Adams noted the growth of a new evolutionary metaphysic of 'Form, Law, Order or Sequence'. Though evolution is almost the least of the problems facing theologians today, Stephen read Darwin as *evidence* confuting orthodox metaphysics; by using this evidence empirically was it not possible to show scientifically that all metaphysical explanations of the cosmos were worthless?

Worthless because, as soon became apparent, diametrically opposed inferences could be drawn from Darwin. Some cursed the 'rigorous logic which wrecked the universe for me and for millions of others'. Some were outraged not because God had been displaced but because God had been Satanized. Some realized the difficulty of guessing at what precise moment in time mankind could be said to have free will and hence a soul for Christ to redeem. On the other hand there were those whose belief in the wonders of Natural Theology – 'O Lord, how manifold are Thy works' – was strengthened by Darwin's description of orchids; and Temple's contribution to *Essays and Reviews* pleaded that theologians had better draw their conclusions from the laws of Nature rather than from the alleged miraculous suspension of those laws. You could counter examples of the imperfection of Nature by examples of the beauty of Nature; the brutality and immorality of Nature, by its far-reaching, far-seeing Design. Yet nothing was ever to be the same again. In countless stained-glass windows, in the greatest works of art in the fifteenth and

---

[1] Not always very happily: A. R. Wallace, the joint discoverer of natural selection, declared that the mechanism of natural selection, which left no room for the creation of the soul, was broken with the emergence of Mind: Mind required a separate act of creation – an argument not very far removed from Max Müller's rebuttal of the principle of natural selection, namely, that language separates men from apes.

sixteenth centuries, in Milton's epics, the old simple story of the Creation to the Last Judgement, the story of God's scheme of salvation, was stamped upon the imagination with all the force that Ghiberti had employed when he cast the reliefs on the bronze doors of the Baptistery in Florence. Even those who had accepted the story as an allegory were forced to ask themselves: what else is allegorical in Christianity?

There was another book, slim and unpretentious, also published in 1859, of which Stephen was an early admirer and which may well have influenced him. This was Fitzgerald's translation of the *Rubáiyát of Omar Khayyám*. Who are we to say, Fitzgerald seemed to ask, that Persian civilization as revealed in this poem is inferior to ours? When Jowett wrote on Plato he followed the old game of reconciling Plato with Christianity and making classical authors safe for British undergraduates and schoolboys to read. But when Pater wrote on Plato, or Symonds wrote on the Renaissance, however much they may seem to us to portray a Greece that never was or a Renaissance which is difficult to recognize, they contrasted the culture of those ages to Victorian Christianity. They suggested that past ages should be judged by their own standards and by the stage of evolution which they had reached. The Victorians were fast discovering other civilizations through excavations and through anthropology. What was evolution but an exploration of the way society is transformed throughout the ages? John Burrow showed that the insights of positivism, conjectural history and the comparative method were all used to explain the existence and ways of life of savages and their relation to modern civilization. The work of the evolutionary anthropologists – McLennan, Tylor and Frazer – belongs to the post-Darwinian era, but already the notion was current, which Darwin was to reinforce, that at different periods in time people had lived in societies possessing values and beliefs which in turn affected their economy, status and kinship systems. People had begun to notice that the same myths and rites animated different religions.[1]

It took time, as we shall see, for the rationalists to draw the inferences from Darwin which they wanted so much to find and which gave them

[1] Eliza Lynn Linton, who was a considerable Victorian bluestocking, grasped this idea in her girlhood. At the age of 17 in 1839 she noticed, reading in the garden, that the story of Nisus and Scylla in Ovid's *Metamorphoses* was strikingly similar to that of Samson and Delilah. 'There shot through my brain these words which seemed to run along the page in a line of light: "What difference is there between any of these stories and those like to them in the Bible? – between the loves of the sons of God for the daughters of men, and those of the Gods of Greece for the girls of Athens and Sparta?" ' This reflection so disturbed her that she collapsed on the grass in a dead faint. Similarly, Darwin in the *Beagle* suddenly realized that the sacred Hindu books, the Veda, were strikingly similar to the Old Testament. These experiences caused both of them eventually to lose their faith. When in the *Grammar of Assent* Newman dubiously argued that the Atonement must be a valid doctrine because we find the belief current among savages, Stephen pointed out that it would be more rational to deduce that Christianity was just another religious phenomenon holding doctrines common to other creeds. Cf. Feuerbach's 'The secret of theology is anthropology'.

new confidence. Stephen thought evolution enabled the rationalists to capture history by extricating them from a logical dilemma. James Mill and Ricardo had deliberately rejected the historical method because for them to admit a single breach in the principle that Nature is uniform would be to allow the intuitionists to storm through it and disrupt the camp. Admit that one race differs from another, or even that the sexes can be distinguished, and these ruffians would be found conjuring up proofs that some races were doomed to perpetual slavery or one sex to perpetual subjection. Mill and Buckle had gaoled themselves. If they admitted that some types were fixed they might have to admit that the types were governed by *a priori* laws; if they regarded all characteristics of a race or class as merely fortuitous, they must declare that man was everywhere the same and only his coat changed.

And here at hand was deliverance. Evolutionists admitted that there were differences between the races and the sexes and they also agreed that an organism had specific qualities: but both the differences and the essential property of the type were in a perpetual state of adaptation. Superficial differences might turn out to be radical differences and vice versa. The rationalist now had a scientific criterion for agreeing with Burke and Coleridge that society was an organism changing slowly in accordance with scientific not transcendental laws.

The notion that history was now becoming a branch of science gathered weight. How do you judge what is true in history? The rationalists answered, study the evidence, which consists of facts, and then see that your account squares with the scientific way of interpreting Nature. No more remarkable example of this way of arguing from evidence exists than the controversy over the Gadarene swine between a former Prime Minister and the most widely known scientist of the day. Huxley declared that the faithful could not have it both ways. Either the Evangelists were fabricating a story when they spoke of Jesus casting out devils and permitting them to enter a herd of swine, who immediately plunged into the sea, or Jesus had wantonly destroyed other men's property. Gladstone rose to the bait. Roused by the suggestion that Jesus might have undermined the fundamental Liberal principle of the sacredness of private property, he declared that this 'accusation against our Lord' was intolerable: the destruction of the swine was legitimate because Jews were forbidden under Mosaic law to keep pigs. Huxley replied at length. He examined the authorities and argued that Gadara was in fact a Hellenic and Gentile town, and therefore the inhabitants had a right to keep pigs; since we might assume that Christ would never have wrongfully harmed such men, we should dismiss the story as false – unless one chose to assume that Christ broke 'the first condition of enduring liberty [which] is obedience to the law of the land'. Further

animadversions on pig-keeping habits in Galilee, the administrative
boundaries, the social structure of Gadara, and Schürer's interpretation
of Josephus, led Huxley to declare that all the best opinion agreed that the
synoptic Gospels were not independent but were founded on a common
source and hence the story rested on legend or the observation of a single
observer; and while, *pace* Hume, there is no a priori objection against the
miracle, such frail evidence for its occurrence was wholly insufficient.
And Huxley added the singular prophecy: 'Whether the twentieth
century shall see a recrudescence of the superstitions of medieval papistry,
or whether it shall witness the severance from the living body of the
ethical ideal of prophetic Israel from the carcase, foul with savage
superstitions and cankered with false philosophy, to which the theologians have bound it, turns upon their final judgement of the Gadara
tale. As for the miracle of the feeding of the five thousand why should we
believe it to be true on contradictory evidence? Would Christians end by
boasting that since faith was not in touch with fact at all, it was therefore
inaccessible to infidel attack?'

This method of testing evidence was continually gaining ground during
the century. By 1903 J. B. Bury was to pronounce in his inaugural lecture
that history was a science, no less, no more; and elsewhere he wrote that if
a historian were a theist he must regard his belief in God as otiose,
'otherwise indeed history could not be a science'. The conviction that the
historian can truthfully deduce from evidence what happened in the past
was expressed in a significant mistranslation of one of Ranke's most
famous passages by G. P. Gooch, the doyen of English historiographers in
the early years of this century. Protesting in 1824 against partisan history,
inspired by what he regarded as the mistaken view that historians should
pass moral judgements, Ranke wrote in the first work of importance he
published, 'People have thought that it was the duty of the historian to
judge the past and instruct the present for the benefit of the future. The
present essay is more modest. *Er will bloss zeigen, wie es eigentlich
gewesen.*' These words, meaning 'It merely wants to show what it was
really like', Gooch translated on one occasion as 'what actually occurred'
and on another as 'events as they actually happened'. To Ranke the
notion of an historian compiling evidence out of facts and interpreting it
scientifically was an illusion. He never doubted that the historian,
bearing, as he should, Hegel in mind, would form a personal interpretation of the evidence even if what constituted evidence was a technical
matter. All he asked was that the historian should consider the past in its
own terms and not try to judge it by inappropriate standards.

By the 1930s virtually no one thought that history was a science, no
less, no more. History consisted of unique and non-recurring events in
which individuals with free will move and have their being. The quest for

accuracy gave way to the quest for verisimilitude, and scientific laws to plausible generalizations. Norman Baynes set out the view of the professionals accurately when he said that, faced with the story that Constantine the Great saw before his victory a cross in the sky, a historian would judge according to his ontological interpretation of life whether or not it appeared and if it did, whether it was sent by God. Or he was entitled to disregard the question. As a *technical* historian he could not determine whether the cross existed. All he could do was to record and test the authenticity of the sources from which the story derives. A century and a half of German biblical criticism had at last taken effect. While Schweitzer might not have ended the quest for the historical Jesus, he showed how enormously complex the quest had become. The shift from source-criticism to form-criticism can be seen as another attempt to deny individuals the determining factor in history and to replace them by a sociological study of the community within which early Christianity took shape. But at any rate it made it difficult for rationalists to hold the same simplistic view of evidence which had been current in England in the nineteenth century.

As we have seen, German historiography was slow to influence British historians. Maitland wrote, 'Then in the nineteenth century came the critical movement. Would Englishmen see and understand what was happening in Germany? Would they appreciate and emulate the work of Savigny and Grimm? It can hardly be said they rose to the occasion.' Maitland was not speaking of the treatment of evidence. What he had in mind was that until the 1860s English historians were uninfluenced by the way the Germans brought into history legal origins and institutions, or the language, folk tales and myths, in which a people express their culture. Only then did the English begin to interpret the history of their own country through land tenure, local government, the administration of justice and the rights and privileges of communities and corporations rather than through Parliament and the constitutional conflict of the seventeenth century. When British historians argued about interpretation in history they did not bother to see how their German colleagues treated evidence because German interpretations of history – i.e. the theme which 'made sense' of the period – were not all that different in German versions of the past from their own. As a moderate Hegelian Ranke saw Britain as the antithesis to the thesis of the centralizing, bureaucratizing, chauvinist creature of the Enlightenment, France, which threatened Protestant northern Europe by its hateful Revolution and dictator Napoleon. Ranke praised Britain for its sturdy tradition of local government which sustained an independent assured ruling class, a bulwark against tyranny and revolution. Britain was a great Protestant power rooted in the Teutonic heritage of folk custom common to both Germans and

Englishmen. To English historians this chimed very well with their own interpretation of their history. Froude might be a conservative, Stubbs a clergyman, Seeley an imperialist and Freeman a fiery liberal, but all subscribed to what Herbert Butterfield immortalized as the Whig interpretation of history in that they subordinated the past to the present in order to tell a story – the story which explained why England had developed as it had. And this too was the inspiration of positivist history. The histories of free thought at the turn of the century by Benn and Robertson were learned examinations of every scrap of evidence which showed how men threw off the yoke of false belief and moved towards the appointed end where all phenomena were examined rationally or in the light of science. Positivist history which had its apogee in Bury was an extreme form of the Whig interpretation of history.

Leslie Stephen was a fully paid-up member of the positivist party; but he was the sort of supporter of whom party whips and hatchet men despair because he was so scrupulously full of qualifications. He quoted with approval the work of two French positivist historians who had pronounced that the aim of history was not to entertain or to sit in judgement but 'to give knowledge pure and simple'. But should history be pure? Were we for instance to ban those imaginative flights of fancy and unforgettable descriptions of human beings which enlivened the pages of Carlyle and Michelet? 'The people [they described], after all, were once alive, and that truth has some bearing upon their history.' He admitted that Grote lacked the professional expertise of German historians but Grote also understood that shifts in social structures brought about political changes. Could history be simple? Stephen replied (not perhaps all that helpfully) that it was important to 'regard history scientifically, though we cannot hope for a complete science of history'. History was governed by 'forces dimly perceived, not capable of accurate measurement' and perhaps utilitarians were rather too ready to 'accept convenient postulates as absolute truths'.

Few men are converted solely by intellectual arguments. John Henry Newman left a marvellous account of his progression to Rome, and who can forget his description of those heavy summer months in 1839 at Oxford when he began to study heresy in the fifth century and found reflected in the mirror of that study the controversies of the sixteenth and nineteenth centuries? 'I saw my face in that mirror, and I was a Monophysite.' But though that was a milestone upon the road to his conversion, he recorded also the string of external events – the Jerusalem bishopric, the reception of Tract 90 – which in the end made him leave the Church of England. Leslie Stephen took priest's orders in the summer of 1859 yet exactly three years later he found himself unable to officiate in Chapel. The chain of ideas which we have been examining certainly drew

him to this pass, but it seems likely that it was not so much Darwin's book
as the reception it got from the educated public which revealed to Stephen
where he stood. Evolution was a familiar enough idea for one who had
read his Comte: but did Darwin who palpably wrote solely as a scientist
deserve to be treated as he was?

'I do not attack Moses, and I think that Moses can take care of himself,'
wrote Darwin, and a year later he wrote to Asa Gray: 'With respect to the
theological view of the question, this is always painful to me. I am
bewildered. I had no intention to write atheistically.' In this he was naïve
and ignored what had happened to his predecessors such as Chambers.
Churchmen of all denominations fell upon him. Good form, middle-
stump Anglicanism (Wilberforce), the High Church (Pusey), Nonconformity (the *North British Review*), liberal Roman Catholicism (the
Rambler), Irish Roman Catholicism (*Dublin Review*), all cut him up.
Among scientists the support of Lyell, Huxley and Hooker was counterbalanced by the attacks of Sedgwick, Owen, Wollaston and Agassiz. The
tone of the intellectual reviews was cool rather than shocked, but the
agitation Darwin's book caused was extreme and it had the effect of
closing the minds as well as the ranks of the orthodox. So when orthodox
opinion had again been ruffled by the mild explorations of *Essays and
Reviews* and Bishop Colenso published his curious calculations throwing
doubt on certain passages in the Pentateuch, Wilberforce seized an
occasion to create an issue on which Evangelists and High Churchmen
could sink their differences and unite against infidelity.

The occasion was the famous meeting of the British Association in the
Oxford Museum at the end of June 1860. Accustomed to manipulate
ecclesiastical machinery, the Great Diocesan, a genial and often attractive
prelate, fell into the trap which awaits men of good humour who become
politicians – he made a joke at the wrong moment. When he asked Huxley
at this meeting which of his grandparents claimed descent from an ape,
the earnestness of Clapham passed in an instant into the hands of his
adversaries. His levity made Belief an issue of rectitude; and this would
not have escaped Stephen. In the same way when the Essayists were
savaged – when Rowland Williams was prosecuted for heresy, Jowett
was disgraced, and the future archbishop Frederick Temple was
admonished by the Archbishop of Canterbury – the moral victory went to
the accused. Temple made an unanswerable reply to Tait when he wrote:
'Many years ago you urged us from the University pulpit to undertake the
critical study of the Bible. You said that it was a dangerous study but
indispensable . . . To tell a man to study, and yet bid him, under heavy
penalties, come to the same conclusions with those who have not studied,
is to mock him. If the conclusions are prescribed, the study is precluded.'
The treatment of Darwin, the Essayists and Colenso brought home to

rationalists the conclusion of the *Essay on Liberty* that it was not the law of the land but social disapproval which sent scientists to the pillory and impeded the March of Mind.

It was all the more galling because nearly everyone who questioned the tenets of orthodoxy lent over backwards to dissociate themselves from infidelity. English scientists, Owen Chadwick recorded, dissociated themselves at that meeting of the British Association from the clumsy American, J. W. Draper, who beat the drum for a war of science against religion in his keynote speech. They thought him a poor scientist and his shopping list of scientific achievements to prove nothing about religion. On the Continent British timidity in such matters was among many intellectuals a byword either for muddle-headed cowardice or for sagacious comprehension that nothing unsettled a society more quickly than to have the foundations of its culture shaken. Why were the rationalists so circumspect?

The Timidity of the Rationalists

Consider the case of the foremost philosopher of evolution in Britain. Herbert Spencer was *not* an other-worldly man. Poetry, mystery, imagination, played no part whatsoever in his life. An evolutionist before Darwin, an analytical psychologist resolving human consciousness into its elementary forms after the fashion of James Mill and Bain and thus denying those 'special faculties' so dear to theologians, Spencer epitomized pseudo-scientific systemizing and *laissez-faire* utilitarianism. To him evolution, so long as it increased personal freedom, was progress, and the state tolerable only so long as it protected private rights, particularly those of property. He was the apogee of the mechanist philosopher. Everything could be explained in terms of force and by the law of conservation of energy all change could be shown to be a process in which less complicated systems gave way to more complicated systems. Nebulae were replaced by solar systems, amoebae by human beings, tribes by nation-states, primitive agricultural economies by the nexus of industrial commerce. Brick by brick he constructed his Synthetic Philosophy to demonstrate how animate and inanimate matter, the individual and society, were related to each other and governed by the same laws. Spencer's cosmogony did not require a God of Design. He was at pains to show that his axioms needed no other proof than the fact that we cannot expel this sense of order (produced by the conservation of energy) from our consciousness; and at this point he might have professed himself an agnostic, in the sense that Leslie Stephen did, by confessing that the ultimate origin of force and matter, and their relation to mind, lay outside human experience. But no; Spencer would have his God. He

e Stephen, aged twenty-eight (1860)

Ready to spring: Julia Margaret Cameron's photograph of Leslie Stephen

azing at extinction: Leslie Stephen by G.C. Beresford, 1902

Above left Minnie Thackeray, in mournin[g] for her father, 1862; photograph by Julia Margaret Cameron

Above Leslie Stephen with Minnie, 1867

Annie Thackeray, 1875

Leslie Stephen with his Alpine guide
Melchior Anderegg, *c*. 1870

slie Stephen with his dog Troy, 1875

Fitzjames Stephen; drawing by G.F. Watts

James Russell Lowell

J.K. Stephen

ia Jackson aged fourteen

Julia Stephen; photograph by
Julia Margaret Cameron

slie and Julia Stephen, 1892

Talland House, St Ives (The Ramsey's house in Virginia Woolf's *To the Lighthouse*)

Leslie Stephen with his daughter Virginia, photographed by G.C. Beresford, 1902

called it the Unknowable. Beyond the finite lay the Infinite of which man had no knowledge though he was conscious of its existence. Beyond all matter lay Energy which could not be increased, diminished or affected by man's actions, and hence lay beyond their control. Spencer wedded these two notions and produced a First Cause which had created and operated the Universe. This was 'a manifestation of an Unknowable Power'; and this Power was defined by calling it 'an Infinite and Eternal Energy whence all things proceed'. What was Spencer's Unknowable? It was not an Hegelian Absolute: for the Absolute was the sum of all existence including all separate and smaller totalities reconciling them with the unique – it was ideally knowable because it was finite – whereas the Unknowable lay outside totality. Sometimes he treated it as a Transcendent Power, a mode of Being higher than human intelligence and will, just as these human attributes are higher than and transcend mechanical motion. Sometimes he treated it as an Immanent Substance into which our consciousness lapsed when we died – for a future life was not, according to Spencer, a credible concept. Spencer's Unknowable might be more remote than Arnold's Eternal Not-ourselves making for Righteousness or Comte's Grand-Etre; but remote or not, it was a God.

Or take the case of W. R. Greg who in 1850–1 published a book called *The Creed of Christendom* which Morley in a characteristic flight of rhetoric declared had shaken 'the fabric of early beliefs in some of the most active minds' at Oxford. Justin McCarthy, however, declared that the book never made one convert or suggested a doubt to anyone, and his testimony is to be preferred since the book was only in its second edition eighteen years after publication. Certainly Greg expressed doubts about the historical truth of the Gospels, but he continued to call himself a Christian – the kind of Christian, Fitzjames Stephen unkindly declared, who appeared to be much like a disciple 'who had heard the Sermon on the Mount, whose attention had not been called to the miracles, and who had died before the Resurrection'. Then there was Buckle who roasted French free-thinkers and declared, as if Gibbon had never lived, that 'in our country the truths of religion are rarely attacked except by superficial thinkers'. And yet by the logic of his writing his God, said Benn, 'like Carlyle's, never did anything and indeed would have fallen in the opinion of his worshipper by any attempt to meddle with such a perfect mechanism as the universe'. The 27-year-old Lecky's desire not to offend when he published his *Rationalism in Europe* was so pronounced that George Eliot described him as one who, while not denying that in certain circumstances and with certain limitations all the radii of a circle are equal to one another, adds that the spirit of geometry must not be pushed too far; or as one who does not know how far he goes but knows that he does not go too far. Not that George Eliot wished to carry a torch. Her novels contained hardly a hint of her loss of faith; and though in intellectual circles she was well known for her translation of Strauss's *Das Leben Jesu*, she declared that she had 'too profound a conviction of the efficacy that lies in all sincere faith, and the spiritual blight that comes with no-faith, to have any negative propagandism'. The Wadham Positivists published nothing until 1859, the *Westminster Review* took care not to outrage clerical opinion, and this policy of reticence continued, broadly speaking, to be accepted until Stephen's time. Small wonder that the American free-thinker, Moncure Conway, was struck by the way in which English rationalists thought it their duty to conceal their views, and noted how James Martineau was censured by Tennyson and Colenso by Matthew Arnold for publishing their opinions.

It is true that ever since the days of the Tractarians at Oxford there had been well-publicized defections and what Victorians called 'unsettling' books. Francis, the brother of John Henry Newman, in his *Phases of Faith* (1842) had attacked Christian dogma as a series of immoral propositions; but he declared himself a theist. Three of Carlyle's disciples, Sterling, Clough and Froude, each caused a mild stir when they abandoned Christianity, but Carlyle himself was regarded as a bulwark against irreligion and rationalism. Harriet Martineau's *Letters on the Laws of Man's Social Nature and Development* (1851) achieved a certain scandalous success, but people dismissed her as a bluestocking. The rationalists were determined not to sell all their shares in an investment which still showed a good return. Even the saint of rationalism was hesitant. In 1844 Mill had written to Comte that 'the time has not yet come when it is possible without prejudice to our cause to make open attacks upon theology'. But Mill's followers were confident that he was an agnostic and might even declare himself to be so. They were to be disillusioned. In 1874, the year after his death, his *Three Essays on Religion* were published which contained as was expected some sharp criticisms of Christian orthodoxy. They also contained an apologia for theism. Rationalists were dismayed to see Mill dispassionately weighing how far Christianity fulfilled inescapable spiritual needs, how far it succeeded, as well as failed, in redeeming man's corrupt consciousness. Scrupulously honest, Mill admitted that there was nothing in human knowledge to disprove the claim for immortality of the soul. The terror of death was a reality and he was not prepared totally to dismiss this panacea even though he himself believed that the only way man could diminish that terror was to improve society so that more human beings could lead happier lives. 'They who have had their happiness can bear to part with existence; but it is hard to die without having lived.' Some critics have seen Mill's hesitations as yet another indication of his well-meant but hopeless attempt to blend Coleridge with Bentham and muddy the waters of rationalism at the very time when they needed clearing. Others have seen in them the mark of a distinction of mind which, however deficient in imagination and impeded in considering morality by pseudo-scientific criteria, was warning his followers that there were more things in heaven and earth than could be dreamt of in his philosophy. The puzzle remains. How was it that in England open opposition to Christianity was so long delayed and left to men of Stephen's generation to make?

G. M. Young described the 1850s as 'a time of preparation: of deep-seated folding, straining and faulting: old strata and new shifting against each other into fantastic and precarious poises'. They were also a time of domestic tranquillity after the stormy and hungry 1840s when revolution seemed to threaten. The reforming zeal of the Whigs and of Peel was exhausted. Parliament dissolved into factions, party ties loosened, pressure groups flourished, great movements and agitations died away and prosperity flourished. Much as in the 1950s, a century later, there was a lull after a rainstorm of reform and in it grew an unspoken agreement between both middle and working class to become more comfortable and more conscious of what they could enjoy in common. The philosophic radicals grew old and disintegrated; the Tractarians were a defeated remnant, their great leader having seceded to Rome; and the evangelicals in the Church grew fat and complacent, no longer a despised body fighting against inhumanity but a powerful party with a keen eye for acquiring sees and advowsons. Respectability reigned – that decent aspiration to show that one lived according to the received customs of the day and accepted constraints willingly as the guarantee of a settled life. Palmerston epitomized the mood, a figure who symbolized hard-working, sound administration, no nonsense abroad and no dogmatism at home, the politics of the possible, not lazy like Melbourne but not divisive like Peel, a man of robust common sense who made no one uncomfortable by displaying brilliance and wit. People in the 1850s and 1860s wanted stability. The great poets and novelists did not picture themselves as estranged from their society: on the contrary they wrote to entertain and edify their fellow citizens and were not ashamed to be didactic. In many walks of life people woke up to the fact that what they were doing affected others and were prepared to accept regulation. The professions organized themselves and codified their articles of association and of conduct. Games such as cricket and football, sports such as racing and boxing, were controlled henceforth by arbitrating bodies. The most powerful of the forces of social control were the most intangible: the influence of home and the head of the family; the notion of gentility – the obligations and prestige of the gentleman who should set the tone for society. But among the institutions which brought stability and decency to society few doubted that the most important were the churches. Ever since the Civil War men had feared fanaticism and religious controversy as an unstable explosive. The unmasking of Guy Fawkes and the Gunpowder Plot was celebrated annually and still found its place in the Book of Common Prayer; and the building of nearly two hundred churches by Bishop Blomfield in London was regarded as more important than the building of prisons or workhouses. Long ago Collins, the Deist, had been asked why he made his servants go to church. He had replied: 'I do it that they may neither rob nor murder me.' Voltaire himself had not wished his opinions to become those of tailors and bootmakers. So if a clergyman stepped out of line, he could expect to be taken to task. Jowett's commentary on the Atonement in his edition of St Paul's Epistles (1855) earned him the humiliation of being forced publicly to subscribe to the Thirty-Nine Articles on his appointment to the Regius Chair of Greek at Oxford. Alfred Benn believed that the attacks on *Essays and Reviews* (1860) were especially virulent because their authors were suspected of holding more subversive views than they printed. The liberal was haunted by the spectre of his own creed. He stood for tolerance; and tolerance meant respect for men's consciences and the multiplication of religions and creeds. So long as the State could change affairs through argument and the due process of law, government would still be respected. But if it permitted law and order to be undermined by too violent and radical agitation, wild spending would destroy property, and it would be only a question of time before the revolutionaries would be supplanted by a tyrant drawing his authority from plebiscites. Was not patriotism rooted in religion and anti-clericalism in democracy? In the first edition of *Culture and Anarchy* Matthew Arnold urged that the leaders of the demonstration which broke down the Hyde Park railings should be hurled from the Tarpeian rock; and in the year of the Paris Commune *The Times* rebuked Darwin for publishing *The Descent of Man* which was like dropping a match into a powder magazine.

Philosophically the rationalists might be strong but politically they were weak. Indeed they hardly existed at all as a political force. How different from the Continent! In Turgenev's *Fathers and Sons* young Arkady Kirsanov, home from the university with his Nihilist friend Bazarov, decides to re-educate his father: his first step is to remove the volume of Pushkin which his father is reading and to lay in his hands Büchner's *Force and Matter*, the famous Bible of materialism which, published in 1855, ran into fifteen editions by 1884. (Arkady, like many young students, thinks he can change the elder generation by giving them the right books to read.) On the Continent, where the Revolution coloured all intellectual configurations, free-thought was an integral part of liberal and socialist theory: a flank force to pin down the clerical wing of the opposing army. The European rationalists fighting autocracy found an appropriate cosmology in the scientific monism forged by the German scientists Haeckel and Büchner. There science became a weapon in the struggle against reaction, gunpowder to blow up the hypocrisies of the existing social order. In 1877 Virchow attacked Haeckel and the Darwinists at a scientific congress at Munich on the grounds that since Social-Democrats supported Darwin, all anti-revolutionaries must renounce him and his works. The conflict between religion and rationalism was submerged beneath the dissonances of a profounder social discord.

In England, on the other hand, free-thought never became specifically associated with a political movement or party. The Tories depended on the Methodist vote until the middle of the century and looked askance at the Tractarians who, had they been encouraged, might have turned religious belief into a serious political issue. The Liberals accepted the support of free-thinking radicals, but they were tied to nonconformity and their most famous leader was a High Churchman. Political alignments cut clean across religious differences. Nor were the politically conscious working class necessarily militant free-thinkers. One of the themes of Halévy's history of nineteenth-century England is how those groups among the lower classes who hated Anglicanism as a weapon of upper-class coercion, found their natural home in the Nonconformist communions, which provided an alternative to the upper-class religion. The free-thinkers themselves were untainted by revolutionary ideas: the patient, ethical humanitarianism of the secularists, who looked to the day when science and knowledge would dissipate want and injustice, belonged to the reformist, not to the revolutionary, tradition of the English working-class movement. The Secularist Society was formed after the collapse of Chartism by Holyoake, the leader of the Co-operative movement. Its most successful member, Bradlaugh, ended his life significantly as a Liberal MP orating against socialism; and Stephen was one of the few upper-middle-class agnostics who came to his defence in 1880 when he was fighting to be admitted to the House of Commons to take his seat. Free-thinkers were never united in a nation-wide body. The middle-class rationalists dissociated themselves ostentatiously from the vulgar outpourings of the secularists. Huxley, a devoted lecturer to working-men's associations, intervened with some reluctance when Foote, the editor of the *Freethinker*, was imprisoned in 1883 under the Blasphemy Laws: though he admitted that he had not read Foote's writings, he took it upon himself to pronounce that rightful freedom was not attacked when a man is prevented from coarsely insulting his neighbours' honest beliefs. George Eliot declared that she had very little sympathy for free-thinkers as a class, and Herbert Spencer and Eliza Lynn

Linton[1] echoed her sentiments. The middle-class rationalists observed in secularism the streak, faint though it was, of social discontent which, they sensed, was different from their own protest, namely that intellectuals must be considered seriously by the political rulers of the country. They were divided from the secularists by those class differences in temperament and education that can be bridged only by intimate friendship or by a common political affinity. The middle-class rationalists apprehended that the political reforms they desired could be achieved within the framework of Liberalism rather than by an alliance with secularism; they could be achieved so long as public opinion was assured that rationalists were not agitators or subversive, but healthy corpuscles in the life-blood of respectable Liberalism. Stephen himself had little contact with the secularists until he became an honorary associate of the Rationalist Press Association. But he was at least among those who protested against Foote's harsh sentence after his trial. Although the rationalists might appear to be better equipped for the intellectual contest, the churches held the political initiative. As Stephen said, they assumed axiomatically that if I hit you, it's zeal, but if you hit me, it's blasphemy.

The morality of the middle-class rationalists was almost as orthodox as that of their opponents. Whereas in Europe Romanticism challenged Christian ethics – in the exotic and profound interpretations of life by Baudelaire, Nietzsche, Tolstoy, Treitschke and Marx – in England the religious revival tamed the second generation of Romantics with a few exceptions such as Swinburne. Insulated from political revolution to a greater degree than Continental intellectuals, Victorian thinkers continued broadly to accept the Protestant ethic, anglicized foreign immigrants such as Goethe and Kant and appeared to be unaware of the spiritual maquis burrowing underground in Europe. This was why the debate on Christianity was conducted in intellectual terms and why it is right to study the philosophic background in such detail.

There was another reason why the critical spirit of enquiry was so long held in check. It was opposed by a force no less strong in mid-Victorian times – the trust in authority. It was to this trust that Newman and the

---

[1] Mrs Lynn Linton (1822–98) was in her youth a radical and agnostic. She oscillated between spiritualism, mesmerism, communism and conservatism, and married her husband (an inoffensive friend of Mazzini's), so she said, on God's express instructions. A. W. Benn commented: 'The gifted lady professed agnosticism with complete sincerity . . . but it was a creed that contrasted rather oddly with her credulous nature.' The most vigorous of her many novels is *Under Which Lord?* in which a Ritualist priest shatters the happy home of an agnostic gentleman by setting his wife against him and kidnapping his daughter whom the priest compels to enter a convent when he himself goes over to Rome. Victorian society would have described the book as 'v'y parful'. She was a voluble anti-feminist, wrote a famous article for the *Saturday Review* entitled 'The Girl of the Period', and dedicated a novel in which she attacked Girton College (where one B A marries a policeman by proposing to him) 'to the sweet girls still left amongst us who have no part in the new revolt but are content to be dutiful, innocent, and sheltered'.

Tractarians appealed, it was to this which the Roman Catholic Church owed so many of its converts. It was to this that young men turned when they wrote to Carlyle or Ruskin pledging their faith in them. It was this that made those Victorian periodicals which provided short answers to the topics of the day so popular. The respect for authority was hardly likely to be diminished when it was matched by the hostility to intellectuals so characteristic of the businessman or industrialist. The longer one studies the first three decades of Victoria's reign the more one realizes how the rationalists were on the defensive, beleaguered by not only the orthodox but by seers, liberals and vigorous champions of common sense who were more concerned to shore up the walls of institutions than to rebuild them to accommodate industrialism and the mounting population.

The young radicals waited gloomily, counting the hypocrisies of their elders. Why did Palmerston contrast Britain's liberties with the authoritarian regimes in Europe and then back the slave-owning South against the North in the American Civil War? And then Palmerston died. In May 1866 there was a run on the banks and, while Matthew Arnold flinched, Stephen urged the demonstrators who marched from Poplar and Whitechapel to Hyde Park not to put their trust in Whig or Tory aristocrats but to be guided by 'the cultivated intellect and talent of the country'. As he wrote in the *North American Review*, this clarion call would hardly have roused the blood of the demonstrators; but Disraeli got the message and parliamentary reform became an issue. When it at length came about and a Liberal government was returned in 1869 which was to open the universities, nullify the payment of church rate and disestablish the Irish Church, the floodgates opened and a torrent of books and articles attacking Christianity poured out of the press. In that year Morley, who had succeeded G. H. Lewes at the age of 28 to the editorship of the *Fortnightly Review*, published Huxley's article 'On the Physical Basis of Life' and Froude followed his lead in accepting similarly outspoken articles in *Fraser's Magazine*. In the 1870s Swinburne's *Songs before Sunrise* (1871) and James Thomson's *The City of Dreadful Night* (1874), Winwood Reade's *The Martyrdom of Man* (1872), the Duke of Somerset's *Christian Theology and Modern Scepticism* (1872), Mill's *Three Essays on Religion* (1874), Walter Cassels's *Supernatural Religion* (1874–7), Romanes's *A Candid Examination of Theism* (1874) were the most prominent books published; there also appeared as articles the contents of Morley's *On Compromise*, Stephen's *Essays in Freethinking and Plainspeaking* and part of *An Agnostic's Apology*, Tyndall's *Belfast Address* (1874), Huxley's *Animal Automatism* (1874) and Clifford's essays. Even Greg's *The Creed of Christendom* began to sell and between 1873 and 1883 went through six editions. In 1877 James Knowles, founder of the Metaphysical Society, established a new review, *The Nineteenth Century*, especially to discuss religion and philosophical questions and in the second half of that year every number of the *Fortnightly* contained an attack on theology. Intellectuals notoriously split up as soon as they show signs of uniting but there was one slogan which kept the radicals together. That was the unity of truth.

The Assertion of the Unity of Truth

The unity of truth was a tenet as much on the tongues of the orthodox as of the rationalists. Dean Buckland, the first professor of geology at Oxford, said: 'Truth can never be opposed to truth.' The Newtonian tradition was so strong because it explained how society was governed by the same laws as obtained in the physical world. Locke suggested that ideas in the mental universe corresponded to Newton's particles in the physical universe. Like the planets ideas were attracted to each other by the law of gravitation. In psychology this was called the principle of the association of ideas where the two springs of action (or Newtonian forces) were observation of the outside world and 'the internal operations of our minds, perceived and reflected by ourselves'. Thus Christian dogma could not be true and at the same time defy the laws of geology or common morality; if it could no longer receive the flood of new ideas pouring down the streams of science and philosophy, then it must be false. The question they asked was: what is the *evidence* for believing this to be true? and evidence was defined as empirical examination of facts. G. M. Young cites Newman's fifth proposition of liberalism as crucial to mid-Victorian thought: that it is immoral for a man to believe more than he can spontaneously receive as being congenial to his mental and moral nature. 'I being what I am, and the evidence being what it is, am disposed more or less strongly to think so-and-so.' This was Mill's legacy.

His bequest bore fruit in the best of all agnostic novels, *The Story of an African Farm*. Olive Schreiner wrote a parable on Mill. A stranger who is passing across the veldt tells the German farm boy, Waldo, the parable of a hunter who spent his life stalking a beautiful white bird, the white bird of Truth, whose reflection he had seen in the lake when shooting wild-fowl soaring above him. He sets snares for the bird, the snares of credulity and a cage of a new creed, until he learns that nothing but Truth can hold Truth. And so he leaves the valleys of superstition and sets out to climb the mountains of Reality. On he climbs till he reaches a vast precipice of stone towering above him. Year after year he cuts steps up the precipice until, old and wizened, he reaches the summit – and sees rising above him a yet higher range. But as he lies dying he consoles himself:

'Where I lie down worn out other men will stand, young and fresh. By the steps that I have cut they will climb . . . They will never know the name of the man who made them. At the clumsy work they will laugh; when the stones roll they will curse me. But they will mount, and on *my* work; they will climb, and by *my* stair! They will find her, and through me! And no man liveth to himself and no man dieth to himself.'

Then slowly from the white sky above, through the still air, there came something falling, falling, falling. Softly it fluttered down, and dropped on to the breast of the dying man. He felt it with his hands. It was a feather. He died holding it.

We can never catch the bird of Truth itself, but we can discover particles of truth so long as we are not decoyed by superstition or sensuality, so long as we are never deterred by the fear that a new truth can endanger society. 'The question must always be, not whether [the disputant's] argument be positive or negative, but whether it is *true*,' pontificated Francis Newman. 'The longer I live', wrote Huxley, 'the more obvious it is to me that the most sacred act of a man's life is to say and to feel, "I believe such and such to be true." ' The hunter was rewarded by the sight of the steps he had cut and the feather that fell into his hands; the hunt itself was unimportant. Lessing had declared that it was the search for Truth that gave life meaning and the hunter happiness, rather than the attainment of truth. Huxley contradicted him. 'I protest that if some great Power would agree to make me always think what is true and do what is right, on condition of being turned into a sort of clock and wound up every morning before I got out of bed, I should instantly close with the offer. The only freedom I care about is the freedom to do right; the freedom to do wrong I am ready to part with on the cheapest terms to anyone who will take it off me.' The passage gains from the Evangelical phraseology. 'My only desire', George Eliot wrote as a young girl, 'is to know the truth, my only fear to cling to error.'

But how could one know what is true? The answer was given in a revealing document by W. K. Clifford, *The Ethics of Belief*. Examine the state of your mind strictly, says Clifford, and renounce the sin of believing what is pleasant. Belief is not a matter of taste. Suppose you accuse a man wrongly, you cannot excuse your statement by protesting that it was made in good faith when in fact you could have easily obtained evidence of his innocence merely by a little hard work. You have behaved dishonourably however sincere your accusation. To plead to a charge of sending an unseaworthy vessel on a voyage that you thought that she was well rigged and sound is no defence. Why did you not find out the facts first? Belief is not a private possession, a 'self-regarding' property, which affects no one else in the community. Our beliefs influence our fellow men and create the world in which posterity will live, and false beliefs poison the air as surely as noxious factory chimneys. We must not accept the traditional answers blindly. Life lays on us a duty to ask questions. Clifford may have recalled the maxim of Jacobi: 'A question rightly asked is a question half answered', and he stressed that it was by asking questions that knowledge has progressed. To stifle questions because they conflicted with an accepted code of belief was wrong and fatal to the development of the human race. This echoed Mill's *On Liberty*. 'No one can be a great thinker who does not recognize that as a thinker it is his first duty to follow his intellect to whatever conclusions it may lead.' But the note had changed by the 1870s. Mill's plea for tolerance was sharpened by his disciples. By all means, said Clifford, let us be tolerant, but do not let us forget our duty to expose error. Whereas Mill seemed almost to forget that belief was related to action, the connection between the two was uppermost in Clifford's mind. To relate belief directly to action was in line with the revision of associationist psychology which Alexander Bain had been making in mid-Victorian times. In *The Senses and the Intellect* (1855) Bain argued that thinking is silent speech or motionless action. All human activity, including thought, is transmitted by nerve-currents which are related to the nerve system of our five senses. Man is a mechanism, and thought is just one of the mechanical processes which connect our actions to our sensations. To feel is to think is to act. Bain defined belief as 'that upon which a man is prepared to act'.

The clearest statement of the new hard-nosed reaction to belief was John Morley's *On Compromise*. Morley did not appeal for toleration of unpopular opinions: he attacked everyone who did not hold them. Morley denounced the sentence from Mill's posthumous essays on theism (though he prudently refrained from mentioning his source) which ran 'a religious belief may be morally useful without being intellectually sustainable'. No matter that Renan had said that ancient beliefs had charm, or that Pattison had argued you needed to see how congenial anachronistic beliefs had once been. Your first duty was to expose error. The trouble was that men and women were congenitally lazy and cowardly and preferred to profess themselves Christians while acting like pagans and thinking as agnostics. Those who sneered at Roman Catholics for taking their beliefs on trust were usually the very men who would never dare dissent from the majority. No one should delude himself that progress was automatic. Unless we discarded or built on the foundations of creeds which could no longer be credited society would stagnate. Morley's prose resembles a municipal garden: it is so intersected with purple passages, so teeming with floribunda roses, begonias and calceolarias that the mind is dazed by the riot of colour. Indeed nearly all the leading free-thinkers rose on lyrical wings to describe the ardour with which they pursued truth. George Eliot after a scene with her father about her refusal to attend church experienced the sensation of joining 'the ranks of that glorious crusade that is seeking to set Truth's Holy Sepulchre free from a usurped domination'. In this apotheosis Huxley soared upwards with Morley when he denounced Mill's contention that 'toleration of error is a good thing in itself, and to be reckoned among the cardinal virtues'. No political, aesthetic or sentimental defence for sham beliefs could be accepted. Huxley was proud to reject the consolation of immortality: 'Had I lived a couple of centuries earlier I could have fancied a devil scoffing at me . . . – and asking me what profit it was to have stripped myself of the hopes and consolations of the mass of mankind. To which my only reply was and is – Oh, devil! Truth is better than much profit!'

The rationalists hardly considered the possibility that 'truths' were of different varieties or that it is convenient to use one set of propositions in one field, but inconvenient to use them in another, e.g. that it is a matter of convenience whether a straight line is defined as the shortest distance between two points or as the line following a ray of light. St Thomas Aquinas, centuries before, had attacked the school of Siger of Brabant for using a similar intellectual device which had been elaborated with singular ingenuity by the great Mohammedan Averroës of Cordoba in his commentaries on Aristotle. Intelligence, reasoned Averroës, falls from God upon man in a series of descending spheres so that the theologian may interpret Scripture allegorically while the common people interpret it literally; and Siger took this doctrine a stage further when he argued that dogmas which were true theologically were not in that form true philosophically. Of the many great contributions to thought which Aquinas made none was so far-reaching as his separation of faith from reason; and thus he too in reconciling the physics and metaphysics of the Ancients admitted a division in thought itself. Of course he wanted to stick faith and reason together as tightly as possible. But what ultimately mattered was to prove the truth of revelation; and since reason had its limits, faith must be the ultimate arbiter. He crushed philosophers who were not content to be theologians first.

Heresies, however, are as resistant to destruction as some viruses are to antibiotics. Double truth reappears over the years in many different forms – most notably in Machiavelli. Clifford could hardly have been expected to be acquainted with the medieval Schoolmen but he was well aware of the significance of the most recent developments in mathematics. He himself had pointed out the fallacy in Kant's contention that space could be proved by the eternal truth of Euclidean geometry to exist independently of our experience, by showing that alternative means of measuring space, such as the non-Euclidean geometries of Lobachevski and Riemann, existed which were as valid as that of Euclid and could be adopted whenever they proved more convenient. His chapter 'On the Bending of Space' in *The Common Sense of the Exact Sciences* prefigured the general theory of relativity. He saw that geometry was not absolutely true but depended on multiple postulates: e.g. Euclid's fourth postulate 'All right angles are equal' itself postulates the principle of elementary flatness. Curiously enough, Newman raised this question. Writing with the dispute between Galileo and the Church in mind, Newman said that we cannot decide who was right until we know precisely what motion is. And he added: 'If our sense of motion be but an accidental result of our present senses, neither proposition is true and both are true, neither true philosophically, both true for certain practical purposes in the system in which they are respectively found.' This was the sentence which made Froude renounce Newman – who was, of course, not trying to make a revolution of logic but attempting to extract himself from a moral difficulty. But that curiously astute though twisted figure Mark Pattison was alive to this problem. In 1878 he delivered a paper to the Metaphysical Society entitled 'Double Truth'.

Stephen was close to Morley in these years and shared his view that the toleration of palpable evils was not always preferable. But he may have been faintly repelled by the rhetoric of his party. 'A love of truth', he wrote of Huxley, 'must be considered, if I may say so, as a regulative rather than a substantive virtue. Abstract truth is rather a shadowy divinity, though a most essential guide in pursuing any great enquiry.' He must have disappointed those who ten years earlier saw him as one of the up-and-coming radicals in Cambridge. By 1874 he found himself unable to vote in the General Election for Gladstone, let alone for Disraeli. He had seen that truth did not prevail in politics. He had seen that men's interests divert them from following truth. Just how far this stalwart supporter of positivist history and philosophy was prepared to deviate now became apparent. For some time he had been working on his history of eighteenth-century thought and in the course of so doing he had come to conclusions which differed from those of Mill and Comte in one crucial respect. He no longer believed that ideas changed society. It was the shifts in society which changed men's ideas.

Chapter Eight

ᘓᘓ ᘓᘓ ᘓᘓ

THE REVELATION OF THE
EIGHTEENTH CENTURY

Stephen's Rehabilitation of the Augustan Age

'To me the Eighteenth Century has nothing grand in it,' wrote Carlyle,

except that grand universal suicide, named French Revolution, by which it
terminated its otherwise most worthless existence with at least one worthy act –
setting fire to its old home and self; and going up in flames and volcanic
explosions in a truly memorable and important manner. A fit termination, as I
thankfully feel, for such a century. Century spendthrift, fraudulent, bankrupt;
. . . What could the poor Century do, but at length admit, 'Well, it is so, I am a
swindler-century, knowing hardly any trade but that in false bills . . . and have
nothing to eat. What remains but that I blow my brains out, and do at length one
true action?' Which the poor Century did; and many thanks to it, in the
circumstances.

Just as Lytton Strachey's friends saw within five years of his death the
appearance of G. M. Young's magisterially omniscient rehabilitation of
the Victorian age, and not long after that the acclamation of the St
Pancras hotel as a luminous relief from the concrete and cladding of
contemporary architecture, so Carlyle lived to see a renaissance of the
century he despised, and a change in architectural fashion. The Queen
Anne revival, a by-product of the pre-Raphaelites, was pioneered by the
Victorian intelligentsia in revolt against over-elaborate Gothic structures
and ponderous stucco buildings, indeed the tyranny of having to build to
a 'style'. In the new revival there was not one prescribed style but a
mixture of themes, Moorish or Jacobean, rooms decorated with blue and
white china or Japanese prints, Chelsea porcelain, Persian carpets and
asymmetrical furniture reflecting the lightness of Sheraton. Red brick
pediments, tipped roofs, weather boarding, gables and fanlights recalled
the domestic style of Queen Anne's time and gave meaning to that phrase
of Swift which Matthew Arnold was to make famous, 'sweetness and
light'. Sidgwick saw to it that the second women's college at Cambridge,
Newnham, was built by his friend Champneys in this style where the

corridors had windows at both ends for cheerfulness in contrast to the spartan spare Girton whose Tudor Gothic buildings designed by Waterhouse urged its inmates to strengthen their moral fibre so that they could prove they could compete intellectually on equal terms with men.

Among the intellectuals who were the protagonists of the new architectural movement were some who were reviving eighteenth-century literature. Voltaire, so repulsive to Carlyle, was praised by Lecky who declared that 'beneath his withering irony persecution appeared not even criminal but loathsome'; and Morley wrote studies in praise of Voltaire, Rousseau and Diderot. In fact Mark Pattison had claims to be the first to rediscover that age with his contribution to *Essays and Reviews* in which he praised the theologians in the sixty years after the Glorious Revolution for trying to find and justify God through reason rather than authority. But the most powerful advocate of using the eighteenth century to illuminate the nineteenth was Leslie Stephen with his articles in the *Cornhill* on Augustan literature and with the classic work which established him as a scholar.

The History of English Thought in the Eighteenth Century began with a critical analysis of the philosophers and theologians of the times. The second volume dealt with the moralists, economists, political theorists and with preachers, poets, novelists and writers; and it ended with a review of the reaction at the end of the century against the age of reason by Methodists, Romantics and the Gothic revivalists. Stephen saw the work as a study in ideas. This had the disadvantage that the Pope of the *Dunciad, The Prologue to the Satires* and *The Rape of the Lock* never appeared on the stage and the poet made his entry solely as the didactic author of the *Essay on Man*, which Stephen rightly thought was not his best work. There was a further disadvantage. Stephen arranged his history according to subject. This meant that individual thinkers were analysed at length in more than one chapter: Hume, for instance, appeared in all twelve. Faintly vexing as this can be, the reader is carried away by Stephen's skill in pursuing an argument or tracing a descent – when for instance he absolved Berkeley from the charge of scepticism by emphasizing the bishop's belief in the necessity of efficient causes, a proposition which he then deftly showed was destroyed by Hume. He did not expect his readers to be acquainted with works covered with the dust of years, and the days are long past when a formidable littérateur such as the Liberal politician, Augustine Birrell, could call a young critic an 'ignorant dog' for not having read Hoadly. But if the reader turns to those pages in Stephen's book which deal with the Bangorian controversy he will enjoy a rollicking account of a man whose 'style is the style of a bore; he is slovenly, awkward, intensely pertinacious, often indistinct, and, apparently at least, evasive . . . We owe, however, a vast debt of gratitude to the bores who have defended good causes, and in his pachydermatous fashion Hoadly did some service by helping to trample down certain relics of the old spirit of bigotry.' Page after page is enlivened by Stephen's gusto, his delight in metaphor, his humour, indeed his sense of fun, and the scholar's delight in exploring byways while never losing sight of his main argument.

That last quotation may suggest that Stephen, like J. M. Robertson or A. W. Benn after him, would have praised in the manner of Comte those thinkers who most nearly presaged the day when religious superstition and metaphysical explanations would vanish and be replaced by the purity of positivist thought. Deists might still be misguided but had they not sloughed off the skin of revealed religion? Paine might be crude but had he not struck a blow for the poor, for liberty and freedom of thought? But Stephen was not an orthodox positivist. Certainly he left no one in doubt that he thought all the complex arguments advanced by the theologians to be riddled with contradictions. Certainly he set out to rescue the English empiricists, Locke, Berkeley and Hume, from Taine's contention that they were insignificant even if he did some injustice to Descartes and Spinoza in the process. Certainly his eye gleamed when he set about a clerical bully such as Warburton who 'led the life of a terrier in a rat-pit worrying all theological vermin . . . probably no man who has lived in recent times has ever told so many of his fellow creatures that they were unmitigated fools and liars'. Warburton was such an ardent servant of Christ that he 'proposed to cudgel his opponents into Christianity and to thrust the Gospel down their throats at the point of a bludgeon'. He used Warburton to satirize the folly of believing that although miracles used once to occur, at a later stage God ordained that Nature should be ruled by law.

But when Stephen considered the Deists he pulverized them, and said that they and their orthodox opponents seemed to him 'to be engaged in a fencing-match rather than in a life-and-death struggle with pointed weapons'. Nor did he spare their faults. He hated Shaftesbury's aristocratic detachment, dismissed Bolingbroke as 'little more than a rake and an intriguer', to attack whom 'would be like criticizing Gothic architecture from the sham cloisters of Strawberry Hill'. He found Mandeville's 'grin simply detestable . . . His brutality and love of paradox revolt us as a display of cynical levity.' It was not only the Deists whom he pursued. The more rational a theologian was the more ready Stephen was to pin him to the wall. Paley's writing, he admitted, was as sharp and cold as ice and it preserved his theology from decay; but only because he froze it. Stephen caused particular offence, at a time when Paley had just replaced Butler as the Christian apologist whose *Evidences* were set for many years to come for the examinations taken by schoolboys entering Oxford and Cambridge, by concluding a devastating analysis with the sentence, 'Had there been a competitive examination for the construction of the best form of reptile, the Almighty artisan would have had every chance of carrying off the prize.' Stephen even had a good word to say for the intuitionists who by insisting on the importance of conscience forced people to ask what the origin of virtuous impulses was: what room had Hume left for conscience, remorse or sin? What, *per contra*, were the utilitarians reduced to saying? That God had spoken from Sinai and had declared to all his creatures that vice was a bad speculation? Like a counsel with a shady financier in the witness box before him, Stephen was quick as a flash onto the language these utilitarians used to illustrate how sordid their prospectus was. If Heaven existed, it seemed unlikely, as Tucker imagined, that it resembled a bank where the security was perfect, the interest enormous and where those sufferers wronged in this world will be rewarded by an angel who will 'privately slip the proper sum into my hand at a time when I least expect it'.

Stephen was too hard on the wretched Deists even though they were intolerably dull. Benn later showed that European thinkers drew ideas from them. Indeed Lechler had shown what influence they had in Germany, laying a train of thought that was to ignite Strauss and Renan; but Stephen ignored him. Stephen, so John Bicknell argued, was trying to have it both ways: if the Deists were to be commended for their strictly intellectual approach to religion he had no right to criticize them for failing to attract the mass audiences which the Methodists drew. When Stephen declared that their 'creed was never alive', did he consider the *Essay on Man* to be petrified? Or Addison's hymn, 'The Spacious Firmament on High', faint? Or did Newton inspire no one? Stephen should have made allowances that in the reign of Queen Anne Deists had to use cautious language, especially as he admitted they had to fight in fetters. He made some modifications in the third edition of his book, but Toland had to wait for Stephen to write his life for the *DNB* to get proper amends. Why did he lean over backwards so far?

To Stephen the Deists were simple-minded optimists. 'A purely optimistic creed always wants any real stamina; for the great stimulant of religious emotions is a profound sense of the evils of human life.' That was why Stephen preferred Bishop Butler to Paley. Butler admitted in the *Analogy* that in this world suffering exists, pain exists, evil exists; and that man's conscience is his best hope of renouncing evil. He praised him for telling men to observe what happened in the world and by analogy learn about God. He praised him for arguing that wickedness or folly brought their own Nemesis: virtuous races would inherit the earth because the feeble or vicious ones would have contravened divine law. He praised him for denying that revealed or natural religion provided a satisfactory explanation for the existence of evil: faith alone was the road to understanding the truths of religion. 'The mere fact of injustice in the world cannot, as Butler sees it, prove justice in the next.' Naturally Stephen wanted to destroy the argument from analogy. What was one to say of a theology in which God made men liable to sin; placed them where they were prone to sin; and damned them everlastingly for sinning? But Butler had a grandeur that the shallow Deists lacked. And so had Johnson. Unlike Johnson Stephen would not have despatched Jean Jacques to the plantations, for he admired him even more than Montesquieu because Rousseau despised the encyclopaedists of the salon. Still, Johnson 'was as good a moralist as a man can be who regards the ultimate foundations of morality as placed beyond the reach of speculation'. In fact the contempt for philosophy exemplified by Johnson was typical of most Englishmen and hence they 'avoided the catastrophe of a revolution'. Johnson embodied Stephen's creed: stick to the facts, clear your mind of cant, don't whine, resist anarchy. His 'morality is not the highest because it implies an almost wilful blindness to the significance of contemporary thought . . . but it expresses the determination to see the world as it is, and to reject with equal decision the optimism of shallow speculation and the morbid pessimism of such misanthropists as Swift.'

Stephen did not sell out his own party. He had two rationalist heroes, Adam Smith and Hume. Smith was a hero in establishing immutable laws of economics: he was the first social scientist, the first to do what Stephen believed must be done for the whole of social behaviour. Hume's morality left something to be desired and he may have held 'a vague belief suggesting that there must be something behind the veil and something, perhaps, bearing a remote analogy to human intelligence'. But Hume was the most powerful assailant of pretentious dogmatism and the timid avoidance of ultimate difficulties so characteristic of his time. Stephen was wrong to assert that Hume denied causality: all Hume said was that it could not be proved. He was right to praise him for the virtue of intellectual candour. No one can read Stephen's volumes without knowing where he stood. He might take Bentley's side against Collins or Burke's against Paine, but what he was determined to show was that taking sides was unhistorical. All men fall into fallacy. Some have more honest or acute or original minds than others. But for Stephen the duty of the historian of ideas was to disentangle the web which thinkers have spun and show where the strands led. He ought to declare which strands were coarse and hempen and led nowhere and which were of the finest silk. If the historian grasps the silken threads he can pull himself into his own times. Like Pope's spider, he 'feels at each thread and lives along the line'.

Stephen was as hard on the ethos of the ruling class and the intellectuals who justified it as he was on the Deists. He exposed the assumption of the aristocracy that they and the adherents of their class alone were destined to rule, and was far from an uncritical admirer of Locke, whose mysterious compact, said Stephen, anticipating C. B. S. Macpherson, was 'the tacit consent of mankind to the inequality of property'. Kings now became the managers of a joint stock company and the Kingdom passed into the hands of a class. Paine had neither the acuteness of mind nor the principles to attract Stephen, but on religion 'with all his brutalities he has the conscience of the hearers on his side' and he 'really feels for the people instead of treating their outcry as so much "puling jargon" '. Of course Stephen would never have come out on the side of the Jacobins, and he tended to lump together Priestley, Price, Paine and Godwin as revolutionaries even though their arguments sprang from widely differing principles. But often enough he showed how a man's beliefs reflected his class interests and were suspiciously near to humbug.

Humbug was what he detested. Paine had denounced the Old Testament as 'a history of wickedness that has served to corrupt and brutalize mankind'. Bishop Watson of Llandaff answered him. Watson, said Stephen,

> went through the regular parade of defence; he compares the massacre of the Canaanites to an earthquake; accounts for the anachronisms in the Pentateuch by later interpolations; and thinks that the young women reserved from the slaughter of the Midianites were not intended for debauchery, but for slavery, a custom everywhere prevalent in early times. He intersperses becoming bursts of indignation with edifying passages of Christian unction and prays for the soul of his opponent. Nothing could be more becoming from a non-resident bishop and professor of divinity.

For similar reasons Stephen did not care for the sentimentalists who preceded the great romantic poets. Sentimentalism was 'a kind of mildew which spreads over the surface of literature' and 'the mood in which we make a luxury of grief'. There was a daily increasing number among the upper classes of rich and idle persons who found the cultivation of the finer feelings to be 'a very amusing luxury'. When reading Richardson we should remember that 'the casuistical moralist passes easily into the prurient analyser of moral hotbeds'. That literary prostitute, Sterne, wept over the miseries of mankind without the smallest desire to diminish any of them. No wonder the stage was left empty for the Methodists to fill it and turn the clock back to the seventeenth century.

Such were Stephen's principles and preferences. But what methods did he use to establish them?

Society the Progenitor of Ideas

The confident ease with which *The History of English Thought in the Eighteenth Century* is written conceals an enigma. It was first spotted by John Bicknell who, reading Stephen's introduction, saw that it described a book considerably different from the one which he in fact wrote. It is primarily – and particularly the first volume – an analysis of the writings of all thinkers of importance, and their writings are examined to see what they said, why they said it and whether what they said was coherent or self-contradictory. Where a thinker went wrong or was inadequate or neglected some major principle or problem – as all thinkers do – how and why did he do it? Stephen asked first whether the writer he was examining was logically consistent: did his argument stand up? Next he asked whether the writer's morality, his notions of right and wrong or of what is valuable and important, withstood scrutiny – the kind of scrutiny which many literary critics have exercised. For instance, does a thinker show that for him the ability to experience joy and endure sorrow is the hallmark of the good man?

Gradually Stephen covers his canvas with figures like Bruegel's personifications of proverbs and parables, figures startlingly full of life and some even as grotesque and pitiful as those Bruegel painted. It is the picture of an endless debate in which each thinker rises from the benches to buttress or refute the last speaker's arguments. Many other matters make their appearance – biographical details, social background material and psychological factors. It is in the classic mode which other historians of ideas in England and America adopted at any rate until well after the Second World War: G. H. Sabine's great textbook on political thought is a notable example.

But this method, Bicknell argued, ran counter to the declaration Stephen made in his introductory paragraphs. He had declared that it was social developments that changed men's ideas, not 'the activity of a few speculative minds. A complete history of thought would have to take into account the social influences, as well as the logical bearing of the varying phases of opinion.' Why did Stephen not follow his own precept? Why did he not reveal the social forces which were moulding what thinkers wrote and why did he not show how changes in social structure brought about changes in intellectual fashion? Instead he ploughed through the illogicalities of each thinker inevitably suggesting that had they been more rigorous they would have had a greater influence upon the way men and women looked at their world.

It was all the odder because not only had Stephen in his review of Buckle shown his hand, but in his introduction and throughout the text he scattered clues for historians to pick up. Mill did not convince him that

truth in the end must prevail: men's interests deflect them from accepting
the truth. Mill was not, of course, entirely wrong in believing that 'each
great man has contributed some permanent element of truth'. Speculation
advances. No creed can survive if it is shown decade after decade to go
contrary to fact. Although the history of thought is not unilinear, it
'moves in a spiral curve'. But progress is far slower than thinkers care to
admit. Different communities, and classes, and sects and trades or
professions reject this discovery or adhere to that fallacy long after
savants think they have settled the matter. Men think, and more
important still they feel, in symbols; and when science engenders a new
idea and destroys their myths, they are aggrieved that science cannot also
invent new symbols, a new metaphor as Tennyson did in *In Memoriam*
for the conception of a child, 'A soul shall draw from out the vast And
strike his being into bounds.' Men cling to creeds long in tatters because
they symbolize things men think important. Nor are thinkers themselves
immune to this condition of humanity. Intent on excising some
monstrous excrescence which for long, like a cataract, has impaired
human vision, they forget how much of the remainder of their thoughts
rests on the common assumptions of the day: so that a thinker in the
future will wonder how he who so clearly diagnosed the disease in the
crystalline lens of his opponent's eye could be so unaware of his own
astigmatism which prevented light focusing on his retina.

Ideas, then, may originate in men's minds but they will come to nothing
unless the social structure shifts and the ideas can germinate in the cracks.
In the first paragraph he wrote, Stephen asked why Hume's writings made
at first so little impression, as if they had crackled into flames beneath
Warburton's insolence and flaked into ashes under Johnson's dogmatic
contempt. Yet within a few years English thought and literature were to
be transformed as if Warburton had never scoffed and Johnson had never
spoken of Hume going to milk the bull because truth would yield him no
milk. 'A cold blast of scepticism seems to have chilled the very marrow of
speculative activity.' How did this occur? Stephen answered: unknown to
us now, or people then, there were thousands of inferior thinkers puzzled
by the very problems Hume considered and coming up with answers like
his own. And this could not have happened unless social conditions had
been favourable to them.

There was another social factor which came into play: the conflict of
classes. In his second volume Stephen described how as statesmen were in
danger of losing only their place at court, and no longer their heads, they
no longer supported poets by taking them into their household. They
turned patronage into a joint stock enterprise whereby they got their
friends to subscribe to a new edition of verses. The poet became the
political follower of the nobleman. But as a new middle-class audience

arose, and the press developed, the nature of patronage and hence of literature changed, and the novel began to grace ladies' tables. The change owed nothing to philosophical enquiry. It was caused by the racial, historical, social and political relations which played upon 'the individual peculiarities of mind and temperament [in ways] which defy all attempts at explanation'. That people grew tired of old forms of literature or were no longer satisfied by old expressions of religion was not because they suddenly developed an interest in the veracity of their logic but because the old social structure was breaking up. 'The change was not due to the gradual growth from below of a new order of ideas displacing the old, as the buds in spring push off the dead leaves of the previous season. A creed dies first at its extremities . . . As society developed, as knowledge extended, and the instincts shaped themselves into new forms, the doctrine broke down', and different classes wearied of this or that until in the end people perceived that they were living in intellectual chaos and a new thinker arose to sort out the mess.

Stephen's greatest contribution to the history of ideas in his time was to argue that different classes used different modes of thought. The *Zeitgeist* was an illusion. Like Mark Pattison he refused to treat the eighteenth century as the age of reason, or even to treat it as the battle of reason against superstition. What satisfied one class left another cold; and the reason why the eighteenth-century rationalists went down before the passion of the Methodists or the visions (and vapours) of the Romantics was because they lost the ability to appeal to a changing public. Stephen had the courage to admit that there would often be an antipathy between the enlightened and the lower classes; but he left no one in doubt of his view that the vulgarization of ideas into slogans was but another form of superstition. He had all the horror of the academic intellectual for those intellectuals in politics who fudge and simplify issues in order to make them acceptable to a mass audience or to the party faithful. That 'leads to downright dishonesty and disregard of the great virtue of intellectual candour'. If the intelligentsia fail to share their beliefs with the mass of the people because, like Voltaire or the Deists, they fear the consequences, revolution is likely to follow.

Why is it that truth and error march hand in hand, why can one who holds the most enlightened views which reach out to our times simultaneously retain beliefs which have long been discarded? Here Stephen played his scientific trump card. Beliefs are governed by the same law which Darwin discovered in Nature. Beliefs which patently contradict the facts of life cannot survive, because the species would perish if it continued to rely on them; but 'an erroneous postulate' may survive so long as it does not imperil the species. 'The progress of the intellect necessarily involves a conflict.' Gradually the race adapts to changing circumstances and men's beliefs conform more nearly to the world of facts and the material wants of society. People begin to question the claims of Christianity to be the unique path to salvation not because they first lose faith in its theology but because 'the extension of commercial activity' reveals that millions of men in India or China believe in other faiths more ancient and no less intricate. In the end it was not Hume nor even the thousands of little Humes who were responsible for the decline in speculative thought in the second half of the century. The social conditions were responsible – and Stephen at the end of his life gave some examples: the absence of any popular ideology as in France; the contentment of people in general with the rule of squire and parson; and the subordination of the Church to the laity.

John Bicknell provided two solutions to the puzzle he set himself. Introductory paragraphs so far from being the first words an author writes are frequently the last. Those paragraphs reflected in fact a change of plan which occurred during the genesis of the book. Maitland showed that Stephen's annotations of the books he read in the sixties became steadily less political and more concerned with religious thought. By 1871 he was planning to write a history of Deism; and he did so to emphasize that, dull as they were and safe as it was to consign them to the dust and the moths, they had cut the ground from under the feet of the orthodox. Unfortunately for them, they could only call metaphysical spirits from the vasty deep whereas Stephen in his generation could hand down the tablets of Darwinian science. Voltaire might be worth a bushelful of them but the English empirical tradition contained the seeds which were to grow and flower in nineteenth-century science. Stephen saw analogies between 'the warfare of science and theology of the nineteenth century and the warfare of reason and dogma in the eighteenth'. In an article he contributed to the *Fortnightly Review* in 1872, Stephen called Shaftesbury the Matthew Arnold of his time, an advanced Broad Churchman, who tried to save morality by abandoning an indefensible theology; Clarke a Dean Mansel invoking not Kant but Descartes, Spinoza and Leibniz to rescue that theology; and Mandeville a precursor (offensive though he was) of Bentham's theory of morals and of Darwin. 'Shaftesbury like Mr Disraeli is plainly "on the side of the angels", and would have taunted Mr Huxley with his great-grandfather the ape. Mandeville replies in the spirit and sometimes with the very arguments of a modern believer in natural selection . . . The world is the scene of a huge struggle of units driven by conflicting passions.' The pressure of those passions caused the social and intellectual changes which others ascribe to Providence. 'The modern man of science and the old reckless cynic agree in the resolution to look facts in the face.' It is true that Stephen did not reprint these breezy analogies in the *History*. But they show why he wrote it.

The second reason Bicknell gives we have already examined. Evangelicalism drove back the rationalists, seemingly recovering all the ground they had won. This could never have happened if logic alone determined men's opinions. That was why Stephen concluded that the impersonal forces of history, not ideas, changed men's minds. How could he have concluded otherwise? To him, and as he thought all dispassionate men, Hume, and after Hume the utilitarians, had won the ideological battle. If they were driven temporarily from the field it must be for other reasons.

We shall see later what weight to give to Stephen's theory of social change and causation in the balance. The notion of thousands of little Humes scattered through the towns of England and Scotland in the second half of the eighteenth century may appear fanciful or even alarming, but Stephen can himself be numbered among the little Marxes who a century later were coming to the conclusion that material forces condition or determine all other forces. Stephen was very far from asserting that economic forces or the means of production are primary, although before the *History* took shape he envisaged writing a work on political economy. Indeed, he would fall back sometimes on such shady concepts as national character or human nature to get himself out of difficulties. But he would have agreed that 'it is not the consciousness of men which determines their existence but on the contrary their social existence determines their consciousness' – he would have agreed even with the word 'determines' because he believed that eventually scientific laws governing human development would be discovered. But the fact that he stood Mill on his head made little impression on his contemporaries.

The Augustan Age the Progenitor of Agnosticism

The reviews which greeted the *History* were predictable. The orthodox had no doubt in which direction the argument led and were pained. The free-thinkers were disappointed. As a Positivist, Cotter Morison was disappointed that the work lacked a European, or indeed a world, dimension: what he meant was that Comte played so little part in the argument. Mark Pattison complained that Stephen did not use the comparative method (always a safe card to play in a review). Stephen's close friend, Croom Robertson, was perplexed that Stephen had not explained why the English were obsessed with morality; for him Stephen had not been dispassionate enough and had been 'over-ready to see the present in the past and to reckon with the long departed as if they were adversaries or allies'. This was certainly not the view of J. M. Robertson who years later deplored Stephen's 'vacillating way of throwing sirloins to Cerberus . . . and of betraying alarm lest the author should be thought to be civil to people whom it has been customary to treat with insolence'. He thought Stephen had been unfair to the Deists and to Paine. In his view the work needed greater breadth of philosophic genius to make it a classic, though he later admitted that it was 'the first massive and scholarly contribution to the critical history of English freethought'. Pattison, too, it must be said, was generous in praise and now had the convenient excuse for abandoning his own study of the eighteenth century. (Stephen in thanking Pattison admitted how vile the index was and excused himself by saying that after his bereavement he 'wanted some mechanized task to occupy my mind. It is bad – I humbly admit'.) Some have accused Stephen of having totally neglected the history of scientific thought – where are Watt and Stephenson, where is Dalton? But an author is entitled to confine himself to the field which he chooses, and the field Stephen tilled was wide enough: he did not have to prefigure Merz's four-volume history of nineteenth-century European thought.

In his usual deprecating way Stephen referred to the *History* in later years as an act of audacity: 'subsequent work, requiring more thorough research, has led me to believe it is very superficial'. It is not superficial but perhaps it tries to do too many things at once; and certainly Stephen had not worked out what he meant when he said that impersonal changes in society dictate changes in ideas. Nor is it clear what he meant by his hope that history would eventually become a science. He accepted the current rationalist interpretation of science as the sole corpus of verifiable knowledge (which is right). But he then went on to declare that it was the only method of description which laid down 'the base to which all other truth in so far as it is discoverable must conform' (which is either a repetition of the first proposition or false). The introductory paragraphs are singularly opaque; and the asides in the second volume show us how puzzled he is to describe the processes he believed to be at work more than how in fact ideas change.

On one charge he must be acquitted. If as Maitland said he had been on a few occasions a little too ready to accept at their face value the criticisms of the orthodox by the *bien-pensants*, his account did not lack that quality by which he set such store: intellectual candour. Moreover, all the time he was writing the *History* and for years after, he was publishing the articles which he was to collect in *Essays in Freethinking and Plainspeaking* and in *An Agnostic's Apology* which could have left no one in doubt about his beliefs. Huxley gave him a name for them. Perceiving, said Huxley, that he was surrounded by men who were certain that 'they had attained a sort of "gnosis" – had, more or less successfully, solved the problem of existence; while I was quite sure I had not and had a pretty strong conviction that the problem was insoluble', he coined the word agnostic.

It suited Stephen better than Huxley. Huxley was certain of too many things. He had already in fact found his own 'gnosis', the scientific metaphysic of the time. Huxley was no bigot. He voted on the School Board for teaching children the Bible because he believed the Authorized Version to be the heritage of Englishmen. (He was less successful as a Fellow of Eton in getting the Provost and Fellows to see that science should also be part of their heritage.) Nor did he, like the German materialists, declare that only Force and Matter existed: he wrote an admirable exposition of Hume and condemned materialism as heartily as dogmatics. But that truth was not all of the same nature never struck him. So in effect he repudiated his own definition of agnosticism and took much of the meaning out of the word by calling it the method of following the intellect fearlessly and of not pretending that conclusions were certain if they were not demonstrable. Arguing with the new authority of science, with his flair for controversy, his articles more widely read, especially among the working class, Huxley was a more famous figure than Stephen. But A. W. Benn had no doubt that it was Stephen who made agnosticism a party name. 'His masterly handling of the dialectical weapons told for much; literary skill and charm told for more; but character and sincerity told for most.'

Stephen revalued the word agnosticism in the currency of the language.[1] He purged the word of Spencerian Unknowables and anti-clericalism. He did not try to prove a particular point in Christian theology to be untrue. Theology and metaphysics were not so much untrue as unreal; they simply did not correspond, he thought, to the impression which totality made upon an educated man's senses. Grasping the wider implications of Darwinism, Stephen constantly returned in English Thought in the Eighteenth Century and in his controversial essays to the impossibility of squaring the circle and constructing a system which would include an other-worldly Omnipotent Power and a rational Supreme Being at work in this world deducible by Natural Theology after the fashion of Paley. He passed from dogma and ontology to epistemology; to the dialectic in which Newman and Maurice defended Christianity; thence to the nature of conviction and morality; and thereby presented agnosticism as a comprehensible response to religion.

What arguments did he use and what effect did they have upon the churches?

[1] The other leading agnostics were Tyndall and Morley, as well as, to a lesser degree, Spencer, Meredith, Winwood Reade and J. R. Green. Tyndall echoed Huxley. Morley was a determined anti-clerical and in 1870 he wrote that it must be an objective to 'disband that sinister clerical army of 28,000 in masks'. He unkindly described the clergy as intellectual eunuchs who had been rendered 'mentally sterile' by the laying-on of hands, a ceremony not unlike the Turkish method of providing 'incomparable guardians of the Seraglio'.

Chapter Nine

CCCCCCCCCC

AGNOSTICISM

The Case Against Christianity

In 1885 the Reverend J. E. C. Welldon was appointed headmaster of Harrow and, preening his feathers, told the Church Congress which he had been invited to address that atheism was gaining ground at Cambridge, a fact all the more deplorable since he had noticed when he had been a Fellow of King's that loss of faith among undergraduates was always followed by loss of morality. Revisiting his old college soon afterwards he was greeted by that devout Christian, Henry Bradshaw, whom Mommsen thought the most impressive scholar he had met in England, with the words, 'Well, Welldon, you lied: and what is worse you knew you lied.' Seven years later G. M. Trevelyan, then a 16-year-old Harrow schoolboy, who had acquired a reputation for mild eccentricity when he was practically the only boy in the school to support the Liberals in the General Election of 1892, refused to be confirmed. 'Quite right, boy', said his housemaster, E. E. Bowen, the author of so many of the Harrow songs; and with the tact and affection for his charges which characterizes the good schoolmaster, did not offer to discuss the matter further. The next year there appeared a book which Trevelyan read as an undergraduate at Cambridge and which did indeed confirm him – in agnosticism. What able and fiery undergraduates think today is not invariably what everyone thinks tomorrow: but even if Trevelyan was to describe himself later in life as an agnostic 'but an Anglican agnostic', within a few years more and more of the intelligent young came to think as he did. The book he read was Stephen's *An Agnostic's Apology*.

When Stephen said that dogmatic Christianity was unreal, he meant that there was no possible way of knowing whether the propositions put forward by theologians were true or false. There was a simple answer to the theologians. You denied that their subject had any right to exist. The agnostic declared that there were limits to human knowledge and that beyond those limits no man had the right to be dogmatic. Had the theologians, who set out to chart the ocean of infinity, settled anything? If you listened to the bedlam within the churches today you would see that on no single point were they agreed. Theologians defined 'the nature of God Almighty with an accuracy from which modest naturalists would shrink in describing the genesis of a black beetle', yet plenty of sincere Christians and fellow theologians disagreed with them. Why should agnostics be ashamed of professing ignorance in matters still involved in hopeless controversy? Even if the theologian called the metaphysician to his aid, he remained confounded. Spinoza told us that God was the First Cause and that he was the cause of all effects down to the most remote: this led us straight to a pantheism in which there was no need of a Revelation, and God became the cause of evil as well as of good. The doctrine of predestination attempted to overcome this difficulty, but whole armies of pious logicians lay sunk in this Serbonian bog; and if the theologian abandoned predestination and argued that the chain of causation was broken by the gift of free will to man, God still remained the source of good and evil, since he alone through bestowing his Grace could make a man good. Either God was not omniscient or else his design was so incomprehensible that men, such as Mansel, had to acknowledge their ignorance so abjectly that they became agnostics in spite of themselves. Nor were the orthodox who deserted reason for Revelation less agnostic. They claimed that intuitively man could know God; but whom God would save and whom he would damn, whether the damned would suffer in hell for ever or for a space of time, whether he would grant his uncovenanted mercies to certain gross sinners, they could not say. Butler admitted in his *Analogy* that both Nature and God appeared to us unjust. Even as Nature wasted millions of seeds in the fertilization of plants and animals, so God wasted millions of souls. Why, then, should we be comforted by the Incarnation? We were told that often in this world the helpless and innocent suffered tortures in order to fit them for the world to come. If that were true of God, what moral being would worship him? In fact the whole workings of the universe were shrouded in total mystery. And yet agnostics who acknowledged this to be so were reviled! Until the time when the orthodox could point to a single truth which they had discovered and which would stand scrutiny, agnostics would be content 'to admit openly, what you whisper under your breath or hide in technical jargon, that the ancient secret is a secret still; that man knows nothing of the Infinite and Absolute; and that, knowing nothing, he had better not be dogmatic about his ignorance'.

The agnosticism of the orthodox should not astonish us. The whole fabric of Christianity is a dream, woven out of the pathetic desires of human beings suffering the miseries of life on earth and perplexed by man's final end. Christianity is distinguished from other religions by the certainty of its message that man shall not die and pass into timeless oblivion but shall live in heaven after a corporeal resurrection. The Christian argues that human existence would be a hideous mockery without this belief. Yet the Jews had no such consolation: God rewarded Job in this life with oxen and asses, and sons and daughters, for his patience. The Christian sought no such recognition: his portion is in the world to come, where he will obtain his reward. His reward – but also his punishment; for the ungodly will descend to hell. What is hell? On this point Christians were by no means agreed. Dean Farrar stated that, if even a part of mankind were to suffer eternally the torments described by Tertullian, or by Dr Pusey, he would ask God to let him perish as the beasts of the field. This did credit to the Dean's heart – is not the doctrine of hell, which condemned to punishment the mass of mankind who were not Christians, abominable? But what of the Dean's head? Apparently he was still willing to propagate a religion the majority of whose priests entertained such a belief. Stephen recalled the remark of his eldest brother Herbert to Fitzjames at Eton: 'If you can enjoy yourself [in heaven] when you think of me and my like grilling in hell-fire, upon my soul, I don't envy you.'[1] If it were admitted that these threats of hell-fire which Catholics had hurled at Protestants and Presbyterians at Socinians, and which had in the past been held to be assured for infidels and unbaptized children – if it were admitted that these threats were the offspring of mistaken zeal, why not admit that the whole fabric of heaven and hell were mistaken zeal as well? Historical Christianity was not a corpus of revealed and unchanging truth; it changed with the times. If hell were to be abolished, or to consist of Judas Iscariot and one or two others, what was to become of heaven? In fact the whole conception of an anthropomorphic God dispensing justice on the Day of Judgement was outworn, and that of heaven and hell unreal.

Not only was the Christian morality of rewards and punishments immoral. It was also anti-social. Christians held rationalists guilty of the sin of materialism, of neglecting spiritual values and of worshipping the carnal. But they were themselves guilty of the vice which Blake condemned. They feared the flesh, identified matter with evil and escaped from the world into asceticism. Marriage was regarded as a concession to frailty, a monastery a better society than the world. The ultimate end of man became the duty to save his soul and not to do his duty in that station to which he was called. The very men who stood accused of materialism were those who had done most for the improvement of mankind.

[1] C. E. Norton referred in a letter to a rebuke administered to Stephen by Carlyle for his lack of reverence. Stephen had written to Norton 'the old prophet loves hell and answered me on the authority of Dante that it was made by Infinite Love. To which I could only reply naturally in the words of the good Briton whose parson assured him that whom the Lord loveth he chasteneth, "I wish he weren't so bloody fond of me." '

(Stephen should not have added that atheists and materialists had led the movement for the prevention of cruelty to animals. It is hard to believe that he did not know that this honour belonged to the Evangelicals.) The churches seemed oblivious to the condition to which industrialism had reduced people. Priests ought not to declare that poverty was a blessing: they ought to show that they wanted to abolish pauperism.

Religious belief also was the parent of intolerance. People argued that there was no harm in the churches supplying what men most desired to hear: consolation was much needed on this earth. Yet this argument conveniently neglected the past in whose annals the churches stood blackened by their lust for persecution. No doubt those days were past. 'The impossibility of organizing an effectual persecution now is admitted,' said Stephen, living seventy years before our times, which witnessed the most terrible of all the persecutions of the Jews. But the authority of the churches was of a different order from that of the other authorities to whom we every day submitted. The authority of science could be checked by analysing its conclusions and premises; the authority of a ruler or assembly was open to the arbitrament, if necessary, of a revolution; but the authority of a church was illimitable for it purported to come from God himself. Perhaps Stephen had in mind Newman's dictum that 'religious error is in itself of an immoral nature'. The Church's dogma was the truth, heretics were those who denied the truth and had to be exterminated; religion was, therefore, a danger to society. Since the truth of any religion could not be proved to the satisfaction of a majority of mankind, since it proved to be, on examination, the offspring of a shot-gun marriage between tribal rites and superstitions, should we not regard all religions with tolerant scepticism? Let man acknowledge authority in matters of opinion only when authority could be demonstrated.

Looking at our past as it stretches behind us in long perspective, we can see that the religious wars of the sixteenth and seventeenth centuries had taught men that to demand conformity without which a state could not survive (*cujus regio eius religio*) was an error. The reverse was true. Unless there was religious toleration the State would be destroyed. Owen Chadwick remarked that Luther's great dictum, 'Here stand I, I can do no other', in the end had to be adopted as binding for most nineteenth-century states. Stephen admitted the longer perspective to be true, but there was quite enough petty persecution around in his time to justify his argument; and while earnest Victorian rationalists would not have been disposed to join fanatical Protestants in crying No Popery, the actions of Pius IX in proscribing liberalism and proclaiming Papal infallibility were to induce that split among the intellectual aristocracy over Irish Home Rule which resulted in numbers of them leaving the Liberal party rather than agreeing with a policy which would put Protestants under Catholic rule. Paradoxically in some countries today the churches, feeble as they are, are almost the sole remaining institution capable of protesting for, even if they cannot protect, the rights of individuals against the State or against tyrannical corporations.

The Atonement and the Resurrection

One doctrine of the Church seemed specially important to the Victorians although to their alarm it began to be regarded as more and more difficult to understand or even to justify. This was the doctrine of the Atonement. Whereas the Incarnation has become for Christians in this century the crucial dogma of the faith, for the Victorians the Atonement, containing within it as it did the promise of redemption and salvation in a world to come, was of supreme importance because it was the key which unlocked discussion on the Four Last Things – heaven, hell, death and judgement. As we have seen, the doctrine of the Atonement in its cruder forms began to be attacked, and so consequently did the cruder exegeses of rewards and punishments. In an age when any child of 10 could have been expected to have witnessed at least one death among his family and cousins, Evangelical tracts declared as a fact that the blessed would recognize each other in Heaven and asked 'Reader, have you a little white-robed warbler in the celestial choir? Are you content to see his face no more for ever?'

But what of hell? For Christians ranging from Newman to the Calvinists it was the place of eternal punishment, a place to which most of mankind seemed likely to go. How many would suffer? Bishop Colenso, it will be remembered, when asked by an intelligent Zulu how many animals had entered the Ark and how much food they required, began a series of statistical enquiries into the Hexateuch such as convinced many outside, and even some bold spirits inside Cambridge, that Wranglers could be simple-minded men. With the same hardihood a Congregationalist minister got down to the figures and calculated that only 10.5 million out of 938 million souls would be saved. The goulish glee of those who chortled over the torments of the damned and played upon the neuroses of the melancholic and hysterical so revolted some sensitive clergy that they reinterpreted the nature of eternal punishment – to the scandal of the orthodox as F. D. Maurice and the Essayists were to discover. Among them was another Congregationalist minister, a young man called Edward White, who in 1844 wrote a book in which he speculated that eternal punishment was not suffering so much as privation and that immortality depended on spiritual regeneration. It was a book which Leslie Stephen's father kept by him.

Whereas in the second half of the twentieth century the Catholic Church has turned to practices which were at the heart of Protestantism, such as the sermon and worship in the vernacular, so in the second half of the nineteenth Protestant churches discovered in the once hated Roman concept of purgatory a way out of their eschatological difficulties. Purgatory seemed almost to have been invented for a world accepting evolution. What could be more apposite than the existence of a place where men and women could learn to repent of their sins and approach sanctification before attaining final communion with God? As for hell, that began to empty rapidly. By the end of the century there were universalists, such as Samuel Wilberforce's son, arguing that unless the God of Love wanted to save all creatures in his creation he could be only limitedly good and limitedly omnipotent: which was absurd.

Geoffrey Rowell traced the course of the flood of speculation in mid-Victorian times about the nature of hell and, as so often happens when a topic becomes too fashionable, the waters ran into the sands of the inevitable disillusion which followed. The theory of universal salvation no doubt brimmed over with compassion. But there had to be a doctrine of hell to remind men how serious the consequences of a life of evil in this world could be, however much those consequences were pictured not as fire and brimstone but as alienation and estrangement from God. At the end of his life Gladstone was alarmed that hell no longer seemed to concern theologians. He might also have noticed that whereas in his youth the immortality of the soul had been accepted as a fact, it was now regarded as open to proof. It was certainly open to doubt; and it is worth while pausing to compare the way in which three agnostics, Huxley, Stephen and the Oxford philosopher F. H. Bradley reacted to the most poignant of all Christian desires.

Huxley spoke very much as the apologist for science. He argued that the soul could not be 'deduced from scientific methods of reasoning from the facts of physical or psychical nature' and that such evidence as exists suggested that immortality was a delusion since 'it is a law of nature that living matter is always dying, is being resolved into its lifeless constituents and cannot live unless it dies'. The immortality of the soul was an assertion of fact contrary to the laws of science and we had no evidence to support it. He let his reader suppose that the laws of science would provide a verifiable proof that immortality was false. But Huxley was also stirred by grief to rise far above such cold arguments. When one of his sons died, Charles Kingsley sent him messages of condolence to which Huxley replied in a letter which was made public in his official biography and much quoted by agnostics. In it he said:

As I stood behind the coffin of my little son the other day, with my mind bent on anything but disputation, the officiating minister read, as a part of his duty, the words 'If the dead rise not again, let us eat and drink, for to-morrow we die.' I cannot tell you how inexpressibly they shocked me. Paul had neither wife nor child, or he must have known that his alternative involved a blasphemy against all that was best and noblest in human nature . . .

Kicked into the world, a boy, without guide or training, or with worse than none, I confess to my shame that few men have drunk deeper of all kinds of sin than I. Happily my course was arrested in time – before I had earned absolute destruction – and for long years I have been slowly and painfully climbing, with many a fall, towards better things. And when I look back, what do I find to have been agents of my redemption? The hope of immortality or of future reward? I can honestly say that for fourteen years such a consideration has never entered my head. No, I can tell you exactly what has been at work. *Sartor Resartus* led me to know that a deep sense of religion was compatible with the entire absence of theology. Secondly, science and her methods gave me a resting place independent of authority and tradition. Thirdly, love opened up to me a view of the sanctity of human nature and impressed me with a deep sense of responsibility.

'If there is any place', wrote Owen Chadwick, 'where the temptation to justify the ways of God to man is misplaced, it is a graveside.'

Stephen, as usual, concentrated on the unreality of the doctrine. It was exceedingly difficult, he argued, to imagine a soul without a body – a difficulty shared by theologians who in the past had consigned souls to an undeniably corporeal hell. Consciousness came to us only through our senses. 'It is impossible', he wrote, 'even to understand emotions in an eternal state where nothing happens.' If we were to believe in the immortality of the soul, why should we not accept the Hindu belief in its pre-existence and therefore in its transmigration? An agnostic should be prepared to admit that the soul might be immortal but he could see no reason why immortality should take the form taught by the Church. Stephen was not much taken with the arguments Huxley used to suggest that the soul could not exist or be immortal. As an agnostic he thought it futile to dogmatize. No doubt scientific statements were true because their conclusions were independently verifiable, but it was as vain to prefer one contention as the other. In his essay 'The Vanity of Philosophizing', Stephen came to agree with Sidgwick who argued in the Metaphysical Society that the field in which empirical enquiry could be used to effect was narrower than commonly supposed.

Stephen believed that the churches deliberately preached heaven and hell to their congregations at all seasons so as to assault their emotions and awaken within them the sense of their sinfulness; and precisely because our emotions are so prone to overrule our intellect, the belief in immortality retained its hold on men's imagination. Yet could anyone who reflected really believe in a life to come? Stephen, too, could speak from the anguish of grief. Shortly after the death of his first wife he asked which of the two spoke the truth from his heart during the service for the

Burial of the Dead: the Psalmist who declared that we fade away like the grass and that to live long was but labour and sorrow? or St Paul with his magnificent rhetoric but tortuous arguments, which sought to convince us against reason that we would rise incorruptible? As he pursued this argument Stephen paused to give his reply.

Standing by an open grave, and moved by all the most solemn sentiments of our nature, we all, I think – I can only speak for myself with certainty – must feel that the Psalmist takes his sorrow like a man, and as we, with whatever difference of dialect, should wish to take our own sorrows; while the Apostle is desperately trying to shirk the inevitable and at best resembles the weak comforters who try to cover up the terrible reality under a veil of well-meant fiction. I would rather face the inevitable with open eyes.

And yet more telling than the indignation of Huxley or Stephen was the disdainful, swift style of F. H. Bradley who hovered high in the skies like an eagle and then swooped to seize an argument in its talons and tear it to pieces. Bradley was the finest Hegelian of the day, McTaggart and Bosanquet included. Indeed he was the most formidable philosopher of the Victorian age. His philosophical writings were incomprehensible to the majority of the reading public but there was something touching yet remorseless in the manner in which one by one he set out the arguments for immortality and one by one dismissed them. Asked whether the soul existed, he wondered how if our finite universe is contained within the Absolute, a finite object could expand to contain a constant and potentially infinite supply of newly created souls. And if people object that the question of survival after death, or even the existence of the soul, should not be based on philosophic conjecture about the nature of the Absolute or the Universe, then he must answer that 'the balance of hostile probability is so large that the fraction on the other side to my mind is not considerable'. But surely man's craving for immortality should be taken into account and find satisfaction? 'That every demand of every kind must, as such, be gratified – this . . . is surely irrational.' But if there was no immortality, then how could strict justice be paramount? 'No, I am sure that is not so. There is a great deal in the universe, I am sure, beyond mere morality; and I have yet to learn, even in the moral world, that the highest law is justice.' But after all, must not pain and sorrow in this world somehow be made good? 'On the whole and in the whole . . . this is fully the case. With the individual . . . it is not the case. . . . I cannot argue that all is wrong if individuals suffer. There is in life always, I admit, a note of sadness; but it ought not to prevail nor can we truly assert that it does so.' But if hopes and fears were to be taken away, would not people be less happy and less moral? 'Perhaps, and perhaps again more moral and more happy . . . Whoever argues that belief in a future life has, on the whole, brought evil to humanity has, at least, a strong case . . . If human beings now are in such a condition that, if they do not believe what is probably untrue, they must deteriorate . . . it is well for a race of beings so out of agreement with their environment to make way for another race constituted more rationally and happily. And I must leave the matter so.'

Bradley did not leave the matter so. He too thought of love and the grave, and he added a footnote.

I have said nothing about the argument based on our desire to meet once more those whom we have loved. No one can have been so fortunate as never to have felt the grief of parting or so inhuman as not to have longed for another meeting after death. But no one, I think, can have reached a certain time of life without finding, more or less, that such desires are inconsistent with themselves. There are partings made by death and, perhaps, worse partings made by life; and there are partings which both life and death unite in veiling from our eyes. And friends that have buried their quarrel in a woman's grave, would they at the Resurrection be friends? But in any case the desire can hardly pass as a serious argument. The revolt of modern Christianity against the austere sentence of the Gospel (Matthew, XXII, 30)[1] is interesting enough. One feels that a personal immortality would not be very personal, if it implied mutilation of our affections. There are those too who would not sit down among the angels, till they had recovered their dog. Still this general appeal to the affections – the only appeal as to future life which to me individually is not hollow – can hardly be turned into a proof.

What is a True or a False Belief?

Religion for Stephen was belief. What did you mean by your beliefs and how and why did we believe statements were true or false?

These questions were the chief subject of discussion in the seventies and particularly in the Metaphysical Society. He had no high regard for this Society, and thought that four out of five members had failed to pass the *pons asinorum* of metaphysics. In philosophy, as in religion, Stephen was something of an agnostic. He was delighted when Charles Francis Adams, son of the American statesman, quoted with approval his aphorism, 'the grave humorists who call themselves historians of philosophy seem to be at times under the impression that the development of the world has been affected by the last new feat of some great man in the art of logical hair-splitting'. Doctor and saint might argue about it and about, but metaphysicians could never disguise the most notorious conjuring trick in theology whereby God, or the Supreme Power, was identified with the anthropomorphic God of the Gospels. Stephen had been taught as a child to treat beliefs in a singularly literal style. At the day-school at Brighton he had heard the headmaster question the boys at prayers. 'Gurney, what's the difference between justification and sanctification? Stephen, prove the

[1] 'For in the resurrection they neither marry, nor are given in marriage, but are as the angels of God in heaven.'

omnipotence of God.' No wonder he detested Ritualism, 'surely the most vapid form of sacerdotalism ever imposed upon effeminate natures'. He feared that man's love of beauty would quench his thirst for truth. 'Admit that the Pope is not, in the plain sense of words, a judge of controversies but a master of ceremonies, and the difficulty [of accepting Christianity] disappears.' Stephen wanted to return to 'the uncomfortable Protestant habit of demanding statements of fact'. It was therefore with some relish that he turned to examine the ripest example of the *mens theologica* in the Catholic Church in England.

Faced with the problem of evil in the world which 'inflicts upon the mind the sense of a profound mystery, which is absolutely beyond human solution', John Henry Newman declared that uninstructed reason could never solve the difficulty. Logic by itself would never convince men of the truth of any statement and the reasons for conviction were too subtle and complex to be expressed in syllogisms. Religious truth could not be expressed in logic. 'Life is not long enough for a religion of inferences, we shall never have done beginning if we determine to begin with proof. Life is for action. If we insist on a proof for everything, we shall never come to action; to act you must assume, and that assumption is faith.' Stephen agreed that Newman showed that we believed countless things on insufficient evidence, but Newman asked us to make not simply an *intellectual* act of belief on the evidence before us, but a *volitional* act; we were guilty of lack of faith if we believed by balancing probabilities. We must believe first – 'the logic has been felt before it is proved'. Stephen answered that if you 'allow conviction to be influenced by the will, you must admit that a belief morally right may be intellectually wrong'. Newman had simply produced out of the hat a logical device for calling an unanswerable objection a 'difficulty'. Moreover, though he was always pouring scorn on the Protestant conscience, he was compelled to appeal to it in the end when he claimed that in man's conscience resided the Illative Sense or 'sensible intuition'. Between Newman's mind and Stephen's yawned a gulf too wide to bridge. Stephen showed where an empiricist cannot accept Catholic dialectic; and he could hardly be expected to agree that propositions for a Catholic were true only when the Church recognized them as such, or take pleasure in Newman's deliberate scepticism which was designed to show that the dynamic of belief was the act of faith. Truth, argued Stephen, was not absolute but conditioned by each age; and though the methods of rational enquiry superseded each other, each generation ought to accept the best obtainable opinion. No doubt evidence struck men in different ways and divergence of belief was inevitable. No doubt what passed for scientific exactitudes in the past were now exploded. But this should lead us to deduce, not that conviction was absurd, but that dogma was absurd and toleration necessary; and we should accept as sound reasoning only that which was capable of being disproved by the very methods which made up its proof. Whatever we might think of the truth of religion, there could be only one arbiter in all disputes: if we abandoned reason we were left at the mercy of prejudice – you may call prejudice faith or intuition, as you will.

But may we not say that our beliefs change? How could the disciple of evolution deny that ideas as well as societies could develop and change their shape while remaining the same species? Newman declared in his 'Essay on Development' that Christian dogma, consisting as it did of perfect truth, could never change; but though changeless it could appear to expand to include newly discovered lesser truths. This assertion outraged Dean Milman, one of the best of the Liberal Anglican historians, and it inspired some of G. G. Coulton's most fiery pamphlets. Stephen contented himself with observing that Newman conveniently abandoned the argument from development directly he observed that the temper of his own age was hostile to Christianity. Instead of concluding that Christianity was ossifying, he declared that the age was sunk in wickedness. Most Broad Churchmen declared without a qualm that theology was not static but changed with the times. The theology of the past might reflect a barbaric morality, but theology had always evolved to become acceptable to future generations. Surely it was self-evident that Scripture had to be reinterpreted.

Stephen admitted that there had always been clergymen such as Tillotson or Burnet or Paley ('of whom it is now the fashion to speak with contempt partly caused by his utter inability to be obscure'), who had declared that the Bible and Prayer Book need not be literally interpreted; and he praised them and their modern followers for their liberalism and sincerity. But how, he asked, could a clergyman get round the Thirty-nine Articles? There they stand – the document of dogmas to which he must subscribe. The second Article says quite clearly that the Atonement was a bargain struck between the Father and the Son. To their credit Broad Churchmen find this repulsive; but how do they reconcile subscription to this article with their conscience? No doubt they can plead some legal quibble but surely in *this* matter one is not morally entitled to take advantage of loopholes in the law. 'The practical tendency of Broad Church teaching is not, as formerly, to convince young men that it is possible to be at once rational and Christian, but to convince them that it is possible to be at once rational and clergymen, which is a very different thing.'

The spectacle of clergymen such as Voysey and J. R. Green quitting the Church after a conscientious struggle to square dogma with history encouraged Stephen in his strictures; and he exposed the weakness in the reasoning of Jowett, Dean Stanley and Kingsley, none of whom was a match for his intellect. But the greatest Anglican theologian of his day, F.D. Maurice, Stephen's old mentor, faced the problem of reinterpreting Christian dogma even if he declared that so far from being a Broad Churchman he belonged to no party in the Church. The Church of England, he thought, was not a sect propagating certain beliefs but a good *position*. It did not balance opinions but united opposites: truth was not a series of compromises between extremes, but the union of these extremes. Since the world was full of problems insoluble by formulae, all dovetailed logical systems of dogma were fallacious. That was the base from which Maurice proceeded to break with the old Evangelical teaching. Man is fundamentally good and sin is an aberration. God created the world in Christ before man's Fall, and Christ is the ground on which humanity rests. Since Christ, not sin, is the basis of human nature, sin is an aberration not a norm; sin is the result of man's folly in trying to live independently of God instead of acknowledging his relation to him in Christ. Evangelicals insisted on personal salvation: Maurice emphasized the salvation of the human race. The Elect were not a set of God's favourites but the whole of humanity restored to its foreordained state of goodness by incorporation into the body of which Christ is the Head. The Bible was not to be interpreted in a fundamentalist sense, but neither was it a set of myths; analytical criticism was at fault when the Bible was treated as a collection of texts and not as the revelation of a Divine Kingdom in which man had a place shown to him by God in Scripture; Scripture explained not only that evil exists but how it was compatible with other facts such as goodness. The Creed meant belief in a Name, not in a set of doctrines. All doctrines were reconciled in that Name. The Thirty-nine Articles protected us from the tyranny of systems and parties by their very ambivalence. Since Christ and not Satan is the Prince of this world, miracles are manifestations of his order, not (*pace* Mansel) violations of order to impress us; they demonstrated that spiritual power is superior to mechanical and the world subject to God and not to Darwinian chance.

Widespread as Maurice's influence was, his attempt to make Christianity at once philosophically and morally acceptable was imperfectly understood by his own contemporaries in the Church. To Stephen he was anathema, and of all theologians whom Stephen handled none got rougher treatment. He portrayed him as intricate, futile, bewildering, a 'melancholy instance of the way in which a fine intellect may run to waste in the fruitless endeavour to force new truth into the old mould'. Sir James Stephen had regarded Maurice's teaching as an attempt to wed 'the gospel to some form of philosophy if so to conceal its baldness. But Paul of Tarsus many years ago forbade the banns'; and his son added that to see Maurice graft Coleridgean metaphysics on to Christianity was like watching the struggles of a drowning creed. Stephen had been justly criticized for writing Maurice's life for the *DNB* and thereby breaking his own rule of obtaining biographers sympathetic to their subject. Why did he lose his sense of equity? Why was he so incensed?

It was the epistemological tangle, the perversion by Maurice of the meaning of meaning, which appalled Stephen. Faced with the difficulty that a loving Father condemned his children to eternal torment, Maurice juggled with words and claimed that 'eternal' had nothing to do with time, a solution which, Stephen said, 'was more satisfactory than intelligible'. Maurice held that eternity has no meaning in this world; it could be used only in relation to God and therefore was not a term of temporal duration. It was a word of quality rather than quantity and was used in this sense by St John, who talked of eternal life and death being known here and now in this world, thus showing that eternal death really meant being severed from the love of God. Very well, says Stephen, we now arrive at the proposition: 'God's punishments are not excessive, for eternity, as we know, has nothing to do with time, and therefore eternal damnation means merely separation from the Eternal.' A theologian will wince at the word 'merely', but Stephen relentlessly asks how this theory differs from the old dogma of hell. Maurice would reply that propositions and dogmas have nothing to do with the matter. We cannot be certain what the word αἰώνιος means, but taking the Gospel message and the course of history as a whole, we may trust in the Larger Hope. To believe firmly that some men go to hell is to acknowledge that Satan and not Christ is Prince of this world.[1] This, says Stephen, means that one 'has to learn not a new set of facts or opinions, but a new mode of thinking'. For Stephen, Maurice had solved nothing. Maurice rejected the old Evangelical theology, but he did not agree with Mill that one could not worship a Being who punished his children. In fact, he had broken with the Unitarian faith, in which he was brought up as a child, because it denied the need for atonement. To say that God was too kind and good to punish men was to have 'a feeble notion of the Divine perfections [and to represent] *good nature* as the highest of them'. For Stephen the problem of the morality of a belief in hell (or separation from God's Love) remained. How can we argue about God except in words and by laying down dogmas? When Maurice said that Christ had revealed himself and not a dogma, we may ask what a revelation of God can be but the revelation of a dogma about God. An anthropomorphic explanation of

---

[1] H. G. Wood admitted that Maurice went too far in declaring that 'eternal', as used in Scripture, had nothing to do with time and that he also forgot that Satan derived his authority from God even if he was not Prince of this world.

God is inevitable, as Maurice admitted when he attacked Mansel's unknowable God; and when Maurice says that we must not confound that which *seems* with that which *is*, we can only answer that what *seems* and *is* are indistinguishable to our relative minds. The confusion between a cognition and an emotion runs through Maurice's work.

Here Stephen stood in the best tradition of rationalist thought; just such a refusal to allow words to carry meanings other than they are given in normal conversation was at the root of G.E. Moore's philosophy at the beginning of this century. Stephen feared that the logic of language as a means of communication would be destroyed. 'Treat believing as a branch of gymnastics and there is nothing, however revolting, which you may not train yourself to swallow.' The crux of his criticism was his refusal to accept Maurice's tenet of the polarity of truth. This enabled Maurice to say that every formula was worthless, but also of infinite value when rightly interpreted. Maurice believed that the facts of history supported Christianity: but watch, said Stephen, how he interprets them. He rejected what he disliked in other creeds and took the remainder as a vital principle because it coincided with his beliefs. 'Rightly interpreted' Buddhism becomes a prayer for the Light of the World. 'Rightly interpreted' the fate of the Gadarene swine is an illustration of the redemption of men from brutish passions. Stephen claimed that Maurice had invented a new tense, 'the conjectural preterite'. Buddhists, Mohammedans, Christians 'will have thought so-and-so', i.e. they did think so 'if Mr Maurice's theories be sound'. For Maurice the desire for a Saviour expressed in other religions proved the truth of Christianity: for Stephen the incompatibility of other religions with Christianity and the lack of evidence that the world was being converted showed that Christianity was merely another product of the human mind and not the supreme truth. The deepest principles, according to Maurice, were those which the schoolman and peasant could both grasp; was not this, asked Stephen, to hold that 'the ultimate criterion of truth . . . comes to be simply that it is the doctrine which satisfies at once a bed-ridden old woman and a high-minded clergyman?'

Maurice had been taught by Coleridge to revere history; but he did not understand the historical movement and was impervious to the current ways of treating the past. (Frederic Harrison complained that he insisted on teaching history in terms of the reigns of kings and never in terms of movements or subjects.) Nevertheless, his modern apologists often defend his treatment of history by arguments derived from Collingwood. Collingwood denied that history was a chain of evidence based on events and facts, hard, concrete and tangible, as Newtonian particles; it was a series of situations impossible to interpret unless we got inside the thought of the past. When this was grasped we would realize that fact was not *followed* by interpretation: every fact was automatically itself interpretation as soon as it was used in narrative or analysis. Objective history was as obsolete as Newtonian physics which presupposed a direct relationship between mathematical fact and reality. Maurice was, therefore, right to reject German biblical source-criticism which, after 200 years of research, still today has not discovered 'the historical Jesus' – for the simple reason that the Gospels are not biographies written by detached observers but an expression of the early Church's faith. Such historians prefer to subject the Gospels to form-criticism which discloses the tradition of the primitive Church. Thus the story of the youth flying naked from the arrest of Christ (Mark XIV, 51–2), which used to be cited as evidence that that young man was an eye witness of the events he later recorded in the Gospel – for who else but Mark would have set down such a trivial incident? – now became a mere parable in Church tradition illustrating the need for courage in the Day of the Lord. It could not purport to answer the unanswerable question: what happened? It could be only a symbol of a Messianic pattern of events. Not, *pace* Strauss, a myth; but a tradition governing the minds of those faithful. Since we can interpret history only through the thought of the past, it is the only ascertainable truth. Stephen argued that a scientific hypothesis, such as the circulation of the blood, was based on a true relation between facts, whereas Maurice's theology was simply an attempt to justify an arbitrary relation between figments. But the form critics declared that Stephen based his arguments on the rationalist fictions of his time. Maurice was correct in appreciating that the divine revelation of the truth was not deducible from 'facts', events or dogmatic propositions.

Indeed the critics and the anthropologists are taking out an injunction today to oust the historians whom they regard as impudent squatters. They deny that historians can ever understand the texts and stories of another era because we are all imprisoned in our own historical situation and the assumptions of our age are our warders. The texts of religion such as the Bible should be interpreted as critics interpret literary masterpieces. Such masterpieces embody myths, and the Bible belongs to a class of writings such as Greek tragedy or *War and Peace* which perpetually renew men's spiritual life. The very fact that a text was regarded for centuries as sacred is good reason for continuing to regard it as a sacred text – not in the sense that it would be impious to examine it but in the sense that it has no meaning other than as a sacred text: it should not be treated as an historical document. The anthropologists are even more dismissive of the historians. They argue that from the time the books of the Bible were written men believed they concealed mysteries and myths within the stories.

These myths are used to explain the rules of behaviour which society endorses. The fact that in the past men gave different explanations is irrelevant; every age uses new techniques to interpret through myth. The anthropologists' interpretation of the Bible and the sacred texts cannot be expected to resemble St Jerome's. The very fact that one part of the Bible contradicts another is further evidence of the density of the social traditions it embodies. The contradictions are simply reflections of different rituals or myths. To attempt to disentangle them and say which is true and which is false is as pointless as unravelling a tapestry and hoping to find the truth of the scene which it depicts.

The question which Stephen posed remains unanswered and is probably unanswerable. Scholars will continue to interpret the historical evidence concerning events in Palestine and their social setting before and after the birth of Christ in such widely differing ways that the historical claims of Christianity will be forever in dispute; and scholars in other fields will declare that the questions Stephen asked are meaningless.

There was another adversary whose analysis of belief Stephen rated considerably higher than Newman's or Maurice's. Are we capable, as Huxley and Clifford claimed, of weighing evidence in an emotional vacuum? Is conviction independent of the will as Stephen suggested? William James did not think so. James gave a turn of the screw to the controversy about belief which was all the more difficult for Stephen to endure because James too was an empiricist. The elder generation of metaphysicians, such as W. G. Ward, had played with the concepts of Mind and Will and so had Bradley. If Tyndall states that Matter contains the promise and potency of all terrestrial life, how, asked Ward, does the will exist? If Huxley argues that man can change Nature by exercising his will, how does a non-material concept play a part in the chain of causation? If Science says that life cannot be spontaneously generated, how is the will spontaneously generated? The rationalists fell back on Hume as their first line of defence. They denied they were materialists. But even if there could be no proof for an inductive truth, experience alone gave data from which to draw *firm* conclusions, and the uniformity of Nature gave us good reasons for not accepting revelations and miracles. The debate resembled a long-range bombardment in which the rationalists, well dug in, were secure and their enemy supplied with the wrong kind of ammunition. But James's right-wing empiricism turned the flank of the rationalist position. James wanted to restore the richness of human experience. He wanted to justify our right to believe. 'Your bogey is superstition,' he wrote to an English rationalist, 'my bogey is desiccation. . . In my essay the evil shape was a vision of "Science" in the form of abstraction, priggishness and sawdust, lording it over all. Take the sterilest scientific prig and cad you know, compare him with the richest religious intellect you know, and you would not, any more than I would, give the former the exclusive right of way.' When agnostics thundered that it was immoral to believe unverifiable statements merely because they gave pleasure, they really wanted to impose laws based 'on nothing but their natural wish to exclude all elements for which they, in their professional quality of logicians, can find no use'. Every man, said James, believes according to his 'willing nature', and if it is in your nature to believe in God, then believe, and realize that your belief is justified.

This does not mean that by believing a thing we make it true. James tried to formulate rules for belief and one of them was that in certain cases where belief and doubt were possible, there was often a greater chance of getting at the truth by believing. Nor should we be dismayed if truths conflict. James substituted relativism and pluralism for the agnostic unity of truth. The world 'is a sort of republican banquet . . . where all the qualities of being respect one another's personal sacredness, yet sit at the common table of space and time'. God is finite, external to the world's evil, not an Absolute and part of a monist determined scheme of things. Just as Pascal, living in a society given to gaming, so James, living in an age of financial gambling, employed against the agnostics the image of the wager.[1]

It [the rationalist theory of belief] is like those gambling and insurance rules based on probability, in which we secure ourselves against losses in detail by hedging on the total run. But this hedging philosophy requires that the long run should be there; and this makes it inapplicable to the question of religious faith as the latter comes home to the individual man. He plays the game of life not to escape losses, for he brings nothing with him to lose; he plays it for gains; and it is now or never with him, for the long run which exists indeed for humanity, is not there for him. Let him doubt, believe or deny, he runs his risk and has the natural right to choose which one it shall be.

To refuse to bet is in fact to bet – you are betting against the field; and that is a negative and mean approach to life.

Stephen reviewed *The Will to Believe* in the *Agnostic Annual* of 1898 and in a letter said of James, 'He is the one really lively philosopher; but I am afraid that he is trying the old dodge of twisting "faith" out of moonshine.' Writing to James towards the end of his life, Stephen said, 'You (as I fancy) say that there is no "conclusive" evidence (I say none of any kind) for a certain belief. You infer that a man has a right to hold either the negative or the positive creed. My reply is that he has a right to hold *neither*. By Agnostic I do not mean a negative creed but an absence of all opinion; and that I take to be the only rational frame of mind.' Stephen was then too old to meet the challenge of pragmatism – which at that date

---

[1] Veblen pointed out that religion and gambling are often associated; he claimed that officers of the Salvation Army comprised a higher proportion of men with a sporting record than the proportion of such men to the aggregate of the community.

was only partially constructed. Pragmatism is the rebellious child of agnosticism. It accepts the agnostic premise that we must not be dogmatic about the unknowable; it also rejects immutable monist religion; but it turns the premise back on its father by arguing that in many cases we ought to believe rather than disbelieve in a God. Why not believe in God? – as a concept it is a deal more satisfactory than other substitutes. And if the unknowable paradoxically grows vaster as scientific knowledge increases, we shall soon be left without any verifiable beliefs (except the most trivial) if we remain agnostics. Stephen did not grasp that pragmatism could be met only by re-examining the nature of such philosophical terms as propositions (which James calls beliefs) and by asking how the truth of these propositions related to objective fact – the method by which agnosticism's younger son, logical positivism, set about bullying its elder brother. He still hoped, like Comte, that scientific principles could be discovered and applied to society. But like any good rationalist he knew that there would always be certain ontological questions which could never be answered satisfactorily by any mode of thought; that they were unanswerable in no way impugned the value of reason, even though the rationalist in cap and gown might not be able to speak so authoritatively. In his review of James's book Stephen suggested that even if the will influences our beliefs, it could be courted by good reasons; and those good reasons should convince unless someone could supply better ones. Deprived of his cane by the psychoanalysts and the mathematical physicists, the stern parent today puts his trust in persuasion.

There was one near-contemporary with whom Stephen could never come to terms. This was Matthew Arnold. How much the difference of a decade can make! Stephen was an undergraduate of the 1850s when to follow Mill seemed to put one on the path to truth. Arnold studied, or rather failed to study, in the 1840s at an Oxford exhausted by the fierce conflicts of the days of the Tractarians when the desperate dissection of propositions led to families and friends dividing – and for what? Arnold did not doubt that if a man took a course reading the writings of Benjamin Franklin, Jeremy Bentham or Herbert Spencer he would find that the Bible had incomparably more power than those sages to teach righteousness, influence his conduct and bring him peace and joy. Unfortunately the dogmas of the Church, its miracles, sacraments and mysteries, no longer stood up to critical enquiry. How then could the saving power of the Gospel be preserved? Arnold answered that the Christian faith could still be believed as true and redemptive if the Bible and Book of Common Prayer were read as literature not as scientific treatises. Double truth again made its appearance. There were two kinds of truth: poetic truth and scientific truth. Bishops were all too often the most guilty in treating religion as a science by insisting on the literal truth of some text or doctrine. Righteousness was what mattered and saved men, not the dogma of the Trinity, or the existence of a First Cause, or miracles which even if they were all true would be irrelevant to Christ's claim to be the Son of God. Immortality must be accepted too as an *Aberglaube*, a part of the mythology of the Church. Immortality was 'the sense of being truly alive which accompanied righteousness'; and if we read the Gospels carefully we would see that Christ time and again tried to correct those who interpreted his words to mean a personal resurrection – death meant the spiritual death which overcomes most of us in this world and which could be conquered only by believing in him.

Whatever may be said of Arnold as a critic, he was no philosopher. Stephen made hay of Arnold the metaphysician. Arnold purported to have discovered a super-law of science deducible from other scientific laws: namely that in science we will find a God or Principle by which all things fulfil the law of their being. This debased Aristotelianism was given no quarter; and Stephen replied that science could tell us only the order in which our sensations occur and could not authorize an intuitively perceived morality to declare itself an absolute morality. By misunderstanding the nature of scientific law, Arnold added modern *Aberglauben* with the left hand as fast as he removed ancient *Aberglauben* with the right. Nor did Bradley spare him. Arnold had unwisely mocked Herbert Spencer by saying that no one was likely to say 'the unknowable is our refuge and strength, our very present help in trouble'. He then went on to define God as the Eternal Not Ourselves that Makes for Righteousness. Arnold was the master in controversy of *de haut en bas*. Bradley addressed him from an even more withering height. In one of the most savage passages he ever wrote Bradley declared that Arnold's concept was simply a fraudulent device 'just as the habit of washing ourselves might be termed the "Eternal not ourselves that makes for cleanliness", or "Early to bed and early to rise" the "Eternal not ourselves that makes for longevity", and so on – that the Eternal, in short, is nothing in the world but a piece of literary clap-trap.' Bradley continued: ' "Is there a God?" asks the reader. "Oh yes," replies Mr Arnold, "and I can verify him in experience." "And what is he then?" "Be virtuous and as a rule you will be happy", is the answer. "Well, and God?" "That is God," says Mr Arnold, "there is no description and what more do you want?" I suppose we do want a good deal more.'

Stephen too said that religion was nothing unless it answered with certainty the perennial questions that troubled men. He thought Arnold indifferent to such questions. Arnold had said of Maurice that he beat the bush without ever starting a hare, and Stephen added of Arnold, 'if he started the hare, he did not quite catch it'. And yet Arnold's later

Christian critics, such as T. S. Eliot and C. S. Lewis, emboldened by such slashing and mauling, did not dispose as easily as they imagined of Arnold's attempt to preserve certain moral habits even when their historical and dogmatic sanction had gone. Graham Hough commented in a wise passage:

It seems commonly to be assumed that there is something peculiarly perverse or wrong-headed about this. The objections vary from Chesterton's crude gibe at 'those who do not have the Faith, and will not have the fun', to T. S. Eliot's more refined eyebrow-raising at Arnold's attempts to make a purely secular culture do the work of religion. It is surely the objections which are wrong-headed. It is not self-contradictory to say, 'this type of conduct is right, though the traditional sanctions for it are wrong.' And if one holds this view it is perfectly reasonable to practise the conduct without any sanctions at all, or to attempt to find new and valid ones.

Religion for Arnold was a matter of right *feeling* as well as right conduct; and what he tried to do was to fill the emotional gap created by rationalism. Arnold never imagined that these questions could be answered with certainty by minds temperamentally *ondoyant et divers*. Arnold's approach to religious, as well as poetic, diction was subtle and delicate. 'To handle these matters properly there is needed a poise so perfect that the least overweight in any direction tends to destroy the balance. Temper destroys it, a crotchet destroys it, even erudition may destroy it. To press to the sense of the thing itself with which one is dealing, not to go off on some collateral issue about the thing, is the hardest matter in the world.' When Stephen wrote in his valediction that Arnold was urging us 'to get rid of prejudices in general, not of any special prejudice', Arnold's departed spirit must have bowed ironically from the fields of asphodel. *That* was exactly what he was doing.

Did He Understand Religion?

Leslie Stephen's encounters which helped him to define agnosticism did not encompass it. All sorts and conditions of men found each in his own way the way out of Christianity and their substitute for it much as in our own time men and women for very different reasons decide to leave the Communist party. Sidgwick, Frederick Myers and the scientist A. R. Wallace tried to find evidence for existence beyond the grave. Frank Miller Turner showed how they and the philosopher James Ward, the gentle George Romanes and the great eccentric Samuel Butler each rejected the scientific naturalism which sustained Stephen's agnosticism. Or there was William Hale White whose confessions were, as befitted one born in the town near which Bunyan was born and imprisoned, puritanical, spiritual and markedly different from those of Rousseau.

Nevertheless it was not only the young George Trevelyan whose thoughts Stephen put into words. For over half a century among intellectuals his controversial essays provided the standard apologia for unbelief. Many men and women – more than is commonly admitted – are not religious. They require no explanation of the order in the universe or the relation of its parts to totality, nor are they perplexed by the mystery behind appearance. Others – Hobbes was one of them – require such an explanation but see no necessity to explain the world in terms of the supernatural: they prefer to explain it in terms of itself. Leslie Stephen demonstrated that such people should not be expected any longer to believe in Christianity. He showed that theologians might define faith but could not secure it. His arguments were not original. They were to be found in Voltaire. In his review of Morley's book on Voltaire Stephen dissociated himself from Voltaire's obscenity and unworthy attacks on virtues which remained virtues still even if the Church happened to praise them, but the very wording of Stephen's arguments paralleled that of Voltaire's *Dictionnaire Philosophique*. It was the clarity and vigour of his prose which convinced people that there were other explanations than those of the Church of man's place in the cosmos.

It is fashionable to dismiss the so-called conflict between science and religion in the nineteenth century as an aberration on the part of churchmen who insisted on literal interpretation of the Bible against which Hooker, the most famous of Anglican theologians, had long ago warned; and as an illusion on the part of the rationalists who mistook a metaphysical explanation of science as science itself. It is true that doctrine can always be accommodated to the latest discoveries of science – at any rate to the satisfaction of theologians. But there was a genuine conflict in the nineteenth as there had been in the thirteenth century. At that time Aristotelian physics and Islamic philosophy appeared to be irreconcilable with orthodox Christian theological and philosophical speculation which in myriad forms derived from St Augustine's works mediated through Platonism. The Church had the good fortune to find within the Dominicans St Thomas Aquinas (and indeed among the Franciscans St Bonaventure), who reconciled the science of the ancients with the teachings of the Fathers of the Church. For instance Aquinas explained the mystery of transubstantiation in the Mass by employing Aristotelian concepts. The substance of the bread and wine was replaced at the elevation of the Host by the substance of Christ, the accidents (or atoms) of the bread and wine remaining untouched and appearing to the eye to be, as they were, unchanged. But it would be wrong to think that Aquinas was at once universally acclaimed. Several of his propositions were condemned, the Franciscans banned his works, his theories of the nature of the soul, of the relationship of form to matter and of the distinction between essence and existence were all scientific explanations which excited violent opposition. His opponents were to be found even among the Dominicans – one of them, Robert Kilwardby, became Archbishop of Canterbury. It can be argued that Kilwardby, Grosseteste and Roger Bacon gave more genuinely scientific answers to certain problems in physics and optics than Aquinas because they stressed the importance of experiment and rejected Aristotle's determinist explanation of Nature. If Aquinas upset the orthodox, there were numbers of philosophers in Paris, ardent Aristotelians or fervent neo-Platonists, who upset them far more. These Schoolmen maintained that what was true for philosophy need not be regarded as true for theology and propagated other more horrible heresies, such as astral determinism,[1] which between 1270 and 1277 were condemned, denounced and for a while extirpated.

In the 1870s there was no Aquinas. Catholic dignitaries, no less than the most fundamentalist Protestants, condemned Darwin as bitterly as many of Aristotle's commentators had been condemned six centuries earlier. The conflict was as real as that which engaged the Schoolmen because the scientists themselves were divided on the issue of natural selection. Catholics denied that Christian dogma needed to be re-interpreted. It remained true *quod semper, quod ubique, quod ab omnibus creditum est*. Stephen rejoiced because to him this was proof that Christiantity was a dying species and that mankind was on the verge of attaining 'enough truth to secure the welfare and progress of the race . . . and throw some light upon the great problem, What is the conception of the universe to which the previous history of inquiry shows that men's minds are gradually conforming themselves as they become more rational?' How far belief may change and a man still call himself a Christian is a matter for much curious speculation. Sidgwick was more sensitive on this matter than Stephen. In an essay entitled 'Clerical Veracity' he agreed with such clerics as Rashdall that the clergy were entitled to read metaphor into Scripture where their forefathers had taken the texts literally; but he declared that the dogmas of the Incarnation and Virgin Birth, about which there is no obscurity in Scripture, must be accepted – at any rate by clergymen. But that is not a criterion which would be accepted by theologians today. Stephen's obsessive pursuit of F. D. Maurice is significant. Did he sense that in Maurice's interpretation of the meaning of words – in his muffled metaphysics, in his conviction that truth could not be expressed in propositions divorced from the act of living – lay the escape route for theologians from the encircling movement by which the generals of the rationalist army were planning to cut off their

---

[1] This heresy arose from the Islamic philosopher, Avicenna, who envisaged a hierarchy of separate intelligences, eternally moving and reaching down to the world. It had to exist because God was capable of creating only that which was immediately outside him, i.e. the heavens.

enemies' retreat? Like a wise commander Maurice determined to fight on ground of his own choosing. It took him and his followers some time to persuade his fellow commanders to change their ground; and by the time they did so they had suffered losses. Skill in changing the meaning of words, which Stephen so deplored, had been carried to such a pitch as to be beyond his imagining. What would Stephen have made of Tillich's famous statement that 'It is as atheistic to affirm the existence of God as it is to deny it'? When Tillich declared that since accurate assertions about the Divine must be made in non-worldly language, it would be more misleading to use words such as Love or Spirit than to use none at all; or that to speculate about a transcendental God would be to denigrate God by bringing him on to the same level as oneself, would not Stephen have exclaimed, A Mansel come to judgement? The use which modern theologians make of Kierkegaard, Heidegger, and existentialist philo-sophy has driven a chasm between the language which they use and that used by rationalists. In vain rationalists demand precision in the use of language: precision according to many theologians is the most fatal of all the progenitors of error.

And yet this is a measure of Stephen's success. Both he and Arnold were trying to demolish clerical intransigence and diminish their confidence in describing God – that terrible confidence which, as Arnold put it, made clergymen appear that they were not only a party to the inner councils of the Trinity but could even describe the colour of the hangings in the council chamber. Stephen predicted clergymen would become agnostics, and today they express ignorance or caution on matters concerning which their Victorian predecessors pronounced anathema. The thunder of the Athanasian Creed is no longer heard on Trinity Sunday and few are the parsons who expound from the pulpit the central dogma of the Church on that day. Miracles are no longer mentioned, their name is never heard; and this in turn shrouds in mystery the greatest of all miracles, the time when the body of Christ rose from his tomb on the third day. The bright clear light in which Heaven was seen in Victorian times is extinguished and men see, if at all, through a glass darkly.

If, however, we ask a different question – did Stephen understand Christianity and the needs it satisfies – we shall get a different answer. A religion is not simply a corpus of truth designed to train men to conduct themselves aright in *this* world. To define religion as Belief is to define it narrowly. When Stephen called the doctrine of the Atonement repulsive he saw a clear concept, the theory of penal substitution; he did not see the mystical purification through suffering which Dostoevsky beheld. He lacked the imagination – and for a rationalist it requires imagination – to enter into the state of mind that believes that history is meaningless without the Incarnation and that even a life of sin is meaningless without a celestial Judge and Lover. God, not just as a father and friend, but as a lover, was incomprehensible to him. He and his fellow agnostics, A. O. J. Cockshut remarked, understood the struggle against temptation, the struggle Tom Brown faced at Oxford or Tennyson depicted in *In Memoriam*. But they did not understand the motives or the fiery emotions of Augustine or Bunyan who struggle for salvation. Stephen's vision of life, as he often admitted, was terrestrial. He did not see it as a vale of mystery, at once splendid, tragic and suffocatingly tedious. Nor did he regard it with the curious interest of the humanist who relates knowledge to his own experience to reveal various truths, many of them conflicting and contradictory. Nor did he understand how men come to believe. The profoundest religious minds have recognized how difficult it is for some men to believe in God and his goodness. They themselves have often come to believe only through doubt and despair: Father Zossima has no reproach for Ivan Karamazov because he sees that Ivan, though blessed with a soul capable of suffering, is prevented by the limitations of his mind from knowing himself. One way some men come to believe is through ritual and the sacraments. For Stephen ritual was mumbo-jumbo. He failed to realize that it suffuses communal emotion and helps a man to adjust himself psychologically to his fellow men.

He did not face, as we shall see, how glad tidings are to be spread or sad tidings to be vindicated. How is truth to be disseminated? How is it to be popularized? How can truth of any kind be conveyed to the mass of ignorant mankind and also to the few wise men? Is there to be one religion or several according to caste? Are we to force the wise to acknowledge falsehoods as truth, or in the interests of truth make religion incomprehensible to the mass of mankind? This is the problem raised by Dostoevsky in the Inquisitor's speech. 'Thou didst promise them the bread of Heaven, but, I repeat again, can it compare to earthly bread in the eyes of the weak, ever sinful and ignoble race of man? . . . Or dost thou care only for the tens of thousands of the great and strong, while the millions, numerous as the sands of the sea, who are weak but love Thee, must exist only for the sake of the great and strong?' The answer a man gives to this question depends on his temperament; as a lapsed Evangelical, Stephen deplored the adulteration of the heavenly bread.

Stephen's notions of good and evil, of right and wrong behaviour, were narrow. He turned his back on the multitude of examples in the Catholic tradition of ambivalent behaviour which deepen our understanding of how curious and various human beings are. Significantly he examined among Catholics Newman and Pascal, the one an Evangelical convert and the other a Jansenist. Stephen took it for granted that the Christian ideal was that of the virtuous man, obeying God's rules (all of which are totally revealed to man), soberly working in the circle of his family, and directed by his conscience to improve the state of the world. The virtuous man behaved as his conscience instructed by his reason told him how to act. But that is not how most people think and feel. They seize on explanations far removed from their true feelings so long as they seem plausible. The greatest Catholic moralists, however, continually emphasize that man's corrupt reason cannot understand God's judgement. Reprobates, publicans and harlots may stand less in awe of the Last Trump than their earthly betters who have fallen into the more deadly sins of pride and pharisaism. To enable men to lead better lives is only one of the objects of Christianity. It demands that men should love God and it acknowledges that there are many gateways into his temple through which men can pass to offer adoration. The offerings of the juggler of Notre-Dame or the Bedford tinker are both acceptable in the sight of God. For Stephen the Catholic Church, though no longer the Scarlet Woman, was nothing but the Father of Lies: not an illuminating judgement.

Nor did he consider the Orthodox Church. He would have found its morality more shocking than Catholicism since the prophets of the Eastern Church often deny that right conduct is essential to the love of God: indeed that preoccupation with conduct and 'the Law' may be a positive hindrance. Both Puritan and Orthodox see conviction of sin as essential to salvation; but the former intends that it shall spur man to mend his ways, the latter to a deeper experience of God's love. In the unwritten sequel to *The Brothers Karamazov*, Dostoevsky intended Alyosha to 'sin his way to Jesus'. The Russian mystics demanded a change of heart not of habits, and suggested that reiterated sin, in any case inevitable, could be valuable if revulsion from sin awakened the sinful heart to a profounder experience of God's grace. When Stephen followed the German Protestant theologian Harnack and dismissed the experiences of the Eastern mystics as 'spiritual narcotics', he ignored those saints and poets who proclaim that intensity of experience, rather than harmony of interests, gives meaning to life, This is not to suggest that Stephen should have abandoned his ideal. But to convince other men to abandon theirs you must first understand them. Ignoring the splendours and glories of religion and the infinite variety of ways in which it corresponds to men's needs, his critique was in this respect poverty-stricken.

If Stephen was successful in justifying agnostics, he was less successful in persuading religiously-minded men who had doubts that the evidence against the truth of Christianity was so strong that they must abandon it. For to persuade such a man, you yourself must understand what religion means to him. This Stephen could not do. Religion may or may not be true but it is a reality: in unemotional language we may say that men experience a variety of pleasurable or painful sensations of great complexity under its influence. And here a confusion in utilitarian psychology put Stephen on the wrong track. Pleasure and pain are not emotions but qualities which emotions sometimes possess. They are not, as Hume thought, synonymous with approval and disapproval. Thus, if you demonstrate that certain religious beliefs will cause a man pain, he may reply that such pain will give him joy, or he may deny that the emotion can properly be described as painful. The utilitarians never touched more than the surface of pleasure and pain. Strange that dedicated to the principle of basing all their conclusions in human experience, they knew so little of its range and variety. Stranger still that Stephen, who declared that all experience comes within reason's province, should not have realized that he who would discuss religion must investigate it. Such a man may hold that God probably does not exist, but he cannot ignore that men have held various ideas of God and that mystics have described their experience of communion with him. Stephen could never have written William James's *The Varieties of Religious Experience* because he did not understand the religious mind.

The Secularization of Society

Stephen prophesied the secularization of society. Was he right?

The sociologists of religion would not be sociologists if they gave a simple answer. Bryan Wilson certainly thought Stephen right. To his mind religious symbols, doctrines and thought, the churches themselves, have declined in importance year by year in this century. They impress people less and fewer think in Christian terms. Ah, say his critics, but does this mean that we must accept the existence of a golden age of faith which Wilson identifies as being Victorian England? Are there not better candidates – what about the fourth century when Constantine established Christianity as the official religion of the Roman Empire and, in so doing, institutionalized it, secularized it, made it no longer the sect of saints and martyrs but gave it temporal power and hence ushered in the secularization of the Christian world? Or the twelfth century when the papacy was at the height of its power and the schoolmen were providing a definitive theology? Or, perhaps, secularization came after the Reformation when the Calvinists taught that salvation is to be sought not in withdrawing from the world, as monks and nuns did, but by pursuing worldly activities under the eye of a transcendental God. Why should the nineteenth century be seen as the summit from which Christianity declines? Such critics, however, lay themselves open to the charge that, if such is the case, Europe has been secularized so often that it is difficult to argue that Christianity ever had any force.

Some sociologists, such as Wilson and Shiner, declare that even in countries such as America where people continue to worship together, the churches are so zealous in the concerns of this world rather than the next that Christianity becomes processed and packaged and theology becomes a form of advertising. But there are others such as Bellah and Robertson who argue that so far from religion legitimizing men's notions of what is good or bad, it has retreated from the world. Christianity, like the family, has lost so many of the functions it once had which have now been taken over by other agencies. Religion has lost its public role and in so doing has lost its authority. But this need not necessarily be taken as evidence of secularization. The very fact that we speak of fundamentalist sects and contrast them with other more prestigious ways of worship suggests that masses of people have reinterpreted Christian dogma, each in his own fashion. The churches have become places where it is convenient to discuss these reinterpretations.

Other sociologists maintain that as organized Christianity has tiptoed into the wings, the centre of the stage has been taken by religious surrogates: psychoanalysis, Marxism, and above all nationalism – indeed any system such as astrology which venerates symbols and concepts. There are also scholars who give a more sophisticated version of Stephen's rationalism – scholars who see religion as the enemy of progress and interpret secularism as the readiness to welcome change. And with this interpretation of the secular goes another. The world no longer is seen to be a world of magic, enchantment, mystery with sacred themes and objects. It becomes a world explicable solely in terms of scientific thought. This was the kind of world Weber feared when he spoke of it being peopled by 'specialists without spirit, sensualists without heart; this nullity imagines it has attained a level of civilization never before achieved'.

Whatever way secularization is defined, there is an irresistible impulse to ask: what caused it? Vernon Pratt took Mill's line that Stephen and the Victorian agnostics persuaded first the highly intelligent to become sceptics and then by degrees others followed. Alasdair McIntyre argued (as Stephen did) that the deteriorating fortunes of the churches were simply a reflection of changes in society; and that if the unspoken agreement between men of different classes on what one meant by good behaviour cracked, that was because there was no longer agreement on the aim of life and its goals. But arguments about causation are tedious. Michael Hill holds the sensible view that secularization cannot be explained by one single cause. Nor is secularization unilinear. At the same time, Hill argues, that some parts of life become secularized, other parts become desecularized. Certainly the total subversion of Christian ethics which Nietzsche preached has not fared well. Nevertheless, whether one considers the part the churches play in people's lives or the hold theology or Christian apologetics have upon people's minds, who can doubt that Stephen's prophecy about English life was true?

In his own day it was different. Victorian life was influenced by the churches because people had fewer choices then and religion was their solace and their entertainment. The churches had a long lead over other institutions in the art of popularization: they provided serious topics for conversation in their sermons, books and tracts. Men and women could identify themselves in the lively in-group of the congregation. Missionaries and revivalism were the entertainment and release from work for the poor. A significant part of the working classes fell under the spell of religion, the lower middle classes were permeated by it. Through the non-conformist communions the poor could protest against the Establishment and the culture of the ruling class. Yet the Anglican Church was in fact performing duties now undertaken by a dozen ministries. However true it may be that the 'submerged tenth' lived untouched by Christianity, as did a sizeable proportion of rakes, Bohemians, demi-mondaines, artists and *revoltés* of all classes, the notorious English Sunday proclaimed to the world that Britain was a nation whose culture was deeply affected by religion.

Today people have far more numerous choices before them when they decide how to spend their leisure. Many of the functions of the Church have been taken over by the State; critics perform the role of priests and deliver the weekly sermon in our favourite newspapers or periodicals; television pundits are our hedgerow preachers; and the rituals of football and sport have supplanted revivalist meetings. The churches are concerned less with the individual's soul than with the world at large and the material welfare of those who are poor or afflicted or live in primitive conditions in poverty-stricken countries. Late in the day they listened to Maurice's other message, that Christians should be socialists, in the sense of caring for the poor man at the rich man's gate. The experience of worker priests and the activities of the World Council of Churches show how difficult it is for an institution which by its nature must be one of the forces of social control to speak for revolution and subversion by the oppressed; but from the tone in which some Protestant churchmen speak one might infer that a Christian who concerns himself first with his relation to God and the state of his immortal soul had sinned – were it decorous to mention the word sin. In countries whose citizens find difficulty in identifying with the society in which they live, many people still tend to regard the churches as yet another alien social institution. Only in totalitarian countries, or in countries rent by civil war, are churches the one conspicuously non-secular refuge.

With the decline of belief in Christian doctrine went the decline in the status and power of the clergy. They were to lose their influence, and in numerous cases their place, on local boards and committees, and finally in Parliament and Whitehall. The more ecumenical and less fanatically sectarian they became, the more they lost their political influence since united they caused much less trouble than when they were divided. Their incomes were reduced by the agricultural depression, and by the time the Church Commissioners began to invest in equities inflation depressed them further. Unlike almost every other group in society they practised admirable self-denial; bishops no longer aspired to be prelates; and they became the poorest of all the professions. The class to which Stephen belonged replaced them. By the end of the First World War the dons had acquired much of the status which formerly the clergy enjoyed, and by the end of the Second World War the dons were set to improve their incomes and their influence as the academic profession and the occupations to which the intelligentsia belonged rose in public esteem. Stephen would have been rightly indignant if anyone had accused him of conducting a campaign against the churches in order to feather his own nest. He lived before the greater part of the intelligentsia had organized itself into pressure groups and in trade unions to improve their standard of living: he had to rely on a patron, George Smith, for employment which enabled him to write. None of this alters the fact that the vacuum which was created by the decline of the clergy was filled by the intelligentsia. As university reform no longer made subscription to the Thirty-Nine Articles obligatory for an academic career, as secular provincial universities grew in number, as the world of letters and periodicals and later broadcasting began to give comfortable financial rewards, the intelligentsia began to form as a class at least as well able to look after their own interests as the clergy at the beginning of the nineteenth century. Like most classes, they were oblivious of the fact that they were doing so.

Stephen had his apocalypse no less than Marx. For Marx the State and the dictatorship of the proletariat would wither away, for Stephen religion would decay and lose its hold over men and women. But towards the end of his life he had his doubts; or rather he had come to believe it might take longer than he thought. In 1900 he wrote: 'Modern evolutionism . . . coincides with the Catholic view so far as it recognizes the social importance of the Churches . . . and parts company with the old "negative" criticism which regarded creeds as simply false and churches as organized impostures.' He came reluctantly to agree that religion corresponded not simply to men's knowledge but to the whole impression made on them by the world. For paradoxically the very scholars, the sociologists whom Stephen believed would be encoding the laws which enabled societies to behave more rationally, were in fact informing their contemporaries that societies could not exist unless their citizens shared common values – and those values were often most poignantly expressed through religions. Much of the mortar which cemented societies together was mixed irrationally with such elements as sacraments and rituals. Religion affected people's behaviour in the market, and it influenced their ideas about law and obligation. So far from following Comte, the new sociologists examining the world as it was and not predicting what it was to become reaffirmed the importance of religion as a component in society.

There was, however, another side to that coin. As the techniques of government and technology developed, men put greater faith in political action than in religion to create a heaven on earth. The secular State precisely because it has so many devices to hand tries to give its citizens greater individuality, a greater number of choices, greater potentialities; who should discover how to do this better than the wise – better than the intellectual aristocracy? People no longer believe religion influences the major political issues of our times. 'We dimly perceive', wrote Norman Birnbaum, 'that our disasters are our collective fault. We are individually and collectively helpless before them, but a sociological rather than a theological view of causation dominates our thinking about our fate – even if, as is mostly the case, our sociology is false.' Stephen too believed that the cure for evils within society could be found only by studying society itself, and that such study would slowly reveal how men could lead better lives. He regarded man as prone to evil but not bound to it; as capable of training himself to prefer virtue to vice – material conditions permitting. He did not believe in the perfectibility of man, or think that evil was caused by priests or kings, or like Hardy by a hostile universe. Nor did he countenance the worship of man and his works like the Comtists or the Aesthetes. A man's actions should be judged in relation to the effect they had on society. When a man sinned he blasphemed not against his Maker but against his fellow men and himself. When Walter Pater was reviewing *Robert Elsmere* he concluded that there were two estimates of life – and it became a fashionable dichotomy for many years – between 'the off-spring of the scientific spirit which is for ever making the visible world fairer and more desirable in mortal eyes; and the estimate of St Augustine'. What was it in Augustine that the agnostics so disliked?

It was his belief in man's being born in and to Original Sin. The belief that Original Sin was a doctrine which tended to lead the best minds to despise man was finely expressed in the most interesting of all Stephen's religious essays, his study of Pascal. Stephen felt an affinity with the Puritanism of Port Royal, with a Catholic who drubbed those Jesuits for making reservations about the first great commandment that man must love God with all his heart and with all his might. 'Love Virtue, she alone is free' was a message which a Clapham heart could receive, and he applauded Pascal for attacking casuistry as a system of morality which divorced actions from those who do them. To be convinced by St Thomas Aquinas, Hooker, Bossuet or Butler, a man must accept their fundamental premises. Alone among the great apologists Pascal met the agnostic on his own ground. Pascal went all the way with the sceptic, and Stephen appreciated in glowing terms the honesty and integrity which led him to frame his great question in the form of a bet. Since man knows nothing and can never know anything even of God, since his reason is frail and his vaunted successes over nature mere vanities, he must bet, with the spectre of death before his eyes, on the probability that God exists. If he is wrong he loses nothing. If he is right he wins all. Pascal did not stop there. He admitted that a man might be unconvinced even by this display of logic and probability. Such a man might remain unable to believe and might doubt whether God would praise him for manufacturing pseudo-belief. Pascal gave him his answer. Submit yourself to the Church, hear Mass and lose your soul in her mysteries. 'Naturellement cela vous fera croire et vous abêtira.'

Stephen then delivered a fine sermon on man's duties.

I see that Pascal's morality becomes distorted; that in the division between grace and nature some innocent and some admirable qualities have got to the wrong side; that Pascal becomes a morbid ascetic, torturing himself to death, hating innocent diversion because it has the great merit of distracting the mind from melancholy brooding, looking upon natural passions as simply bad ... distrusting even the highest of blessings, love of sisters and friends, because they take us away from the service of the Being who, after all, does not require our services; consecrating poverty instead of trying to suppress it; and finally, renouncing the intellectual pursuits for which he had the most astonishing fitness, because geometry had no bearing upon dogmatic theology. The devotion of a man to an ideal which, however imperfect, is neither base, sensual, nor anti-social, which implies a passionate devotion to some of the higher impulses of our nature, has so great a claim upon our reverence that we can forgive, and even love, Pascal. We cannot follow him without treason to our highest interests.

By appealing to his heart and begging him to abase his reason Pascal was prohibiting man to discover those reasons which turn mere intellectual inclination into deep conviction. Instead of reconciling the heart and the head Pascal separated them and called one of them error. He left 'not a final solution but a problem: How to form a system which shall throughout be reasonable and founded upon fact, and yet find due place and judicious guidance for the higher elements?'

Whether Leslie Stephen formed such a system we shall see; but he convinced any fairminded man that agnostics were not by definition evil. The reader will remember his dogged credo when he lost his faith: 'I now believe in nothing to put it shortly, but I do not the less believe in morality etc. etc. I mean to live and die like a gentleman if possible.' For some years yet clergymen such as Welldon or the Reverend Noah Porter might thunder that 'sooner or later this agnostic without hope will become morose and surly, or sensual and self-indulgent', etc. etc., but fewer and fewer believed them or stigmatized agnostics in public life. The phraseology, indeed, which agnostics used in affirming that their conduct would equal, if not surpass, in rectitude that of the devout, strikes one as somewhat rhetorical. A fortnight before they were married Lord Amberley, Bertrand Russell's father, wrote to Kate Stanley:

> For if I fail in love and kindliness, you will not: therefore it shall be mine to elaborate theories in written arguments, but it shall be yours to prove by daily, constant example, that Christian virtues in their purest, their most perfect, form may exist apart from the remotest tincture of Christian dogma. Thus shall we strive to increase the charity of men to each other, and mitigate their bitterness. And we will not demand Toleration only at the hands of our friends but much more, Justice. They shall do us Justice. Let them be shocked and pained at first if it must be so . . . but when the first violence of their surprise or their resentment is over, we will ask them if, after all, we are worse than other men; we will ask them to confess, if not at once by the force of reason, then later by the force of facts, that the fruits of the spirit may be granted to those who have flung off the ancient creeds as chaff, and stand upright, pure and noble without their aid!
> We will ask them: yes! and they shall confess it!

Confession would be wrung from a society amazed by agnostic punctiliousness. Had not a Cambridge don said of Sidgwick's resignation from Trinity, 'though we kept our own fellowships without believing more than he did, we should have felt that Henry Sidgwick had fallen short if he had not renounced his'. The fallen children of the Evangelicals kept up the old standards. Mrs Lynn Linton, as ever melodramatic, related how George Cruikshank was not a whit less severe than Zachary Macaulay when he told her that she personally was responsible for the drunken men and women in the London streets whom they saw as they walked home after supper. She protested: 'but he insisted on it, and hung those ruined souls like infernal bells about my neck, tinkling out my own damnation, because at supper I had drunk a glass of champagne from which he had vainly tried to dissuade me!'

Visiting the casino at Homburg George Eliot exclaimed that 'Hell is the only right name for such places', and she rejoiced to hear that a young woman who had staked her fortune on the tables would no longer be able to indulge her pleasure as next year the place was to be closed. The agnostic, however, did not lead the good life for his own self-satisfaction but to benefit society as a whole. We could not avoid influencing our fellow-men. 'For good or for evil,' wrote Frederic Harrison, 'the inevitable chain is set in motion. By every word we have spoken, every act we have done, we have helped to accomplish some decision, to clear a problem, to form a character, to strengthen or weaken some brother or sister.' They lived with the fate of future generations hanging over their heads. 'How pleasant it would be each day to think, To-day I have done something that will tend to render future generations more happy', mused the naturalist Richard Jefferies. Mallock hit the note in his *New Republic* when he made an earnest guest say to his host that it was more moral to do good for Good's own sake than for God's: selfishness would then perish and be replaced by altruism. Altruism – the word which Comte invented – was the final virtue. W. K. Clifford denied that altruism was the same as piety. 'It is not doing good to others as others, but the service of the community by a member of it, who loses in that service the consciousness that he is anything different from the community.' 'Your happiness', he added, 'is of no use to the community, except in so far as it tends to make you a more efficient citizen.'

All this was as uplifting as clerical unction. But Stephen was faced with the question which the vast majority of the fairminded men asked who admitted that individual agnostics could lead honourable lives: what will happen to society if the sanctions of religion are discarded? What sanctions can take their place?

Chapter Ten

THE MORAL SOCIETY

Can There Be a Substitute for Religion?

Ever since men began to explain to themselves the nature of the society in which they lived, they have been puzzled by the fact that, fragile as it appears to be, society still holds together. Divided by their loyalties to their kin, by class, by race, by institutions, by economic rivalries and pressure groups, and by their interpretations of what is sacred or good or politically desirable, men and women find themselves faced with different obligations. Various value systems compete for their allegiance and the claims of the systems often conflict. What holds society together?

The Victorians were much exercised by this question and in the hungry 1840s some despaired and believed that the rapid urbanization of the country had destroyed so many of the bonds which for so long had bound human beings together that the State would soon disintegrate. The philanthropists who organized prison visiting, almoners, college lecturing, young men's associations, working men's institutes, fallen women's societies, chimney sweeps' protection, Sunday schools, ragged boys' schools and a host of other movements were moved partly by compassion. But they were moved much more by the deliberate intention of inducing the working class to adopt the virtues of cleanliness, punctuality, sobriety, thrift and care for the aged. Some historians write as if the ruling classes institutionalized these virtues as forms of social control. The new police force and the poor law between them would ensure that potential revolutionaries would be detected in their wrongdoing and held either in prisons or in the bastilles of the workhouse. What were schools but repressive institutions designed to geld or splay children, what were hospitals but devices for incarcerating the poor so that doctors could experiment upon them and use the results of those experiments to improve the health of the ruling classes, what were asylums but prisons for those whom the middle classes were embarrassed to have at home, who might not in fact be clinically disturbed but merely enraged by the hypocrisies and repressions of the patriarchal society in which they found themselves?

None of these contentions stands scrutiny. In any society the ruling classes exercise social controls and orchestrate them to harmonize with their own interests. But within these classes there are conflicts of interest. As a result they cannot exercise authority unanimously. And there is another reason why such speculations are vain. The working classes had minds of their own. If their children went to schools which church and chapel set up, the children, as often as not, let the grave moralizing of their betters slide off their backs. What is more, numbers of families preferred to diminish their insubstantial incomes by paying fees to vocational schools where deference was at a discount. The working-class families often accepted the services the middle classes provided because they found them useful, but they did not supinely respond to middle-class socialization. They had their own culture, xenophobic, deeply distrustful of change particularly in work habits, but ready at once to support each other. Family feeling was strong; so was loyalty to the street where one lived. They had their own ways of socialization – the pub, the club, professional games and sport. Nor did most of them require instruction from their superiors to improve their lot, to save, to lead orderly lives in which self-respect and self-help played their part in keeping them out of the dreaded workhouse. For the poor, as even the most superficial Victorian moralizers recognized, were not a single body any more than the ruling classes were: among them were many who wanted to climb the social ladder by freely adopting so-called middle-class values and regarded hospitals and schools as agencies which helped them to do so. Nor were the upper classes so superior that they regarded themselves as beyond improvement. They may not have been the first target for those who sponsored the prevention of cruelty to children but they certainly were in the minds of those who fought for the prevention of cruelty to animals. Readers of Anna Sewell's *Black Beauty* will not have forgotten the heartless society lady who ordered Ginger's bearing-rein to be shortened hole after hole so that her carriage horses should hold their heads higher.

Society cannot function without some form of compulsion upon individuals from childhood to the grave. Yet the compulsion is not always consciously exercised by those in power to gain more power. Custom, convention and ancient habits constrain social groups and individuals as much as the law, the police and the army. But there was certainly one form of social control which went back to time immemorial, and that was religion; and if the kind of charity which was dispensed by fervent evangelicals in George Eliot's or Trollope's novels was more concerned with power to coerce than the haphazard charity of parsons of the old

Low and Slow party in the Church, religion was still regarded as the most effective way to mollify the urban proletariat. There were clergy who deplored that Erastian sentiment which sanctified the rich man in his castle, the poor man at his gate, God made them high and lowly and ordered their estate. Kingsley in his *Letters to Chartists* declared, 'We have used the Bible as if it were a mere special constable's handbook – an opium-dose for keeping beasts of burden patient while they were being loaded . . . We have told you that the Bible preached the rights of property and the duties of labour, when (God knows!) for once it does that, it preaches ten times over the *duties of property* and the *rights of labour*.' If Marx was the first, he was not alone in using this famous simile. The Tractarians too denounced as immoral Paley's definition of virtue, 'the doing good to mankind, in obedience to the will of God, and for the sake of everlasting happiness'. But the Church was still regarded, particularly in the countryside, as the arm of the secular law, and Christianity (as Bentham recognized) the sanction which forced men to be righteous.

It was not as strong an arm as it once had been. It could still invoke the blasphemy laws to silence obstreperous unbelievers, but it had to rely more on the power of social disapproval than on legal powers. The Church of England was too rent by its own disputes to command obedience from the laity nor even on some issues from its own clergy; and the dissenting congregations in their millions were further evidence of the limits to its power to command allegiance. Throughout the century the Church of England continued to be edged aside – and ironically a High Churchman, Gladstone, did most to alter its status within the State. But, however much some regretted that the old writ of squire and parson no longer ran through so much of the kingdom, practically none would have gone as far as that cold fanatic in France, Joseph de Maistre. Here was a man who really believed that religion was by far the most important force of social control. To him the chain of authority descended from God, and unless the State was in league with the Catholic Church, its repressive power would be unsanctified and ineffective. The main secular deterrent – the hangman – derived his power ultimately from God and the Church. Men by their nature were rebels against God, corrupt, feeble and dissolute, whose wicked acts brought retribution on their children. They needed perpetually to be reminded by war and personal suffering of the anarchy which their pride and subversive trust in reason threatened to unleash. No society could exist without a state, no state without sovereignty, no sovereignty without infallibility, no infallibility without God. Protestantism epitomized for de Maistre man's folly in challenging authority with his conscience; and liberals, intellectuals, above all scientists, were hateful and disruptive. Only the authority of the Catholic Church in its most absolutist and transmontane emanation could strike terror and obedience into the seething population of a modern state.

Despite de Maistre's ferocity and loathing of mankind, his premise was not lost on the rationalists in France. They concluded that religion, indeed sacerdotalism, fulfilled a need. Saint-Simon for all his originality had few followers in his lifetime; but no sooner had he died than those few that remained supplied what they felt to be missing in his work. A sacred college of apostles was founded, a church with branches in six departments began to flourish, and no sooner had it taken root than it split, dividing on that pregnant topic on which so many sects have foundered – free love and the place of women. The warm scenes of enthusiasm and agape which the extravagant eloquence of Père Enfantin aroused led to one disciple falling into convulsions and another into a trance, to awake endowed with the gift of prophesy. A retreat by Enfantin into a semi-monastic state in Ménilmontant, where husbands were separated from wives and distinguished *polytechniciens* put aside their set-squares and drawing-boards to weed the garden or polish the floor, presented the appropriate setting to design refulgent vestments including a waistcoat which buttoned from behind and no one could put on without help from someone else – a symbol of the interdependence of human beings. As extravagance succeeded extravagance the inevitable occurred, and Enfantin and his disciples were arraigned in the Palais de Justice where with equal inevitability they threw the court into confusion. Enfantin pronounced, 'I judge, I cannot be judged.' The court took a different view, and sentenced him to be fined and jailed for a year. There, awaiting the arrival of a female Messiah, Enfantin devised a new calendar and organized the spread of his gospel in the provinces by intrepid young disciples. But on his release he interested himself in more secular speculations such as the construction of a Suez Canal, and watched the ripples of the Saint-Simonian movement grow fainter upon the sea of events.

With such a spectacle before his eyes Auguste Comte might have been expected to have displayed extreme caution before promulgating a new religion. But religion was the keystone of his system; and Comte was too like Saint-Simon in character to resist the challenge. Not only did he borrow a sizeable part of Saint-Simon's ideas on science, the progress of thought and the structure of society, but he rivalled him in vanity and egoism. Both men lived on the generosity of their friends, both separated from their wives, both attempted to commit suicide, both were convinced that within a few years the schemes they had devised for reorganizing society would be realized in every detail. But only Comte could have continued to live off his wife's earnings as a prostitute after he had left her and could have contrived to quarrel with most of his benefactors so that she continued to have to support him as best she could and encourage him by attending his lectures. Comte saw the function of religion more through the eyes of de Maistre than the Saint-Simonians. Believing that Protestantism, liberalism and democracy were evil, he praised the Roman Catholic Church for demanding obedience and exercising authority. Unlike Enfantin, Comte found his female Messiah in the person of Clothilde de Vaux whose husband had deserted her and with whom he became besotted. She did not attend his lectures, insisted on their relationship remaining unspotted as she preferred another admirer, and her early death less than two years after they met gave Comte an object to worship, lent dignity to his intentions and absurdity to their realization. His best interpreter, Littré in France, and his best ambassador, Mill in England, both lamented the excessive precision with which Comte defined the theology and liturgy of the new faith. But Littré was wrong to describe them as aberrations: from his earliest days Comte had envisaged his philosophy of science to be the prolegomena to the construction of a new European polity sustained by morality. Since morality was meaningless unless it sprang from the heart, men must adore and worship Humanity.

What did the worship of Humanity mean? Comte left no one in doubt. Europe was to be split up into small republics, each ruled by a triumvirate of bankers; wealth was to be concentrated into the hands of the few; the workers were to be guaranteed a minimum wage and a seven-roomed house; priests were to act as industrial relations officers; and the recalcitrant were to be quelled by public denunciation. The destinies of the Continent would be guided by the High Priest of Humanity who, strangely enough, was to be Monsieur Comte. Widowhood was to be perpetual, divorce with one exception impossible, and chastity to be preserved during the first three months of marriage. The calendar was to be recast, each day and month consecrated to a great human benefactor. The Comtist mythology was elaborate and symbolic. The Earth should be regarded as an animated object called *Le Grand Fétiche*; Space, *Le Grand Milieu*, represented Fatality. 'Our images of all sorts,' noted Mill, 'down to our geometrical diagrams, and even our ciphers and algebraic symbols, should always be figured to ourselves as written in space, and not on paper or any other material substance. Monsieur Comte adds that they should be conceived as green on a white ground.' Womanhood was the source of love; Positivist saints might be worshipped *provided* they were women; and in order to develop compassionate propensities to the full, priests were to be compelled to marry and imbibe (like Bishop Proudie) rich draughts of female affection. Prayer, which was to occupy two hours of every day, did not consist in asking for favours but in effusing or pouring out emotion ('Effuse as much as you like,' commented the Secularist, J. M. Robertson, 'but why call it prayer?'). Sacraments and festivals there were in abundance, culminating in the last, seven years after death, when the priest delivered public judgement on the departed who, if found worthy, might be removed from the public cemetery to *le bois sacré*.

Indeed, Comte emphasized that the *Grande-Etre* of Humanity was not the sum of human beings past and present, but 'only those who are really capable of assimilation, in virtue of a real co-operation on their part in furthering the common good'. Humanity meant those who had helped mankind advance in acquiring knowledge, wisdom and welfare. Faithful animals would join the Elect before 'human manure'. Aves and Paternosters would be supplanted by their Positivist equivalents; the Virgin Mother replaced as an object of adoration by Madame Clothilde de Vaux, who was to personify Humanity but was neither a virgin nor a mother; the Sign of the Cross by placing the hand in succession upon the three chief organs, those of Love, Order and Progress. (Comte was speaking phrenologically.) 'This *may* be a very appropriate way of expressing one's devotion to the Great Being,' commented the exasperated Mill, 'but anyone who had appreciated its effect on the profane reader would have thought it judicious to keep it back till a considerably more advanced stage in the propagation of the Positivist Religion.' But Comte believed that this stage was at hand. In 1862 he would invite the Vicar-General of the Jesuits to a conference which would force all those who still believed in God to become Catholics and the remainder Positivists. The High Priest of Humanity would touch 60,000 francs a year . . .

And yet Comte was not totally absurd. Exactly the same problem troubled Plato who knew that the sophisticated Athens of his day could no longer interpret the meaning of life through the stories of Zeus and the Olympian gods and goddesses; and at the end of his life Plato in the *Laws*, like Comte, advocated a state religion with the death penalty for heretics. Some distinguished scholars, such as Owen Chadwick and Basil Willey, have praised Comte for the nobility of his acknowledgement that some sort of religion is a necessity. At the time, however, the majority of Comte's followers regarded the Positivist religion as a disaster and it was not surprising that when Richard Congreve determined to preach theological Comtism in 1879, more than half of his tiny band of adherents seceded, led by Frederic Harrison. Leslie Stephen, as may be imagined, was not impressed by Comte's reckless ingenuity. He did not intend to replace one false religion by another.

Someone else, however, was pressing the claims of another contender to be the supreme form of social control. That was Leslie's own brother and his client was the law. Fitzjames had studied de Maistre. Naturally he rejected de Maistre's demand for total submission to the Catholic

Church, but he was not all that far from de Maistre in believing that among all the functionaries of the State there is one of immense importance – the hangman. Fitzjames thought little of the agnostic dictum that altruism would replace selfishness and man would lose himself in working for the community. No doubt, said Fitzjames, individual agnostics lived pure high-minded lives. But society could not exist without a moral law; the essence of a law was the sanction; and the gushing humanitarianism of the Comtists was no sanction. Remove the Christian sanction, which compelled the wicked to conform, and you were left with nothing but man's naked selfishness. Fitzjames believed in original sin hardly less passionately than de Maistre. To base morality on appeals to man's better nature was to be sentimentally blind. Nor was he without support for this view among rationalists. Huxley agreed with him. 'As to whether we can fulfil the moral law, I should say hardly any of us. As there are men both physically cripples, and intellectually idiots, so there are some who are morally cripples and idiots and can be kept straight not even by punishment. For these people there is nothing but shutting up, or extirpation.'

What, then, asked Fitzjames, was the principle that in fact governed society? Not freedom as Mill thought, but coercion. Examine society and see how in subtle economic and social forms coercion enforced certain moral standards. Mill was wrong in trying to divide actions into 'other-regarding' acts which affect other people and 'self-regarding' acts which for practical purposes affect only ourselves, and with which the State has no right to interfere. Mill had to admit that since no man is an island, practically every action would harm or benefit someone else: surely Frederic Harrison was far nearer the truth in arguing that every action harmed or helped a brother or sister. This was why the State could not avoid enforcing the moral code. Nevertheless, the State could not make men virtuous, and it would be intolerable if, like the seventeenth-century Calvinists, it tried to do so. Some other exterior mystical force was needed. If Christianity was dying what could it be?

Fitzjames's scheme to give morality claws and teeth was to invest the Law with new majesty. The Law of the Prophets must be replaced by the Law of England; punishment meted out by the courts must supplant the torments of hell and be transmogrified into social revenge. The degree of moral indignation with which society views a particular crime should determine the punishment, and judgement would appear as a terrifying visitation of human wrath in place of the divine anger by which men were no longer awed. This doctrine of retributive punishment was taken a step further in F. H. Bradley's idealist philosophy which conceived the criminal willing his own punishment. Now, this idea is relevant in the world of the individual soul which is the province of the novel; Mihail, who confesses to Father Zossima that he has murdered the woman he loved, wills his own punishment; Dinah Morris tried to induce the same state of mind in Hetty Sorrel; Billy Budd's captain is faced with the perfect Hegelian dilemma; and Koestler's old communist, Rubashov, finally accepts his own execution as just. But is this conception relevant to English law? Perhaps; public indignation for lòng prevented the abolition of the death penalty for murder, and Fitzjames understood better than Leslie the social tensions which generate political emotion and sweep aside the papery plans of reformers. His argument descended from a distinguished lineage, being derived partly from Machiavelli but owing most to St Augustine and Hobbes. Man, so the arguments runs, is unalterably selfish and his wants conflict with the desires of other selfish men. He cannot perform even an unselfish act without retaining a tough little nut of selfishness within him; for if he were wholly unselfish, he would be trampled underfoot by the ruthlessness of the rest of mankind. Thus individual selfish egoisms all war against each other, and society resembles a carnage of struggle and competition. Hence the object of government is not to make men good but to prevent them from doing too much evil. Fitzjames held that man was a compound of Good and Evil in a Heraclitean world of antinomies; and therefore to suppose that appeals to liberty and humanitarianism would change human nature was ridiculous. Fitzjames was enraged by the Positivists' ignorance of human nature. Allegedly scientific, they reeked of superstition. Had not Huxley called the goddess of Humanity, 'as big a fetish as ever nigger first made and then worshipped'? Mill, too, had satirized Comte's religion, but was not Liberty, Fitzjames asked, as great a fetish as the object of his satire? 'Discussions about liberty', wrote Fitzjames, 'are either misleading or idle unless we know who wants to do what, by what restraint he is prevented from doing it, and for what reasons it is proposed to remove that restraint.' Freedom will not make men righteous. To argue that altruism must replace selfishness was to be as absurd as a physicist arguing that the object of mechanics was to alter the law of gravitation. Man has to be coerced to show his better nature.[1]

Fitzjames regarded himself as the true disciple of Bentham, and Mill as an apostate. Certainly the principle of utility is not inconsistent with Hobbism: the interpretation of what is useful will change with each

[1] Fitzjames's comments on the Positivists were withering – he called them a Ritualistic Social Science organization – but he was unjust. They were one of the few countervailing forces to Mill and classical economics. Frederic Harrison's Order and Progress (1875) was the one political treatise in the tradition of rationalism (other than the works of the English pre-Marxists) which challenged laissez-faire and argued that the duty of the State was to promote a moral society even if this led to State interference. 'It was Harrison', wrote Beatrice Webb, 'who first explained to me the economic validity of Trade Unionism and factory legislation; and taught me to resist the current depreciation of the medieval social legislation.'

interpretation of human psychology. Fitzjames took a gloomy, Mill a bright, view of man the political animal. Mill really believed in the perfectibility of man and spoke with scorn of those who regard perfectibility as a mere dream: such men, he said, were usually those who feel that it would afford them no pleasure were the dream to be realized. Fitzjames was certainly numbered among them. Even more than his brother he delighted in the struggle itself. That, not progress, was what gave meaning to life. He wrote:

> The *Great Eastern*, or some of her successors, will perhaps defy the roll of the Atlantic, and cross the seas without allowing their passengers to feel that they have left the firm land. The voyage from the cradle to the grave may come to be performed with similar facility. Progress and science may, perhaps, enable untold millions to live and die without a care, without a pang, without an anxiety. They will have a pleasant passage, and plenty of brilliant conversation. They will wonder that men ever believed at all in clanging fights, and blazing towns, and sinking ships, and praying hands; and, when they come to the end of their course, they will go their way, and the place thereof will know them no more. But it seems unlikely that they will have such a knowledge of the great ocean on which they sail with its storms and wrecks, its currents and icebergs, its huge waves and mighty winds, as those who battled with it for years together in the little craft which, if they had few other merits, brought them who navigated them full into the presence of time and eternity, their Maker and themselves, and forced them to have some definite views of their relations to them and to each other.

This contempt for the days of perfectibility, and total scepticism that such days would ever dawn, made Fitzjames, who did not believe in Christianity any more than Leslie, continue to go to church and urge that Christian sanctions should be preserved as long as possible. Nor was Fitzjames alone in this belief. When the German materialist, Ludwig Büchner, rallied Darwin on his silence about the religious issue, he was shocked to hear his host doubt whether the masses were ripe for atheism.

'My brother is preaching to the world at a great rate,' wrote Leslie Stephen to Holmes in 1873, 'and I regret to say that I don't much approve of some of his sentiments. Oddly enough, he has been, in my opinion, a good deal corrupted by old Carlyle.' He may have thought Carlyle influenced Fitzjames in regarding as immaterial whether Christianity was true. Writing in the *Saturday Review* eighteen months before the publication of *The Origin of Species*, Fitzjames had asked: 'What difference can it make whether millions of years ago our ancestors were semi-rational baboons?' The same facts were always with us: how they came to be with us was another question of minor importance. Leslie certainly thought Fitzjames was persuaded by Carlyle to despise humanity at large, and he particularly disliked his brother's justification of retributive justice which revolted all good Benthamites. Should society,

Leslie asked, pander to those who want to enjoy contemplating a criminal suffer? Sometimes the law has to take account of a criminal's state of mind but it should not express the judgement of God – or of society acting as God – upon the criminal.

Indeed was the law so relevant, as Fitzjames thought? The law carried less weight than it had done in the seventeenth century. The mid-Victorian prescription for a sound society differs almost as much from ours as from the Elizabethan. The Elizabethans thought that the commonweal depended on the system of church government; in Stephen's time it was thought to depend, not on the form in which God was obeyed and worshipped, but on the moral health of each individual in society. The individual was an atom bombinating among other atoms and exerting a force for good or evil over his fellow men. Possessing a soul he could choose freely between right and wrong. Hence society could improve only in so far as each member was regenerated. Law, literature, commerce, voluntary societies, such as churches or trade unions, were judged by the influence they exerted over the individual. Did such and such a reform promote the virtues of self-help, thrift, family sanctity? Did not the ballot weaken moral courage? Did a factory act destroy by compulsion that free moral choice essential to a healthy society by forcing owners to be good? Prohibit the sale of liquor and what merit would there be in not getting drunk? – had not Archbishop Magee said, when asked to sign the temperance pledge, that it would be better for England to be free than England compulsorily sober? Whereas in our time harmony in society is thought to depend on the nation's economic structure, and reforms are measured by the amount they are supposed to increase the material welfare of the people, in Stephen's time self-improvement was regarded as the cure for social ailments. A society which relied for its stability upon legal compulsion, pains and penalties was a bad society.

In his younger days Leslie was apt to fall back on agnostic bombast and demand to know how we could prejudge the future when 'we are only laying the foundations of the temple and know not what will be the glories of the completed edifice'. His fellow agnostics were always reminding each other of their duty 'to busy themselves', as G. R. Bithell put it in the customary swollen rhetoric, 'in the observation, colligation and classification of phenomena with the ultimate aim of discovering the invariable law and order which operates through the universe of mind, intellect and emotion. If he succeeds all is well: if he fails wholly or partly he must pay the penalty; and the bitterest portion of that penalty will sometimes be the reflection that children yet unborn will be made to suffer for his delinquencies.' Certainly the agnostics recognized that Locke had reason on his side when he said that the taking away of God, even in thought alone, dissolved everything. They had to demonstrate that good conduct would not disappear when the sanctions of religion were cleared away because they rested on something which was really eternal, man's sense of right and wrong. Good would replace God, morality Christianity, and he who lost his faith would find it. But how were they to demonstrate it? What was the modern equivalent of theology? Surely it was ethics; and that was why in the second half of the century theists and agnostics such as Mill, Green, Martineau, Spencer, Sidgwick, Bradley, Huxley and Stephen turned to the study of ethics in order to find a sanction to replace heaven and hell.

Henry Sidgwick was the philosopher whom Stephen might have been expected to find most sympathetic. He too had resigned his fellowship at Cambridge on the grounds that he could no longer call himself an Anglican, but he did not become an agnostic. Of all the free-thinkers Sidgwick had the most open mind. His impartiality was so excessive that it cost Maitland his fellowship at Trinity. Sidgwick, who was an elector, was so impressed by Maitland's work, with whose conclusions he agreed, that he voted against him. But it was Maitland who praised Sidgwick's lectures. 'He always gave us of his very best; not what might be good enough for undergraduates . . . but the complex truth just as he saw it, with all those reservations and qualifications, exceptions and distinctions which suggested themselves to a mind that was indeed marvellously subtle, but was showing its wonderful power simply because, even in a lecture room, it could be content with nothing less than the maximum of attainable and communicable truth.' Sidgwick spent his life, whether in the Society for Psychical Research or in the Metaphysical Society, searching for new evidence that God did or did not exist, and at the end of it he inclined ever so gently to the view that he did. He irritated the agnostics by constantly seeing both sides of the question. 'Sidgwick', said Stephen after a meeting of the Metaphysical Society, 'displayed that reflective candour which in him becomes at times a little irritating. A man has no right to be so fair to his opponents.' Indeed in 1898 Walter Raleigh described Sidgwick's role as that of a referee in the duel fought between Faith and Doubt.

This combat was prolonged and was neither bloody nor decisive. Indeed, so inconclusive was it, that at times it was impossible to distinguish whether the combatants, inextricably entangled with each other, were exchanging blows, or costumes, or compliments. One reason for the mild character of the fray (which perhaps diminished its interest merely as a spectacle) was no doubt to be found in the extremely weak state of health of both the protagonists. The Faith that fought on the one side reminds one of the faith of a Unitarian acquaintance of mine. 'We Unitarians', he said, 'believe, as you know, in only one God, and often we have the greatest difficulty in believing even in Him.' The Doubt that fought on the other was an equal antagonist. Moreover, so extreme was their respect for each other, that they could hardly be induced to stop shaking hands that the battle might begin. Sidgwick's decision as referee . . . was to this effect: that the duel was to be lamented only if it should prove decisive, that so long as it proved indecisive it must necessarily continue and must necessarily be of the greatest utility, and that in the nature of things it must always be indecisive. Some dissatisfaction arose on this judgement but it was met by Sidgwick with an offer to award the victory to Faith on condition that he should be allowed to define Faith . . . His actual definition, so far as it can be compounded from his remarks, introduced a new and useful subtlety of qualification. 'Faith', he said, 'is the quality whereby we should be enabled to believe that which we might know to be untrue, could we know anything to be untrue, which, by the operation of Doubt, we cannot.' The most decisive result of the whole affair was the unanimous admiration that was expressed for the skill and impartiality of the referee.

Sidgwick was still admired as the advocate of many good causes in Cambridge; but his ethics seemed to Moore to be inhuman, and the young Keynes writing to Lytton Strachey complained, 'There is no doubt about his moral goodness. And yet it is all so dreadfully depressing – no intimacy, no clear-cut, crisp boldness.'

In the paper which ruffled Stephen Sidgwick had maintained that physics and metaphysics were not as distinct as the rationalists imagined; and in an address to the Society for Psychical Research he claimed that 'the whirligig of time brings round his revenges and . . . the new professor is "but old priest writ large" in a brand-new scientific jargon'. A continuous process of reasoning led Sidgwick to believe that unless God existed, the structure of ethics, as he understood it, was contradictory. He did not conclude, *donc Dieu existe*, but merely stated the dilemma. For him there were two conflicting ethical principles: the duty to do good impartially to others and the duty to seek one's own good. Both altruistic and egoistic duties lie unconditionally upon each of us, yet they must conflict because in many cases they will simultaneously dictate different courses of action. How can these two principles be reconciled? We all know, Sidgwick argued, that it is really *better* to work for the good of others. The only inducement to be altruistic is the assurance that happiness sacrificed in this life will be made up to us in the next life; so that in the long run we will not have minimized our egoistic happiness by our altruistic behaviour. The universe includes, not only this world, but the next, and Sidgwick saw them both as a single ethical system. Thus if God does exist, there appears to be rule in unity itself. If, on the other hand, God does not exist and the soul is not immortal, yet another ontological mystery must be admitted; and we need not be ashamed of this incoherence in ethical thought since scientists themselves have to admit inconsistencies between various scientific principles.

Sidgwick had not solved anything by his first postulate. For even if God exists, it does not alter the fact that the two principles are logically incompatible. To throw in a postulate is to disguise the fact that you have abandoned the search for a coherent ethical system. This, however, was not the marrow of Leslie Stephen's criticism. He objected not to Sidgwick's logic but to his whole approach to ethics. It was the approach of an academic philosopher – and he judged that approach to have failed. Sidgwick declared that morality was reasonable: a man always had a reason for what it was morally right for him to do: the commonsense morality of the day was sensible and required little revision. Such revision as was needed could be made acceptable by philosophers supplying reasons. Pose any practical problem and reason could come up with a practical answer. This was so because philosophers could establish a 'method' in ethics – the title of his treatise – which would convince men that on the whole happiness and pleasure were identical. It was at this point that Sidgwick's fatal impartiality intervened. He could not convince himself that, if the promotion of pleasure was a reasonable pursuit, each of us who pursued it could be persuaded to change his mind, abandon his own selfish interpretation of pleasure and agree on a common policy in order to improve society.

The sight of Sidgwick trying and failing to establish that reasonable and right conduct are identical made Stephen conclude that abstract ethics landed the enquirer in the metaphysical bog of free will. Philosophers for ever failed to distinguish between the cause for an opinion which was held by society and the reasons which men gave for holding that opinion. In an ideal mind they would be identical; but men, by and large, accepted the moral code of the day and invented reasons for acceptance afterwards. The moral philosopher must drop what Stephen loosely called metaphysics – Sidgwick strictly speaking was not a metaphysician; he must turn sociologist.

The first thing to do, Stephen concluded, was to turn ethics into a science. Apply evolution to ethics; and then you will see how morality has developed and why its laws have to be acknowledged. The moral philosopher can hardly doubt 'the indisputable truth that mankind is engaged in a perpetual struggle for existence with the consequent crushing out – as we must try to hope – of the weakest and the worst'. Philosophers should show that the differences between intuitionists and utilitarians were purely verbal. The Kantian categorical imperative was binding on every society: a society which disobeyed it perished. The utilitarian principle of the greatest happiness of the greatest number was equally valid because that was simply another way of putting the truth that individual desires have to be subsumed under the general injunction to behave in a way which promotes the species.

Stephen turned to evolutionary ethics because he thought that there was no need to find a *new* sanction to replace heaven and hell; the sanction had always been inherent in the cosmic process. He thought he had made a major discovery.

Stephen's Evolutionary Ethics

The nineteenth-century poets rejoiced that Nature had thrown off her disguise. No longer was she the mechanically perfect, rationally ordered, Newtonian universe. No longer did Nature work for the benefit of man to the glory of the Deity, no longer did the stars rejoice in Reason's ear and sing that the hand that made them was divine. To each poet now Nature appeared in a different light. Wordsworth admitted, and Stephen commended his admission, that while men were helped and healed by Nature, they would find evil as well as good within her. Baudelaire thought the dualism in Nature was so marked that different men saw not the same but different Natures.

> L'un t'éclaire avec son ardeur,
>   L'autre en toi met son deuil, Nature!
> Ce qui dit à l'un: Sépulture!
> Dit à l'autre: Vie et splendeur!

Some went further and asserted that Nature delighted in her wickedness. Sade's doctrine that evil was the Natural Law was reiterated by Swinburne:

> Nature averse to crime? I tell you, nature lives and breathes by it; hungers at all her pores for bloodshed, aches in all her nerves for the help of sin, yearns with all her heart for the furtherance of cruelty . . . Unnatural is it? Good friend, it is by criminal things and deeds unnatural that nature works and moves and has her being . . . if we would be at one with nature, let us continually do evil with our might.

For Goethe ethics and Nature were for ever divorced:

> Denn unfühlend
> Ist die Natur:
> Es leuchtet die Sonne
> Über Bös' und Gute,
> Und dem Verbrecher
> Glänzen wie dem Besten
> Der Mond und die Sterne.[1]

For Leconte de Lisle Nature was ethically neutral, dispassionate, neither sad nor joyful. If you will visit Nature, forget tears and laughter, empty your heart of such human emotions as forgiveness and rancour;

---

[1] 'For Nature does not feel: the sun shines upon the wicked and good alike, and the criminal as well as the best of men sees the brightness of the moon and the stars.'

only then will you be able to understand her and *goûter une suprême et morne volupté.*

> Viens! Le soleil te parle en paroles sublimes;
> Dans sa flamme implacable absorbe-toi sans fin;
> Et retourne à pas lents vers les cités infimes
> Le coeur trempé sept fois dans le néant divin.

Philosophers seldom listen to poets. The confusion and alarm among the poets should have stimulated philosophers to consider whether analogies between nature and ethics, or between Natural Selection and social forces, were in any way apposite; when popular confusion on some issue arises, critical philosophers might be expected to analyse the relevance of the questions that are being asked and shift the controversy into another key. But such was not the case. Here is yet another instance of the indebtedness of Victorian thinkers to the eighteenth-century philosophic tradition. They adhered to their forebears' treatment of evolution. Just as, broadly speaking, Voltaire and Paley took an optimistic, and Dr Johnson and Butler a pessimistic, view of Nature's processes, so on the one hand Spencer, and on the other Huxley, explained men's relation to Nature in the time-honoured manner. Determined to preserve the unity of truth, they continued to treat all experience in the same terms.

Herbert Spencer is the best known exponent of evolutionary ethics. He denied that there is a necessary antinomy between natural and social laws. He had defined Evolution as the development of all Being from the homogeneous or less complex to the heterogeneous or more complex. Thus the more highly developed a society became, the more highly civilized would be its moral code and behaviour. Why? Because the same process by which variations in the species were transmitted enabled man unconsciously to inherit certain fundamental moral intuitions. But there was a proviso. Man must preserve within his environment a free society at peace with other societies. So long as he did this these moral intuitions would become more highly developed as each generation bequeathed to the next the accumulated experience of what was most useful in producing good. Spencer's ethics depended, therefore, on a theory which orthodox biologists have scouted for many years, namely the inheritance of acquired characteristics. As a corollary to transforming Natural Selection into the Survival of the Fittest, Spencer went on to proclaim that the rule of life was that the weakest went to the wall and that the weakest were the worst.

But for Spencer ethics was a mere sideline. He was engaged on a more momentous task – the construction of a sociology of progress in which, like a spider, he spun laws out of his own guts. Long before the web was

woven, it had ceased to catch living matter. The circle of Stephen's friends
produced more vigorous evolutionists. For instance, in the first issue of
Mind Frederick Pollock pleaded that ethics was the social equivalent of
the scientific process of natural selection. In another article W. K. Clifford
reasoned that man's conscience had the function of the preservation of
society in the struggle for a future existence. Then there was Bagehot who
sub-titled one of his books *Thoughts on the Application of Natural
Selection and Inheritance to Political Society* and who concluded that
'those nations which are the strongest tend to prevail over the others; and
in certain marked peculiarities the strongest tend to be the best'. But it was
really Sidgwick's attempt to revitalize utilitarian ethics which 'set me
thinking when it failed to make me think with him'. Stephen hoped to
disarm his critics by saying that if giants had built a foundation for the
subject, 'even dwarfs may add something to the superstructure of the
great edifice of science'. What, then, is *The Science of Ethics* about?

The book opens by arguing that ethical treatises such as Sidgwick
wrote lead the reader into linguistic quagmires. We must look beyond
traditional ethics. We must also look beyond the individual to the
community. That is where the ethical process is at work. It works through
the race (by race Stephen meant Caucasian, Negroid, etc., distinguishing
morality, a property of the race, from habit or custom, properties of the
nation). The race forms a 'social tissue' through which normal qualities
are transmitted. This tissue is composed of individuals just as anatomical
tissue is composed of cells. Society therefore is an organism of living tissue
held together by molecular chains of institutions and by the values which
by and large men accept. Why do they accept them? Does not each
institution produce its own distinctive moral code and, if so, how are they
integrated? They are integrated by the family. It is the family which
indoctrinates children with notions of right and wrong and, if family life
is healthy, the life of the race is ensured.

There is always bound to be a conflict between the institutional values
and the demands of society as a whole. But there is a regulator. The law of
Natural Selection compels mankind to become efficient in all walks of life
including that of conduct. So social mutations take place. They are caused
by new technology, or by new political institutions, or by cultural
advances, indeed even by intellectual discoveries such as the realization
that morality no longer rests on supernatural religious sanctions.
Stephen, therefore, ends up in the position, paradoxical for the author of
The History of English Thought in the Eighteenth century, that ideas are
not a reflection but actually a cause of social change and that those
societies which permitted intellectual freedom would be the more likely to
survive: savage societies, he concluded, perished partly because such
freedom was proscribed. In fact evolution can be seen as a process which

in politics tends towards constitutional government: the changes in Parliament and the legal system enshrined in the British constitution had preserved the vigour of the nation. Stephen, as a true nineteenth-century Cobdenite liberal, insisted that the struggle for survival was not a struggle between nations. Soon the nations, accustomed to the benefits of free exchange of commodities and ideas, would outlaw war. It is the human race which struggles to survive, not the nations. This struggle may 'occasionally lead to an internecine struggle between nations.' A nation survives by destroying its neighbour. But this is no longer the case 'in any moderately civilized state of the world . . . War decides how races are to be grouped, not which race is to survive.' We may raise our eyebrows, but Stephen clarifies his meaning. 'A conquest is the extinction of a political organization, and the commonest result is that the qualities of the resulting group are determined as much by the conquered as by the conquerors. The race is not extirpated but incorporated.'

Morality, then, is generated by social pressure and keeps the social tissue alive: if it grows faint, the tissue perishes and the race is threatened with extinction. In other words a moral rule states a condition of social welfare. For instance, intemperance can be proved scentifically to produce a state of disease in both the individual and society; thus we can prove that courage, benevolence and, with minor reservations, truthfulness and justice are logical necessities. All are essential conditions of social existence. Reason and morality are linked. It is reasonable to be moral because to be moral is socially useful. At this point Stephen marries Darwinism to John Stuart Mill. Utilitarianism possesses 'a core of inexpugnable truth', for what is social welfare but another name for utility? Certain types of behaviour are dubbed virtuous when they are recognized by society to be useful because they preserve the race. Right and wrong are terms expressing reverence for certain rules that existed long before man developed a true moral sense. Utilitarianism, however, has been till now an ethic of pure expediency in that it denies that evil can 'be objectionable as evil or good desirable as good [because it argues that] we must consider morality as a means to some ulterior end'.

In Stephen's ethics conduct, considered as a necessary part of social welfare, becomes more than a matter of expediency. It is a vital principle in the survival of the race. It is not a simple calculus of Benthamite self-interest. The right kind of social behaviour serves the interest of the social organism and requires the individual at times to sacrifice his self-interest. Economic competition, says Stephen in line with Alfred Marshall, can crush an individual, but his sacrifice benefits his environment, and the society in which he lives is better adapted to meet the challenges of the future. There could be no innovation without competition, and it is a rule of life that some succeed and some fail.

Nevertheless, Stephen adds, reverting to the true faith, though the utilitarians are wrong in explaining goodness solely in terms of happiness, social ethics show that the general happiness of the people is the ultimate standard. Health and happiness coincide – not absolutely of course and therefore all efforts in the manner of Sidgwick to prove virtue and happiness identical resemble attempts to square the circle – but, by and large, the current morality produces happiness.

This is the sanction we seek. There can be no sanction such as Fitzjames or Sidgwick demanded. The moralist can point out what things are beneficial and can explain what virtue and vice are, but he can never give a bad man a reason for being good; he can give only good people reasons for being good. Virtue resides within man; and if a man's nature is corrupt, intrinsic reasons for good conduct do not exist. Belief in God and the fear of hell are not real sanctions, but theological superstructures built upon the hard facts of social ethics. Why do the Churches put it about that drunkards may be damned? Because originally drunkenness was seen to be socially evil. 'The limiting and determining cause of the moral objection to vice is in all cases measured by the perception of the social evils which it causes.' In fact these supernatural sanctions, like hell, have always been avoidable because such imaginary penalties can be warded off by equally imaginary remedies such as prayer, absolution or conversion. Thus there is no ultimate motive for good conduct but that of social welfare. Science itself is not the basis of morality but a method of demonstrating that the only basis is the old basis and that the rules governing human conduct have been and will be always the same.

Stephen's book was reviewed by Sidgwick – a review which, he admitted, 'gave some twinges to my vanity', and he was pained to be chided for failing to acknowledge his debt to Comte because he had 'a higher estimate of him than most people do'. He simply thought that 'the evolutionists have made his theory workable and have brought it into a quasi-scientific state more than he could do'. But to Stephen's chagrin few thought his book had changed anything. Then eleven years later someone gave tongue on evolution and ethics whom Stephen would have liked dearly to have endorsed his views. This was T. H. Huxley who in his old age had roused himself to deliver the Romanes Lecture at Oxford. The lecture took a view diametrically opposed to *The Science of Ethics*. Huxley described his lecture as 'really an effort to put the Christian doctrine that Satan is the Prince of this world upon a scientific foundation'. Huxley denied that the Fittest was necessarily the Best. In any case 'social progress means a checking of the cosmic process at every step and the substitution for it of another, which may be called the ethical process: the end of which is not the survival of those who may happen to be the fittest in respect of the whole of the conditions which obtain, but of those who are ethically the best'. We must not imitate but combat the cosmic process. Huxley in fact destroyed his case when in the *Prolegomena*, which he published before the body of his essay, he conceded that there was no real resemblance between human society and the process which adapts living beings to current conditions in the state of nature. That should have disposed of the matter. But Huxley had not answered the question: is there a moral law in human society which will make men do good even when the sanctions of religion vanish? Of course he announced with his accustomed vigour that there was such a law. Yes, men of every age and country have lamented that the wicked flourish as the green bay-tree while the righteous beg for bread, but this was an illusion. Science told us that morality was 'a real and living belief in that fixed order of nature which sends social disorganization upon the track of immorality, as surely as it sends physical diseases after physical trespasses. And of that firm and lively faith it is her high mission to be priestess.' 'The gravitation of sin to sorrow', he wrote on another occasion, 'is as certain as that of the Earth to the Sun and more so . . . nay it is before us all in our own lives, if we had but the eyes to see it.' Huxley's faith lay in the Immortality of Force and Matter and 'in a very unmistakable *present* state of rewards and punishments for all our deeds'. Where have we heard that somewhat strained tone of voice before? Is not George Eliot saying, 'I have not observed that beastliness, treachery and parricide are the direct way to happiness and comfort on earth'?

This time Stephen was puzzled as well as pained. He could not see why Huxley did not accept that actions inspired by the highest motives could in fact be wrong and disastrous for the race. Suppose you disburse charity indiscriminately you will multiply beggars. Does that mean that by exercising a moral quality (charity) you will diminish the nation's vigour? Certainly not. Charity remains a virtue but that charity which fosters a degraded class must be called immoral. Or again, if it can be demonstrated, as Alfred Marshall can, that protection destroys the new technologies which will make goods cheaper and that collectivism produces greater evils than unbridled individualism, can we not regard it as proven that to induce the working class to become thrifty, sober and prudent is better than paying whole armies of inspectors to enforce regulations about their hours of labour? From this he did not think Huxley would differ.

Stephen went on to say that he could not accept Huxley's version of the cosmic process as 'an internecine struggle of each against all'. If that were true how had there been progress? The more moral the race, the more harmonious and better organized, the better it is fitted for holding its own. Stephen agreed that the most civilized race was also the most formidable in war. But, he said, by now skating on thin ice, the white race

held its own not by brute force but by justice, humanity and intelligence –
and these qualities do not weaken the brute force when such a quality is
required. The equality of man is a dream. But it is not a dream because of
natural inferiority. Neither the descendants of the criminal or the poet
inherit their vices or virtues. Similarly negroes are not inherently lazy.
They are lazy because they were slaves. They became slaves because they
were inferior in their development to the white man – and it was
incumbent upon the whites now to show their moral qualities and give the
tribes in Africa land of their own and the power of self-government. 'I am
not so anxious to see the whole earth covered by an indefinite
multiplication of the cockney type.' The whites could not take over the
whole of Africa – though Stephen had to admit they might encroach on
what was left to the Africans. Sometimes one feels that Stephen plods on
and on unaware of the fact that the further he marches the longer grow his
lines of communication and the more vulnerable he is to attack. Huxley –
for once – did not reply; and the next year they both had the satisfaction
of condemning Benjamin Kidd's *Social Evolution* for daring to argue that
non-rational conduct such as adherence to religious forms and codes
could protect society from rampant individualism. Kidd's book, too, is
forgotten. Its single insight was incorporated in Durkheim's work on
sociological method which immediately followed it. But it is more
acceptable to modern sociologists than Stephen's treatise.

The Fallacies of Evolutionary Ethics

Stephen deserves some praise. He had had the courage to break with the
tradition which nurtured him. He was not an egoistical hedonist. He
maintained that men do whatever is easiest for them to do. Some men
sacrificed their own happiness to that of others for various reasons – that
they feared public opinion or had been brought up by high-minded
parents. But it was a real sacrifice and it hurt: it was disingenuous to say
that *really* they were happier in making it.

Nevertheless, if we have to consider his treatise as a contribution to
ethics, it is worthless. It simply expresses an opinion about a scientific
hypothesis and relates it to ethics by scientific analogies. You may prefer
T. H. Huxley's theory that it is our duty to combat the cosmic process to
Stephen's theory that we ought to go along with it; or you may agree with
the Austrian sociologist Gumplowicz, who published *Der Rassenkampf*
the year after Stephen's book, and saw the evolutionary process in terms
of war between races, nations and groups. But your preference will
depend on your temperament and the society and community in which
you live and move – in logic there is not a penny to choose between them
because they are of the same class of argument. Evolutionary ethics are

fraudulent. They solve the main problems by evading them. Ethics tell us what we ought to do, they deal with problems of obligation; evolutionary ethics tell us nothing about obligation. Just as one sees that sneak of a concept – the transformation of men seeking their own pleasure being identical with seeking each other's pleasure – being kicked out through the front door, to our dismay we see the wretch sidling in through the back door. Altruism is now not a conscious act but an unconscious process effected by Evolution.

Stephen expressly denied that men were ever under an obligation to act in a particular way. Why should a man feel under a moral obligation when Nature is doing the job for him? Conscience in Stephen's ethics became 'the utterance of the public spirit of the race, ordering us to obey the primary conditions of its welfare'. The law Do This became Be This. Directly you substitute the phrase, You Must Do This for You Ought to Do This, ethics ceases to be ethics. Morality has been gelded and all its potency removed. Follow Stephen's argument and you can see that he doubles back on his tracks on the question of conscience. Right conduct, he says, is dictated by the conscience, and the greatest moral reformers are those whose consciences will not let them rest. Naturally they are dissatisfied with the moral code of society because the majority of mankind prefer peace even at the price of condoning evil. ' "Be good if you would be happy" seems to be the verdict even of worldly prudence; but it adds in an emphatic aside "Be not too good." ' That is why men who break with the world for the world's good must expect to suffer pain. But how does Stephen square these platitudes with his definition of conscience as 'the utterance of the public spirit of the race'? This, of course, is the very point where ethics come in; and at this very point Stephen breaks off.

Stephen believed that his conclusions derived from scientific premises, but when we examine how he relates facts to values, the scientific part of the argument obviously does not affect the conclusions at all. Social Health and Happiness coincide – but how? Virtue and Happiness though not identical are complementary – in what way? The 'scientific' parts of the argument cancel each other out before we get to the point where ethics begin. When Stephen applies the principle of Natural Selection to human conduct, he is unaware that he is faced with a choice: are we to concentrate on the brutal competition of the process or on the advantages which society gains from this process of change? When Stephen says that right and wrong are names given to rules that existed before man had a moral sense, is he saying that it is right for a tribe faced with starvation to migrate and pillage the territory of another tribe? When he says that moral rules are statements of a condition of social welfare what does he mean by 'welfare'? Hopeless to enquire – all the terms are used in just as 'oily and saponaceous' a way as theological terms are used: one cannot grasp them – 'like an eel they slip through your fingers and straight are nothing'.[1] They evade the question why one way of acting should be considered better than another and how goodness relates to right conduct. When Stephen says that the moral code on which social welfare depends changes as society evolves, he does not tell us why nor how high-minded men are entitled to break the code in order to make it 'higher'. It is not evolution which sanctifies our conception of right and wrong; it is the very reverse – morality gives meaning to such words as 'progress' and 'welfare' and hence to the interpretation given by Stephen to the term 'evolution'. The most devastating criticism of this kind of ethics was made by G. E. Moore in *Principia Ethica* when he showed that the structure of evolutionary ethics was built on the assumption that 'to be more evolved' is synonymous with 'better'. Writing of Spencer, Moore said, '*If* he could establish that amount of pleasure is always in direct proportion to amount of evolution, *and also* that it was plain what conduct was more evolved, [his theory] *would* be a very valuable contribution to the science of Sociology; it would even, if pleasure were the sole good, be a valuable contribution to Ethics.' On examination there is no *logical* connection at all between moral standards and the evolutionary process.

Why did Stephen fail as a moral philosopher? He took enormous trouble to organize the argument of his book, but in retrospect it shares the same failing as did his son-in-law's work: Leonard Woolf's *Principia Politica*. It rambles. Sometimes he ends up where he started because in making numbers of admissions he destroys the premise he is striving to establish. All sorts of admirable sentiments are deployed in each of these books, but the logical bonding fails to take place. Sidgwick had been prolix, over-subtle and ill-organized, but *The Method of Ethics* analysed logical terms and epistemological and psychological questions and therefore showed the reader what he meant and how he inferred. Stephen fell into the error of the amateur in thinking that preoccupation with problems of logical inference was mere academic logomachy. A bold attack from the flank would scatter them. He believed, for instance, that he had shown that the conflict between intuitionists and utilitarians was unreal; and that they were reconciled by his acceptance of both the standard of utility and the principle that virtue resides within a man. Had he considered what questions the two schools were seeking to answer he would have seen that they were sharply opposed, since utilitarians (Mill, Sidgwick and later Moore) all believe that the goodness of a state of

---

[1] These were the words in which Lord Chancellor Westbury described Samuel Wilberforce's protest against the Privy Council's rejection of the process for heresy against Rowland Williams in 1861 when Westbury was said to have 'dismissed Hell with costs'. The words were a malicious play on Wilberforce's nickname, Soapy Sam.

affairs is the primary ethical concept and that rightness of actions is a derivative concept, while religious or Kantian ethics hold that the rightness and wrongness of actions ('What is it my duty to do?') is primary. Mill thought that the goodness of a state of affairs meant pleasantness; Sidgwick that although goodness did not mean pleasantness, it was an a priori truth that all good states were pleasant; and Moore, whose Principia Ethica appeared a few months before Stephen died, that there were many characteristics other than pleasantness of a state of affairs which make it good – all a moral philosopher could do was to give a partial list of such characteristics.

Stephen was making the social sciences do the work of religion. Evolution replaces God. Evolution is the Creator, Man his child; Evolution is an Immanent God or Process at work within the world. Just as a belief in God comforted Newman and reconciled him to the spectacle of evil in the world, so Stephen was comforted by the belief that morality was created and sanctioned by Evolution. Despite his long explanation that no sanction exists which will compel an evil man to do good, he was at pains to show that the sanction really resides in the development of civilization, and that evil men and societies perish (go to hell) according to the Law. This is not discreditable. A man should have the right to express how in his view he relates to the world. William James did so, as did others who did not require his finite God. Turgenev merely said, 'My faith is in civilization, and I require no further creed.' He acknowledged that this attitude was a faith, and though he did not define it, he knew that it involved him in certain moral and intellectual implications. We should not blame Stephen for seeking, and in his evolutionary ethics finding, comfort. To seek reassurance that the scheme of things is somehow rational and 'makes sense' is common enough among men. Did not Jonathan Edwards in the end find Predestination 'infinitely pleasant, bright and sweet'? Some analytic philosophers obtain a similar reassurance when they declare that these unpleasant problems can be spirited away by showing that they arise from confusions in the logic of language. Even historians derive comfort from the study of history by setting the hopes and frustrations of their times in perspective beside those of other civilizations in the past and future.

But Stephen wanted not only comfort but certitude in the realm of the uncertain. And this he had asserted was unobtainable. Isaiah Berlin has analysed the fallacies that lie behind a recurrent desire by philosophers to obtain infallible knowledge of incorrigible propositions (e.g. Locke's simple ideas or Mill's sensations or Russell's atomistic use of words) – propositions beyond which it is logically impossible to go and which, they tell us, are the one spring of all knowledge. Stephen's evolutionary law of morality – though it is born of the same desire for certainty – can hardly be regarded in this light. Stephen desired not just the discovery of a basic proposition on which a science of knowledge could be founded, but a law which would govern the moral relations of the individual to society – and this, Stephen had declared while destroying orthodox metaphysics, could never be found. It is this desire to find metaphysical sanctions which gives Victorian agnosticism the appearance of a new nonconformist sect. The power of religion over the very minds which denied it emerges nowhere more subtly than in Stephen's evolutionary ethics.

The Science of Ethics as Sociology

If *The Science of Ethics* is worthless as ethics, is there something to be said for it as sociology? For many years now sociologists have been discarding the two main notions which Comte and writers of Stephen's generation popularized – namely that society is the same everywhere and at every time and that there can be a general theory of society or a single law or explanation governing human behaviour. In the eighteenth century Condorcet made the most explicit, in the nineteenth Marx the most famous, and in the twentieth Talcott Parsons the most impenetrable, attempt to do so. In such theories the factual and the causal are inextricably tangled with the historical and the normative. The dis-agreement between Stephen and Huxley resembles in miniature the disagreement between Marxists and functionalists in our time. Marxists take as proved that conflict between the classes is irrevocable and caused by the iron laws of economic determinism, whereas functionalists consider that the roles which different groups and people play in society produce a fundamental harmony which arises from people's needs and cannot be otherwise. Each side uses the evidence used by the other. According to Marxists apparent identity of interest is produced by a mere ideological distortion. According to the functionalists conflict is merely the release or resolution of tensions – a process which enables societies to adjust and change. But in fact there is no evidence by which either could convince the other. The dispute reflects two visions of life or philosophies of history.

Stephen and other social Darwinists similarly believed that they had discovered laws which governed society – laws analogous to, sometimes derived from, the laws of physics, chemistry and biology. They too argued from an abstraction called Man to an abstraction called Society which embraced all societies. In one sense Stephen resembled the functionalists with his excessive concern for moral solidarity and his anxiety that any deviation from the determined path of evolution would be at mankind's peril. Despite all Stephen's talk about introducing scientific method and his genuine distrust of metaphysics (by which he meant not just political theories which invoke the sanctions of religion but theories based on rights or on equality), his book was innocent of any empirical reasoning. Blue Books, surveys such as Mudie-Smith's *The Religious Life of London*, or Mayhew's work on working-class conditions, never impinged upon him. Nor did the work of the early anthropologists who were already beginning to collect examples of primitive cultures to argue from facts in the way Stephen advocated but did not follow. Not being a scientist Stephen was uninterested in the *mechanism* of change in biology and therefore neglected this problem in his sociology. As Sidgwick said in his review, the natural selection of social tissue could not explain exactly how the changes during the past two thousand years took place.

In another sense Stephen resembled the Marxists. When he declared that truthfulness was good because it promoted social welfare, he should have made his readers ask whether everything which promotes welfare was necessarily good. Who is to decide *at the time* that a particular course of action will promote social welfare? And how are they to decide? Every orthodox Marxist would argue that the dialectic has given man the answer. 'Objectively' what may appear false or wrong is in fact true and right because it will ultimately 'promote social welfare'. But how can one know for certain what promotes social welfare? Who is to judge? To the communist there is only one answer: the Party. Stephen had his answer. Not politicans who are locked in their party shibboleths. Not Oxford and Cambridge dons – 'to find people who believe honestly in antiquated prejudices, we must go to the people who have been trained to believe them'. The best forecasters will be the most intelligent and least prejudiced and most open-minded men, who have won their place in society through open competition, not patronage. In other words the new intelligentsia – who look suspiciously like Stephen himself. But do not scoff: like the Marxists they are not without guidance. Comte invented the sociology of knowledge and from this we can learn, and hence apply, the laws of progress. It will be remembered that Comte acknowledged grudgingly that there could conceivably be a few additions to the sum of knowledge in his day – not many, but a few. The map of knowledge was spread before us and some corrections of detail no doubt would be vouchsafed. So the second answer that Stephen gave was that we must apply and amplify the scientific laws which govern society. Could he give an example? What an advantage would have been gained, explained Stephen, 'if our grandfathers would have looked at the French Revolution scientifically . . . the true moral, as we all see now, was that England should make such reforms as would obviate the danger of a similar catastrophe at home. The moral which too many people drew was that all reforms should be stopped; with the result that the evils grew worse and "social strata" more profoundly alienated.' This is a sensible and defensible historical interpretation of the period from 1789 to 1832, but there is nothing 'scientific' about it as he used that word. What Stephen really means is that it is 'reasonable'. But there is, as Stephen knew only too well, no reason why intelligent people should not come to widely differing views about what is efficacious or conduces to welfare, nor why they should not fall into fearful error.

Nor is there any likelihood that the historical process will remain virtually immutable as Comte and the Marxists have argued. It is all too evident that proletarian class-consciousness has changed because the circumstances of the proletariat in Europe have changed for the better since Marx wrote. Marxists produce numbers of explanations why this should be so. Mass culture has stupefied the working class and sapped their revolutionary ardour. Not only increasing misery but increasing bewilderment will put the tinder to the twigs. When working-class men and women realize how alienated they are, how estranged from their world and its products, from their rulers, from each other – their own mates – then they will demand that the corrupt political and economic structure, capitalism, which inflicts this misery on them, must be brought to an end. Nevertheless these explanations do not meet the most deadly criticism which sociologists of knowledge bring against those who declare that laws governing progress or the way to create a better society have been discovered, as Stephen believed. This is the criticism that all systems of thought relate to their times. As times change the system has to change – or even has to be discarded. Suppose we take Stephen's defensible contention that the refusal to introduce some measure of parliamentary reform before 1832 deepened class divisions in Britain. Suppose we apply this criterion to his own political beliefs. Is it not equally true to say that Stephen's opposition to the welfare legislation which was introduced at last by Lloyd George deepened class divisions and strengthened the syndicalism which has afflicted Britain throughout the twentieth century? Or again let us ask why Stephen opposed so vigorously anything which diminished competition or provided through taxation social insurance. It was, of course, because he believed that the classical economists had discovered the first of those immutable social laws which he as a sociologist was longing to establish. In fact men's grasp of the principles governing the welfare of their society is far less certain than their grasp of the principles employed to categorize actions as right or wrong.

And yet it is always possible that a pulse still beats in Stephen's sociology and it is not as dead as it looks. W. G. Runciman argues that there is still life in Marxist, functional and evolutionary theories. They are developed by the interplay of deductive reasoning and empirical observation, and though by now too many examples of human behaviour for which they cannot account have piled up, it may well be that the survival of the fittest or the social relations of production can still partially explain past events. Stephen's belief that indiscriminate charity will damage the social tissue can be thrown away leaving the original thesis still valid. 'Dated and complacent as they may have come to seem, theories of a unilinear progression from militant to industrial society, or from an Asiatic to an ancient to a feudal to a bourgeois to a socialist mode of production, or from a theological to a metaphysical to a positivist age, or from promiscuity to polygamy to monogamy, or from status to contract, or from animism to science could perfectly well have turned out to stand up better than they have against the reported evidence now available.' In his treatise on social theory Runciman argued – though with immensely greater sophistication, logical rigour and insight – Leslie Stephen's contention that even if the variables and imprecision of social data do not permit us to operate with the same confidence as physicists or chemists, there is nothing in that data which generically debars it from being examined by the methods of science. If schemes such as those of Spencer and Stephen are invalidated and have been superseded because societies evolve in a different fashion from that which they predicted, their mode of reasoning is still as valid as that of Darwin in biology. Evolution will not, as Leslie Stephen thought, reveal with a wave of the wand how societies change their structure; but it can throw out a few suggestions which can be tested, some of which might even be accepted as likely to be true.

Stephen held most emphatic views on what was for him the most important social institution: the family. He was himself a typical example of the Hajnal pattern of marriage common to Western Europe in which marriage is delayed until the married couple, either by increasing earnings, or by saving, or by uniting fortunes, can achieve economic independence and live in a separate home. We have already seen what an uncompromising protagonist he was of the patriarchal family in his own life, and he had no doubt that anything which shook the family, such as adultery, must shake society. In this he was at one with virtually all educated opinion. G. M. Young declared that there were two institutions in Victorian England which the age accepted as almost divinely sanctioned – representative institutions and the family. The family 'was perhaps the clue to the Victorian paradox – the rushing swiftness of its intellectual advance and the tranquil evolution of its social and moral ideals. The advance was in all directions outwards, from a stable and fortified centre'. Shaftesbury thought 'there can be no security to society, no honour, no prosperity, no dignity at home, no nobleness of attitude towards foreign nations, unless the strength of the people rests upon the purity and firmness of the domestic system. Schools are but auxiliaries.' The family's head was unquestionably the father and Leslie Stephen noted that Henry Fawcett's relationship with his father – which was that of affectionate comradeship – was exceptional in that more usually (as in his own case) 'affection is coloured by deference and partial reserve'. Fathers might often be absent or remote, but they were sovereigns supported in every wish by their consort – unless, of course, the consort established a matriarchy; and in the urban evangelical home in which Stephen grew up fathers admonished and exhorted their sons when they were away at school in frequent letters. The sons learnt to be stoical, reserved, independent and to value comradeship and loyalty.

Stephen claimed that mankind had advanced from polyandry and the capture of women to 'monogamy and comparative sexual equality'. He did not believe that the equality could be more than comparative; and this belief he considered was endorsed by scientific evidence. A few years after *The Science of Ethics* appeared the biologist Patrick Geddes published *The Evolution of Sex*, in which he argued that cell metabolism determined the difference between the sexes. Masculinity at the level of the cell was characterized by the dissipation, femininity by the conservation, of energy. Male cells by their catabolic function transmitted variations, female cells by their anabolic function maintained stability in the new life they supported. From this flowed male aggressiveness: 'the hungry active cell becomes flagellate sperm' while female passivity flowed from the quiescent well-fed cell which became an ovum. No political or technological change could alter the male and female temperament; 'what was decided by the prehistoric *Protozoa* cannot be annulled by act of parliament'. And so at a time when Zola's social realism was challenging romantic notions of love, Geddes declared that his researches suggested that while the capacity of human beings to feel passion was deepening so was their sense of moral order.

Geddes, like Stephen, believed that the growing influence of women would increase altruism and diminish male egoism; and that this influence would be exerted first and foremost upon their children in the home. A new era of co-operation in society was dawning. But it would be a false dawn unless the separate sex roles for male and female were understood and followed. If females became male activists, or if they usurped specifically male positions in society, they would fly in the face of scientific laws. Women were not confined to the home because they were less strong than men. They worked at menial tasks because men expended energy in bursts of physical or cerebral activity, whereas women being passive stored their energy and had greater patience, appreciation of subtle detail and intuition. So Geddes set out his scientific justification for the familiar Victorian typology of the sexes.

In recent years the nuclear family, still more the patriarchal family, has been much derided. Anthropologists, historians and feminists who desire

a freer society for women in which wives are not chained to their home
and can compete for jobs on equal terms with men, in which divorce is
regarded as normal and in which children are not repressed by parental
tyranny, have argued that in primitive societies more extended kinship
systems are customary; or that marriages in medieval and Renaissance
times were arranged for dynastic or financial reasons; or that romantic
love and the family as the Victorians knew it was a product of capitalism.
At various times rulers, philosophers and theologians have denounced the
family, both State and churches regarding it as too tenacious a rival for
the duties which they conceive are owed to them. One of Charles
Kingsley's favourite villains was the Roman Catholic priest who in-
sinuated himself into the family through the confessional and broke up
the family by setting wives against husbands and by inducing daughters to
break filial obedience and enter convents. More prosaic demographic and
historical studies do not sustain this denigration of the nuclear family.
Stephen was right in thinking that the family has always been the primal
unit in ancient as well as advanced societies. He was right to believe that
love, affection and loyalty between its members are more the norm than
repression and hatred. He was right to sense that the family preserves
privacy and hinders the State and its innumerable agencies encroaching
and dictating how its members shall live. He recognized that evolutionary
theory entailed an understanding of social structure.

On the other hand he can hardly be called a sociologist of the family.
He assumed that family stability depended on the conscious decisions of
its members and on tradition. He showed little understanding that it also
depended on impersonal demographic factors. The fertility and mortality
rates and the social conditions of marriage affect the relationship of the
young to the old and of kith to kin. Longevity combined with low fertility
means fewer cousins and more great-aunts and uncles and grandparents;
and that in itself will change the pattern of domestic life. Concern with
facts, and the dreary, long-drawn-out search for the facts, do not come
easily to moralists, and Stephen's way of arguing from general principles
to justify his own beliefs and prejudices was normal in Britain on such
subjects as divorce until the second half of the twentieth century.
Stephen's article, for instance, on the 'redundancy of women' is sad stuff,
a classic example of looking at a problem solely in economic terms and
concluding that since the expense of keeping up an establishment deters
men from marrying until early middle age, fewer footmen and butlers
should be employed. It took more imagination than Stephen had to see
that a century of education, of birth-control and of rising living standards
would transform the relationship between the sexes. But although few
possessed that imagination, numbers of his contemporaries, men and
women, possessed the faith in women's intelligence and abilities which he

lacked. Singular irony that Leslie Stephen's daughters were figures in the revolution in manners which discarded the conventions of the Victorian family in which they were brought up.

The Man of the Left

Where, then, did Leslie Stephen stand in relation to the great divisions in politics? He was without question a man of the Left. He may have liked manly fellows, but he called Henry VIII a tyrant. He had no use for the aristocracy or the ruling classes in England. On the great moral division in politics he believed that though many people were wicked or weakly foolish, human beings should be treated as equal in dignity and as potentially good. His life was witness to his rejection of man as the creature of original sin and therefore requiring to be curbed, and sometimes repressed, by authority which alone prevented society from becoming solitary, poor, nasty, brutish and short. He would have nothing to do with his brother's belief in the value of retributive punishment. To take pleasure in the sufferings of a criminal because he has caused suffering was to him to justify drawing and quartering. His sister said he lived in his study and never met the poor. Maybe; but he despised those who rejoice in their separation from the poor and regard them as a species outside their own society.

He was a man of the Left, but despite the distance he put between himself and Fitzjames he did not belong to the anarchic or to the soft-centred Left. He thought that if we have discovered some of the laws which ensure progress, they should be enforced. He did not agree with Archbishop Magee. 'A nation in which everyone was sober,' Stephen wrote, 'would be a happier, better and more progressive, though a less diversified, nation than one in which half the members were sober and the other half habitual drunkards.' He considered the *Essay on Liberty* an aberration. Mill was advocating 'the apotheosis of anarchy'. Authority in itself was not evil. Instead of being justified by appeals to some arbitrary tradition or other it should take its stand on reason. If it could do so sensible men would not be deterred from enforcing the laws of progress by appeals to abstract rights or liberty. 'We have improved, and improved by imbibing some of the scientific doctrine.' Equality meant equality of opportunity, not refusal to distinguish between the incompetent and the able. When people asked what are we to do with our boys, what they really meant was what are we to do with our fools. Equality implied not that all boys should be found a snug billet in life but that every boy should be allowed to compete on equal terms. In his meritocracy Stephen resembled other authoritarians of the Left: Saint-Simon, Bentham, and the Webbs.

Stephen was a man of the Left at a precise date – at the time of the second Reform Bill. People who are not in politics or actively concerned with current issues tend to get stuck in the grooves they cut when they were young or in early middle age. Stephen was uncompromising in what he regarded as the sentimentalities of Ruskin and socialism because he believed that the truths of classical economics were irrefutable. He wrote:

A study of the good old orthodox system of Political Economy is useful in this sense, even where it is wrong; because at least it does give a system, and therefore forces its opponents to present an alternative system, instead of simply cutting a hole in the shoe where it pinches, or striking out the driving wheel because it happens to creak unpleasantly. And I think so the more because I cannot but observe that whenever a real economic question presents itself, it has to be argued on pretty much the old principles, unless we take the heroic method of discarding argument altogether. I should be the last to deny that the old Political Economy requires careful revision and modification . . . but . . . it does lay down principles which require study and consideration, for the simple reason that they assert the existence of facts which are relevant and important in all the most vitally interesting problems of today.

But technical changes were taking place in the subject when he was in his fifties though submerged in the drudgery of the Dictionary. Jevons's work on the theory of marginal utility which appeared in 1871 had passed him by, and it would have been easy to overlook Marshall's little book on *The Economics of Industry* published in 1879. But *The Principles of Economics*, which came out in 1890, was such a major revision of classical economics that Stephen should have noticed it. Inaugural lectures by professors are read only by other professors, but Marshall enunciated in his a new outlook which those who had learnt their economics from Fawcett should have taken to heart. 'Ricardo and his chief followers', wrote Marshall, 'did not make clear to others, it was not even quite clear to themselves, that what they were building up was not universal truth, but a machinery of universal application in the discovery of a certain class of truths . . . [Economics] is not a body of concrete truth, but an engine for the discovery of concrete truth.' Stephen thought political economy to be concrete truth, and thus became the kind of positivist who used argument to preserve instead of change the status quo.

Marshall had abandoned ethics for economics because economics became for him the subject which could best explain morality. The other theorist of the new Liberalism was a political theorist. T. H. Green abandoned utilitarianism because he could not find in it the justification for the collectivist legislation which he had concluded was essential if poverty was to be tempered. Stephen acknowledged in a letter to Charles Eliot Norton that Green 'though a Hegelian was a man of power'; but his three-volume *English Utilitarians* was written as if Green had never lived. By a cruel irony the new Liberalism was conceived in the last place where according to Stephen's calculations it should have been. Green was a pupil of Jowett, and the Balliol men who were taught by him or by Caird or Nettleship learnt to ask how far the State should help citizens to lead the good life and how far – if at all – they could live morally without acknowledging that they were part of an organism to which they owed allegiance. Having introduced Green as an undergraduate to German philosophy, Jowett characteristically did all he could to snub and thwart him, when as a fellow and later professor Green taught Idealist metaphysics in language Jowett was not alone in finding incomprehensible. (Jowett did not regard Idealism as heresy: what disturbed him was the fear that Balliol men infected by such stuff would fail to get a good class in the Schools. It is pleasing to speculate whether Stephen's sense of outrage in a fine scholar being hampered and ridiculed publicly in his search for truth would have overcome his contempt for Idealist philosophy.) But there it was: Balliol taught Asquith, Lansdowne, Milner, Curzon, Broderick and Grey, to name only a few, to modify the political stereotypes of the second Reform Bill days. Other Balliol men learnt a new doctrine of social service from Arnold Toynbee and became early supporters of Fabian socialism. The new words in fashion were no longer happiness and liberty but self-realization creating freedom. Stephen, it will be remembered, had not ignored the absurdities of egoistical hedonism in utilitarian doctrine and had boldly admitted that altruism meant what it said: the sacrifice of one's own pleasure to give others pleasure. Fabians such as Shaw contradicted him. Shaw praised Ibsen for saying that altruism meant not self-sacrifice but self-realization. How antiquated Stephen looks when, in the spirit of the Charity Organization Society, he declared that 'the essential condition of all social improvement is not that we should have this or that system of regulations, but that the individual should be manly, self-respecting, doing his duty as well as getting his pay, and deeply convinced that nothing will do any permanent good which does not imply the elevation of the individual in his standards of honesty, independence and good conduct'! How wise Beatrice Webb was to understand that poverty had to be studied statistically if its hideous shape was to be dented and diminished!

Yet how wise was she? Like Stephen she belonged to the hard Left. Conduct came to mean for her the social behaviour of groups and the degree of self-sacrifice an individual should make in the service of the community ('Asquith is deplorably slack, Grey is a mere dilettante, Haldane plays at political intrigue and has no democratic principle, Perks is an unclean beast.'). This girl of Radical nonconformist stock, who described in *My Apprenticeship* the moral dilemma in which she found herself living without vocation or creed, and severed by her father's wealth and comfortable upper-middle-class milieu from the purposive groups in society; who set out to discover her function in life and the secrets of human nature among her poor dissenting relations in a mill-town; who, like Stephen, thought that the religious faith which gave so many of the poorer classes their sense of honesty, industry and value was certain to decline and needed to be replaced by some new gospel of conduct – this girl became the woman whose life, despite the triumph at large of Fabianism, was in detail a series of political defeats at the hands of Lloyd George, MacDonald and the rest owing to her lack of knowledge of human nature and the sources of power. Priding herself on her hard-headedness she became as much a prisoner of political doctrine as Stephen ever did and in the end came to believe that the moral problems which had once inspired her had been solved in the Soviet Union under Stalin. Leslie Stephen cannot be said to be impressive as a political thinker. But he recognized his limitations and, in order to show how human beings could lead the good life without belief in God, he concentrated on the individual and analysed through biography and the novel the virtues and the vices.

Chapter Eleven

✿✿✿ ✿✿✿ ✿✿✿

MORALITY THROUGH BIOGRAPHY

Biography to Replace Casuistry

Ethics resemble a conduit constructed to carry water to the right place. Morality is like a great river, turbulent, foaming, perilous, scouring every bend in the banks of life. You will never discover the source of this river, Stephen acknowledged, by following utilitarian ethics. The source is not hedonism. It is man's conscience. Christians believe that man's sense of right and wrong is awakened only by the grace of God who, unwilling to abandon his children, speaks through their conscience and thus is the author of all good deeds in the world. Agnostics deny that God needs to be invented to prove that men have the power to recognize good from evil. Nevertheless they face a challenge. The religious regard morality not as a foaming torrent but a trickle which barely moistens the cracked mud of the river-bed. To dispel this illusion the agnostic must not rely on wise saws and modern instances, abstract principles of conduct, which indeed are parched and juiceless. He must show how rich a thing it is to live the good life; how some ways of life are richer than others; and how joy comes from following the richest and how the richest alone avails in sorrow. But could this possibly be done?

Not by following the first Christian moralists, the Fathers of the Church. The early Fathers had written treatises about prudence, fortitude and the other virtues; you could see the result in modern times if you took up a volume of Emerson. Stephen had been unimpressed when Lowell took him to see the New England sage, and years later summing up Emerson's achievements he concluded that it was not enough to find effective utterance for the 'simplest truths'. 'The difficulty of the task', Stephen wrote, 'is proverbial . . . Proverbs, says Emerson, are statements of an absolute truth, and thus the sanctuary of the intuitions. They are, indeed, absolute statements of truth; and for that reason, as Sancho Panza might have pointed out, you can always quote a proverb on each side of every alternative.' Emerson had fallen between two stools: he had neither erected a system of morality nor shown morality in action. Morality withered if it was reduced to the reiteration of noble principles.

The Church itself had soon found the need for something more dynamic; and between the fifth and seventh centuries penitential works began to be written which related moral principles to men's actions. But it was not until the seventeenth century that a new kind of moral theology emerged to meet the excesses of Puritanism. If you were tormented like Christian in *The Pilgrim's Progress* and cried out, 'What must I do to be saved?', was it obligatory to abandon wife and children, put your fingers in your ears and run from the City of Destruction? Was it not possible to live in the world of getting and gaining and yet lead a holy life? Indeed it was, replied the theologians of the Counter-Reformation and the Anglican Church. The Jesuits and Dominicans were not the only masters of casuistry. In England Robert Sanderson and Jeremy Taylor were renowned for their skill in this art of bringing general moral principles to bear on individual cases: Taylor regarded his treatise on casuistry, *Ductor Dubitantium*, as more important than his famous books on *Holy Living* and *Holy Dying*. Casuistry got a bad name because priests extended what was called Probabilism, the doctrine that you should feel free to follow an opinion which endorsed a particular course of action provided there was some probability it was right. You might do so even though an opposing opinion which was endorsed by the law was even more probably correct. Morality, Stephen thought, did not consist in answering teasers such as whether it was right to lie in order to save a man's life. We needed some other medium.

Biography and fiction were the media Stephen found. Biography is a way of catching morality as it flies: it deals with real men and dispenses with the fallacious eighteenth-century method of setting up a fictitious Moral Man, the counterpart of Economic Man. Biography is especially illuminating if the subject is a writer. A man's attitude to life is expressed through his books, and a novelist peoples a world which he implicitly judges, a fictitious world no doubt, but a world in which each individual is placed in a different moral predicament. Casuists depersonalize conduct, reduce it to a set of principles, and imply that virtue consists in discharging duties imposed by a code of behaviour. The novelist assesses a man's motives and by what may be called his moral aroma. Sainte-Beuve styled himself a naturalist of souls and for him the question was: how do men live? But a biographer should go one step further and ask: how should men live? Biography and fiction replaced the confessional.

Few biographers have been more intent than Stephen to place their subject in his age. True to his principles he saw human beings as the children of their heredity and environment. Biographers who explained a man by calling him a genius or a hero lacked historical sense. 'What are called achievements are really the events upon which through some accident of fortune [a statesman] has been allowed to inscribe his name.' You could not know a man unless you understood his age; and then you saw that 'great men are only the brightest stars in a brilliant constellation'. There was above us all an eternal code of behaviour, but no valid estimate of a man could be made unless you recognized that in every age morality was subject also to a 'municipal law' which reflected the customs and conventions of the times.

But the biographer was not a social scientist. He was concerned with character, the art of producing a speaking likeness. 'To possess that power a man must be a bit of what is harshly called a cynic' – he must not judge human beings by the ten commandments but against the customs of the times. Each of us is vulnerable. Thomas Fuller was not 'quite free from the weakness of the moderate man'. We are all of a piece and Macaulay was wrong to portray people as a bundle of dazzling paradoxes. 'Nobody can really be a contradiction,' Stephen thought. 'The apparent contrast states the problem which it is the function of the good analyser to solve.' If a man was a writer, you could resolve the contradictions by reading his works: the book was the author. 'We receive the same advantage from reading Scott's printed words that we should have received from his spoken words.' Donne's life was one long problem in casuistry, and the task of his biographer was to resolve the reader's perplexity and to judge how sincere Donne was. To do this you needed sympathy for your subject: often you learnt to love a man through his books. That was why the best biographies were written by an intimate friend; and that is how despite his lack of knowledge of the law and of Indian finance or the postal service Stephen justified the biographies he wrote of his brother and of Fawcett.

Sympathy, affection, intimacy are all desirable but they are also impediments to truth. Time and again Stephen asked – can you not praise the dead without telling lies? Isaak Walton used 'the rose-colour a little too freely'; Spedding weakened the case for Francis Bacon by defending him against every imputation. Each of us in fact has the defects of our merits and the biographer harms his hero unless he admits this. If Boswell had suppressed Johnson's irritability, we would not have been so touched by Johnson's tenderness. Autobiographies were a delight, for no one, said Stephen, living before our times, ever wrote a dull one. But spare us 'the last new terror in life, the habit of reminiscing in which everyone is invited to explain what a genial and charming creature he is, how thoroughly he appreciates his contemporaries and how superior he is to any desire for popular praise'.

Stephen wanted biography to be concise as well as truthful. 'It does not follow that because I want fact, not fiction, I therefore want all the facts, big and small; the poet's washing bills, as well as the early drafts of great works.' Stephen had no use for the two- or three-decker life and letters. His longest biographies ran to a single volume and his most characteristic work was the biographical essay and entry to the *DNB*. He spent long hours in the British Museum and enjoyed the chase. His bibliography of Pope is two hundred lines long and he was meticulous about editions; but he was not the equal of Lee in research. American scholarship – Lewis on Horace Walpole, Pottle on Johnson and Boswell, Marchand on Byron, Ray on Thackeray, Haight on George Eliot – has set new standards in biographical research; and Stephen could never have spared the time to hunt for material on that scale. He read letters – considered them as indispensable to a good biography – but he rarely quoted from them. What he did relish was an anecdote. He would tell one, however limited his space, to bring his man alive. His friend James Payn, he recalled, 'went to the Derby and for lack of funds rode back on a hearse; and on one famous occasion, he raised the eight pence necessary to take him and a friend back to Woolwich by preaching from a tub while his friend went round with the hat'. Biography was resurrection not exhumation.

We want the truth . . . but not too much of the truth. In reading the letters of Robert and Elizabeth Browning Stephen said he felt like an eavesdropper, and after circling round the point, as a dog does before curling up before the fire, he concluded that some excisions ought to have been made. If a man had lived with a mistress, his biographer should say so; but he wanted no revelations about sexual experiences. Why should one write about the dead? Cynics told one that no one ever wrote except for money, but there was a higher purpose. A man's virtues should live after him and might inspire the living. Fawcett's masculine independence and generous sympathy or Fitzjames's strong and noble character might yet influence their countrymen. Pompous? Plutarch, that prince of biographers, would have agreed with Stephen.

Moral and Immoral Man

So in his biographies and criticism Stephen illustrated moral and immoral man. He began by dividing human beings into men and women. The distinction has a biological justification but is quite fatal to the understanding of character. On this issue Plutarch flatly disagreed. For him 'man's virtues and woman's virtues are one and the same', but for Stephen men must be manly and women womanly. Stephen's ideal man was beset with many temptations, sometimes falling but always painfully drawing himself upward and out of youthful folly, determined that the worst that could befall would not break his spirit. Dr Johnson and Fielding were men. Trollope was 'as sturdy, wholesome, and kindly a being as could be desired', and the way he accepted the world, even his appalling schooldays, must be admired, when 'a more sensitive and reflective nature [would have revolted] against morality in general or [met] tyranny by hypocrisy and trickery'. On the other hand, manliness was not a synonym for John Bull, and Stephen twitted Hawthorne and Taine for claiming that Englishmen must be hewn into this shape. Hawthorne even fell into the error of suggesting that Nelson was not a typical Englishman. Stephen did not bother to argue the point. No truer Englishman of course ever existed, he 'was of the same breed as Cromwell, though his shoulders were not so broad'; mysteriously Stephen ignored the feminine qualities of this Dostoevskian admiral.

He stopped short of pushing the distinction to absurdity. Having tossed and gored Coventry Patmore, a close friend of his future mother-in-law, much to her distress, he wrote to apologize – and to explain.

I do think C. P. effeminate. Every man ought to be feminine, i.e. to have quick and delicate feelings; but no man ought to be effeminate, i.e. to let his feelings get the better of his intellect and produce a cowardly view of life and the world. I dislike George Herbert because he seems to me always to be skulking behind the Thirty-Nine Articles instead of looking facts in the face, and C. P. has found a refuge which I dislike still more heartily. Want of clearness *is* a fault in poetry as in everything else, and so is a tendency to conceits.

Stephen thought there was plenty of evidence that men and women were morally different beings. Women novelists could hardly ever portray a man. He called Charlotte Brontë's Rochester 'a spirited sister of Shirley's', Paul Emmanuel 'a true woman, simple, pure, heroic and loving', George Eliot's Tito 'thoroughly and to his fingers' ends a woman', and Daniel Deronda a creation in whom 'the feminine vein becomes decidedly the most prominent'. Adam Bede was a thorough man, yet if he 'had shown less Christian forbearance to young Squire Donnithorne, we should have been more convinced that he was of masculine fibre throughout'. Since Adam knocks the young squire down for carrying on with Hetty, Stephen's standard of masculinity was certainly high. Yet though he held that these blemishes detracted from the novels as works of art they strengthened his estimate of these women novelists as women. Charlotte Brontë, though sadly unaware of Rochester's moral failings, was not to be pilloried: Rochester was the longing of a woman for a strong man, and her work as a whole showed that she did not lack 'true purity and moral elevation'. Though George Eliot possessed a masculine intelligence, she was a real woman, not that most offensive of all beings, a bluestocking – a feminine prig: her greatest creative triumphs were those of suffering women and her favourite theme was what might be called, 'speaking with proper reserve', woman in need of a manly confessor. Women must lean on men for help, and we should pardon George Eliot's unmanly cringing from criticism because it was incited by the desire to be protected by her husband. But the androgynous was nearly always dangerous: Richardson's garrulousness was feminine, and Cleopatra, so we are told, had 'an abundant share of the masculine temperament'; Rousseau's longing for enjoyment was as effeminate as his shrinking from pain. And was there not something intrinsically ridiculous in the notion that Keats was killed by the *Quarterly*? Why should a poet howl under the lash, and his admirers continue to howl, merely because the walls of Jericho did not at once fall down before him? Byron's contempt for Keats was more to the point than Shelley's 'musical moan'. If Keats was killed by criticism then the only sane reaction is pitying contempt. After all, is the universe so much the worse for it? Can't we 'rub along tolerably without another volume or two of graceful rhymes'? While millions are starving in body and soul, we cannot afford to waste many tears 'because a poet's toes have been trampled in the crush'. As for those creatures who hover between the sexes, Stephen averred that (making allowances for the robuster manners of the eighteenth century) Cobham had expressed the proper way of treating 'milksops' when he spat in Hervey's hat.

The opposite of masculine is not feminine but morbid. Morbidity implies the refusal to be manly or feminine; it is to permit carnal desire or horror of the world to dominate and pervert the character. Stephen sometimes seems to use the word to mean almost any emotion not kept rigidly in control. 'Pope was amongst the most keenly sensitive of men . . . Sensitive, it may be said, is a polite word for morbid.' One cannot read the *Dunciad* without spasms of disgust. 'Pope's morbid sensibility perverts his morals till he accepts the worst of aristocratic prejudices and treats poverty as in itself criminal.' Swift, a terrible example of extreme morbidity, committed the treason of cursing his affections instead of lamenting the injury to them, and was so tormented by an extreme personal fastidiousness, that he vented his anger in filthy abuse. Donne, like Swift, wrote filth from remorse: his love poems exhibit a morbid tendency. The emotion which inspired *In Memoriam* was, if not morbid, at least abnormal: the loss of a college friend should hardly cause such immoderate agony and prolonged depression. Rousseau has a morbid tendency to introspection and a morbid appetite for happiness. Balzac's artistry is ruined by his morbid tendencies, by his delight in horrors on which no healthy imagination would dwell. What could be more revealing than the behaviour of Balzac's aristocratic ladies who are first morbidly sentimental about their lovers, and then turn to the saccharine of religion and retire into convents? If we compare Crabbe with Balzac, we shall of course agree that the scene of repentance which Crabbe contrives at the end of *The Brothers* is less true and effective than Balzac's treatment of a similar scene; but then Crabbe is healthy – there is nothing morbid about *him*. Why in Massinger's plays do we enter an unnatural country where goodness is praised but wholesome common sense absent? Because Massinger's morality is morbid: it can hardly be said that he helps us to 'recognize more plainly than we are apt to do the surpassing value of manliness, honesty, and pure domestic affection'.

What did Stephen mean by the terms masculine and morbid? His first criterion for the good life was sexual purity, and when alluding to it, Stephen wrote at the top of his voice. Man can be saved from himself by woman: feminine innocence will rouse man from sensuality – this is how eternal womanhood, thought Stephen, interpreting Goethe literally (and wrongly), will draw man upwards. Unless we eradicate 'brutalizing and anti-social instincts', the institutions of marriage and the family will perish. Hence all social forces must be directed to the inculcation of chastity; and since art is a persuasive force, the artist too must play his part. Balzac's novels 'breathe an unwholesome atmosphere', and his cynical assurance that success in marriage depends on the wife coolly practising the arts of keeping a husband reminds one of the brashness of a lad fresh from college. On the contrary, love 'not only affords the discipline by which men obtain the mastery over themselves, but reveals to them the true theory of their relation to the universe'.

The second canon of masculinity was to accept life. Stephen did not mean quite what Carlyle meant by the Everlasting Yea. Fulminating as the sentence he passed on the promiscuous was it was a mere twitter compared to the curses Carlyle scattered on mankind. Of his talks with Carlyle he said, 'I felt something like the editor of a Saducee's gazette interviewing John the Baptist.' According to Stephen those who accepted life fell into two camps. There were first those who saw man as a loving, hating, instinctive animal using his reason as a mask to disguise his passions and defining virtue as whatever maximized pleasure. Swift was a general in this army, and Bentham and Byron in their different ways commanded a corps in it. They might be cynics but they stuck to facts. The other camp thought that reason would reveal the laws to which mankind would ultimately conform. Their apogee was Godwin: but they included far finer minds such as Plato or Aristotle, or Descartes and Condorcet, and many poets and intellectuals who wanted to leave the world a better place than they found it. Somehow a synthesis must be found to unite these two parties. 'The great aim of moral philosophy is . . . to end the divorce between reason and experience.'

There is no doubt which of the two Stephen preferred. Those who faced facts cleared the mind of cant and exposed shams. Sham was born of either sentimental hypocrisy (Sterne) or faking (Defoe) or deliberate blindness and determination to live in a private world grotesquely remote from reality (Shelley). The sincere man fought for his beliefs. Stephen found de Quincey full of 'effeminate prejudices and mere flippancies draped in elaborate rhetoric', lapped in reactionary dreams of the sanctity of Church and State, pouring out his spleen on radicals and the French but quite unwilling to rouse himself from his opium slumber and write a first-rate book. Candour was a great virtue. 'No cowardice is ever pardonable because it is never pardoned by the facts.' He called Defoe a vigorous liar, Pope an unparalleled liar and Newman . . . well, Newman was disingenuous. 'The foundation of all excellence, artistic or moral, is a vivid perception of realities and a masculine grasp of facts.' *Wuthering Heights* was a 'kind of baseless nightmare' because of Emily Brontë's feeble grasp of external facts, 'which we may read with wonder and with distressing curiosity, but with even more pain than pleasure or profit'. Stephen distinguished between those who taught us to accept facts and those who sneered at them. La Rochefoucauld merely concocted smart sayings – 'the wisdom which he affects is very easily learnt' – whereas Johnson or Burke declared that though men were less just than they should be, they were more generous than the cynics allowed. Man's blind instincts were far from being invariably bad. To belong to the first school of moralists was not to be a reactionary: the man who accepted facts could change the world. Were we to bestow the same praise on men who did good to their fellows as on Shelley whose poetry 'is not the passionate war-cry of a combatant in a deadly grapple with the forces of evil, but the wail of a dreamer . . . whose wrath is little more than the futile, though strangely melodious, crackling of thorns'?

Stephen's third touchstone was the acceptance of sorrow. Byron might have a masculine grasp of facts but his verse (which 'resembles too often the maudlin meditation of a fast young man over his morning's soda-water') did little more than play with sorrow. 'A true man ought not to sit down and weep with an exhausted debauchee . . . He has to work as long as he has strength; to work in spite of, even by strength of, sorrow, disappointment, wounded vanity, and blunted sensibilities; and therefore he must search for some profounder solution for the dark riddle of life.' 'The waste of sorrow', wrote Stephen after the death of his first wife,

is one of the most lamentable forms of waste. Sorrow too often tends to produce bitterness or effeminacy of character . . . [It] is deteriorating so far as it is selfish. The man who is occupied with his own selfish interests makes grief an excuse for effeminate indulgence in self-pity . . . The man who has learnt habitually to think of himself as part of a greater whole, whose conduct has been habitually directed to noble ends, is purified and strengthened by the spiritual convulsion. His disappointment, or his loss of some beloved object, makes him more anxious to . . . be content with the consciousness of honest work, instead of looking for what is called success.

The intellectual has spoken: so much for the glittering prizes.

The Concessions of Compassion

At this point one feels as if in Anstey's disturbing novel, *Vice Versa*, one is back again at school trembling before a terrifying and ludicrous headmaster. But Stephen was not naïve. He recognized that the conscience, though for him the supreme faculty of the soul, could not be its sole faculty. Men are moved by other motives often hidden from themselves. Writing of Johnson, Stephen said, 'Conversation was to him not merely a contest but a means of escape from himself.' Trust in a father was an excellent thing in daughters but in Elizabeth Barrett's case it amounted to self-deception. 'Popularity is more often significant of the tact which makes a man avoid giving offence than of the warm impulses of a generous nature.' He could distinguish between a failing and a vice, and understood that a good man may sometimes have a weak character. Vanity was 'a quality to which moralists have never done justice'; it was a craving for sympathy and confidence in the sincerity of one's fellows: it was the inverse side of a man's philosophy of life, the value he set on certain qualities of mind and character which he believes to be his own: most vain men were vain of qualities which they did not possess or possessed in a lower degree than they fancy. Colley Cibber's vanity was at any rate frank. It 'implies unfeigned self-complacency quite unalloyed to self-deception'. He also knew that men deceive themselves un-consciously even in their most obvious frauds. 'When [Coleridge's letters] expound a vast scheme for a *magnum opus*, or one of the various *magna opera* which at any time for thirty years were just ready to issue from the press, as soon as a few pages were transcribed, we perceive, after a moment, that they are not the fictions of the begging-letter writer, but a kind of secretion, spontaneously and unconsciously evolved to pacify the stings of remorse.' This is marvellously acute. Stephen understood that there are different levels of morality and that prigs are men who fail to distinguish between them. Sir Charles Grandison reminded him of those 'beefy and corpulent angels whom the contemporary school of painters sometimes portray. No doubt they are angels, for they have wings and are seated in the clouds; but there is nothing ethereal in their whole nature.' Grandison's virtue was trivial because he gave the same weight to every moral decision, whether it was the treatment of his horses or his wife; Stephen's last word on him was: 'It should have been inscribed on his tombstone, "He would not dock his horses' tails." ' Scott's debts were forgiven seventy times seven because he had a noble heart. Whereas in Richardson virtue means standing out for the higher price, Fielding for all his laxity made us love virtue for its own sake. Stephen would not blame a man for pitching his morality in too low a key provided he was convinced that the man knew the score. He might have been expected to approve Johnson's dictum that Chesterfield taught the morals of a whore and the manners of a dancing master, but instead he praised Chesterfield for thinking that morality was a subject for cool enquiry, for asking what the conditions for success in public life were and giving a common-sense reply. Benvenuto Cellini was a monstrous egoist and tempestuously violent. But Stephen preferred him to that model of propriety, Lord Herbert of Cherbury, who was so absurdly vain that he found his own sweat aromatic. If, said Stephen, you demand that everything be always judged in relation to moral standards, as Carlyle did, you defeat your own end: the ceaseless pursuit of morality leads to a narrow vision of life because it neglects qualities which make life worth living.

Such insight reassures the reader and implies that Stephen will not take a man at face value. When he first wrote about Swift he said he 'had not the power or the nobility of nature to become a true poet or philosopher or reformer'. But he later came to pity Swift because his egoism was neither petty nor vain and because his philanthropy kept breaking through his misanthropy. 'The misery of dependence was burnt into his soul.' Contemplating Swift Stephen stood in awe before 'the spectacle of a nature of magnificent power struck down, bruised and crushed under fortune, and yet fronting all antagonists with increasing pride, and comforting itself with scorn even when it can no longer injure its adversaries'. Pope tried Stephen to the limit – he 'did not love good women as a man of genius ought', he was the incarnation of the literary spirit, pock-marked with stinginess and spleen. Pope's literary man-oeuvres disgusted him and the publication of his correspondence, in which Pope traduced the dying Swift, was a disgusting transaction; the only apology one could make for it was 'that Pope did not know at starting how many and what disgraceful lies he would have to tell'. Eventually Stephen found an excuse. How much this malignant dwarf must have suffered from his stunted appearance! Did not Pope's reason direct his passions to a worthy end, did not his morality rest on good sense, and good motives inspire his religion? 'He was at bottom . . . a man of really fine nature, affectionate, generous and independent; unfortunately, the better nature was perverted by the morbid vanity and excessive irritability which led him into his multitudinous subterfuges.'

Even more strenuous was his attempt to find some palliative for the spiteful, quarrelsome, frivolous intriguer, Horace Walpole, scarcely for Stephen a congenial spirit. And yet he took pleasure in displaying Walpole's tolerance, scepticism and shrewdness, and sympathized with his hatred of dullards and boors. A man of his sensibilities and acumen had reason to sneer at the world he lived in. Walpole was more than a personage, he was an interesting phenomenon:

There is an intermediate class of men who are useful as sensitive barometers to foretell coming changes of opinion. Their intellects are mobile if shallow; and perhaps their want of serious interest in contemporary intellects renders them more accessible to the earliest symptoms of superficial shiftings of taste. They are anxious to be at the head of fashions in thought as well as in dress, and pure love of novelty serves to some extent in place of genuine originality. Amongst such men Walpole deserves a high place; and it is not easy to obtain a high place even amongst such men. The people who succeed best at trifles are those who are capable of something better . . . [Walpole's] peevish anxiety to affect even more frivolity than was really natural to him, has blinded his critics to the real power of a remarkably acute, versatile, and original intellect. We cannot regard him with much respect, and still less with much affection; but the more we examine his work, the more we shall admire his extreme cleverness.

Cleverness! It is not often that we hear this quality praised by Stephen's contemporaries. Time and again when you think Leslie Stephen is going to pass a conventional judgement, his sense of the oddity of life saves him. So does his sense of humour, which made his *DNB* articles so readable. 'Austin thought it his duty to be as dry as Bentham, and discharged that duty scrupulously.' 'Coleridge was an excellent talker if allowed to start from no premises and come to no conclusions.' 'Nobody', he said of Macaulay, 'can hit a haystack with more certainty.' Thomas Newton 'combined good domestic qualities with the conviction that the whole duty of a clergyman was to hunt for preferment by flattery'. The young St John 'soon became conspicuous for such qualities as are typical of the heroes of Congreve's comedies'. 'Everybody, I hold, is a bore to some people, but Godwin was one of the unlucky people capable of boring all round.' 'Criticism of Burns is only permitted to Scotsmen of pure blood.' He had a great love of eccentrics which he indulged in the *DNB*. The clergyman William Whiston 'amused great men by his frank rebukes' and believed in 'anointing the sick with oil . . . that the Tartars were the lost tribes . . . that the millennium would begin in twenty years . . . that Mary Toft [a neighbour] had been foretold in the book of Esdras' and that Prince Eugène had been predicted in the Apocalypse. Another clergyman wrote a learned work comparing the Apocalypse to Homer and Sophocles and thereby 'verified the old saying as to the result of such studies by afterwards becoming deranged'. Stephen cherished such parsons.

Stephen, then, was magnanimous, but he reserved a hell for one type of man. That was the careless Gallio: the indifferent, easy-going man who consciously shirked his moral responsibilities – Tolstoy's Stepan Arkadyevitch Oblonsky. Such a man was Sterne whose duplicity and sentimentalism made him in Stephen's phrase a literary prostitute. Sterne cultivated fineness of feeling with a direct view to the market, inducing his readers to weep over the plight of a donkey more than over the plight of a man. Sterne was careful to convey the impression that all his faults sprang from his candour and impulsiveness – a judicious device 'by which a man reconciles himself to some very ugly actions'. It was a device which

> provides by anticipation a complete excuse for thoughtlessness and meanness. If he is accused of being inconstant, he points out the extreme goodness of his impulses; and if the impulses were bad, he argues that at least they did not last very long. He prides himself on his disregard to consequences even when the consequences may be injurious to his friends. His feelings are so genuine for the moment that his conscience is satisfied without his will translating them into action ... He can call an adversary a dirty fellow, and is very proud of his generous indiscretion. But he is also capable of gratifying the dirty fellow's vanity by high-flown compliments if he happens to be in the enthusiastic vein; and somehow the providence which watches over the thoughtless is very apt to make his impulses fall in with the dictates of calculated selfishness. He cannot be an accomplished courtier, because he is apt to be found out; but he can crawl and creep for the nonce with anyone. In real life such a man is often as delightful for a short time as he becomes contemptible on a longer acquaintance.

What a searching condemnation of the man who is on the make! On the make, not in a ruthless cold-hearted adamant fashion which by its very precision compels an unwilling tribute to conscious clear-headedness; but on the make in the sense of having it both ways, preening oneself on being an honest carefree fellow, yet always in fact having an eye to the main chance. To Stephen, as to Bloomsbury, being on the make was one of the nastier vices; and according to Stephen, it was often the result of that conscious indifference to morality which is the unforgivable sin. So long as a man had a good heart or a 'firm grasp of facts', he was redeemable. For instance, a man might be pardoned for breaking a moral law which he refused to recognize as binding, provided his action proceeded from an open heart; but if he announced that questions of value did not concern him, he was not only a stupid liar – for value is implicit in all our actions and opinions – but a worthless coward in that he had abdicated in the face of the most difficult, but the most meaningful, challenge presented by life.

But what could Stephen make of Rousseau who tried to justify his 'hideous avowals of downright depravity' by arguing, 'like all senti-mentalists', that the exaltation of the immediate sensation was to be the rule of life? He began by asking a pertinent question: what happens if you respond immediately to what you feel? You have to invert normal thought. Rousseau had to invent a metaphysic which defied common sense by arguing that everything was right in a transcendental sense because everything in an actual sense was wrong. Man was everywhere in chains and the chains made him free. Abuse of the emotions brought its own reward. You could not live by feeling alone, and if you tried to do so you developed abnormally – the emotions grew malignantly like tumours and emaciated the spirit which gave them life. Rousseau constantly protested that he was in love; but he was not in love with a beloved object so much as in love with love itself. Here Stephen not only made a sound judgement on Rousseau but also an act of imaginative insight into the psychology of the promiscuous. He might not appreciate the shades of distinction perceived by the French moralists – for example by Madame de La Fayette or Constant or Stendhal. But he was aware that if you made a habit of falling in love with different people, one after another, you became obsessed with the chase and with the sensation of falling under the spell rather than caring for the beloved. The sensation becomes more important than the person who excites the sensation, and the beloved becomes a mere excuse for setting in motion a sequence of feelings. The enjoyment of these feelings and not the beloved becomes the end of love. But that was not his final judgement on Rousseau. For Stephen, Rousseau was the nonpareil of autobiographers, the master of nostalgia. He 'chewed the cud of past delight . . . . Even his affectations are instructive.' Once again Stephen conquered his instinctive dislike and without modifying his categories of judgement acknowledged Rousseau's unique candour.

Time and again Stephen declined to pronounce a verdict of guilty on sexual deviants. He did not overlook the matter: he said in the *DNB* that George Eliot's union with George Henry Lewes 'placed her in many ways in a false position'. But tempestuous marriages or affairs were nearly always ascribed to temperament. Where Scott or Fielding or Burns was concerned, their failings were as nothing in his view compared with their generosity, kindliness and great-heartedness. He tested the springs of action for pollution. If a man's motives were sound, he advised the reader to acquit. If he was mean, if he were spiteful, if he intrigued or was a brazen liar or malicious or cruel or venomous or vindictive, then Stephen said so without indignation but he scratched around (as he did in the case of Pope) to find some redeeming features.

Who then would be saved? Above all men, thought Stephen, Dr Johnson. Johnson, who hated cruelty and injustice as much as anarchy; who despised optimism and found the world miserable but never whined; who called ugly things by their right names, attacked the cant of calling luxury bad or poverty 'want of riches'; who overcame the torments of his youth and the temptations of Grub Street. Johnson might have rejected life but he accepted it; no one had a firmer grasp of facts; no one ever had a more open heart. To dwell on Johnson's manners or his rudeness is to be trivial – what do they matter beside his profound goodness of heart? For Johnson was humble – he did not judge people by their earthly attainments but loved poor creatures like Levett. Opposed as Stephen was to Johnson's religion, torysim, method of reasoning, manners and habits, no man so unreservedly won his praise and affection.

These saving clauses follow naturally from his social philosophy. They are not a sauce ladled over his moral principles to disguise the taste of the meat. For if man was the product of his environment and heredity, 'temperament and circumstance, not logic, make the difference between a pessimist and an optimist'. That was why human beings did not always behave as well as they should. In some cases like Trollope or James Payn they behaved so well one could scarcely imagine how they overcame the horrors of their early days. Carlyle, he said, made the error of thinking that morality was the sole condition of all excellence, and for that reason sneered at Scott for 'writing impromptu novels to buy farms with' and 'harmlessly amusing indolent and languid men'. If geniuses were simply men and women who had the gift to express more forcibly than their contemporaries what society wanted and needed, they were by that amount less responsible for the harm they did. And this his daughter suggested was the way he justified to himself his own behaviour.

The Limitations of Stephen's Moral Sensibility

And yet this is not how Stephen's essays read. Analysis can smoothe away the difficulties, but the difficulties were always present in his mind and his doubts and hesitations disturb the reader. Round and round goes the dog on the hearth rug before it settles cocking an ear against trouble. Stephen was upset that, as he put it, aesthetic considerations should affect one's moral judgement. Gibbon appeared to have solved the problem of living so satisfactorily that his life had an appeal which seemed to put it beyond the reach of moral judgement. The *spectacle* of Swift was so awe-inspiring that comment seemed cruel. How could one censure Colley Cibber who positively enjoyed exposing his own failings or Rousseau declaring he had nothing to be ashamed about? Fielding was a special trial to him. Fielding's books did not show that vice necessarily led to moral disintegration. He came perilously near to saying that good instincts were everything and that a moral code strangled spontaneity. Accept this and vice only became objectionable when complicated by cruelty or hypocrisy. Should Fielding be condemned? Stephen, who wanted to acquit him, gave it up. 'Really to know the man, we must go to his books.' And to pardon the 'stains' in his books we must go to the man whose life showed his goodness of heart. Then again Defoe's crooks 'always seem to speak like steady respectable Englishmen and never seem to be tortured by remorse'. Thumping crooks rarely are. But why should he be worried when he said so sensibly, 'Until you admit that human nature is in some sense a contradictory compound, and can take delight in the queer results which grow out of the [antagonisms in a man's nature], you are hardly qualified to be a student of autobiography.' When looking at the *spectacle* of man we 'take delight in the queer results'. Exactly. But then it follows that the palm should be awarded to Sainte-Beuve, the naturalist of souls, and we should no longer consider judgement to be the most important act of the moralist.

Stephen seemed to admit that this was so when he wrote about Coleridge. C. R. Sanders once took Stephen to task for the way he went on about Coleridge. 'That old sinner S.T.C. . . . forever wasting his time in aimless talk', muddling his intellect by religion, admiring George Herbert's poetry, 'part of a craze which possessed all his set at that time', had been attacked by Stephen for being a slave to opium, deserting his wife, plagiarizing the Germans, failing to realize his potentialities, thinking nebulously and opposing the eighteenth-century spirit of common sense. In fact Stephen's essay is an excellent example of the art of making reservations, yet leaving no one in doubt where he stood on the moral issue. He started by ridiculing his own utilitarian outlook, by deploring attempts to judge Coleridge by rule of thumb, and declined to answer direct whether the author of *The Ancient Mariner* was entitled to break the ten commandments. But he then pointed out that the apologists who argued that Coleridge's wretched wife was at fault were attempting to save his character by abusing her. As Coleridge was a slave to opium and lay in bed all day except for the hours when he was laying his heart at the feet of another woman, Stephen concluded, 'to speak of all this as a moral excuse for Coleridge is unmanly . . . If a man of genius condescends to marry a woman, and be the father of her children, he must incur responsibilities.' He takes note of these facts and 'leaves anybody who pleases to do the moralizing', and offers this judgement about the privilege of genius. 'Don't be his brother-in-law, or his publisher, or his editor, or anything that is his if you care twopence – it is probably an excessive valuation – for the opinion of posthumous critics.' 'But again,' Stephen continued, 'I would avoid moralizing. Opium ruined Coleridge's power of will, never very strong, his home life, and all but ruined his intellectual career. But there is also this to be said, that at his worst Coleridge was both loved and eminently lovable. His failings excited far more compassion than indignation.' Stephen praised without reserve Coleridge's recognition that the morality of a poem lies in its total effect upon the imagination, and rightly called him the seminal mind of the age. He asked us to pity the man whose vast promise and power in youth ran all but hopelessly to waste, and to recollect that his nature was kind and generous. One of the finest passages Stephen wrote, said John Timmerman, was when he contrasted the reputations of Coleridge and James Mill, contemporaries for sixty years. 'Coleridge', he said, 'was indolent, fitful, dawdling, impulsive, dependent, shirking his social duties; Mill was assiduous, laborious, temperate, self-denying, fulfilling his social obligations beyond the letter; yet, Coleridge died in the "odour of sanctity" whereas Mill died "amidst shrugs of respectable shoulders". ' Stephen let the irony sink in.

His moralizing is made up of this curious mixture of strenuous assertion and scepticism of his own judgements. His style of self-deprecation and take-it-or-leave-it does not disarm the reader so much as bewilder him. What is this man asking us to believe? The next thing the reader wonders is whether Stephen's judgements are prejudices. Stephen let his anti-clerical prejudices out on a run in numbers of *DNB* articles on clergymen, and most readers would be willing to make allowance for them. But when he declared 'to recommend contemplation in preference to action is like preferring sleeping to waking' and one remembers some of the most influential moralists who persuade others by a curious faculty of emanating wisdom, the judgement appears ridiculous. Was it his prejudice that women novelists cannot draw convincing portraits of men that was responsible for the inadequate entry – a bare four columns in the *DNB* – for Jane Austen? His moral categories were decidedly Anglo-American. Although he read French and German with ease, the only European writers he tangled with were Pascal, Voltaire, Rousseau and Balzac. What would he have made, one asks, of that Byronic cad, the Hero of Our Times, Lermontov's Pechorin? – who is indeed something more than a cad. Experience abroad upsets our tidy western notions of good and evil as E. M. Forster discovered when he wrote *A Passage to India*. On occasions Stephen in his essays resembles a man being end-played at the bridge table. He concedes trick after trick to his opponents as he admits the vices, follies and hypocrisies of the man he seeks to defend, until the moment comes when he is thrown in, triumphantly claims two tricks for the man's good qualities, and then discovers to his dismay that his next lead will inevitably give the declarer game and rubber. He could never bring himself to admit that great writers are often horrible men. It was too painful a contradiction; and yet the biographer has to resolve it. His determination to 'get a speaking likeness', to paint a portrait of a static figure, prevented him from seeing human beings *in movement* and from appreciating that change, variety, evanescence, even contradiction itself, were inseparable from living.

He was never more wayward in flicking away revelations of fact than when he dealt with sexual conduct. The Victorian code on sexuality was intended to debrutalize society, and Stephen, though he shared these ideals, was far less puritanical than W. R. Greg or Morley and no more severe than Arnold. Arnold loathed French 'lubricity' and believed that the idolization of fornication had undermined the State and brought the

French to their knees at Sedan. But he understood the relation of morality to sex far more clearly than Stephen. He realized that it was no good the will commanding the flesh to resist the enormously powerful drive of lust. To bark orders at our sexual impulses 'only irritates opposition in the desires it tries to control'. Stephen called Angelo in *Measure for Measure* a hypocrite; but Angelo was not merely a hypocrite but a man suddenly overcome by a desire more powerful than his own will – a wicked desire, of course, but a desire that must be understood. Stephen might have checked himself had he remembered his *Phaedrus* in which Plato compared the soul to a team of horses driven by the charioteer of the will, the one white and noble representing man's higher aspirations, and the other horse black and ferocious representing his lower passions. Plato allowed that even though the souls of men were run away with by the black horse, they might learn from sexual passion the rule of love and honour and grow wings to begin their upward journey to the light. Arnold was a humanist enormously well read in Indian as well as European literature and he brought to bear on moral questions a mind which had ruminated for years on what religion does to help men live a good life. Moral philosophy is a dignified matron and some elderly gentlemen such as Marcus Aurelius have led her to the altar; the rest of us require someone much more attractive if we are to resist temptation. But at Cambridge Stephen had read mathematics.

The moralist who is also a humanist must resemble Baudelaire's *hypocrite lecteur – mon semblable – mon frère*. He must put himself into the shoes of other men and understand why it is so difficult to do good. He has got to dig deeper. He has got to explain why all the actions of someone who actively promotes good are so intolerable to his beneficiaries – he must explore unconscious as well as conscious motive, for instance that determination to impose one's will or to extract gratitude or to discomfit enemies or to patronize which can poison the most admirable actions. He has to consider such virtues as mercy and meekness. When Stephen contrasted the popular response to the death of Coleridge and the death of James Mill, he may have felt that there was no need to draw a moral. It was, however, this reluctance to discuss what human beings are really like which diminishes Stephen's worth as a moralist. Perhaps he felt that he had no need to do so because he had a shelf of textbooks to hand which would make the point for him. The novel is the textbook for the *connoisseur de belles âmes* because it is not concerned with the rules and laws and customs which govern behaviour but with the nature of men and women who obey or break them. What kind of a literary critic, then, was Stephen, the first English critic to turn from poetry and consider the novel which with grand opera was the nineteenth century's greatest gift to the life of the imagination?

Chapter Twelve

❦❦❦

MORALITY AND LITERATURE

The Duties of Author and Critic

Leslie Stephen deserves to be remembered as a critic for two achievements. He was the first Englishman to consider the novel as seriously as the critics had treated poetry at a time when novels were still dismissed as light entertainment suitable only for the boudoir or, if French, suitable only for the smoking-room. Stephen's task was all the more difficult as some of the greatest masterpieces of English literature were appearing as he wrote. He was also one of the first Englishmen to argue that the character and demands of the reading public influenced literary expression. He explained changes in taste by unravelling social relationships, and liberated the history of literature by suggesting that it was more than a search for influences and movements. No one before him in England had made it quite so evident how intimately literature was bound up with the customs, manners, money-sense and the unspoken assumptions of different classes in society. Characteristically he shrugged off his achievement. ('I hope and believe I have said nothing original.')

When a man first begins to write, the literary rows current at the time often force him to ask himself where he stands. The phrase 'art for art's sake' had been coined by Cousin and Constant in France in the years after Waterloo, but it was not until Swinburne popularized it in his book on Blake that shivers ran down the spine of honourable men. John Morley had already exhausted almost every epithet of loathing in reviewing Swinburne's poems and now Robert Buchanan denounced what he called the Fleshly School of poetry. The row showed Stephen where he stood.

He was unhesitatingly against Swinburne. Stephen believed a critic should ask himself whether the work he read was a good moral influence and pass judgement accordingly. In a number of articles written as editor of the *Cornhill* Stephen considered the nature and function of criticism. When aesthetes told him that there was no such thing as a moral or an immoral book, the metaphors of the penal system leapt to his lips. If a man delighted in corrupting others we should, if the law allows, lock him up or give him six months on the treadmill. But 'if, for any reason, legal punishment is impossible, the critic should step in and administer the lash with the full strength of his arm. The harder he hits and the deeper he cuts the better for the world . . . If a man really has the impudence to say that immorality is right because it is artistic, he is either talking nonsense or proposing a new law of morals which is too absurd to require confutation.'

Having severed the aesthetes' jugular Stephen next plunged his knife into their guts. They thought the function of criticism was to enthuse. Nothing could be more deplorable. *Nil admirari* is a sentiment highly praised in Cambridge, and if Horace is right in saying it can make a man happy and keep him so, Stephen should have been a happy man. He thought Dickens had enjoyed applause too much and it had killed him; and he called Arnold's proposal for an Academy 'where men of letters would crown each other' part of the twaddle which turned 'the whole literary world into one gigantic clique'. He found even so sober a contemporary as R. H. Hutton of the *Spectator* 'a little too anxious to show quick appreciation of merit'. No wonder Thomas Hardy thought Stephen's approval 'disapproval minimised'.

Is criticism then simply a matter of a forthright assertion of moral principles? By no means. Stephen – no one will be surprised – declared that gush or censure should be replaced by scientific judgement. As he developed his theme he modulated from the major and became more subtle. In 1873 Taine's *History of English Literature* appeared. In it Taine claimed that the criteria he adopted were scientific and therefore applicable to all literature. Surely this should have pleased Stephen. But no; John Gross has called Stephen's review of that book 'one of the most devastating things he ever wrote: on page after page he showed how brutally the Frenchman had to torture the facts in order to make them fit his preordained theories.'[1] Stephen asked critics to be as dispassionate as the naturalist who ticketed a fossil in a museum. But ticketing a fossil did

---

[1] For all his positivism Stephen had a keen nose for detecting what he believed were the pretensions of science. Praising the Arctic explorer Nansen for his courage, he remarked that his scientific results – the mapping of an utterly useless region – were really a pretext for a fine display of manliness rather as the fox was the pretext for a gallop across difficult country. But in these days, he said, scientific aims had become as sacrosanct as any action which could 'cover itself under a religious mask. The Royal Society and the Salvation Army are objects at which one may not even smile.'

not mean giving it a ticket. 'Nothing is easier than to put the proper label on a poet, to call him "romantic" or "classical" and so on . . .' He said that he could use words like reaction as easily as his neighbours but 'the only thing I find difficult is to look wise when I use them, or to fancy that I give an explanation when I have adopted a classification.' Stephen admitted that scientific critics would blunder but even blunders helped posterity come to that definitive verdict which it passed in the end on every work. Johnson's attack on *Lycidas* was outrageous yet much of it was undeniably true. 'I would welcome a good assault on Shakespeare which was not prompted by a love of singularity.' All Stephen's essays, even on the authors he loved best, sum up judicially the faults as well as the merits of their works. That was his hall-mark. He stated as unequivocally as it can be stated that not all tastes are equally good any more than morality is simply subjective or political principles rationalizations of naked power. He was right to do so.

This modulation from the word 'scientific' is the key to Stephen's criticism. Taken by themselves the *Cornhill* articles on the function and criteria of criticism are excessively dogmatic. But he never reprinted them in his collected works. Why? Was it not because he came to realise that criticism cannot be expressed in *ex cathedra* statements? Principles emerge only from the act of criticism itself. Stephen realized that it was mistaken to pose the bald question whether a poem was moral: one ought to ask whether it was 'developed by invigorating and regenerating processes'. And having given that answer is it not likely that he realized that such generalizations are not all that helpful? They remind one of F. R. Leavis's strident appeals to 'life' and 'health'. This is what happens when people demand clear-cut manly answers to oblique and intricate questions. When once asked 'Why ought one to do what is right?' or 'What is the intellectual basis of ethics?' or some such question which is oblique but the questioner thought was direct, Wittgenstein answered: 'This is a terrible business – just terrible! You can at best stammer when you talk of it.'

Stephen had accused the Broad Churchmen of emptying hell so that only Judas Iscariot was left in it, but, as we have seen, he was something of a Broad Moralist himself. In one of the four *Cornhill* articles he declared that the critic should flay any writer who encouraged people to admire cynicism or delight in cruelty even if he had the talents of a Shakespeare or a Raphael or a Mozart. But then he went on to say that no one who 'corrupted the social atmosphere' could possibly have had their talents. By definition a genius could not produce an immoral work. This reminds one of Wilde during his fatal cross-examination by Carson in the witness-box acknowledging that although there was no such thing as a moral or an immoral book, a good book was well, and a bad book ill, written. Critics who state unequivocally where they stand usually if they are wise circle round the spot. Stephen by inference dissociated himself from Morley and Buchanan. He thought they had given the game away by suggesting that it was only in an ideal world that virtue triumphed. Surely one did not have to accept Balzac's word that the powerful and wicked always succeed and the good and simple are invariably crushed? And equally one did not have to accept that a good novel was one in which the hero was rewarded with a legacy and the villain with the gallows. One of the troubles with Dickens was his habit of making his villains so black that they were 'fit only for starvation in hollow trees'. In his old age Stephen concluded, 'Edifying morality is as easy as lying.'

Inevitably one contrasts Stephen with Arnold and as inevitably one concludes that Arnold was the finer critic. René Wellek is, of course, right to say that Stephen was no disciple of Arnold. Not for him the breadth of reference which enabled Arnold to appeal from the French savants to the Greeks and thence to the *Gita*. Not for him the marvellous contrasts of one poet with another. He distrusted even while he admired Arnold's sensibility. He could not pass over the famous phrase about poetry being a criticism of life without a sigh; and he made the obvious riposte that if poetry was to replace what passed then for religion and philosophy it could hardly be at the same time criticism. But Stephen's generosity and good judgement vanquished his suspicion of the fop. Too many of Arnold's critics, he said, were dim-wits who could not distinguish between an epigram and a philosophical dogma. Arnold's criticism would have to be taken into account by every man who believed in civilizing the coming world. Like Arnold he conceived that the critic should be a moralist. Like Arnold he thought the critic's function was to judge. Like Arnold he wanted poets to express simple and great truths. Stephen preferred the long majestic flight of a Virgil or a Milton to contemporary poets who rose on the wings of an ode or a lyric to express the emotion of some vague mood and soon fluttered to earth. He resented Tennyson's pretensions to being a bard. In the *Idylls* he seemed 'not so much to be inspired by an overmastering idea as to be looking about for appropriate images to express certain ethical and religious sentiments'. How different from Gray's *Elegy* in which content and expression were in perfect harmony, and the difficulty of feeling rightly had been mastered as easily as the difficulty of finding words to express the feeling. He wanted characters in novels to resemble Weber's Ideal Types. Fielding and George Eliot made you feel that the thoughts and passions of their characters were reflections of what men and women at all times have thought and felt; but Charlotte Brontë made you feel Paul Emmanuel was someone who gave real lectures in Brussels on a particular date.

To get some idea of Stephen's power as a critic at his best compare his essay on Wordsworth with those by Arnold, Mill, Hutton, Bagehot, Lowell and Church. Mid-Victorian taste placed Wordsworth just below Shakespeare and Milton. Stephen was no exception but his essay is the best of the lot. Arnold determined to rescue Wordsworth from the Wordsworthians and had mocked Stephen for saying that the poet was 'a prophet and a moralist as well as a mere singer'. But modern criticism has vindicated Stephen. He did not admire Wordsworth merely because his ethics were 'capable of systematic exposition'. Stephen knew very well, as is shown in a letter he wrote to Morley, that a philosophy of life has more poetry in it than logic; but one test of the excellence of poetry was the depth of a poet's understanding of good and evil. In his essay he showed how Wordsworth's greatness depended upon his power of mind as well as his strength of feeling. Extract the philosophy from a poem, and you have one way of testing its value. Poets feel that the world is out of joint. Byron and Shelley thought that since they could not mend it, there was no point in searching for an answer to the riddle of life. Wordsworth did not give up the search. Of course he did not find the answer to the riddle. But he found a way of reconciling experience with a theory of existence. He did so because he was one of those rare natures in whom head and heart harmonized. You may think his attempt to answer the riddle was misconceived, fallacious or deluded. Children do not habitually have intimations of immortality, and Nature devours her offspring as well as heals them. And yet Wordsworth's poetry struck to the heart. Why? It did so because he could evoke what a child may experience and how a man can learn from sorrow. Do we not tire eventually, asked Stephen, of 'musical moans' that love, spring and joy fade and die, that today is not yesterday and that everything is not as it should be? Wordsworth had felt these emotions but related them to the facts and suggested how we could come to terms with them. Contemplation healed the mind but contemplation was the prelude to action, not a substitute for it. Alone among his contemporaries Wordsworth understood that men should make something from their despondency instead of abandoning themselves to it. This essay is Stephen's finest contribution to literary criticism.

His second contribution to the study of literature was really original. Stephen will be remembered longest for declaring that you could not judge literature unless you had related it to the times. Before you could understand Dante, Stephen argued, you had to analyse the political and social struggles in which he took part. Matthew Arnold thought that Puritanism was responsible for the decline of verse drama. Stephen argued it was not enough to talk of a reaction in taste. Drama had declined because the relationship between the court and the middle class had changed. Drama came to represent the views of those who were opposed to the Parliamentarians. Literary forms follow the character of the literary class and since authors generally write with a view to being read, one genre is replaced by another as the reading public changes. For instance, eighteenth-century poetry began by being didactic because rationalism governed taste as well as philosophy. How could lyric poetry flourish when it would have been ridiculed by the wits of the town? But the middle classes were providing a wider market for books than the London circle of wits who read the *Tatler* and the *Spectator*. One of these wits, Edward Young, disappointed in the chase for patronage, was struck by the idea that the declamations about liberty, simplicity and integrity which fell from the lips of Thomson or Wilkie or Glover, snugly provided for by patrons, were pompous pieties. The wit turned moralist, caught sight of Wesley and wrote his *Night Thoughts*. It was not enthusiasm for religion so much as his disappointment in being spurned by a patron which inspired Young. Just at this time Johnson too was changing his feathers and began to preach the morality of Richardson and Young. Whereas until the fall of Robert Walpole literature was inextricably mixed with politics, it was now passing into the hands of men of a lower social class, leaving Horace Walpole, who had conversed in his youth with Addison and Pope and treated them as his social equals, to bewail that with the single exception of Gray literature was no longer written by gentlemen.[1] Communication between the author and reader was changing all the time. By and large human nature was a constant: that is why we are still moved by Chaucer today: but how far was it a constant and how did the values in part imposed upon us by our own society affect our appreciation? Stephen entreated critics to realize that an author responded to the world in which he found himself. They should judge him in relation to that world and not to an abstract world created by the critic himself.

Stephen's Reputation

There has never been much doubt that, second only to Arnold, Leslie Stephen was the outstanding critic of late Victorian times. If one wants to read Victorian criticism on the eighteenth century would one turn to John Morley? No sound can be heard today from that once melodious bell. Does one consult David Masson or Henry Morley who thought literature enabled one to understand our island story, or Dowden and Courthorpe who maintained that literature followed an historical trend and oscillated between collectivism and individualism? There are curios such as Eneas

[1] Stephen found in his family a successor who related the arts to society. His grandson, Quentin Bell, examined the way in which social forces govern fashion in dress and dictate changes in fashion. *On Human Finery* (1947) attempted by modifying the concepts Veblen used in *The Theory of the Leisure Class* to subsume the 'municipal' laws which govern fashion in any period under a general system.

Sweetland Dallas who had come across William Hamilton's notion of the unconscious but like an old fogey confronting a computer did not know what to do with it. Dallas too claimed criticism was a science – *The Gay Science* was the title of his second book – but since he thought a student 'of poesy must learn to sol-fa through the emotions', one can see that his definition of scientific criticism was hardly that of Stephen. Dallas resembled a hostess who has set out tables and chairs but has forgotten to provide music or supper for the guests. Can Arthur Symons or J. A. Symonds stand comparison with Stephen's judicious, sensible, searching exposures? Among the editors and critics of periodicals only Bagehot could hold a candle to Stephen.

But where exactly does Stephen stand in the history of criticism? Have his standards of criticism any life left in them ? Certainly one influential school of criticism thought so and shortly before the Second World War a battle was joined over his body which resembled in violence the struggle for the corpse of Patroclus on the plain of Troy.

In 1937 Desmond MacCarthy delivered the Leslie Stephen Lecture in Cambridge, and chose Stephen as his subject. He called Stephen the least aesthetic of critics. Stephen discoursed more about human nature and morals than about art; and his puritanism made him declare that the reader could not respond wholeheartedly unless the author showed that he 'has been moved himself'. No marvel then that Stephen was blind to the peculiar delight in reading Sterne which MacCarthy said is evoked by Sterne's 'elegant ambiguity' towards emotion, 'a state of mind (Shandyism) in which we enjoy together the pleasures of extravagant sensibility, and a feeling that nothing much matters.' Happy as many of Stephen's observations were, he could not record a thrill or communicate any emotion he had derived from literature. Yes, he was dispassionate and hated loose enthusiasm; but he was so swayed by his reverence for certain qualities, such as those of domestic affection, that the equilibrium of his criticism was upset. This, in effect, led Stephen 'in whom the exercise of the intellect was a passion' to make judgements which amounted to little more than saying 'Be good, sweet maid, and let who will be clever.'

Two years later Queenie Leavis replied. She stigmatized MacCarthy's praise as an insult to Stephen's memory and declared that what MacCarthy condemned as critical defects were virtues. Stephen was to be praised for not recording thrills, for despising aesthetic criticism and for believing that criticism was 'a process of the intelligence'. He was also to be praised for thinking, like Henry James, that the value of a work of art depends on the quality of the writer's make-up. 'Art is not immoral,' she said tartly, 'and everything is not as valuable as everything else.' Stephen's contempt for eulogy was to be commended and his belief in reason led him to the sound conclusion that poets who preached should have a mature understanding of life. MacCarthy had questioned the merits of Stephen's scientific criticism. His analyses of novelists told us as little of the value of a novel as a naturalist in describing a beast threw light on its value to man. On the contrary, said Queenie Leavis, Stephen told us its exact value because he appealed to a 'serious' view of life and attended to the writer's idiom and technical devices instead of attempting to find some aesthetic theory to justify his taste. She described MacCarthy's lecture as 'an insolent performance' and claimed that if the study of humanities at Cambridge 'has any justification for existing it is in standing in the eyes of the great world – as it does – for a critical position descended from Leslie Stephen and antagonistic to Mr MacCarthy.'

What are we to make of this? The battle for Stephen's body was merely one episode in the long war which the Leavises fought against Bloomsbury, and like most wars, while it was being fought the combatants were enveloped in propaganda. It is, for instance, important to realise that MacCarthy's verdict on Stephen was also a verdict on criticism itself. Virginia Woolf's respect for her father's writing was greater than MacCarthy's but he spoke for both Stephen's daughters who, in their role as artists, possessed first-hand experience of the mystery of creation: they painted and wrote as part of the artistic revolution called modernism which proclaimed the freedom of art from the rules and conventions of conservatoires or academies and upper-middle-class taste. They agreed with Arnold that a nation's culture lay in the hands of an intellectual élite. They agreed with him that it was the duty of this élite to spread sweetness and light. But they denied that the main purpose of criticism was to judge that this work was better than that. What sense could you make of the post-symbolist poets or the experimental novel by applying Arnold's criteria of judgement? Indeed what understanding of literature as art would you get if you insisted that poetry was a criticism of life? Arnold did not praise Pope, who unquestionably did criticize life; no wonder he did not praise Sappho or Catullus. The professors of literature such as W. P. Ker, who despised criticism as literary chatter masquerading as aesthetics, were no better. They spent their time, said Lytton Strachey, trying to prove Racine inferior to Shakespeare. They were neglecting the most important duty of the critic: to discover the essence of the work, what gave it singularity, what made the author tick. The critic must defer to the artist. His works were children of a unique imagination and experience. Since no critic could be infallible or impartial, why spin webs of orthodoxy and lay down elaborate critical canons? E. M. Forster declared that novelists could not be fitted into simple categories. Virginia Woolf pleaded that the critic ought to concern himself with the creative act, the birth-pangs, the struggle of the artist to solve certain technical problems. 'It is the critic's business,' said Raymond Mortimer, successor to Desmond MacCarthy as literary editor of the *New Statesman*, 'to discover and expose the merits and defects of a work;' but he adds a significant qualification: 'after this analytic process he must remember that the work itself is a synthesis, in which the defects are frequently inseparable from the merits.' Reading Homer or Blake or Proust should be an emotional as well as an intellectual experience. Criticism should be the homage paid to creators by the uncreative. What could it be but a branch of *belles-lettres*, an illumination of art by a civilized mind (civilization having been defined – possibly – by Clive Bell) inviting the reader to accept certain conclusions?

Paradoxically enough it was also in the years between the wars that Cambridge broke with academic convention and for the first time treated English literature not as a branch of philology or as a history of genres and influences. It was treated as a subject for criticism; and I. A. Richards made Cambridge criticism famous for his attempt to bring psychology and logic to bear on meaning and on the reader's response to poetry. For him the first question was: can we agree on criteria which will enable us to evaluate a poem? Yet most of the Cambridge critics were in those days far nearer to Bloomsbury than Richards. The founding professor, Quiller-Couch, had said that it was his intention in 1900 when he compiled the *Oxford Book of English Verse* to 'preserve at least some faint thrill of the emotion through which [the poem] had to pass before the Muse's lips let it fall, with however exquisite deliberation'. The object of criticism – at any rate of teaching literature – should be to convey how to live 'not with lily in buttonhole, but with a sense, too vivid to grow old, of the perpetual oddity, yet beauty of life'. The Cambridge critics used Richards's techniques of practical criticism, but for them communication – why it is that we respond to a work of art – came first, evaluation of the work second. The wily Tillyard spun theories about poetry direct or oblique; Joan Bennett analysed the Metaphysicals and Virginia Woolf; and the bizarre Mansfield Forbes would burst into song to illustrate his meaning. By 1929 Richards had himself abandoned the quest for a theory of value in favour of close reading of the text to reveal texture, pattern, symbolism, and the like, particularly after his most gifted pupil had discovered in reading literature seven types of ambiguity. '*Critical* certainties,' he said, 'convictions as to the value, and kinds of value, of kinds of poetry, might safely and with advantage decay, provided that there remained a firm sense of the importance of the critical act of choice, its difficulty, and the supreme exercise of all our faculties that it imposes'; and he added: 'The lesson of all criticism is that we have nothing to rely upon in making our choices but ourselves. The lesson of good poetry seems to be that, when we have understood it, in the degree in which we can order ourselves, we need nothing more.'

But in London a voice more authoritative than Richards was to be heard. T. S. Eliot's distinction of mind, his immense influence as a poet, his dismissal of fashionable liberalism for austere Anglo-Catholicism or of Russell for F. H. Bradley and T. E. Hulme and his habit of rejecting argument by persuasion in favour of argument by assertion made his criticism unique. Arnold had quoted Sainte-Beuve: 'In France the first consideration for us is not whether we are amused and pleased by a work of art or mind, nor is it whether we are touched by it. What we seek above all to learn is, whether *we were right* in being amused with it, and in applauding it, and in being moved by it;' and Eliot took his *pièce justificative* also from France when at the beginning of *The Sacred Wood* he quoted Remy de Gourmont: *Ériger en lois ses impressions person-nelles, c'est le grand effort d'un homme s'il est sincère.*' Eliot pronounced certain works to be more serious than others: Villon's *Testament* more serious than *In Memoriam* and (singular judgement!) *Amos Barton* than *The Mill on the Floss.* The *hauteur* of Eliot's *Criterion*; his devastating dismissal of romanticism; and his destruction of the pantheon which Victorian and Georgian critics had erected, appealed to the young and served as a model for a new generation of critics such as Edgell Rickword or Geoffrey Grigson; and above all for the Leavises.

In *Scrutiny* F. R. and Q. D. Leavis assembled a group of like-minded critics who were to establish once and for all which authors were significant, important and valuable and which were trivial, over-valued and unworthy of serious study. Whereas the word 'serious' used by Eliot had meant the possession of a citadel of belief, Catholicism, from which to set off perceptions to advantage, the Leavises used 'serious' in the Evangelical sense to mean a concern with moral problems. Disciples had to acquire not only a habit of mind but the method of expressing the mind at work. They had to learn to write a prose which fused Arnold's irony with Lawrence's furious denunciation of the modern world and Eliot's habit of assertion and refusal to engage with his opponents' arguments; above all, with Henry James's celebrated convoluted way of conveying what was not in order to insinuate what was. Only then were they permitted to amplify their masters' conclusions and find additional arguments for 'placing' poets and writers definitively. The only justi-fication for studying an author's craftsmanship was to expose his morality through his style. A writer's personality, his life, was irrelevant. The only personality a writer possessed was his writings. Criticism as elegant writing, *belles-lettres*, was detestable, 'substitute-creation', evil and conceited egoism. Criticism in fact was the only discipline which could save the nation's culture; and it could do so partly by exposing how Bloomsbury's claim to be cultured and civilized was the fraudulent claim of a despicable upper-middle-class coterie. Perhaps they recalled

Stephen's denunciation of literary cliques. *Scrutiny* was not to be a coterie; and they showed it was not by dissociating themselves publicly from their colleagues in Cambridge and rounding on their most ardent supporters for the clumsiness of their praise.

The Leavises also had a theory of English culture. For them the life of the rural world in which speech was natural and vigorous had been overcome by machine civilization, suburban falsities and the glitter of upper-class civilities. The natural robust response to language had been gelded by the jargon of advertisers. Queenie Leavis's first book had claimed to show why the reading public preferred one kind of fiction to another, and throughout her life she praised Leslie Stephen for asking why bad poets won renown in their lifetime or best-sellers became unreadable. She applauded him for pouring cold water on that hard-worked word 'originality'. The most original writers were those who spotted what line in the tradition they inherited was the best to explore. At a time when Marxist criticism was gaining ground Queenie Leavis could point to Stephen's conviction that literature was not illuminated by relating it to a theory about social development whether by Taine or Marx. Here was a critic who declared that you could not praise a novel sensibly unless you showed how it was superior to its second and third rate contemporaries even though they might have sold better or been more highly esteemed when they first appeared. Here was a critic prepared to discriminate among the works of the famous, even to 'place' novels. 'We were grateful to Leslie Stephen,' she said, 'not so much for what he wrote – that was considerable – as for what he stood for, implied and pointed to.' Was he not a forerunner of the Leavises who rejected false Benthamite psychological pseudo-science such as Ivor Richards's 'appetencies'? Did he not say that the critic should study the country's culture and judge whether it inspired or impeded the production of masterpieces – and did not this point to her book *Fiction and the Reading Public*?

At first sight there can scarcely be any doubt that Queenie Leavis had the better of the battle for Stephen's body. She should incidentally have noticed that MacCarthy was limping from a self-inflicted wound. In picking up a rock to hurl at Stephen's reputation MacCarthy dropped it on his toes. Stephen, he said, would be the last to see evidence of Pope's genius in such a line as 'Die of a rose in aromatic pain'. Unfortunately for him, the work of Pope's Stephen knew best was *An Essay on Man* and he quoted this very line in his *Cornhill* article 'Thoughts on Criticism by a Critic' as an example of extreme (and probably morbid) poetic sensibility. There was an ominous gap in MacCarthy's armour despite the fact that he had allies. It was all very well for A. E. Housman delivering in 1933 his Leslie Stephen Lecture on 'The Name and Nature of Poetry' to remark (his target was Ivor Richards) that the bristling of his beard was a better guide than criticism to what was poetic. It was beside the point that David Garnett reviewing MacCarthy with an air of insufferable complacency said that Stephen 'quite rightly in my opinion wrote disparagingly of literary criticism. He was not well fitted for it, and he was wasted on it.' But the fact was that the Cambridge school had been founded in order to discover what could profitably be said about English literature and inevitably this led to discriminating between one poem and another, this writer and that. To exclude judgement meant that literary criticism was unlike any other branch of the humanities, history, language or philosophy. If the processes of thought which enabled scholars in those subjects to distinguish between this and that were valid, similar processes were valid for criticism; to deny that was to deny that critical concepts had any meaning not only for literature but for all the humanities. Judgement is integral to the spirit of liberal inquiry. The liberal insists that opinions must not be advanced by unworthy methods: not that all opinions are equally valuable. On those who like MacCarthy distrusted judgement, Lionel Trilling delivered a memorable *obiter dictum*. To refuse, as E. M. Forster did, he said, to conquer by the intellect a province which for so long had been subject to the vagaries of taste, was the wrong kind of liberalism. It 'seems to carry itself to the extreme of anarchy, a liberalism shot through with a sentimentally-literal Christian morality. It is laissez-faire to the ultimate . . . a contradiction of the Western tradition of intellect which believes that by making decisions, by choosing precisely, by evaluating correctly it can solve all difficulties.' To refuse to use the will to solve problems is to shirk the responsibility that is borne by every man of intellect and courage.

The Other Side of the Coin

And yet a niggling doubt remains. Why did Queenie Leavis picture Stephen as John the Baptist, a forerunner of he who was to come? Advent Sunday is not Christmas Day so perhaps something in his criticism discomfited her. Perhaps after all she had not seen MacCarthy off the battlefield.

Anyone who reads Stephen's criticism today is bound to be struck by how little attention he pays to language, imagery, symbols and models. Stephen treated them as mere matters of craftsmanship. He could draw a contrast between Fletcher whose metre produced 'a kind of monotonous sing-song' and Massinger where 'the metre is felt enough and only just enough to give a more stately step to rather florid prose.'[1] In a nine-line

---

[1] In his famous essay on Massinger T. S. Eliot called Stephen's work 'a formidable destructive analysis' though he added that Stephen had not put Massinger 'finally and irrefutably in place'.

quotation from *Hellas* he could spot an obvious use of the *Tempest*'s imagery but could miss a line echoing a phrase from *King Lear*; and such cases of textual analysis were rare. When Pope's delicacies confronted him he could only say, 'The value of all good work ultimately depends on touches so fine as to elude the sight.' Indeed it is far from clear whether he thought Pope wrote poetry. To explain why Johnson's judgement of *Lycidas* was wrong would be 'to go pretty deeply into the theory of poetic expression'. Stephen stayed on the bank and kept dry. He left Coleridge's melody 'to critics of finer perception and a greater command of superlatives' and declared that when Arnold claimed to detect Celtic or Teutonic or Norman elements in English literature he was 'going a little beyond his tether'. It is unkind or does one not hear an echo of the fatuous Mr Brooke in *Middlemarch*: 'I went into science a good deal myself at one time; but I saw it would not do . . . the fact is human reason may carry you a little too far . . . but I saw it would not do. I have always been in favour of a little theory: we must have a little thought: else we shall be landed back in the dark ages.'

Lytton Strachey thought that only such an eminent Victorian would have dared to make the cool observation that, since he found Donne's poetry indigestible, he would write only about Donne's life. It was as if an historian were to write of Columbus and preface his remarks by saying he would say nothing about the great explorer's geographical discoveries because geography bored him. In his bewilderment Stephen concluded that poetic excellence could be measured by the genuineness of the poet's sincerity (by which he apparently meant the depth of his emotion). But how could this be tested? In desperation he cried aloud for an Ithuriel spear to distinguish true sentiments from false. Since no spear materialized, he declared: 'It is best to look at each poet by himself. We need only distinguish between the sham and the genuine article; and my own method of distinguishing is a simple one. I believe in poetry which learns itself by heart.' Or, as he put it in a less naïve moment, 'the thing had to be said just as it was said.' Then, shaking his head, he admitted that all these tests were as personal as any he had condemned in Arnold.

This is not an impressive spectacle; and Desmond MacCarthy saw at a glance that Stephen had lost a piece of equipment as a critic. Ithuriel had come on parade without his spear. What was the critic for if not to tell us why certain lines have power to move? No theory of value could be spun without unravelling the thread which connects words and ideas. 'Poetry, my dear Degas, is made not with ideas, but with words,' and though no one any longer would use Mallarmé's epigram in defence of a theory of 'pure poetry', ideas and emotions cannot be separated from the imagery in which they are expressed. J. W. Mackail tried to explain his failure by claiming that Stephen had no touch of poetry in him: the logic was odd seeing that Mackail twitted him for being too much a Wordsworthian to appreciate Pope. Leslie Stephen loved poetry in the way that men before the First World War did. Poetry in those days was music. It was an incantation to be chanted, as anyone who listens to the earliest gramophone recordings can tell. Stephen had thousands of lines by memory and would recite Kipling and Newbolt as readily as Milton and Wordsworth. Poetry was his breviary, his matins, terce and compline, his book of magic spells. He had only to read once a new set of verses which touched him and they were added to his prayers. What priest as he whispers his office to himself pauses to analyse the rhythms of the general confession or the cadences in the prayer of Saint Chrysostom? Only once in his essay on Defoe did he analyse language – the tricks by which that great journalist produced an impression of reality. He hated gossip about books and to have concerned himself with the imagery a poet used may have seemed to him a profanity of the arcane. He failed to see that language is the germ from which grows a writer's world, his character and his moods. Language, not morality, makes authors survive. If it were not so why should many serious novelists fail whose morality has been exemplary? Why does Evelyn Waugh succeed while L. H. Myers does not?

A critic is as great as his perceptions. It is not their rhetoric but their perceptions which make judicial critics such as T. S. Eliot or F. R. Leavis worth reading, as anyone who glances at their lesser disciples can see. As with all judicial critics Stephen's bag after a battue over the fields of literature was mixed. The essay on 'Shakespeare as a Man' was commonplace though better than that of Bagehot; the psychopathic nature of Oliver Wendell Holmes's novels, which explore perversions of character, passed him by; and one is astonished to learn that Balzac's characters are naturalistic, the work of a patient Dutch artist painting every hair on the head and wrinkle on the face with photographic accuracy. There has always been a good deal to be said against the Brontës and Stephen said most of it. Charlotte's hero in *Jane Eyre* was 'the personification of a true woman's longing (may one say it now?) for a strong master'. Unfortunately she did not realize that Rochester behaved not as a rake but a sneak and portrayed him 'as knowing as little of the world as she did: so far from being simple and masculine he is as self-conscious as a lady at her first appearance in society.' There is something deficient in a critical judgement which concludes that Charlotte Brontë could hardly be put in 'the highest rank amongst those who . . . can help us to clearer conceptions'; and there is something bizarre about a critic who declares that *Wuthering Heights* was a baseless nightmare whose author had such a feeble grasp of external facts that its only parallel in English literature was with Jacobean dramas such as *The Revenger's*

Tragedy. Not all Stephen's polite bows to the sisters could mask his condescension. Who ever supposed the Brontës should be judged by the standard one applies to George Eliot? Consider his judgement of the two greatest novelists of his day. In the *DNB* he recorded that 'if literary fame could be safely measured by popularity with the half-educated, Dickens must claim the highest position among English novelists.' Dickens, he thought, showed little real depth or tenderness of feeling and 'his amazing powers of observation were out of all proportion to his powers of reflection.' He wrote 'for readers who cannot take a joke until it has been well hammered into their heads', and his characters were caricatures. These judgements were not eccentric. They remained for several generations the stock response of intellectuals with a very few exceptions, such as G. K. Chesterton. To them Dickens was a best-seller fit for their nursery, not for their drawing-room or study. Neither Henry James nor the aesthetes turning their hearts to stone to avoid laughing at the death of Little Nell were any likelier to give Dickens a serious hearing. It was not until Edmund Wilson and Humphry House acclaimed him in the 1940s that the tide began to turn.

One of Stephen's misjudgements is particularly illuminating. He thought *Bleak House* showed a decline in Dickens's powers induced probably by overwork. 'The humour is often forced, and the mannerism more strongly marked; the satire against the court of chancery, the utilitarians, and the "circumlocution office" is not relieved by the irresistible fun of the former caricatures, nor strengthened by additional insight. It is superficial without being good-humoured.' Is the son of Sir James Stephen taking his revenge? Possibly. But Stephen brought exactly the same objection against George Eliot's later novels. He thought them as powerful as ever: the description of Lydgate 'engulfed by the selfish persistence of his wife, like a swimmer sucked down by an octopus . . . is so lifelike that one reads it with a sense of acute bitterness. And as in *Daniel Deronda*, though I am ready to confess that Mordecai and Daniel are to my mind intolerable bores, I hold the story of Grandecourt and Gwendolen to be, though not a pleasant, a singularly powerful study . . . Only one cannot help regretting the loss of that early charm.' The indescribable glow which illuminated the earlier writing had gone. When Stephen resented Dickens's and George Eliot's failure to display charm or be pleasant, he was really resenting their maturity.

One might think that he would have praised that alarmingly precise moralist Jane Austen, or at least have been interested in Fanny Price or Emma. But no; he thought her horizon confined by the garden wall and the Pump Room at Bath. 'I never, for example, knew a person thoroughly deaf to humour who did not worship Miss Austen. [Such people] like her because her humour (to use a vulgar, but the only, phrase) is drawn so excessively mild . . . She is absolutely at peace with her comfortable world.' How much at heart an Arnoldian he was! Great themes, the grand style, heroic deeds were what Stephen wanted in the novel. That was why Scott was the novelist he never tired of re-reading – *Guy Mannering, The Heart of Midlothian* and *Waverley*. As the critic who had begged his colleagues to relate literature to society he praised Scott for showing how each character, even a beggar such as Edie Ochiltree, had his place in society. He persuades us that it hardly matters that Scott's historical romances prove to be made of plaster of Paris or that his plots are devices in which the heroes and heroines are shuffled into the wings while his lawyers, bailies, gentry, smugglers and peasants move centre stage. But then Stephen spoils it. He finds in Scott a quality he admired in Stevenson – a streak of boyishness which he is not ashamed to acknowledge in himself. An 'invincible boyishness' he tells us is a prominent characteristic of genius. This is not reassuring.

Literary criteria resemble those shady characters who assume an alias. In the place of those aesthetic descriptions 'subtle', 'bitter' and 'tender' which Stephen banned we find the ominous words 'masculine' and 'morbid' appearing. The critic cannot avoid using shorthand terms of praise and distaste; but he ought not to *think* in shorthand. Sincerity was so near to Stephen's heart that he accepted without question Arnold's distinction between 'genuine' poetry and poetry conceived in the wits: of which Eliot observed that there is not one kind of poetry but many. This was the kernel of MacCarthy's reservation when he said that Stephen had missed the point of Sterne's surrealist world where time loses its meaning.

Unlike his first great work, *English Literature and Society in the Eighteenth Century* is not a work of scholarship. He wrote these lectures as he lay dying and he had never had the time to work systematically in libraries to test his theories and give those that survived that overwhelming conviction of truth generated by the evidence which the great scholar conveys. For instance when he explained why literature was no longer written by gentlemen in the second half of the eighteenth century, he did not explain how it again came to be written by ladies and gentlemen such as Fanny Burney and Byron. The book is really a collection of hints by a fine literary journalist. Unfortunately it had a dire effect upon Queenie Leavis. *Fiction and the Reading Public* did not lack courage or industry. What it lacked was scholarship. The idyllic picture of society from Elizabethan to Georgian times which she painted to contrast with the hideous industrial class-ridden society of her times is unrecognizable to an historian; and her misreadings and omissions in ephemeral literature made her draw erroneous conclusions about the reading public. Her idealization of an Arcadian past with which to whip the sins of the present was no part of Stephen's work; but the ease with which he put forward untested generalizations deluded her.

His contribution to learning would have been immeasurably greater had he worked out the implications of relating literature to society as the historians of the German Renaissance had done. Yet when we follow what happened to criticism under Gundolf or under Marxist inspiration in Germany, we are struck not by the limitations of Stephen's insights, we are struck by their common sense. Whatever may be said against the Leavises' analysis of English culture and their denunciation of advertising and the media, it was not the child of a comprehensive system of ideas such as Stephen had condemned in Taine. In the hands of the heirs of the German Renaissance mass culture, and hence the reading habits of the public, became a symptom of a far greater social malaise. Mass culture, so the neo-Marxists of the Frankfurt *Institut für Sozialforschung* in exile in New York argued, was the opium which stupefied the working class and robbed them of their revolutionary ardour. The exact opposite view was taken by Terry Eagleton. He thought the concern of Stephen and the Leavises for evaluation to be a bourgeois strategy: literary studies should analyse society instead of reading literature for its own sake: the study of masterpieces was counter-revolutionary because it reinforced bourgeois patterns of thought. Raymond Williams urged his Cambridge colleagues to 'drop their narrow criteria of literature and evaluate the songs and speech of the semi-literate'. Evaluation, as Stephen and the Leavises had defined it, taught the young to think of literature as sacred texts unsuitable for the profane working class. Popular taste, the cinema, television and tapes ought to be the first concern of the critic. The critic should speak for all social classes and not just for those who regarded literature as the proper study for the élite.

Even stranger were the turnings taken by the sociolinguists such as Lacan. They declared that people behave in response to a succession of signals, signs, codes and symbols. It was an illusion to imagine that we had freedom of choice; and therefore it was wrong to think of a novelist creating work through his imagination. A novelist merely responded to the social structure of the times. Study therefore the pattern of his impulses and the symbols he used, and you will be able to establish the genetic code of his writings with the same certainty as a molecular biologist. The critic would never discover the laws governing human behaviour if he allowed himself to be deluded by facts. Facts were not indisputable truths. They were manufactured by the bourgeois to defend their own modes of thought. Theory, not facts, clinched the argument for changing society, and theory could be understood by joining the élite who had learnt to use the new language. Lost in the thickets of discussing literature in terms of strategies, reification, praxis and deconstruction the reader may well feel that there is something to be said for the English empirical tradition which Stephen exemplified and for his belief in facts.

Yet in fact dozens of admirable books have appeared, some of them by highly intelligent Marxists, others by those holding implicitly conservative or liberal interpretations of society. To take two examples: there was Ian Watt's unforgettable work on the rise of the novel and the way Defoe through Robinson Crusoe unconsciously exposed the entrepreneurial assumptions of the society of his day – the relations of master and servant, the obligations to save and spend, the rights of the individual and the duties he did or did not owe to his fellow citizens. Or there was John Barrell who did exactly what Stephen had hoped would be done for the century he loved when he showed how Smollett suggested in *Roderick Random* that a gentleman may be defined by his occupation and by the way he meets and makes his fortune rather than through gentle birth. Or when he showed that disputes about grammar and correct speech have political overtones and we see Johnson defending the usages of polite and learned society against Paine and Wordsworth who wanted to write the English spoken in the provinces and John Clare exclaiming 'grammar in learning is like tyranny in government – confound the bitch I'll never be her slave.' Books such as these would have rejoiced Stephen's heart.

Stephen laid down one critical canon which was specifically repudiated by the Leavises. He always related the life of the writer to his works and would have regarded the separation of the two as absurd. He would not have accepted F. R. Leavis's contention that characters in novels are merely illustrations of the moral qualities which sustain the novel, still less that the character of the writer exists only in his books. And suddenly one is struck by something odd. Is it a trick of the light or is this forerunner carrying the colours not of the Leavises but of Bloomsbury's stables? Who is this telling us that the true arbiter of literature is not the critic but the Common Reader? Who is saying, 'I do not accept with satisfaction the apparently implied doctrine that poets can be satisfactorily arranged in order of merit. We cannot give so many marks for style and so many for pathos or descriptive power'? Tennyson and Browning could both be admitted to be excellent without enquiring which was absolutely the better. To ask whether *Adam Bede* or *The Heart of Midlothian* was the greater novel was a silly question: they were incomparable. Stephen praised Walter Raleigh as a critic because he began with a spontaneous love of the poet, used his learning to reveal new beauties and deepen old and was impartial in his analysis: little of the hanging judge there. John Gross reminded us that the Leavises who were so fond of quoting Stephen's dictum 'really the value of second rate literature is nil' conveniently overlooked another dictum, 'all books are good, that is to say there is scarcely any book that may not serve as a match to fire our enthusiasm'; and he reminded us also that while neither statement is to be taken literally it is the most natural thing in the world to feel in certain moods that only a handful of writers are ultimately worth bothering with, and at other times a diet of nothing but the classics would be intolerable.

It is not merely that Stephen anticipates Bloomsbury judgements. In the essays on Balzac which he and Raymond Mortimer wrote, both agreed that Balzac lived vicariously in an imaginary world; that for him dream and reality were the same; that his view of human nature was nonsensical; that society could not be divided into virtuous fools and clever knaves; that his stories were improbable but thrilling; that his ceaseless explanations were intolerable; but that the incredibilities vanished as his vigour and intensity swept the reader away. Compare their tone of voice. Compare Stephen's 'Bishops indeed have fallen upon evil days; they no longer enjoy the charming repose of the comfortable dignitaries of the eighteenth century. But I should dearly like a deanery'; with Raymond Mortimer's 'I am one of the diminishing band who dearly love a bishop . . .' Dover Wilson hinted at the debt which Strachey owed to Stephen's sinewy style, and in biography he used Stephen's technique to describe a crisis of mind. Consider Stephen's irony at Froude's expense. 'Froude was roused to a resentment against poor Queen Elizabeth. She would not be a heroine. She got upon his nerves. She cared nothing for creeds . . . Instead of putting herself at the head of European Protestantism her whole policy was to play off the two Catholic powers against each other with lying promises;' and though at bottom her purpose was ' "moderately upright" she had no nice sense of honour to raise difficulties.' Strachey carried this teasing ridicule several stages further when he enveloped Freeman with ridicule. Ridicule, which modern literary critics find so shocking, bubbles through Stephen's high-spirited description of William Godwin's novels or through his grave interest that Emerson had discovered an Olympian British philosopher called Mr Wilkinson. How irreverent to see a whole essay devoted to the vivacity that Landor was a model sixth-form boy only with 'an unusually strong infusion of schoolboy perversion'. How right to entreat Disraeli to be a little less serious and to spare us Sidonia. '*Coningsby* wants little but a greater absence of purpose to be a first-rate novel.' How characteristic of Bloomsbury to endorse Pope's conclusion that most people praise humour because gentle dullness ever loves a joke! 'Can you not read Falstaff's story of the men in buckram without bringing tears to the eyes? Rabelais is a great name. Can anybody deliberately sit down and laugh "over a jolly chapter" of Rabelais unless he has laboriously qualified himself for the purpose?' No, to be a humorist you must be so excessively manly that like Swift you raise 'the propriety of converting Irish babies into an article of food'.

He had the gift of taking an attribute such as vanity in his hands like a jewel and tossing it to and fro so that it caught the light. He could crystallize a piece of analysis into an aphorism, as when he said that to appreciate the rustic humour which Scott or George Eliot retail 'we require not a new defect of logic but a new logical structure'. His criticism is full of such comments. On Balzac: 'He did not so much invent characters and situations as watch his imaginary world, and compile the memoirs of its celebrities.' On Pope's emotion which 'came in sudden jets and gushes, instead of in a continuous stream'. On the *Epistle to Arbuthnot* in which Pope 'seems to be actually screaming with malignant fury . . . The most abiding sentiment – when we think of him as a literary phenomenon – is admiration for the exquisite skill which enabled him to discharge a function, not of the highest kind, with a perfection rare in any department of literature.' That was a sentence which Strachey quoted in his Leslie Stephen Lecture on Pope; and he quoted too that line about the aromatic rose – perhaps Virginia Woolf had told him it was one of her father's favourites.

On one matter he differed from MacCarthy and Bloomsbury. He would not make a shrine of art or regard the artist as its priest. Henry James was a welcome friend but Stephen could never have said 'it is art that *makes* life, makes interest, makes importance for our consideration and application of these things, and I know of no substitute whatever for the force and beauty of its process.' Stephen's daughter was no great admirer of James, but she too turned to the inner life for the moral vision, the moment of apprehension. The outer life was shapeless, baffling and disheartening. It was redeemed by visions of beauty and goodness which occasionally gave it meaning – though the meaning was ultimately inexpressible. She showed what values she admired, she expressed her contempt and rage at a world in which all powers and principalities and decisions were taken by men, particularly when those decisions led to war. But how to relate the rights of women, or socialism, or pacifism or anti-imperialism to something larger than the individual consciousness was an insoluble mystery – and possibly a nasty mystery. Like many of us she was more interested in the personalities of politicians than in their policies. She was not interested in day-to-day issues, in the way her husband was as he argued over the wording of manifestoes or the clauses of parliamentary bills in the sweaty committee rooms of the Labour Party. 'We've been sitting in the dark and listening to the Band and having a terrific argument about Shaw. I say he only influenced the outer fringes of morality. Leonard says the shop girls wouldn't be listening to the Band with their young men if it weren't for Shaw. I say the human heart is touched only by the poets. Leonard says rot, I say damn. Then we go home. Leonard says I'm narrow. I say he's stunted . . . How does one come by one's morality? Surely by reading the poets . . .' Her father would have agreed that to read the poets strengthened morality; but he did not regard politicians as so obtuse, governments so wicked and conventions so stupid that politics was reduced to protest. For him social duties were not tyrannous impostures.

He did not hold the creative writer's life in high esteem. 'Literature,' he wrote, 'is, in all cases, a demoralising occupation, though some people can resist its evil influences. It is demoralising because success implies publicity. A poet has to turn himself inside out by the very conditions of his art, and suffers from the incessant stimulants applied to his self-consciousness.' In a bleak and, it should be said, an off moment, Stephen asked whether art itself was not a luxury to which men had no right while crime and disease were rampant in the world. Like Plato he was disturbed that art is not true. 'All fiction is really a kind of lying.' Do the lives of the poets endorse the Ruskinian canon: By their fruits ye shall know them?

Why this sudden gloom? Lytton Strachey put his finger on the trouble. Stephen 'frankly despised the whole business' – the world of authors, critics and bookmen. We must be scientific and give criticism what dignity we can: but like Bloomsbury he thought criticism had little value. Stephen would have nothing to do with the modern cant which declares that a writer by reading a powerful critic can be put on the right lines. 'After all what does a real genius ever learn from a critic? There is, it seems to me, only one good piece of advice which a critic can give to an author, namely, that the author should dare to be himself.' He advised Thomas Hardy never to read critics but to read the writers 'who give ideas and don't prescribe rules'. He even at times doubted the value of his own method. Did not 'Hazlitt's enthusiasm bring out Congreve's real merits with a force of which a calmer judge would be incapable'? Such scepticism is typical of Stephen's determination to be honest but it makes his literary criticism undeniably less impressive. Nor is it as well written as his biographies. The intelligent, sensible paragraphs trot on, like the second subject of the finale of Schubert's Great C Major. The concise biographer sometimes becomes garrulous. In their essays on Balzac Stephen made some two dozen points in over eleven, Mortimer in under five thousand words. We recognize his voice at once: but it does not woo or command us. It is not solely the dialectical force of the critic that convinces readers. The elegance of impressionist critics, such as Forster or Virginia Woolf, can also make art more important.

The battle between Queenie Leavis and Desmond MacCarthy has receded into the past. On the plain of Troy 'The dragon wing of night o'erspreads the earth, And stickler-like the armies separates.' Critics now fighting on other parts of the field. Stephen is too ecumenical a figure to be captured by any faction. He may not have been a great critic. With characteristic candour he acknowledged that Arnold and Sainte-Beuve were his superiors. Like a mathematician whose axioms are too reasonable, his judgements are too conventional, too much in line with the sensible, intelligent taste of his times; and his hesitating theory of criticism falls short of that architectonic of judgement a great critic should make. But there is something impressive in the way that he unhesitatingly accepts the duty to judge and at the same time does not hide, in his frequent allusions to the priggishness of the young, his contempt for the moralizers who are determined to establish a reign of the saints over the benighted, so characteristic of the Evangelical party in his time and of self-righteous activists in ours.

His final word on criticism was this. It is a pastime. If you engage in it, apply your mind to it, be as precise as you can, and judge authors and books by their moral content. But don't give yourself airs or think that you have done anything important. The whole of criticism is not worth a groat when weighed against a work of art or an original philosophical treatise; and these works in their turn are valuable in the degree to which they help mankind to see truth clearer and to live better.

Chapter Thirteen

𐂷𐂷𐂷

CONCLUSION

The Integrated Intellectual

Each of us, however gentle or wasted our life, has a place in history, usually as the nameless representative of some class or status group or movement. Leslie Stephen thought he would be lucky if he were a footnote in history. A footnote to what?

If some of those who study our country's culture are to be believed, he was either one of the last survivors of a dying breed of literary men or among the first of the modern stereotype, the alienated intellectual. It is becoming a conventional truth among these analysts that those in literary life, indeed many intellectuals, became alienated from their society after 1870. They turned away, so it is said, from public issues and distanced themselves from the reading public with which their predecessors such as Dickens and Thackeray had been in such close rapport. They became convinced that art and intellectual life, such as scientific research, were superior to the ordinary life of making and spending money. Aestheticism was one manifestation of the change. The Pre-Raphaelites rejected middle-class notions of art. Writers wanted simultaneously to be above the rout yet to be able to appeal to some authoritative institution where standard of taste and scholarship were validated. The craving for an academy was another sign of the change. An academy could take the form of the short-lived periodical of that name or of the British Academy. Or it materialized in the movement to reform the ancient and to found the civic universities. As the universities at last became centres of research men of letters dwindled in size and the professoriate strode like giants over the land. Intellectuals no longer sought to be sages like Carlyle or seers like Ruskin: their ideal was to form a minority culture in opposition to the culture of the rest of the population. They intended to distance themselves from the vulgarity of those who had money and the brutality of those who had none. What better retreat than the self-governing universities where they could devote themselves snugly to their own research and would be judged by their ability to manipulate the scholarly techniques of their discipline?

But why should the literary intelligentsia have felt so alienated? Partly, so this theory runs, because of the growing power of the scientists. Just as the Romantics had popularized the idea of the artist as genius writing under the spell of his specially sensitive imagination as a counterweight to the saucy claims of the political economists and philosophic radicals, so Arnold set his concept, culture, against the pretensions of Huxley and the natural scientists. To preoccupy oneself with those habits of mind and judgement which constituted culture was to set oneself apart from the Barbarians, Philistines and the Populace. Who could view his society with optimism when the agricultural depression was destroying the stable paternalism of the gentry and implicitly endorsing the morality of Mr Bottles the manufacturer? Soon the upper and commercial classes began to merge to form a class of conspicuous consumers. Moreover the fortunes of the intelligentsia were threatened by the fracture of the reading public. A vast working-class readership had emerged and the solid middle-class readership was declining and becoming debauched. Mudie's and W. H. Smith would not market the products of the intelligentsia. Their new pessimism did not sell. After Stephen who but Bernard Shaw, Lionel Johnson and W. E. Henley could make a living as intellectual journalists? Knowledge itself fractured and became professionalized. The popular history of Macaulay and Buckle was succeeded by the weighty tomes of Stubbs and Tout. By definition a professional could be indifferent to public demand or taste because he did not live by selling the products of his thought: he had his university post. The new scientific community were as much advocates of science for science's sake as the aesthetes were of art for art's sake. They had no use for applied science nor for the needs of industry. Only fundamental research was respectable – another sign of the rejection not only of the values of the market-place but of any sense of responsible relation to society. Self-isolation is another form of alienation.

According to this theory, then, Leslie Stephen resembles a stranded porpoise, washed up on the sands of time, a specimen of that failing species, the man of letters, a philistine whose very hostility to the aesthetes reflected his antiquated belief that art had moral purpose. But before we accept this judgment should we not examine the theory?

Directly we do so we see that its apologists have to qualify their conclusions so often as almost to negate them. For they have to admit that the intelligentsia and a sizeable proportion of the literary world were not more 'alienated' from their society, indeed in some ways less, than were Dickens, Thackeray or Carlyle, all of whom were savage critics of their world. Only a handful were aesthetes or followed the model of French intellectuals and writers. Ruskin tilled the soil, Pater sowed the seed and Wilde reaped the harvest; but no one could describe Oscar as at odds with society – he enjoyed its company and applause too much. Swinburne was a Bohemian and Symonds for obvious reasons preferred to live abroad; but neither regarded himself as ostracized and both continued to converse with ease within the intelligentsia. Ruskin was at odds with society; but a seer who denounced democracy and preferred an aristocracy of the nobility, the merchants and manufacturers, and scholars and artists to rule was hardly subversive. Like Carlyle the public read him with admiration and even public schoolboys such as the egregious Beetle scoured *Fors Clavigera* for quotations which would fortify them to endure the pieties of prefects and housemasters. Ruskin's disciple, William Morris, was indeed subversive, a man who not only rejected the commercialization of society but most of the remedies his fellow socialists proposed for controlling the means of production and distributing the products: yet the public read him too. But when we listen to Wells's refreshing cheek and contempt for deference or his fellow Fabian Bernard Shaw declaring with the utmost cordiality that his desire to exterminate the rich was equalled only by his detestation of the poor, we realize we are in the company of men who have settled for their lot, however many plans and stratagems and policies they invent for transforming the world they live in. They are no more revolutionaries than the aesthetes were *poètes maudits*. Hardy was alienated from God but not from his fellow men or from the past. Those marvellous critics of society, Henry James and Conrad, were thoroughly at home in it. The only writers of note who join Morris in standing apart, and each does so in a way unique to him and him alone, are Gerard Manley Hopkins, Gissing and Samuel Butler. The character of intellectual life at the turn of the century, so far from being deflationary and depressed, was expansive and confident in its criticisms and its remedies, confident that opponents would take hard knocks with spirited joviality, fertile in producing schemes to reform the world and accepting that few of them would survive adolescence.

In fact it is not until the First World War that we find evidence, as distinct from signs and portents, of that annihilating weariness and disgust with modern life which can fitly be described as alienation; and not until after the Second World War can one speak of dons replacing men of letters as the arbiters of culture and taste. The generation of Bookmen who succeeded Stephen – Andrew Lang, Gosse and Henley or the crushingly learned Collins and Saintsbury – were intellectually not in his class. But Chesterton, Arnold Bennett, Orage, T. S. Eliot, Murry and Grigson were inspired journalists and editors more influential, stimulating or profound than any contemporary professor of literature. So far from the natural Victorian sympathy between audience and author disappearing, England remained a country where scholars did not disdain to write in a style intelligible to the common reader. Intellectuals sold the product of their thought or supplemented their income by taking unexacting jobs with not insuperable difficulty at a time when publishing, periodicals and newspapers were at their zenith. Nor did the intelligentsia distance themselves from the common herd so that between them and the world of government there yawned an abyss. If Gladstone and Lowe were members of the Metaphysical Society, Balfour, Asquith and the Souls even in the most brutally plutocratic days of Edwardianism were hosts to learning; and there were always the clubs and salons where intellectuals could merge with the Establishment. A young English intellectual might, and frequently did, hesitate after taking his first degree before deciding to try for a university post or take the examination for entry to the administrative class of the civil service. He was not likely to feel more than is usual at that age that the times were out of joint in a country where reform was possible, when the civil service at home and in India and the professions including the academic profession were open to him and when, as is true of all countries, an old boy network could help him clamber up the side of the ship and on to the deck. It was as well that they were open. For many years to come there were few permanent posts in the civic universities other than those of the professors. For many years the fellowships at Oxford and Cambridge were occupied by sound college tutors, often learned and good teachers but not noted for their contributions to scholarship. 'The "problem of the intellectual" insofar as it is a subject of scholarly inquiry,' wrote Sheldon Rothblatt, 'arises from a concern with *fin de siècle* radical movements, both right and left, and with the social and political condition of Jews in France, Germany and Eastern Europe.' The alienated and deracinated intellectual was not a phenomenon in Stephen's lifetime nor in the years following his death.

So far from Stephen taking the role of the last of the grand old men of letters, he can easily be seen as in the vanguard of those who gave literary studies professional standards with his insistence on more rigorous standards in criticism and rules to prevent biography turning into hagiography. It is true that he thought his status group the intelligentsia deserved more power and political influence, but he was sceptical of Arnold's claims for culture. To argue that culture should take the place of normal social judgement and replace the values of the machine age was to him pretentious and probably pernicious. Culture could not be divorced from the market place and the laws of political economy. The clerisy in his eyes was not to be confused with and confined to *littérateurs*. It certainly changed in composition during his lifetime but not because most of its members became dons. The real change was the displacement of the clergy. When Stephen was young it was considered natural that works of learning, not merely theological treatises and collections of sermons, but historical, literary and philosophical work would be undertaken by clergymen: the Rolls series was largely compiled by them. He himself as editor of the *DNB* had often to rely on such excellent contributors as Canon Ainger. He lived to see the learned as well as learning secularized.

The Man of Virtue

Leslie Stephen was, then, a representative, not an aberrant, figure. He was an eminent Victorian and to call him that is to distinguish him from those few who, eminent as they were, were not and seemed to have strayed into Victoria's reign by mistake: Disraeli, Bagehot, Meredith, Pater and Samuel Butler. If in his early middle age he was somewhat too fierce a radical and too sardonic and silent in manner, his achievements and character changed men's opinion of him and he ended revered by many and respected by all his peers. What could signalize his apotheosis on Parnassus more clearly than his acceptance of the invitation to reply to the toast of literature and the arts at the annual Royal Academy dinner? He epitomized the right kind of success for those of his calling. He left on his death a decent sum of £15,000 and his house in Kensington exactly reflected his standing: not fashionable like Mayfair or Belgravia, nor artistic with a hint of raffishness like Chelsea, nor dowdy like Bayswater. Some would say he had luck in his patron. He had a patron as many of those who are in the civil service or academic life have, an older colleague who takes a fatherly interest in promoting their protégé's career – even if in theory they belong to a profession in which one rises solely by merit. But not everyone could have handled George Smith, who knew his own mind and spoke it. Stephen's selflessness, capacity for hard work and straight dealing bound his proprietor to him. Neither sought to patronize or intrude upon the other. It was, after all, just such a relationship as proprietors try to establish with publishers and editors today.

What power and success did he have? By worldly standards hardly any. He could be persuaded to drop a line here or put in a word there for young men in whom he believed. But he let the Cambridge connection drop, loyal though he was to those who survived from the days when he was a young don. Manipulation, pulling wires, influencing people and institutions, using the growing respect in which he was held to angle for appointments to boards of trustees or to learned bodies, lobbying ministers, discovering which levers to pull and which women to cultivate, was foreign to his nature. Some intellectuals enjoy ingratiating themselves with those who hold the strings of power; others, with the gift of fascinating them, get swept into streams which they seem powerless to avoid and sometimes drown there. Stephen had no desire to move outside his station and did not enjoy much moving within it. He did not exploit his moderate success as editor of the *Cornhill* or prestigious success as editor of the *D N B*. But neither did he opt out. If honours and invitations came, he accepted them with grace; but he scorned to seek them.

People spoke well of him because he was palpably indifferent to worldly success. For one with so caustic a mind he was magnanimous in his dealings with his fellow men. Revenge, envy and malice were beneath him. He loved his friends and scorned to injure his enemies. He would lash the vice but spare the sinner. Despite his dictum that no one could be composed of contradictory qualities and that a man was all of one piece, character and work together, he nearly always distinguished between failings in achievements and failings of character. He would have had no sympathy with literary critics who take the written word as the sole evidence for a man's worth; and he would have detested the custom in our day of denigrating a fellow writer's work through his character. To probe for a failing and having detected the spot to inflict a personal wound and through the use of a snide phrase to infect the wound and then exult as the pus exudes, would have repelled him. He did not hesitate to expose impostors but he did not try to kill them with ridicule. Stephen was scrupulous in controversy; deflation was his precept, the salute to genius his practice. His virtues were the simple virtues. Anti-imperialist and anti-chauvinist though he was, he was proud of his country, proud of being British and a descendant of beer-drinking and beef-eating John Bulls, proud too of England as the home of civil and religious liberty, a philistine but not a fanatical country, a tolerant country ready to give asylum to European revolutionaries or to Jews flying from pogroms. He was proud of his family but no snob. He would have thought it absurd to boast about his forebears. At the same time he thought a man should wield authority, particularly in his family. Duty and diligence were high on his list of virtues; you owed duties to your family, your country, your employer and the institutions to which you belonged. Self-indulgence, self-advertisement and self-interest he found particularly displeasing. For all that he thought that the educated classes should govern the country, he found his fellow intellectuals exasperating and he considered the clever among the young usually to be callow prigs. Better the simple-hearted athlete such as Harry Hughes.

He did not believe morality to consist of rules. It is a way of life learnt unconsciously first in the family and then in other social institutions. The only way to challenge the prevailing code of conduct was to give good reasons why such change was desirable. Never appeal to religious or other extra-ethical considerations to gain your point. To accept a traditional way of behaviour, to know how to decide certain questions in order to act rightly, and to submit this way to rational criticism readily are hallmarks of a good moralist. He was a man with a conscience, not with something on his conscience; and his own behaviour testified that his morality was not constructed out of propositions and principles but was a reflection of his personality and a tradition.

At times he said in irony that his most characteristic quality – and failing – was his philistinism. He did his best to do justice to Arnold though at heart he thought him a fop. 'I must confess that as a good Philistine I often felt, and hope I profited by the feeling, that he had pierced me to the quick, and I submitted to his castigations as I have to submit to the probings of a dentist – I knew they were for my good. And I often wished, I must also confess, that I too had a little sweetness and light that I might be able to say such nasty things of my enemies.' You can see that Arnold's shafts hurt. But Stephen did not like to admit that Arnold was totally serious; Arnold may have made the old dragon philistinism wince but 'he recognized the monster was after all a most kindly monster at bottom'. Arnold, of course, did nothing of the sort. It has been argued that Stephen enjoyed posing as a philistine so as to expose the follies of both aesthetes and philistines. But throughout his writing you can sense how vapid he thinks the concept of culture is and how his instincts made Henley and Stevenson particularly sympathetic to him.

His morality was to be decisively rejected after the First World War and by many intelligent people before it. Such rejection was inevitable. It will happen to the morality which supplanted his. Morality becomes institutionalized in society. The particular set of virtues which at any given time are valued above others get inculcated by schoolteachers, by journalists and publicists, by pundits and clergymen. Gradually they seep into government. The more a morality becomes accepted as an ideal and is consciously taught, the more it becomes debased and vulgarized. Stephen's stern virtues became institutionalized in the teachings of the late-Victorian public schools, obsessed by athletic success, praising scholarship but despising the intellect, and teaching boys to control their deeper emotions so tightly that they strangled them. But the fact that the sterner virtues he believed in became over the years shop-soiled by others should not blind us to the fact that for all their sternness they are still virtues.

The Scholar and Rationalist

How good a scholar was he? A good scholar is one who not only cuts a trail through some thicket of knowledge, but does not misdirect the generations of scholars to come. Great minds, driven by powerful imaginations, construct new systems and apparently change the thought of their generation; but their books have a curious way of being disregarded after a short passage of time. Frazer's *Golden Bough* was an epic; but what modern anthropologist builds on it today? Stephen's *English Thought in the Eighteenth Century* is not an epic; but because Stephen states plainly what he is doing and sets himself a limited objective, scholars today are helped by his book. They continue to take it from the shelf because he made his own approach so clear. He despised obscurity and practised clarity. As a result, those who disagree can state the grounds of their disagreement with the respect of men talking to their equal. No serious explorer of eighteenth-century thought and literature should ignore Stephen's pioneer work. He had read so widely in eighteenth-century prose and entered so completely into the minds of those writers that the points he makes are too numerous and sensible to be disregarded. It is also interesting that when John Plamenatz made his subtle critique of the utilitarians, it was to Stephen's three volumes that he turned rather than to more recent critics as a reference for manoeuvre. Even theologians benefit from the clarity of Stephen's arguments: he gives them every opportunity to confound him, there are no weasel-words, no camouflage and deception.

Leslie Stephen was an amateur scholar, a Victorian gentleman such as Darwin or Acton whose critical apparatus and techniques are now outdated. He was not a popularizer. Whatever major subject he tackled such as eighteenth- or nineteenth-century thought, he read the original works of the obscurest thinkers. But he did not turn aside to break a lance with other scholars in the field or tell his tale by reference to the literature. There was not all that number of learned articles to which to turn. Nor did he write in the language which professional colleagues construct and which so often resembles a forest of abstract nouns, intersected by critical approaches, in which the common reader for sheer weariness lays himself down and dies. Stephen had the good fortune to be able to write as he pleased and he seized his opportunity and wrote in a lucid, natural prose, solid without being heavy, ironical without being flashy as it coaxes the reader along the road on an easy, gentle rein.

Neverthless if we ask where he himself stands among nineteenth-century thinkers the answer at first sight is unimpressive. Like most intellectuals Stephen accepted one of the broad philosophic interpretations of phenomena – in his case utilitarianism. He picked some holes in it but could not mend them or build a new road. F. W. Bateson, who saw him as someone at war with Blake's Nobodaddy, praised him for refusing to follow the genealogical path in the history of ideas, tracing an idea back through time and never asking whether it made sense or not. Stephen did so ask. So he did; but he did not ask himself all that often why ideas he thought preposterous had lasted so long and what dilemmas in human existence they claimed to explain.

Stephen did not appreciate how immense was the challenge to the British empirical tradition posed by the ideas of the German Renaissance. German philosophers, historians and sociologists asked questions which were fundamental to the interpretation of life and which in England were brushed aside as unanswerable. ('Easy all! Hard word there. Smith, what does it mean? I don't know, says Smith. No more, don't I. Paddle on all.') German thought undermined Stephen's universe in which unchangeable scientific laws existed which could be used to interpret social relationships in the same way as they explained physics and biology; in which mind and matter were one and the same thing and it was only a question of time before all phenomena in the world could be analysed; and in which, above all, human behaviour could be interpreted either in terms of rational self-interest or by determinist principles. The answers which German thinkers gave to the questions they posed were varied and contradictory, and many of them were far from convincing; and that was partly why the confident British empiricists went on their way oblivious of Fichte's sparkling interpretation of nationalism, unaware of Marx, undeterred by the temporary vogue at the end of the nineteenth century for Bradley's and Bosanquet's re-vamping of Hegel. Bertrand Russell was the most original British philosopher since Hume and the greatest British logician since Occam, but when he considered social and moral problems he still wrote as if they could be solved by the simple application of reason without a thought for the structure of society and its institutions even though his prose resounded with imprecations against men for behaving irrationally. He wrote as if Max Weber had never lived. Stephen's reaction to the German Renaissance set an example to his successors. He rightly praised its seriousness and chided those who ignored it. He rightly refused to surrender to it and abandon the well-sited empirical position. But he also refused to examine the defences of that position and mend the gaps in them. Only a few in this century such as Collingwood and Oakeshott took the challenge seriously and tried to construct a new philosophical base independent of German or empirical traditions. Only recently have empirical moralists begun to abandon utilitarianism or to reinterpret it as Richard Wollheim did in his Leslie Stephen Lecture on morality which in its ingenuity and subtlety came to conclusions which Stephen himself would have regarded as immeasurably perverse and shocking.

A rationalist is a bad life if one wants to insure against the short memory of posterity. His ideas soon become so remote that he is remembered only for his defective logic. Muddlers such as the imaginative Coleridge; intricate thinkers such as F. D. Maurice, who defeat objections to their argument by developing a highly personalized dialectic;

prophets, seers, even charlatans, have a longer life than the rationalist whose reputation is soon spotted with the death-tokens of a rare article or reference in a work of learning. Nearly everything Stephen wrote which could claim to be a contribution to thought would have to be reinterpreted today. But a rationalist, such as Stephen, welcomes the extinction of his reputation: to him his future insignificance is a sign that others have built on his work and profited by his blunders. The life, which is unimpressive to posterity, is in his view a life well spent in destroying superstition. There is little doubt that Stephen regarded his assault upon God and the theologians to be his most important contribution to the intellectual life of his times. But like almost all his contemporaries he drew certain conclusions, which he thought were logical, and which we would think were not inferred logically; and he demanded that every true proposition should be shown to be logically necessary, which we do not. When Stephen said that theology was unreal and had no right to exist, he confused an ethical reflection (that theology is a waste of time) with a logical inference (that theology is logically improper). Theology, however, is a mode of reasoning as valid as other modes of reasoning; as a human activity it is not unreal, nor are its rules dissimilar to those which govern other activities such as jurisprudence; and there is no *logical* reason why men should not use this mode of reasoning, if they please.

It is an error to consider rationalism as an icy, unemotional creed, hostile to all that is poetic, imaginative, generous and ardent. What people condemn as mechanical and unsubtle is the deceptive simplicity of a hurdler who has mastered his technique and glides forward scarcely seeming to rise or fall. Success is impossible without hours of training. It is the intense difficulty of excelling and of conquering matter by mind and the challenge to succeed where others have failed, that captivates the young. The discipline is severe, the mood cool, the reward beyond price. The discipline declares war upon rhetoric, phrase-making, hypnotism, and on all those contrivances which spellbinders and mountebanks employ to impose upon a credulous world. The mood is that of a man standing on the beach, the vast uncharted sea of phenomena stretching before him to the horizon, who turns to his fellows and says: *cras ingens iterabimus aequor.* The reward is the possession of a part of truth itself. The rationalist has no hope of conveying an impression of the whole of truth which an artist can sometimes create. Nor would he be satisfied with a subtle impression of experience which, by its very restraint and horror of drawing conclusions, leaves us nevertheless with an uncanny awareness of how events and people are shaped. He claims to discover truths that are independent of personal whim, solid and substantial, capable of acceptance by all dispassionate men of good will. And if this is an illusion – if in fact such truths can never be proved to exist and if all truth is interpretation, all reality appearance – then it is an illusion absolutely necessary for the increase of knowledge and the dissipation of envy, hatred and fear, the enemies of man's happiness and greatness.

The rationalist is often an optimist. The discovery of truths satisfies his self-esteem. He believes they will light the way to a wiser, happier future, and this fires him with the ardour and eloquence that he is popularly supposed to lack. He too has his vision: the vision of the present forging the shape of the future. Yet in reality the rationalist's vision is tragic. For if he is honest he knows that his hopes will be dashed. The crassness of human stupidity, the evils corrupting society, the dreary aimless courses of peoples and governments, exasperate and frustrate him and whisper that tyranny, misery and calamity are the eternal lot of man. And so, unable to remould the scheme of things nearer to his heart's desire, the rationalist works on, now in this vineyard or in that, trying to bring order into one small corner of the chaos to which he inescapably belongs. The belief that order can be created, and the realization that his own efforts will change little in the world, are the two central facts in his experience that dignify and ennoble him.

Leslie Stephen held to this faith and was proud to acknowledge his debt to the past. He reminded his contemporaries that not they, but their eighteenth-century forebears, had mapped the paths to truth. 'I would never abuse', he wrote, 'the century which loved common sense and freedom of speech, and hated humbug and mystery; the century in which first sprang to life most of the social and intellectual movements which are still the best hope of our own; in which science and history and invention first took their modern shape; the century of David Hume, and Adam Smith, and Gibbon, and Burke, and Johnson, and Fielding, and many old friends to whom I aver incalculable gratitude.' This historical sense of belonging to a tradition of thought, in which each man had contributed something, but had also erred, and in which philosophical speculation was kept close to earth by common sense and a generous morality, saved Stephen from the vices of ratiocination. He was a rationalist but never a progressive. The progressive shovels all human experience into the machine of the mind and processes it with a scientific method. He has invested in reading and wants a quick return from his money. Hence he searches about for a few fashionable theories which will explain facets of life; without theories he would be unable to progress. Stephen was sceptical of theories but believed in methods which put the individual in the right relation to the facts. He thought that books widened the mind but that quality of mind depended on character and moral education; and progress for him was an incalculable and slow-motioned operation.

He did not destroy theology and he was, of course, only one of a multitude of influences which were disposing people to change their habits of mind towards the Christianity which the churches then taught. But on one issue he made his mark. Stephen was determined to separate ethics from religion. If you have to argue that you prefer one course of action to another because it is in accordance with God's will, then you accept Newman's contention that logic becomes a matter of feeling, not of proof. Dogmatic or closed systems of thought lead men to make wrong moral decisions. They may then justify persecution or poverty because to do so follows some dogma or arbitrary rule, and justify evil on grounds which purport to be moral but are in fact religious. Stephen justified the divorce between faith and reason.

Nevertheless, the positive contributions men make are often less important than the intangible impression which they leave behind them. Material results are only one criterion of good, and if it is asked what image Stephen left behind for future generations to admire and follow, perhaps the best epitaph was written by Lowes Dickinson.

It does not become a Cambridge man to claim too much for his university, nor am I much tempted to do so. But there is, I think, a certain type, rare, like all good things, which seems to be associated in some peculiar way with my alma mater. I am thinking of men like Leslie Stephen . . . like Henry Sidgwick, like Maitland, like one [Frank Ramsey] who died but the other day with all his promise unfulfilled. It is a type unworldly without being saintly, unambitious without being inactive, warm-hearted without being sentimental. Through good report and ill such men work on following the light of truth as they see it; able to be sceptical without being paralysed; content to know what is knowable and to reserve judgement on what is not. The world could never be driven by such men, for the springs of action lie deep in ignorance and madness. But it is they who are the beacon in the tempest, and they are more, not less, needed now than ever before. May their succession never fail!

NOTES AND REFERENCES

I have included in these notes supplementary information for which there was no space available in the text. For convenience I have abbreviated the titles of certain of Leslie Stephen's works and F. W. Maitland's biography, as follows:

AA	An Agnostic's Apology and Other Essays, 1893
DNB	Dictionary of National Biography
EFP	Essays on Free Thinking and Plain Speaking, 1873
Eng. Thought 18th Cent.	The History of English Thought in the Eighteenth Century, 2 vols, 1902 (First Edition 1876)
Eng. Util.	The English Utilitarians, 3 vols, 1900
HL	Hours in a Library, 3 vols, 1909
Life	F. W. Maitland, The Life and Letters of Leslie Stephen, 1906
Life of Sir JFS	The Life of Sir James Fitzjames Stephen, 1895
Lit. and Soc. 18th Cent.	English Literature and Society in the Eighteenth Century, 1904
MB	Sir Leslie Stephen's Mausoleum Book, ed. Alan Bell, 1977
SB	Studies of a Biographer, 2 vols, 1898; 2 vols, 1902
Sci. Eth.	The Science of Ethics, 1882
SEI	Some Early Impressions, 1924
Sketches	Sketches from Cambridge by a Don, 1865
SRD	Social Rights and Duties, 2 vols, 1896

Other works of all authors are given in full with dates of editions; unless otherwise stated, editions quoted are printed in the United Kingdom.

The main collections where Stephen material is to be found are: in England, at the Cambridge University Library; in the United States, at the Houghton Library, Harvard University, at Duke University Library, and at the Berg Collection, New York Public Library. These I have abbreviated in the notes to Camb, Harvard, Duke, Berg.

The number in the left-hand margin refers to the page in the text.

PREFACE

p. xi 'for another': H. A. L. Fisher, F. W. Maitland (1910), p. 13.
'environment': Life, p. 6.

CHAPTER ONE

THE EARLY YEARS

p. 2 **'amazement'**: Quoted in the typescript of George Smith's unpublished autobiography now in the National Library of Scotland. I am indebted to Alan Bell for this reference.

'if possible': *Life*, pp. 144–5.

p. 3 **'serviceable'**: Anthony Trollope, *The Duke's Children* (1880), Ch. VIII.

of intellect: My original article is to be found in *Studies in Social History*, ed. J. H. Plumb (1955), 'The Intellectual Aristocracy', pp. 243–87. See also Paul Bloomfield, *Uncommon People* (1955); Francis Galton and Edgar Schuster, *Noteworthy Families* (1906).

p. 4 **'even the Roman Catholic'**: J. Stephen, *Essays in Ecclesiastical Biography* (1849), II, p. 313. This is still the best account of the Clapham Sect. J. Telford, *A Sect that Moved the World* (1906) is not helpful. See also F. von Hayek's introduction to Henry Thornton, *An Enquiry into the Nature and Effects of the Paper Credit of Great Britain*, 1802 (1939 ed). Cf *infra*, pp. 376–9.

'level of his speech': Thornton, op. cit., p. 293.

p. 5 **'favoured class'**: J. K. Stephen, *The Living Languages: A Defence of the Compulsory Study of Greek at Cambridge* (1891), p. 47. I am indebted to Jane Marcus for this reference. Jane Marcus, 'Liberty, Sorority, Misogyny', in *The Representation of Women in Fiction*, ed. Carolyn Heilbrun and Margaret Higonnet, Selected Papers from the English Institute, 7, (Baltimore 1983). The full passage reads: 'We are dealing with an *intellectual aristocracy*. Either as a reward for the industry, rapacity or good luck of an ancestor, immediate or remote, or as a reward for their own sterling and unaided qualities, the young men who present themselves at Cambridge to take the first step toward a degree, have obtained entrance into a favoured class: their degree will be a certificate that they have availed themselves of admission to that class . . . and it is for those on whom these benefits have been conferred to show in after life that they are, what they ought to be, the intellectual flower of the nation. If they are not, it is their own fault.'

p. 6 **west-country families**: I am indebted to the researches of Gary Boyd Roberts whose paper, 'One Further Examination into the Intellectual Aristocracy of Great Britain', made me modify my original article. The Babingtons clearly led a different life from that of the Macaulays. But the fact that they were descended from a Duchess of Norfolk who was a great-great-granddaughter of Edward I is not strictly relevant. Many middle-class families can find an ancestor among the medieval nobility. That in itself never guaranteed that the aristocracy would have regarded them as gentlefolk. Those who lived in cities could hardly aspire to be regarded as gentry. Penniless children of the gentry slip into the middle classes, daughters with handsome dowries derived from trade marry into the peerage. Evelyn Waugh had the better of his exchange with Nancy Mitford when he observed that good manners is

the word by which the English describe the social behaviour of those
who are socially above them and which they copy to distinguish
themselves from those below them. For an authoritative discussion of
the subject see Shirley Robin Letwin, *The Gentleman in Trollope*
(1982).

p. 6   **status group:** I originally followed T. H. Marshall's definition of class as
the key to conduct because it defines the way men and women are
treated by their contemporaries, and how reciprocally they treat others.
Sociological Review, XXVI, January 1934, p. 60. Cf. Marshall in *Class
Conflict and Social Stratification* (1938), pp. 97 seq., where he defines
class as a force 'that unites into groups people who differ from one
another, by overriding the differences between them . . . and teaches
the members of a society to notice some differences and to ignore
others when arranging persons in order of social merit'. I have argued
in the past that if Warner and Lunt, *Yankee City Series, Vol. II: The
Status System of a Modern Community* (Yale 1942), proves anything,
it is that analyses of class made in terms of behaviour are too
complicated to apply formally to modern highly civilized societies and
that for the present 'class' can be used only to convey an impression of
a solidity more pronounced than that defined by the term 'group'.
     Nevertheless, the multiplicity of definitions of class in recent years
has persuaded me that W. G. Runciman's plea that Weber's termi-
nology is the most capacious and accurate and should be accepted. See
W. G. Runciman, *Social Science and Political Theory* (1969), pp. 135–
43, 193–5. According to this definition the intellectual aristocracy
belong to the middle class because they share middle-class processes of
production, distribution and exchange. But they are a separate status
group because their style of life and status in society is distinct and
marked off from other groups.

p. 7   **gentlemanly behaviour:** Ibid., pp. 62–73.
     in the world: The genealogy of the Stephens is set out in the *Memoirs of
James Stephen*, ed. M. M. Bevington (1954) and in Quentin Bell,
Virginia Woolf (1972), I. See also *Proc. Medico-Legal Society of
Victoria* (1953–4), 'Lines of Communication' by C. H. Fitts.
     memoirs: The story of Jem Stephen's early years is taken from Bevington,
op. cit.

p. 8   **'This is an error':** *Life of Sir JFS*, p. 12. Bevington points out that both
in the biography of his father and in the *DNB* Leslie Stephen omitted
the date of William Stephen's birth and leaves the reader to infer that
he was the legitimate son of James and Anna Stephen. No doubt Leslie
thought that discretion required concealment; but it is also true that an
adequate explanation would require more space than was warranted.
Bevington concludes: 'the skill with which the omission is made is a
thing to be admired', Bevington, op. cit., pp. 366 ff.
     God's favour: Bevington, op. cit., p. 300.
     'my heart has bled!': Ibid., pp. 110, 164.
     shining face: Ibid., p. 154.

p. 9   **'zealous abolitionist':** Ibid., p. 17.
p. 10   **'scientific knowledge':** *Life of Sir JFS*, pp. 31–2.
     fn. Venns: For an account of the Venn family see John Venn, *Annals of a
Clerical Family* (1904).

p. 11   'devilishly like it': *Life of Sir JFS*, p. 49. Cf. D. M. Young, *The Colonial Office in the Early Nineteenth Century* (1961).

p. 12   'sentimentalist and moralist': *Life of Sir JFS*, p. 33.
'was the cause': Reginald G. Wilberforce, *The Life of Samuel Wilberforce* (1881), II, p. 412.
'not a simple man': *Life of Sir JFS*, p. 43.

p. 13   'not been formed': *Ideas and Beliefs of the Victorians*, ed. Harman Grisewood (1949).

p. 14   'domestic bonds': Caroline Emilia Stephen, *Sir James Stephen* (1906), p. 144, quoted by Jane Marcus, op. cit.
'the human race': C. E. Stephen, op. cit., pp. 5, 45.
'my child': Ibid., p. 112.
Downing Street: Ibid., p. 154.
'desires to be praised': Maitland Add. MS, Camb.
"short-fingered man": *Journal of Modern History* XXXI, Sept. 1959, 'The Retirement of a Titan: James Stephen 1847–50', by John M. Ward, p. 190.
'generation': C. E. Stephen, op. cit., p. 68.

p. 15   castle-building: Ibid., p. 10.
'awfully' . . . 'knell': Ibid., pp. 61–3.
'affection': Maitland Add. MS, Camb.

p. 16   'mind': Maitland, Add. MS, Camb.

p. 17   'married you': *Life of Sir JFS*, p. 63.
'smoked again': Ibid., p. 61.

p. 18   'taken out of him': *Life*, p. 29.
fn. 'active and simple': C. E. Stephen, *The First Sir James Stephen* (1906), p. 76.
home town: A. D. Coleridge, *Eton in the Forties* (1896), p. 23.

p. 19   phenomenal: *Life of Sir JFS*, p. 79.
'perfect devil': Coleridge, op. cit., p. 42.

p. 20   philology: The real instigator of academic and disciplinary reform in the English public schools was Samuel Butler (grandfather of the author), Headmaster of Shrewsbury from 1798 to 1836; under his teaching the Shrewsbury boys won a far higher number of prizes and honours at Cambridge in proportion to their numbers than the alumni of any other school. Hawtrey continually sought Butler's advice for reforms at Eton, many of which the Provost opposed – such as the system of half-yearly examinations whereby boys were deemed fit to move up the school. Kennedy carried on Butler's tradition at Shrewsbury and despite his choleric temperament achieved a fabulous list of classical successes among his pupils; his celebrated Latin Grammar was imposed on all public schools by the Public Schools Commission. It was he who argued before the Commissioners that a public school's duty was to prepare boys for the university, not to serve as a local school for the townspeople. See J. B. Oldham, *Headmasters of Shrewsbury School, 1552–1908* (1937).
'expressionless countenances': C. A. Bristed, *Five Years in an English University* (3rd ed, 1873), p. 337.
broaden their knowledge: For an account of Hawtrey's reforms see H. C. Maxwell-Lyte, *History of Eton College* (1889), pp. 401–9, 473.
fn. 'laugh about?': Coleridge, op. cit., pp. 293–4.

'uneasiness on the subject': *Edinburgh Review* LXXXI, Jan. 1845, p. 228.

'in the world': *Life of Sir JFS*, p. 81.

p. 21 boy's taste: Thomas Balston, *Dr Balston at Eton* (1952), p. 57.

by the Public School Commissioners: Maxwell-Lyte, op. cit., p. 479.

'law of Nature': *Life of Sir JFS*, pp. 79–80.

'impressive phenomenon': *Cornhill Magazine* XXVII, March 1873, p. 290, 'Thoughts of an Outsider: The Public Schools'. Cf. *Fraser's Magazine* IX, March 1874, p. 326, 'University Endowments' (unsigned), [by L. Stephen]. 'People educated at our old public schools sometimes seem to fancy that boys have been created in order to add to the glories of Eton and Winchester, instead of admitting the opposite point of view.'

p. 22 a poem in *Punch*: Oldham, op. cit., p. 76.

bare bottom exposed: *SB* III, p. 258. *Life*, pp. 34–5.

on their sons by prefects: Charles Oman, *Memories of Victorian Oxford* (1941), pp. 35–8. James Sabben-Clare, *Winchester College* (1981), pp. 44–5.

'their memory': This is quoted from a second article on the public schools which Stephen did not publish. Stephen rarely spoke of Eton but he allowed his son Thoby to sit the examination for entry to College. Only because he came too low down on the list for him to be certain of a vacancy did he go to Clifton. (Stephen probably judged that he could not afford to send him as an Oppidan.)

'end to them': *Cornhill* XLV, 1882, p. 236, 'Senior Wranglers' [by LS].

p. 23 'married state': *Life of Sir JFS*, p. 81.

'Christian simplicity': Ibid., p. 81.

'in the face of all spectators': 'The Public Schools', *Cornhill*, op. cit., p. 285. Cf. *SB* II, pp. 127–8.

'shiver when I think of it': Letter from LS to Julia Stephen, 25 March 1887, Berg.

p. 24 fn. poll-examination: D. A. Winstanley, *Early Victorian Cambridge* (1940), pp. 216–18.

intellectual vigour: 'The Public Schools', *Cornhhill*, op. cit., p. 235.

p. 25 forty-four and a half hours work in all: W. W. Rouse Ball, *Cambridge Papers* (1918), 'The History of the Mathematical Tripos', p. 300. Cf. Winstanley, op. cit., p. 160.

different questions: Rouse Ball, op. cit., pp. 301–2.

p. 26 'two hours and a half': Bristed, op. cit., p. 126. C. A. Bristed was an American who entered Trinity College in 1840, became a scholar and, after missing two years from ill-health which weakened his chances of obtaining a good degree, was placed second in the second class of the Classical Tripos in 1845. His book on Cambridge, written for the American public, is by far the best near-contemporary account of Stephen's Cambridge, being full of fascinating detail and accurate in its account of the curricula and regulations of the university. Bristed greatly admired the accuracy of Trinity classical scholarship though he thought that Cambridge, in other ways intellectually superior to Harvard, lagged behind an American university in oratory and in morals. His book is superior to W. Everett's *On the Cam* (1866), a series of lectures delivered in Boston in more elaborate and rhetorical form and far less informative.

five thousand pounds in all: *Sketches*, p. 38.

p. 27   top of the examination: Rouse Ball, op. cit., pp. 308–9.

fn. 'this year': Winstanley, op. cit., p. 411.

'leaving it': *Sketches*, p. 107. Cf. *SEI*, pp. 28–30.

honeymoon: J. E. B. Mayor, *Isaac Todhunter, In Memoriam* (1884), p. 25.

p. 28   fn. with Stephen's help: D. A. Winstanley, *Unreformed Cambridge* (1935), p. 229. H. Gunning, *Reminiscences* (1854), II, p. 28. *Cambridge University Commission and Report* (1852), pp. 180–82. H. E. Malden, *History of Trinity Hall* (1902), p. 241. Stephen held a bye-fellowship, a type of fellowship which originated in the difficulty experienced in estimating, after any considerable accession of wealth, what was the proper sum the College should pay in respect of the newly-founded fellowship and by how much the stipend of the old fellowships should be increased. They were used as stepping-stones by young men to the dignity of a full fellowship. (See *Commission*, op. cit., pp. 187–8.)

'without boldly taking his part': *Life*, p. 48.

p. 29   'another reason': Letter from Henry Jackson to F. W. Maitland, 30 May, 1905. Maitland MS Camb. Not Noel, elected on 1857.

flesh and blood: G. M. Trevelyan, in an introduction to the 1932 edition of *Sketches*, notes that Stephen never mentions the vigorous intellectual life of Trinity and St John's; but it is not true to suggest, as Winstanley does, that he knew only small-College life. Stephen had friends in both these great colleges and the entrée to the best intellectual sets through his brother's and his cousins' friends. His own friends in undergraduate days were the two Diceys, Frank Coleman (a cousin of Herbert Duckworth), F. V. Hawkins, Howard Elphinstone and W. F. Robinson, none of whom he saw much of later in life. Cf. *Life*, p. 74.

'incapable body': Letter to C. E. Norton, 8 Oct. 1898, Harvard.

'Well struck Parson': *Life of Sir JFS*, p. 34.

p. 30   athletics match: See *Empire Review* II, 1902, p. 656, for an account by P. M. Thornton of Stephen's part in starting the University sports.

'clergymen from Cambridge': *Life*, p. 63.

quality of pleasure: An interesting article by P. E. Vernon on the psychology of rowing is to be found in *The British Journal of Psychology* XVIII, Jan. 1928, pp. 317–31.

p. 31   rowing coaches: Sir Charles Dilke, who rowed in the 1864 Head of the River crew, greatly admired Stephen as a coach. So did Lord Justice Romer.

'to row': *British Sports and Pastimes*, ed. A. Trollope (1868), 'Rowing' by Leslie Stephen, p. 244.

'cohesive': Ibid., p. 249.

'my comrades': Odyssey, Bk XI, pp. 77–8.

p. 32   'the mark': *Life*, p. 72.

'he would have done so': *Life*, p. 60.

p. 33   munching: G. F. Browne, *The Recollections of a Bishop* (1915), p. 102.

out of mischief: *Fraser's Magazine* II, Dec. 1870, 'Athletic Sports and University Studies', by L. Stephen, p. 696. Cf. Winstanley, *Early Victorian Cambridge*, pp. 416, 421; and *Life*, p. 58. A novel written on this very theme is T. Hughes, *Tom Brown at Oxford* (1861).

Cf. *Journal of the History of Ideas* XIII, 1952, 'Victorian Anti-Intellectualism' by Walter Houghton.

'set up': 'Athletic Sports . . .', op. cit., p. 692.

pretty thickly: Bruce Haley, *The Healthy Body and Victorian Culture* (1978), p. 225.

p. 34 'very dissolute in 1860': Letter from Henry Jackson to F. W. Maitland, 11 Jan. 1905, Maitland Add. MS. Camb.

'common pump': D. A. Winstanley, *Later Victorian Cambridge* (1947), p. 151. Stephen's comment was that six weeks after a poll-man had gone down he would be unable to distinguish between a pump and a siphon. Cf. L. Stephen, *The Poll Degree from a Third Point of View* (1863), p. 2.

'muscular Christianity': *Life*, p. 77.

trapeze of the intellect: Cf. L. Stephen, *Life of Henry Fawcett* (1885), pp. 90–93.

p. 35 'honour triposes': *Flysheet*, 28 May 1864, *University Papers*, H.C.1, quoted by Winstanley, Later Victorian Cambridge, pp. 153–4. Cf. *The Poll Degree . . .*, p. 14.

young men: *Fraser's*, 'Athletic Sports . . .', op. cit., pp. 691–704.

'intellectual cultivation above everything': Ibid., p. 703.

p. 36 Church and State: Cf. Stephen's remark that Cambridge should not be turned into an École Normale, because it existed to raise the general tone of instruction among the highly-educated classes and to keep the learned professions in touch with the university, and to 'hold out, even to the aristocracy, a hope of improving their minds amongst us' (*The Poll Degree . . .*, pp. 8–9).

cactus?: The duty of a university, thought Stephen, was not to make men work but to put them in the way of, and to encourage, study (ibid., p. 4). The Cambridge system meant a constant disposition to esteem all kinds of knowledge in proportion to their capacity for testing men's abilities. *Fraser's Magazine* LXXVII, Feb, 1868, p. 149, 'University Organization', by a Don (L. Stephen). Stephen had no faith in lectures as a method of instruction. He noted sardonically when delivering the first course of Clark lectures that his audience consisted largely of young ladies from Newnham and Girton colleges who in his opinion could have acquired all that he had to say from two or three books in half the time. Cf. Virginia Woolf's inherited contempt for lectures (*The Death of the Moth* (1942), p. 146).

p. 37 'independent course of study': 'University Organization', op. cit., pp. 142–3.

'improve their minds': Ibid., p. 137.

attached to them: 'Cambridge men have been accustomed so long to associate improvement in education with increased competition in examinations' (ibid., p. 153). Stephen also attacked the system of prizes and sinecure posts: 'the Head of a College would not be missed if he sank into the earth for fifty weeks a year' (ibid., pp. 143–4).

notoriously narrow minded: D. A. Winstanley took the occasion offered by a reprint of *Sketches from Cambridge* (1932 edn) to trounce Stephen for the unfairness of his judgements on his university (see *Cambridge Review* 54, 17 Feb. 1933, p. 259). He complains that Stephen makes no mention of the reform movement which had already

8

LESLIE STEPHEN

swept away many abuses; that he jeers at Fellows and Tutors for
their failure to research; that, as G. M. Trevelyan pointed out (see
supra) he is disdainfully silent about the brilliant literary and classical
sets; and that he writes in spite against the place which he had just
quitted. There are two points to be made here. The first is on the facts.
Anyone who reads Winstanley's researches on nineteenth-century
Cambridge will remark how slow and confused was the reform
movement and how the Colleges continually hampered it. Winstanley
ignores Stephen's articles in *Fraser's* and does no justice to his good
sense. A man like Stephen who was ahead of his time should not be
attacked for his foresight. It is also true that the standard of Cambridge
scholarship *in Stephen's time* was low by comparison with that of the
greatest European universities. Stephen did not ignore the Apostles or
other sets but wrote about them at length in his biographies of
Fitzjames Stephen and Henry Fawcett and in *Some Early Impressions*
which gives a more general picture of his undergraduate days and
dilates at length upon the literary taste of Cambridge (pp. 33–44). This
leads one to the second point, which is more serious, for it raises the
question of whether scholars can maintain a sense of proportion.
Stephen called his book *Sketches*. It was not intended to be an accurate
history of all aspects of university life. It was written after a well-
known pattern of which the next best known example is *Sketches of
Cantabs*, by John Smith of Smith Hall, Gent. (1849) (almost certainly
by John Delaware Lewis, see *DNB* and *Dictionary of Anonymous and
Pseudonymous Literature* by Halkett and Laing). These books were
intended to give amusing portraits of dons and undergraduates, and
they succeeded. You may dislike their jocular tone or disapprove of
their values, but you cannot sensibly attack their accuracy. Why should
they be measured by a standard suitable for Ph.D theses? Why break a
butterfly on the wheel of scholarship?
'in the eighties': *Life*, p. 76. See also, in addition to the two articles cited
above, *Fraser's Magazine* IV, Sept. 1871, p. 269, 'The Future of
University Reform', and IX, March 1874, p. 323, 'University
Endowments', both by Stephen.

p. 38   an Englishman: H. E. Roscoe, *Life and Experiences* (1906), pp. 63–4.
'humble exterior': *Life*, pp. 70–71. Cf. J. A. Mangan, *Athleticism in the
Victorian and Edwardian Public School* (1981), p. 110.
'battle in the world': *Sketches*, p. 81.
'that's all I want': T. Hughes, *Tom Brown's Schooldays*, (1857), Ch. IV.

p. 39   'bachelor's degree': *SEI*, p. 34.
'aspirations of mankind': *HL* III, p. 321. See *Julian Bell, Essays, Poems
and Letters*, ed. by Quentin Bell (1938). Happily all Stephens are
always being filled with the urge to write about themselves and their
family, with the result that from the Master in Chancery's memoir to
the present day we have one hundred and fifty years of published
history of this family. Cf. Peter Stansky and William Abrahams *Journey
to the Frontier* (1966). Stephen was not hostile to originality in the
young, which he defined as an irresistible desire for display; he admired
the man who was not afraid to make a fool of himself and respected
those who were not afraid to be laughed at. *Sketches*, pp. 65–7.

Philosophic Radicals: *Life of Henry Fawcett*, pp. 23–5.

'rest of the species': Ibid., p. 95. Cf. *Life*, p. 170.

p. 40   of the visit: *Life of Henry Fawcett*, p. 85.

fn.: 'Clearly not responsible': T. Thornley, *Cambridge Memories* (1936), pp. 40–41. Cf. F. A. Keynes, *Gathering up the Threads* (1950), p. 53. Stephen in one of his more charitable moments called Mrs Geldart a vulgar old washerwoman and the greatest fool in the world.

'six hours a day': Letter to Henry Jackson from F. W. Maitland, 4 Sept. 1905, Maitland Add. MS, Camb.

'cleared the air': Letter to F. W. Maitland from Henry Jackson, 15 March 1904, Maitland Add. MS, Camb.

p. 41   'I am a parson': Letter from C. B. Clarke to F. W. Maitland, Maitland Add. MS, Camb.

he distrusted him: Letter to Henry Jackson from F. W. Maitland, 27 Jan. 1905, Maitland Add. MS, Camb.

p. 42   'he would have been burnt': M. Holroyd, *Memorials of the Life of G. E. Corrie, D. D.* (1890), p. 277.

fn. 'not he': G. F. Browne, *St Catharine's College* (Univ. of Cambridge College Histories), (1902), p. 223.

p. 43   'for granted': *Life*, pp. 150–51.

'apologetics': Letter from Edward Dicey to F. W. Maitland, 1 Sept. 1904. Maitland Add. MS, Camb.

p. 44   'all right': Letter from Caroline Stephen (Milly) to F. W. Maitland, 8 Jan. 1905. Maitland Add. MS, Camb.

'supporting me': *MB*, p. 3. *Life*, p. 132.

'thousand hours': *Sketches*, p. 22. *SEI*, p. 45.

exceptional: *SEI*, p. 70.

'nobody will': *Life*, p. 159. The book is identified by Maitland as C. W. King, *The Gnostics and Their Remains* (1864).

p. 45   *his* fellowship: Letter to C. E. Norton, 3 March 1874, Harvard.

a mockery: J. H. Newman, *Apologia pro Vita Sua* (1864), p. 120.

rejected: In an article on Lytton Strachey in *Horizon* XV, Feb. 1947, p. 92, John Russell states that the Agnostics bequeathed to Bloomsbury a 'legacy of honest and tormented doubt'. This is a false description of the state of mind of Stephen, Huxley, Spencer, Morley and Meredith or of Sidgwick's theism. The agonized scepticism of Clough and of the young J. A. Froude can be found again in G. J. Romanes who, before his death, was again received into the Church – or, of course, in Robert Elsmere. But the new fashion in unbelief was not one of doubt or agony.

toy: *Life*, p. 24.

'sacred truth': *MB*, p. 8.

suicide: Virginia Woolf, British Library Add. MSS 61973. He spoke of suicide later to his wife. Letter from LS to Julia Stephen, 6–15 June 1890 and 29 Jan. 1893, Berg.

'night': Letter from Sir Robert Romer to F. W. Maitland, 29 Nov. 1904. Maitland Add. MS, Camb.

p. 46   family: Ibid.

'come out': Letter from Caroline Stephen to F. W. Maitland, 8 Jan. 1905, MS. cit.

p. 47   'religious belief': Winstanley, *Later Victorian Cambridge*, p. 40.

CHAPTER TWO
MAKING A REPUTATION

p. 48   'any visible sensation': *Life*, pp. 158–9.
         pleasant a place for a bachelor: Cf. *HL* III, pp. 106–8.
p. 49   eighteenth century thought: *Twentieth Century*, Dec. 1952, pp. 513–25,
         Gertrude Himmelfarb, 'Mr Stephen and Mr Ramsay: the Victorian as
         intellectual', twits Stephen for being an English gentleman and hence
         no true intellectual. 'His calling came too easily to him. For if to be an
         intellectual is as easy as breathing, it can be no more remarkable than
         breathing.' To the English politics and religion were a game;
         Gladstone and Newman took each seriously and hence were regarded
         as outsiders. 'The good agnostic was a good sportsman', and hence in
         A Bad Five Minutes in the Alps the philosopher yields to the sportman.
         Stephen like other Victorian scholars was an amateur – a professional
         writer, yes, but not a New York intellectual.
p. 50   'misanthrope': LS to Julia Stephen, 7 March 1888. See John Bicknell, 'Mr
         Ramsay was Young Once', Comn. to *MLA*, 29 Dec. 1982.
         'graveyard': 'Senior Wranglers' [by LS], *Cornhill* XLV, 1882, p. 227.
         'Americans': LS to C. E. Norton, 6 June 1878, Harvard.
         thought this odd: Katherine C. Hill, 'Virginia Woolf and Leslie Stephen.
         A Study in Mentoring and Literary Criticism', Columbia University
         PhD thesis, 1979, p. 25.
p. 51   the faithful: *Life of Sir JFS*, p. 129.
         fn. **Mr Cunningham:** G. W. E. Russell, *A Short History of the Evangelical
         Movement* (1915), p. 117.
         Saturday Review: M. M. Bevington, *The Saturday Review, 1858–68*
         (New York 1941), p. 381, lists Leslie Stephen's articles written for the
         paper; four were identified by a marked file copy which had belonged
         to Fitzjames; two by Leslie himself; and the remainder by Bevington.
         See *Review of English Studies* III, 1952, pp. 244–62, 'Weekly
         Reviewing in the Eighteen-Sixties' by J. D. Jump.
         Cornhill: Stephen described the *Cornhill* at this time as 'an unprecedented
         shillingsworth – limited to the inoffensive'. J. W. Robertson Scott, *The
         Story of the Pall Mall Gazette* (1950), p. 69.
         'pressure': *MB*, p. 87.
p. 52   'root and branch men': F. W. Hirst, *Early Life and Letters of John
         Morley* (1927), I, p. 45. Cf. J. Morley, *Recollections* I (1917), p. 117.
         Froude: Maitland identifies on p. 171 fn. of the *Life* all Stephen's articles
         in *Fraser's* including those not republished, but he decides not to make
         conjectures about some articles written during 1866–9 on the grounds
         that other men were writing in much the same free-thinking style, and
         because Stephen had decided not to reprint his earlier work. John W.
         Bicknell identifies the review of W. E. H. Lecky's *History of European
         Morals* (LXXX, Sept. 1869, pp. 273–84) as being by Stephen.
         '(for the North)': *The History of the Times* (1939), II, p. 365.
p. 53   'to England': Ibid., p. 376.

'makes four': *Life*, p. 113.
'his pictures': Ibid., p. 120.
indigenous: Cf. *Essays on Reform* (1867), 'On the Choice of
  Representatives by Popular Constituencies', by LS, pp. 86–123.
p. 54 'public crime': *Life*, p. 127.
'due authority': *The Times on the American War*, by LS (1865), pp. 7–8.
  Stephen's closely reasoned analysis of *The Times*'s policy during the
  war in just over a hundred pages is a brilliant forensic argument. He
  accused the paper justly of crass ignorance, vacillation and oscillation
  between different policies (p. 33), apologizing for slavery and
  dissimulating on the issue of emancipation (p. 41), and he had great
  fun at the expense of its military correspondent who, even when
  Sherman reached the coast, was still prophesying ruin for the North
  (pp. 81–9).
Wolstenholme: Virginia Woolf drew the character of Mr Carmichael in
  To the Lighthouse from Wolstenholme. In old age he became
  something of a bore and Stephen irritated his family by asking the
  lonely old bachelor to stay in Cornwall with them for the holidays and
  then, finding his company tedious, leaving wife and daughters to
  entertain him. Wolstenholme was present on the summer holiday in
  Cornwall (see *To the Lighthouse*, Part III), of which Stephen wrote to
  C. E. Norton, 21 Sept. 1899, 'I have lost the power of holiday making'.
  Harvard.
p. 55 'vulgar we are': *New Letters of J. R. Lowell* (1932) ed. M. A. De Wolfe
  Howe and C. E. Norton. I, p. 403.
'Mr Howells': Van Wyck Brooks, *The Flowering of New England* (1936),
  p. 315, fn.
'you are making: *Letters of J. R. Lowell* (1894), II, P. 503.
p. 56 godfather . . . to Virginia: *New Letters of J. R. Lowell* p. 292; cf. also
  p. 268.
'the most lovable of men': *Life*, p. 129.
'needless outrage': Letter from L. Stephen to C. E. Norton, dated 15 June
  1903, Harvard. In a letter of 3 April 1883, to Norton, he bemoans the
  'poor old man' whose 'noble qualities' are forgotten.
'caught in the act': Van Wyck Brooks, op. cit., p. 518, fn.
phraseology is identical: Compare *Life*, p. 181, with *New Letters . . .*,
  p. 317.
'go along with him altogether': *Letters of J. R. Lowell*, II, p. 186; cf. also
  p. 166, 'I confess to a strong lurch towards Calvinism . . . that
  strengthens as I grow older'.
'think of it': Ibid., I, p. 420.
immigrants: Ibid., p. 496.
p. 57 'the cost of fools': Ibid., p. 179.
'who ever was?': Ibid., p. 178; see also p. 274.
'will hurt me somehow': Ibid., pp. 258–9. Cf. V. L. Parrington, *The
  Romantic Revolution in America, 1800–1860* (New York 1927),
  p. 461.
'shutting of the eyes': *Letters of J. R. Lowell*, II, p. 141.
old ship of Faith: Ibid., p. 143. Cf. H. E. Scudder, *J. R. Lowell* (1901), II,
  p. 176. Cf. Lowell's comment on Stephen's essay 'Are We Christians?'
  'I think I should say that you lump *shams* and *conventions* too solidly

together in a common condemnation. All conventions are not shams
by a good deal, and we shall soon be Papuans without them.' *Letters*
op. cit., II, p. 109.
'literature as a holiday': Van Wyck Brooks, op. cit., p. 523. This
assessment of Lowell's writing (pp. 311–22, 514–15) is more
reasonable than V. L. Parrington's unnecessarily harsh judgement (op.
cit., pp. 460–72). Parrington's partiality for hundred per cent American
literature of the Mark Twain variety leads him to depreciate the value
of the aristocratic New England tradition.
Oxford and Cambridge: see Christopher Harvie, *The Lights of
Liberalism* (1976), p. 11.

p. 58   'European intelligence': *Essays on Reform*, op. cit., p. 87.
connected with the aristocracy: *Macmillan's Magazine* XV, April 1867,
p. 531.
remotely in sight: *Fortnightly Review* 24, 1875, 'The Value of Political
Machinery' by LS, pp. 836–52.
'clever arithmetical dodges': *Macmillan's*, op. cit., pp. 529–36.
'spasmodic change': *Fortnightly Review*, op. cit., p. 838.

p. 59   'virtue of self-respect': Ibid., p. 839.
'were necessary': *Fortnightly Review* 23, 1875, 'Order and Progress' by
LS, p. 834.
'great evils of the time': *Essays on Reform*, op. cit., p. 125.
sustained it: Cf. Harvie, op. cit., p. 143.
'scientific truth': *Fortnightly Review*, 14 Sept. 1873, p. 314. Quoted by
John Bicknell in 'Mr Ramsay Was Young Once', Comn. to *MLA*, 29,
Dec. 1982.

p. 60   'narrowing': *Fraser's*, 9 June 1874, p. 688.
become friends: *Life*, p. 246.
condemned as cowardly: In a letter to C. E. Norton, Stephen scoffs at
Sir G. O. Trevelyan for carrying on his uncle's tradition of Whig
history whereby all Americans in the eighteenth century are
God-fearing angels and the only good Englishmen were Burke and Fox.
See also *SB* I, pp. 174–8, for Stephen's estimate of politics.
'outrageous cynicism': *SB* III, p. 163.
'particular case': *Nineteenth Century Review* LI, Jan. 1902, 'The Good
Old Cause', by L. Stephen, p. 23. Cf. Virginia Woolf, *Night and Day*
(1938 edn), Ch. VII, p. 100.
'laws governing social development': This insight enlivens the second
chapter (which is on Stephen's thought) of the forthcoming book –
Jeffrey Paul von Arx, *Progress and Pessimism: Religion, Politics and
History in Late Nineteenth-Century Britain*.

p. 61   'old don': *Life*, p. 179.
'pea in a pod': Ibid., p. 194.

p. 62   'getting into': *The Letters and Private Papers of W. M. Thackeray*, ed.
Gordon N. Ray (1946), IV, p. 230.
'beloved in return': Gordon N. Ray, *Thackeray, The Age of Wisdom*
(New York 1958), II, p. 354.
'corkscrew' questions: Letter from Minny Stephen to Fitzjames Stephen,
2 March 1870, Duke. (*MB*, p. 10, has 'corkscrewing questions'.)
fixed: *Life*, p. 181.
'Onslow Gardens': *MB*, p. 11.

'assembled': *Life*, p. 196.

p. 63   'weak mind': Letter from LS to Anny Thackeray, 10 July 1867, Duke.

'had with her': Letter from Minny Stephen to Anny Thackeray, 29 July 1867, Duke.

'window': Letter from Minny Stephen to Blanche Warre-Cornish, 19 July 1867, Duke.

'miserable': Letter from Minny Stephen to Milly Stephen, 24 July 1867, Duke.

'scrumptious': Minny Stephen to Fitzjames Stephen, 10 April 1870. Duke.

'laughter': *Life*, pp. 190–91.

'oh': Ibid., p. 189.

'benevolent people': Letter from LS to Anny Thackeray.

natural affections: *MB*, p. 17.

p. 64   ear: Letter from Minny Stephen to Fitzjames Stephen, 18 Nov. 1870, Duke.

confidence: See A. Thackeray, *Old Kensington* (1873), for a portrait of Minny Thackeray in the character of Dolly. For a sketch of Lady Ritchie see Virginia Woolf, *The Moment* (1947), pp. 156–8. For an excellent biography see Winifred Guérin, *Anny Thackeray Ritchie* (1981).

applaud: *MB*, p. 13.

at any rate: Ibid., p. 14.

p. 65   'genius': Ibid., pp. 14–15.

'chilling criticism': Ibid., p. 23.

'aggressor': *MB*, p. 23.

mankind: Ibid., p. 23.

dining-room: E. Gosse, *Books on the Table* (1921), pp. 293–8. *Life*, pp. 268–9. Cf. Virginia Woolf, 'Leslie Stephen', *The Captain's Death Bed* (1950), pp. 67–73.

p. 66   papists: *Life*, p. 224.

Cornhill: See *Texas University Studies in English* XXXII (1953), pp. 67–95, 'Leslie Stephen and the *Cornhill Magazine*, 1871–82' by Oscar Maurer. Also Robertson Scott, op. cit., pp. 94–7 *passim*. Since Thackeray's retirement Frederick Greenwood, who was also editor of another of Smith's ventures, the *Pall Mall Gazette*, G. H. Lewes, Dutton Cook, dramatist and novelist, and Smith himself had taken a hand in the editing. Stephen handled contributors better than Thackeray who had been too lenient. Robertson Scott says that Stephen wrote so freely that he would sometimes put other initials than his own to his articles. In fact Stephen signed nothing in the *Cornhill* except a piece on Lowell (XXXI, 1875), initialled F. T., in order to give Lowell the impression that he was widely read. Of his *Cornhill* style, Meredith wrote, 'the only sting in it was an inoffensive humorous irony that now and then stole out for a roll over, like a furry cub, or the occasional ripple on a lake in grey weather'. Under Stephen's editorship, Gosse, Stevenson, Henley, Mrs Lynn Linton, Mrs Oliphant, Hardy, Henry James and Meredith first contributed. See also Wilfrid Meynell (*Academy* LXVI, 27 Feb. 1904, p. 221) for an account of Stephen as an editor.

'their turn': Maurer, op. cit., p. 81.

p. 67   'religion?': *Life*, p. 258.

to fame: Maurer criticizes me (op. cit., p. 68) for saying that the editorship was for Stephen a sideline; and in view of the work which the editorship entailed he is clearly right. But Stephen's main concern was his own writing and reading, and his later acknowledgement that the fall in circulation in part was due to his lack of rapport with the public suggests that it never engaged his mind as fully as editorial policy did other successful editors.

'the publisher': SB, I, p. 35. Quoted by Maurer, op. cit., p. 67.

censorship of the market: Maurer, op. cit., pp. 80–89. See also *Studies in Bibliography* XII (1959), pp. 21–40, ' "My Squeamish Public": some problems of Victorian Magazine Publishers and Editors', by Oscar Maurer.

p. 68   **'tomorrow night':** Letter from LS to Minny, 16 Sept. 1872, Duke.

a child: *Life*, pp. 275–7.

fiction: Maurer, 'Leslie Stephen and the *Cornhill* . . .', p. 89. Oscar Maurer argues with spirit that Stephen was well aware of the absurdities of Victorian prudery and that his own reservations sprang from his justifiable conviction that morality and literature cannot be divorced. I still adhere to my view that both in the argument of the *Science of Ethics* and in his literary criticism – though still more in his letters – Stephen struck an answering chord to Victorian puritanism. Certainly W. E. Norris, *Cornhill* XXVIII, Jan. 1910, 'Leslie Stephen as editor', complains bitterly of Stephen's fear of Mrs Grundy.

p. 69   **'pleasant':** M. Veley, *A Marriage of Shadows* (1888), Introduction by L. Stephen, p. x.

p. 70   **'desired to separate':** Quoted by John Gross, *The Rise and Fall of the English Man of Letters* (1969), p. 17.

'Charles I': *Life*, p. 202.

p. 71   **'my race!':** Ibid., p. 297.

'parsons': Ibid., p. 235.

blood money upon it: Ibid., p. 299.

'years before': Letter from LS to Anny Thackeray, June 1874.

birthday: *MB*, p. 22.

p. 72   **'has gone':** *Life*, p. 256.

amendment: *MB*, p. 432.

p. 73   **'ruin':** The phrase Vanessa Bell remembered. Cf. Quentin Bell's *Virginia Woolf* I, p. 63.

p. 74   **'usefully employed':** Letter from LS to Anny Thackeray, 29 April 1875.

p. 75   **'waste time . . . denunciation':** *MB*, p. 32. Stephen was not alone in his revulsion. Millais exploded with all the indignation of a Victorian paterfamilias, 'Preposterous! It must not be. It shall not be.' Hester Thackeray Fuller and Violet Hammersley, *Thackeray's Daughter* (Dublin 1951), p. 151.

'unsympathetic third person': Letter from LS to Anny Thackeray, 5 May 1877.

'over-demonstrativeness': Letter from LS to Anny Thackeray, 4 April 1877.

p. 76   **'of the chancel':** Fuller and Hammersley, op. cit., p. 152.

'a gorilla': Ibid., p. 159.

'cantankerous outside': Letter from LS to Anny Ritchie, 1 May 1899.

Annunciation: Julia's good looks descended. A BBC television producer, having seen a photograph by Mrs Cameron of Julia at this age, tried to find her counterpart. He engaged a girl who bore a remarkable likeness: to his astonishment – and to hers – he found that he had engaged Julia's great-granddaughter, Virginia Bell.

Pattle sisters: The sisters married, respectively, General Mackenzie, Henry Thoby Prinsep, H. V. Barley, J. W. Dalrymple, Lord Somers, Charles Henry Cameron and Dr Jackson. Dr Jackson was a nonentity; 'somehow', wrote Stephen (MB p. 26), 'he did not seem to count as fathers generally count in their families'; he married Maria Pattle in Calcutta in 1837. The Pattle sisters were granddaughters on their mother's side of the Chevalier de l'Etang, a page of Marie Antoinette who emigrated to India after the French Revolution. See Quentin Bell, Virginia Woolf (1972), I, pp. 14–17. The Jacksons had a son who died in infancy and three daughters, Adeline who married Henry Halford Vaughan, Mary who married Herbert Fisher and Julia who married first Herbert Duckworth and secondly Leslie Stephen. Vaughan, who showed no affection for his wife, was Professor of History at Oxford, from which post he retired to write a *magnum opus*; he later gave out that it had been destroyed by a housemaid's carelessness, but it was suspected that he had himself torn it up. He published three volumes of commentaries on Shakespeare described by Stephen as 'most singular instances of misapplied ingenuity', and of which one bookseller said that the only man who ever bought a copy from him was Disraeli. Fisher was tutor to the Prince of Wales and father of H. A. L. Fisher and Florence, wife of F. W. Maitland.

p. 77   'smart to me': MB, p. 30.
fn. 'rummy effect': Robertson Scott, op. cit., p. 87.
Holman Hunt . . . Woolner: Hunt and Woolner married two sisters and when Hunt's wife died, he married the third sister in the family. This second marriage led to a quarrel between the two men for both had secretly adored her; and the reason for this adoration (so Stephen relates) was said to be that she resembled Julia Jackson and was indeed often mistaken for her. Ibid., pp. 28–9.
'jealousy': MB, p. 35.
'shipwreck': Ibid., p. 40.

p. 78   'thirty-one': L. Tolstoy, *War and Peace*, VI, Ch. 1–3.
'revival': MB, p. 47.
'with Julia!': MB, p. 47.
'would marry': MB, p. 48.

p. 79   'silly': LS to Julia Duckworth, 5 April 1877, Berg.
'deserve it': Ibid., 8 April 1877, Berg.
'philosopher': Ibid., 10 April 1877, Berg.
'impracticable': MB, p. 51.
'dead heart': Ibid., p. 53.
'pin in it': Ibid., p. 52.

p. 80   'they have got': Letters from LS to Julia Duckworth, 18 and 19 July 1877, Berg.
'unctuous way': Ibid., 10 Aug. 1877. Cf 18 Aug. 1877, Berg.
'amongst eggs': Ibid., 18 Aug. 1877, Berg.
'have not': Ibid., 27 July 1877, Berg.
'burnt to death': Ibid., 21 July 1877, Berg.

'vast intellect': *MB*, p. 65.

p. 81   'not yet married': *MB*, p. 57. A full account of their courtship will be
found in John D. Bicknell, *Dearest Julia, Dearest Leslie* (unpublished),
which includes all the letters of those years.
'happiness': Fuller and Hammersley, op. cit., pp. 155–6.

CHAPTER THREE
THE MAN OF LETTERS

p. 82   'adores her': Ibid., *MB*, p. 80.
'your mother': Virginia Woolf, *The Captain's Death Bed* (1950), p. 73.
'ought to be': LS to Julia Duckworth, 7 August 1877, Berg; *MB*, p. 53.
Stephen begins the *Mausoleum Book* by saying: 'I wish to write mainly
about your mother. But I find in order to speak intelligibly it will be
best to begin by saying something about myself.'

p. 83   Stephen's editorship: See A. W. Brown, *The Metaphysical Society* (New
York 1947), pp. 221–2. The first issue in January 1860 sold 110,000
copies. James Payn attributed the drop in sales under Stephen to 'the
failure of the literary and especially the classical essay to attract the
public', and to the increased readableness of the daily and weekly press.
He guaranteed to make the *Cornhill* popular and Smith reduced its
price to sixpence; but the sales still fell. Cf. J. W. Robertson Scott, *The
Story of the Pall Mall Gazette* (1950), pp. 69, 96.
Nineteenth Century: Oscar Maurer, 'Leslie Stephen and the *Cornhill
Magazine*, 1871–82', *Texas University Studies in English*, XXXII
(1953), pp. 70–1.
'commercial sense': Ibid., p. 72.
unsophisticated: James Payn, *The Backwater of Life* (1899). Introduction
by L. Stephen, p. xxxv. Payn was a Cambridge friend of Stephen and
much liked in society: G. W. E. Russell dedicated his *Collections and
Recollections* to his memory. He wrote sixty-nine novels and candidly
admitted that he wrote that much because 'I should not get so much for
one first-rate book as I do for three second-rate ones.'
Dictionary of National Biography: Material for the passage on Stephen
and the *DNB* has been drawn from the *DNB*; *SB* I, pp. 1–36; *Life*, pp.
383, 385, 387, 390, 394; *DNB* (1912–21), 'Memoir of Sir Sidney Lee';
Robertson Scott, op. cit., Ch. XXI, pp. 243–50. See also *Times Literary
Supplement*, No. 2498 (misprinted 2968), 16 Dec. 1949, p. 819; and
16 Dec. 1977, p. 1478, Alan Bell, 'Leslie Stephen and the DNB', for
further comment on the original conception of the Dictionary and its
fulfilment.

p. 84   'concise': *Quarterly Review* 157, April 1884, p. 229.
'body': Quoted by Alan Bell. Letter to C. E. Norton, 13 April 1884,
Harvard.

p. 86   'anything like original investigation': John Kenyon, *The History Men*
(1983), p. 196.

'PhD degree': A. W. Brown, op. cit., p. 223.

Sidney Lee: Stephen preferred him to Gosse's candidate, Hall Caine, to Thomson Cooper who had already devilled for him, and to F. J. Furnivall who having put forward Lee's name then put forward his own.

p. 87 **made a fortune:** Maurer, op. cit., pp. 69–70.

general perversity of things: *Cornhill*, 10 May 1901, p. 59, 'George Smith' by Leslie Stephen.

p. 88 **trade unionists:** *London Review of Books* III, 3–16 Dec. 1981, 'British Worthies' by David Cannadine, pp. 3–6. Virginia Woolf with perhaps excessive satire observed that no lives of maids are to be found in the *DNB*. *Three Guineas* (1938), p. 296.

p. 89 **'a guide to the wanderer':** Louise Creighton, *Life and Letters of Mandell Creighton* (1906), I, p. 372.

'not necessarily a moral crime': Ibid., p. 374.

The Two Mad Chicks: John Johnson Timmerman, 'Sir Leslie Stephen as a Biographer' (1948), Appx I, pp. 277–9. Northwestern University Dissertation.

p. 90 **succeeding generation:** This was the view of the Harrow schoolmaster and climber, John Stogdon, quoted in Arnold Lunn, *Switzerland and the English* (1944), p. 148.

'worship': L. Stephen, *The Playground of Europe* (1910), p. 39. See Stephen's article, 'Alpine Climbing', in *St. Paul's Magazine* I, Jan. 1868, pp. 470–85, in which Stephen ruminates on the changing attitude to mountains as a study in the history of thought. 'The history of mountaineering is, to a great extent, the history of the process by which men have gradually conquered the phantoms of their imagination.' This is quoted by W. R. Irwin, *Queen's Quarterly* 53 (1946), p. 338.

Albert Smith: Smith gave a popular course of lectures in the Egyptian Hall, Piccadilly, in the early 1850s which ran for three years and did much to popularize climbing. Cf. Oscar Browning, *Memories of Sixty Years* (1910), p. 93.

p. 90 **four pounds each:** C. Hudson and E. Kennedy, *Where there's a Will there's a Way* (1856), p. 142. Cf. p. xiv. It was at this time that country sports were becoming expensive and more and more the preserve of the upper classes. The cost of mountaineering, which in the 1850s was about one pound a day, however, rose sharply in the 1870s, partly due to the development of hotels and other comforts and the cost of guides. Cf. A. Willis, *Wandering Among the High Alps* (1937 edn), p. 234.

Alpine Club: The Alpine Club was composed mostly of professional men of the upper-middle classes. C. S. Bennett, in an unpublished paper on the Club in this period, which he generously put at my disposal, calculated that in the first twenty years of the Club's existence, there were 432 members of whom 149 were lawyers, 103 businessmen, 70 dons and schoolmasters, 37 clergymen, 31 officers of the army or navy and 30 civil servants.

Alpine Journal: Stephen also translated H. Berlepsch, *Die Alpen in Natur und Lebensbildern dargestellt*. He contributed to *Peaks, Passes and Glaciers*; F. Galton, *Vacation Tourists* and *Notes of Travel in 1860*; and to *British Sports and Pastimes*, ed. A. Trollope (1868).

exploration: The English Alpinists sometimes saw themselves as Livingstone or Burton or Wills (cf. Frederic Harrison, *My Alpine Jubilee* (1908), p. 120): but though they plugged this theme, no systematic work was carried out as was done by the Deutsche und Oesterreichische Alpenverein in the Eastern Alps.

amateur: *Playground*, op. cit., p. 76 seq. *Life*, p. 96, however, suggests that he did sometimes climb without guides. He also occasionally struck a poor guide. (See Leslie Stephen, *Men, Books and Mountains*, ed. S. A. O. Ullmann (1956), pp. 187–8.)

fn. host: *Life*, pp. 96–7. *Playground*, p. 1.

himself: Irwin, op. cit., p. 341, takes Stephen's sage warnings against racing too literally. The precept that mountaineers should reduce dangers not exploit them was always trotted out by Stephen; but he enjoyed danger and exposed himself to it as all Alpinists do.

p. 91   **'self-satisfaction':** J. Ruskin, *Sesame and Lilies* (Library Edition, 1905) XVIII, Lecture I, §35, p. 90.

'sulkily silent': *Life*, p. 308.

'science': *Playground*, pp. 108–9.

resigned from the Club: Lunn, op. cit., pp. 138, 156. T. G. Bonney attacked Stephen's attitude in the *Alpine Journal* VII, May 1875, p. 223, as 'sheer Philistinism'. The quarrel and resignation have been followed by similar lamentable incidents in the history of this contentious club.

Olive Schreiner: Unpublished MS by Mrs W. K. Clifford.

'mountains!': *Life*, p. 92.

p. 92   **'morning':** G. F. Browne, *The Recollections of a Bishop* (1915), p. 102.

'en silence': *Life*, p. 99.

so speedily: *EFP*, pp. 192–3.

p. 93   **for it:** Ibid., pp. 194–5.

'to retreat': *Life*, p. 92. Cf. Frederic Harrison, op. cit., p. 21, 'I never saw a fresh peak but I thirsted to stand on it.'

'he was that rock': Bruce Haley, *The Healthy Body and Victorian Culture* (1978), p. 253.

p. 94   **'meeting':** *Quarterly Review* CI, April 1857, pp. 285–323, 'Pedestrianism in Switzerland', quoted in W. A. B. Coolidge's edition of J. D. Forbes, *Travels* (1900), p. 473. Forbes was the author of the first detailed book in English relating to exploration in the High Alps and is the link between the Genevese scientist de Saussure and the founder of the Alpine Club.

freemasonry: Cf. C. D. Cunningham and W. de W. Abney, *The Pioneers of the Alps* (1887), p. 25.

'money': *Life*, p. 220.

Religion: T. Carlyle, *Past and Present*, Bk III, Ch. 12, Centenary edn, 1896, p. 200. C. S. Bennett noted the large number among the first mountaineers who were Old Rugbeians. The school motto, he observed, is *Orando, laborando*.

'accomplish it': J. Tyndall, *The Glaciers of the Alps* (1860), pp. 73–4. The spirit of sanctifying play through work inspired both mountaineers and rowing men. Tyndall wrote of a climb up Mont Blanc: 'To some such bodily exertion is irksome, to some painful in the extreme, while to others it imparts the increasing flow of life and energy which is the source of a pleasure fully appreciated by all who, like one or two of our party, could row in a boat on which is depicted the motto "*Labor ipse voluptas*".' Tyndall was referring to E. S. Kennedy who was a don at Caius College.

ennobling pursuit: *Playground*, p. x of 1946 edition.

p. 95 'a rope'?: Ullmann, op. cit., pp. 192–3.

'day's raid': Ibid., pp. 208–9.

'people': Ibid., p. 211.

'mosquitoes': Ibid., p. 207.

p. 96 'take it for': *Playground*, p. 109. Stephen's jocular jokes, alas, have been inherited by too many literary Alpinists and form part of their stock in trade.

rococo imagery: Stephen made play with Ruskin's misanthropy which, he averred, influenced his attitude to the Alps. 'The most eloquent writer who, in our day, has transferred to his pages the charm of Alpine beauties shares in many ways Rousseau's antipathy for the social order. Mr Ruskin would explain better than anyone why the love of the sublimest scenery should be associated with a profound conviction that all things are out of joint, and that society can only be regenerated by rejecting all the achievements on which the ordinary optimist plumes himself. After all, it is not surprising that those who are most sick of man as he is should love the regions where man seems smallest.' *HL*, II, p. 205.

p. 97 'shall be!': *Playground*, pp. 273–5.

possibilities: For other assessments of Stephen as a mountaineer see C. E. Engel, *A History of Mountaineering in the Alps* (1950); C. W. F. Noyce, *Scholar Mountaineers* (1950); and Ronald Clark, *The Victorian Mountaineers* (1953).

Sunday Tramps: *Cornhill*, NS XXIV, Jan. 1908, J. Sully, 'Reminiscences of the Sunday Tramps'. Stephen resigned the leadership in 1891 and went out for his last tramp in 1894. Sully comments (p. 88) on the intimate friendship which these walks bred.

fn. 'climbing?': Unpublished MS of Mrs W. K. Clifford.

p. 98 *not* going to visit: *Holmes–Laski Letters*, ed. Mark DeWolfe Howe (1953), II, p. 1408.

'in front': Letter of Mrs W. K. Clifford to Vanessa Stephen, 2 Feb. 1906.

'bore you are': Virginia Woolf, *Moments of Being*, ed. Jeanne Schulkind (1976), p. 143.

'to me': *MB*, p. 30.

p. 99 due east: A. Birrell, *More Obiter Dicta* (1924), p. 4.

'prisoner': F. W. Hirst, *Early Life and Letters of John Morley* (1927), I, pp. 165–6. The 'refusal to magnify an incident into an event' was Augustine Birrell's comment. *Holmes–Laski Letters*, II, p. 937.

toadied to them: Letters from LS to C. E. Norton, 18 April 1873 Harvard; to Edmund Gosse, 18 April 1877; to Julia Stephen, 27 July 1877, Berg; to George Eliot, 8 Jan. 1878; to Graham Balfour, 21 Oct. 1901; and to Henry Jackson, 9 July 1901. Maitland Add. MS Camb.

'stupid but kindly': LS to Julia Stephen, undated? summer 1878, Berg.

'civilization': LS to Edward Dicey, 10 Oct. 1867, Maitland, Add. MS Camb.

'to dinner': Virginia Woolf, Add. MSS 61973, British Library.

p. 100 'to the play': Ibid.

said and felt there: Ibid.

'listened to': Ibid.

p. 101 'good sense': *Life*, p. 362.

'powers of sympathy': *Holmes–Laski Letters*, I, p. 493.

'literary gents': Letter from F. W. Maitland to Henry Jackson, 20 Feb. 1905, Maitland Add. MS, Camb.

'every way': Letter from LS to Anny Ritchie, 27 Sept. 1898.

'care for me': *MB*, p. 66.

p. 102 'sink into the earth': Ibid. p. 60.

'joydé': Ibid. p. 85.

to be inescapable: *Pall Mall Gazette*, 4 Oct. 1879. I am indebted to Martine Stemerick for letting me see her unpublished dissertation, 'Virginia Woolf and Julia Stephen: the Distaff side of History', in which this reference appears.

'post tonight': *Moments of Being*, p. 38.

p. 103 'the well': Mrs Leslie Stephen, *Notes for Sick Rooms* (1883), p. 3. See *New Feminist Essays on Virginia Woolf*, (1981) II, Jane Marcus, 'Virginia Woolf and her Violin: Mothering, Madness and Music'.

'scientific world': Ibid., p. 5.

Mrs Ramsay: I am indebted to Alexander Zwerdling for showing me in draft two chapters of his book on Virginia Woolf and drawing my attention to these unpublished essays in the Washington State University Library, II, 4–5.

p. 104 exhausted Julia: Jane Marcus, op. cit.

'into the water': *Moments of Being*, p. 39.

'each other': Ibid., p. 57.

p. 105 'disastrous results': Ibid., p. 54.

'be cold': Ibid., p. 37.

p. 107 'over London': Add. MSS 61973 British Library.

p. 108 'Lighthouse': Ibid.

harbour: Ibid. Cf. *Moments of Being*, p. 115.

'appreciating them': Leonard Woolf, *Sowing* (1960), pp. 180–2. Stephen did not discard friends when they found themselves in difficulty.

p. 109 'either side': Add. MSS 61973 British Library.

'little teeth gleam': LS to Julia Stephen, 6 Oct. 1886, Berg.

'certainly intelligent': LS to Julia Stephen, 3 Aug. 1893, Berg.

'never like being beaten': Letter from Mrs W. K. Clifford to F. W. Maitland. Maitland Add. MS, Camb.

p. 110 ' "quarter of a century" ': Letter from C. B. Clarke to F. W. Maitland. Maitland Add. MS, Camb.

'truth and liberty': 'Women and Scepticism' (by LS), *Fraser's Magazine* LXVIII, Dec. 1863, p. 697.

'learned professions': 'The Redundancy of Women' (by LS), *Saturday Review*, 24 April 1869, p. 546.

'hot potato': Letters from LS to Julia Stephen dated 20, 21, 22 Jan. and 4 Feb. 1887, Berg.

Beatrice Potter: Beatrice Webb, *Our Partnership*, ed. Barbara Drake and Margaret Cole (1975), pp. 361–2.

p. 111 'than the dictionary': *SB* I, p. 29.

'anything else': Quoted by Alan Bell, *The Times Literary Supplement*, 16 Dec. 1977, p. 1478.

crush him: It is from this time that Stephen's handwriting deteriorated so badly that misprints, which he failed to notice, appear frequently in his articles in periodicals. *Cornhill* XXVIII Jan. 1910, 'Leslie Stephen as editor' by W. E. Norris, p. 48, relates how Stephen completed a sentence, in which Swift compared something to beef without mustard, with the words, 'in a letter to Arbuthnot', these words were deciphered by the printer as 'or wine without nuts'.

'into slips': *Life*, pp. 394, 397.

for their benefit: Letter from LS to Austin Dobson, 17 May 1887, Berg.

p. 112   'third-rate work': Letter from LS to Julia Stephen, 31 March 1884, Berg.

'wasted myself': Letter from LS to Julia Stephen, 4 Sept. 1884, Berg.

'out of you': Letters from LS to Julia Stephen, 18 Oct. 1884 and 21 April 1885, Berg.

state of mind: Letters from Julia Stephen to George Smith, 1 Jan. 1885, 2 Jan. 1887, 23 Nov. 1888, Berg.

'ghastly manner': Letter from LS to Julia Stephen, 5 Feb. 1886, Berg.

'excitement and misery': *MB*, p. 89. Cf. Letter from LS to V. Welby, 22 Nov. 1890, Maitland Add. MS, Camb. See Julia Stephen's unpublished essay on 'The Servant Question', Washington State University Library.

'now have done Young': Quoted by Alan Bell, op. cit.

earn a living by journalism: LS to Julia Duckworth, 18 July 1877, and to Julia Stephen, 26 Oct. 1891, Berg.

p. 113   gratification: W. Raleigh, *Samuel Johnson* (1907), p. 3.

'presence': Thomas Hardy to Sidney Lee, 22 Nov. 1906, Bodleian.

retarded: Laura Stephen died in 1946 aged 76.

p. 114   sword-stick: *Moments of Being*, pp. 98–9.

bedroom: Ibid., p. 84.

p. 115   'useless words': Letter from F. W. Maitland to LS, 9 May 1895, Camb.

as Stephen's love did?: Cf. E. M. Forster, *Marianne Thornton* (1956), p. 71.

revives: *SRD* II, pp. 243–56.

'unvisited tombs': George Eliot, *Middlemarch*, Bk VIII (1872 edn), pp. 370–1.

p. 116   'protest': *Moments of Being*, p. 94.

'is happy': Ibid., p. 101.

need have been: Ibid., p. 106.

'called in': Quentin Bell, *Life of Virginia Woolf* (1972), I, p. 45.

'denunciations of father': Monks House draft A/5 (c), quoted by Martine Stemerick, op. cit.

p. 117   'developing into insanity': George H. Savage, *Insanity and Allied Neuroses: Practical and Clinical* (Philadelphia 1884), quoted by Jane Marcus, op. cit. See Bruce Haley, op. cit., p. 47, where he quotes Stephen.

'out of their minds': Jane Marcus, op. cit.

the attack: Letters from G. T. Worsley to Julia Stephen, 6 and 20 March, 4 April 1894, quoted in Stemerick, op. cit.

digest: Monks House draft A/5 (c), quoted in ibid.

his concern: Ibid.

p. 118   'skeleton like me': Letter from LS to Julia Stephen, 3 Feb. 1886, Berg.

Thoby . . . Clifton: One should not deduce that Stephen preferred Clifton

to Eton. See *Supra* p. 355. He sent his younger son to Westminster as
a day boy because he was delicate. Letter from LS to Julia Stephen, 22
July 1894, Berg.
'impractical': Letter from LS to C. E. Norton, 25 Aug. 1895, Harvard.
Cf. letter from LS to Julia Stephen, 29 Jan. 1894, Berg.

p. 119   'frustration': *Moments of Being*, pp. 124–5.
'jealousies': *The Letters of Virginia Woolf*, ed. Nigel Nicolson and Joanne
Trautmann (1976), II, p. 247. *PMLA* 96, 1981, Katharine Hill,
'Virginia Woolf and Leslie Stephen: History and Literary Revolution',
p. 361.
'health to learning': Letter from LS to Julia Duckworth, 19 July 1877,
Berg.
'she can ever do now': Letter from LS to Julia Duckworth, 18 July 1877,
Berg.

p. 120   'utterly': Letter from LS to Julia Duckworth, 19 July 1877, Berg.
'highest nature': Julia Stephen, 'The Servant Question', op. cit., quoted by
Stemerick, op. cit.

p. 121   'on my education': Add. MSS 61973 British Library.
Hyde Park Gate News: Phyllis Rose, *Women of Letters* (New York
1978), p. 11.
beautiful, dutiful and altruistic: *MB*, p. 59.
which way to turn: *PMLA* 97 (1982), Louis de Salvo, letter to editor,
pp. 103–4.

p. 122   make up her mind: *Moments of Being*, p. 122, Quentin Bell, op. cit., I,
p. 72.
as Julia had had with Stella: See Frances Spalding, *Vanessa Bell* (1983).
'come out right': Letter from LS to Julia Duckworth, 18 Aug. 1877, Berg,
quoted by Martine Stemerick, 'The Patriarch as Prologue', *PMLA*, Dec.
1982.
'proper place': *The Nineteenth Century* VI, Dec. 1879, 'Mistress and
Servants' by Caroline Emilia Stephen, pp. 1051–2.
but for Laura?: I am grateful to Martine Stemerick for bringing this
matter to my notice.

p. 123   invited: Max Beerbohm's tale that 'Leslie Stephen was struck out, Canon
Ainger included, after a troubled pause, as being an authority on Lamb'
is in character but inaccurate. *Geoffrey Madan's Notebooks*, ed. J. A.
Gere and John Sparrow (1981), p. 99.

p. 124   'vain': Letter from R. B. Haldane to Miss Virginia Stephen, Feb. 1904,
Maitland MS Cambridge.
'follow': Virginia Woolf, *The Diary of Virginia Woolf*, ed. Anne Olivier
Bell (1980) 3 May 1897.
'Johnson': *Life*, p. 486. Quoted by John Gross, *The Rise and Fall of the
English Man of Letters* (1969), p. 87.

p. 125   'without me': *MB*, p. 112.
Ode on the Nativity: Quentin Bell, op. cit., I, p. 86.
goal: W. H. Thompson, *Huxley and Religion* (1905), p. 67.
'exciting topics': Letter to C. E. Norton, 26 June 1898, Harvard. Cf. J. H.
Morgan, *Morley* (1924), pp. 180–81.
'in Nature': *Letters of George Meredith* (1912), II, p. 555 (14 Feb. 1904).
twice in church: Letter from Frederick Pollock to F. W. Maitland, 26 Feb.
1904, Add. MS Camb.

CHAPTER FOUR
WHAT WAS HE REALLY LIKE

p. 126   **of her own class:** Virginia Woolf wanted her sister to approve every novel
she wrote but her verdict on *To the Lighthouse* mattered more than on
any of the others. She was on tenterhooks until she heard from Vanessa
– who treated it as a wonderful portrait of her mother and never
mentioned that of her father. *Diaries*, III, p. 135; *Letters*, III, pp. 572,
375–83. See 'Fountains of Ink, Fountains of Joy: The Psychological
Influence of Leslie Stephen on Virginia Woolf as Fictionalized in *To the
Lighthouse*', by Jane Lilienfeld, Assumption College, Worcester, Mass.
　　The best short articles on Stephen's character which appeared on his
death were those of Frederic Harrison in *Cornhill* LXXXIX, April
1904, p. 433, reprinted in *Realities and Ideals* (1908), and of Frederick
Pollock, *Independent Review* III, June 1904, pp. 48–60. Since then
articles have been remarkably scarce. A 1907 reprint of *EFP* has an
essay by James Bryce and Herbert Paul on Stephen's life and work, but
it does not amount to much. A. C. Lyall, *Studies in Literature and
History* (1915), and J. E. Courtney, *Freethinkers in the Nineteenth
Century* (1920), comment briefly on his career as an agnostic and
moralist. Sidney Lee republished in *Elizabethan and other Essays*
(1928) his Leslie Stephen lecture of 1911, which gives a personal
recollection of their collaboration on the *DNB*. S. T. Williams, *London
Mercury* 8, Oct. 1923, pp. 621–34, considers Stephen as an essayist.
E. Gosse, *Silhouettes* (1925), pp. 319–26, claims that Stephen has been
unfairly forgotten as a critic. Desmond MacCarthy's *Leslie Stephen*
(1937), which he delivered as the Leslie Stephen lecture for that year,
and Q. D. Leavis's reply to it are dealt with in Ch. Twelve below. Alan
Bell's excellent introduction to his edition of the *Mausoleum Book*
stimulated interest in Stephen and among the reviews the best in Britain
was by Stuart Hampshire, *The Times Literary Supplement*, 10
February 1977. See also *Biography* 4, Spring 1981, 'Virginia Woolf
and Biography', by J. Gindin, and 'Virginia Woolf and Autobiography',
by G. Griffin.
　　'first-rate man': Virginia Woolf, *To the Lighthouse* (1927 edn), p. 17.
　　'tyranny in him': Ibid., pp. 255–62, 306.
p. 127   **'human decency':** Ibid, p. 54.
　　'little drama': Ibid., pp. 256–7.
　　masculine nature: *HL* III, p. 162
p. 128   **'easily bored':** Leila Luedeking, 'Strifes, Divisions and Fibers of Being: the
Psychological Impact of Leslie Stephen on Virginia Woolf' (Washington
State University Library).
　　'live them down': *MB*, pp. 57–8.
　　'I ever saw': *MB*, p. 68.
　　'commit suicide': *MB*, p. 89.
p. 129   **'the mind':** C. E. Stephen, *The Service of the Poor*, (1871) p. 71.
　　'little book of hers': *MB*, p. 55.
　　'the effect of unkindness': Letter from C. E. Stephen to F. W. Maitland.

Add. MS, Camb.

'plums nearer together': Letter from G. Loppé to F. W. Maitland. Add. MS, Camb.

p. 130   **'is done'**: Quoted by Jane Marcus, 'The Niece of a Nun: Virginia Woolf, Caroline Stephen and the Cloistered Imagination', *Virginia Woolf: A Feminist Slant* (Nebraska 1983) p. 9.

The Egoist: In Ch. II of *The Egoist* Meredith describes Vernon Whitford, who was drawn from Stephen, in the well-known phrase, 'Phoebus Apollo turned fasting friar'. Readers of *The Egoist*, however, have been misled by Crossjay Patterne's encomium of his tutor to the effect that one could depend upon him because he was 'always the same', e.g. 'If ever a man was all of a piece it was Stephen', F. W. Knickerbocker, *Free Minds: John Morley and His Friends* (1943), p. 15.

a woman likes: Virginia Woolf, Add. MSS 61973 British Library.

whole story: Q. D. Leavis in *Scrutiny* VII, March 1939, p. 405, 'Leslie Stephen – Cambridge Critic' takes it as a final judgement and calls it a 'brilliant study in the Lytton Strachey manner of a slightly ludicrous, slightly bogus, Victorian philosopher, (which) has somehow served to discredit Leslie Stephen's literary work'. It is difficult to see how the agonizing description of the state of mind of a daughter in regard to her father could be conceived to be in the Lytton Strachey manner; or indeed, that Virginia Woolf was preoccupied with debunking her father's character. In an attempt to score a point against Bloomsbury, Q. D. Leavis omitted to mention the complementary portrait of Stephen as Mr Hilbery in *Night and Day*, and was apparently unaware of the article in *The Times*.

The Times: Reprinted in Virginia Woolf, *The Captain's Death Bed* (1950), pp. 67–73.

Pater's sister: LS to C. E. Norton, 21 July 1899, Harvard.

p. 131   **fifteen**: 'Virginia Woolf and Leslie Stephen: A Study in Mentoring and Literary Criticism' by Katherine Hill, Diss., Columbia University, p. 131. The diary is in the Berg Collection.

'twice': *The Letters of Virginia Woolf*, op. cit., IV, p. 26.

'villain': *Life*, p. 474.

'discomfited': *The Captain's Death Bed*, p. 70.

'genuine': Ibid., p. 69.

dissected and discarded: C. E. Norton expressed surprise that Stephen should have defended Gosse when the latter was flayed by the *Nation* for inaccuracy. Stephen admitted that Gosse was fussy and conceited and not 'in a high rank among friends'; but Gosse had been kind to him and should be protected. Letter from LS to Norton, 27 April 1900, Harvard.

'referred to': Add. MSS 61973 British Library.

p. 132   **'unhealthily'**: Quoted in *PMLA* LXX, June 1955, pp. 548–52, 'To the Lighthouse Again' by Frank Baldanza.

'morality, sex': Virginia Woolf, *The Death of the Moth* (1942), pp. 150–51.

'understand'; The quotations in this and the following paragraph are from Add. MSS 61973, British Library.

p. 134   **'to the world'**: *MB*, p. 96.

pause: Cf. the same honesty in C. Oman, *On the Writing of History*,

(1939), pp. 218–20.

'old work': *SB* II, p. 158. C. E. Norton gave a different but, I think, less satisfactory explanation of Stephen's lack of inner purpose. In *Letters*, ed. S. A. Norton and W. Howe, (1913), I, p. 436, he writes: 'Struck as usual with Stephen's intellectual sincerity and liberality, and with that temper of indifference to one's own influence, a certain inertness, which, I fancy, is common to men of delicate and fastidious sensibilities and of philosophic disposition, who find themselves in creed and in motive out of harmony with their generation.'

'own legs': I. S. Turgenev, *Fathers and Children*, Ch. XXI.

'own being': Emily Brontë, *Wuthering Heights*, Ch. IX.

p. 135 'resemblance to her father': The comparison is worked out minutely by Katherine Hill, op. cit.

'like me I feel': LS to Julia Stephen, 25 Jan. 1891, Berg.

'tremendous': *The Letters of Virginia Woolf*, op. cit., III, p. 374, 13 May 1927.

'give her some hints': LS to Julia Stephen, 30 July 1893, Berg.

on his daughter: *PMLA* 96, 1981, 'Virginia Woolf and Leslie Stephen: History and Literary Revolution', by Katharine C. Hill, pp. 351–62. In *PMLA* 97, 1982, pp. 103–6, Katherine Hill replies to her critics and demolishes them. Cf. Leila Luedeking, *Virginia Woolf's Exposure to Leslie Stephen's Books, 'Hours in a Library'*: Washington State University Library.

'inconceivable': *The Diary of Virginia Woolf*, op. cit., III, p. 208. 28 Nov. 1928.

'emotional wastebaskets': Phyllis Rose, *Woman of Letters* (New York 1978), p. 19.

p. 136 'borders of sanity': Virginia Hyman, 'Concealment and Disclosure in Sir Leslie Stephen's *Mausoleum Book*', *Biography* III, p. 127.

'leads to decay': Quoted by Hyman, op. cit., p. 126, *Sci. Eth.*, p. 165.

'cling to life': Sigmund Freud, 'Mourning and Melancholia' (1917), in The Complete Psychological Works of Sigmund Freud ed. Jas Strachey, XIV, p. 237, quoted in Katherine Hill's dissertation, op. cit., p. 37.

possibility: LS to Julia Stephen, 6–15 June 1890 and 29 Jan. 1893, Berg.

p. 137 'weekly accounts': Katharine Hill dissertation, p. 51.

'growing old?': Frontispiece to Clive Bell, *Old Friends* (1956).

p. 139 decreed: See Donna Arzt, 'Psychohistory and Its Discontents', *Biography* I (Summer 1978), p. 22ff. Richard Ellmann, 'That's Life', *New York Review of Books* XVII (June 1971), p. 4. Cf. Jean O. Love, *Virginia Woolf: Sources of Madness and Art* (1978) which argues that Virginia internalized Stephen's concepts of masculinity and femininity and raged inwardly at her inability to reconcile them within herself.

p. 140 'to God': 'The Evangelical Discipline' by Charles Smyth, *Ideas and Beliefs of the Victorians*, ed. Harman Grisewood (1949), p. 100.

p. 141 hospital: *Life*, p. 126.

slaughter: Ibid., p. 436. Stephen spoke strongly against the cant of supposing that the Crimean War had regenerated England. *SB* II, p. 237; and *HL* III, p. 50.

'agreeable': Letter from LS to Mrs W. K. Clifford, 4 Sept., 1884, Harvard.

p. 142 'by him': *SB* Leslie Stephen, II, p. 72.

'good degree': *Men, Books and Mountains*, ed. S. A. O. Ullmann (1956), p. 213.

'in their heads': *Sketches*, p. 84. R. E. Sencourt misjudges Stephen's humour when he writes, 'Nothing of a joke appealed to him but the sardonic in it.' Cf. Sencourt, *Life of Meredith* (1920), p. 192.

'suggest to me': *Sketches*, p. 6.

'Paddle on all': Ibid., p. 119.

p. 143 'antipathy instead': Florence Hardy, *Early Life of Thomas Hardy* (1928), p. 238.

'never changed': *Life*, p. 273.

p. 144 'swept them a curtsey': *The Captain's Death Bed*, p. 71. Hyperbole, of course.

nannies and park-keepers: See Stephen's appreciative references, *SB* I, p. 29 fn.

protection: Letter from LS to Anny Ritchie, 10 Sept. 1898, Berg.

'sonnet to express the fancy': J. O. Bailey, *The Poetry of Thomas Hardy* (North Carolina, Chapel Hill, 1970) p. 281. The sonnet first appeared in Maitland's *Life*.

CHAPTER FIVE

EVANGELICALISM

p. 146 Salvation Army: See G. Kitson Clark, *The Making of Victorian England* (1962), pp. 147–205.

were remarkable: J. S. Reynolds, *The Evangelicals at Oxford* (1953), pp. 90–93.

Oxford Movement: David Newsome, *The Parting of Friends* (1966), pp. 12–15. Y. Brilioth, *Evangelicalism and the Oxford Movement* (1934), *passim*. The best contemporary assessments of the Evangelicals as a party are in W. J. Conybeare, *Essays Ecclesiastical and Social* (1855), pp. 57–164, and an article in *Macmillan's Magazine* III, Dec. 1860, 'The Evangelical Clergy'. A short and suggestive bibliography on Evangelicalism may be found in C. Smyth, 'The Evangelical Movement in Perspective', in *Cambridge Historical Journal* VII, 1943, pp. 160–74. Owen Chadwick, *The Victorian Church* (1966), I, pp. 440–68, and John Kent, *The Age of Disunity* (1966), are also excellent.

'spiritual dynamics': Sir J. Stephen, *Essays in Ecclesiastical Biography* (1849), II, p. 358.

p. 147 attributes: Newsome, op. cit., p. 47. An apparent inconsistency obtrudes upon the Evangelical scheme of salvation as preached by Simeon and the Calvinists. If God predestines a man to be among the elect, why should we evangelize the unredeemed, who are either irretrievably lost or will at some time during their lives turn to God and show signs of their election? Calvinists, like disciples of other necessitarian creeds, stand in danger of antinomianism – the antinomy of a determinate decree of election consequent upon a limiting of Divine Grace to the elect, and of a universal appeal to human free will, as if predestination did not exist. It was this doctrine which Wesley rejected, when he declared that God's grace was not limited, but for all men. The Wesleyan evangelist must spread God's word in order to melt the hearts of men frozen with sin which, when melted, could close with God's offer of salvation. Wesley's Arminianism – though, of course, it finds itself in difficulties in other fields of theology – is a satisfactory logic for the administration of redemption. How then are we to explain the views of the Calvinist Evangelicals?

They held first that no man could say who were the elect, even less that he himself was for certain numbered with them. Thus he must seek out the elect and awake them to their destiny. He must evangelize to spread God's glory and show how many, in fact, he was prepared to pardon and receive. He must evangelize to make sure that he himself did not slip from grace. He must evangelize for every moment of his time was accountable to God; and in what more godly way could he spend his hours? Though many would for ever remain deaf to the Gospel call, many would be awakened to their real mission in life, and so the rule of God's saints on earth would be achieved with greater speed. The Church of England had always been at pains to moderate its Calvinist doctrines. Article XVII is explicitly Calvinist, and the English delegates to the Synod of Dort signed its canons. Yet they were able to interpret them liberally without straining their conscience, and indeed the Synod itself inclined to an Infralapsarian rather than to the Supralapsarian interpretation of predestination preferred by Calvin. Richard Baxter taught a Calvinism which held that God provided salvation for all men, some of whom he elects and others whom he leaves without the necessary grace of repentance and faith (which none of us have the right to claim), and that thus we have great need of evangelizers. Simeon appears to have been oblivious to the difficulty. He was of course aware of the degrading controversy in which Toplady engaged against Wesley on predestination and rightly saw that the work of evangelizing was not furthered or edified by such debates. For a discussion of the matter from the Wesleyan point of view see W. B. Page, *A Compendium of Christian Theology* (1877), II, pp. 340–57. Cf. *Eng. Thought 18th Cent.*, II, pp. 426–8.

in peril of death: H. Venn, *Complete Duty of Man* (1779, 3rd edn), Chs 7–9. *Eng. Thought 18th Cent.*, II, p. 431.

p. 148 experienced God's grace: Cf. J. G. McKenzie, *Psychology, Psychotherapy and Evangelicalism* (1940), pp. 21 seq.

p. 149 train their conscience: Newsome, op. cit., p. 50.
'my uniform reply': Moncure Conway, *Autobiography* (1904), I, p. 396.
'breast of a Nobleman': *Victorian Studies* V, Sept. 1961, 'The Clapham Sect: Some Social and Political Aspects' by David Spring, p. 46.

p. 150 than when reading it: Chadwick, op. cit., p. 442.
Invisible Church: *Journal of Theological Studies* X, 1959, 'The Evangelicals and the Established Church in the Early Nineteenth Century' by G. F. A. Best, p. 70.
'unsteepled places of worship': R. I. and S. Wilberforce, *Life of William Wilberforce* (1838), I, p. 248.
'a light and trifling clergyman': Best, op. cit., p. 71.
'account of my stewardship': Ibid., p. 77.

p. 151 'derived': C. E. Stephen, *The First Sir James Stephen* (1906), pp. 181–3.
p. 152 fn odious: *Life*, pp. 133–4.
p. 153 'humbled mind': G. W. E. Russell, *The Household of Faith* (1902), pp. 226–7.
'praise': Ibid., p. 226.
'notice it': E. M. Forster, *Abinger Harvest* (1936), p. 242.
p. 154 'approximation to truth': *SRD* II, p. 244.
'grave and cheerful complacency': Sir J. Stephen, *Essays in Ecclesiastical Biography* (1849), II, p. 305.
p. 155 'each other': Quoted by Newsome, op. cit., p. 11.
'Evangelicals': G. W. E. Russell, *A Short History of the Evangelical Movement* (1915), p. 124.
'his own absolver': Ibid., p. 83.
'poetical taste . . . for many a year': C. E. Tonna, *Personal Recollections* (1841), pp. 24–5.
'kept under with a firm hand': W. H. B. Proby, *Annals of the Low Church Party* (1888), I, p. 386.
devotional books: Benjamin Gregory, *Autobiographical Recollections* (1903), pp. 119–44.
p. 156 'work of the flesh': *Macmillan's Magazine*, op. cit., pp. 114, 120.
'spiritual good': F. Close, *Sermons* (1842), p. 149.
truth for its own sake: V. F. Storr, *Freedom and Tradition* (1940), p. 29.
right relation to God: R. W. Dale, *The Old Evangelicalism and the New* (1889), pp. 19–26. Cf. Dale, *The Evangelical Revival* (1880), pp. 4–8, 24.
ignorance of the world: A. P. Stanley, *Life and Correspondence of Thomas Arnold* (1880), I, p. 246 fn.
Christ as the broker: See W. E. Gladstone, *Gleanings* (1879), VII, p. 222; and J. Tulloch, *Movements in Religious Thought* (1885), p. 51, on Whateley's attack on Hervey, the author of *Meditations among the Tombs*, for trying to explain the incomprehensible mystery of the Atonement in terms of abstract justice. Cf. F. P. Cobbe, *Broken Lights* (1865), pp. 36–7.
was its undoing: Cf. F. D. Maurice: 'The Evangelical preaching has been deficient in reverence because it has been deficient in depth', *Life of F. D. Maurice* (1884), I, p. 335.
Persecution Company Ltd: Russell, op. cit., p. 114.
p. 157 'momentous a subject': Best, op. cit., pp. 75–6 fn.
fn 'hounds': Anon. (G. W. E. Russell), *Collections and Recollections by One who has Kept a Diary* (1898), p. 251.
p. 158 strong upon him: T. Mozley, *Reminiscences Chiefly of Oriel College and the Oxford Movement* (1882), I, p. 99.
Shaftesbury: E. E. Kellett, *As I Remember* (1936), p. 149 fn.
'philosophi vita': G. M. Trevelyan, *Sir G. O. Trevelyan, A Memoir* (1923), p. 15.
Austin: C. E. Stephen, op. cit., p. 90. *Life of Sir JFS*, p. 75.
'soundness of her anchorage': J. Stephen, op. cit., II, p. 309.
'inquiry': *Life of Sir JFS*, pp. 127–8. Cf. the Rev John Newton, 'I shall preach, perhaps, very usefully upon two opposite texts, while kept apart; but if I attempt nicely to reconcile them, it is ten to one if I don't begin to bungle.' C. Smyth, op. cit., p. 163.

Record: The *Record* first appeared in 1828 and after six months of disastrous sales was saved by Haldane, who gave a 'new acrimony to religious controversy' as the *Christian Observer* noted. Sumner, the first Evangelical archbishop of Canterbury, commented, 'The conduct of the *Record* is execrable'. See G. R. Balleine, *A History of the Evangelical Party in the Church of England* (1908), pp. 206 *seq.*

p. 159   remaining a clergyman: A. V. Dicey, *Memorials* (1925), p. 139. Dicey wrote, in 1895, about the Stephen brothers: 'I am more and more convinced that [Leslie] will live far longer as a writer than his brother. Leslie, whether successful or not, is always trying to ascertain the truth; Fitzjames Stephen is always trying to show somebody else's error; and he often obtains his successes as a controversialist by first misrepresenting, though honestly, the meaning of his opponent, and then confuting an opinion which no one really holds.'

'my wife reads': Letter dated Leeds 1 April 1875. A. W. Brown, *The Metaphysical Society* (New York 1947), p. 132, states that Fitzjames stopped attending church in 1869; and in a letter dated 22 November 1879 Fitzjames declared that he never went to church except on circuit. Vanessa Bell, however, recollected her uncle and aunt coming to lunch on Sundays on their way back from church, and as his wife continued to remain an orthodox Christian, Fitzjames would not have wanted to make a demonstration.

'discernment': F. H. Skrine, *Life of Sir William Hunter* (1901), p. 214. I am indebted to Eric Stokes for this reference. See *Life of Sir JFS*, p. 221.

p. 160   'than dull': *DNB* (1922–30), p. 261.

'faith': J. M. Keynes, *Two Memoirs* (1949), pp. 84, 97.

p. 161   practical politics: Leonard Woolf, *Sowing* (1960), p. 149. But see Robert Skidelsky, *John Maynard Keynes* (1983), I, Ch. 6 for an excellent analysis of this issue.

'contemplating': Desmond MacCarthy, *Portraits* (1949 edn), pp. 164–5.

p. 162   'spirits . . . and sweet': *HL* I, pp. 284, 291.

p. 163   'head': *Life of Sir JFS*, pp. 309–10.

complicated subject: See H. Butterfield, *The Whig Interpretation of History* (1931), Ch. 3, esp. pp. 54–63. The connection between puritanism and empirical science in the seventeenth century deserves more careful examination before generalizations such as that of Stephen can be made. It is, however, significant that of those foundation members of the Royal Society about whose religious beliefs we have evidence, over 60 per cent had puritan or parliamentary affiliations during the Civil War; and all the ten original Enquirers who met in 1645 and subsequently formed the nucleus of the Royal Society, were puritans.

p. 164   'shackles': T. H. Huxley, *Collected Essays* (1894), V. p. 13.

CHAPTER SIX
BRITISH RATIONALISM

p. 167   *marxisant* **interpretations of life:** I do not wish to imply that in the
nineteenth century all French savants remained impervious to Hegel.
Cousin and the eclectic school dominated official education from 1830
to the middle of the century, and a legion of schoolmasters would have
popularized their ideas which had a good deal in common with
German idealism in spite of a facade of psychological analysis. The
method of teaching philosophy through its history provided students at
least with a bowdlerized version of Hegel's thought; and this influence
can be traced in Renan's *L'Avenir de la Science* and in Vigny's
Destinées. Gratry accused Renan, Scherer and Vacherot of being
Hegelians and indeed brought about the dimissal of Vacherot in 1851
from the Ecole Normale. Scherer wrote an article on 'Hegel et
l'Hegelianisme' in the *Revue des Deux Mondes*, 15 Feb. 1861, which is
supposed to have influenced Mallarmé when he was writing his *Notes*
for a thesis on aesthetics and language (see L. J. Austin, 'Mallarmé et le
rêve du livre', *Mercure de France*, 1 Jan. 1953). Scherer paid tribute to
an Italian called Véra who published his *Introduction à la Philosophie
de Hegel* in 1855 and translated the *Logic* in 1859.

p. 168   **'was always what he is now':** Voltaire, *Essai sur les Moeurs et l'Esprit des
Nations* (Paris 1785), p. 32, quoted by Isaiah Berlin, *Vico and Herder*
(1976), p. 197.

p. 169   **a deplorable society:** See Nicholas Boyle's review of *The Secularisation of
the European Mind in the Nineteenth Century* by Owen Chadwick, in
Cambridge Review, 7 May 1976, pp. 149–52.

p. 170   **'the spice, Hegel':** Quoted by J. H. Randall, *The Making of the Modern
Mind* (1940), pp. 414–15.
  the curriculum less narrow: Boyle, op. cit., p. 152.

p. 171   **'who was grave':** H. P. Liddon, *Life of E. B. Pusey* (1894), I, p. 74 fn.
  the higher criticism: Ibid., p. 164. See also A. W. Benn, *The History of
English Rationalism in the Nineteenth Century* (1906), I, pp. 341–5.
  studied Vico: Duncan Forbes, *The Liberal Anglican Idea of History*
(1952) *passim*. See also Isaiah Berlin, op. cit., *passim*.

p. 172   **American history . . . Carlyle:** *Life*, p. 73.
  'we can at present produce': *Life*, pp. 228, 231–2.
  'dislikes me': LS to C. E. Norton, 29 Dec. 1873. Cf. *Life*, pp. 377–8.
  'of his disciples': *Cornhill* XLVI (1882), pp. 602–12, 'The Decay of
Literature'. On the relation between Carlyle and the Utilitarians see
E. E. Neff, *Carlyle and Mill* (New York 1924).
  'vehiculatory gear': T. Carlyle, *The Life of John Sterling* (1851), Ch. VIII.
  European thought: See E. R. Bentley, *The Cult of the Superman* (1947),
esp. Ch. 1–3.
  'the highest value': *Eng. Util.*, III, p. 477.

p. 173   **in historic phenomena:** *Edinburgh Review* LXXIX, Jan. 1844, pp. 1–31.
How much Mill was influenced by Comte may be judged by the fact

that he cited Larcher, Carlyle and Guizot as representing Comte's three stages in historiography.

Dorothea Krook: The four studies referred to are Basil Willey, *Nineteenth-Century Studies* (1949), pp. 141–86; F. R. Leavis, *Mill on Bentham and Coleridge* (1950), pp. 1–38; Raymond Williams, *Culture and Society 1780–1950* (1958), pp. 49–70; Dorothea Krook, *Three Traditions in Moral Thought* (1959), pp. 181–201. I have tried to mediate between the conflicting claims and criticisms of Mill's contributions in these books in an essay in *The English Mind*, ed. Hugh Sykes Davies and George Watson (1964), 'John Stuart Mill' by Noel Annan, pp. 219–39. Some of the arguments in that article are repeated here.

p. 174 **German thought and literature:** See *SB* II, pp. 35–70 for Stephen's research into 'the Importation of German' between 1760 and 1820.

'drowsy indifference': *Eng. Thought 18th Cent.*, I, p. 372.

Feuerbach: e.g. Rosemary Ashton, *The German Idea* (1980).

analysable way: *Political Theory* 10, Aug. 1982, pp. 333–4, Shirley Robin Letwin, 'Matthew Arnold, Enemy of Tradition'.

p. 175 **'an ass . . . poor Kant would be about':** *Life*, p. 172.

'his system': *Life of Sir JFS*, p. 123.

'Aristotle': *SE* I, p. 76.

'swear by': M. Carré, *Phases of Thought in England* (1949), p. 312, quoted from D. Masson, *Recent British Philosophy* (1867), p. 8. Cf. Thomas Hardy, *The Times* 21 May 1906, who says he knew Mill by heart as a young man.

p. 176 **'bang one another':** J. Locke, *Essay Concerning Human Understanding* (1690), IV, 17.6.

use for the syllogism: Cf. O. A. Kubitz, *Development of John Stuart Mill's System of Logic* (Illinois 1932) (Illinois Studies in the Social Sciences, XVIII).

p. 177 **'higher up':** *Letters of J. S. Mill*, ed. H. S. R. Elliot (1910), II, Appx A.

p. 178 **'escape our knowledge':** Locke, op. cit., I, 1.6, quoted by Carré, op. cit., p. 288.

'by ourselves': Locke, op. cit., II, 1.2.

p. 179 **'from within':** J. S. Mill, *System of Logic*, VI, 10.8. For a comparison of Comte's and Mill's positivism see T. Whittaker, *Reason and Other Essays* (1934), pp. 48–55. Stephen analyses the *System of Logic* with customary clarity in *Eng. Util.* III, pp. 75–157.

'inevitably lead to discovery': William Whewell, *Novum Organum Renovatum* (1855), p. 44, quoted by Shirley Robin Letwin, *The Pursuit of Certainty* (1965), p. 278.

from axioms in mathematics and logic: Whewell held that while numerous instances of cause and effect might prove the generality of an induction they could not prove its universal application: that could be achieved only by employing in Cartesian style the additional use of the necessary truths of arithmetic and geometry. Mill replied that geometry is never more than approximately true and that the truth of arithmetic depended on the convention that every unit is exactly the same size as every other which again in real life was not true. As regards geometry Mill was to receive support from contemporary mathematicians when non-Euclidian geometry penetrated to England;

as regards arithmetic, contemporary mathematical opinion was against him, cf. Kronecker's dictum: 'Integral numbers are made by God; everything else is the invention of man.' (Sir W. Dampier, *A History of Science* (4th edn, 1948), p. 465.) Mill appreciated that geometry, if studied as a branch of pure mathematics, must by hypothetical – it can be true only if studied as a branch of physics; but he did not realize that arithmetic is continuous with pure logic and independent of experience. Mill contradicted his own argument on number (contained in *Logic* III, 11, 14), in Ch. VII of the *Examination of Sir W. Hamilton's Philosophy*, curiously enough at the instance of a peculiarly fallacious argument by Fitzjames Stephen in his review of Mansel's metaphysics (republished in *Essay by a Barrister*). See an interesting note by C. E. Whitmore, 'Mill and Mathematics', *Journal of the History of Ideas* VI, Jan. 1945, pp. 109–12.

p. 180 'to accede to the new doctrines': Quoted by R. Wellek, *Immanuel Kant in England, 1793–1838* (1931), p. 26.

p. 181 'negative part of Kant': Ibid., pp. 134–5.
economic laws and moral obligation: Carré, op. cit., p. 341. For W. G. Ward see A. W. Brown, *The Metaphysical Society* (1947), pp. 56–9.
'more than Walpole himself': *Eng. Util.*, III, p. 381.

p. 182 'what is *me*?': M. Nédoncelle, *La Philosophie religieuse en Grande Bretagne de 1850 à nos jours* (Paris 1934), p. 35.
'with each other': H. L. Mansel, *The Limits of Religious Thought* (1858), p. 89.
fn. **Christian:** T. H. S. Escott, *Social Transformation of the Victorian Age* (1897), p. 398.
'un maître': Nédoncelle, op. cit., p. 36.
F. D. Maurice: The theological controversy between Mansel and Maurice is admirably discussed in *1859: Entering an Age of Crisis*, ed. P. Appleman, W. A. Madden and M. Wolff (Indiana 1959), pp. 63–80, 'The Limits of Religious Thought: the Theological Controversy' by R. V. Sampson.

p. 183 fingers: Nédoncelle, op. cit., p. 75, quoted from S. Pringle-Pattison, *Scottish Philosophy* (1885), p. 177.
'end of it': L. Huxley, *Life and Letters of T. H. Huxley* (1900), I, p. 202.
'I will go': J. S. Mill, *An Examination of Sir William Hamilton's Philosophy* (1878 edn), p. 129.
'defended': J. M. Keynes, Essays in Biography (1933), p. 163.

p. 184 dialectical whirligig: *Sketches*, p. 138.
clear the mind: See F. Pollock, *For My Grandson* (1931), p. 64, on disinterested Cambridge discussion.
fn. 'bees': J. Pope-Hennessy, *Monckton Milnes* (1949), I, p. 24.

p. 185 'polish': *Sketches*, p. 139.
humbug: *SB* II, pp. 126 ff.

p. 186 'opinions': Ibid. II, pp. 156–7.
old Fellow: E. Abbott and L. Campbell, *Life and Letters of Benjamin Jowett* (1897), II, p. 149.
'play-acting': C. Oman, *Memories of Victorian Oxford* (1941), p. 235.
politics: He snatched Arnold Toynbee from Pembroke ('Balliol, sir, is a kidnapping College.'), Abbott and Campbell, op. cit., p. 65.
'obstruction': Ibid., p. 213.

p. 187   **his day:** Part of Jowett's opposition to research was inspired by his mid-Victorian liberal hatred of sinecures.

'**hate learning!':** Ibid., p. 132.

'**merit':** Oman, op. cit., p. 234. Other interesting studies on Jowett, in addition to those cited *supra et infra* are A. C. Swinburne, *Studies in Prose and Poetry* (1894), A. M. Fairbairn in *Contemporary Review* LXXI, March 1897, and G. M. Young, *Daylight and Champaign* (1937).

'**masculine':** *SB* II, p. 124. Stephen often praised Jowett in his articles e.g. 'Jowett did more than any other to stimulate the intellect of the rising generation.' *Fraser's Magazine* II, Dec. 1870, p. 700.

'**early years':** Ibid., p. 157.

but sincere: See Stephen's admirable analysis of Jowett on the Atonement, ibid., pp. 134–5.

p. 188   '**a dodge':** Abbott and Campbell, op. cit., I, p. 131.

truth at all: Cf. A. H. Sayce, *Reminiscences* (1923), p. 87, who agrees with Stephen's judgement on Jowett. Jowett's remark that study for its own sake is a waste of time enraged Mark Pattison, who replied by describing Oxford as 'a lively municipal borough'.

'**them all':** *SB* II, p. 143. Jowett, Stephen argued, abandoned metaphysics on having remarked that they should be studied 'to enable the mind to get rid of them'. He based his defence of Christianity on common-sense rationalism and history; but he abandoned his base as soon as he had settled in and appealed to 'mystery'. He did not rely on Hegel or Coleridge or on old style intuitionism. So why should he complain when attacked by Christians who thought that he was sinking the ship or leading, in Carlyle's phrase, 'an exodus from Houndsditch'.

the stake: A. Birrell, *More Obiter Dicta* (1924), pp. 8–9.

'**a rope':** *Life*, p. 114.

p. 189   '**quite a genius':** Abbott and Campbell, op. cit., I, p. 342.

'**of roguery':** *SB* II, p. 153.

that God: *Ideas and Beliefs of the Victorians* ed. Harman Grisewood, (1949), pp. 403–9.

and fiction: *SB* II, p. 152. James Payn, *The Backwater of Life*, Introduction by L. Stephen, pp. xix–xx.

'**especial province':** E. Hodder, *Life and Work of the First Earl of Shaftesbury* (1886), III, p. 166.

'**not reason at all':** *SB* II, p. 282.

'**warm hearts':** Quoted from Marshall's Inaugural Lecture of 1885 by J. M. Keynes, op. cit., p. 255.

'**impartial enquiry':** *SB* III, p. 103.

fn. is serious: Cf. *Fraser's Magazine*, NS IX, June 1874, 'Mr Ruskin's Recent Writings' by L. Stephen. Huxley, too, took time off to defend classical economics and establish still more strongly his reputation for respectability. Cf. his article on Henry George, *Collected Essays* (1901), IX, pp. 147–87, 'Capital – the Mother of Labour'.

p. 190   '**other subjects':** *Sketches* pp. 32–3

'**my Father's':** T. Carlyle, *Sartor Resartus* Chapter IX.

'**in scientific form':** *Eng. Util.* II, p. 381.

CHAPTER SEVEN
THE RHETORIC OF TRUTH

p. 192   **pronunciation:** Charles Fourier, *Oeuvres Complètes* (1841–45), V, pp. 57–8, 158–62, quoted by Alexander Gray, *The Socialist Tradition* (1946), pp. 188–90.

p. 193   **Burdin:** R. Flint, *Philosophy of History* (1893), p. 585.
she died: Gordon S. Haight, *George Eliot* (1968), p. 546. See M. Quinn, *Memoirs of a Positivist* (1924), p. 38.
Positivist: *Life*, pp. 172, 352. Stephen probably had in mind the influence of the Wadham Positivists. Richard Congreve, the founder of Positivism in England, was a Fellow and Tutor of Wadham College and later leader of a set of Wadham men who were undergraduates in the later 1840s: Frederic Harrison; Edward Beesly, afterwards Professor of History at University College London, chairman of the First International and editor of the trade union newspaper, the *Beehive*; and J. H. Bridges, editor of Roger Bacon's *Opus Maius*. George Eliot and Meredith were active sympathizers, and Morley admitted that at one time he was not far off a formal union with the Positivist church (*Recollections* (1917), I, p. 69). Other adherents were Godfrey and Vernon Lushington, Henry Crompton, the Liverpool ship owner, J. K. Ingram, the Irish economist, Cotter Morison, the historian and Patrick Geddes, the scientist. But the faithful never numbered more than about three hundred and J. E. McGee, *A Crusade for Humanity* (1931), p. 184, almost certainly overestimates their following.

p. 194   **at all:** The opium analogy was used by the English Positivist, J. H. Bridges. See Basil Willey, *Nineteenth-Century Studies* (1949), p. 189, who regards Comte as a cultural aberration.

p. 195   **intelligentsia:** E. H. R. Pease, *History of the Fabian Society* (1925), p. 14.

p. 196   **'morality-intoxicated man':** J. S. Mill, *Auguste Comte and Positivism* (1865), p. 139. See 1975 edn, ed. Gertrud Lenzer, p. xl.
agnostic faith: Owen Chadwick, *The Victorian Church* (1966), p. 237.
'lose sight of them': *Fraser's Magazine* LXXX, Sept. 1869, p. 273.

p. 197   **explanation of the tendency:** 'An Attempted Philosophy of History', *Fortnightly Review*, NS XXXVII (1 May 1880), p. 695. See also *DNB* article on Buckle. See Giles St Aubyn, *A Victorian Eminence* (1958), a lively biography of Buckle.
'no explanation at all': Ibid., p. 691.
'day after tomorrow': Ibid., p. 673.

p. 198   *The Great Chain of Being:* Any summary, so short as that *infra*, of so influential a book must be inadequate. For a *résumé* of articles on pre-Darwinian evolutionary theories, see P. P. Wiener, *Evolution and the Founders of Pragmatism* (1949), p. 245.

p. 199   **fully perfected:** See Stephen on Pope's metaphysics, *HL* I, p. 122.

p. 200   **fn. its advocates:** L. Huxley, *Life and Letters of T. H. Huxley* (1900), I, pp. 168–71.

p. 201   **'non-scholastic meanings':** *Nation* XX, 4 March 1875, Chauncey Wright

'Sir Charles Lyell (1797–1875)' pp. 146–7.

fn. **men from apes:** A. W. Benn, *The History of English Rationalism in the Nineteenth Century* (1906), II, p. 167.

Immanence: See C. C. J. Webb, *A Study of Religious Thought in England from 1850* (1933) for an account of the Immanentist movement. In *Stones of Stumbling* (1893), pp. 207–27, Tollemache speaks of personal immortality not being literally true, but as being a process by which we are gathered back to God and *in* God.

'**or Sequence':** *The Education of Henry Adams* (1928), p. 231.

worthless?: For an excellent analysis of the teleological and mechanistic inferences in the *Origin of Species* see Gertrude Himmelfarb, *Darwin and the Darwinian Revolution* (1959), pp. 277–89, 320–39.

p. 202 *Omar Khayyám: 1859: Entering an Age of Crisis,* ed. Philip Appleman, W. A. Madden and M. Wolff (Indiana 1959), 'Science, Religion and the Critical Mind' by Noel Annan, pp. 31–50.

modern civilization: John Burrow, *Evolution and Society: A Study in Victorian Social Theory* (1966).

different religions: Cf. Evans Bell, *Task of Today* (1852), which compares the Bible and the Koran; and *A Was I Hind or A Voice from the Ganges* (anon.) (1861), which dilates on mistranslations in Scripture.

fn. **Eliza Lynn Linton:** G. S. Layard, *Mrs Lynn Linton: Her Life, Letters and Opinions* (1901), p. 36.

fn. **Darwin:** *Life and Letters of C. Darwin* (1887), I, Ch. 8, esp. pp. 307–8.

fn. **other creeds:** *EFP*, p. 98.

fn. '**anthropology':** L. Feuerbach, *The Essence of Christianity*, trans. Marian Evans (1881), p. 270.

p. 203 **coat changed:** *Fortnightly Review* 1880, op. cit., pp. 678–80.

both ways: T. H. Huxley, *Collected Essays* (1894) V, pp. 206, 303–8.

p. 204 **infidel attack:** Ibid., IV, p. 217.

'**be a science':** J. B. Bury, *Selected Essays*, ed. H. Temperley (1930), p. 33.

'**gewesen':** L. von Ranke, *Geschichte der romanischen und germanischen Völker von 1494 bis 1514* [Leipzig] (1874), Vorrede vii. The words were translated by G. P. Gooch as 'what actually occurred' in *History and Historians in the Nineteenth Century* (1913), and as 'events as they actually happened', in *Cambridge Modern History* XII, Ch. XXVI, p. 824. The famous phrase was coined as a protest against historians, such as Leo, who assigned to history 'the task of judging the past, of instructing the present for the benefit of the future'. See *The Times Literary Supplement*, Nos. 2519, 2521, 2522 of May–June 1950, in the last number of which Gooch supported his translation by arguing that Ranke's pictorial sense was so weak and, like most writers before 1848, his sociological interest so little developed, that it would be inappropriate to suggest that he had any feeling for what 'the past was really like'.

p. 205 **generalizations:** *Cambridge University Studies*, ed. Harold Wright (1933), 'History' by R. E. Balfour, pp. 186, 197.

disregard the question: N. H. Baynes, *Constantine the Great and the Christian Church* (1930), p. 9. Cf. *Journal of Theological Studies* I, pp. 24–37, 'Some Current Conceptions of Historiography and their Significance for Christian Apologetics' by N. Sykes for a discussion of this problem.

'rose to the occasion': F. W. Maitland, *Collected Papers*, III, p. 455, quoted by J. W. Burrow, *A Liberal Descent, Victorian Historians and the English Past* (1981), p. 119.

p. 206 **Germans and Englishmen:** Charles E. McClelland, *The German Historians and England* (1971), pp. 96–102. I have also consulted Eduard Fueter, *Geschichte der neueren Historiographie* (Munich, 1936); Friederich Meinecke, *Die Entstehung des Historismus* (Munich, 1936) and Klaus Dockhorn, *Der Deutsche Historismus in England* (Göttingen, 1949).

'pure and simple': *Eng. Util.*, III, p. 338.

'upon their history': Ibid., p. 339.

'convenient postulates': Ibid., p. 344.

Monophysite: J. H. Newman, *Apologia pro Vita Sua* (1864), Part V, p. 209.

p. 207 **where he stood:** Gertrude Himmelfarb, op. cit., p. 372, argues that Stephen was not converted dramatically by the publication of the *Origin* and cites the fact that he continued to remain a clergyman long after the date of 1862 when he resigned his tutorship. I have explained in Chapter One, p. 45, why I consider this view to be wrong. Perhaps Gertrude Himmelfarb was misled by J. M. Keynes, *Essays in Biography* (1933), pp. 161–2, where Keynes suggests that Mill's *Examination of Sir W. Hamilton's Philosophy* was the decisive factor in the loss of faith by James Ward, Alfred Marshall, Sidgwick and Leslie Stephen who in 1865 'was still an Anglican clergyman'. Technically Stephen still remained a clergyman until 1875, but Mill's book can have done no more than confirm him in his agnosticism. Maitland suggests that Stephen had not read Mill's *Logic* by 1855 when he was ordained deacon, and notes that Sir James Stephen had foreseen how 'dangerous' it was (*Life*, p. 135); but Stephen had certainly read it by 1859 when he was ordained priest.

Stephen admired Darwin, but, though he met him (*Life*, pp. 360, 488–9), was too modest and diffident to do more than make his acquaintance. Darwin did not know Stephen well enough to spell his name correctly when Stephen's article on the theological implications of his work appeared in *Fraser's Magazine* in 1871. Writing to Chauncey Wright, the American naturalist and philosopher, Darwin adds a postscript. 'Do you ever see *Fraser's Magazine*? There is a startling article on Divinity and Darwinism by, I suppose, Y. L. Stevens, who married one of the Miss Thackerays.' (*Journal of the History of Ideas* VI, 1945, p. 34, 'Chauncey Wright, Darwin and Scientific Neutrality', by P. P. Wiener.)

Stephen refers to the Wilberforce-Huxley debate in *SB* III. He also cited J. R. Green's intense indignation with Wilberforce in the *Letters of John Richard Green* (1901) which he edited. Green, who had been influenced by Ritualism as a youth and had taken Holy Orders with some misgivings, was just on his way to his first curacy under Mrs Humphry Ward's future father-in-law in the East End of London when it occurred. He followed Stanley's Broad Church party for a time but took the opportunity afforded by ill health (he had contracted tuberculosis) to resign his living in 1869 and, in order to avoid giving pain to his former friends, made no public avowal of his agnosticism (p. 71). He seems still to have been undecided for in 1871 he declared that he did not know until he had seen the Voysey judgment whether he would be able to take further preferment (p. 281). 'He seems to have thought that for a gentleman who openly denied the doctrine of the Trinity to be deprived of his living was an unjust or at least an injudicious restriction on clerical liberty' (Benn, op. cit., II, p. 345); at all events he broke with the Broad Church on this issue. In his *Short History of the English People* he affirmed his faith in mid-Victorian radicalism in bringing 'every custom and tradition, religious, intellectual and political, to the test of pure reason' (1889 edn, p. 605).

'atheistically': Appleman *et al.*, op. cit., 'Darwin and Clerical Orthodoxy' by Basil Willey, pp. 56–60. This essay should be set against Gertrude Himmelfarb's account of the reception of Darwin's book in Himmelfarb, op. cit., pp. 221–35.

ranks of the orthodox: Himmelfarb, op. cit., p. 252.

'the study is precluded': Randall Davidson and W. Benham, *Life of A. C. Tait* (1891), I, p. 291. The Vatican was in similar difficulties, see Owen Chadwick, *Catholicism and History: the opening of the Vatican archives* (1978).

p. 208   Draper: Chadwick, *The Secularization of the European Mind*, pp. 161–3.
p. 209   'all things proceed': A. W. Benn, op. cit., II, pp. 225–6.

was a God: Agnostics were divided on the question of whether to deify the Unknowable, cf. Huxley's remark to a friend, 'the more I think of it the more I am convinced that there must be something at the bottom of it all'. (George Forester, *The Faith of an Agnostic* (1902), p. 81.) Cf. L. Büchner's condemnation of agnostics, 'Faith in the Unknowable is the distinctive feature of Agnosticism,' (*Last Words on Materialism*, trans. J. McCabe (1901), pp. 116, 149) which Forester thinks is unfair. Büchner declared that absolute existence without manifestation was non-existence, but Forester maintained that there might be a manifestation unknown to us. Büchner's Force and Matter might be two sides of the same thing which we call God.

'active minds' at Oxford: Benn, op. cit., II, p. 66.

after publication: J. McCarthy, *Reminiscences* (1899), II, p. 325.

'the Resurrection': *Life of Sir JFS*, p. 213.

'superficial thinkers': H. T. Buckle, *History of Civilization* (1857), I, p. 694. Cf. *Fortnightly Review* NS XXVII, May 1874, pp. 672–95, in which Stephen censures Buckle for this remark. Nevertheless even Stephen did not go far enough for J. M. Robertson who criticizes this review in his work on Buckle. Stephen noted ruefully on the proof copy of his article, 'I think he may have found a blot or two'.

'as the universe': Benn, op. cit., II, p. 177.

go too far: G. Eliot, *Essays and Leaves from a Note-book* (1884), p. 201, quoted by Benn, op. cit., p. 247.

p. 210   'negative propagandism': J. W. Cross, Life and Letters of George Eliot (1885), II, pp. 343. Joan Bennett, *George Eliot, Her Mind and Her Art* (1948), Ch. IV, gives an excellent account of George Eliot's agnosticism.

publishing their opinions: M. Conway, *Autobiography* (1904), II, pp. 47–8. An account of the works of minor rationalists during the 1850s is given by T. H. Bastard, *Scepticism and Social Justice* (1877). They show how far the rationalists were on the defensive and what lines of advance they were exploring. See also A. W. Brown, *The Metaphysical Society* (New York, 1947), pp. 122–3.

'attacks upon theology': *Lettres inédites de John Stuart Mill à Auguste Comte*, ed. L. Lévy-Bruhl (1899), p. 307. Cf. pp. 403, 447. See *On Liberty* (1859), Ch. II, pp. 97–8, where Mill writes 'Opinions contrary to those commonly received can only obtain a hearing by studied moderation of language, and the most cautious avoidance of unnecessary offence, from which they hardly ever deviate, even in a slight degree, without losing ground', i.e. the interests of truth and justice demand restraint. This reticence led to a serious misunderstanding between Mill and Carlyle over the former's religious views: see *Letters of J. S. Mill*, ed. H. S. R. Elliot (1910), I, pp. 87–93.

'without having lived': J. S. Mill, *Three Essays on Religion* (1874), p. 119.

p. 211   **in his philosophy:** e.g. Gertrude Himmelfarb in her edition of *Essays on Politics and Culture by J. S. Mill* (New York, 1962). Shirley Robin Letwin, *The Pursuit of Certainty* (1965) is one of the best hostile accounts of Victorian rationalism. On J. S. Mill see pp. 203–318.

'precarious poises': G. M. Young, *Daylight and Champaign* (1937), p. 161.

p. 212   **'nor murder me':** 'Tendencies in Religious Thought in England 1688–1750' by Mark Pattison, p. 274, Quoted by J. W. Bicknell, *Diss.*

than they printed: A. W. Benn, *Modern England* (1908), pp. 326–7.

powder magazine: E. R. Brown, *Studies in the Text of Arnold's Prose* (1942), p. 23, quoted in J. W. Bicknell, 'The Neglected Band of Victorian Intellectual Historians' (dissertation), p. 24; John Morley, *On Compromise* (1874), p. 13.

p. 213   **Virchow:** W. Boelsche, *Haeckel, His Life and Work*, trans. J. McCabe (1906), pp. 145 and 171. Darwin was regarded in conservative scientific circles in Germany as an anarchist blowing up the work of a generation of careful classifiers, *vide* the speech of the Professor of Zoology at Göttingen at the scientific congress of 1863.

Blasphemy Laws: J. M. Robertson, *A Short History of Freethought* (1899), pp. 385–9, gives an account of the major prosecutions.

honest beliefs: *Life and Letters of T. H. Huxley*, II, p. 343. Max Müller, delivering a Hibbert lecture entitled 'Atheism a Spectre' before Dean Stanley in the Jerusalem Chamber at Westminster Abbey, drew a distinction between religious and vulgar atheism. Vulgar atheists baited priests. M. Conway, op. cit., II, p. 365.

Herbert Spencer: S. Dark and R. S. Essex, *The War against God* (1937), p. 73.

p. 214   **and Eliza Lynn Linton:** G. S. Layard, op. cit., pp. 243, 334–46.

fn. **'credulous nature':** Ibid., p. 202.

it's blasphemy: *SB* III, pp. 202–4.

p. 215   **pledging their faith in them:** Walter E. Houghton, *The Victorian Frame of Mind 1830–1870* (1957), pp. 101–2.

p. 216   **'opposed to truth':** *The Bridgewater Treatises* (1836), W. Buckland, 'Geology and Mineralogy', I, p. 595. The same tribute to truth was paid by the father of the historical movement in Germany. Niebuhr, who declared that his researches into Roman history had been helped by his studies of the 'New Rome', Great Britain, wrote, 'In laying down the pen we must be able to say in the sight of God, "I have not knowingly nor without earnest investigation written anything which is not true."' (G. P. Gooch, *History and Historians . . .* , op. cit., p. 19.)

'reflected on by ourselves': J. Locke, *Essay Concerning Human Understanding* (1690), II, 1.2.

p. 217   **'but whether it is *true*':** *Fortnightly Review* XIV, Dec. 1873, pp. 741–2. F. W. Newman was reviewing the 3rd edition of Greg's *The Creed of Christendom*.

'such and such to be true': *Life and Letters of T. H. Huxley*, I, p. 217.

'take it off me': T. H. Huxley, *Collected Essays* (1894), I, p. 192. Cf. W. McNeile Dixon, *The Human Situation* (1942), p. 342.

'cling to error': Cross, op. cit., I, p. 103.

The Ethics of Belief: W. K. Clifford, *Lectures and Essays* (1901), II, pp. 163–205.

p. 218   **'to whatever conclusions it may lead':** J. S. Mill, *On Liberty*, Ch. II, p. 62.

'is prepared to act': A. Bain, *The Senses and the Intellect* (4th edition, 1894), pp. 356–8. See M. Carré, *Phases of Thought in England* (1949), pp. 316–17, who explains this point in greater detail.

'intellectually sustainable': Basil Willey, op. cit., p. 281.

p. 219   **'usurped domination':** Cross, op. cit., I, p. 106. George Eliot told Jowett that she was never a Comtist but as they were a poor unfortunate sect she would never renounce them. (E. Abbott and L. Campbell, *Life and Letters of Benjamin Jowett* (1897), II, p. 182.) She continued to subscribe to Positivist funds until her death.

'cardinal virtues': *Life and Letters of T. H. Huxley*, I, p. 358.

'much profit!': Ibid., p. 217. Cf. Carlyle, *Frederick the Great* (Complete Works, 1897–1901, VIII), p. 240. 'The vital all-essential point, what we may call the heart's core of all Creeds which are human, human and not simian or diabolic . . . that it is not allowable, that it is dangerous and abominable, to attempt believing what is not true.'

Even Jowett approved of a lady who wrote to him saying, 'We Liberals should not talk about Freedom, but about truth – that is the flag under which to fight.' (Abbott and Campbell, op. cit., I, p. 299.)

p. 220   **proved more convenient:** Clifford, op. cit. II, 'The Philosophy of the Pure Sciences', pp. 301–409.

'respectively found': J. H. Newman, *Sermons chiefly on the Theory of Religious Belief* (1844), pp. 350–51. AA, pp. 179–80. J. A. Froude, *Nemesis of Faith* (1904), p. 172.

alive to this problem: See A. W. Brown, *The Metaphysical Society* (1947), pp. 85–90, for an analysis of Pattison's paper.

'pursuing any great enquiry': SB III, p. 196. Note the revolt of Henry Adams against this devotion to truth by the Darwinists. He wrote of himself in the 1860s: 'Henry Adams was one of the first of an infinite series to discover and admit to himself that he did not care whether truth was, or was not, true. He did not even care that it should be proved true, unless the process were new and amusing. He was a Darwinian for fun.' *The Education of Henry Adams* (1928), pp. 231–2.

390

LESLIE STEPHEN

CHAPTER EIGHT
THE REVELATION OF THE EIGHTEENTH CENTURY

p. 221 'circumstances': T. Carlyle, *History of Friedrich II of Prussia, called Frederick the Great* (1858–65), I, pp. 11–12.

p. 222 on equal terms with men: See Mark Girouard, *Sweetness and Light: the 'Queen Anne' Movement 1860–1900* (1977).
'loathsome': W. E. H. Lecky, *The Rise of the Spirit of Rationalism in Europe* (1865), II, pp. 71–2, quoted by John W. Bicknell, 'The Neglected Band of Victorian Intellectual Historians' (dissertation). For other studies see Oscar Maurer, *Texas University Studies in English* (1944), 'Pope and the Victorians', pp. 211–39.
all twelve: See the review in the *Athenaeum*, 25 Nov. 1876, p. 682.
destroyed by Hume: J. W. Bicknell, *Diss* (Cornell 1950).
Hoadly: Raymond Mortimer, *Channel Packet* (1942), p. 194.

p. 223 'spirit of bigotry': *Eng. Thought 18th Cent.*, II, p. 153.
'bludgeon': Ibid., I, pp. 345–7.
'pointed weapons': Ibid., I, p. 157. See Bicknell, op. cit., pp. 186–203.
'Strawberry Hill': *Eng. Thought 18th Cent.*, II, p. 170.
'cynical levity': Ibid., II, p. 40.

p. 224 'the prize': Ibid., I, p. 411. Bicknell cites an article by the Rev John Hunt as characteristic of orthodox reaction: op. cit., pp. 249 ff.
virtuous impulses: Ibid., II, p. 16.
'least expect it': Ibid., II, p. 119.
intolerably dull: *Fraser's Magazine*, NS V (1872), p. 683, quoted by Bicknell, *Diss*. op. cit., pp. 136 ff.
fight in fetters: Bicknell, op. cit., pp. 203–11.
'evils of human life': *Eng. Thought 18th Cent.* I, p. 170.

p. 225 shallow Deists lacked: Bicknell notes that Butler's argument from faith, which made him a favourite of Newman and the Tractarians, so alarmed the dons that Whewell substituted Paley for Butler as a set book in the Littlego in 1838; and Pattison followed suit at Oxford in 1860 (Mark Pattison, *Memoirs*, (1885) pp. 134–5). Bicknell, op. cit., p. 218.
'Swift': *Eng. Thought 18th Cent.*, II, p. 376.
'human intelligence': Ibid., I, p. 342.

p. 226 'inequality of property': Cf. Neal Wood, *The Politics of Locke's Philosophy* (California, 1983), pp. 143–8, 158–60.
'"puling jargon"': *Eng. Thought 18th Cent.*, II, pp. 63–4, 264.
'brutalise mankind': T. Paine, *The Age of Reason* (1793), I, p. 13.
'professor of divinity': *Eng. Thought 18th Cent.*, I, p. 464.
'very amusing luxury': Ibid., p. 437.

p. 227 he in fact wrote: John W. Bicknell, 'Leslie Stephen's "English Thought in the Eighteenth Century": A Tract for the Times', *Victorian Studies* VI (Dec. 1962).
notable example: G. H. Sabine, *History of Political Thought* (1937).
'phases of opinion': *Eng. Thought 18th Cent.*, I, p. 13.

p. 228 'element of truth' . . . 'spiral curve': Ibid., I, p. 3.
'its being into bounds': Tennyson, *In Memoriam*, Epilogue.
'speculative activity': *English Thought 18th Cent.*, I, p. 2.

p. 229 'attempts at explanation': Ibid., II, p. 330.
'broke down': Ibid., II, pp. 382–3.
modes of thought: Bicknell, *Diss.* p. 430.
'intellectual candour': *Eng. Thought 18th Cent.*, I, p. 9.
'a conflict': Ibid., I, pp. 4–5.

p. 230 'commercial activity': Ibid., I, p. 13.
to the laity: *Lit. and Soc. 18th Cent.*, pp. 106–8.
'eighteenth': Bicknell, *Victorian Studies*, op. cit., pp. 112–13.
'in the face': *EFP*, pp. 270–74, quoted by Bicknell, op. cit., p. 115.

p. 231 'determines their consciousness': Karl Marx, *Introduction to the Critique of Political Economy*.
'adversaries or allies': *Mind*, (1876) II, p. 366. Bicknell summarizes the reviews in *Diss.* (Cornell 1950), pp. 435–57.

p. 232 'with insolence': J. M. Robertson, *The Dynamics of Religion* (1926), pp. 62–3. But see his *A History of Freethought in the 19th Century* (1929), p. 406.
'I humbly admit': Letter from LS to Mark Pattison, 2 Dec. 1876, Bodleian.
where is Dalton?: Not only Robertson but Bicknell too makes this point (Bicknell, *Diss.*, p. 458). John Theodore Merz. *A History of European Thought in the Nineteenth Century* (1914), 4 vols.
'very superficial': *Life*, p. 282.
'insoluble': T. H. Huxley, *Collected Essays* (1894), V. pp. 238–40. Huxley came to define agnosticism, however, as no more than a method of thought, i.e. empirical enquiry. It 'is not a creed but a method. . . . Positively the principle may be expressed: In matters of the intellect, follow your reason as far as it will take you, without regard to any other consideration. And negatively: In matters of the intellect do not pretend that conclusions are certain which are not demonstrated or demonstrable. That I take to be the agnostic faith, which if a man keep whole and undefiled, he shall not be ashamed to look the universe in the face, whatever the future may have in store for him.' (Ibid., pp. 245–7.)
R. C. Churchill in *English Literature and the Agnostic* (1944) claimed (pp. 17–18) Shakespeare, Jonson, Dryden, Swift, Pope, Fielding, Gibbon, Burke, Coleridge, Wordsworth, Burns, Peacock, Lamb, Byron, Hunt, de Quincey, Hazlitt, Keats, Shelley, Arnold, Mark Rutherford and Jefferies as agnostics. Only the last-named qualifies. This is sheer idiocy: to use the term agnostic in this fashion is to make a useful word meaningless.

p. 233 too many things: Huxley, op. cit., V, pp. 238, 245–8, 313–34. Huxley admitted he did not like saying that anything was unknowable.
'told for most': A. W. Benn, *The History of English Rationalism in the Nineteenth Century* (1906), II, p. 386.
fn. 'masks': Ibid., II, p. 356.
fn. 'Seraglio': Quoted by W. Staebler, *The Liberal Mind of John Morley* (Princeton 1943), p. 48. Cf. W. K. Clifford, *Lectures and Essays* (1901), II, p. 237. 'I can find no evidence that seriously militates

against the rule that the priest is at all times and in all places the
enemy of all men.' I have not included Clifford among the agnostics.
He should be classed as an atheist. He looked to the day when we
should have as good evidence for the non-existence of God as we have
now for the non-existence of a large planet between the earth and
Venus; he also prognosticated that physiology would prove the
existence of 'mind-stuff' and so end the dichotomy between mind and
matter. But Clifford also believed in something he called 'cosmic
emotion', and Morley thought some religion of some kind was a
necessary postulate for human happiness.

CHAPTER NINE
AGNOSTICISM

p. 234 **'knew you lied'**: L. P. Wilkinson, *A Century of King's 1873–1972* (1980),
p. 10.
discuss the matter further: G. M. Trevelyan, *Autobiography of an
Historian* (1949), p. 9. See Humphrey Trevelyan, *Public and Private*
(1980), p. 150.
Agnostic's Apology: From a conversation with the author. Trevelyan
enormously admired Stephen and in his young days joined the Sunday
Tramps.

p. 235 **'black beetle'**: *AA*, p. 5.
appeared to us unjust: Cf. Stephen's reply to an article by Gladstone who
criticized his writing on Butler. See Gladstone's article in *Nineteenth
Century* XXXVIII, Nov. 1895, pp. 715–39, and XXXIX, Jan. 1896,
pp. 106–22, for Stephen's reply.
'his ignorance': *AA*, p. 41.
not astonish us: Stephen noted A. J. Balfour's admission, 'I do not suggest
that the doctrine of the Incarnation supplies any philosophical solution
of [the problem of evil in the world]', and annotated his copy of the
Foundations of Belief with the sardonic word 'Modest'. Stephen's copy
of Balfour's book is to be found in the London Library where he
succeeded Tennyson as President in 1892.
man's final end: *AA*, 'Dreams and Realities', pp. 86–126.

p. 236 **beasts of the field**: Ibid., p. 98.
such a belief: Stephen had no love for Farrar, and writing to Norton on
the death of Dean Stanley, for which he expressed real regret, said that
he feared Farrar would be the next Dean of Westminster since he 'is
just the man to impose upon a rhetorician like Gladstone'. (LS to C. E.
Norton, 26 July 1881, Harvard.)
'don't envy you': *Life of Sir JFS*, p. 84.
fn. 'fond of me': LS to C. E. Norton, 16 Nov. 1873, Harvard; cf. *Letters
of C. E. Norton* ed. S. A. Norton and Howe (1913), II, p. 19.

p. 237 **parent of intolerance**: *AA* 'Poisonous Opinions', pp. 242–337.
'now is admitted': *AA*, p. 274.

'immoral nature': J. H. Newman, *Essay on Development* (1878), p. 357. could be demonstrated: *EFP*, p. 352.

most nineteenth century states: Owen Chadwick, *The Secularization of the European Mind in the Nineteenth Century* (1975), pp. 21–3.

p. 238   'for ever?': Quoted by Geoffrey Rowell, *Hell and the Victorians* (1974), p. 9. 'The Recognition of Friends in Heaven: a Symposium' (1866), p. 112.

souls would be saved: Ibid., p. 16.

kept by him: Ibid., pp. 188–9. James Stephen, *Essays in Ecclesiastical Biography* (1853), II, pp. 502–3.

p. 239   to concern theologians: Ibid., p. 3. W. E. Gladstone, *Studies Subsidiary to the Works of Bishop Butler* (1896), pp. 199–201.

'unless it dies': T. H. Huxley, 'The Physical Basis of Life', *Fortnightly Review*, Feb. 1869, reprinted in *Lay Sermons* (1880).

p. 240   'sense of responsibility': L. Huxley, *Life and Letters of T. H. Huxley* (1900), I, p. 220, reviewed by Stephen in *Nineteenth Century* XLVIII, December 1900, pp. 905–18, reprinted in *SB* III, pp. 188–219. Stephen refers to the letter to Kingsley in *SB* III, p. 212.

'a graveside': Owen Chadwick, op. cit., p. 260.

'nothing happens': *AA*, p. 152 *passim*.

commonly supposed: *SRD* II, pp. 208–23.

p. 241   'open eyes': *AA*, pp. 91–2.

p. 242   'leave the matter so': F. H. Bradley, *Appearance and Reality* (1916 edn), pp. 501–9.

'into a proof': Ibid., fn. p. 509.

pons asinorum of metaphysics: Berkeley of course. The first paper on 12 June 1877 was on 'Belief and Evidence', and the second on 11 March 1879 on 'The Uniformity of Nature'. The one argues that although false beliefs may satisfy those who act on them, we must not let our assent outrun evidence, for that would create a dangerous precedent; the other that we cannot conceive nature to be anything but uniform or we would be faced with a negation of thought. See A. W. Brown, *The Metaphysical Society* (New York 1947), pp. 135–6, 221–3, 333, 335.

'hair-splitting': *Life*, p. 417. The quotation is to be found in *AA*, p. 309.

p. 243   'omnipotence of God': *Life of Sir JFS*, p. 73.

'effeminate natures': *EFP*, p. 7.

'the difficulty disappears': Ibid., p. 51.

'statements of fact': Ibid., p. 48.

'beyond human solution': J. H. Newman, *Apologia pro Vita Sua* (1864), p. 378.

'is faith': J. H. Newman, *Grammar of Assent* (1889), pp. 94–5. *Eng. Util.*, III, p. 495. *AA*, p. 223.

'intellectually wrong': *Eng. Util.*, III, p. 496 *et seq.* Perhaps the best contemporary answer to Stephen on Newman's theory of belief is R. H. Hutton, *Cardinal Newman* (1891), Ch. V. Stephen's analysis of Newman's thought is fully considered in Regina Tangl, *Leslie Stephens Weltanschauung* (1961) (unpublished doctoral dissertation at the University of Hamburg), pp. 54–111.

p. 244   fiery pamphlets: Two good examples of Coulton's dialectic are *St. Thomas Aquinas on the Elect and the Reprobate* (1927) and *Infant Perdition in the Middle Ages* (1922).

'inability to be obscure': *EFP*, p. 37.

sincerity: Ibid., 'The Broad Church', pp. 7, 26. C. E. Raven, *Christian Socialism* (1920), p. 81, complained that Stephen accused F. D. Maurice and Broad Churchmen of being cheats. This did not do justice to Stephen's constant attempt to acknowledge the sincerity of the Broad Church and at the same time make his point that they were (unconsciously) deceiving themselves intellectually and morally.

'a very different thing': Ibid., p. 40.

p. 245   F. D. Maurice: For this passage, I have drawn on A. R. Vidler, *Witness to the Light* (New York 1948); H. G. Wood, *F. D. Maurice* (1950); *Victorian Studies* III, March 1960, pp. 227–48, 'F. D. Maurice and the Victorian Crisis of Belief' by Olive Brose; and Philip Appleman *et al.* (ed.), *1859: Entering an Age of Crisis* (Indiana 1959), pp. 63–80, 'The Limits of Religious Thought: the Theological Controversy' by R. V. Sampson.

a good *position*: Quoted by Vidler, op. cit., p. 208, from *The Kingdom of Christ* (Everyman edn), II, p. 329.

the Head: Ibid., p. 52.

contemporaries in the Church: See Vidler, op. cit., pp. 1–5; and Wood, op. cit., pp. 1–12, for diverse contemporary opinion on Maurice's teaching.

'the old mould': *EFP*, p. 20. Cf. C. R. Sanders, 'Sir Leslie Stephen, Coleridge and Two Coleridgeans', *PMLA* LV, Sept. 1940, in which Stephen's references to F. D. Maurice are collected. See also *Fortnightly Review*, NS XV, May 1874, pp. 595–617, 'Mr Maurice's Theology', by L. Stephen; and *Eng. Util.*, III, pp. 453–62. *Life*, pp. 240–41.

forbade the banns: *Life of Sir JFS*, p. 127.

p. 246   Maurice's life: C. E. Raven, op. cit., p. 77 fn.

'than intelligible': *SEI*, p. 66.

'from the Eternal': *Fortnightly Review*, op. cit., pp. 614–15.

'merely': Wood, op. cit., p. 100, comments that this word shows the great gap between the two minds.

the Larger Hope: Cf. Hallam Tennyson, *Tennyson, A Memoir* (1897), I, p. 322, in which Tennyson expresses disappointment that the translation of the Revised Version had not changed 'everlasting' into 'aeonian' or some such word.

fn. Prince of this world: *Fortnightly Review*, op. cit., pp. 606–7, 609. Wood, op. cit., pp. 102–4: a most scrupulous assessment of the worth of Stephen's criticism will be found at pp. 77–128 which, though it naturally differs from mine, treats Stephen honestly.

'mode of thinking': *Fortnightly Review*, op. cit., p. 610.

'highest of them': *Life of F. D. Maurice*, ed. Frederick Maurice (1883–4), II, p. 15, quoted by Wood, op. cit., p. 29.

p. 247   'to swallow': *EFP*, p. 152.

'conjectural preterite': *Fortnightly Review*, op. cit., p. 605.

'high-minded clergyman': Ibid., p. 615.

p. 248   fact and reality: See *Cambridge Journal* II, Feb. 1949, pp. 288–300, 'Some Reflections on a Contemporary Problem Raised by Science and Religion', by I. T. Ramsey, which puts the anti-positivist view clearly, though I think it to be misleading in its sketch of nineteenth-century historiography.

only ascertainable truth: On form criticism I have found M. Dibelius, *From Tradition to Gospel*, trans. B. L. Woolf (1934), most helpful; also B. M. Easton, *The Gospel before the Gospel* (New York 1928), and A. Schweitzer, *The Quest of the Historical Jesus*, trans. W. Montgomery (1910).

p. 249   the will exist?: J. Tyndall, *Fragments of Science* (1899), p. 191. For Ward's argument see A. W. Brown, op. cit., pp. 56–9.

p. 250   'right of way': R. B. Perry, *The Thought and Character of William James* (1936), II, pp. 246–7.

'find no use': William James, *The Will to Believe and Other Essays in Popular Philosophy* (1897), pp. 10–11.

'space and time': Ibid., p. 270. See Jacques Barzun, *A Stroll With William James* (1983), pp. 83–108 for some wise reflections on pragmatism and truth.

fn. of the community: T. Veblen, *The Theory of the Leisure Class* (1899), pp. 297–8.

'which one it shall be': W. James, op. cit., pp. 94–5, fn.

Agnostic Annual: This periodical was edited by Charles Watts from the 'Propaganda' of Rationalism at Johnson's Court in 1884. Most of the articles are of an inconceivable dullness; the best are by F. J. Gould, G. R. Bithell, Edward Clodd and J. McCabe. Stephen in his review reiterates his thesis that our intellect and not our will disposes us to believe one way or another. He defended Clifford against James's charge that he was more eager to avoid error than find truth by claiming that Clifford merely held that certain hypotheses explain facts better than their rivals and of these we should take notice. Of course, Clifford went far further than this. James and Stephen also diverged on the nature of fact. James, echoing Feuerbach, found that faith created facts and that a sceptic should deny only the worth of the facts of Christianity. Stephen asserted that so far as religion depended on assertions of fact it was clear that the facts were not dependent on our wishes but on logic.

'out of moonshine': *Life*, p. 445. In the same letter to C. E. Norton there is a characteristic comment by Stephen on Santayana, which Maitland excluded. Stephen detected an illogicality in Santayana, who had said that nothing is objectively impressive. 'How the devil should it be? Nothing impresses which does not impress.'

'frame of mind': LS to William James, 15 Feb. 1898, Harvard.

p. 251   peace and joy: M. Arnold, *Literature and Dogma* (1893), Ch. X, Section 3, p. 185.

p. 252   accompanied righteousness: Ibid., Ch. XII, Section 4, p. 224. See Dorothea Krook, *Three Traditions of Moral Thought* (1959), Ch. VIII.

'help in trouble': M. Arnold, op. cit., p. 31.

a good deal more: F. H. Bradley, *Ethical Studies* (1927, 2nd edn), pp. 317–18 fn. Both Stephen and James Martineau (*An Ideal Substitute for God* (1978), pp. 8–12, 24–5; and *SB*, II, p. 312) were on to this point. By far the best account of Arnold's religious views is, of course, Lionel Trilling, *Matthew Arnold* (1949), pp. 317–68, which meets many of the points Stephen raised.

'catch it': *SB*, II, p. 120. R. H. Hutton took the same line as Stephen upon Arnold's religion from a Christian standpoint in *Contemporary*

Thought and Thinkers (1894), I, p. 217, 'Mr. Arnold must choose between two alternatives. He must evaporate the whole . . . or he must take the personal language about God as straightforwardly as he takes the moral language about man. It is not criticism at all, it is playing fast and loose with language in the most ridiculous manner, to regard the long series of passionate appeals to God . . . as mere effort of poetry while all the words describing the moral conceptions of men are interpreted with scientific strictness'; see *PMLA* LVI, 1941, 'R. H. Hutton' by Gaylord C. Le Roy, for a useful article on Hutton's criticism.

p. 253 'valid ones': G. Hough, *The Last Romantics* (1949), p. 136. Cf. G. M. Young, *Daylight and Champaign* (1937), p. 250.

'in the world': M. Arnold, *On Translating Homer, Last Words* (1862), p. 10.

'special prejudice': *SB*, II, pp. 95–6 seq.

sustained Stephen's agnosticism: Frank Miller Turner, *Between Science and Religion* (Yale 1974).

p. 254 *Dictionnaire Philosophique*: Floyd Clyde Tolleson, 'The Relation between Leslie Stephen's Agnosticism and Voltaire's Deism', *Dissertation Abstracts* XV (1955), pp. 2218–19. In his criticism of Voltaire, Stephen followed his brother. 'It is perfectly obvious to every competent observer that to treat religious controversies with the contempt which Voltaire on all occasions displayed for them, is merely to show ignorance and shallowness.' *Horae Sabbaticae* (1892), II, p. 240.

p. 255 'more rational': *AA*, p. 241.

by clergymen: H. Sidgwick, *Practical Ethics* (1898), pp. 142–77. Morley took Stephen's line on this matter; cf. *On Compromise* (1874), pp. 72–6.

p. 256 'to deny it': Paul Tillich, *Systematic Theology* (1953), I, p. 263.

come to judgement: *Religion and Culture*, ed. Walter Leibrecht (New York 1959), pp. 3, 35.

through a glass darkly: Appleman et al., (ed.), op. cit., 'Science, Religion and the Critical Mind' by Noel Annan, p. 50.

p. 257 struggle for salvation: A. O. J. Cockshut, *The Unbelievers* (1964), p. 95.

p. 258 'spiritual narcotics': *AA*, pp. 159, 167.

p. 259 declined in importance: Bryan R. Wilson, *Religion in Secular Society* (1966).

had any force: Michael Hill, *A Sociology of Religion* (1973), pp. 232–3.

p. 260 a form of advertising: *Journal of Religion* XLV, 1965, 'Towards a Theory of Secularization' by Larry Shiner, pp. 279–95.

retreated from the world: Roland Robertson, *The Sociological Interpretation of Religion* (1970); *American Sociological Review*, 29 June 1964, 'Religious Evolution' by Robert N. Bellah, pp. 358–74.

'never before achieved': Max Weber, *The Protestant Ethic and the Spirit of Capitalism* (1930), p. 182, quoted in Michael Hill, op. cit., p. 245.

others followed: Vernon Pratt, *Religion and Secularization* (1970).

its goals: A. McIntyre, *Secularization and Moral Change* (1967).

single cause: Michael Hill, op. cit., p. 263.

p. 262 hold over men and women: *AA*, pp. 194–203, 234–9. Algernon Cecil, *Six Oxford Thinkers* (1909), pp. 83–4, makes the point that Stephen always assumed that what was fittest to survive was necessarily the best.

'organised impostures': *The Nineteenth Century: a Review of Progress* (1901), 'Evolution and Religious Conceptions' by L. Stephen, p. 380.

p. 263 'sociology is false': *Frontier II* (1959), pp. 8–13, 'An Agnostic Looks at the Church' by Norman Birnbaum.

'in mortal eyes': W. Pater, *Essays from 'The Guardian'* (1905), p. 69, quoted by G. Hough, op. cit., p. 155.

p. 264 'abêtira': *SB*, II, p. 277. Arnold in the preface to *God and the Bible* (1875), p. xii, exclaims about this phrase, 'Did ever a great reasoner reason so madly?'

'our highest interests': *SB*, II, p. 281.

'higher elements': Ibid., p. 284; cf. *AA*, pp. 338–80, *EFP*, pp. 360–62.

p. 265 'if possible': *Life*, pp. 144–5.

'and self-indulgent': G. R. Bithell, *The Creed of a Modern Agnostic* (1883), p. 147, where he quotes a pamphlet by the Rev. Noah Porter entitled 'Agnosticism: a Doctrine of Despair'.

'they shall confess it!': *The Amberley Papers*, ed. Bertrand and Patricia Russell (1937), I, p. 341.

'renounced his': J. W. Cross, *Life and Letters of George Eliot* (1885), III, p. 214.

'tried to dissuade me!': G. S. Layard, *Mrs Lynn Linton: Her Life, Letters and Opinions* (1901), p. 87.

'name for such places': Cross, op. cit., III, p. 170. Cf. Esther, sister of F. D. Maurice, rejoicing in the fact that some children who had been kept by their parents from going to church for fear of catching measles, had succumbed. 'I am *very glad* they are so ill; it is a well-deserved punishment.' Augustus Hare, *Story of My Life* (1896), I, pp. 202–3.

p. 266 'brother or sister': F. Harrison, *The Creed of a Layman* (1908), p. 89. Cf. W. K. Clifford, *Lectures and Essays* (1901), II, p. 169, 'An awful privilege, an awful responsibility, that we should help to create a world in which posterity will live.' Arnold and Morley admired Turgot for being 'filled with an astonished, awful, oppressive sense of the *immoral thoughtlessness* of men; of the heedless, hazardous way in which they deal with things of the greatest moment to them; of the immense incalculable misery which is due to this cause'. J. Morley, *Biographical Studies* (1923), p. 90. The responsibility for their utterances hung just as heavily upon those who had abandoned their faith as on Christians. Cf. Francis Newman, 'It is a sad thing to have printed erroneous fact. I have three or four times contradicted and renounced the passage . . . *but I cannot reach those I have misled.*' (F. N. Sieveking, *Francis Newman* (1909), p. 342.) What is this but an echo of his brother? 'A man publishes an irreligious or immoral book, afterwards he repents and dies. . . . Shall *he* be now dwelling in Abraham's bosom, who hears on the other side of the gulf the voice of those who curse his memory as being the victims of his guilt?' (5th University Sermon, 'On Justice as a Principle of Divine Governance'. Quoted by G. W. Faber, *Oxford Apostles* (1936), p. 260.

'more happy': R. Jefferies, *The Story of My Heart* (1883), p. 120.

than for God's: W. H. Mallock, *New Republic* (1877), Bk. I, Ch. IV, p. 83.

'efficient citizen': W. K. Clifford, op. cit., II, p. 94.

398   LESLIE STEPHEN

CHAPTER TEN
THE MORAL SOCIETY

p. 268   **in which they found themselves?**: See Michel Foucault, *Histoire de la Folie à l'Age Classique* (Paris 1972) and R. D. Laing and A. Esterson, *Sanity, Madness and the Family* (1965) for an expression of this point of view. See also the critique by Lawrence Stone, *New York Review of Books* 16 Dec. 1982 and the subsequent exchange between Foucault and Stone in the issue of 31 March 1983.
            helped them to do so: F. M. L. Thompson, 'Social Control in Victorian Britain', *Econ. Hist. Rev.* XXXIV, May 1981, pp. 189–208.
p. 269   **'the *rights of labour*'**: Charles Kingsley, 'Letters to Chartists', *Politics for the People* (1848), 27 May 1848, p. 58 and 17 June 1848, pp. 136–7.
            'everlasting happiness': W. Paley, *Moral and Political Philosophy*, Bk I, Ch. VII (*Coll. Works*, 1838, III, p. 20).
            de Maistre: I am indebted to Isaiah Berlin for letting me see his unpublished lecture on de Maistre.
p. 270   **the sea of events**: See A. J. Booth, *Saint-Simon and Saint-Simonism* (1871), pp. 85–233, which gives a spirited account of the movement. Cf. Alexander Gray, *The Socialist Tradition* (1946), pp. 160–8.
            resist the challenge: J. S. Mill, *Auguste Comte and Positivism* (1865), pp. 139–40.
            in every detail: Booth, op. cit., p. 78. Cf. *The Essential Comte*, ed. Stanislav Andrevski (1974), pp. 7–8.
p. 271   **'on a white ground'**: Mill, op. cit., p. 194.
p. 272   **'the common good'**: A. Comte, *Catechism of Positivist Religion*, trans. by R. Congreve (1858), p. 74.
            and Progress: Ibid., p. 143.
            'Positivist Religion': Mill, op. cit., pp. 154–5.
p. 273   **'extirpation'**: L. Huxley, *Life and Letters of T. H. Huxley* (1900), II, p. 306.
            brother or sister: Frederic Harrison, *The Creed of a Layman* (1908), p. 89.
            the moral code: J. F. Stephen, *Liberty, Equality, Fraternity* (1873), p. 131 and pp. 158–88. Cf. B. Lippincott, *Victorian Critics of Democracy* (1938), pp. 134–66.
p. 274   **Machiavelli**: See Machiavelli, *Discourses on the First Decade of Titus Livius*, Bk I, Ch. 12, for a disquisition on the utility of religion.
            Hobbes: Fitzjames Stephen's essay on Hobbes in *Horae Sabbaticae* (1892), II, pp. 1–54, is more illuminating than Leslie's book on Hobbes in the English Men of Letters Series: Fitzjames had studied philosophic conservatism – see the essays on de Maistre in the third volume.
            'made and then worshipped': *Life and Letters of T. H. Huxley*, I, p. 301.
            that restraint: *Liberty, Equality, Fraternity*, p. 182.
            fn. he was unjust: Ibid., p. 122.
            fn. 'social legislation': B. Webb, *My Apprenticeship* (1929), p. 145.
p. 275   **realized**: Mill, *Speech on Perfectibility* (1828), reprinted in OUP World's

Classics edition of *Autobiography* (1924), p. 290. Huxley was at one
with Fitzjames: he thought it monstrous to dangle the prospect of
perfectibility in the face of mankind when they lived within a solar
system in which life would for certain be extinguished according to the
second law of thermodynamics. (*Collected Essays* (1894), IX, p. 44.)
and to each other: *Essays by a Barrister* (by J. F. Stephen) (1862), pp.
318–19.
ripe for atheism: L. Büchner, *What is Materialism?* (1897), p. 147.
'old Carlyle': *Life*, pp. 230–31.
'semi-rational baboons': Quoted in *Life of Sir JFS*, p. 375.

p. 276   upon the criminal: *SRD* II, pp. 55–93.
compulsorily sober: Speech in the House of Lords, 8 May 1873.
'the completed edifice': *EFP*, p. 360. A comparison between the views of
the two brothers, as expressed in *EFP* and *Liberty, Equality, Fraternity*,
was made by Henry Holbeach in *St Paul's Magazine* XIV, Feb. 1874,
pp. 193–220.
'his delinquencies': *Agnostic Annual* (1896), article by G. R. Bithell.

p. 277   voted against him: G. G. Coulton, *Fourscore Years* (1943), p. 324.
'communicable truth': H. A. L. Fisher, *F. W. Maitland* (1910), p. 8.
sides of the question: See A. W. Gore's tribute in *Henry Sidgwick – A
Memoir* (1906), p. 557.
'to his opponents': *Life*, pp. 333–4.

p. 278   'impartiality of the referee': The quotation is from an unpublished paper
by Walter Raleigh (1898).
Moore . . . Keynes: *The Philosophy of G. E. Moore*, ed. P. A. Schlipp,
(1942), pp. 16–17; R. F. Harrod, *The Life of John Maynard Keynes*
(1951), pp. 116–17. Bertrand Russell, however, continued to admire
Sidgwick (*Unpopular Essays* (1950), p. 214).
'scientific jargon': A. W. Brown, *The Metaphysical Society* (New York
1947), p. 246. Cf. *Henry Sidgwick – A Memoir*, Appx II, pp. 608–15.
was contradictory: *Henry Sidgwick*, op. cit., pp. 600–608. Cf. *Mind*,
NS X, Jan. 1901, pp. 1–17, 'Henry Sidgwick', by L. Stephen. *Hibbert
Journal* XXXVII, Oct. 1938, pp. 25–43, 'Henry Sidgwick', by C. D.
Broad. Broad considered Sidgwick's mistaken appeal to the nature of
scientific postulates in *Five Types of Ethical Theory* (1930),
pp. 244–56.

p. 279   'weakest and the worst': *Fraser's Magazine*, NS XI, March 1875, p. 325,
'Sidgwick's Methods of Ethics' by L. Stephen.

p. 280   divine: Joseph Addison, 'The spacious Firmament on High'.
Baudelaire: *Les Fleurs du Mal* (1857).
'do evil with our might': A. C. Swinburne, *William Blake, a Critical
Essay* (1906), p. 175 fn., quoted by Mario Praz, *The Romantic Agony*
(1933), pp. 283–4.
Goethe: Goethe, *Das Göttliche*.
de Lisle: Leconte de Lisle, *Midi*.

p. 282   for a future existence: W. K. Clifford, *Lectures and Essays*, (1901) II,
p. 169.
'tend to be the best': W. Bagehot, *Physics and Politics* (1873), p. 43.
'think with him': *Sci. Eth.*, p. vi.
'edifice of science': Ibid., p. ix.
composed of cells: Ibid., p. 120.

p. 283   'is to survive . . . incorporated': Ibid., p. 124.
a condition of social welfare: Ibid., p. 450.
'inexpugnable truth': Ibid., p. 356.
'some ulterior end': Ibid., p. 358.
challenges of the future: Greta Jones, *Social Darwinism and English Thought* (1980).

p. 284   'evils which it causes': *Sci. Eth.*, p. 460.
'vanity . . . most people do': *Life*, pp. 351–2.
'more than he could do': *Mind* X, Jan. 1901, p. 4 fn.
'a scientific foundation': *Life and Letters of T. H. Huxley*, II, p. 359.

p. 285   'ethically the best': T. H. Huxley *Collected Essays* (1894), IX, p. 81.
'mission to be priestess': Ibid., p. 146.
'the eyes to see it': *Life and Letters of T. H. Huxley*, II, pp. 219–20.
'all our deeds': Ibid., I, p. 241.
'comfort on earth': George Eliot, *Essays and Leaves from a Note-book* (1884), p. 62.
'for holding its own': *SRD* I, p. 250 (first printed in *Contemporary Review* LXIV, Aug. 1893, p. 168).

p. 286   'quality is required': Ibid., p. 168.
'the cockney type': Ibid., pp. 245–6.
rampant individualism: Greta Jones, op. cit., p. 122, provides a useful introduction to the development of social Darwinism in Britain, but there is some truth in Roger Bannister's criticism of her book that the term becomes in her hands so protean that the moral and intellectual evolutionism of Stephen is seen to be a forerunner of the functionalists and collectivists – which it was not (*Victorian Studies* 25, Winter 1982, pp. 250–51).

p. 287   'conditions of its welfare': *Sci. Ethics*, pp. 350–1.
'not too good': Ibid., p. 418.
'breaks off': *Queen's Quarterly* 55, 1948, pp. 450–63, contains a useful article by J. A. Irving on 'Sir Leslie Stephen, Evolution and Ethics'. There is also an admirably concise exposure of evolutionary ethics in *Cambridge Journal* I, May 1948, pp. 465–73, 'World-Stuff and Nonsense', by S. E. Toulmin, to which I am indebted.

p. 288   'contribution to Ethics': G. E. Moore, *Principia Ethica* (1929 edn), p. 54.

p. 289   'no further creed': Quoted by B. Bosanquet, *The Civilization of Christendom and Other Studies* (1893), I, p. 63.
'bright and sweet': *HL*, I, p. 284.
spring of all knowledge: Isaiah Berlin, *Concepts and Categories* (1978), pp. 56–80.

p. 290   cannot be otherwise: W. G. Runciman, *Social Science and Political Theory* (1969), p. 122.

p. 291   empirical reasoning: *SRD* I, pp. 49–54.
trained to believe them: Ibid., p. 71.
profoundly alienated: *SRD* I, p. 64.

p. 292   to be discarded: For a brief and illuminating discussion of this problem see Runciman, op. cit., pp. 162–75.

p. 293   'evidence now available': W. G. Runciman, *A Treatise on Social Theory* (1983), I. p. 214.
methods of science: *SRD* I, pp. 54, 58. Runciman, *Treatise* op. cit., pp. 215–22.

the nuclear family: *Household and Family in Past Time*, ed. Peter Laslett and Richard Wall (1972); *The Family in Interdisciplinary History*, ed. Theodore K. Rabb and Robert I. Rothberg (1971); Ferdinand Mount, *The Subversive Family* (1982); G. R. Elton, 'Happy Families', *New York Review of Books*, 14 June 1984, pp. 39–41.

'fortified centre': G. M. Young, *Portrait of an Age*, ed. G. Kitson Clark (1977), p. 154.

'are but auxiliaries': C. Potter, 'The First Point of the New Charter, Improved Dwellings for the People', *Contemporary Review* XVII, Nov. 1871, pp. 555–6, quoted in *The Victorian Family*, ed. Anthony S. Wohl, 1975, p. 9.

p. 294   'partial reserve': Leslie Stephen, *Life of Henry Fawcett* (1885), p. 45, quoted by David Roberts, 'The Paterfamilias of the Victorian Governing Classes'. Wohl, op. cit., p. 74.

'sexual equality': *Sci. Eth.*, p. 133.

'flagellate sperm': Patrick Geddes, *The Evolution of Sex* (1889), pp. 115–17. For an account of Geddes's ideas see Jill Conway, 'Stereotypes of Femininity in a Theory of Social Evolution', *Victorian Studies* XIV, Sept. 1970, pp. 47–62.

'act of parliament': Geddes, op. cit., p. 247.

p. 295   and enter convents: Elaine Showalter, 'Family Secrets and Domestic Subversion: Rebellion in the Novels of the 1860s', Wohl, op. cit., pp. 101–18.

social structure: J. W. Burrow, *Evolution and Society: A Study in Victorian Social Theory* (1966), pp. 193–4.

pattern of domestic life: 'Love, Loss and Family Advantage' by Rosalind Mitchison, *London Review of Books* 5, 1–14 Sept. 1983, pp. 3, 5.

should be employed: *Saturday Review*, LXVII, 24 April 1889.

p. 296   drawing and quartering: *SRD* II, pp. 92–3.

'habitual drunkards': 'Social Macadamization', *Fraser's Magazine* LXXXVI (1872), p. 150.

scientific doctrine: *SRD* I, p. 65.

our fools: Ibid., p. 138.

'equal terms': *Sci. Eth.*, p. 133.

p. 297   'problems of today': *SRD* I, pp. 131–2.

'the discovery of concrete truth': Quoted by J. M. Keynes, *Collected Works, Essays in Biography* (1972), X, p. 196.

p. 298   as if Green had never lived: *Life*, p. 379. Letter from LS to Charles Eliot Norton, 4 March 1883, Harvard. Klaus Dockhorn, *Die Staatsphilosophie des englischen Idealismus* (Bochum, 1937), especially Part II, 'Die Wirkung der Lehre', is interesting and informative on the extent of Green's influence on particular individuals.

finding incomprehensible: Melvin Richter, *The Politics of Conscience: T. H. Green and his Age* (1964), pp. 141–58.

not self-sacrifice but self-realization: E. R. Bentley, *Bernard Shaw* (New York 1947), Ch. I *passim*.

'independence and good conduct': *SRD* I, p. 219.

'an unclean beast': B. Webb, *Our Partnership* (1948), p. 232.

p. 299   poor dissenting relations in a mill-town: F. R. Leavis in his useful introduction to *Mill on Bentham and Coleridge* (1950) rightly shows

that there is a line of descent through Mill and George Eliot to Beatrice
Webb, but is careful not to carry the argument further than the years of
My Apprenticeship (1926). For had he done so and drawn attention to
her endorsement of Stalinism his argument would have been seen to be
specious.

CHAPTER ELEVEN
MORALITY THROUGH BIOGRAPHY

p. 301   'every alternative': *SB* IV, pp. 136–8.
p. 302   'inscribe his name': *HL* III, p. 223.
            'brilliant constellation': *Cornhill* XIX, June 1869, 'Idolatry by a Cynic'
            (by LS), p. 697.
            customs and conventions of the times: *Lit. and Soc. 18th Cent.*, p. 6.
            'harshly called a cynic': *SB* III, p. 168.
            'weakness of the moderate man': *DNB* entry Thomas Fuller.
            'analyser to solve': *National Review* XXXIX, April 1902, 'James
            Spedding' by Leslie Stephen, quoted by John Johnson Timmerman, 'Sir
            Leslie Stephen as a Biographer', *Diss.* Northwestern University (1948),
            p. 70.
            'from his spoken words': *Cornhill* XXXII, July 1875, 'Art and Morality',
            p. 96.
            'how sincere Donne was': *SB* III, p. 38. John Carey, *John Donne, Life,
            Mind and Art* (1981) is mainly concerned with Donne's sincerity.
            'rose-colour a little too freely': *HL* III, p. 174.
            every imputation: *SB* I, p. 178.
            touched by Johnson's tenderness: Leslie Stephen, *Samuel Johnson* (1878),
            p. 93. Cf. *SB* III, p. 232; *Life*, pp. 231, 242; *HL* III, p. 221.
            'desire for popular praise': *SB* III, p. 31.
            concise as well as truthful: *National Review* XXII, 1893, 'Biography' (by
            LS), p. 180.
p. 303   'great works': *SB* III, p. 28.
            Lee in research: J. J. Timmerman, op. cit., pp. 214–15.
            'went round with the hat': James Payn, *The Backwater of Life* (1899),
            with an introduction by Leslie Stephen.
            excisions ought to have been made: *SB* III, pp. 13, 32.
            sexual experiences: Stephen declared that men of the world would admit
            that some matters were too intimate to reveal. *SB* IV, pp. 160–7; James
            Payn, op. cit., p. xi.
            influence their countrymen: L. Stephen, *Life of Henry Fawcett* (1885),
            p. 468; *Life of Sir JFS*, p. 481.
            'one and the same': Plutarch, *Moralia*, trans. F. C. Babbit (Harvard 1931),
            p. 475, quoted by Glenn D. Paige, *Biography* 6, Spring 1983, p. 186.
p. 304   'as could be desired': *SB* IV, p. 205.
            'and trickery': Ibid., p. 176.

'not so broad': *HL* I, pp. 164–5.

'a tendency to conceits': *Life*, pp. 314–15.

'sister of Shirley's': Ibid., III, p. 21.

'heroic and loving': Ibid., p. 18.

'a woman' ': L. Stephen, *George Eliot* (1902), p. 139.

'the most prominent': *HL* III, p. 206.

'masculine fibre throughout': Ibid., p. 207.

'moral elevation': Ibid., p. 23.

of a manly confessor: Ibid., p. 207.

p. 305   by her husband: *George Eliot*, op. cit., pp. 145 f.

'masculine temperament': *HL* II, p. 155. Landor exhibits a 'masculine simplicity', ibid., p. 294.

'trampled in the crush': *Cornhill* XXXIV, Nov. 1876, 'Thoughts on Criticism by a Critic' (by LS), p. 558.

spat in Hervey's hat: *HL* I, p. 328.

'a polite word for morbid': *Eng. Thought 18th Cent.*, Ch. XII, p. 350.

'in itself criminal': *Lit. and Soc. 18th Cent.*, p. 134.

filthy abuse: L. Stephen, *Swift* (1909), p. 31.

a morbid tendency: *SB* III, p. 47.

prolonged depression: Ibid., II, pp. 228–9.

appetite for happiness: *HL* III, p. 236. The text reads 'retrospection', a misprint, I believe, for 'introspection'.

retire into convents: Ibid., I, p. 213.

p. 306   nothing morbid about *him*: Ibid., II, p. 54 ff.

'pure domestic affection': Ibid., p. 159.

draw man upwards: Stephen took the final lines of *Faust* in the normal Victorian sense, that eternal womanhood ennobles man and improves him. Goethe, however, was describing the two principles which govern life: the masculine which is active and creative but for those very reasons destructive and sinful, and the feminine which is passive, loving, suffering and redeeming. Both are needed in the world. Thus Faust, the sinful man, is saved by Gretchen's love and sacrifice. Faust is admitted to Heaven for Gretchen's sake, because she has atoned for his sins through her love. Goethe's idea was religious, not ethical.

'anti-social instincts': *Cornhill* XXXII, July 1875, 'Art and Morality' (by LS), p. 94.

'an unwholesome atmosphere': *HL* I, pp. 211–13. Cf. L. Stephen, *Pope* (1914 edn), p. 14.

'relation to the universe': *HL* III, p. 35.

'interviewing John the Baptist': *National Review* XLII (1903), p. 422.

'reason and experience': *HL* II, p. 258.

p. 307   'draped in elaborate rhetoric': Ibid., I, p. 250.

never pardoned by the facts: *Eng. Thought 18th Cent.*, II, p. 315.

'a masculine grasp of facts': *HL* II, p. 160.

'more pain than pleasure or profit': Ibid., III, p. 25.

'easily learnt': Ibid., II, p. 174.

'crackling of thorns': Ibid., III, pp. 90–91.

'soda-water': Ibid., II, p. 261.

the dark riddle of life: Ibid., p. 262.

'what is called success': Ibid., p. 279.

p. 308   hidden from themselves: Ibid., III, p. 264.
            'escape from himself': Ibid., II, p. 27.
            amounted to self-deception: *SB* III, pp. 23–7.
            'impulses of a generous nature': *Pope*, op. cit., p. 46.
            a lower degree than they fancy: *SB* II, p. 73; *HL* III, pp. 239–40;
                Johnson, op. cit., p. 86.
            'unalloyed to self-deception': *HL* III, p. 237.
            'the stings of remorse': Ibid., p. 330.
            'their whole nature': *HL*, I, p. 74. *Lit. and Soc. 18th Cent.*, p. 162.
            'dock his horses' tails': Ibid., pp. 70–71.
p. 309   his own sweat aromatic: J. J. Timmerman, op. cit., p. 119. *HL* III, p. 235.
            'philosopher or reformer': *Eng. Thought 18th Cent.*, II, p. 374.
            'burnt into his soul': Timmerman, op. cit., p. 144.
            'injure its adversaries': *Swift*, op. cit., p. 185. Cf. *Pope*, op. cit., pp. 158,
                210.
            'as a man of genius ought': *HL* I, p. 114.
            'his multitudinous subterfuges': *DNB* entry Alexander Pope.
p. 310   'his extreme cleverness': *HL* I, p. 350.
            'discharged that duty scrupulously': Ibid., III, p. 318. See Timmerman,
                op. cit., p. 170.
            'come to no conclusions': *HL* II, p. 67.
            'haystack with more certainty': Ibid., p. 327.
            'preferment by flattery': *DNB* entry Thomas Newton.
            'heroes of Congreve's comedies': *DNB* entry Henry St John.
            'boring all round': *SB* III, p. 114.
            'to Scotsmen of pure blood': *DNB* entry Robert Burns.
            'in the Apocalypse': *DNB* entry William Whiston.
            'becoming deranged': *DNB* entry William Cooke.
            one type of man: Quoted by John D. Bicknell, *Diss.*, from *Eng. Thought
                18th Cent.*, II, p. 443, and *HL* III, p. 140.
p. 311   'on a longer acquaintance': *HL* III, pp. 160–61.
            'firm grasp of facts: *HL* II, p. 256.
            presented by life: Ibid., p. 226.
p. 312   'his affectations are instructive': Ibid., II, p. 199.
p. 313   'a pessimist and an optimist': *AA*, p. 177.
            of their early days: *SB* IV, pp. 160–67; James Payn, op. cit., p. xi.
            'indolent and languid men': *HL* III, p. 258.
            less responsible for the harm they did: 'Idolatry' (by LS), *Cornhill
                Magazine* XIX 1869, p. 697; 'Heroes and Valets' (by LS), ibid., XXXV
                (1897), pp. 45–55; *Sci. Eth.*, p. 145.
            one's moral judgement: ibid., pp. 79, 236–7, 247; *SB* I, pp. 148–9;
                George Eliot, op. cit., p. 204.
            'go to his books': *HL* II, p. 172.
            'tortured by remorse': Ibid., I, p. 15.
p. 314   'a student of autobiography': Ibid., III, p. 233. Cf. ibid., p. 264.
            spirit of common sense: C. R. Sanders, 'Sir Leslie Stephen, Coleridge and
                Two Coleridgeans', *PMLA* LV, Sept. 1940, p. 795. *Life*, pp. 315, 318.
            'more compassion than indignation': *HL* III, pp. 326–9.
p. 315   'shrugs of respectable shoulders': *Eng. Util*, II, p. 38 *passim.* Quoted by
                Timmerman, op. cit., p. 143 fn.

the judgement appears ridiculous: *HL* II, p. 271.
inseparable from living: *National Review* XXII (1893), p. 174.
no more severe than Arnold: Cf. W. R. Greg, *Literary and Social
Judgements* (1869), esp. pp. 146–84, 'French Fiction: The Lowest
Deep', in which the novels of Victor Hugo, Eugène Sue, A. Dumas and
Georges Sand are unsparingly attacked. 'The inspiration of French
fiction – the source from which flow half its deformities, its vile
morality and its vitiated taste – is the *craving for excitement* that has so
long been characteristic of the nation' (p. 150). After declaring that 'of
course we can give no quotations' (p. 155), he proceeds to quote
liberally from their works, and is particularly irate that God is
mentioned as the mainstay of a religion of 'affection and emotion',
never as a Guide, a Governor and the apex of a Creed (p. 182). Greg
has also some hard words for Kingsley's preoccupation with sex (pp.
133–5). For Morley see his famous review of Swinburne's poetry in
Saturday Review XXII, 4 Aug. 1866, pp. 145–7.

p. 316 **'tries to control':** Quoted by L. Trilling, *Matthew Arnold* (1949 edn),
p. 347, from M. Arnold, *St Paul and Protestantism* (1870, 2nd edn),
p. 49.
Angelo . . . a hypocrite: *HL* II, p. 156.
Phaedrus . . . lower passions: *Phaedrus*, pp. 255, 256 D.

CHAPTER TWELVE
MORALITY AND LITERATURE

p. 317 **'said nothing original':** *Lit. and Soc. 18th Cent.*, p. 26.
p. 318 **nature and function of criticism:** The important articles in the *Cornhill*
are 'Art and Morality', XXXII, 1875, pp. 91–101; 'Thoughts on
Criticism by a Critic', XXXIV, 1876, pp. 556–69; 'The Moral Element
in Literature', XLIII, 1881, pp. 34–50; 'The Decay of Literature',
XLVI, 1882, pp. 602–12.
'require confutation': op. cit., 'Art and Morality', pp. 91–2. The
aesthetes were not as dogmatic as Stephen suggests. Pater admitted
that art could be morally irresponsible and also a powerful influence.
Walter Pater, *Plato and Platoism* (Library ed. 1910), p. 269.
to enthuse: Stephen urged critics to 'smite pretenders', *Cornhill* XIX,
1869, p. 579, 'A Cynic's Apology'; what is odd is that he took
Macaulay to task for wasting powder and shot on that wretched poetic
charlatan Robert Montgomery, *Cornhill* XXXIV, 1876, p. 562.
a happy man: Horace, *Epistles*, l.VI.1
killed him: *Cornhill* XLIII, 1881, p. 701, 'Authors for Hire'.
'crown each other . . . gigantic clique': *Life*, p. 454; *Cornhill* XXXV,
1877, p. 679, 'Genius and Vanity'.
'quick appreciation of merit': *Saturday Review* XXXI, 1871, p. 214,
quoted by S. A. O. Ullmann, *Diss.*, op. cit., p. 444.
'disapproval minimised': Florence Hardy, *Early Life of Thomas Hardy*

(1928), p. 223.
'his preordained theories': John Gross, *The Rise and Fall of the Man of Letters* (1969), p. 86. Cf. *SB* II, p. 81; *HL* III, p. 6.
fn. 'may not even smile': *International Journal of Ethics* VIII, October 1897, p. 5, 'Nansen' by Leslie Stephen.
a fossil in a museum: *HL* III, p. 1. Cf. *Cornhill* XLVI, 1882, 'The Study of English Literature', pp. 486–508.

p. 319   'have adopted a classification': Ibid., p. 338. Cf. ibid., II, p. 46, where Stephen says that the scientific method depends on observation not on *a priori* theories. 'The true business of the critic is to discover from observation what are the conditions under which a book appeals to our sympathies, and, if he finds an apparent exception to his rules, to admit that he has made an oversight, and not to condemn the facts which persist in contradicting his theories.' Cf ibid., II, pp. 83 and 167.
'on every work': Stephen took Johnson to task for thinking that criticism was judging whether an author 'had infringed or conformed to established rules and [for passing] sentence accordingly.' *Lit. and Soc. 18th Cent.*, pp. 3–4. G. U. Ellis in *Twilight on Parnassus* (1939), pp. 63–89, chooses to attack Stephen on the grounds that it is valueless to consider the sociological aspect of literature, since poets are influenced not by their 'age' but by other poets. He accuses Stephen of thinking that the poet owed more to the Reform Bill than to Apollo, and of suggesting that the middle class, so far from often ruining authors by imposing their prejudices and taste upon them, raised the standard of literature by extending the reading circle. The argument is not worth considering since Stephen made no such claims and to rend one book from the corpus of his criticism and to cite it as the essence of the whole is ludicrous, though not perhaps suprising from a critic who discerns the quality which makes the nineteenth century unique is that it was 'an acquisitive age'. Cf. Stephen's ironical treatment of the very method of which Ellis complains, *HL* II, p. 83.
'prompted by a love of singularity': *HL* II, p. 25.
naked power: *National Review* XXV, 1895, 'The Choice of Books' by Leslie Stephen.
'invigorating and regenerating processes': Ibid., p. 101.
'stammer when you talk of it': *Science and Ethics*, ed. C. H. Waddington (1942), p. 7.
have had their talents: op. cit., 'Art and Morality', p. 93. Cf. *Cornhill* XLIII, 1881, 'The Moral Element in Literature'.

p. 320   that virtue triumphed: *HL* II, pp. 160–1.
invariably crushed: *SRD* II, p. 173, quoted by Ullmann, op. cit., p. 129.
the villain with the gallows: Cf. Richard Stang, *The Theory of the Novel in England 1850–1870* (1959), p. 75.
'starvation in hollow trees': James Payn, op. cit., p. xxxv.
'is as easy as lying': SEI, p. 171.
no disciple of Arnold: Wellek, op. cit., p. 185. But surely T. S. Eliot was right to say that Stephen, Symons, Symonds, Pater and Myers all adopt most of Arnold's assumptions. T. S. Eliot, *The Use of Poetry and the Use of Criticism* (1933), p. 115.
'an epigram and a philosophical dogma': SB II, p. 83.
'civilizing the coming world': ibid., pp. 104, 109.

'ethical and religious sentiments': SB II, pp. 202–3.
to express the feeling: *HL* III, p. 109.

p. 321 'a mere singer' . . . 'systematic exposition': *HL* II, p. 256. *Essays in Criticism*, II, op. cit., pp. 148–54.
understanding of good and evil: *Life*, p. 396.
strength of feeling: *HL* II, p. 252.
in which he took part: Ibid., pp. 11–12.

p. 322 Richardson and Young: Ibid., p. 153.

p. 323 'to sol-fa through the emotions': René Wellek, *A History of Modern Criticism* (1966), p. 146.
'moved himself': D. MacCarthy, *Leslie Stephen* (1937), p. 16.
'nothing much matters': Ibid., p. 15.
'be clever': Ibid., p. 44.
'as everything else': *Scrutiny*, VII, March 1939, p. 407, 'Leslie Stephen – Cambridge Critic', by Q. D. Leavis.

p. 324 its value to man: MacCarthy, op. cit., p. 46.
'antagonistic to Mr. MacCarthy': Q. D. Leavis, op. cit., p. 406.
Sappho or Catullus: Lytton Strachey, *Characters and Commentaries* (1933), 'A Victorian Critic', p. 193.
literary chatter . . . were no better: Lord Strang, *Home and Abroad* (1956), pp. 30–6.
inferior to Shakespeare: Lytton Strachey, *Books and Characters* (1922), 'Racine', pp. 3–30.

p. 325 'inseparable from the merits': Raymond Mortimer, *Channel Packet* (1942), p. 57.
'exquisite deliberation': *The Oxford Book of English Verse*, ed. Arthur Quiller-Couch (1900), Introduction.
'beauty of life': 'English Literature' by F. L. Lucas, *University Studies Cambridge*, ed. Harold Wright (1933), p. 293. It is there that Lucas gives testimony to Quiller-Couch's 'charm and literary honesty'.
'we need nothing more': I. A. Richards, *Practical Criticism* (1929), pp. 299–305, 351.

p. 326 'moved by it': Matthew Arnold, *Essays in Criticism* (1895 edition), I, p. 48.
The Mill on the Floss: T. S. Eliot, *The Sacred Wood* (1923), p. 43.

p. 327 'implied and pointed to': Q. D. Leavis, op. cit., p. 404.
Fiction and the Reading Public: Q. D. Leavis, *Collected Essays* (1983), I, pp. 11–13.
'in aromatic pain': MacCarthy, op. cit., p. 20.
poetic sensibility: 'Thoughts on Criticism by a Critic', op. cit., p. 558.

p. 328 to what was poetic. . . . 'wasted on it': A. E. Housman, *The Name and Nature of Poetry* (1933); *New Statesman and Nation* XIV, Aug. 1937, p. 221.
'solve all difficulties': Lionel Trilling, *E. M. Forster* (1944), pp. 147–8 and 140–1.
'rather florid prose': *HL* II, p. 144, quoted by Ullmann, op. cit., pp. 421–2.
fn. 'irrefutably in place': T. S. Eliot, *The Sacred Wood* (1923), p. 123.

p. 329 *King Lear*: Ibid., p. 82. The line 'By which they have been, are, or cease to be' recalls *King Lear*, I, 1, 115.
'so fine as to elude the sight': Leslie Stephen, *Alexander Pope* (1880), p. 197.

'theory of poetic expression': *Johnson*, op. cit., p. 189.

'command of superlatives' . . . 'beyond his tether': *HL* III, p. 198; *SB* II, pp. 81–2.

'in the dark ages': George Eliot, *Middlemarch*, Book I, Chapter 2.

geography bored him: Lytton Strachey, *Characters and Commentaries*, op. cit., p. 189.

depth of his emotion: *HL* I, p. 101.

'learn itself by heart': *SB* II, pp. 81–2. Cf. Algernon Swinburne, *William Blake*, Chapter XIV, pp. 214–18, 'The test of the highest poetry is that it eludes all tests.'

'but with words': G. H. W. Rylands, *Words and Poetry* (1928), p. xi.

p. 330   to appreciate Pope: J. W. Mackail, *Pope* (1919), pp. 7–14. Cf. Francis Thompson, *Sir Leslie Stephen as a Biographer*, in which Thompson calls Stephen natively prosaic and unimaginative. 'Throughout his writing one cannot but be conscious of a certain hardness, a lack of moist light', which is only partly counterbalanced by a strenuous fairness of mind permitting him to reach the aesthetic in poetry in a 'reflex way'. Thompson called Stephen's essay on Arnold the best ever written by a critic on an author with whom he was not in native sympathy. Thompson's essay pronounces upon Stephen the judgement of the young in the 1890s.

Milton and Wordsworth: *Life*, pp. 475–6.

photographic accuracy: *HL* I, pp. 190–1.

'first appearance in society': *HL* III, pp. 21–3.

'clearer conceptions': Ibid., pp. 27–8.

p. 331   *Revenger's Tragedy*: Ibid., p. 25.

'highest position among English novelists': *DNB*, quoted by John Gross, op. cit., p. 88. Cf. *Cornhill* XLIII, 1881, 'The Moral Element in Literature', p. 36.

'superficial without being good-humoured': Ibid.

'loss of that early charm': *HL* III, pp. 213, 216.

p. 332   'her comfortable world': *Cornhill* XXXIII, 1876, 'Humour', p. 324.

'had his place in society': *HL* I, p. 152.

a prominent characteristic of genius: *SB* IV, p. 210 ff.

where time loses its meaning: Cf. T. S. Eliot, *The Use of Poetry and the Use of Criticism* (1933), p. 98.

erroneous conclusions about the reading public: Q. D. Leavis, *Fiction and the Reading Public* (1932), pp. 175–77. *Vide* Gertrude Himmelfarb, *The Idea of Poverty* (1984), p. 450 fn.

p. 333   bourgeois patterns of thought: Terry Eagleton, *Literary Theory* (1983).

'speech of the semi-literate': *London Review of Books* 5, 1983, 'Cambridge English and Beyond' by Raymond Williams.

p. 334   to his fellow citizens: Ian Watt, *The Rise of the Novel* (1967).

for the century he loved: John Barrell, *English Literature in History 1730–80: An Equal, Wide Survey* (1983).

'pathos or descriptive power': *SB* II, p. 81; *HL* III, p. 6.

little of the hanging judge there: *SB* IV, p. 90.

p. 335   classics would be intolerable: John Gross, op. cit., p. 89.

'dearly love a bishop': *SEI*, p. 98; Mortimer, op. cit., p. 18.

a crisis of mind: J. Dover Wilson, *Two Critics of Wordsworth* (1939), pp. 20–1.

'to raise difficulties': *SB* III, p. 226.

'of schoolboy perversion': *HL* II, p. 313.

'a first-rate novel': Ibid., p. 107. Note Stephen's delight when John Byrom's biographer felt he had to excuse Byrom's verses on the fight between Figg and Sutton by declaring that it was not 'a brutal prize-fight' but 'an ultra vigorous assault at arms': the line, remarked Stephen, seems hard to draw; SBI, p. 91. The finest extravaganzas occur in *SB*, *SEI* and *Sketches*.

'qualified himself for the purpose': *Cornhill* XXXIII, 1876, p. 320.

p. 336   'a new logical structure': *HL* III, p. 202. Note the way Stephen exposes the deficiencies of de Quincey's humour (HL I). He demanded that 'the imaginative humorist must in all cases be keenly alive to the "absurdity of man"; he must have a sense of the irony of fate, of the strange interlacing of good and evil in the world, and of the baser and nobler elements of human nature' (HL III, p. 159).

'memoirs of its celebrities': Ibid., I, p. 188. The text reads 'memories' – a misprint, I think, for 'memoirs', which, like numerous other misprints, Stephen never corrected.

'a continuous stream': *Pope*, p. 189.

'beauty of its process': *The Letters of Henry James*, ed. Percy Lubbuck, pp. 503–8 (letter from Henry James to H. G. Wells, 10 July 1915). Cf. Dorothea Krook, *The Ordeal of Consciousness of Henry James* (1962), pp. 409–10.

the moment of apprehension: *The Letters of Virginia Woolf 1912–22*, ed. Nigel Nicolson and Joanne Trautman (1976), II, p. 67.

ultimately inexpressible: Joan Bennett, *Virginia Woolf* (1945), ch. IV.

than in their policies: *Virginia Woolf Miscellany* (Spring 1983), 'Virginia Woolf, Her Politics', by Quentin Bell.

'by reading the poets': Nicolson and Trautman, op. cit., p. 529, Quoted by Jane Marcus, 'Tintinnabulations', in *Marxist Perspectives*, 5 January 1979.

p. 337   'applied to his self-consciousness': *SB* III, pp. 31–2 ff.

'a kind of lying': *HL* III, p. 143.

'despised the whole business': Lytton Strachey, op. cit., pp. 188–9.

'dare to be himself': *George Eliot*, p. 147.

'and don't prescribe rules' *Life*, p. 290. Stephen thought that 'Saint-Beuve and Mat. Arnold (in a smaller way) are the only modern critics who seem to me worth reading – perhaps, too, Lowell.'

'a calmer judge would be incapable': *HL* II, p. 88. Cf. 'Your impartial critic or historian is generally a man who leaves out of account nothing but the essential', ibid., p. 132.

... five thousand words: Ibid., I, pp. 186–220; Mortimer, op. cit., pp. 7 and 46–57.

stickler-like the armies separates: *Troilus and Cressida*, V, 8, 18.

CHAPTER THIRTEEN
CONCLUSION

p. 339   after 1870: See T. W. Heyek, *The Transformation of Intellectual Life in Victorian England* (1982), especially Chs 7 and 8, and Frank M. Turner's review of this book in *Victorian Studies*, Summer 1983, pp. 465–6. Cf. Raymond Williams, *Culture and Society 1780–1950* (1959); Jerome Buckley, *The Victorian Temper: A Study in Literary Culture* (1951); Walter Houghton, *The Victorian Frame of Mind 1830–1870 (1957)*.

p. 340   as intellectual journalists: Heyek, op. cit., p. 202.

p. 341   any contemporary professor of literature: John Gross, *The Rise and Fall of the Man of Letters* (1969), pp. 132–245.

p. 342   'Eastern Europe': Sheldon Rothblatt, Review article, *History of Education* XII, Sept. 1983, pp. 222–5.

p. 345   'such nasty things of my enemies': SB II, p. 97.
'kindly monster at bottom': Ibid., p. 113.

p. 346   for manoeuvre: J. Plamenatz, *The English Utilitarians* (1949).
made sense or not: *New Statesman* LXV, 21 June 1963, pp. 945–6.

p. 347   by determinist principles: Cf. H. S. Hughes, *Consciousness and Society* (1958), chs 1 and 2.
behaving irrationally: Noel Annan, *The Curious Strength of Positivism in English Political Thought* (1959), Hobhouse Memorial Lecture, pp. 17–18.
perverse and shocking: Richard Wollheim, *The Sheep and the Ceremony* (1979), which considers the relationship between morality and ritual or aesthetic sensibility and does indeed make use of the ideas of the German Renaissance (in this case those of Freud) in reinterpreting utilitarianism.

p. 348   profited by his blunders: Cf. *Cornhill* XXXIV, 1876, 'Thoughts on Criticism by a Critic', p. 566.
theology is logically improper: S. E. Toulmin, *The Place of Reason* in *Ethics* (1950), considers this matter in Chs 11–14.

p. 349   'incalculable gratitude': *HL* III, p. 338.

p. 350   'never fail!': Quoted by J. M. Keynes, *Collected Works* (1972), X, p. 340.

THE WORKS OF
LESLIE STEPHEN

An Agnostic's Apology and Other Essays. 1893
Alexander Pope. English Men of Letters. 1880
English Literature and Society in the Eighteenth Century. Ford Lectures, 1903,
  1904
The English Utilitarians. 3 vols, 1900
Essays on Freethinking and Plainspeaking. [Collected edn] 1905
George Eliot. English Men of Letters. 1902
The History of English Thought in the Eighteenth Century. 2 vols, 1876, 1902
Hobbes. English Men of Letters. 1904
Hours in a Library. 1874, 1876, 3 vols. 1909
Life of Henry Fawcett. 1885
The Life of Sir James Fitzjames Stephen. 1895
The Playground of Europe. 1871, 1910, 1936
The Poll Degree from a Third Point of View. 1863
Samuel Johnson. English Men of Letters. 1878
The Science of Ethics. 1882
Sketches from Cambridge. 1st edn 1865, by 'A Don.', 1932
Social Rights and Duties. Addresses to Ethical Societies. The Ethical Library,
  2 vols, 1896
Some Early Impressions. 1924
Studies of a Biographer. [Collected edn] 4 vols, 1898, 1907
Swift. English Men of Letters. 1882
The "Times" on the American War: A Historical Study. 1865 [Initialled]

INDEX

Ives house, 107–8; liking for young people, 108; on women's emancipation and role, 109–10, 144, 295; English Men of Letters biographies, 110–13; delivers Clark Lectures, 111; scholarship, 111, 345–50; overwork and breakdown, 111–12, 129, 137; literary achievements, 112–13, 124; scholarly honours, 113, 123; grief at Julia's death, 114–16; takes house in Hindhead, 116; exploits Stella Duckworth, 116–17; decline, 118; appointed Trustee of National Portrait Gallery, 122; deafness, 122; offered KCB, 123; cancer, 124; death and cremation, 125, 343; portrayed by Virginia Woolf, 126–8, 132; sentimentality and emotional dependence, 127–8, 141, 144; portrayed in Meredith's *Egoist*, 130, 374; claims recognition as genius, 133–4; psychological analysis of, 134–8, 140; Evangelicalism, 141, 146–7, 152 *fn*, 153–4, 162; hypersensitivity and will, 141–5; humour, 141–2; on family and ethics, 154, 293–6; on Protestantism, 163–4; and German philosophy and history, 169–70, 172–5, 185, 347; and Mill, 173, 175, 178; and Kantianism, 183; criticises Jowett, 187–9; and Comtism, 195–7, 272; on Buckle, 197; and Darwinian evolution, 201–3, 207, 233, 293; positivism, 206; and secularists, 214, 343; and political demonstrators, 215; on Truth, 220; on 18th c. 222–5, 229; criticises Deists, 223–6, 233; criticises ruling classes, 226, 228; and history of ideas, 227–30; concern with religious thought, 230; and immortality of soul, 239–41; and belief, 242–6, 251, 254–9; criticises Maurice, 245–6, 255; reviews W. James, 250–1; attacks Arnold, 251–3; anti-clericalism, 256; and ritual, 257; lacks understanding of religious mind, 257–9; prophesies secularisation of society, 259–66; on Pascal, 263–4; ethics, 277, 279, 282–7, 290; criticises Sidgwick, 278–9; and Natural Selection, 282–3, 287; and Huxley's ethics, 284–5; and general theory of society, 290–2; political stance, 296–9; as biographer, 300–11; respect for masculinity, 303–4; on conscience, 308; and sexual morality, 315–16; as literary critic, 316, 317–38;

on morality in literature, 317–9; essay on Wordsworth, 321; MacCarthy on, 323; Q. D. Leavis on, 327; and poetry, 328–31; ridicule in, 335; place as intellectual, 339–44; virtues, 343–5; rationalism, 348–9; handwriting, 371 *see also* authors' names; and titles of LS's own works

Stephen, Nancy (Anne; *née* Stent; LS's grandfather's first wife), 8–9

Stephen, Thoby (LS's son), 5, 102, 108, 117–19, 123, 159 *fn*, 355, 371–2

Stephen, Vanessa *see* Bell, Vanessa

Stephen, Virginia *see* Woolf, Virginia

Sterling, John, 174, 210

Sterne, Laurence, 226, 306, 310–11, 323

Stevenson, Robert Louis, 65, 67, 75, 99, 332, 345, 363

Stogdon, John, 367

Storr, Anthony, 137–8

Storr, Vernon Faithfull, 156

Story of an African Farm (Schreiner), 216

Strachey, James, 159 *fn*

Strachey, Lytton, 159 *fn*, 221, 324, 329, 335–7

Strachey, Marjorie, 159 *fn*

Strachey, Oliver, 159 *fn*

Strachey, Ray (*née* Costelloe), 5

Strauss, David F., 52, 170, 174, 210, 224, 248

Stubbs, William, Bishop, 206, 340

Studd, Peter, 107

'Substitution for the Alps, A' (LS), 95

Sully, James, 67–8, 97

Sumner, John Bird, Archbishop, 379

Sunday Tramps, 97–8

Sunderland, Thomas, 184 *fn*

'Sunset on Mont Blanc' (LS), 96–7

Supernatural Religion (Cassells), 215

Sutton, Ned, 408

Swift, Jonathan: LS writes life of, 111; on sweetness and light, 221; morbidity, 305–6; egoism, 309, 313; humour, 335

Swinburne, Algernon Charles: and religious revival, 214–15; on morality of nature, 280; on 'art for art's sake', 317; criticised by Morley, 317, 405; criticised by LS, 318; bohemianism, 341; on poetry, 408

Sydney-Turner, Saxon, 159 *fn*

Symonds, John Addington, 5, 67, 83, 108, 202, 323, 341

Symonds, Madge (JAS's daughter), 108

Symons, Arthur, 323

System of Logic (Mill), 175, 181, 193, 200